Volume 8

Critical Studies on
Black Life and Culture

Advisory Editor
Professor Henry-Louis Gates
Afro-American Studies, Yale University

Alain Locke. Courtesy of Moorland–Spingarn Research Center, Howard University, Washington, D.C.

THE CRITICAL TEMPER OF ALAIN LOCKE
A Selection of His Essays on Art and Culture

Jeffrey C. Stewart

GARLAND PUBLISHING, INC. • NEW YORK & LONDON
1983

Library of Congress Cataloging in Publication Data

Locke, Alain LeRoy, 1886–1954.
   The critical temper of Alain Locke.

   (Critical studies on Black life and culture ; v. 8)
   Bibliography: p.
   Includes index.
   1. Afro-American arts—Addresses, essays, lectures.
I. Stewart, Jeffrey C., 1950-   II. Title.
III. Series.
NX512.3.A35L62   1983   700'.8996073   80–9046
ISBN 0–8240–9318–6

Printed on acid-free, 250-year-life paper
Manufactured in the United States of America

For my father

CONTENTS

Acknowledgments   xi
List of Illustrations   xv
Introduction   xvii

RENAISSANCE APOLOGETICS
  Editor's Note   3

  Harlem   5
  Enter the New Negro   7
  Youth Speaks   13
  The Art of the Ancestors   15
  Harlem Types   17
  Our Little Renaissance   21
  Beauty Instead of Ashes   23
  Art or Propaganda?   27
  Beauty and the Provinces   29

POETRY
  Editor's Note   33

  Emile Verhaeren   35
  Color—A Review   39
  Review of *The Weary Blues*   41
  The Negro Poets of the United States   43
  The Poetry of Negro Life   47
  Sterling Brown: The New Negro Folk-Poet   49
  Propaganda—or Poetry?   55
  Spiritual Truancy   63

DRAMA
  Editor's Note   69

  Steps Toward the Negro Theatre   71
  Goat Alley   75
  Max Rheinhardt Reads the Negro's Dramatic Horoscope   77
  The Negro and the American Stage   79
  The Drama of Negro Life   87
  Broadway and the Negro Drama   93

MUSIC
  Editor's Note   101

  Roland Hayes: An Appreciation   103
  The Technical Study of the Spirituals—A Review   107
  Toward a Critique of Negro Music   109
  Negro Music Goes to Par   117
  Spirituals   123

AFRICAN ART
  Editor's Note   129

  A Note on African Art   131
  Art Lessons from the Congo   137
  A Collection of Congo Art   139
  African Art: Classic Style   149

CONTEMPORARY NEGRO ART
  Editor's Note   159

  To Certain of Our Philistines   161
  The Art of Auguste Mambour   163
  More of the Negro in Art   167
  The American Negro as Artist   170
  Foreword to Contemporary Negro Art   181
  Advance on the Art Front   185
  Up Till Now   191

RETROSPECTIVE REVIEWS
  Editor's Note   197

  1928: A Retrospective Review   201
  This Year of Grace: Outstanding Books of the Year in Negro Literature   205
  We Turn to Prose: A Retrospective Review of the Literature
      of the Negro for 1931   209
  Black Truth and Black Beauty: A Retrospective Review of the Literature of
      the Negro for 1932   215
  The Saving Grace of Realism: Retrospective Review
      of the Negro Literature of 1933   221
  The Eleventh Hour of Nordicism: Retrospective Review of the Literature
      of the Negro for 1934   227
  Deep River: Deeper Sea: Retrospective Review of the Literature of the
      Negro for 1935   237
  God Save Reality! Retrospective Review of the Literature of the Negro: 1936   245
  Jingo, Counter-Jingo and Us. Retrospective Review of the Literature
      of the Negro: 1937   257
  Freedom Through Art: A Review of Negro Art, 1870–1938   267
  The Negro: "New" or Newer: A Retrospective Review of the Literature of the
      Negro for 1938   271
  Dry Fields and Green Pastures   285
  Of Native Sons: Real and Otherwise   299
  Who and What Is "Negro"?   309
  Reason and Race: A Review of the Literature of the Negro for 1946   319
  A Critical Retrospect of the Literature of the Negro for 1947   329
  Dawn Patrol: A Review of the Literature of the Negro for 1948   337

Wisdom *de Profundis*: The Literature of the Negro, 1949   351
Inventory at Mid-Century: A Review of the Literature of the Negro for 1950   363
The High Price of Integration: A Review of the Literature of the Negro for 1951   375
From *Native Son* to *Invisible Man*: A Review of the Literature
    of the Negro for 1952   385

RACE AND CULTURE

Editor's Note   397

The American Temperament   399
Race Contacts and Inter-Racial Relations   407
The Ethics of Culture   415
The Concept of Race as Applied to Social Culture   423
American Literary Tradition and the Negro   433
The Negro's Contribution to American Art and Literature   439
The Negro's Contribution to American Culture   451
The Negro in the Three Americas   459
The Negro in the Arts   471

Endnotes to Editorial Notes   477
Further Reading   481
Index   483

ACKNOWLEDGMENTS

Thanks are due and acknowledgments made to the following people, publishers, and institutions for their permission to reprint copyrighted material in this anthology.

The Albany Institute of Art and History for "Up Till Now," the introduction to *The Negro Artist Comes of Age*, Albany Institute of History and Art, January 3–February 11, 1945. Exhibition and accompanying catalogue.

The Baltimore Museum of Art for "Foreword," *Contemporary Negro Art*, Baltimore Museum of Art, February 3–19, 1939. Exhibition and accompanying catalogue.

The Barnes Foundation, Merion, Pennsylvania, for photographs of art in "The Art of the Ancestors," *Survey Graphic* 53 (March 1, 1925): 673; and "A Note on African Art," *Opportunity* 2 (May 1924): 136–137.

Mr. Richmond Barthé for photographs of his sculpture.

Mrs. Anna Jones Bernard, White Plains, New York, for the photographic reprint of Winold Reiss's portrait, "A Woman Lawyer."

Mr. Arnold Braithwaite for "The Negro Poets of the United States" in *Anthology of Magazine Verse 1926 and Yearbook of American Poetry*. Edited by William S. Braithwaite. (Sesquicentennial Edition.) Boston: B.J. Brimmer Co., 1926, pp. 143–151.

Dr. Arthur Huff Fauset for "Spirituals." Comments by Dr. Alain Locke accompanying the program of spirituals on Friday evening, December 20, 1940, presented by the Library of Congress in commemoration of the 75th Anniversary of the 13th Amendment to the Constitution of the United States.

Mr. Elton Clay Fax for "Self-Portrait," a drawing first published in "Advance on the Art Front" in *Opportunity* (May 1939).

The *Journal of Negro Education* for "The Negro's Contribution to American Culture," 8 (July 1939): 521–529; "The Negro in the Three Americas," 13 (Winter 1944): 7–18.

The Moorland–Spingarn Research Center, Howard University, for "Beauty and the Provinces," *The Stylus* (June 1929): 3–4; "The Concept of Race as Applied to Social Culture," *The Howard Review* 1 (June 1924): 290–299; "The Ethics of Culture," *Howard University Record* 17 (January 1923): 178–185; and miscellaneous photographs and playbills from the Alain Locke Papers and Photograph Collections of the Research Center.

The Museum of Art and Archaeology, University of Missouri–Columbia. Reprints of Winold Reiss's drawings, "Harlem Boy" and "Harlem Girl." Gift of Mr. W. Tjark Reiss.

National Museum of American Art (formerly the National Collection of Fine Arts), Smithsonian Institution, for the photographic reprint of Malvin Gray Johnson's "Self-Portrait." Gift of the Harmon Foundation.

National Portrait Gallery, Smithsonian Institution, Washington, D.C., for photographic reprints of Winold Reiss's portraits of Roland Hayes and Paul Robeson.

The National Urban League for the following articles which first appeared in *Opportunity*: "*Color*—A Review," *Goat Alley*, "Max Rheinhardt Reads the Negro's Dramatic Horoscope," "Roland Hayes: An Appreciation." "The Technical Study of the Spirituals—A Review," "Toward a Critique of Negro Music," "Negro Music Goes to Par," "A Note on African Art," "To Certain of Our Philistines," "The Art of Auguste Mambour," "More of the Negro in Art," "1928: A Retrospective Review," "This Year of Grace: Outstanding Books of the Year in Negro Literature," "We Turn to Prose: A Retrospective Review of the Literature of the Negro for 1931," "Black Truth and Black Beauty: A Retrospective Review of the Literature of the Negro for 1932," "The Saving Grace of Realism: Retrospective Review of the Negro Literature of 1933," "The Eleventh Hour of Nordicism: Retrospective Review of the Literature of the Negro for 1934," "Deep River: Deeper Sea: Retrospective Review of the Literature of the Negro for 1935," "God Save Reality! Retrospective Review of the Literature of the Negro: 1936," "Jingo, Counter-Jingo and Us: Retrospective Review of the Literature of the Negro: 1937," "The Negro: 'New' Or Newer: A Retrospective Review of the Literature of the Negro for 1938" "Dry Fields and Green Pastures," "Of Native Sons: Real and Otherwise," "Who and What Is 'Negro'?" These are reprinted with the permission of the National Urban League.

Phylon and Atlanta University for the following articles which first appeared in *Phylon*: "Reason and Race: A Review of the Literature of the Negro for 1946," "A Critical Retrospect of the Literature of the Negro for 1947," "Dawn Patrol: A Review of the Literature of the Negro for 1948," "Wisdom *de Profundis*: The Literature of the Negro, 1949," "Inventory at Mid-Century: A Review of the Literature of the Negro for 1950," "The High Price of Integration: A Review of the Literature of the Negro for 1951," "From *Native Son* to *Invisible Man*: A Review of the Literature of the Negro for 1952." These are reprinted through the courtesy of *Phylon* and Atlanta University.

Mr. W. Tjark Reiss for photographic reprints of Winold Reiss's portraits, "The Poetess," "Mother and Child," "Two Harlem Girls," and "A College Lad."

Mr. James Lesesne Wells for the photographic reprint of "The Wanderers."

PERSONAL ACKNOWLEDGMENTS

I wish to thank the following people who contributed to this volume. In 1976, Henry Louis Gates, Jr., suggested I begin collecting materials for this volume, which he and Paul Wright successfully lobbied for at Garland Publishing. Marie Ellen Lacarda brought the project to conclusion, along with Julia Johnson, Ralph Carlson, and Rita Quintas of Garland. Russell Miller supported my request for research funds from Tufts University, which allowed further collection of materials. Lorn Foster encouraged me to apply for the National Research Council–Ford Foundation fellowship, which enabled me to complete the project.

The staff of the Moorland–Spingarn Research Center at Howard University was exceedingly helpful. The director, Michael R. Winston, helped secure permission to reprint articles from Howard University publications and provided numerous helpful comments. The curator, Thomas C. Battle, allowed last-minute photocopying from the Alain Locke Papers. William J. Scott produced remarkable reproductions from aging photographs and gave much needed advice and support. Esme Bhan provided encouragement, guidance in the Locke Papers, and wise counsel. Marcia Battle Bracey tracked down innumerable photographs. Deborra Richardson read Locke's music criticism and offered useful information, while Paul Coates gave sound editorial advice. Alex T. Rapheal III did a superb job of photocopying articles and essays.

Thanks are also due the following persons: Richmond Barthé for his encouragement; John W. Blassingame for his support; Ellen Cummings for her suggestions, typing, and contributions beyond the call of duty; Carl Faber for comments on early drafts of the Contemporary Negro Art section; Lucinda Gedeon for information on black artists; Jacqueline Goggin for reading and commenting on early drafts of the Contemporary Negro Art section; Shane Gregory for secretarial assistance and suggestions about the design of the volume; Helen A. Harrison for information on the 1939 New York World's Fair; David Levering Lewis for reading the draft of the entire manuscript and several helpful comments; Michelle Pacifico for references to the New Negro Alliance; Richard Powell for comments on the visual arts; E. Curmie Price for many helpful ideas and references; W. Tjark Reiss for assistance in locating photographs of Winold Reiss's work; Roy Rosenzweig for reading early drafts, comments on the introduction, and last-minute references; Fath Davis Ruffins for reading and commenting on the first and the last drafts of the introduction; Anthony Ruiz for goading; Ladislas Segy for his interpretation of African art and its significance for Alain Locke; John Edgar Tidwell for many suggestions and helpful leads; and John S. Wright for arguing vigorously for Locke's changing views of art in the 1930s, and for his good humor.

Special thanks, however, are due Lawrence Lee Jones, whose editorial guidance, suggestions on the design of the volume, and unflagging support made this volume possible.

ILLUSTRATIONS

1.	Alain Locke	frontispiece
2.	Roland Hayes by Winold Reiss	4
3.	Young Africa by Walter Von Ruckteschell	11
4.	Paul Robeson by Winold Reiss	12
5.	Yoruba	15
6.	Dahomey (Bronze)	15
7.	Soudan-Niger	15
8.	Baoulé	15
9.	Harlem Girl by Winold Reiss	17
10.	Mother and Child by Winold Reiss	18
11.	The Poetess by Winold Reiss	18
12.	Harlem Boy by Winold Reiss	19
13.	A Woman Lawyer by Winold Reiss	19
14.	Two Harlem Girls by Winold Reiss	19
15.	A College Lad by Winold Reiss	20
16.	Cast list of the Howard Players, with Charles S. Gilpin	70
17.	Emperor Jones by Aaron Douglas	83
18.	Brutus Jones by Aaron Douglas	84
19.	Playbill of *Native Son* by Paul Green and Richard Wright	92
20.	Birth of the Spirituals by Richmond Barthé	102
21.	Zouenouia—13th Century	133
22.	Modigliani—stone	134
23.	Bakuba Ointment Box	139
24.	Throne-Stool (Primitive Kasai)	140
25.	Bapende Mask	141
26.	Throne-Stool (Primitive Badjok)	141
27.	A Kasai Dance Mask Belgian Congo	142
28.	Bakuba Ceremonial Cup (#1 of 2)	144
29.	Bakuba Ceremonial Cup (#2 of 2)	144
30.	Bakuba Sword	145
31.	Plain Pattern Cups	146
32.	Kasai Fetish (Slave Carrying Chief)	147
33.	Fetish Statuette (Primitive Kasai)	147
34.	Carved Buffalo Drinking Horn (Bakuba)	148
35.	Figure of Man, Baoulé, Ivory Coast	150
36.	Relief with Hunter, Benin, British Nigeria	151
37.	Terracotta Head, Yoruba, British Nigeria (plaster cast)	151
38.	Man's Head, Benin, British Nigeria	152
39.	Figure of Young Woman, Pahouin, Border of Spanish Guinea	152

40. Head Rest, Urua, Belgian Congo   153
41. Mask, Grassland Bamendjo, Cameroon   154
42. Four-faced Mask, Mpongwe, French Congo   154
43. Fetish with Calabash and Shells, Urua Belgian Congo   155
44. Two Public School Teachers by Winold Reiss   160
45. From a painting by Auguste Mambour   164
46. The Old Servant by Edwin A. Harleston   170
47. Self-Portrait by Lillian Dorsey   172
48. Meditation by Malvin Gray Johnson   173
49. Old Snuff-Dipper by Archibald T. Motley   174
50. Sonny by William H. Johnson   174
51. Landscape by Hale Woodruff   175
52. The Wanderers by James Lesesne Wells   175
53. Mother and Daughter by Laura Wheeler Waring   176
54. Chester by Sargent Johnson   178
55. Mask of Boy by Richmond Barthé   178
56. The Breakaway by Richmond Barthé   178
57. West Indian Girl by Richmond Barthé   178
58. The Mother by Richmond Barthé   185
59. Self-Portrait by Malvin Gray Johnson   187
60. A Seated Figure by Ronald Moody   187
61. Self-Portrait by Elton Clay Fax   188
62. Blanche by Richmond Barthé, and Mr. Barthé   189
63. From the book jacket of Slaves Today   211
64. From the book jacket of God Sends Sunday   212

INTRODUCTION

Critic, educator, philosopher, Dr. Alain LeRoy Locke (1885–1954) was a major interpreter of Afro-American culture from the 1920s to the 1950s. Through his anthologies, essays, introductions, and his activities as a promoter, patron, and publisher, Locke gave depth and coherence to the study of black culture in the twentieth century. Known primarily for his role in the Negro Renaissance, a black literary and visual arts movement of the 1920s, Locke gave black art its "critical temper" by correlating the artistic and creative possibilities of the black experience with its social and political realities.

When *The New Negro* was published in 1925, Locke gained national prominence as both the editor and a contributor to this collection of essays, poems, short fiction, and artwork on contemporary urban black life. His essays stated dramatically the ideals of the Renaissance, which he defined as an artistic awakening of racial self-consciousness and a collective self-renewal for black people. He introduced the work of Langston Hughes, Countee Cullen, Claude McKay, Jean Toomer, Paul Robeson, Zora Neale Hurston, and Aaron Douglas to a national audience as evidence of the "New Negro"—Locke's term for a generation of young black writers and artists whose creative vitality promised to bring a new appreciation of Afro-American contributions to American culture.

Yet when *The New Negro* was republished in 1968, few of the new generation of young blacks knew of the small, refined black philosopher, who after editing this volume had produced numerous articles, anthologies, and speeches documenting the African presence in the world. When readers searched for more of his work, they found it scattered among a variety of journals, magazines, and collections, a testament to his effectiveness as a publicist but a hindrance to easy access to his thought. A pressing need arose for a collection of Locke's published writings both before and after *The New Negro*. This volume is a response to that need.

A more important goal of this collection is to record the development of his theory of art and culture and his notion of art as an alternative political strategy. Locke felt the purpose of culture and art was to educate and thus redefine the meaning of blackness in Western society. He believed that not only is our sense of beauty learned from our culture but our ideas about race are, too.

The point of a black arts movement was to provide society with a new view of blackness through Afro-American art and culture and thus mitigate racism. Racism was learned, and therefore could be unlearned, instead of perpetuated by culture. New social conditions could produce a "New Negro" who looked at himself or herself differently through art and culture.

Locke shared the faith of early twentieth-century black American intellectuals such as Carter G. Woodson, W.E.B. Du Bois, and Charles S. Johnson that through black contributions to history, politics, and sociology, intellectuals could shape the valuation of blacks in American society. Locke's theory of culture is actually the most explicit statement of the intellectual foundations of contemporary Afro-American studies. The difference between Locke and other black intellectuals of the period is that he wrestles with the Afro-American experience as an artistic rather than a political enterprise, and that makes him interesting today.

Locke argued that by turning to art, rather than politics, the discussion of the Afro-American question could be advanced beyond the stalemate of black protest, white backlash, and racial conflict. Locke recognized that Afro-American thought had become stagnant in the aftermath of World War I. Progressivism had lost popular support for social and political reform, while black protest had made race into a permanent obstacle to further dialogue between blacks and whites.

By focusing on art, Locke believed he could substitute a positive for a negative conception of race by drawing attention to past and present Negro contributions to American culture. Just as American literary realists such as Carl Sandburg, Vachel Lindsay, and William Carlos Williams sought to make America more expressive through poetry, Locke believed that a core of talented black writers and artists such as Langston Hughes, Claude McKay, Jean Toomer, Zora Neale Hurston, Aaron Douglas, and Roland Hayes could make the Afro-American experience evocative in a way it could never be as simply a political problem.

This belief became the motive for his advocacy of a Negro Renaissance during the 1920s. Locke announced that a new spirit of humanism, racial consciousness, and artistic freedom was sweeping Afro-American life. Harlem was the intellectual capital of this spiritual emancipation, although after 1925, cities such as Chicago, Philadelphia, Cleveland, and Washington, D.C., experienced their own "renaissances." While Locke credited the black masses with urbanizing the black population, he saw the talented, educated artists of the race as the vanguard of the Renaissance.

Locke began the 1920s with the notion that only elite artists could make the kind of liberating art he wished produced; toward the end of the 1920s, he became more aware of, and sympathetic to, the "folk art" of the people. As his taste for the decadent, decorative art of the Harlem school began to wane, he predicted that a more naturalistic art rooted in the folk culture of the masses would follow.

His prediction came true in the 1930s. Beginning with southern realism in the early thirties and culminating in the "proletarian art" toward the end of the decade, Afro-American art bloomed anew in the work of a new half-generation of writers such as Sterling Brown, Richard Wright, and Frank Marshall Davis. Moreover, black music, drama, and visual arts achieved in the thirties the productivity which Locke had promised in the 1920s.

Locke's critical views changed over the years as well. No longer shackled with establishing the legitimacy of Afro-American art, in the 1930s Locke became a surer, bolder, and more controversial critic. Less tolerant of gradualism by the late 1930s, he embraced the militant protest art of the Popular Front Era, emphasizing that art should be a tool of liberation for all the people, not a divertissement for the elite.

With the post–World War II crusade against segregation, Locke saw a renewed role for art to condition Americans against intolerance and racism. While gratified by the emergence of such writers as Myron O'Higgins, Ann Petry, James Baldwin, and Ralph Ellison, Locke also heralded the work of South African Alan Paton and the Haitian writer, Willard Motley, as evidence that black art, now soundly democratic, must become international.

Some critics may charge that Locke changed his views to fit the political fashion. I believe that rather than adopting the beliefs of his times, Locke adapted his theory to the changing political and intellectual climate. As a historical critic, Locke conceived of Afro-American art and culture as passing through tightly organized phases in an on-going, evolutionary process. His conception of an eternally changing culture allowed Locke to change his own views, and yet maintain the core of his theory that art and culture could condition Americans against racism.

While Locke's views changed over time—and the reader should be aware of that—even more important are the continuities and tensions in his thought. Throughout his career, a tension in his views on art remains between his desire to create a popular, usable art for all the people, and his own grounding in a European high art for the elite. As the son of one of the educated black middle-class families of Philadelphia, Locke had imbibed an aesthetic and Edwardian culture by attending Harvard, Oxford, and the University of Berlin shortly after the turn of the century. Locke never lost his love for European art forms, and despite his appreciation of black folk culture, he persisted in his belief that Afro-American folk forms could be transformed into high art.

Tensions remain in Locke's views of culture as well. As a cultural pluralist, Locke was committed to the notions of the equality of all cultures and the right of all peoples to maintain their own values, lifestyles, and heritage. Yet Locke was not able to eliminate completely the notion of qualitatively ranked cultures from his thought. His appreciation for certain forms of black folk culture, such as the spirituals, rested on his belief that aspects of Afro-American folk culture were superior to white American culture.

Moreover, Locke never defined precisely the relationship of Afro-American culture to the larger American whole. At times he spoke of black culture as if it were a separate entity in American life with strong African antecedents. At other times, he portrayed black American culture as merely an idiomatic strain of an integrated American culture. Thus, while he worked to establish a black intellectual and cultural tradition, he also saw the fulfillment of that task in the eventual integration of black art into the mainstream of American art.

Yet such tensions in Locke's thought make him interesting today. Locke is the quintessential intellectual, who plays with ideas, is able to entertain contrasting views of the situation, and seems caught between assimilation and racialism, integration and nationalism, elitism and populism in a way that both reflects and engages the problem in a refreshing way. What Locke has to say about the relation of subcultures to dominant cultures, the social uses of art, and the problem of alienation for the black artist and intellectual are relevant today because as a nation we remain ambivalent about these questions.

Alain Locke tempered these tensions with a commitment to finding in art and culture a political strategy to combat racism and its negative effects. Locke believed that both whites *and* blacks need an art which will liberate them from the brainwashing of American racism. By moving the discussion of blacks from the periphery to the center of the cultural debate over what is an American, Locke worked to convince white Americans of the humanity of blacks at a time when that was seriously questioned. Without sacrificing his belief that all art should be beautiful, Locke encouraged artists to forge an art which both reflects and redefines what it means to be Afro-American. Locke never backed away from his belief that art and culture have a powerful role to play in shaping our attitudes towards race in contemporary life. It is this theory which makes him an important thinker today.

I have organized this collection topically to provide easy access to Locke's views. The essays in each section are arranged chronologically and are preceded by editorial notes which contain biographical information on Alain Locke. The spellings and citations for most of the captions for the illustrations from the original articles, though out of date, have been retained for insight into Locke's perspective on African and Afro-American art.

The first section, Renaissance Apologetics, presents Locke's writings inaugurating his racial program in art. As this developed at a different pace in each field, the next five sections, Poetry, Drama, Music, African Art, and Contemporary Negro Art, present a representative selection of Locke's published writings on these subjects.

The next section, Retrospective Reviews, reproduces the entire body of Locke's annual reviews of Afro-American creative and sociological literature. Beginning in 1929 and ending in 1953, these reviews show Locke's changing views over time. The last section, Race and Culture, provides a selection of his more scholarly essays on the cultural underpinning of his writings on art. In this section, the reader will find evidence of how Locke revised his portrait of Afro-American culture throughout his career.

I hope this collection of Locke's essential writings will spark a reevaluation of him as a thinker. Perhaps it will also stimulate a new generation to create its own renaissance. For as Locke wrote in his introduction to *Four Negro Poets*, "To [Jean] Toomer, slavery, once a shame and stigma, becomes a spiritual growth and transfiguration, and the torturous underground groping of one generation the maturing and high blossoming of the next."

RENAISSANCE
APOLOGETICS

Alain Locke was born in Philadelphia on September 13, 1885.[1] He excelled as a student, entering Harvard College in 1904 during its "Golden Age." Locke was exposed to teachers like Barrett Wendell, who stressed the importance of national tradition in literature, and classmates like Van Wyck Brooks, who was envisioning an American renaissance of letters. Graduating from Harvard with an A.B. in English and Philosophy in 1907, Locke went to Oxford as the first black American Rhodes Scholar. After further graduate study at the University of Berlin, Locke returned to the United States, and in 1912 began teaching at Howard University in Washington, D.C. Although Locke became a Professor of Philosophy, he remained interested in the arts. When a group of young black writers emerged in the Northeast during the 1920s, Locke found an opportunity to promote a renaissance of Afro-American letters.[2]

In 1924, Paul Kellogg, editor of *Survey Graphic*, a prominent journal of social reform, asked Locke to contribute a series of essays to a special issue devoted to the new writers. Locke was also responsible for selecting a collection of black poetry, short fiction, essays, and visual arts for this number, entitled "Harlem: Mecca of the New Negro." The first five essays presented here appeared in this special edition of March 1, 1925.[3]

In the first essay, "Harlem," Locke revives the term "renaissance," which W.E.B. Du Bois, the black editor of *The Crisis*, the journal of the National Association for the Advancement of Colored People, used in 1920 in connection with black literature.[4] Locke takes the notion of a black renaissance a step further in "Harlem" by relating black art to social change in the black community. The most visible social change for blacks, according to Locke, is the "Great Migration" from South to North, or as Locke puts it, "from medieval America to modern."

Blacks are searching for a new vision of the black experience, Locke argues in the next essay, "Enter the New Negro." Black intellectuals were rejecting outworn strategies of accommodation and protest, thereby "achieving something like a spiritual emancipation." The younger writers, he argues in "Youth Speaks," communicate this new intellectual mood, which, Locke hopes in "The Art of the Ancestors" will provoke an artistic exploration of the past. With the photo essay "Harlem Types," Locke lets the black experience speak directly to his audience.

I have titled this section "Renaissance Apologetics" because the essays answered criticism of the movement by both whites and blacks in the 1920s. Six months after the appearance of the Harlem number of the *Survey Graphic*, Locke published *The New Negro*, an expanded book version of the periodical anthology. *The New Negro* was well received within the reform movement, as might be expected, but outside reaction was mixed. One white critic, Ernest Boyd, wrote, "as a revelation of a great renaissance of Negro art and literature it [*The New Negro*] is no more convincing than the momentary vogue of the 'Charleston.'"[5] In answer to Boyd and other white critics, Locke wrote "Our Little Renaissance" in 1927.

Immediate black response was generally favorable, but by 1928, even former allies such as Du Bois and the NAACP became critical. Du Bois charged that art should be propaganda first, and beauty second. Allison Davis, writing in *The Crisis*, criticized the Harlem writers for representing "the Negro as essentially bestialized by jazz and the cabaret." Davis contended that some of the Harlem writers were exploiting decadence to reap profits from the vogue in "things Negro." A deeper concern was that realistic portraits of lower class Negro life would be damaging to the Negro image.[6]

Locke counters these charges with "Beauty Instead of Ashes," his best defense of the writers; "Art or Propaganda?" is his best defense of art as an alternative to protest. To charges that Harlem received too much attention as the hub of black creativity, he responded with "Beauty and the Provinces" in 1929.

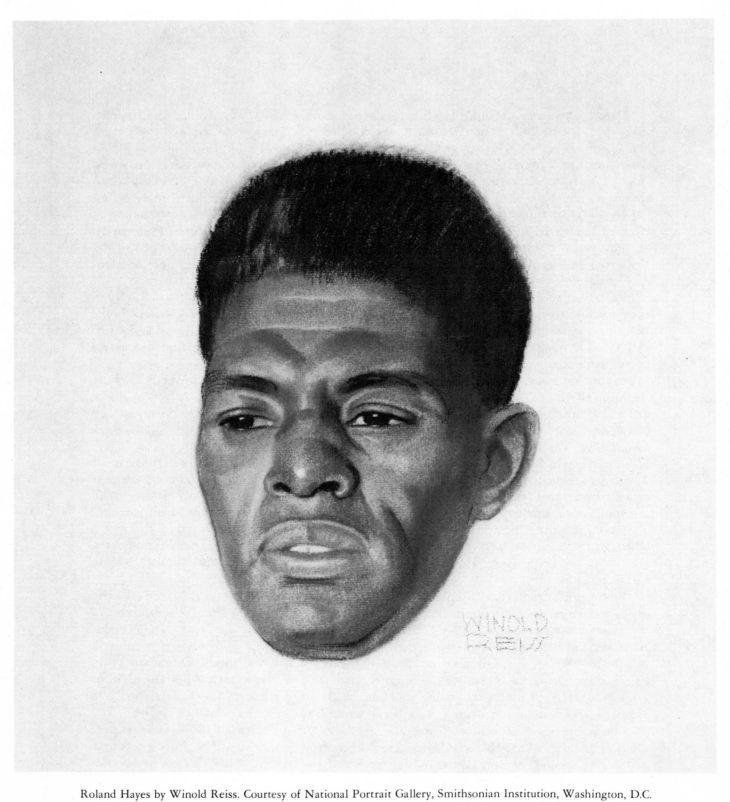

Roland Hayes by Winold Reiss. Courtesy of National Portrait Gallery, Smithsonian Institution, Washington, D.C.

HARLEM

IF we were to offer a symbol of what Harlem has come to mean in the short span of twenty years it would be another statue of liberty on the landward side of New York. It stands for a folk-movement which in human significance can be compared only with the pushing back of the western frontier in the first half of the last century, or the waves of immigration which have swept in from overseas in the last half. Numerically far smaller than either of these movements, the volume of migration is such none the less that Harlem has become the greatest Negro community the world has known—without counterpart in the South or in Africa. But beyond this, Harlem represents the Negro's latest thrust towards Democracy.

The special significance that today stamps it as the sign and center of the renaissance of a people lies, however, layers deep under the Harlem that many know but few have begun to understand. Physically Harlem is little more than a note of sharper color in the kaleidoscope of New York. The metropolis pays little heed to the shifting crystallizations of its own heterogeneous millions. Never having experienced permanence, it has watched, without emotion or even curiosity, Irish, Jew, Italian, Negro, a score of other races drift in and out of the same colorless tenements.

So Harlem has come into being and grasped its destiny with little heed from New York. And to the herded thousands who shoot beneath it twice a day on the subway, or the comparatively few whose daily travel takes them within sight of its fringes or down its main arteries, it is a black belt and nothing more. The pattern of delicatessen store and cigar shop and restaurant and undertaker's shop which repeats itself a thousand times on each of New York's long avenues is unbroken through Harlem. Its apartments, churches and storefronts antedated the Negroes and, for all New York knows, may outlast them there. For most of New York, Harlem is merely a rough rectangle of commonplace city blocks, lying between and to east and west of Lenox and Seventh Avenues, stretching nearly a mile north and south—and unaccountably full of Negroes.

Another Harlem is savored by the few—a Harlem of racy music and racier dancing, of cabarets famous or notorious according to their kind, of amusement in which abandon and sophistication are cheek by jowl—a Harlem which draws the connoisseur in diversion as well as the undiscriminating sightseer. This Harlem is the fertile source of the "shufflin'" and "rollin'" and "runnin' wild" revues that establish themselves season after season in "downtown" theaters. It is part of the exotic fringe of the metropolis.

Beneath this lies again the Harlem of the newspapers—a Harlem of monster parades and political flummery, a Harlem swept by revolutionary oratory or draped about the mysterious figures of Negro "millionaires," a Harlem preoccupied with naive adjustments to a white world—a Harlem, in short, grotesque with the distortions of journalism.

YET in final analysis, Harlem is neither slum, ghetto, resort or colony, though it is in part all of them. It is—or promises at least to be—a race capital. Europe seething in a dozen centers with emergent nationalities, Palestine full of a renascent Judaism—these are no more alive with the spirit of a racial awakening than Harlem; culturally and spiritually it focuses a people. Negro life is not only founding new centers, but finding a new soul. The tide of Negro migration, northward and city-ward, is not to be fully explained as a blind flood started by the demands of war industry coupled with the shutting off of foreign migration, or by the pressure of poor crops coupled with increased social terrorism in certain sections of the South and Southwest. Neither labor demand, the boll-weevil nor the Ku Klux Klan is a basic factor, however contributory any or all of them may have been. The wash and rush of this human tide on the beach line of the northern city centers is to be explained primarily in terms of a new vision of opportunity, of social and economic freedom, of a spirit to seize, even in the face of an extortionate and heavy toll, a chance for the improvement of conditions. With each successive wave of it, the movement of the Negro migrant becomes more and more like that of the European waves at their crests, a mass movement toward the larger and the more democratic chance—in the Negro's case a deliberate flight not only from countryside to city, but from mediaeval America to modern.

The secret lies close to what distinguishes Harlem from the ghettos with which it is sometimes compared. The ghetto picture is that of a slowly dissolving mass, bound by ties of custom and culture and association, in the midst of a freer and more varied society. From the racial stand-

Survey Graphic 53, no. 11 (March 1, 1925): 629–630.

point, our Harlems are themselves crucibles. Here in Manhattan is not merely the largest Negro community in the world, but the first concentration in history of so many diverse elements of Negro life. It has attracted the African, the West Indian, the Negro American; has brought together the Negro of the North and the Negro of the South; the man from the city and the man from the town and village; the peasant, the student, the business man, the professional man, artist, poet, musician, adventurer and worker, preacher and criminal, exploiter and social outcast. Each group has come with its own separate motives and for its own special ends, but their greatest experience has been the finding of one another. Proscription and prejudice have thrown these dissimilar elements into a common area of contact and interaction. Within this area, race sympathy and unity have determined a further fusing of sentiment and experience. So what began in terms of segregation becomes more and more, as its elements mix and react, the laboratory of a great race-welding. Hitherto, it must be admitted that American Negroes have been a race more in name than in fact, or to be exact, more in sentiment than in experience. The chief bond between them has been that of a common condition rather than a common consciousness; a problem in common rather than a life in common. In Harlem, Negro life is seizing upon its first chances for group expression and self-determination. That is why our comparison is taken with those nascent centers of folk-expression and self-determination which are playing a creative part in the world today. Without pretense to their political significance, Harlem has the same role to play for the New Negro as Dublin has had for the New Ireland or Prague for the New Czechoslovakia.

It is true the formidable centers of our race life, educational, industrial, financial, are not in Harlem, yet here, nevertheless, are the forces that make a group known and felt in the world. The reformers, the fighting advocates, the inner spokesmen, the poets, artists and social prophets are here, and pouring in toward them are the fluid ambitious youth and pressing in upon them the migrant masses. The professional observers, and the enveloping communities as well, are conscious of the physics of this stir and movement, of the cruder and more obvious facts of a ferment and a migration. But they are as yet largely unaware of the psychology of it, of the galvanizing shocks and reactions, which mark the social awakening and internal reorganization which are making a race out of its own disunited elements.

A railroad ticket and a suitcase, like a Bagdad carpet, transport the Negro peasant from the cotton-field and farm to the heart of the most complex urban civilization. Here, in the mass, he must and does survive a jump of two generations in social economy and of a century and more in civilization. Meanwhile the Negro poet, student, artist, thinker, by the very move that normally would take him off at a tangent from the masses, finds himself in their midst, in a situation concentrating the racial side of his experience and heightening his race-consciousness. These moving, half-awakened newcomers provide an exceptional seed-bed for the germinating contacts of the enlightened minority. And that is why statistics are out of joint with fact in Harlem, and will be for a generation or so.

HARLEM, I grant you, isn't typical—but it is significant, it is prophetic. No sane observer, however sympathetic to the new trend, would contend that the great masses are articulate as yet, but they stir, they move, they are more than physically restless. The challenge of the new intellectuals among them is clear enough—the "race radicals" and realists who have broken with the old epoch of philanthropic guidance, sentimental appeal and protest. But are we after all only reading into the stirrings of a sleeping giant the dreams of an agitator? The answer is in the migrating peasant. It is the "man farthest down" who is most active in getting up. One of the most characteristic symptoms of this is the professional man himself migrating to recapture his constituency after a vain effort to maintain in some Southern corner what for years back seemed an established living and clientele. The clergyman following his errant flock, the physician or lawyer trailing his clients, supply the true clues. In a real sense it is the rank and file who are leading, and the leaders who are following. A transformed and transforming psychology permeates the masses.

When the racial leaders of twenty years ago spoke of developing race-pride and stimulating race-consciousness, and of the desirability of race solidarity, they could not in any accurate degree have anticipated the abrupt feeling that has surged up and now pervades the awakened centers. Some of the recognized Negro leaders and a powerful section of white opinion identified with "race work" of the older order have indeed attempted to discount this feeling as a "passing phase," an attack of "race nerves," so to speak, an "aftermath of the war," and the like. It has not abated, however, if we are to gage by the present tone and temper of the Negro press, or by the shift in popular support from the officially recognized and orthodox spokesmen to those of the independent, popular, and often radical type who are unmistakable symptoms of a new order. It is a social disservice to blunt the fact that the Negro of the Northern centers has reached a stage where tutelage, even of the most interested and well-intentioned sort, must give place to new relationships, where positive self-direction must be reckoned with in ever increasing measure.

As a service to this new understanding, the contributors to this Harlem number have been asked, not merely to describe Harlem as a city of migrants and as a race center, but to voice these new aspirations of a people, to read the clear message of the new conditions, and to discuss some of the new relationships and contacts they involve. First, we shall look at Harlem, with its kindred centers in the Northern and Mid-Western cities, as the way mark of a momentous folk movement; then as the center of a gripping struggle for an industrial and urban foothold. But more significant than either of these, we shall also view it as the stage of the pageant of contemporary Negro life. In the drama of its new and progressive aspects, we may be witnessing the resurgence of a race; with our eyes focussed on the Harlem scene we may dramatically glimpse the New Negro.

ENTER THE NEW NEGRO

IN the last decade something beyond the watch and guard of statistics has happened in the life of the American Negro and the three norns who have traditionally presided over the Negro problem have a changeling in their laps. The Sociologist, The Philanthropist, the Race-leader are not unaware of the New Negro, but they are at a loss to account for him. He simply cannot be swathed in their formulae. For the younger generation is vibrant with a new psychology; the new spirit is awake in the masses, and under the very eyes of the professional observers is transforming what has been a perennial problem into the progressive phases of contemporary Negro life.

Could such a metamorphosis have taken place as suddenly as it has appeared to? The answer is no; not because the New Negro is not here, but because the Old Negro had long become more of a myth than a man. The Old Negro, we must remember, was a creature of moral debate and historical controversy. His has been a stock figure perpetuated as an historical fiction partly in innocent sentimentalism, partly in deliberate reactionism. The Negro himself has contributed his share to this through a sort of protective social mimicry forced upon him by the adverse circumstances of dependence. So for generations in the mind of America, the Negro has been more of a formula than a human being —a something to be argued about, condemned or defended, to be "kept down," or "in his place," or "helped up," to be worried with or worried over, harassed or patronized, a social bogey or a social burden. The thinking Negro even has been induced to share this same general attitude, to focus his attention on controversial issues, to see himself in the distorted perspective of a social problem. His shadow, so to speak, has been more real to him than his personality. Through having had to appeal from the unjust stereotypes of his oppressors and traducers to those of his liberators, friends and benefactors he has subscribed to the traditional positions from which his case has been viewed. Little true social or self-understanding has or could come from such a situation.

But while the minds of most of us, black and white, have thus burrowed in the trenches of the Civil War and Reconstruction, the actual march of development has simply flanked these positions, necessitating a sudden reorientation of view. We have not been watching in the right direction; set North and South on a sectional axis, we have not noticed the East till the sun has us blinking.

Recall how suddenly the Negro spirituals revealed themselves; suppressed for generations under the stereotypes of Wesleyan hymn harmony, secretive, half-ashamed, until the courage of being natural brought them out—and behold, there was folk-music. Similarly the mind of the Negro seems suddenly to have slipped from under the tyranny of social intimidation and to be shaking off the psychology of imitation and implied inferiority. By shedding the old chrysalis of the Negro problem we are achieving something like a spiritual emancipation. Until recently, lacking self-understanding, we have been almost as much of a problem to ourselves as we still are to others. But the decade that found us with a problem has left us with only a task. The multitude perhaps feels as yet only a strange relief and a new vague urge, but the thinking few know that in the reaction the vital inner grip of prejudice has been broken.

With this renewed self-respect and self-dependence, the life of the Negro community is bound to enter a new dynamic phase, the buoyancy from within compensating for whatever pressure there may be of conditions from without. The migrant masses, shifting from countryside to city, hurdle several generations of experience at a leap, but more important, the same thing happens spiritually in the life-attitudes and self-expression of the Young Negro, in his poetry, his art, his education and his new outlook, with the additional advantage, of course, of the poise and greater certainty of knowing what it is all about. From this comes the promise and warrant of a new leadership. As one of them

Survey Graphic 53, no. 11 (March 1, 1925): 631–634.

has discerningly put it:

We have tomorrow
Bright before us
Like a flame.

Yesterday, a night-gone thing
A sun-down name.

And dawn today
Broad arch above the road we came.
We march!

This is what, even more than any "most creditable record of fifty years of freedom," requires that the Negro of today be seen through other than the dusty spectacles of past controversy. The day of "aunties," "uncles" and "mammies" is equally gone. Uncle Tom and Sambo have passed on, and even the "Colonel" and "George" play barnstorm roles from which they escape with relief when the public spotlight is off. The popular melodrama has about played itself out, and it is time to scrap the fictions, garret the bogeys and settle down to a realistic facing of facts.

FIRST we must observe some of the changes which since the traditional lines of opinion were drawn have rendered these quite obsolete. A main change has been, of course, that shifting of the Negro population which has made the Negro problem no longer exclusively or even predominantly Southern. Why should our minds remain sectionalized, when the problem itself no longer is? Then the trend of migration has not only been toward the North and the Central Midwest, but city-ward and to the great centers of industry—the problems of adjustment are new, practical, local and not peculiarly racial. Rather they are an integral part of the large industrial and social problems of our present-day democracy. And finally, with the Negro rapidly in process of class differentiation, if it ever was warrantable to regard and treat the Negro en masse it is becoming with every day less possible, more unjust and more ridiculous.

The Negro too, for his part, has idols of the tribe to smash. If on the one hand the white man has erred in making the Negro appear to be that which would excuse or extenuate his treatment of him, the Negro, in turn, has too often unnecessarily excused himself because of the way he has been treated. The intelligent Negro of today is resolved not to make discrimination an extenuation for his shortcomings in performance, individual or collective; he is trying to hold himself at par, neither inflated by sentimental allowances nor depreciated by current social discounts. For this he must know himself and be known for precisely what he is, and for that reason he welcomes the new scientific rather than the old sentimental interest. Sentimental interest in the Negro has ebbed. We used to lament this as the falling off of our friends; now we rejoice and pray to be delivered both from self-pity and condescension. The mind of each racial group has had a bitter weaning, apathy or hatred on one side matching disillusionment or resentment on the other; but they face each other today with the possibility at least of entirely new mutual attitudes.

It does not follow that if the Negro were better known, he would be better liked or better treated. But mutual understanding is basic for any subsequent cooperation and adjustment. The effort toward this will at least have the effect of remedying in large part what has been the most unsatisfactory feature of our present stage of race relationships in America, namely the fact that the more intelligent and representative elements of the two race groups have at so many points got quite out of vital touch with one another.

The fiction is that the life of the races is separate, and increasingly so. The fact is that they have touched too closely at the unfavorable and too lightly at the favorable levels.

While inter-racial councils have sprung up in the South, drawing on forward elements of both races, in the Northern cities manual laborers may brush elbows in their everyday work, but the community and business leaders have experienced no such interplay or far too little of it. These segments must achieve contact or the race situation in America becomes desperate. Fortunately this is happening. There is a growing realization that in social effort the cooperative basis must supplant long-distance philanthropy, and that the only safeguard for mass relations in the future must be provided in the carefully maintained contacts of the enlightened minorities of both race groups. In the intellectual realm a renewed and keen curiosity is replacing the recent apathy; the Negro is being carefully studied, not just talked about and discussed. In art and letters, instead of being wholly caricatured, he is being seriously portrayed and painted.

To all of this the New Negro is keenly responsive as an augury of a new democracy in American culture. He is contributing his share to the new social understanding. But the desire to be understood would never in itself have been sufficient to have opened so completely the protectively closed portals of the thinking Negro's mind. There is still too much possibility of being snubbed or patronized for that. It was rather the necessity for fuller, truer, self-expression, the realization of the unwisdom of allowing social discrimination to segregate him mentally, and a counter-attitude to cramp and fetter his own living—and so the "spite-wall" that the intellectuals built over the "color-line" has happily been taken down. Much of this reopening of intellectual contacts has centered in New York and has been richly fruitful not merely in the enlarging of personal experience, but in the definite enrichment of American art and letters and in the clarifying of our common vision of the social tasks ahead.

The particular significance in the reestablishment of contact between the more advanced and representative classes is that it promises to offset some of the unfavorable reactions of the past, or at least to re-surface race contacts somewhat for the future. Subtly the conditions that are moulding a New Negro are moulding a new American attitude.

However, this new phase of things is delicate; it will call for less charity but more justice; less help, but infinitely closer understanding. This is indeed a critical stage of race relationships because of the likelihood, if the new temper is not understood, of engendering sharp group antagonism and a second crop of more calculated prejudice. In some quarters, it has already done so. Having weaned the Negro, public opinion cannot continue to paternalize. The Negro today is inevitably moving forward under the control largely of his own objectives. What are these objectives? Those of his outer life are happily already well and finally formulated, for they are none other than the ideals of American institutions and democracy. Those of his inner life are yet in process of formation, for the new psychology at present is more of a consensus of feeling than of opinion, of attitude rather than of program. Still some points seem to have crystallized.

UP to the present one may adequately describe the Negro's "inner objectives" as an attempt to repair a damaged group psychology and reshape a warped social perspective. Their realization has required a new mentality for the American Negro. And as it matures we begin to see its effects; at first, negative, iconoclastic, and then positive and constructive. In this new group psychology we note the lapse of sentimental appeal, then the development of a more positive self-respect and self-reliance; the repudiation of social dependence, and then the gradual recovery from hyper-sensitiveness and "touchy" nerves, the repudiation of the double standard of judgment with its special philanthropic allowances and then the sturdier desire for objective and scientific appraisal; and finally the rise from social disillusionment to race pride, from the sense of social debt to the responsibilities of social contribution, and offsetting the necessary working and commonsense acceptance of restricted conditions, the belief in ultimate esteem and recognition. Therefore the Negro today wishes to be known for what he is, even in his faults and shortcomings, and scorns a craven and precarious survival at the price of seeming to be what he is not. He resents being spoken for as a social ward or minor, even by his own, and to being regarded a chronic patient for the sociological clinic, the sick man of American Democracy. For the same reasons, he himself is through with those social nostrums and panaceas, the so-called "solutions" of his "problem," with which he and the country have been so liberally dosed in the past. Religion, freedom, education, money—in turn, he has ardently hoped for and peculiarly trusted these things; he still believes in them, but not in blind trust that they alone will solve his life-problem.

Each generation, however, will have its creed and that of the present is the belief in the efficacy of collective effort, in race cooperation. This deep feeling of race is at present the mainspring of Negro life. It seems to be the outcome of the reaction to proscription and prejudice; an attempt, fairly successful on the whole, to convert a defensive into an offensive position, a handicap into an incentive. It is radical in tone, but not in purpose and only the most stupid forms of opposition, misunderstanding or persecution could make it otherwise. Of course, the thinking Negro has shifted a little toward the left with the world-trend, and there is an increasing group who affiliate with radical and liberal movements. But fundamentally for the present the Negro is radical on race matters, conservative on others, in other words, a "forced radical," a social protestant rather than a genuine radical. Yet under further pressure and injustice iconoclastic thought and motives will inevitably increase. Harlem's quixotic radicalisms call for their ounce of democracy today lest tomorrow they be beyond cure.

The Negro mind reaches out as yet to nothing but American wants, American ideas. But this forced attempt to build his Americanism on race values is a unique social experiment, and its ultimate success is impossible except through the fullest sharing of American culture and institutions. There should be no delusion about this. American nerves in sections unstrung with race hysteria are often fed the opiate that the trend of Negro advance is wholly separatist, and that the effect of its operation will be to encyst the Negro as a benign foreign body in the body politic. This cannot be—even if it were desirable. The racialism of the Negro is no limitation or reservation with respect to American life; it is only a constructive effort to build the obstructions in the stream of his progress into an efficient dam of social energy and power. Democracy itself is obstructed and stagnated to the extent that any of its channels are closed. Indeed they cannot be selectively closed. So the choice is not between one way for the Negro and another way for the rest, but between American institutions frustrated on the one hand and American ideals progressively fulfilled and realized on the other.

There is, of course, a warrantably comfortable feeling in being on the right side of the country's professed ideals. We realize that we cannot be undone without America's undoing. It is within the gamut of this attitude that the thinking Negro faces America, but the variations of mood in connection with it are if anything more significant than the attitude itself. Sometimes we have it taken with the defiant ironic challenge of McKay:

> Mine is the future grinding down today
> Like a great landslip moving to the sea,
> Bearing its freight of debris far away
> Where the green hungry waters restlessly
> Heave mammoth pyramids and break and roar
> Their eerie challenge to the crumbling shore.

Sometimes, perhaps more frequently as yet, in the fervent and almost filial appeal and counsel of Weldon Johnson's:

> O Southland, dear Southland!
> Then why do you still cling
> To an idle age and a musty page,
> To a dead and useless thing.

But between defiance and appeal, midway almost between cynicism and hope, the prevailing mind stands in the mood of the same author's To America, an attitude of sober query and stoical challenge:

> How would you have us, as we are?
> Or sinking 'neath the load we bear,
> Our eyes fixed forward on a star,
> Or gazing empty at despair?
>
> Rising or falling? Men or things?
> With dragging pace or footsteps fleet?
> Strong, willing sinews in your wings,
> Or tightening chains about your feet?

More and more, however, an intelligent realization of

the great discrepancy between the American social creed and the American social practice forces upon the Negro the taking of the moral advantage that is his. Only the steadying and sobering effect of a truly characteristic gentleness of spirit prevents the rapid rise of a definite cynicism and counter-hate and a defiant superiority feeling. Human as this reaction would be, the majority still deprecate its advent, and would gladly see it forestalled by the speedy amelioration of its causes. We wish our race pride to be a healthier, more positive achievement than a feeling based upon a realization of the shortcomings of others. But all paths toward the attainment of a sound social attitude have been difficult; only a relatively few enlightened minds have been able as the phrase puts it "to rise above" prejudice. The ordinary man has had until recently only a hard choice between the alternatives of supine and humiliating submission and stimulating but hurtful counter-prejudice. Fortunately from some inner, desperate resourcefulness has recently sprung up the simple expedient of fighting prejudice by mental passive resistance, in other words by trying to ignore it. For the few, this manna may perhaps be effective, but the masses cannot thrive on it.

FORTUNATELY there are constructive channels opening out into which the balked social feelings of the American Negro can flow freely.

Without them there would be much more pressure and danger than there is. These compensating interests are racial but in a new and enlarged way. One is the consciousness of acting as the advance-guard of the African peoples in their contact with Twentieth Century civilization; the other, the sense of a mission of rehabilitating the race in world esteem from that loss of prestige for which the fate and conditions of slavery have so largely been responsible. Harlem, as we shall see, is the center of both these movements; she is the home of the Negro's "Zionism." The pulse of the Negro world has begun to beat in Harlem. A Negro newspaper carrying news material in English, French and Spanish, gathered from all quarters of America, the West Indies and Africa has maintained itself in Harlem for over five years. Two important magazines, both edited from New York, maintain their news and circulation consistently on a cosmopolitan scale. Under American auspices and backing, three pan-African congresses have been held abroad for the discussion of common interests, colonial questions and the future cooperative development of Africa. In terms of the race question as a world problem, the Negro mind has leapt, so to speak, upon the parapets of prejudice and extended its cramped horizons. In so doing it has linked up with the growing group consciousness of the dark-peoples and is gradually learning their common interests. As one of our writers has recently put it: "It is imperative that we understand the white world in its relations to the non-white world." As with the Jew, persecution is making the Negro international.

As a world phenomenon this wider race consciousness is a different thing from the much asserted rising tide of color. Its inevitable causes are not of our making. The conse-

quences are not necessarily damaging to the best interests of civilization. Whether it actually brings into being new Armadas of conflict or argosies of cultural exchange and enlightenment can only be decided by the attitude of the dominant races in an era of critical change. With the American Negro his new internationalism is primarily an effort to recapture contact with the scattered peoples of African derivation. Garveyism may be a transient, if spectacular, phenomenon, but the possible role of the American Negro in the future development of Africa is one of the most constructive and universally helpful missions that any modern people can lay claim to.

Constructive participation in such causes cannot help giving the Negro valuable group incentives, as well as increased prestige at home and abroad. Our greatest rehabilitation may possibly come through such channels, but for the present, more immediate hope rests in the revaluation by white and black alike of the Negro in terms of his artistic endowments and cultural contributions, past and prospective. It must be increasingly recognized that the Negro has already made very substantial contributions, not only in his folk-art, music especially, which has always found appreciation, but in larger, though humbler and less acknowledged ways. For generations the Negro has been the peasant matrix of that section of America which has most undervalued him, and here he has contributed not only materially in labor and in social patience, but spiritually as well. The South has unconsciously absorbed the gift of his folk-temperament. In less than half a generation it will be easier to recognize this, but the fact remains that a leaven of humor, sentiment, imagination and tropic nonchalance has gone into the making of the South from a humble, unacknowledged source. A second crop of the Negro's gifts promises still more largely. He now becomes a conscious contributor and lays aside the status of a beneficiary and ward for that of a collaborator and participant in American civilization. The great social gain in this is the releasing of our talented group from the arid fields of controversy and debate to the productive fields of creative expression. The especially cultural recognition they win should in turn prove the key to that revaluation of the Negro which must precede or accompany any considerable further betterment of race relationships. But whatever the general effect, the present generation will have added the motives of self-expression and spiritual development to the old and still unfinished task of making material headway and progress. No one who understandingly faces the situation with its substantial accomplishment or views the new scene with its still more abundant promise can be entirely without hope. And certainly, if in our lifetime the Negro should not be able to celebrate his full initiation into American democracy, he can at least, on the warrant of these things, celebrate the attainment of a significant and satisfying new phase of group development, and with it a spiritual Coming of Age.

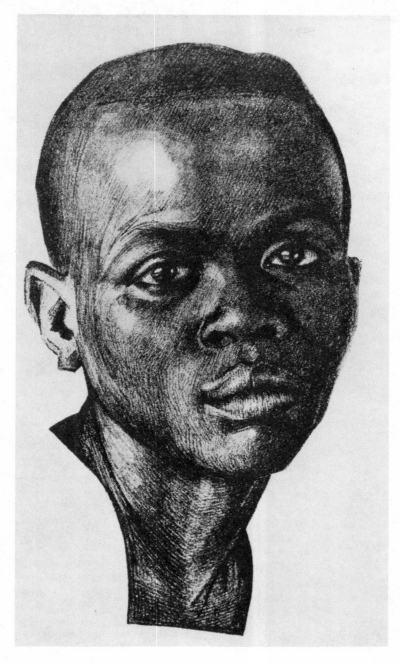

Young Africa. Drawn by Walter Von Ruckteschell. Courtesy of Moorland–Spingarn Research Center, Howard University, Washington, D.C.

Paul Robeson by Winold Reiss. Courtesy of National Portrait Gallery, Smithsonian Institution, Washington, D.C.

YOUTH SPEAKS

WE might know the future but for our chronic tendency to turn to age rather than to youth for the forecast. And when youth speaks, the future listens, however the present may shut its ears. Here we have Negro youth, foretelling in the mirror of art what we must see and recognize in the streets of reality tomorrow.

Primarily, of course, it is youth that speaks in the voice of Negro youth, but the overtones are distinctive; Negro youth speaks out of an unique experience and with a particular representativeness. All classes of a people under social pressure are permeated with a common experience; they are emotionally welded as others cannot be. With them, even ordinary living has epic depth and lyric intensity, and this, their material handicap, is their spiritual advantage. So, in a day when art has run to classes, cliques and coteries, and life lacks more and more a vital common background, the Negro artist, out of the depths of his group and personal experience, has to his hand almost the conditions of a classical art.

Negro genius today relies upon the race-gift as a vast spiritual endowment from which our best developments have come and must come. Racial expression as a conscious motive, it is true, is fading out of our latest art, but just as surely the age of truer, finer group expression is coming in—for race expression does not need to be deliberate to be vital. Indeed at its best it never is. This was the case with our instinctive and quite matchless folk-art, and begins to be the same again as we approach cultural maturity in a phase of art that promises now to be fully representative. The interval between has been an awkward age, where from the anxious desire and attempt to be representative much that was really unrepresentative has come; we have lately had an art that was stiltedly self-conscious, and racially rhetorical rather than racially expressive. Our poets have now stopped speaking for the Negro—they speak as Negroes. Where formerly they spoke to others and tried to interpret, they now speak to their own and try to express. They have stopped posing, being nearer to the attainment of poise.

The younger generation has thus achieved an objective attitude toward life. Race for them is but an idiom of experience, a sort of added enriching adventure and discipline, giving subtler overtones to life, making it more beautiful and interesting, even if more poignantly so. So experienced, it affords a deepening rather than a narrowing of social vision. The artistic problem of the Young Negro has not been so much that of acquiring the outer mastery of form and technique as that of achieving an inner mastery of mood and spirit. That accomplished, there has come the happy release from self-consciousness, rhetoric, bombast, and the hampering habit of setting artistic values with primary regard for moral effect—all those pathetic over-compensations of a group inferiority complex which our social dilemmas inflicted upon several unhappy generations. Our poets no longer have the hard choice between an over-assertive and and appealing attitude. By the same effort, they have shaken themselves free from the minstrel tradition and the fowling-nets of dialect, and through acquiring ease and simplicity in serious expression, have carried the folk-gift to the altitudes of art. There they seek and find art's intrinsic values and satisfactions—and if America were deaf, they would still sing.

But America listens—perhaps in curiosity at first; later, we may be sure, in understanding. But—a moment of patience. The generation now in the artistic vanguard inherits the fine and dearly bought achievement of another generation of creative workmen who have been pioneers and path-breakers in the cultural development and recognition of the Negro in the arts. Though still in their prime, as veterans of a hard struggle, they must have the praise and gratitude that is due them. We have had, in fiction, Chestnutt and Burghardt Du Bois; in drama, Du Bois again and Angelina Grimke; in poetry Dunbar, James Weldon Johnson, Fenton and Charles Bertram Johnson, Everett Hawk-

Survey Graphic 53, no. 11 (March 1, 1925): 659–660.

13

ins, Lucien Watkins, Cotter, Jameson; and in another file of poets, Miss Grimke, Anne Spencer, and Georgia Douglas Johnson; in criticism and *belles lettres,* Braithwaite and Dr. Du Bois; in painting, Tanner and Scott; in sculpture, Meta Warrick and May Jackson; in acting Gilpin and Robeson; in music, Burleigh. Nor must the fine collaboration of white American artists be omitted; the work of Ridgeley Torrence and Eugene O'Neill in drama, of Stribling, and Shands and Clement Wood in fiction, all of which has helped in the bringing of the materials of Negro life out of the shambles of conventional polemics, cheap romance and journalism into the domain of pure and unbiassed art. Then, rich in this legacy, but richer still, I think, in their own endowment of talent, comes the youngest generation of our Afro-American culture: in music, Diton, Dett, Grant Still, and Roland Hayes; in fiction, Jessie Fauset, Walter White, Claude McKay (a forthcoming book); in drama, Willis Richardson; in the field of the short story, Jean Toomer, Eric Walrond, Rudolf Fisher; and finally a vivid galaxy of young Negro poets, McKay, Jean Toomer, Langston Hughes and Countée Cullen.

These constitute a new generation not because of years only, but because of a new aesthetic and a new philosophy of life. They have all swung above the horizon in the last three years, and we can say without disparagement of the past that in that short space of time they have gained collectively from publishers, editors, critics and the general public more recognition than has ever before come to Negro creative artists in an entire working lifetime. First novels of unquestioned distinction, first acceptances by premier journals whose pages are the ambition of veteran craftsmen, international acclaim, the conquest for us of new provinces of art, the development for the first time among us of literary coteries and channels for the contact of creative minds, and most important of all, a spiritual quickening and racial leavening such as no generation has yet felt and known. It has been their achievement also to bring the artistic advance of the Negro sharply into stepping alignment with contemporary artistic thought, mood and style. They are thoroughly modern, some of them ultra-modern, and Negro thoughts now wear the uniform of the age.

But for all that, the heart beats a little differently. Toomer gives a folk-lilt and ecstasy to the prose of the American modernists. McKay adds Aesop and irony to the social novel and a peasant clarity and naïveté to lyric thought, Fisher adds Uncle Remus to the art of Maupassant and O. Henry. Hughes puts Biblical fervor into free verse, Hayes carries the gush and depth of folk-song to the old masters, Cullen blends the simple with the sophisticated and puts the vineyards themselves into his crystal goblets. There is in all the marriage of a fresh emotional endowment with the finest niceties of art. Here for the enrichment of American and modern art, among our contemporaries, in a people who still have the ancient key, are some of the things we thought culture had forever lost. Art cannot disdain the gift of a natural irony, of a transfiguring imagination, of rhapsodic Biblical speech, of dynamic musical swing, of

cosmic emotion such as only the gifted pagans knew, of a return to nature, not by way of the forced and worn formula of Romanticism, but through the closeness of an imagination that has never broken kinship with nature. Art must accept such gifts, and revaluate the giver.

Not all the new art is in the field of pure art values. There is poetry of sturdy social protest, and fiction of calm, dispassionate social analysis. But reason and realism have cured us of sentimentality: instead of the wail and appeal, there is challenge and indictment. Satire is just beneath the surface of our latest prose, and tonic irony has come into our poetic wells. These are good medicines for the common mind, for us they are necessary antidotes against social poison. Their influence means that at least for us the worst symptoms of the social distemper are passing. And so the social promise of our recent art is as great as the artistic. It has brought with it, first of all, that wholesome, welcome virtue of finding beauty in oneself; the younger generation can no longer be twitted as "cultural nondescripts" or accused of "being out of love with their own nativity." They have instinctive love and pride of race, and, spiritually compensating for the present lacks of America, ardent respect and love for Africa, the motherland. Gradually too under some spiritualizing reaction, the brands and wounds of social persecution are becoming the proud stigmata of spiritual immunity and moral victory. Already enough progress has been made in this direction so that it is no longer true that the Negro mind is too engulfed in its own social dilemmas for control of the necessary perspective of art, or too depressed to attain the full horizons of self and social criticism. Indeed, by the evidence and promise of the cultured few, we are at last spiritually free, and offer through art an emancipating vision to America. But it is a presumption to speak further for those who have spoken and can speak so adequately for themselves.   A. L.

THE ART OF THE ANCESTORS

Dahomey (Bronze).

FROM one of the best extant collections of African art, that of the Barnes Foundation of Merion, Pennsylvania, come these exemplars of the art of the ancestors. Primitive African wood and bronze sculpture is now universally recognized as "a notable instance of plastic representation." Long after it was known as ethnological material, it was artistically "discovered" and has exerted an important influence upon modernist art, both in France and Germany. Attested influences are to be found in the work of Matisse, Picasso, Modigliani, Archipenko, Lipschitz, Lembruch and others, and in Paris centering around Paul Guillaume, one of its pioneer exponents, a coterie profoundly influenced by the aesthetic of this art has developed.

Masterful over its material, in a powerful simplicity of conception, design and effect, it is evidence of an aesthetic endowment of the highest order. The Negro in his American environment has turned predominantly to the arts of music, the dance, and poetry, an emphasis quite different from that of African culture. But beyond this as evidence of a fundamental artistic bent and versatility, there comes from the consideration of this ancient plastic art another modern and practical possibility and hope, that it may exert upon the artistic development of the American Negro the influence that it has already had upon modern European artists. It may very well be taken as the basis for a characteristic school of expression in the plastic and pictorial arts, and give to us again a renewed mastery of them, a mine of fresh motifs, and a lesson in simplicity and originality of expression. Surely this art, once known and appreciated, can scarcely have less influence upon the blood descendants than upon those who inherit by tradition only. And at the very least, even for those not especially interested in art, it should definitely establish the enlightening fact that the Negro is not a cultural foundling without an inheritance.   A. L.

Soudan-Niger.

Baoulé.

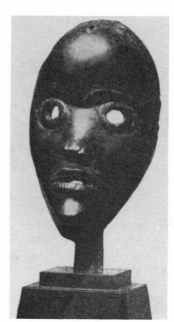

Yoruba.

Survey Graphic 53, no. 11 (March 1, 1925): 673.
Photos on this page courtesy of the Barnes Foundation, Merion, Pa. Photos by Moorland–Spingarn Research Center, Howard University, Washington, D.C.

Harlem Girl. Courtesy of Museum of Art and Archaeology, University of Missouri–Columbia. Gift of Mr. W. Tjark Reiss.

HARLEM TYPES—
PORTRAITS BY WINOLD REISS

HERE and elsewhere throughout this number, Winold Reiss presents us a graphic interpretation of Negro life, freshly conceived after its own patterns. Concretely in his portrait sketches, abstractly in his symbolic designs, he has aimed to portray the soul and spirit of a people. And by the simple but rare process of not setting up petty canons in the face of nature's own creative artistry, Winold Reiss has achieved what amounts to a revealing discovery of the significance, human and artistic, of one of the great dialects of human physiognomy, of some of the little understood but powerful idioms of nature's speech. Harlem, or any Negro community, spreads a rich and novel palette for the serious artist. It needs but enlightenment of mind and eye to make its intriguing problems and promising resources available for the stimulation and enrichment of American art.

Survey Graphic 53, no. 11 (March 1, 1925): 651–653.

Mother and Child. Courtesy of Mr. W. Tjark Reiss.

The Poetess. Courtesy of Mr. W. Tjark Reiss.

CONVENTIONS stand doubly in the way of artistic portrayal of Negro folk; certain narrowly arbitrary conventions of physical beauty, and as well, that inevitable inscrutability of things seen but not understood. Caricature has put upon the countenance of the Negro the mask of the comic and the grotesque, whereas in deeper truth and comprehension, nature or experience have put there the stamp of the very opposite, the serious, the tragic, the wistful. At times, too, there is a quality of soul that can only be called brooding and mystical. Here they are to be seen as we know them to be in fact. While it is a revealing interpretation for all, for the Negro artist, still for the most part confronting timidly his own material, there is certainly a particular stimulus and inspiration in this redeeming vision. Through it in all likelihood must come his best development in the field of the pictorial arts, for his capacity to express beauty depends vitally upon the capacity to see it in his own life and to generate it out of his own experience.

WINOLD REISS, son of Fritz Reiss, the landscape painter, pupil of Franz von Stuck of Munich, has become a master delineator of folk character by wide experience and definite specialization. With ever-ripening skill, he has studied and drawn the folk-types of Sweden, Holland, of the Black Forest and his own native Tyrol, and in America, the Black Foot Indians, the Pueblo people, the Mexicans, and now, the American Negro. His art owes its peculiar success as much to the philosophy of his approach as to his technical skill. He is a folk-lorist of the brush and palette, seeking always the folk character back of the individual, the psychology behind the physiognomy. In design also he looks not merely for decorative elements, but for the pattern of the culture from which it sprang. Without loss of naturalistic accuracy and individuality, he somehow subtly expresses the type, and without being any the less human, captures the racial and local. What Gauguin and his followers have done for the Far East, and the work of Ufer and Blumenschein and the Taos school for the Pueblo and Indian, seems about to be done for the Negro and Africa: in short, painting, the most local of arts, in terms of its own limitations even, is achieving universality.

Harlem Boy. The Museum of Art and Archaeology, University of Missouri–Columbia. Gift of Mr. W. Tjark Reiss.

A Woman Lawyer. Courtesy of Mrs. Anna J. Bernard, first Black woman lawyer in New York.

Two Harlem Girls. Courtesy of Mr. W. Tjark Reiss.

A College Lad. Courtesy of Mr. W. Tjark Reiss.

OUR LITTLE RENAISSANCE

NOW that the time has come for some sort of critical appraisal, what of our much-heralded Negro Renaissance? Pathetically pale, thinks Mr. Mencken, like a candle in the sunlight. It has kindled no great art: we would do well to page a black Luther and call up the Reformation. Fairly successful, considering the fog and soot of the American atmosphere, and still full of promise—so "it seems" to Mr. Heywood Broun. I wonder what Mr. Pater would say. He might be even more sceptical, though with the scepticism of suspended judgment, I should think; but one mistake he would never make—that of confusing the spirit with the vehicle, of confounding the artistic quality which Negro life is contributing with the Negro artist. Negro artists are just the by-products of the Negro Renaissance; its main accomplishment will be to infuse a new essence into the general stream of culture. The Negro Renaissance must be an integral phase of contemporary American art and literature; more and more we must divorce it in our minds from propaganda and politics. Otherwise, why call it a renaissance? We are back-sliding, I think, into the old swamp of the Negro problem to be discussing, as we have been of late, how many Negro artists are first-rate or second-rate, and how many feet of the book-shelf of leather-bound classics their works to date should occupy. According to that Hoyle, the Grand Renaissance should have stopped at the Alps and ought to have effected the unification of Italy instead of the revival of Humanism.

To claim the material that Negro life and idiom have contributed to American art through the medium of the white artist may seem at first unfair and ungracious; may even be open to the imputation of trying to bolster up with reenforcements a "wavering thin line of talent." But what is the issue—sociology or art—a quality of spirit or complexions? The artists in question themselves are gracious enough, both in making their acknowledgements to the folk spirit, and in asserting the indivisible unity of the subject-matter. Only recently, confirming her adoption of Negro material as her special field, Mrs. Peterkin has said: "I shall never write of white people; to me their lives are not so colorful. If the South is going to write, what is it they are going to write about—the Negro, of course." Still more recently, the distinguished author of *Porgy* applauds shifting the stress from the Negro writer to the "Negro race as a subject for art" and approves of "lifting the material to the plane of pure art" and of making it available to the American artist, white or Negro, "as native subject-matter." And if there is any meaning to the term universal which we so blithely and tritely use in connection with art, it must be this. There is no other alternative on the plane of art. Indeed, if conditions in the South were more conducive to the development of Negro culture without transplanting, the self-expression of the "New Negro" would spring up just as one branch of the new literature of the South, and as one additional phase of its cultural reawakening. The common bond of soil and that natural provincialism would be a sounder basis for development than the somewhat expatriated position of the younger school of Negro writers. And if I were asked to name one factor for the anemic and rhetorical quality of so much Negro expression up to the present, I would cite not the unproved capacities of our authors but the pathetic exile of the Negro writer from his best material, the fact that he cannot yet get cultural breathing space on his own soil. That is at least one reason for the disabilities of the Negro writer in handling his own materials with vivid and intimate mastery.

More and more the younger writers and artists are treking back to their root-sources, however. Overt propaganda now is as exceptional as it used to be typical. The acceptance of race is steadily becoming less rhetorical, and more instinctively taken for granted. There was a time when the only way

Reprinted in *Ebony and Topaz: A Collectanea*, ed. Charles S. Johnson. Freeport, N.Y.: Books for Libraries Press, 1971, pp. 117–118. Originally published in 1927.

out of sentimental partisanship was through a stridently self-conscious realism. That attitude stripped the spiritual bloom from the work of the Negro writer; gave him a studied and self-conscious detachment. It was only yesterday that we had to preach objectivity to the race artist to cure the pathetic fallacies of bathos and didactic approach. We are just beginning perhaps to shake off the artifices of that relatively early stage; so to speak the Umbrian stiffness is still upon us and the Florentine ease and urbanity looms just ahead. It is a fiction that the black man has until recently been naive: in American life he has been painfully self-conscious for generations—and is only now beginning to recapture the naivete he once originally had. The situation is well put in a stanza of Mae Cowdery's poem—"Goal,"

> I must shatter the wall
> Of darkness that rises
> From gleaming day
> And seeks to hide the sun.
> I will turn this wall of
> Darkness (that is night)
> Into a thing of beauty.
>
> I will take from the hearts
> Of black men—
> Prayers their lips
> Are 'fraid to utter,
> And turn their coarseness
> Into a beauty of the jungle
> Whence they came.

So, in the development of the materials of Negro life, each group of artists has a provincialism to outgrow; in the one case narrowness of vision; in the other, limiting fetters of style. If then it is really a renaissance—and I firmly believe it is, we are still in the hill-town stage, and the mellowness of maturity has not yet come upon us. It is not to escape criticism that we hold it thus; but for the sake of a fair comparison. The Negro Renaissance is not ten years old; its earliest harbingers cannot be traced back of the beginning of the century; its representative products to date are not only the work of the last three or four years, but the work of men still in their twenties so far as the producing artists are concerned. Need we then be censured for turning our adjective into an affectionate diminutive and for choosing, at least for the present, to call it hopefully "our little renaissance"?

BEAUTY INSTEAD OF ASHES

LIKE a fresh boring through the rock and sand of racial misunderstanding and controversy, modern American art has tapped a living well-spring of beauty, and the gush of it opens up an immediate question as to the possible contribution of the soil and substance of Negro life and experience to American culture and the native materials of art. Are we ever to have more than the simple first products and ground flow of this well-spring, and the fitful spurt of its released natural energies, or is the well-head to be drummed over and its resources conserved and refined to give us a sustained output of more mature products and by-products?

To produce these second-process products is the particular *raison d'être* of a school of Negro poets and artists, and what most of our younger school really mean by an "acceptance of race in art" is the consciousness of this as an artistic task and program. Its group momentum behind the individual talent is largely responsible, I think, for the sudden and brilliant results of our contemporary artistic revival. The art movement in this case happens to coincide with a social one—a period of new stirrings in the Negro mind and the dawning of new social objectives. Yet most Negro artists would repudiate their own art program if it were presented as a reformer's duty or a prophet's mission, and to the extent that they were true artists be quite justified. But there is an ethics of beauty itself; an urgency of the right creative moment. Race materials come to the Negro artist today as much through his being the child of his age as through his being the child of his race; it is primarily because Negro life is creatively flowing in American art at present that it is the business of the Negro artist to capitalize it in his work. The proof of this is the marked and unusually successful interest of the white writer and artist in Negro themes and materials, not to mention the vogue of Negro music and the conquest of the popular mind through the dance and the vaudeville stage. Indeed in work like that of Eugene O'Neill, Ridgely Torrence, and Paul Green in drama, that

of Vachel Lindsay and a whole school of "jazz poets," and that of Du Bose Heyward, Julia Peterkin, Carl Van Vechten, and others in fiction, the turbulent warm substance of Negro life seems to be broadening out in the main course of American literature like some distinctive literary Gulf Stream. From the Negro himself naturally we expect, however, the most complete and sustained effort and activity. But just as we are not to restrict the Negro artist to Negro themes except by his own artistic choice and preference, so we are glad that Negro life is an artistic province free to everyone.

The opening up and artistic development of Negro life has come about not only through collaboration but through a noteworthy, though unconscious, division of labor. White artists have taken, as might be expected, the descriptive approach and have opened up first the channels of drama and fiction. Negro artists, not merely because of their more intimate emotional touch but also because of temporary incapacity for the objective approach so requisite for successful drama and fiction, have been more effective in expressing Negro life in the more subjective terms of poetry and music. In both cases it has been the distinctive and novel appeal of the folk life and folk temperament that has first gained general acceptance and attention; so that we may warrantably say that there was a third factor in the equation most important of all—this folk tradition and temperament. Wherever Negro life colors art distinctively with its folk values we ought, I think, to credit it as a cultural influence, and as in the case of Uncle Remus, without discrediting the interpreter, emphasize nevertheless the racial contribution. Only as we do this can we see how constant and important a literary and artistic influence Negro life has exerted, and see that the recent developments are only the sudden deepening of an interest which has long been superficial. After generations of comic, sentimental, and *genre* interest in Negro life, American letters have at last dug down to richer treasure in social-document studies like "Birthright" and "Nigger," to problem analysis like "All God's Chillun Got Wings," to

The Nation 126 (April 18, 1928): 432–434.

23

a studied but brilliant novel of manners like "Nigger Heaven," and finally to pure tragedy like "Porgy" and "Abraham's Bosom." Negro intellectuals and reformers generally have complained of this artistically important development—some on the score of the defeatist trend of most of the themes, others because of a "peasant, low-life portrayal that misrepresents by omission the better elements of Negro life." They mistake for color prejudice the contemporary love for strong local color, and for condescension the current interest in folk life. The younger Negro artists as modernists have the same slant and interest, as is unmistakably shown by Jean Toomer's "Cane," Eric Walrond's "Tropic Death," Rudolph Fisher's and Claude McKay's pungent stories of Harlem, and the group trend of *Fire*, a quarterly recently brought out to be "devoted to younger Negro artists."

These critics further forget how protectively closed the upper levels of Negro society have been, and how stiffly posed they still are before the sociologist's camera. Any artist would turn his back. But in the present fiction of the easily accessible life of the many, the few will eventually find that power of objective approach and self-criticism without which a future school of urbane fiction of Negro life cannot arise. Under these circumstances the life of our middle and upper classes is reserved for later self-expression, toward which Jessie Fauset's "There Is Confusion," Walter White's "Flight," and James Weldon Johnson's "Autobiography of an Ex-Colored Man" are tentative thrusts. Meantime, to develop the technique of objective control, the younger Negro school has almost consciously emphasized three things: realistic fiction, the folk play, and type analysis, and their maturing power in the folk play, the short story, and the *genre* novel promises much for the future.

Though Negro genius does not yet move with full power and freedom in the domain of the novel and the drama, in the emotional mediums of poetry and music it has already attained self-mastery and distinguished expression. It is the popular opinion that Negro expression has always flowed freely in these channels. On the contrary, only recently have our serious artists accepted the folk music and poetry as an artistic heritage to be used for further development, and it is not quite a decade since James Weldon Johnson's "Creation" closed the feud between the "dialect" and the "academic" poets with the brilliant formula of emancipation from dialect plus the cultivation of racial idiom in imagery and symbolism. Since then a marvelous succession of poets, in a poetry of ever deepening lyric swing and power, have carried our expression in this form far beyond the mid ranks of minor poetry. In less than half a generation we have passed from poetized propaganda and didactic sentiment to truly spontaneous and relaxed lyricism. Fifteen years ago a Negro poet wrote:

> The golden lyre's delights bring little grace,
> To bless the singer of a lowly race,
> But I shall dig me deeper to the gold—
> So men shall know me, and remember long
> Nor my dark face dishonor any song.

It was a day of apostrophes and rhetorical assertions;

Africa and the race were lauded in collective singulars of "thee's" and "thou's." Contrast the emotional self-assurance of contemporary Negro moods in Cullen's

> Her walk is like the replica
> Of some barbaric dance,
> Wherewith the soul of Africa
> Is winged with arrogance

and the quiet espousal of race in these lines of Hughes

> Dream singers,
> Story tellers,
> Dancers,
> Loud laughers in the hands of Fate,
> My people.

It is a curious thing—it is also a fortunate thing—that the movement of Negro art toward racialism has been so similar to that of American art at large in search of its national soul. Padraic Colum's brilliant description of the national situation runs thus: "Her nationality has been a political one, it is now becoming an intellectual one." We might paraphrase this for the Negro and say: His racialism used to be rhetorical, now it is emotional; formerly he sang about his race, now we hear race in his singing.

Happily out of this parallelism much intuitive understanding has come, for the cultural rapprochement of the races in and through art has not been founded on sentiment but upon common interests. The modern recoil from the machine has deepened the appreciation of hitherto despised qualities in the Negro temperament, its hedonism, its nonchalance, its spontaneity; the reaction against over-sophistication has opened our eyes to the values of the primitive and the importance of the man of emotions and untarnished instincts; and finally the revolt against conventionality, against Puritanism, has fought a strong ally in the half-submerged paganism of the Negro. With this established reciprocity, there is every reason for the Negro artist to be more of a modernist than, on the average, he yet is, but with each younger artistic generation the alignment with modernism becomes closer. The Negro schools have as yet no formulated aesthetic, but they will more and more profess the new realism, the new paganism, and the new vitalism of contemporary art. Especially in the rediscovery of the senses and the instincts, and in the equally important movement for re-rooting art in the soil of everyday life and emotion, Negro elements, culturally transplanted, have, I think, an important contribution to make to the working out of our national culture.

For the present, Negro art advance has one foot on its own original soil and one foot on borrowed ground. If it is allowed to make its national contribution, as it should, there is no anomaly in the situation but instead an advantage. It holds for the moment its racialism in solution, ready to pour it into the mainstream if the cultural forces gravitate that way. Eventually, either as a stream or as a separate body, it must find free outlet for its increasing creative energy. By virtue of the concentration of its elements, it seems to me to have greater potentialities than almost any other single contemporary group expression.

Negro artists have made a creditable showing, but after all it is the artistic resources of Negro life and experience that give this statement force.

It was once thought that the Negro was a fine minstrel and could be a fair troubadour, but certainly no poet or finished artist. Now that he is, another reservation is supposed to be made. Can he be the commentator, the analyst, the critic? The answer is in process, as we may have shown. The younger Negro expects to attain that mastery of all the estates of art, especially the provinces of social description and criticism, that admittedly mark seasoned cultural maturity rather than flashy adolescence. Self-criticism will put the Negro artist in a position to make a unique contribution in the portrayal of American life, for his own life situations penetrate to the deepest complications possible in our society. Comedy, tragedy, satire of the first order are wrapped up in the race problem, if we can only untie the psychological knot and take off the somber sociological wrappings.

Always I think, or rather hope, the later art of the Negro will be true to original qualities of the folk temperament, though it may not perpetuate them in readily recognizable form. For the folk temperament raised to the levels of conscious art promises more originality and beauty than any assumed or imitated class or national or clique psychology available. Already our writers have renewed the race temperament (to the extent there is such a thing) by finding a new pride in it, by stripping it of caricaturish stereotypes, and by partially compensating its acquired inferiority complexes. It stands today, one would say, in the position of the German temperament in Herder's day. There is only one way for it to get any further—to find genius of the first order to give it final definiteness of outline and animate it with creative universality. A few very precious spiritual gifts await this releasing touch, gifts of which we are barely aware—a technique of mass emotion in the arts, a mysticism that is not ascetic and of the cloister, a realism that is not sordid but shot through with homely, appropriate poetry. One wonders if in these sublimated and precious things anyone but the critic with a half-century's focus will recognize the folk temperament that is familiar today for its irresistibly sensuous, spontaneously emotional, affably democratic and naive spirit. Scarcely. But that is the full promise of Negro art as inner vision sees it. That inner vision cannot be doubted or denied for a group temperament that, instead of souring under oppression and becoming materialistic and sordid under poverty, has almost invariably been able to give America honey for gall and create beauty out of the ashes.

ART OR PROPAGANDA?

RTISTICALLY it is the one fundamental question for us today.—Art or Propaganda. Which? Is this more the generation of the prophet or that of the poet; shall our intellectual and cultural leadership preach and exhort or sing? I believe we are at that interesting moment when the prophet becomes the poet and when prophecy becomes the expressive song, the chant of fulfillment. We have had too many Jeremiahs, major and minor;— and too much of the drab wilderness. My chief objection to propaganda, apart from its besetting sin of monotony and disproportion, is that it perpetuates the position of group inferiority even in crying out against it. For it lives and speaks under the shadow of a dominant majority whom it harangues, cajoles, threatens or supplicates. It is too extroverted for balance or poise or inner dignity and self-respect. Art in the best sense is rooted in self-expression and whether naive or sophisticated is self-contained. In our spiritual growth genius and talent must more and more choose the role of group expression, or even at times the role of free individualistic expression,—in a word must choose art and put aside propaganda.

The literature and art of the younger generation already reflects this shift of psychology, this regeneration of spirit. David should be its patron saint: it should confront the Phillistines with its five smooth pebbles fearlessly. There is more strength in a confident camp than in a threatened enemy. The sense of inferiority must be innerly compensated, self-conviction must supplant self-justification and in the dignity of this attitude a convinced minority must confront a condescending majority. Art

cannot completely accomplish this, but I believe it can lead the way.

Our espousal of art thus becomes no mere idle acceptance of "art for art's sake," or cultivation of the last decadences of the over-civilized, but rather a deep realization of the fundamental purpose of art and of its function as a tap root of vigorous, flourishing living. Not all of our younger writers are deep enough in the sub-soil of their native materials,— too many are pot-plants seeking a forced growth according to the exotic tastes of a pampered and decadent public. It is the art of the people that needs to be cultivated, not the art of the coteries. Propaganda itself is preferable to shallow, truckling imitation. Negro things may reasonably be a fad for others; for us they must be a religion. Beauty, however, is its best priest and psalms will be more effective than sermons.

To date we have had little sustained art unsubsidized by propaganda; we must admit this debt to these foster agencies. The three journals which have been vehicles of most of our artistic expressions have been the avowed organs of social movements and organized social programs. All our purely artistic publications have been sporadic. There is all the greater need then for a sustained vehicle of free and purely artistic expression. If HARLEM should happily fill this need, it will perform an honorable and constructive service. I hope it may, but should it not, the need remains and the path toward it will at least be advanced a little.

We need, I suppose in addition to art some substitute for propaganda. What shall that be?

Harlem 1 (November 1928): 12.

Surely we must take some cognizance of the fact that we live at the centre of a social problem. Propaganda at least nurtured some form of serious social discussion, and social discussion was necessary, is still necessary. On this side: the difficulty and shortcoming of propaganda is its partisanship. It is one-sided and often prejudging. Should we not then have a journal of free discussion, open to all sides of the problem and to all camps of belief? Difficult, that, —but intriguing. Even if it has to begin on the note of dissent and criticism and assume Menckenian scepticism to escape the commonplaces of conformity. Yet, I hope we shall not remain at this negative pole. Can we not cultivate truly free and tolerant discussion, almost Socratically minded for the sake of truth? After Beauty, let Truth come into the Renaissance picture,—a later cue, but a welcome one. This may be premature, but one hopes not,— for eventually it must come and if we can accomplish that, instead of having to hang our prophets, we can silence them or change their lamentations to song with a Great Fulfillment.

BEAUTY AND THE PROVINCES

OF THE many ways of defining the provinces, after all there is none more reliable than this—capitals are always creative centers, and where living beauty is the provinces are not. Not that capitals are always beautiful, but they are always, at the least, the meccas of the beauty seekers and the workshops of the beauty-makers. Between capital and province, many draw the distinction merely of pomp and power: for them it is where the king lives, where the money barons thrive, where the beau-monde struts. While this is superficially true, after all a capital that is not a center of culture is no capital at all, and must look to its laurels if it cannot buy or borrow sufficient talent to become so. One of the first missions of a new metropolis is the quest for genius; it is as inevitable as the passion of sudden wealth for jewels. In a country like ours that still lives primarily on borrowed culture, the metropolis becomes the market-place for genius and its wares, and with its tentacles of trade and traffic captures and holds the prize.

It was those same forces that have made New York the culture-capital of America, which made Harlem the mecca of the New Negro and the first creative center of the Negro Renaissance. Older centers of what was thought to be culture resented the parvenu glory of careless, congested, hectic Harlem. But though many a home-town ached to be robbed of the credit for its village Homer, it was inevitable. It was also just. For oftener than not genius was starved, despised and even crucified in the home-town, but by the more discerning judgment and quickened sensibilities of the capital was recognized, stimulated, imitated, even though still perhaps half starved. In this way more than one Negro community has been forced to pay its quota of talent as tribute, and then smart under the slur of being lumped with the provinces. There has been only one way out—and that, to compete for creative talent and light a candle from the central torch. Even the hill towns of Italy, veritable nests of genius, had to yield first to Florence and then to Rome.

The current cultural development of Negro life has been no exception. But now as the movement spreads and beauty invades the provinces, it can be told—at least without offense. Chicago, Philadelphia, Boston, Washington, Nashville, Atlanta—is this the order, or shall we leave it to the historian?—have in turn had their awakening after nightmares of envy and self-delusion. For culture, in last analysis, is a matter not of consumption but of production. It is not a matter of degrees and diplomas, or even of ability to follow and appreciate. It is the

The Stylus (June 1929): 3–4.

capacity to discover and to create. Thereby came the illusion which has duped so many who cannot distinguish between dead and living culture, between appreciation and creativeness, between borrowed spiritual clothes and living beauty—even if living beauty be a bit more naked.

For the moment, we are only concerned with Washington—that capital of the nation's body which is not the capital of its mind or soul. That conglomeration of Negro folk which basks in the borrowed satisfactions of white Washington must some day awake to realize in how limited a degree Washington is the capital of the nation. A double tragedy, this of the city of magnificent distances, tragically holding to its bosom the illusion that it is not provincial. In spite of its title, its coteries, its avenues, it is only a candidate for metropolitan life, a magnificent body awaiting a soul. And but for the stultification of borrowed illusions, Negro Washington would have realized that it contains more of the elements of an intellectual race capital proportionately than the Washington of political fame and power. It is in its way a greater and more representative aggregation of intellectual and cultural talent. Had this possibility been fully realized by the Washington Negro intelligentsia a decade or so ago, and constructively striven after, Washington would have out-distanced Harlem and won the palm of pioneering instead of having merely yielded a small exodus of genius that went out of the smug city with passports of persecution and returned with visas of metropolitan acclaim.

One may pardonably point with pride—with collective pride and not too ironic satisfaction—to certain exceptions, among them the pioneer work of Howard University in the development of the drama of Negro life and the Negro Theater. Close beside it should be bracketed the faith of which this little magazine is a renewed offshoot—the pioneer foundation at Howard University in 1913 of THE STYLUS, a group for creative writing, with the explicit aim at that comparative early date of building literature and art on the foundation of the folk-roots and the race tradition. Since then over a score of such drama and writing groups have sprung up—the Writers' Guild of New York, Krigwa of New York and elsewhere, the Scribblers of Baltimore, the Gilpins of Cleveland, the Quill Club of Boston, the Philadelphia group that so creditably publishes *Black Opals*, the several Chicago groups from the Ethiopian Folk Theater to the most promising drama group of the present "Cube Theater," the Writers' Guild of Fisk, the Dixwell Group of New Haven, the Ethiopian Guild of Indianapolis, the recently organized Negro company of the Dallas players in far Texas. The very enumeration indicates what has been accomplished in little more than a decade. The provinces are waking up, and a new cult of beauty stirs throughout the land.

But it is not enough merely to have been a pioneer. THE STYLUS and the Howard Players must carry on—vitally, creatively. The University, at least, can be—should be—a living center of culture; both of that culture which is the common academic heritage and of that which alone can vitalize it, the constant conversion of our individual and group experiences in creative thought, and the active distillation of our hearts and minds in beauty and art. The path of progress passes through a series of vital centers whose succession is the most significant line of human advance. A province conscious of its provinciality has its face turned in the right direction, and if it follows through with effort can swerve the line of progress to its very heart.

ALAIN LOCKE.

POETRY

Locke was not content with the life of a university professor. The emergence of young poets Countee Cullen, Claude McKay, Jean Toomer, and Langston Hughes in the 1920s drew Locke out of his ivory tower into the bohemian life: he became part of a coterie of poets who met in Harlem cabarets, attended poetry readings, and corresponded about poetry. Locke provided encouragement, financial assistance, and reviews of their work. Though not a poet himself, Locke was welcomed into the circle as a friend and sponsor, or as he termed himself, "a philosophical mid-wife to a generation of younger Negro poets."[1]

Locke was acquainted with the literary avant-garde before the 1920s, as evidenced by the first essay, "Emile Verhaeren," published in *The Poetry Review* in 1917. Emile Verhaeren, a Belgian poet, met Locke's demand that modern poetry not escape from society, but instead take up "the task, ancient and perennial in some respects, of getting the real world into the microcosm of art without shattering either one or the other."

Locke searched for an Afro-American poet who would give expression to the black American experience. The next essays, "*Color*—A Review" (1926) and a review of *The Weary Blues* (1926), celebrate the first books of poetry by Countee Cullen and Langston Hughes, respectively. Locke hails them as "representative" poets, who express their time, their milieu, and their race, as only great artists can. In "The Negro Poets of the United States" (1926) and the introduction to his anthology, *Four Negro Poets* (1927), Locke argues that with the pool of 1920s poets, a "Poetry of Negro Life" has come of age.

After 1927, Locke increasingly saw Afro-American poetry as grounded in the language and experience of the common people. He believed that Hughes was the poet laureate of the race because of Hughes's immersion in, and identification with, the folk experience of the black masses. By 1934, however, Locke had parted company with Hughes, and had become enthused with another poet, Sterling Brown, a colleague at Howard.[2] In "Sterling Brown: The New Negro Folk-Poet" (1934), Locke deems Brown a more direct voice and "a closer student of folk life."

Locke wanted a poetry which balanced artistic excellence with social consciousness. In "Propaganda—or Poetry?" (1936), Locke chastises "proletarian poetry" for being "drab, prosy and inartistic," while praising the younger poets of the 1930s for working toward a blend of class and race consciousness in their poetry.

While the poets of the 1930s suffered from an excess of social consciousness in Locke's opinion, the 1920s poets, in retrospect, suffered from too little. Toomer had abhorred being labeled a black poet in *The New Negro*, while McKay and Cullen resented Locke's imposition of race consciousness on their work.[3] When McKay published his autobiography, *A Long Way from Home,* in 1937, that enabled Locke, through his stinging review, "Spiritual Truancy," to issue a postmortem not only on McKay's career, but on the 1920s poets in general.

EMILE VERHAEREN

Not as a pioneer merely, but as a constant devotee throughout all the other changes in his art, Verhaeren, so lately and lamentably gone, is to be accounted the greatest exponent of modernism in poetry. In so styling him, we rate as the really vital modernism in the art, not the cult of sheer modernity of form and mood,—the ultra-modernism in which the poetic youth exults, but that more difficult modernity of substance which has as its aim·to make poetry incorporate a world-view and reflect the spirit of its time. The task,—ancient and perennial in some respects, of getting the real world into the microcosm of art without shattering either one or the other, was of unusual difficulty in Verhaeren's day. No life has been harder to transmute into art than modern life, and in no art so difficult as in that of poetry. Yet this was the master-passion of Verhaeren's temperament and the consummate achievement of his work. Once achieved—and it must be remembered that Verhaeren's modernism was wrested from the fin-de-siécle aestheticism of a decadence that deliberately despaired of a solution of this problem—the whole movement, of which the ultra-modernistic phases are still with us, was made possible. To assert that Verhaeren's modernity is a bit old-fashioned and somewhat superceded now, as is so much the mode, is therefore but to emphasize his parental relation to the whole idea. Indeed let us venerate the more, if as the young radicals have hinted, it is the dowager-muse whom we must console.

With fiction and drama in the throes of naturalism, poetry at the time of Verhaeren's début had renounced life, and was in full retreat toward the cloister or that other asylum of the eighties, the ivory towers. And it was his own instinctive and passionate love of the real in poetry, not Zola's or Lemmonier's creed, that sent him like a jealous and desperate lover in pursuit. And who can doubt in the light of what has subsequently happened in modern poetry, the comparative success of Verhaeren above all others in this respect, if he will but picture, let us say, Maeterlinck ecstatically returning from the convent with the maiden's veil; Verhaeren, with less grace but more triumph, from the ivory towers with the damsel herself? It was this effort that produced the crude defiant realism of *Les Flamandes* (1883), and the vigorous protests of *L'Art Moderne*. Though somewhat in excess of his nature, as the later poems show, these early pronouncements were a creed from which in principle Verhaeren never radically departed, and out of which modernistic realism in poetry takes its origin. There was proved to be something else between what poets then regarded their only alternative,—that of a pagan or a religious aestheticism.

For Verhaeren himself, however, the appeal to the realism of his native art, a fugitive sojourn with his stolen bride at the boisterous inn of Teniers, was but a temporary refuge. The ivory towers avoided, it was not so easy to flee the cloister. Training, association, and above all the trend of thought at the time, forced the issue upon him. Yet it seems unwarranted to construe *Les Moines* (1885), as so many critics have, as a recantation of modernism on Verhaeren's part. A reaction from realism it undoubtedly was, but it is to Verhaeren's credit that he never confounded modernity with a particular technique or a particular type of subject. *The Monks* is a modernistic as *Les Flamandes*. His familiarity and sympathy for what he is dealing with conceals the iconoclasm; his is a reverent vandalism. "Dwellers, long before death in a mystic and extra-human world" and "You who alone still hold, upright, your dead God over the modern world" are written not in the mood of retreat, but of recall. Trailing humanity as ever, Verhaeren cathecizes it in the heart of the cloister, and chides it there for solving the problems of life in an artificial, selfish, and futile way Having disdained aestheticism, he rejects asceticism

The Poetry Review 2 (January 1917): 41–43.

too. The place of poetry he says in the splendid apostrophe, *Aux Moines,* is in its own temple in the midst of life, and not with

> "Men of a dead and distant day,—men
> Broken but living still,—poets, too,
> Who cannot bear with us the common lot."

Reverently, Verhaeren shuts the door to the Middle Ages.

The trials and labours of this course, Verhaeren seems to have realized, in anticipation; then later in painful actuality. The temple of modern art was to be sought in an immense and towering chaos. And being the universe itself, the problem was not to find a place for it, but to find a place in it for the poet. *Les Soirs* (1887), *Les Débacles* (1888), and *Les Flambeaux noires* belong to the working out of this problem, and to his own period of stress. Stéfan Zweig makes much of this phase as a record of personal struggle; it is as significant, or more so, as a journal of the mal du siécle. An Amiel's Journal of its time, nowhere will a more exact or sincere testament be found than in this group of poems of what art was passing through in those years. It was the doubting period in poetry, when poets were sure of nothing but their own inner experiences, and of these in a morbidly subjective way. No depth or variety of this experience did Verhaeren leave unexplored,—

> "I, too, would have my crown of thorns,
> Each thought a thorn upon the brow,"—

but while the symbolists revelled in their subjectivity, Verhaeren strove mightily against it as the besetting solipsism he must escape to reach a vitally modern art.

> "The world itself is most disdained of all,
> And hands that hope to seize the light
> Stretch toward the vague and unattainable."

For he found no satisfaction in a phantom or an exiled beauty of the inner world, it withered like an exotic flower in his fevered hands. Groping toward what is real and vital in the world at large, he says of himself, "I have been a coward and have fled into a world of futile egoism." Out of the polar darkness of this experience, like Henley, Verhaeren saw a new vision, not Henley's indomitable self however, but the redeeming World. Like Henley's though, Verhaeren's discovery was made in the heart of the metropolis, where the necessity of finding an excuse for life is if anywhere imperative. In life as it showed itself there, most crude and common, but most real, Verhaeren grasped a new objective, that was not merely the release he desired from subjectivism, but a new world for poetry to conquer.

The place of the City in Verhaeren's poetry is as a symbol of this achievement. It dominates both of his great trilogies, — *Les Campagnes Hallucinees* (1893), *Les Villages Illusoires* (1895), *Les Villes Tentaculaires* (1896), and *Les Forces Tumulteuses* (1902), *La Multiple Splendeur* (1906), and *Les Rythmes Souverains* (1910). Symbolizing modern life

for him, it stands for an attitude and treatment of subject which he carries throughout his art. The light source of his vision, it determines all the values of his art: we find it by the shadows it casts even when it is out of the picture, as in the depiction of what he not equivocally calls Illusory Villages and Ghostly Countrysides,—since they too must be keyed to his standard of art,—the real, the throbbingly actual,—which first revealed itself to him as an artistic criterion in the life of the Tentacular Cities. It is obviously not the city as such,—indeed Verhaeren never quite escaped his old preoccupation with peasant folk and country life in all their Flemish provinciality,—but the city as a symbol, a point of view, behind which we glimpse Verhaeren's real gods, Humanity and Force.

The force he idealizes perhaps, but never the subject. It is a strange art, this vast untiring and exultantly descriptive realism, in which the style of Verhaeren seems all his earlier career to have been developing, at last finds an appropriate subject matter. Realism in fact never attained a completer triumph than in these depictions, genre pictures in themselves, but set in an epical series and moving with an epical force. Like the poem of Lucretius, it lacks only heroes to make it an epic. Indeed it is the way Lucretius would have written of modern life. For the hero is an infinite energy, as big in the atom as in the mass, suffusing everything, and carrying life with or without its will to its destiny: the divinity of the world is its moving energy, and the divinity in man the cosmic enthusiasm of it all. Nature and man, city and countryside, emotion and fact, seem thus in the same perspective are manifestations of a force as significant in the atom as in the aggregate. Yet so endowed with the life force is everything,—the very motions of the atoms and the dust so significant,—that out of an apparent materialism, an ardent vitalism is brought.

The humanism that is the counterpart of this worldview is indeed a rare emotion. Verhaeren only at times achieves it. His style records a perilous quest for it. On this score he is not to be judged by the style of his earlier or even of his middle period. In the one, he dehumanized man in a cold relentless portraiture and a mechanistic interpretation: in the other, he overanimated nature, and by a sheer rout of the pathetic fallacy, seems to have put into inanimate life all he took out of the human subject. Contrast the hard brush stroke of his portraits, presenting men "grim, course, and bestial, as they are," with his mood-saturated description of inanimate things, the "tower clocks staring in dumb amazement," "evenings crucified and agonizing in the west" and his notorious snow and rain, the one "cold with loveliness, warm with hate" and the other "long fingered, tearing to shreds the tattered firmament." The achievement comes eventually only in his best art, in a resolution of this odd contrast as in the lines,—

"Thus are poor hearts,—with lakes of tears within them,
Pale,—as the tombstones of the cemetery.

Thus are poor shoulders,—with toil more weighted down
And burdened than their hut-roofs in the valleys."

We then see that Verhaeren's purpose was not a paradoxical technique, in which the usual emphasis is reversed by pictorializing man and poetizing nature, but a purpose, only gradually realized and revealed, to break the barrier between them that even the flood of romanticism had left intact. Life, for Verhaeren at this later stage, is what man and nature share in common: out of a deeper penetration into each, a new relevancy comes. By welding his figures to their backgrounds, like Rodin scarcely freeing them from the rock, he gains his essential purpose, which is to exhibit in an art free from conventional illusion and sentimental overemphasis, the underlying vitalism of the universe.

Style for Verhaeren was thus the corollary of his content and message. His periods of style follow his philosophy, and the form, determined as Zweig so aptly says by "inner necessity," is the genuine idiom of his thought. Whether traditional or free in metre, symbolist or realistic in his imagery, Verhaeren, unlike so many modern poets, is never exploiting a technique or a form merely. His style accordingly in all its phases seems inevitable, dictated by the idea,—and all great style must be inevitable. This element more than any other, as with Whitman, gives Verhaeren greatness: defying classification, it puts their poetry above that of the schools. Strangely similar indeed, in spite of all differences of overtone, is the fundamental groundnote of Whitman's and Verhaeren's poetry. The catholic response vibrating to everything, the rhapsodic fling, the cosmic emotion and exultant vitalism in the poetry of each proclaims a striking spiritual kinship between them, which if rightly interpreted establishes their common paternity in the age. Easy to recognize, this modernism is none the less hard to define. What is it of which we feel that the style is but the shadow and reflection? Both poets are terribly explicit about it, yet for all their dogma, it is by no means clear. Democracy triumphant, the ethics of fervour, the religion of humanity, the cult of cosmicality, emotional pantheism, Dionysan neo-paganism,—all this and more it has been termed without a really satisfying caption. For Whitman and Verhaeren it was all one living creed—but their followers have had to cast lots and part their garments. Competent criticism has recently traced the idea in a half dozen or more contemporary schools, each stressing but an aspect, yet one apparently important enough for further emphasis and elaboration. The poetry of Dynamism, the most considerable of these, but catches the physics of the philosophy; while many, like "Effrénéisme," the Paroxystes, Totalistes, Synchronists, Vorticists and what not, catch only the mannerism of the style. And we should not flatter ourselves that because we lack these *isms* in our literary discourse, we are free from the unfortunate sectarianism that has befallen this great idea. With its greatest exponents, a single ideal dominates all the aspects of the idea: with Whitman a thoroughgoing *eleutherianism* or Libertism, if you will; with Verhaeren, a consistent pan-Vitalism in which, giving the philosophy of the *élan vitale* a place in poetry, he celebrates the cosmic energy and its onrushing goal. To Whitman belongs the credit of discovery, the sounding of these new notes; to Verhaeren, their linking up and blending into something of a harmony. The modern dithyramb, like the ancient, has a philosophy of life, a religion, back of it: thus there was always in poetry for Verhaeren an almost religious and pæanizing strain that finds its climax in his most famous line, "O race of Man, bound to the golden stars."

If any proof were needed that this is the persistent and fundamental note in Verhaeren, its presence in the personal lyrics where it is least to be expected, would finally prove the matter. The sequence of *Les Heures Claires* (1896), *Les Heures D'Après-Midi* (1905), and *Les Heures du Soir* (1911), into which the enigma of the universe scarcely intrudes, is dominated by the same point of view and philosophy. Though personal, we find Verhaeren interpreting his own private experience in the same cosmic way: love for him, even in his own life, is not an individual force or will or destiny, but a supra-human force moving to a destiny beyond the stars.

"No sooner lip to lip, than we are fraught
With sun-lit fervour that o'erpowers,
As though two gods within us sought
A godlike union in these souls of ours;
Ah, how we feel divinity is near—
Our hearts so freshened by their primal might
Of light,
That in their clarity the universe shines clear.
Ah, joy alone, the ferment of the earth,
Doth bring to life and stir
To far, illimitable birth;
As there above, across the bars
Of heaven, where voyage veils of gossamer,
Are born the myriad-flowering stars."

"Exaltation is this gift of thine,"—a line from another of these poems makes clear the derivation of it all; this ecstatic orphism which has so subtly grown up out of its opposite in modern life as the religion of the mysteries cropped out of a more sober paganism. But in Verhaeren, it is really a fine frenzy, steadied in a cosmic vision, and uttered " in all clarity." Here perhaps is the necessary balm for the eroticism of contemporary poetry. A message yet unheard, it may eventually be one of Verhaeren's greatest contributions.

The social aspects of Verhaeren's poetry have always been overemphasized, very naturally, but somewhat unjustifiably. In the social disillusionment through which we are passing, and which involves so many of the ideals with which Verhaeren affiliated, it is well to recognize that back of the social creeds is a personal philosophy that may be their ultimate justification. Practically, as it seems now, Verhaeren has been robbed by circumstance of his greatest triumph, the achievement of Europeanism. Coming into French literature, with an essentially Teutonic temperament, he mediated much of what was common to these two cultures, and to the time and the larger aspects of modern life. There is no hedging the fact that racial difference made possible his achievement. Technically even, the rhapsodic rhythm and the form of free verse are foreign to French verse and the Gallic spirit, and the advance of French poetry in the last twenty years has been due considerably to the foreign yeast in the loaf,—Verhaeren's subtle infusion having been one of the most efficacious. Ideally too, there has been a fusion of notions,—the deification of Force and Change, essentially Teutonic, with the humanitarian and cosmic scope so typical of the Gallic conception. Verhaeren was one of the great Europeans, who did much to fuse alien cultures in terms of their common problems; for his contributions have been so assimilated as to seem native. The elements that have discorded in practice have blended acceptably and permanently in a personal type of philosophy. Still the disillusionment of the social creed is keen, and may reverse the values, making the laureate of Belgium, the Verhaeren of Toût la Flandre, greater than Verhaeren, apostle of Europeanism. As either, Verhaeren himself would be, as he says of his countrymen in Ceûx de Liege, "secure beyond all praise." Yet properly speaking, cosmopolitanism of culture goes with the cosmic scope of his philosophy. Because of its deep humanitarianism, his nationalism is as big as his cosmopolitanism. His work closed as it began on the note of vibrant nationalism. It is to be pitied though that in the last stage war broke the serenity of mood in which he could see and say that, "Life goes on its cyclic way, and though man suffers, Nature seems to be carving a new face for her eternity." Modernists of all stripes could not forsee that the "transvaluation of all values" they were clamoring for was not the work of philosophy or art, but the travail and destiny of an age. Perhaps Verhaeren's superlative claim is this representativeness he has gained by incorporating in his poetry the issues of the age; but if it should prove that through war men can attain a unity of which they could only dream in peace, then the prophet in Verhaeren will contest the poet's fame.

COLOR—A REVIEW

LADIES and gentlemen! A genius! Posterity will laugh at us if we do not proclaim him now. COLOR transcends all the limiting qualifications that might be brought forward if it were merely a work of talent. It is a first book, but it would be treasurable if it were the last; it is a work of extreme youth and youthfulness over which the author later may care to write the apology of "juvenilia," but it has already the integration of a distinctive and matured style; it is the work of a Negro poet writing for the most part out of the intimate emotional experience of race, but the adjective is for the first time made irrelevant, so thoroughly has he poetized the substance and fused it with the universally human moods of life. Cullen's own Villonesque poetic preface to the contrary, time will not outsing these lyrics.

The authentic lyric gift is rare today for another reason than the rarity of poetic genius, and especially so in contemporary American poetry—for the substance of modern life brings a heavy sediment not easy to filter out in the poetic process. Only a few can distill a clear flowing product, Housman, de la Mare, Sara Teasdale, Edna St. Vincent Millay, one or two more perhaps. Countee Cullen's affinity with these has been instantly recognized. But he has grown in sandier soil and taken up a murkier substance; it has taken a longer tap-root to reach down to the deep tradition upon which great English poetry is nourished, and the achievement is notable. More than a personal temperament flowers, a race experience blooms; more than a reminiscent crop is gathered, a new stalk has sprouted and within the flower are, we believe, the seeds of a new stock, richly parented by two cultures. It is no disparagement to our earlier Negro poets to say this: men do not choose their time, and time is the gardener.

Why argue? Why analyze? The poet himself tells us

> Drink while my blood
> Colors the wine.

But it is that strange bouquet of the verses themselves that must be mulled to be rightly appreciated. Pour into the vat all the Tennyson, Swinburne, Housman, Patmore, Teasdale you want, and add a dash of Pope for this strange modern skill of sparkling couplets,—and all these I daresay have been intellectually culled and added to the brew, and still there is another evident ingredient, fruit of the Negro inheritance and experience, that has stored up the tropic sun and ripened under the storm and stress of the American transplanting. Out of this clash and final blend of the pagan with the Christian, the sensual with the Puritanically religious, the pariah with the prodigal, has come this strange new thing. The paradoxes of Negro life and feeling that have been sad and plaintive and whimsical in the age of Dunbar and that were rhetorical and troubled, vibrant and accusatory with the Johnsons and MacKay now glow and shine and sing in this poetry of the youngest generation.

This maturing of an ancestral heritage is a constant note in Cullen's poetry. *Fruit of the Flower* states it as a personal experience:

> My father is a quiet man
>   With sober, steady ways;
> For simile, a folded fan;
>   His nights are like his days.
>
> My mother's life is puritan,
>   No hint of cavalier,
> A pool so calm you're sure it can
>   Have little depth to fear.
>
> And yet my father's eyes can boast
>   How full his life has been;
> There haunts them yet the languid ghost
>   Of some still sacred sin.
>
> And though my mother chants of God,
>   And of the mystic river,

COLOR, by COUNTEE CULLEN. Harper & Brothers, New York. $2.

Opportunity 4 (January 1926): 14–15.

I've seen a bit of checkered sod
  Set all her flesh aquiver.

Why should he deem it pure mischance
  A son of his is fain
To do a naked tribal dance
  Each time he hears the rain?

Why should she think it devil's art
  That all my songs should be
Of love and lovers, broken heart,
  And wild sweet agony?

Who plants a seed begets a bud,
  Extract of that same root;
Why marvel at the hectic blood
  That flushes this wild fruit?

Better than syllogisms, *Gods* states the same thing racially:

I fast and pray and go to church,
  And put my penny in,
But God's not fooled by such slight tricks,
  And I'm not saved from sin.

I cannot hide from Him the gods
  That revel in my heart,
Nor can I find an easy word
  To tell them to depart:

God's alabaster turrets gleam
  Too high for me to win,
Unless He turns His face and lets
  Me bring my own gods in.

Here as indubitably as in Petrarch or Cellini or Stella, there is the renaissance note. What body of culture would not gladly let it in! In still more conscious conviction we have this message in the *Shroud of Color*:

Lord, not for what I saw in flesh or bone
Of fairer men; not raised on faith alone;
Lord, I will live persuaded by mine own.
I cannot play the recreant to these;
My spirit has come home, that sailed the
  doubtful seas.

The latter is from one of the two long poems in the volume; both it and *Heritage* are unusual achievements. They prove Mr. Cullen capable of an unusually sustained message. There is in them perhaps a too exuberant or at least too swiftly changing imagery, but nevertheless they have a power and promise unusual in this day of the short poem and the sketchy theme. They suggest the sources of our most classic tradition, and like so much that is most moving in English style seem bred from the Bible. Occasionally one is impressed with the fault of too great verbal facility, as though words were married on the lips rather than mated in the heart and mind, but never is there pathos or sentimentality, and the poetic idea always has taste and significance.

Classic as are the fundamentals of this verse, the overtones are most modernly enlightened:

The earth that writhes eternally with pain
Of birth, and woe of taking back her slain
Laid bare her teeming bosom to my sight,

And all was struggle, gasping breath, and fight.
A blind worm here dug tunnels to the light,
And there a seed, tacked with heroic pain,
Thrust eager tentacles to sun and rain.

Still more scientifically motivated, is:

Who shall declare
  My whereabouts;
Say if in the air
  My being shouts
Along light ways,
  Or if in the sea
Or deep earth stays
  The germ of me?

The lilt is that of youth, but the body of thought is most mature. Few lyric poets carry so sane and sober a philosophy. I would sum it up as a beautiful and not too optimistic pantheism, a rare gift to a disillusioned age. Let me quote at the end my favorite poem, one of its best expressions:

THE WISE.

Dead men are wisest, for they know
How far the roots of flowers go,
How long a seed must rot to grow.

Dead men alone bear frost and rain
On throbless heart and heatless brain,
And feel no stir of joy or pain.

Dead men alone are satiate;
They sleep and dream and have no weight,
To curb their rest, of love or hate.

Strange, men should flee their company,
Or think me strange who long to be
Wrapped in their cool immunity.

REVIEW OF *THE WEARY BLUES,*
BY LANGSTON HUGHES

I believe there are lyrics in this volume which are such contributions to pure poetry that it makes little difference what substance of life and experience they were made of, and yet I know no other volume of verse that I should put forward as more representatively the work of a race poet than *The Weary Blues*. Nor would I style Langston Hughes a race poet merely because he writes in many instances of Negro life and consciously as a Negro; but because all his poetry seems to be saturated with the rhythms and moods of Negro folk life. A true "people's poet" has their balladry in his veins; and to me many of these poems seem based on rhythms as seasoned as folk songs and on moods as deep-seated as folk ballads. Dunbar is supposed to have expressed the peasant heart of his people. But Dunbar was the showman of the Negro masses; here is their spokesman. The acid test is the entire absence of sentimentalism, the clean simplicity of speech, the deep terseness of mood. Taking these poems too much merely as the expressions of a personality, Carl Van Vechten in his debonair introduction wonders at what he calls "their deceptive air of spontaneous improvisation." The technique of folk song and dance are instinctively there, giving to the individual talent the bardic touch and power. Especially if Hughes should turn more and more to the colloquial experiences of the common folk whom he so intimately knows and so deeply loves, we may say that the Negro masses have found a voice, and promise to add to their natural domain of music and the dance the conquest of the province of poetry. Remember—I am not speaking of Negro poets, but of Negro poetry.

Poetry of a vitally characteristic racial flow and feeling then is the next step in our cultural development. Is it to be a jazz product? The title poem and first section of *The Weary Blues* seem superficially to suggest it. But let us see:

> And far into the night he crooned that tune.
> The stars went out and so did the moon.

Or this:

> Sing your Blues song,
> Pretty baby.
> You want lovin'
> And you don't mean maybe.
>
> Jungle lover. . . .
> Night black boy. . . .
> Two against the moon
> And the moon was joy.

Here—I suspect yet uncombined—are the two ingredients of the Negro poetry that will be truly and beautifully representative: the rhythm of the secular ballad but the imagery and diction of the spiritual. Stranger opposites than these have fused to the fashioning of new beauty. Nor is this so doctrinaire a question as it seems, when considering a poet who has

New York: Alfred A. Knopf, 1926. *Palms* (October 1926): 24–26.

gone to the cabaret for some of his rhythms and to the Bible for others.

In the poems that are avowedly racial, Hughes has a distinctive note. Not only are these poems full of that passionate declaration and acceptance of race which is a general characteristic of present-day Negro poets, but there is a mystic identification with the race experience which is, I think, instinctively deeper and broader than any of our poets has yet achieved.

"The Negro Speaks of Rivers" catches this note for us most unmistakably:

> I've known rivers;
> I've known rivers ancient as this world and older than the flow
>   of human blood in human veins.
>
> My soul has grown deep like the rivers.
>
> I bathed in the Euphrates when dawns were young.
> I built my hut near the Congo and it lulled me to sleep.
> I looked upon the Nile and raised the pyramids above it.
> I heard the singing of the Mississippi when Abe Lincoln
>   went down to New Orleans, and I've seen its muddy
>   bosom turn all golden in the sunset.
>
> I've known rivers;
> Ancient, dusky rivers.
>
> My soul has grown deep like the rivers.

Remembering this as the basic substratum of this poetry, we may discriminatingly know to what to attribute the epic surge underneath "its lyric swing, the primitive fatalism back of its nonchalance, the ancient force in its pert colloquialisms, the tropic abandon and irresistibleness of its sorrow and laughter."

No matter how whimsical or gay the poet may carry his overtones after this, or how much of a bohemian or happy troubadour he may assume to be, we will always hear a deep, tragic undertone pulsing in his verse. For the Negro experience rightly sensed even in the moods of the common folk is complex and paradoxical like the blues which Hughes has pointed out to be so characteristic, with their nonchalant humor against a background of tragedy; there is always a double mood, mercurial to the artist's touch like an easily improvised tune. As our poet himself puts it:

> In one hand
> I hold tragedy
> And in the other
> Comedy,—
> Masks for the soul.
>
> Laugh with me.
> You would laugh!
> Weep with me,
> Would you weep!
>
> Tears are my laughter.
> Laughter is my pain.
> Cry at my grinning mouth,
> If you will.
> Laugh at my sorrows's reign.

THE NEGRO POETS OF
THE UNITED STATES

NEGRO poets and Negro poetry are two quite different things. Of the one, since Phyllis Wheatley, we have had a century and a half; of the other, since Dunbar, scarcely a generation. But the significance of the work of Negro poets will more and more be seen and valued retrospectively as the medium through which a poetry of Negro life and experience has gradually become possible. Just such retrospective value and importance mainly has the entire earlier period of American literature itself, which for so considerable a time even after 1776, remained a provincial body of tradition and culture. America's cultural autonomy can as yet claim no sesqui-centennial, — the ink is still damp on our spiritual Declaration of Independence. By still slower but not unrelated processes have the various secondary bodies of the American tradition and experience come to cultural maturity and representative expression; but as they do, it becomes all the more apparent that the scheme of our culture is a confederation of minority traditions, a constellation of provinces, and not a national sun concentrated in one blazing, focal position. And among these, inevitably distinct by virtue of its peculiar social and cultural focus, whirls the gradually incandescent orb of the Negro's group thought and experience.

In the context of an established literature of New England and a metropolitan East, of a semi-established literature of the South and Middle West, and of an insurgent poetry of the Far West, and the Southwest, a Negro poetry and literature is no anomaly or exception. Even more distinctly (and in time we hope as proudly exclusive) of this area has American life been set apart and intensified as a group experience; social isolations and pressure have welded it into more than a local or sectional unity, and a cultural focus of peculiar range and dignity has thus been generated. It is out of the peculiarity of the experience rather than any uniqueness of inherent nature that this world of Negro thought and emotion has been created, but it needs only the glowing combustion of genius moving through it to reveal a new star in the American firmament, — a body of the first cultural magnitude.

Therefore I maintain that the work of Negro poets in the past has its chief significance in what it has led up to; through work of admittedly minor and secondary significance and power a folk-consciousness has slowly come into being and a folk-tradition has been started on the way to independent expression and development. Phyllis Wheatley chirping however significantly in the dawn of the American Revolution about

The muse inspire each future song!
Still, with the sweets of contemplation bless'd,
May peace with balmy wings your soul invest!
But when these shadows of time are chas'd away,
And darkness ends in everlasting day,
On what seraphic pinions shall we move,
And view the landscapes in the realms above?
There shall thy tongue in heav'nly murmur flow,
And there my muse with heav'nly transports glow —

has only a distant promise. She was race-conscious but not race-minded. And later when for two generations or more Negro poets rhymed out their "moral numbers" and pleaded for freedom, sometimes in creditable, sometimes in puerile quatrains that echoed Whittier and Mrs. Hemans, although the acceptance of race was passionate, it was

Anthology of Magazine Verse 1926 and Yearbook of American Poetry, sesquicentennial edition, ed. William S. Braithwaite. Boston: B.J. Brimmer, 1926, pp. 143–151.

abstract and rhetorical. Theirs was the opposite excess of being so race-minded that they
were race-bound. That verse of any treasurable
value at all was produced under these conditions
is an evidence of a musical and imaginative
endowment beyond the ordinary. George Horton,
Albery Whitman, Frances Watkins Harper at
least established our poetic literacy, and nourished
the ambition of a singing people to master the
provinces of language. They were well-recognized
in their day, perhaps as exceptions, but at least
not as Phyllis Wheatley was, as a controversial
prodigy. Further they compared not unfavorably
with all but their greatest contemporaries, in outlook, theme and diction so similar as to have
incurred from many quarters the charge of "sheer
unoriginal imitativeness." Be that as it may,
except for their preoccupation with the topic
of freedom and the notes of sentimental appeal
and moral protest, — both popular enough in
American poetry at large in their day, one cannot
say that there was anything inherently racial
about their poetry either in the derogatory or the
favorable sense. The second step up Parnassus
had simply been from the foothold by Negroes
to the half-way lodging of a poetry about the
Negro cause and question.

Poetry of Negro life itself, poetry that was in
any true sense racially expressive, was still unat-
tained at the time of emancipation and for at
least three decades after. Later the causes of this
may stand out more clearly. But this much is
certainly clear; — no such social satisfaction and
stimulus came into Negro life with emancipation
as accompanies normal political freedom; the
concrete realities of reconstruction could by no
means fill in and vivify the abstract Abolitionist
hopes or realize the roseate anti-slavery dream.
The poetic impulse was checked by steep social
disillusionment, by the dint of moral momentum
it plodded on in hortatory moods and accents,
fifing platitudes "to cheer the weary traveller."
Tracts in verse and sermons in couplets were the
typical result. Then eventually came the time
when the hectic rhetoric and dogged moralism had
to fall back in sheer exhaustion on the original
basis of cultural supply. Through Dunbar, — part
of whose poetry nevertheless, reflects the last stand
of this rhetorical advance, Negro poetry came
penitently back to the folk-tradition, and humbled
itself to dialect for fresh spiritual food and raiment.
It is for this reason, as Stanley Braithwaite has so
discerningly put it, that Dunbar's poetry closes
one age and begins another. Paul Laurence Dunbar definitely accomplished three significant things.

The first was to have brought the work of a Negro
in poetry to general public attention and acceptance; and thus to have emancipated the Negro
artist from his special reading clientele of pet
friends and sympathizers. His second was to have
established the idea of folk-expression; a priceless
boon even at the great cost of having shackled
Negro poets for over a generation to the limitations and handicaps of dialect. The third accomplishment was to have given fresh impetus
to lyric expression; free singing from a free heart.
This makes Dunbar the Robert Burns of our
race tradition.

Dunbar had scores of imitators, some of them
like Holloway, Carmichael, Daniel Webster Davis,
and Ernest Shackleford, poets of some real talent
and inspiration. But they were as handicapped as
their predecessors, though in a different way.
They plead in dialect; the peasant became a moral
stalking-horse for their generation just as for the
previous generation the ideals of freedom and
humanity had been. They were thus hopelessly
minor and secondary in outlook and accomplishment, befogged again by the mists of the Negro
problem. Almost contemporaneously however,
isolated individuals were manœuvring towards
the main roads of poetry: Carruthers, McClellan,
Joseph Cotter, Sr., held back somewhat by the
dilemma of dialect, — wishing not to desert the
race spiritually but at the same time not to be
hampered by the Dunbar tradition, which was
gradually deteriorating from minstrelsy, to buffoonery. Significant in title and accomplishment,
there came, in 1917, James Weldon Johnson's
"Fifty Years and Other Poems." Cultural perspective had come, and with it the depth and
articulateness of major poetry; Negro poetry in
the year of America's entry into the Great War,
through the work of Roscoe Jameson, Claude
McKay and James Weldon Johnson was linked
up with the main stream and tradition of English
poetry, and on an esthetic rather than a moral
basis began to attain universality and by right to
claim general attention.

In the very act of discarding dialect and the
hectic rhetorical assertion of race, Negro poetry
became at one and the same time more universal
and more racial, finding a strange peace and ease
in what had given it most inquietude. For in
becoming less self-conscious, it became more
naïvely and beautifully expressive, like music.

Blown by black players on a picnic day.

The poetry of protest and social analysis still
continued, as the vibrant verses of the same poet,

Claude McKay, so often attest, but even in this vein contemporary Negro poetry has achieved the dignity of self-esteem and the poise of self-confidence. Of the race spirit, as of McKay's dancer, it can be said —

> To me she seemed a proudly swaying palm
> Grown lovelier through passing through a storm—

To the freedom of heart, freedom of mind and spirit had to be joined before conditions conducive to great poetry were achieved. Negro poets now began to accept race not as a duty but a privilege, and to find joy and inspiration not in the escape from handicaps, but in the mastery of experience. McKay can sing of America,

> Although she feeds me bread of bitterness
> I love this cultured hell that tests my youth,—

and Cullen, reaching out through the race experience to the sense of a group heritage and tradition, expresses this growing spiritual conquest still more positively: —

> Lord, not for what I saw in flesh or bone
> Of fairer men; not raised on faith alone;
> Lord, I will live persuaded by mine own.
> I cannot play the recreant to these:
> My spirit has come home, — that sailed the
>   doubtful seas.

In the work of the younger Negro poets since 1918, though there is no unity of style or a school, there is this ever-increasing unity of spirit and sense of tradition. It has come about in spite of a startling increase in the numbers of our poets, and their varied affiliations with the richly differentiated technique of the modern schools of poetry. More than this, a comparable gain in technical competence and distinctive excellence of performance has come about in recent years. Readers of this *Anthology* and of the general and special magazines, familiar already with the names of McKay, Georgia Douglas Johnson, Anne Spencer, Angelina Grimke, Jean Toomer, Langston Hughes, and Countée Cullen, will know and concede that Negro genius has shared liberally in the renaissance of American poetry and made a substantial and distinctive contribution to it. Indeed, contemporary American poets, engaged in spite of all their diversities of outlook and technique in a fundamentally common effort to discover and release the national spirit in poetry, have sensed a kindred aim and motive in Negro poetry, and have turned with deep and unbiassed interest to Negro materials as themes and Negro idioms of speech and emotion as artistic inspiration. While not limiting themselves to the special province, which is peculiarly and intimately their own, the young Negro poets have become quite unanimous in spirit and purpose to develop

this folk tradition into full artistic expression and cultural recognition. This gives their work the significance and impetus of a definite artistic movement. Special organs of journalistic and literary expression, specific prize-awards and contests as those now conducted annually under the auspices of the Negro journals, *Opportunity* and *The Crisis*, feed the movement and to some extent give it critical direction. Of late a new crop of poets is hatched annually, and names of fresh promise constantly appear, — Gwendolyn Bennett, Arna Bontemps, Frank Horne, Helene Johnson, — to mention only a few. But the significance of this is not so much in the fact that more poetry has been produced in less than a decade than the yield of over a century and a half, but that better poetry and a philosophy of art have also come. From the bathos of sentimental appeal and the postures of moralizing protest, Negro poets have risen to the dignity and poise of self-expression. Freed from the limitations of dialect that made the technique of the nursery rhyme tolerable, they have not only achieved a modernism of expression, but are attempting to develop new characteristic idioms of style. In place of the persistent and oppressive race consciousness, they have in part acquired the dignity of race spokesmanship and in part re-achieved the enviable naïveté of the slave-singers. More than all else, especially in its promise for the future, they have won that artistic acceptance of life which makes great art possible.

Can it be doubted? At least the contemporary Negro poets have no hawk shadow of doubt over their attempts to sing and soar; they are writing today poetry of national distinction and value, but poetry none the less full of a vitally characteristic racial flow and feeling, inspired by the belief that a people that can give its sorrow enduring musical expression can make its soul powerfully articulate. There is more than subjective ecstasy in Cullen's,

> This is my hour
> To wax and climb,
> Flaunt a red flower
> In the face of time.

And the lyric sincerity and insight of her generation are in Helene Johnson's

> Ah, little road all whirry in the breeze,
> A leaping clay hill lost among the trees,
> The bleeding note of rapture streaming thrush
> Caught in a drowsy hush
> And stretched out in a single singing line of dusky song.
> Ah little road, brown as my race is brown,
> Your trodden beauty like our trodden pride,
> Dust of the dust, they must not bruise you down.
> Rise to one brimming, golden, spilling cry!

THE POETRY OF NEGRO LIFE

With this generation of Negro poets, a folk temperament flowers and a race experience bears fruit. Race is often a closer spiritual bond than nationality and group experience deeper than an individual's: here we have beauty that is born of long-suffering, truth that is derived from mass emotion and founded on collective vision. The spiritual search and discovery which is every artist's is in this case more than personal; it is the epic reach and surge of a people seeking their group character through art.

So, significant as these four poets are in their separate individualities among their American contemporaries,—and they notably are—with their common racial background behind them they have still deeper meaning and wider human interest. Though their poetry ranges through all possible themes, it is therefore no spiritual distortion or misrepresentation that their more racially distinctive poems have been selected for this little anthology. For the present-day Negro poet regards his racial heritage as a more precious endowment than his own personal genius, and to the common legacy of his art adds the peculiar experiences and emotions of his folk. For McKay, Africa's past is not an abandoned shamble but a treasure trove:

> 'My soul would sing forgotten jungle songs . . .
> I would go back to darkness and to peace
> But the great western world holds me in fee
> And I may never hope for full release
> While to its alien gods I bend my knee.'

To Toomer, slavery, once a shame and stigma, becomes a spiritual process of growth and transfiguration, and the tortuous underground groping of one generation the maturing and high blossoming of the next. Of this dark fruit of experience he says:

> 'One plum was saved for me; one seed becomes
> An everlasting song, a singing tree
> Caroling softly souls of slavery.'

In Cullen's *Shroud of Color*, the vision is one of loyalty, group pride and confidence; a revelation of destiny as that of a chosen people:

> 'Lord, I will live persuaded by mine own,
> I cannot play the recreant to these:
> My spirit has come home, that sailed the doubtful seas.'

And Langston Hughes, with a quite ecstatic sense of kinship with even the most common and lowly folk, discovers in them, in spite of their individual sordidness and backwardness, the epic quality of collective strength and beauty.

> Dream-singers all,—
> Story-tellers all,—
> Singers and dancers,
> Dancers and laughers,
> Loud-mouthed laughers in the hands of Fate.
> My people.

Yet with all their racial representativeness, these poets are of their time and nation. In major magnitude instead of minor twinkling, they help make the brilliance of contemporary American poetry. They are modernists among the moderns, and reflectors of common trends and current tendencies. McKay's proud spirit links our newly insurgent race pride and consciousness with the rebel poetry of radical thought and social criticism. Jean Toomer's probing into the sub-soil of Southern life is only a significant bit of the same plowing under of Reconstruction sentimentalism that has yielded us a new realistic poetry of the South. The work of Countee Cullen shares the polished lyricism of Sara Teasdale, Edna St. Vincent Millay and Robert Frost as much as it does the exuberant flow of an awakening Negro life. And Hughes, Dunbar of his generation, brings to his portrayal of his folk not the ragged provincialism of a minstrel but the descriptive detachment of a Vachel Lindsay and a Sandburg and promises the democratic sweep and universality of a Whitman.

Since Weldon Johnson's *Creation*, race poetry does not mean dialect but a reflection of Negro experience true to its idiom of emotion and circumstance. But through these younger poets, the Negro poet becomes as much an expression of his age as of his folk. In the chorus of American singing they have registered distinctive notes whose characteristic timbre we would never lose or willingly let lapse; however more and more they become orchestrated into our national art and culture.

Four Negro Poets, ed. Alain Locke. New York: Simon & Schuster, 1927, pp. 5–6.

STERLING BROWN:
THE NEW NEGRO FOLK-POET

MANY critics, writing in praise of Sterling Brown's first volume of verse, have seen fit to hail him as a significant new Negro poet. The discriminating few go further; they hail a new era in Negro poetry, for such is the deeper significance of this volume (*The Southern Road*, Sterling A. Brown, Harcourt Brace, New York, 1932). Gauging the main objective of Negro poetry as the poetic portrayal of Negro folk-life true in both letter and spirit to the idiom of the folk's own way of feeling and thinking, we may say that here for the first time is that much-desired and long-awaited acme attained or brought within actual reach.

Almost since the advent of the Negro poet public opinion has expected and demanded folk-poetry of him. And Negro poets have tried hard and voluminously to cater to this popular demand. But on the whole, for very understandable reasons, folk-poetry by Negroes, with notable flash exceptions, has been very unsatisfactory and weak, and despite the intimacy of the race poet's attachments, has been representative in only a limited, superficial sense. First of all, the demand has been too insistent. "They required of us a song in a strange land." "How could we sing of thee, O Zion?" There was the canker of theatricality and exhibitionism planted at the very heart of Negro poetry, unwittingly no doubt, but just as fatally. Other captive nations have suffered the same ordeal. But with the Negro another spiritual handicap was imposed. Robbed of his own tradition, there was no internal compensation to counter the external pressure. Consequently the Negro spirit had a triple plague on its heart and mind—morbid self-consciousness, self-pity and forced exhibitionism. Small wonder that so much poetry by Negroes exhibits in one degree or another the blights of bombast, bathos and artificiality. Much genuine poetic talent has thus been blighted either by these spiritual faults or their equally vicious over-compensations. And so it is epoch-making to have developed a poet whose work, to quote a recent criticism, " has no taint of music-hall convention, is neither arrogant nor servile "—and plays up to neither side of the racial dilemma. For it is as fatal to true poetry to cater to the self-pity or racial vanity of a persecuted group as to pander to the amusement complex of the overlords and masters.

I do not mean to imply that Sterling Brown's art is perfect, or even completely mature. It is all the more promising that this volume represents the work of a young man just in his early thirties. But a Negro poet with almost complete detachment, yet with a tone of persuasive sincerity, whose muse neither clowns nor shouts, is indeed a promising and a grateful phenomenon.

By some deft touch, independent of dialect, Mr. Brown is able to compose with the freshness and

Negro Anthology, reprint ed. Nancy Cunard. New York: Negro Universities Press, 1969, pp. 111–115. Originally published in 1934 (pp. 88–92).

naturalness of folk balladry—*Maumee Ruth, Dark O' the Moon, Sam Smiley, Slim Green, Johnny Thomas,* and *Memphis Blues* will convince the most sceptical that modern Negro life can yield real balladry and a Negro poet achieve an authentic folk-touch.[1]

Or this from *Sam Smiley* :

> The mob was in fine fettle, yet
> The dogs were stupid-nosed, and day
> Was far spent when the men drew round
> The scrawny wood where Smiley lay.
>
> The oaken leaves drowsed prettily,
> The moon shone benignly there;
> And big Sam Smiley, King Buckdancer,
> Buckdanced on the midnight air.

This is even more dramatic and graphic than that fine but more melodramatic lyric of Langston Hughes :

> Way down South in Dixie
> (Break the heart of me!)
> They hung my black young lover
> To a cross-road's tree.

With Mr. Brown the racial touch is quite independent of dialect; it is because in his ballads and lyrics he has caught the deeper idiom of feeling or the peculiar paradox of the racial situation. That gives the genuine earthy folk-touch, and justifies a statement I ventured some years back : " the soul of the Negro will be discovered in a characteristic way of thinking and in a homely philosophy rather than in a jingling and juggling of broken English." As a matter of fact, Negro dialect is extremely local—it changes from place to place, as do white dialects. And what is more, the dialect of Dunbar and the other early Negro poets never was on land or sea as a living peasant speech; but it has had such wide currency, especially on the stage, as to have successfully deceived half the world, including the many Negroes who for one reason or another imitate it.

Sterling Brown's dialect is also local, and frankly an adaptation, but he has localised it carefully, after close observation and study, and varies it according to the brogue of the locality or the characteristic jargon of the *milieu* of which he is writing. But his racial effects, as I have said, are not dependent on dialect. Consider *Maumee Ruth* :

> Might as well bury her
> And bury her deep,
> Might as well put her
> Where she can sleep. . . .
>
> Boy that she suckled
> How should he know,
> Hiding in city holes
> Sniffing the " snow "?[2]
>
> And how should the news
> Pierce Harlem's din,
> To reach her baby gal
> Sodden with gin?
>
> Might as well drop her
> Deep in the ground,
> Might as well pray for her,
> That she sleep sound.

That is as uniquely racial as the straight dialect of *Southern Road* :

> White man tells me—hunh—
> Damn yo' soul;
> White man tells me—hunh—
> Damn yo' soul;
> Got no need, bebby,
> To be tole.

---

[1] This exquisite poem is in the Poetry section.   (This refers to Nancy Cunard's book [Editor's note].)

[2] Cocaine.

If we stop to inquire—as unfortunately the critic must—into the magic of these effects, we find the secret, I think, in this fact more than in any other : Sterling Brown has listened long and carefully to the folk in their intimate hours, when they were talking to themselves, not, so to speak, as in Dunbar, but actually as they do when the masks of protective mimicry fall. Not only has he dared to give quiet but bold expression to this private thought and speech, but he has dared to give the Negro peasant credit for thinking. In this way he has recaptured the shrewd Aesopian quality of the Negro folk-thought, which is more profoundly characteristic than their types of metaphors or their mannerisms of speech. They are, as he himself says,

> Illiterate, and somehow very wise,

and it is this wisdom, bitter fruit of their suffering, combined with their characteristic fatalism and irony, which in this book gives a truer soul picture of the Negro than has ever yet been given poetically. The traditional Negro is a clown, a buffoon, an easy laugher, a shallow sobber and a credulous christian ; the real Negro underneath is more often an all but cynical fatalist, a shrewd pretender, and a boldly whimsical pagan ; or when not, a lusty, realistic religionist who tastes its nectars here and now.

> Mammy
> With deep religion defeating the grief
> Life piled so closely about her

is the key picture to the Negro as christian ; Mr. Brown's *When the Saints Come Marching Home* is worth half a dozen essays on the Negro's religion. But to return to the question of bold exposure of the intimacies of Negro thinking—read that priceless apologia of kitchen stealing in the *Ruminations of Luke Johnson*, reflective husband of Mandy Jane, tromping early to work with a great big basket, and tromping wearily back with it at night laden with the petty spoils of the day's picking :

> Well, taint my business noway,
> An' I ain' near fo'gotten
> De lady what she wuks fo',
> An' how she got her jack;
> De money dat she live on
> Come from niggers pickin' cotton,
> Ebbery dollar dat she squander
> Nearly bust a nigger's back.
>
> So I'm glad dat in de evenins
> Mandy Jane seems extra happy,
> An' de lady at de big house
> Got no kick at all I say—
> Cause what huh " dear grandfawthaw "
> Took from Mandy Jane's grandpappy—
> Ain' no basket in de worl'
> What kin tote all dat away. . . .

Or again in that delicious epic of *Sporting Beasley* entering heaven :

> Lord help us, give a look at him,
> Don't make him dress up in no nightgown, Lord.
> Don't put no fuss and feathers on his shoulders, Lord.
>   Let him know it's heaven,
> Let him keep his hat, his vest, his elkstooth, and everything.
> Let him have his spats and cane.

It is not enough to sprinkle " dis's and dat's " to be a Negro folk-poet, or to jingle rhymes and juggle popularised clichés traditional to sentimental minor poetry for generations. One must study the intimate thought of the people who can only state it in an ejaculation, or a metaphor, or at best a proverb, and translate that into an articulate attitude, or a folk philosophy or a daring fable, with Aesopian clarity and simplicity—and above all, with Aesopian candor.

The last is most important; other Negro poets in many ways have been too tender with their own, even though they have learned with the increasing boldness of new Negro thought not to be too gingerly and conciliatory to and about the white man. The Negro muse weaned itself of that in McKay, Fenton Johnson, Toomer, Countee Cullen and Langston Hughes. But in Sterling Brown it has learned to laugh at itself and to chide itself with the same broomstick. I have space for only two examples: *Children's Children*:

> When they hear
> These songs, born of the travail of their sires,
> Diamonds of song, deep buried beneath the weight
> Of dark and heavy years;
> They laugh.
>
> They have forgotten, they have never known
> Long days beneath the torrid Dixie sun,
> In miasma'd rice swamps;
> The chopping of dried grass, on the third go round
> In strangling cotton;
> Wintry nights in mud-daubed makeshift huts,
> With these songs, sole comfort.
>
> They have forgotten
> What had to be endured—
> That they, babbling young ones,
> With their paled faces, coppered lips,
> And sleek hair cajoled to Caucasian straightness,
> Might drown the quiet voice of beauty
> With sensuous stridency;
>
> And might, on hearing these memories of their sires,
> Giggle,
> And nudge each other's satin-clad
> Sleek sides.

Anent the same broomstick, it is refreshing to read *Mr. Samuel and Sam*, from which we can only quote in part:

> Mister Samuel, he belong to Rotary,
> Sam, to de Sons of Rest;
> Both wear red hats like monkey men,
> An' you cain't say which is de best. . . .
>
> Mister Samuel die, an' de folks all know,
> Sam die widout no noise;
> De worl' go by in de same ol' way,
> And dey's both of 'em po' los' boys.

There is a world of psychological distance between this and the rhetorical defiance and the plaintive, furtive sarcasms of even some of our other contemporary poets—even as theirs, it must be said in all justice, was miles better and more representative than the sycophancies and platitudes of the older writers.

In closing it might be well to trace briefly the steps by which Negro poetry has scrambled up the sides of Parnassus from the ditches of minstrelsy and the trenches of race propaganda. In complaining against the narrow compass of dialect poetry (dialect is an organ with only two stops—pathos and humor), Weldon Johnson tried to break the Dunbar mould and shake free of the traditional stereotypes. But significant as it was, this was more a threat than an accomplishment; his own dialect poetry has all of the clichés of Dunbar without Dunbar's lilting lyric charm. Later in the *Negro Sermons* Weldon Johnson discovered a way out—in a rhapsodic form free from the verse shackles of classical minor poetry, and in the attempt to substitute an idiom of racial thought and imagery for a mere dialect of peasant speech. Claude McKay then broke with all the moods conventional in his day in Negro poetry, and presented a Negro who could challenge and hate, who knew resentment, brooded intellectual sarcasm, and felt contemplative irony. In this, so to speak, he pulled the psychological cloak off the Negro and revealed, even to the Negro himself, those facts disguised till then by his shrewd protective mimicry or pressed down under the dramatic mask of living up to what was expected of him. But though McKay sensed a truer Negro, he was at times too indignant at the older sham, and, too, lacked the requisite native touch—as of West Indian birth and training—with the local color of the American Negro. Jean Toomer went deeper still—I should say higher—and saw for the first time the glaring paradoxes and the deeper ironies of the situation, as they affected not only the Negro but the white man. He realised, too, that Negro idiom was anything but trite and derivative, and also that it was in emotional substance pagan— all of which he convincingly demonstrated, alas, all too fugitively, in *Cane*. But Toomer was not enough of a realist, or patient enough as an observer, to reproduce extensively a folk idiom.

Then Langston Hughes came with his revelation of the emotional color of Negro life, and his brilliant discovery of the flow and rhythm of the modern and especially the city Negro, substituting this jazz figure and personality for the older plantation stereotype. But it was essentially a jazz version of Negro life, and that is to say as much American, or more, as Negro; and though fascinating and true to an epoch this version was surface quality after all.

Sterling Brown, more reflective, a closer student of the folk-life, and above all a bolder and more detached observer, has gone deeper still, and has found certain basic, more sober and more persistent qualities of Negro thought and feeling; and so has reached a sort of common denominator between the old and the new Negro. Underneath the particularities of one generation are hidden universalities which only deeply penetrating genius can fathom and bring to the surface. Too many of the articulate intellects of the Negro group—including sadly enough the younger poets—themselves children of opportunity, have been unaware of these deep resources of the past. But here, if anywhere, in the ancient common wisdom of the folk, is the real treasure trove of the Negro poet; and Sterling Brown's poetic divining-rod has dipped significantly over this position. It is in this sense that I believe *Southern Road* ushers in a new era in Negro folk-expression and brings a new dimension in Negro folk-portraiture.

PROPAGANDA—OR POETRY?

AS the articulate voices of an oppressed minority, one would naturally expect the work of Negro poets to reflect a strongly emphasized social consciousness. That is the case, if gauged by their preoccupation with the theme of race. But whereas the race consciousness factor has been strong for obvious reasons, more generalized social-mindedness has been relatively weak in Negro poetry, and until recently the form of it which we know today as class-consciousness has been conspicuously absent.

Before broaching an interpretation, let us look at the facts. Negro expression from the days of Phyllis Wheatley was pivoted on a painfully negative and melodramatic sense of race. Self-pity and its corrective of rhetorical bombast were the ground notes of the Negro's poetry for several generations. The gradual conversion of race consciousness from a negative sense of social wrong and injustice to a positive note of race loyalty and pride in racial tradition came as a difficult and rather belated development of spiritual maturity. This and its group analogue—a positively toned morale of group solidarity—was the outstanding feature of Negro development of the post-World War period. I would not recant my 1925 estimate of this, either as a symptom of cultural maturity or as a sign of a significant development in the Negro folk consciousness. However, I would not confuse this upsurging of race consciousness with a parallel maturing of social consciousness, such as seems recently to be taking place. I do think, however, that the Negro could only be spurred on to the development of social consciousness in his creative expression through the previous intensification and change of tone of his racial consciousness.

But for a long while it was quite possible for the Negro poet and writer to be a rebel and protestant in terms of the race situation and a conforming conventionalist in his general social thinking. Just as it was earlier possible for many Negroes to be anti-slavery but Tory, rather than Whig in their general politics. The average Negro writer has thus been characteristically conservative and conformist on general social, political and economic issues, something of a traditionalist with regard to art, style and philosophy, with a little salient of racial radicalism jutting out in front—the spear-point of his position. Many forces account for this, chief among them the tendency the world over for the elite of any oppressed minority to aspire to the conventionally established values and court their protection and prestige. In this the Negro has been no exception, but on that very score is not entitled to exceptional blame or ridicule.

There is an additional important factor in accounting for the lack of social radicalism in the Negro's artistic expression. This comes from the dilemma of racialism in the form in which it presents itself to the American Negro. Let me state it, with grateful acknowledgements, in the words of Rebecca Barton's admirable but little known study, "Race Consciousness and the American Negro."*

*Busck Press; Copenhagen, 1934.

Race 1 (Summer 1936): 70–76, 87.

"The Negroes have no distinctive language to help foster their uniqueness. Their religion is the same fundamentally as that of the white group. There is no complete geographical isolation or centralization in one part of the country. On leaving their particular community they find themselves in a white world which suggests that the only claim they have for being a distinctive group is their color, and that this is nothing to arouse pride. Their manners, habits and customs are typically American, and they cannot escape from a certain economic and cultural dependence on the white people. They have not as much inner content to nurture their separate group life in America as national groups composed of immigrants from the Old World. Too great insistence upon withdrawing into their race would be an unhealthy escape, and would damage the chances of group efficiency by a balanced adjustment to the larger environment. . . . On the other hand, race values are too important not to preserve, and if the Negroes tried to identify themselves completely with white America, they feel that there would be a cultural loss. The skepticism as to any uniqueness of race temperament which has biological roots may be justified, but there is plenty in the distinctive social experience of the group to account for it and to give it tangible substance. The solution becomes one of being both a Negro and an American. It is the belief of many that this middle course can be taken, that the Negro can still be his individual self and yet cooperate in American life. If the building up of some group tradition is encouraged only as long as it is harmonious with fuller participation in national culture, then it can be a center from which creative activity can radiate. From this point of view, 'the racialism of the Negro is no limitation or reservation with respect to American life; it is only a constructive effort to build the obstructions in the stream of his progress into an efficient dam of social energy and power'."

It is this flaming dilemma that has narrowed and monopolized the social vision of the Negro artist. Race has been an obsession with him, and has both helped and hampered his spiritual progress. However, it is absurd to expect him to ignore it and cast it aside. Any larger social vision must be generated from within the Negro's race consciousness, like the adding of another dimension to this necessary plane of his experience. The deepening social consciousness of Negro poets actually follows this expected course, from its earliest beginning even to the present.

As early as 1914, Fenton Johnson flared out with a mood of emotional revolt and social indictment that was half a generation ahead of its time. Johnson went much further than the usual rhetorical protest against social injustice; he flung down a cynical challenge and a note of complete disillusionment with contemporary civilization. His contemporaries were too startled to catch the full significance of "Tired" and "The Scarlet Woman."

Tired

I am tired of work; I am tired of building up somebody else's civilization.

Let us take a rest, M'Lissy Jane.

I will go down to the Last Chance Saloon, drink a gallon or two of gin, shoot a game or two of dice and sleep the rest of the night on one of Mike's barrels.

You will let the old shanty go to rot, the white people's clothes turn to dust, and the Calvary Baptist Church sink to the bottomless pit.

You will spend your days forgetting you married me and your nights hunting the warm gin Mike serves the ladies in the rear of the Last Chance Saloon.

Throw the children into the river; civilization has given us too many. It is better to die than it is to grow up and find out that you are colored.

Pluck the stars out of the heavens. The stars mark our destiny. The stars marked my destiny.

I am tired of civilization.

The Scarlet Woman

Once I was good like the Virgin Mary and the Minister's wife.

My father worked for Mr. Pullman and white people's tips; but he died two days after his insurance expired.

I had nothing, so I had to go to work.

All the stock I had was a white girl's education and a face that enchanted the men of both races.

Starvation danced with me.

So when Big Lizzie, who kept a house for white men, came to me with tales of fortune that I could reap for the sale of my virtue I bowed my head to Vice.

Now I can drink more gin than any man for miles around.

Gin is better than all the water in Lethe.

Claude McKay's vibrant protests of a few years later deserve mention, although in social philosophy they are no more radical because the indignation is fired by personal anger and the threat of moral retribution. McKay was a rebel, but an individualistic one. And so, for the most part was Langston Hughes, except in his later phase of deliberate proletarian protest. In his earlier poetry, Hughes has a double strain of social protest; the first, based on a curious preoccupation (almost an obsession) with the dilemma of the mulatto, and the other, a passionate description of the suppressed worker. But in both, Hughes' reaction is that of an ironic question mark or the mocking challenge of a folk laughter and joy which cannot be silenced or suppressed. "Loud-mouthed laughers in the hands of Fate": Hughes throws his emotional defiance into the teeth of oppression. He rarely extends this mood to systematic social criticism or protest, often suggests, instead of a revolutionary solution, emotional defiance and escape—as in

Cross

My old man's a white old man
And my old mother's black.
If ever I cursed my white old man
I take my curses back.

If ever I cursed my black old mother
And wished she were in hell,
I'm sorry for that evil wish
And now I wish her well.

My old man died in a fine big house.
My ma died in a shack.
I wonder where I'm gonna die,
Being neither white nor black?

and

A bright bowl of brass is beautiful to the Lord.
Bright polished brass like the cymbals
Of King David's dancers,
Like the wine cups of Solomon.
        Hey, boy!
A clean spittoon on the altar of the Lord. . . .
At least I can offer that.

This is hardly more socialistic than Countee Cullen's well-turned epigram

For a Certain Lady I Know

She even thinks that up in Heaven,
Her class lies late and snores,
While poor black Cherubs rise at seven
To do celestial chores.

or Waring Cuney's

The Radical

Men never know
What they are doing.
They always make a muddle
Of their affairs,

They always tie their affairs
Into a knot
They cannot untie.
Then I come in
Uninvited.

They do not ask me in;
I am the radical,
The bomb thrower,
I untie the knot
That they have made,
And they never thank me.

These were the moods of 1927-31; and though they are not Marxian or doctrinal, their emotional logic is significantly radical. They have one great advantage over later more doctrinal versification—they do have poetic force and artistry.

Right here we may profitably take account of an unfortunate insistence of proletarian poetry on being drab, prosy and inartistic, as though the regard for style were a bourgeois taint and an act of social treason. Granted that virtuosity is a symptom of decadence, and preciosity a sign of cultural snobbishness, the radical poet need not disavow artistry, for that is a hallmark of all great folk-art. The simplicity, calm dignity and depth of folk art have yet to be constructively considered by the bulk of the proletarian exponents of our present scene. This decline in poetic force, terseness and simplicity is noticeable in the majority of the overtly radical Negro poetry. In his later poems that more directly espouse the cause of the masses. Langston Hughes, for example, is much less of a poet; he is often merely rhetorical and melodramatic rather than immersed in the mood. "Scottsboro Limited" (1932) marks with him the definite transition from the folk concept to the class concept. But instead of the authentic folk note, the powerful and convincing dialect, the terse moving rhythm of his lyric and his "blues" period, or the barbed and flaming ironies of his earlier social challenge, we have turgid, smouldering rhetoric, rimed propaganda, and the tone of the ranting orator and the strident prosecutor. I have two criticisms in passing, made in the interests of effective expression of the very reactions in question and the radical objectives themselves. The fire of social protest should flame, not smoulder; and any expression on behalf of the Negro masses should exhibit the characteristic Negro folk artistry.

That is why we should scan the horizon for the appearance of a true spokesman for the black masses, an authentic voice of the people. As yet, he seems not at hand. But a succession of younger poets points in his direction. Richard Wright, Frank Marshall Davis, Sterling Brown show a gradually nearer approach to the poetry that can fuse class consciousness with racial protest, and express proletarian sentiment in the genuine Negro folk idiom. And with this we approach a really effective and probably lasting poetry. Even Hughes moves on between 1933 and 1935, from the turgid tractate drawl of his "Letter to the Academy" (1933):

"But please—all you gentlemen with beards who are so wise and old, and who write better than we do and whose souls have triumphed (in spite of hungers and wars and the evils about you) and whose books have soared in calmness and beauty aloof from the struggle to the library shelves and the desks of students and who are now classics—come forward and speak upon
The subject of the Revolution.

We want to know what in the hell you'd say?" to the terser, homelier, more effective "Ballad of Roosevelt":

The pot was empty,
The cupboard was bare.
I said, Papa
What's the matter here?
"I'm waitin' on Roosevelt, son,
Roosevelt, Roosevelt,
Waitin' on Roosevelt, son."

But when they felt those
Cold winds blow
And didn't have no
Place to go—
Pa said, "I'm tired
O' waitin' on Roosevelt,
Roosevelt, Roosevelt,
Damn tired o' waitin' on Roosevelt."

Similarly, much of Richard Wright's poetry is mere strophic propaganda, little better for being cast in the broken mold of free verse than if it were spoken in plain pamphlet prose. Of course, this is not always so. "I Have Seen Black Hands," for all its obvious Whitman derivation, is powerful throughout, and, in several spots, is definitely poetic. The final strophe, lifted out of the descriptive potpourri of the earlier sections by a really surging rhapsodic swell, is convincing and exceeds propagandist dimensions:

"I am black and I have seen black hands

Raised in fists of revolt, side by side with the white fists of white workers,
And some day—and it is only this which sustains me—
Some day there will be millions and millions of them,
On some red day in a burst of fists on a new horizon!"

But Wright is capable of the still finer, though entirely non-racial note of

"Everywhere,
On tenemented mountains of hunger,
In ghetto swamps of suffering,
In breadline forest of despair,
In peonized forest of hopelessness
The red moisture of revolt
Is condensing on the cold stones of human need."

Frank Howard Davis, of Chicago,* for all that he boasts of a "perch on Parnassus" and confesses an urge "to take little, pale, wan, penny-apiece words and weave them into gay tapestries for beauty's sake," has an etcher's touch and an acid bite to his vignettes of life that any "proletarian poet" or Marxian critic might well envy and emulate. For he speaks of

Black scars disfigure
    the ruddy cheeks of new mornings in Dixie
    (lynched black men hanging from green trees)
Blind justice kicked, beaten, taken for a ride and left for dead
    (have you ever heard of Scottsboro, Alabam?)
Your Constitution gone blah-blah, shattered into a thousand pieces like a broken mirror
Lincoln a hoary myth
    (how many black men vote in Georgia?)
Mobs, chaingangs down South
Tuberculosis up North
--so now I am civilized
What do you want, America? . . . .

Kill me if you must, America
All at once or a little each day
It won't matter. . . .

Yet today is today
Today must be emptied like a bucket before it dries into history
Today is an eagle, lingering a while, ready to fly into eternity,
Today I live
Today I tell of black folk who made America yesterday, who make America now
Today I see America clawing me like a tiger caged with a hare

*Black Man's Verse; Black Cat Press, Chicago, 1935, $3.50.

Today I hear discords and crazy words in the
   song America sings to black folk
So today I ask—
What do you want, America?

How different, even in the similarity of theme,
is this from James Weldon Johnson's pale
rhetoric of yesterday:
    "How would you have us—
    As we are,
    Our eyes fixed forward on a star?
    Or clanking chains about your feet?"

No more apt illustration could be given of
the change in the last fifteen years of the tone
and gamut of the Negro poet's social consciousness. But let us follow Frank Davis a step further in his social analysis which is as accurate
as his social description is trenchant: from his
"Georgia's Atlanta:"

As omnipresent as air
are the Complexes
reminding white folk of superiority
keeping black folk subdued.
God
it so happens
either sleeps in the barn
or washes dishes for the Complexes.

Black Shirts—B.Y.P.U.'s
Ku Klux Klan—Methodist Conventions
Colleges—chaingangs
Millionaires—Breadlines
and taxes for the poor
(out of every dollar . . . .
take twenty five cents
to feed the Complexes
who keep white folk, black folk separate).

"Yas suh—Yas suh"
"You niggers ain't got no business bein' out past
   midnight"
"I know it's so . . . a white man said it"
"That black gal you got there, boy, is good
   enough for any white man. 'Is she youah wife
   or youah woman? . . ."
"S'cuse me, Boss"
"You niggers git in th' back of this streetcah or
   stand up"
"We's got seats reserved for you white folks at
   ouah church Sunday night"
"He's a good darky"
"I know'd mah whitefolks'd git me outa dis
   mess from killin' dat no good nigguh"
"I've known one or two of you Nigras who were
   highly intelligent."

These, in case you don't know, are extracts
   from the official book on race relations as
   published by the Complexes.

Is it necessary to call attention to the even-
handed, unsparing chastisement meted out to
white and black alike? Or to the unanswerable
realism? Or to the devastating irony, or the
calm courage? For all its sophisticated underpinning, I construe this as more instinctively and
idiomatically an expression of Negro social protest than an officially proletarian screed. It
comes from the vital heart of the Negro experience and its setting; it smacks neither of Marx,
Moscow nor Union Square.

Similarly undoctrinated, and for that reason,
in my judgment, more significant and more
effective, are Sterling Brown's recent poems of
social analysis and protest. The indictment is
the more searching because of its calm poise and
the absence of melodramatic sweat and strain.
Not all of Mr. Brown's poems reach this altitude, but the best do. So that where the earlier
Negro poetry of protest fumes and perorates,
these later ones point, talk and reveal: where
the one challenges and threatens, the other en-
lightens and indicts. Today it is the rise of
this quieter, more indigenous radicalism that is
significant and promising. Doubly so, because
along with a leftist turn of thought goes a real
enlargement of native social consciousness and
a more authentic folk spokesmanship. Judged
by these criteria, I find today's advance point in
the work of Sterling Brown. Without show
of boast or fury, it began in the challenge of
"Srong Men":
"Walk togedder, chillen,
   Dontcha git weary . . . .
They bought off some of your leaders.
You stumbled, as blind men will . . .
They coaxed you, unwontedly soft-voiced . . .
You followed a way
Then laughed as usual.
They heard the laugh and wondered;
Uncomfortable;
Unadmitting a deeper terror . . .
The strong men keep a-comin' on
Gittin' stronger . . . ."

Later there was the unconventional appeal of
"Strange Legacies" to the folk hero, uncon-
quered in defeat:
"John Henry, with your hammer;
John Henry, with your steel driver's pride,
You taught us that a man could go down like
   a man,
Sticking to your hammer till you died.
Brother, . . .
You had what we need now, John Henry.
Help us get it."

But in yet unpublished poems, the proletarian implications of "Mr. Samuel and Sam" become more explicit as the color line and its plight are definitely linked up with the class issue:

"Listen, John Cracker:
Grits and molasses like grease for belts
Coffee-like chicory and collards like jimson,
And side-meat from the same place on the hog
Are about the same on both sides of the track.

Listen, John, does Joe's riding ahead in the
    'Jimmy'
Sweeten so much the dull grits of your days?
When you get where you're going, are you not
    still
John, the po' cracker, Joe, the po' nig?"

And profounder, still, the calm indictment of his "Decatur Street", entirely within the black Ghetto physically, but underscoring it as but a segment of a common American tragedy:

The picture of content should be complete
I sing the happy pickaninnies
Underneath the Georgia moon . . . .

M'ole man is on de chaingang
Muh mammy's on relief

Down at the Lincoln Theatre, little Abe is set
    free again,
Hears music that gets deep-down into his soul:
"Callin' all cars,—callin' all cars," and the pro-
    longed hiss—
"Black Ace, Black Ace!"   And his thin voice
    screams
When the tommy-guns drill and the bodies fall,
"Mow them down, mow them down—gangsters
    or "G" men
So long as folks get killed, no difference at all,
So long as the rattling gun-fire plays little Abe
    his song.

And the only pleasure exceeding this
Will come when he gets hold of the pearl-
    handled gat
Waiting for him, ready, at Moe Epstein's.
Gonna be the Black Ace hisself before de time
    ain't long.

Outside the theatre he stalks his pa'dner,
Creeps up behind him, cocks his thumb,
Rams his forefinger against his side,
"Stick 'em up, damn yuh," his treble whines.

The squeals and the flight
Are more than he looked for, his laughter peals.
He is just at the bursting point with delight.
Black Ace. "Stick 'em up, feller . . . I'm the
    Black Ace."

Oh to grow up soon to the top of glory,
With a glistening furrow on his dark face,
Badge of his manhood, pass-key to fame.
"Before de time ain't long," he says,
"Lord, before de time ain't long."

The young folks roll in the cabins
    on the floor
And in the narrow unlighted streets
Behind the shrouding vines and lattices
Up the black, foul allies, the unpaved roads
Sallie Lou and Johnnie Mae play the spies,
Ready, giggling, for experiments, for their un-
    formed bodies
To be roughly clasped, for little wild cries,
For words learned of their elders on display.
"Gonna get me a boy-friend," Sallie Lou says.
"Got me a man already," brags Johnnie Mae.

This is the schooling ungrudged by the state,
Short in time, as usual, but fashioned to last.
The scholars are apt and never play truant.
The stockade is waiting . . . and they will not
    be late.

Before, before the time ain't very long.

In the stockade: "Little boy, how come you
    hyeah?"
"Little bitty gal, how old are you?"
"Well, I got hyeah, didn't I?—Whatchu keer!"
"I'm goin' on twelve years old."

Say of them then: "Like Topsy, they just grew."

It is not enough to think of this as a modern equivalent of "the slave in the dismal rice-swamp" and the Abolitionist moral threat of "Woe be unto ye!" For here it is the question of a social consciousness basic, mature, fitted not to the narrow gauge of the race problem but to the gauge and perspective of our whole contemporary scene. In such a mould poetic and artistic expression can be universal at the same time that it is racial, and racial without being partial and provincial.

A recent writer, of doctrinaire Marxist leanings, insists that as a matter of strict logic the racial note and the class attitude are incongruous. So the proletarian poet should not be a racialist; and the common denominator of the art of our time is to be the "class angle." I think, in addition to documenting some notable changes in the social consciousness of recent Negro poets, the burden of this evidence is against such a doctrinaire conclusion and in favor of a high compatibility between race-conscious and class-conscious thought. The task of this younger literary generation is not to ignore or eliminate the race problem, but to broaden its social dimensions and deepen its universal human implications. And on the whole, at least so far, the more moving expression seems to have come from the side of the racial approach broadened to universality than from the poetry conceived in doctrinaire Marxist formulae and applied, like a stencil, to the racial problem and situation. The one has the flow and force of reality and the vital tang of life itself; the other, the clank and clatter of propaganda, and for all its seriousness, the hollow echoes of rhetoric. The Negro poet has not so long outgrown the stage of rhetoric; let us hope that the new social philosophy will not stampede our artists into such a relapse. Especially, since the present prospects are that some of the finest and most effective expressions of social protest in contemporary art will come from the younger Negro poet and his colleagues.

SPIRITUAL TRUANCY

When in 1928, from self-imposed exile, Claude Mc Kay wrote *Home to Harlem*, many of us hoped that a prose and verse writer of stellar talent would himself come home, physically and psychologically, to take a warranted and helpful place in the group of "New Negro" writers. But although now back on the American scene and obviously attached to Harlem by literary adoption, this undoubted talent is still spiritually unmoored, and by the testimony of this latest book, is a longer way from home than ever. A critical reader would know this without his own confession; but Mr. Mc-Kay, exposing others, succeeds by chronic habit in exposing himself and paints an apt spiritual portrait in two sentences when he says: "I had wandered far and away until I had grown into a truant by nature and undomesticated in the blood"—and later,—"I am so intensely subjective as a poet, that I was not aware, at the moment of writing, that I was transformed into a medium to express a mass sentiment." All of which amounts to self-characterization as the unabashed "playboy of the Negro Renaissance".

Real spokesmanship and representative character in the "Negro Renaissance",—or for that matter any movement, social or cultural,—may depend, of course, on many factors according to time and circumstance, but basic and essential, at least, are the acceptance of some group loyalty and the intent, as well as the ability, to express mass sentiment. Certainly and peculiarly in this case: otherwise the caption of race is a misnomer and the racial significance so irrelevant as to be silly. We knew before 1925 that Negroes could be poets; what we forecast and expected were Negro writers expressing a folk in expressing themselves. Artists have a right to be individualists, of course, but if their work assumes racial expression and interpretation, they must abide by it. On this issue, then, instead of repudiating racialism and its implied loyalties, Mr.

New Challenge 2 (Fall 1937): 81–85.

Mc Kay blows hot and cold with the same breath; erratically accepting and rejecting racial representatives, like a bad boy who admits he ought to go to school and then plays truant. It is this spiritual truancy which is the blight of his otherwise splendid talent.

Lest this seem condemnation out of court, let us examine the record. If out of a half dozen movements to which there could have been some deep loyalty of attachment, none has claimed Mc Kay's whole-hearted support, then surely this career is not one of cosmopolitan experiment or even of innocent vagabondage, but, as I have already implied, one of chronic and perverse truancy. It is with the record of these picaresque wanderings that Mc Kay crowds the pages of *A Long Way from Home*. First, there was a possible brilliant spokesmanship of the Jamaican peasant-folk, for it was as their balladist that Mc Kay first attracted attention and help from his West Indian patrons. But that was soon discarded for a style and philosophy of aesthetic individualism in the then current mode of pagan impressionism. As the author of this personalism,—so unrecognizable after the tangy dialect of the Clarendon hill-folk,—

> *'Your voice is the colour of a robin's breast*
>
> *And there's a sweet sob in it like rain,*
>
> *Still rain in the night among the leaves of the trumpet tree'*

Mc Kay emigrated to our shores and shortly adopted the social realism and racial Negro notes of *Harlem Shadows* and *The Harlem Dancer*. These were among the first firmly competent accents of New Negro poetry, and though an adopted son, Mc Kay was hailed as the day-star of that bright dawn. However, by his own admission playing off Max Eastman against Frank Harris and James Oppenheimer, he rapidly moved out toward the humanitarian socialism of *The Liberator* with the celebrated radical protest of *If We Must Die;* and followed that adventuresome flourish, still with his tongue in his cheek, to Moscow and the lavish hospitality and hero-worship of the Third Comintern. Then by a sudden repudiation there was a prolonged flight into expatriate cosmopolitanism and its irresponsible exoticisms. Even Mc Kay admits the need for some apologia at this point. Granting, for the sake of argument, that the "adventure in Russia" and the association with *The Liberator* were not commitments to some variety of socialism (of this, the author says:—"I had no radical party affiliations, and there was no reason why I should consider myself under any special obligations to the Communists . . . I had not committed myself to anything. I had remained a free agent . . .") what, we may reasonably ask, about the other possible loyalty, on the basis of which the Russian ovation had been earned, viz,—the spokesmanship for the proletarian Negro? In the next breath, literally the next para-graph, Mc Kay repudiates that also in the sentence we have already quoted:—"I was not aware, at the moment of writing, that I was transformed into a medium to express a mass sentiment." Yet the whole adventuresome career between 1918 and 1922, alike in Bohemian New York, literary Harlem and revolutionary Moscow, was predicated upon this assumed representativeness, cleverly ex-ploited. One does not know whether to recall Peter before the triple cock-crow or Paul's dubious admonition about being "all things to all men". Finally, in the face of the obvious Bohemianism of the wanderings on the Riviera and in Morocco, we find Mc Kay disowning common cause with the exotic cosmopolitans,—"my white fellow-expatriates", and claiming that "color-consciousness was the fundamental of my restlessness". Yet from this escapist escapade, we find our prodigal racialist returning expecting the fatted calf instead of the birch-rod, with a curtain lecture on "race salvation" from within and the necessity for a "Negro Messiah", whose glory he would like to celebrate "in a monument of verse".

Even a fascinating style and the naivest egotism cannot cloak such inconsistency or condone such lack of common loyalty. One may not dictate a man's loyalties, but must, at all events, expect him to have some. For a genius maturing in a decade of racial self-expression and enjoying the fruits of it all and living into a decade of social issues and conflict and aware of all that, to have repudiated all possible loyalties amounts to self-imposed apostasy. Mc Kay is after all the dark-skinned psychological twin of that same Frank Harris, whom he so cleverly portrays and cari-catures; a versatile genius caught in the ego-centric predicament of aesthetic vanity and exhibitionism. And so, he stands to date, the *enfant terrible* of the Negro Renaissance, where with a little loyalty and consistency he might have been at least its Villon and perhaps its Voltaire.

If this were merely an individual fate, it could charitably go unnoticed. But in some vital sense these aberrations of spirit, this lack of purposeful and steady loyalty of which Mc Kay is the su-preme example have to a lesser extent vitiated much of the talent of the first generation of "New Negro" writers and artists. They inherited, it is true, a morbid amount of decadent aestheticism, which they too uncritically imitated. They also had to reckon with "shroud of color". To quote Countee Cullen, they can be somewhat forgiven for "sailing the doubtful seas" and for being tardily, and in some cases only half-heartedly led "to live persuaded by their own". But, with all due allowances, there was an unpardonable remainder of spiritual truancy and social irresponsibility. The folk have rarely been treated by these artists with unalloyed reverence and unselfish loyalty. The commitment to racial materials and "race expression" should be neither that of a fashionable and profitable fad nor of a condescending and missionary duty. The one great flaw of the first decade of the Negro Renaissance was its exhibition-ist flair. It should have addressed itself more to the people them-selves and less to the gallery of faddist Negrophiles. The task confronting the present younger generation of Negro writers and artists is to approach the home scene and the folk with high serious-ness, deep loyalty, racial reverence of the unspectacular, unmelo-dramatic sort, and when necessary, sacrificial social devotion. They must purge this flippant exhibitionism, this posy but not too sincere racialism, this care-free and irresponsible individualism.

The program of the Negro Renaissance was to interpret the folk to itself, to vitalize it from within; it was a wholesome, vigor-ous, assertive racialism, even if not explicitly proletarian in concep-tion and justification. Mc Kay himself yearns for some such thing, no doubt, when he speaks in his last chapter of the Negro's need to discover his "group soul". A main aim of the New Negro move-ment will be unrealized so long as that remains undiscovered and dormant; and it is still the task of the Negro writer to be a main agent in evoking it, even if the added formula of proletarian art be necessary to cure this literary anaemia and make our art the nourish-ing life blood of the people rather than the caviar and cake of the artists themselves. Negro writers must become truer sons of the people, more loyal providers of spiritual bread and less aesthetic wastrels and truants of the streets.

DRAMA

Locke had a deep and abiding love of the theater. As a student, he was an avid theater-goer, primarily to the Hollis Street Theatre in Boston and the variety theaters in London. But when Locke came to Washington, D.C., in 1912, blacks were only permitted in segregated sections of the legitimate theaters. Locke maintained his interest in the theater at Howard University, where, together with Montgomery Gregory, the head of the Drama Department, he revived the Howard Players, a nationally renowned theater group.[1]

In a finely crafted essay, "Steps Toward the Negro Theatre" (1922), Locke proposes Howard as the center for a national Negro theater. Like other black intellectuals of the period, he reacted against the negative images of blacks presented in the commercial theater, which had revived the minstrel tradition in the black musical comedies of the early twentieth century. In a privately endowed theater, Locke argues, black playwrights and actors will be free to create a drama that will stimulate the self-conscious development of a race.

Serious dramatic treatment of black life by white playwrights is also needed; in "Goat Alley" (1923), Locke's review of Ernest Culbertson's play of the same name, he acknowledges, however, that the results are not always successful. To Locke, this play exposed the pitfall of a realistic portrayal of the Negro: "plays of this character must either be inevitably and spontaneously racial, or else produce a painful impression of having been written to show the Negro up."

The next essay, "Max Rheinhardt Reads the Negro Dramatic Horoscope" (1924),[2] shows what a stumbling block the "image of the Negro" remained for black promoters of the drama such as Locke and Charles S. Johnson, the editor of *Opportunity*, the journal of the National Urban League. This remarkable interview with Max Reinhardt, the Swedish director and playwright, reveals Locke's bias against black vaudevillian actors, whom Reinhardt believed were the great innovators of modern theater.

In "The Negro and the American Stage" (1926), Locke reverses himself, and accepts Reinhardt's main contentions, reprinting much of the earlier article in a new forum, the *Theatre Arts Monthly*, a white drama journal. Taken together, "Max Rheinhardt Reads the Negro Dramatic Horoscope" and "The Negro and the American Stage" stand as a revealing self-portrait of Locke as a black intellectual torn between his bourgeois background and the modernist ideas of drama to which he is exposed.

Later that year, Locke published in *Theatre Arts Monthly* his boldest critique of protest drama, "The Drama of Negro Life" (1926). Here he disparages "problem plays" like Eugene O'Neill's *All God's Chillum Got Wings*, but welcomes Willis Richardson's *Chip Woman's Fortune* as a portent of mature folk drama. "Later no doubt, after it [Negro drama] learns to beautify the native idioms of our folk life and recovers the ancestral folk tradition, it will express itself in a poetic and symbolic style of drama that will remind us of Synge and the Irish Folk Theatre or Ansky and the Yiddish Theatre."

In the final essay, "Broadway and the Negro Drama" (1941), Locke criticizes Broadway for not systematically developing the Negro theme. The old claim that people would not pay for serious black drama was refuted not only by the commercial successes of serious Broadway shows about blacks, but by the success of off-Broadway and Federal Theatre Project productions. Rarely, however, did these productions find their way to Broadway.

AFRICAN FIRE DANCE
ARRANGED BY OTTIE GRAHAM

Ottie Graham, Sadye Spence, Willie Finkley, Sara Pelham, Eltinge Holmes,
Arliner Young, Beatrice Walker, Dorothy Gillam, Georgia Washington,
Martha Jones, and Ethel Jones.

THE HOWARD PLAYERS
WITH
CHARLES S. GILPIN

THE EMPEROR JONES
A PLAY IN EIGHT SCENES BY EUGENE O'NEILL

Persons of the Play in Order of Appearance

AN OLD NATIVE WOMAN   -   -   Eunice Matthews

HARRY SMITHERS, a white trader   -   *Jasper Deeter*
   Alston Burleigh

BRUTUS JONES, EMPEROR   -   -   *CHARLES GILPIN*
   George Williams

THE LITTLE FORMLESS FEARS   -   -

JEFF   -   -   -   -   Walter W. Goens

THE NEGRO CONVICTS: Harold Bledsoe, Purvis J. Chesson, Carl
   Garner, Richard S. McGhee, John Erskine.

THE PRISON GUARD   -   -   John H. Broadnax

THE PLANTERS: Bernard Walton, John H. Broadnax, Walter W. Goens

THE SPECTATORS: Marcelle Brown, Martha Jones, Beatrice Walker
   Arliner Young, Clyde Mobley, Ethel Jones

THE AUCTIONEER   -   -   Harold Bledsoe

THE SLAVES: Harold Bledsoe, Purvis Chesson, Carl Garner, Richard
   McGhee, John Erskine, Richard Alston

THE CONGO WITCH DOCTOR   -   Bernard Pryor

THE CROCODILE GOD   -

LEM, A NATIVE CHIEF   -   Richard McGhee

SOLDIERS, ADHERENTS OF LEM: Harold Bledsoe, Purvis Chesson,
   Carl Larner, John Erskine, and Richard Alston

Cast list from the program for *The Emperor Jones* performed by the Howard Players, with
Charles S. Gilpin. Courtesy of Moorland–Spingarn Research Center, Howard University, Washington, D.C.

STEPS TOWARD THE NEGRO THEATRE

CULTURALLY we are abloom in a new field, but it is yet decidedly a question as to what we shall reap—a few flowers or a harvest. That depends upon how we cultivate this art of the drama in the next few years. We can have a Gilpin, as we have had an Aldridge—and this time a few more —a spectacular bouquet of talent, fading eventually as all isolated talent must; or we can have a granary of art, stocked and stored for season after season. It is a question of interests, of preferences:—are we reaping the present merely or sowing the future? For the one, the Negro actor will suffice; the other requires the Negro drama and the Negro theatre.

The Negro actor without the Negro drama is a sporadic phenomenon, a chance wayside flower, at mercy of wind and weed. He is precariously planted and still more precariously propagated. We have just recently learned the artistic husbandry of race drama, and have already found that to till the native soil of the race life and the race experience multiplies the dramatic yield both in quality and quantity. Not that we would confine the dramatic talent of the race to the fence-fields and plant-rooms of race drama, but the vehicle of all sound art must be native to the group—our actors need their own soil, at least for sprouting. But there is another step beyond this which must be taken. Our art in this field must not only be rescued from the chance opportunity and the haphazard growth of native talent, the stock must be cultivated beyond the demands and standards of the market-place, or must be safe somewhere from the exploitation and ruthlessness of the commercial theatre and in the protected housing of the art-theatre flower to the utmost perfection of the species. Conditions favorable to this ultimate development, the established Negro Theatre will alone provide.

In the past, and even the present, the Negro actor has waited to be born; in the future he must be made. Up till now, our art has been patronized; for the future it must be endowed. This is, I take it, what we mean by distinguishing between the movement toward race drama and the quite distinguishable movement toward the Negro Theatre. In the idea of its sponsors, the latter includes the former, but goes further and means more; it contemplates an endowed artistic center where all phases vital to the art of the theatre are cultivated and taught—acting, playwriting, scenic design and construction, scenic production and staging. A center with this purpose and function must ultimately be founded. It is only a question of when, how and where. Certainly the time has come; everyone will admit that at this stage of our race development it has become socially and artistically imperative. Sufficient plays and sufficing talent are already available; and the awakened race consciousness awaits what will probably be its best vehicle of expansion and expression in the near future.

Ten years ago it was the theory of the matter that was at issue; now it is only the practicabilities that concern us. Then one had constantly to be justifying the idea, citing the precedents of the Irish and the Yiddish theatres. Now even over diversity of opinion as to ways and means, the project receives the unanimous sanction of our hearts. But as to means and auspices, there are two seriously diverse views; one strenuously favoring professional auspices and a greater metropolitan center like New York or Chicago for the Negro Theatre; another quite as strenuously advocating a university center, amateur auspices and an essentially educational basis. Whoever cares to be doctrinaire on this issue may be: it is a question to be decided by deed and accomplishment—and let us hope a question not of

The Crisis 25 (December 1922): 66–68.

hostility and counter-purpose, but of rivalry and common end.

As intended and established in the work of the Department of the Drama at Howard University, however, the path and fortunes of the latter program have been unequivocally chosen. We believe a university foundation will assure a greater continuity of effort and insure accordingly a greater permanence of result. We believe further that the development of the newer forms of drama has proved most successful where laboratory and experimental conditions have obtained and that the development of race drama is by those very circumstances the opportunity and responsibility of our educational centers. Indeed, to maintain this relation to dramatic interests is now an indispensable item in the program of the progressive American college. Through the pioneer work of Professor Baker, of Harvard, the acting and writing of plays has become the natural and inevitable sequence, in a college community, of the more formal study of the drama. Partly through the same channels, and partly as a result of the pioneer work of Wisconsin, college production has come to the rescue of the art drama, which would otherwise rarely get immediate recognition from the commercial theatre. And finally in its new affiliation with the drama, the American college under the leadership of Professor Koch, formerly of North Dakota, now of the University of North Carolina, has become a vital agency in community drama, and has actively promoted the dramatization of local life and tradition. By a threefold sponsorship, then, race drama becomes peculiarly the ward of our colleges, as new drama, as art-drama, and as folk-drama.

Though concurrent with the best efforts and most significant achievements of the new drama, the movement toward Negro drama has had its own way to make. In addition to the common handicap of commercialism, there has been the singular and insistent depreciation to stereotyped caricature and superficially representative but spiritually misrepresentative force. It has been the struggle of an artistic giant in art-engulfing quicksands; a struggle with its critical period just lately safely passed. Much of this has been desperate effort of the "bootstrap-lifting kind," from the pioneer advances of Williams, Cole, Cook, and Walker, to the latest achievements of "Shuffle Along." But the dramatic side has usually sagged, as might be expected, below the art level under the imposed handicap. Then there has been that gradual investment of the legitimate stage through the backdoor of the character rôle; the hard way by which Gilpin came, breaking triumphantly through at last to the major rôle and legitimate stardom. But it is the inauguration of the Negro art drama which is the vital matter, and the honor divides itself between Burghardt DuBois, with his "Star

of Ethiopia", staged, costumed, and manned by students, and Ridgeley Torrence, with his "Three Plays for a Negro Theatre." In the interim between the significant first performances and the still more significant attempts to incorporate them in the Horizon Guild and the Mrs. Hapgood's Players, there was organized in Washington a Drama Committee of the N. A. A. C. P. which sponsored and produced Miss Grimké's admirable pioneer problem-play, "Rachael," in 1917. Between the divided elements of this committee, with a questionable paternity of minority radicalism, the idea of the Negro Theatre as distinguished from the idea of race drama was born. If ever the history of the Negro drama is written without the scene of a committee wrangle, with its rhetorical climaxes after midnight—the conservatives with their wraps on protesting the hour; the radicals, more hoarse with emotion than effort, alternately wheedling and threatening—it will not be well-written. The majority wanted a performance; the minority, a program. One play no more makes a theatre than one swallow, a summer.

The pariah of the committee by the accident of its parentage became the foundling and subsequently the ward of Howard University. In its orphan days, it struggled up on the crumbs of the University Dramatic Club. One recalls the lean and patient years it took to pass from faculty advice to faculty supervision and finally to faculty control; from rented costumes and hired properties to self-designed and self-executed settings; from hackneyed "stage successes" to modern and finally original plays; and hardest of all progressions, strange to relate, that from distant and alien themes to the intimate, native and racial. The organization, under the directorship of Professor Montgomery Gregory of a Department of Dramatics, with academic credit for its courses, the practical as well as the theoretical, and the fullest administrative recognition and backing of the work have marked in the last two years the eventual vindication of the idea. But from an intimacy of association second only to that of the director, and with better grace than he, may I be permitted to record what we consider to be the movement's real coming of age? It was when simultaneously with the production of two original plays on race themes written in course by students, staged, costumed, and manned by students, in the case of one play with the authoress in rôle, there was launched the campaign for an endowed theatre, the successful completion of which would not only give the Howard Players a home, but the Negro Theatre its first tangible realization.

As will already have been surmised from the story, the movement has, of course, had its critics and detractors. Happily, most of them are covered by that forgiveness which goes out spontaneously to the opposition of the short-sighted. Not they, but their eyes, so to speak, are to blame. Rather it has been amazing, on the other hand, the proportion of responsiveness and help that has come, especially from the most prominent proponents of the art drama in this country; names too numerous to mention, but representing every possible section of opinion—academic, non-academic; northern, southern, western; conservative, ultra-modern; professional, amateur; technical, literary; from within the university, from the community of Washington; white, black. Of especial mention because of special service, Gilpin, O'Neil, Torrence, Percy Mackaye, DuBois, Weldon Johnson, and the administrative officers of the University; and most especially the valuable technical assistance for three years of Clem Throckmorton, technical director of the Provincetown Players, and for an equal time the constant and often self-sacrificing services of Miss Marie Forrest in stage training and directing, services recently fitly rewarded by appointment to a professorship in the department. But despite the catholic appeal, interest and co-operation it is essentially as a race representative and race-supported movement that we must think of it and that it must ultimately become, the best possible self-expression in an art where we have a peculiar natural endowment, undertaken as an integral part of our higher education and pursuit of culture.

The program and repertoire of the Howard Players, therefore, scarcely represent the full achievement of the movement; it is the workshop and the eventual theatre and the ever-increasing supply of plays and players that must hatch out of the idea. The record of the last two years shows in performances:

1920-21—

"Tents of the Arabs"—Lord Dansany.

"Simon the Cyrenean"—Ridgeley Torrence.

"The Emperor Jones"—Guest performance with Charles Gilpin at the Belasco; student performance at the Belasco.

Commencement Play, 1921-22—

"The Canterbury Pilgrims"—Percy Mackaye. Repetition of first bill in compliment of the delegates to the Washington conference on Limitation of Armaments.

"Strong as the Hills" (a Persian play)—Matalee Lake.

Original Student Plays—

"Genefrede,"—a play of the Life of Toussaint L'Ouverture—Helen Webb.

"The Yellow Tree"—DeReath Irene Busey.

Commencement Play—

"Aria de Capo"—Edna St. Vincent Millay.

"The Danse Calinda"—a Creole Pantomime Ms. performance — Ridgeley Torrence.

A movement of this kind and magnitude is, can be, the monopoly of no one group, no one institution, no paltry decade. But within a significant span, this is the record. The immediately important steps must be the production of original plays as rapidly as is consistent with good workmanship and adequate production, and the speedy endowment of the theatre, which fortunately, with the amateur talent of the university, means only funds for building and equipment. I am writing this article at Stratford-on-Avon. I know that when stripped to the last desperate defense of himself, the Englishman with warrant will boast of Shakespeare, and that this modest Memorial Theatre is at one and the same time a Gibraltar of national pride and self-respect and a Mecca of human civilization and culture. Music in which we have so trusted may sing itself around the world, but it does not carry ideas, the vehicle of human understanding and respect; it may pierce the heart, but does not penetrate the mind. But here in the glass of this incomparable art there is, for ourselves and for the world, that which shall reveal us beyond all propaganda on the one side, and libel on the other, more subtly and deeply than self-praise and to the confusion of subsidized self-caricature and ridicule. "I saw Othello's visage in his mind," says Desdemona explaining her love and respect; so might, so must the world of Othello's mind be put artistically to speech and action.

Stratford-on-Avon, August 5, 1922.

GOAT ALLEY,
BY ERNEST HOWARD CULBERTSON

Goat Alley, a serious three act play of Negro life, comes to us with a wonderful introduction. Mr. Ludwig Lewisohn vouches for it most interestingly; but we do not share the impressario's enthusiasm for the performance. If the play is to be praised at all, it must be rather for its intentions than for its achievements, more for its promise, even from the same author, than for actual contribution. One somehow expects, both from its preface and sub-title,—'A Tragedy of Negro Life,' something more essentially racial than he gets from this play by Mr. Culbertson. Especially after reflection does it seem rather to be a tragedy of the slums, with Negro characters thrown in. One does not wish for sentimental reasons to dissociate conditions or disclaim types that actually exist among Negroes as among others, and that may, by virtue also of conditions, exist among them in undesirable proportion. However, the basic framework of plot, motivation, and character, has so little in it that is essentially or peculiarly racial that one is forced to wonder why Mr. Culbertson chose Negro dialect and characterization for his theme. This is a play of the tragic, sordid sort that is happening the world over in the life of the submerged classes. Caught in the double mesh of poverty and the snares of her own loose past, Lucy Belle, the heroine, is gradually bound down to her fate,—death at the hands of the only man to whom she has tried to be faithful. His suspicions, placated over and again, cannot stand the last revelation of her perfidy, which she resorts even to infanticide to hide. As much, —indeed more than ever the victim of circumstances in this, she cannot avail herself of his easy, good-natured credulity any longer. Relentlessly the human and the physical forces of the underworld bear her down.

A tragedy as sordid as this has to seem inevitable or it leaves the painful impression of gratuitous and unnecessary exposure of the rags and bones of life, not to speak of its sores. After the labored exposition, we know that it is only a question of time before Lucy Belle's fate will overtake her. But though it is Mr. Culbertson's evident intention to make this a tragedy of the inevitable struggle, the movement of the play, except the fine inevitableness of her acceptance of the designing lodger, Chick the Barber, proceeds too much like the mechanical turn of the thumb-screw. Or, to change our figure, one too often feels as one follows the incidents, that a Pinkertonian playwright, rather than fate, has 'stacked the cards' against Lucy Belle. Old man Pocher's ready-packed valise offsets the finest scene in the play, every reentrance of Lizzie Gibbs, the jealous rival, weakens her dramatic value,

at the last she seems merely the agent of the dramatist; again the revelation of the infanticide is clumsily amateurish. We are not ungrateful, but Goat Alley is a practice-piece: there is a greater tragedy there in solution than the author's art has been able to release.

Mr. Culbertson nevertheless has aimed seriously, perhaps overseriously at his problem. The play properly belongs to the newer movement and the newer attitude in the serious portrayal of the life of the Negro which have so decidedly come about in the last few years. Such an attitude, realistic rather than sentimental, seriously and scientifically analytic, is today a prerequisite for vital work or for serious consideration. Mr. Culbertson at least has this. According to Mr. Lewisohn, he began rehearsals of Goat Alley in a dingy little hall on a side street. "The actors were, with one exception, amateurs colored working people who gave their time and services for the sake of what they felt to be an artistic expression of the life of their race. The author had no sociological intention; he had no ambition to be a propagandist. He had not even a special interest in the racial problem. He thought that he had come upon an action that has the quality of tragic inevitableness. He thought, furthermore, that tragedy does not reside in pomp and circumstance, but in the profound realities of human helpfulness and human suffering, and that poor Lucy Belle struggling to maintain her spiritual integrity in Goat Alley was a protagonist worthy of the sternest art and the largest sympathy." From this point of view, Goat Alley is of considerable interest and promise.

Eventually out of the very material which Mr. Culbertson has opened up must come fine realistic tragedy. And it will come as soon as we learn how to cross-section scientifically the race life at this point, and regard it more with the eye of pity than of scorn, more from the point of view of interest than of problem-hunting or problem-solving. Such drama will leave the race problem precisely where it stood or stands; it is not the business of plays to solve problems or to reform society. But plays of this character must either be inevitably and spontaneously racial, or else produce a painful impression of having been written to show the Negro up. It is the distortion of the average social perspective in race matters which is primarily responsible for this, and only the finest and most accurate regauging of the true human perspectives in art can escape the effect of it. For this reason, mistakenly or not, the intelligenzia of the Negro people want uplift plays. They are wrong, I think, in wanting them to the exclusion of plays of other types, as well as

Opportunity 1 (February 1923): 30.

wrong in complaining when others do not write them. More representative sections of our race life have their tragedies, their comedy and satire too, for that matter, —but it must be remembered that these sections are socially and artistically accessible only to ourselves. More plays then, of all kind, but especially those by Negro authors, seem to be the only solution of the art problem produced by having for so long a time artificially restricted the portrayal of the life of the Negro in the arts. One of the soundest and most constructive ways out of the distortions of social prejudice will be through this correction of its reflected distortions in the conventions of the arts.

MAX RHEINHARDT READS THE NEGRO'S DRAMATIC HOROSCOPE

MAX RHEINHARDT has always been a prophet in the theatre,—and the things which he has foreseen and helped come to realization have matured so quickly and vigorously as to make his own work of ten or fifteen years back almost old-fashioned in comparison with the advanced contemporary art of drama which, we must always remember, his work has so largely made possible. Perhaps no one could have a more pronounced "sixth sense" with respect to drama or a more dependable knack of finding new veins of dramatic possibilities. When, therefore, we learned that Director Rheinhardt of "The Miracle" had expressed keen interest in the work of the Negro actors whom he had seen in his visit to New York last season, we were naturally most anxious to have a first hand opinion. Max Rheinhardt must be interviewed. The opportunity was missed at Salzburg; and again, by the accidents of travel, at Vienna; and the trail eventually led back to New York and the second season. From the beginning it was not the usual interview. Charles Johnson and I found our subject too willing to be in any sense the usual victim. It was not a tribute to us so much as to the subject in which we were interested that this rather busy and inaccessible man was anxious to talk with us. Indeed, our first engagement was excused on the ground that there wasn't sufficient time to talk over so important a subject adequately. A second visit found us very much in the predicament of the fisherman who catches other fish than he was fishing for: obviously we ourselves were about to be interviewed. And we were,—but that is not our story. Then the springy, inquisitive, experimental mind of the man came back at us,— with what he apologetically called "mere impressions," but what the reader will instantly recognize as penetrating and quite prophetic observations.

"Yes, I am very interested,—it is intriguing,

very intriguing, these musical comedies of yours that I have seen. But, remember, not as achievements, not as things in themselves artistic, but in their possibilities, their tremendous artistic possibilities. They are most modern, most American, most expressionistic. They are highly original in spite of obvious triteness, and artistic in spite of superficial crudeness. To me they reveal new possibilities of technique in drama, and if I should ever try to do anything American, I should build it on these things."

We didn't enthuse. What Negro who stands for culture with the hectic stress of a social problem weighing on the minds of an over-serious minority could enthuse? Liza, Shuffle Along, Runnin' Wild! We had come to discuss the possibilities of serious Negro drama, of the art—drama, if you please. Surely Director Rheinhardt was a victim of that distortion of perspective to which anyone is liable in a foreign land. But then, the stage is not a foreign land to Max Rheinhardt. He has the instinct of the theatre,—the genius of the producer who knows, if anyone knows, what is vital there. So we didn't protest, but raised brows already too elevated perhaps and shrugged the shoulder that carries the proverbial racial chip. Herr Rheinhardt read the gestures swiftly.

"Ah yes, I see—you view these plays for what they are, and you are right; I view them for what they will become, and I am more than right. I see their future. Why? Well, the drama must turn at every fresh period of creative development to an aspect which has been previously subordinated or neglected, and in this day of ours we come back to the most primitive and the most basic aspect of drama for a new starting point, a fresh development and revival of the art,—and that aspect is pantomime,—the use of the body to portray emotion. And your people have that art—it is their forte—it is their special genius. At present it is prostituted to farce, to trite comedy,—but the

Opportunity 2 (May 1924): 145–146.

technique is there, and I have never seen more wonderful possibilities. Yes, I should like to do something with this material. If I knew more about it I certainly would do something with it. Somebody must demonstrate its fresh artistic value. Now it is exploited, when will it be utilized?"

Now we understood. Baronial hotel arm-chairs moved as lightly and as instinctively as ouija-boards. Understanding made a circle, and the interview was ended though the conversation continued thrice as long.

"No, not the story, not the acting in the conventional sense, not the setting, not even the music, and certainly not the silly words; but the voices, the expressive control of the whole body, the spontaneity of motion, the rhythm, the bright emotional color. These are your treasures—no, not yours only,—these are American treasures."

"But how, Mr. Rheinhardt, are we to develop these,—especially in the face of exploitation?"

"Only you can do it, you yourselves. You must not even try to link up to the drama of the past, to the European drama. That is why there is no American drama as yet. And if there is to be one, it will be yours. That is my advice, that is my feeling about this. I would gladly help. I would gladly do something just to show what can be technically developed out of such material. But I would have to saturate myself with the folk-spirit, and really this requires the Negro dramatist eventually."

"'Eventually,'—why, we have already many plays of Negro life, some promising Negro playwrights, several attempts at a Negro theatre, a college department of dramatics."

"That is interesting, most interesting—but I am afraid of that sort of a thing. It is too academic. I fear there is too much imitation in it. My last word is, be original—sense the folk-spirit, develop the folk-idiom,—artistically, of course, but faithfully; and above all, do not let that technique of expression which is so original, so potential, get smothered out in the imitation of European acting, copied effects.

"With such control of body, such pantomime, I believe I could portray emotion as it has never been portrayed,—pure emotion, almost independently of words or setting. It is really marvelous. You are perhaps too near to see it."

We terminated the interview in deference to Mr. Rheinhardt's engagements,—he was still talking, still "intrigued," as he kept putting it. And to our "Thank you's," his reply was: "Not at all, gentlemen. On the contrary, I must thank you for an opportunity of expressing an opinion about the possibilities of Negroes and for an occasion to learn more of what is actually being done toward developing these fine resources of American art." So when it was reported by the *N. A. A. C. P. Press Service* that "Max Rheinhardt, one of the foremost theatrical producers of Germany, who recently stage a monster production of 'The Miracle' in New York, has recently praised the art of the American Negro, in an interview cabled to the *Chicago Daily News*," two amateur but ardent race journalists had the exhilaration of having been "back-stage" on that.

THE NEGRO AND
THE AMERICAN STAGE

IN the appraisal of the possible contribution of the Negro to the American theatre, there are those who find the greatest promise in the rising drama of Negro life. And there are others who see possibilities of a deeper, though subtler influence upon what is after all more vital, the technical aspects of the arts of the theatre. Certainly the Negro influence upon American drama has been negligible. Whereas even under the handicaps of second hand exploitation and restriction to the popular amusement stage, the Negro actor has considerably influenced our stage and its arts. One would do well to imagine what might happen if the art of the Negro actor should really become artistically lifted and liberated. Transpose the possible resources of Negro song and dance and pantomime to the serious stage, envisage an American drama under the galvanizing stimulus of a rich transfusion of essential folk-arts and you may anticipate what I mean. A race of actors can revolutionize the drama quite as definitely and perhaps more vitally than a coterie of dramatists. The roots of drama are after all action and emotion, and our modern drama, for all its frantic experimentation, is an essentially anemic drama, a something of gestures and symbols and ideas and not overflowing with the vital stuff of which drama was originally made and to which it returns for its rejuvenation cycle after cycle.

Primarily the Negro brings to the drama the gift of a temperament, not the gift of a tradition. Time out of mind he has been rated as a "natural born actor" without any appreciation of what that statement, if true, really means. Often it was intended as a disparaging estimate of the Negro's limitations, a recognition of his restriction to the interpretative as distinguished from the creative aspect of drama, a confinement, in terms of a second order of talent,

Theatre Arts Monthly 10 (February 1926): 112–120.

to the status of the mimic and the clown. But a comprehending mind knows that the very life of drama is in dramatic instinct and emotion, that drama begins and ends in mimicry, and that its creative force is in the last analysis the interpretative passion. Welcome then as is the emergence of the Negro playwright and the drama of Negro life, the promise of the most vital contribution of our race to the theatre lies, in my opinion, in the deep and unemancipated resources of the Negro actor, and the folk arts of which he is as yet only a blind and hampered exponent. Dramatic spontaneity, the free use of the body and the voice as direct instruments of feeling, a control of body plastique that opens up the narrow diaphragm of fashionable acting and the conventional mannerisms of the stage—these are indisputably strong points of Negro acting. Many a Negro vaudevillian has greater store of them than finished masters of the polite theatre. And especially in the dawn of the "synthetic theatre" with the singing, dancing actor and the plastic stage, the versatile gifts of the Negro actor seem peculiarly promising and significant.

Unfortunately it is the richest vein of Negro dramatic talent which is under the heaviest artistic impediments and pressure. The art of the Negro actor has had to struggle up out of the shambles of minstrelsy and make slow headway against very fixed limitations of popular taste. Farce, buffoonery and pathos have until recently almost completely overlaid the folk comedy and folk tragedy of a dramatically endowed and circumstanced people. These gifts must be liberated. I do not narrowly think of this development merely as the extension of the freedom of the American stage to the Negro actor, although this must naturally come as a condition of it, but as a contribution to the technical idioms and resources of the entire theatre.

To see this rising influence one must of course look over the formal horizons. From the vantage of the advanced theatre, there is already a significant arc to be seen. In the sensational successes of *The Emperor Jones* and *All God's Chillun Got Wings* there have been two components, the fine craftsmanship and clairvoyant genius of O'Neill and the unique acting gifts of Charles Gilpin and Paul Robeson. From the revelation of the emotional power of the Negro actor by Opal Cooper and Inez Clough in the Ridgeley Torrence plays in 1916 to the recent half successful experiments of Raymond O'Neill's Ethiopian Art Theatre and the National Ethiopian Art Theatre of New York, with Evelyn Preer, Rose MacClendon, Sidney Kirkpatrick, Charles Olden, Francis Corbie and others, an advanced section of the American public has become acquainted with the possibilities of the Negro in serious dramatic interpretation. But the real mine of Negro dramatic art and talent is in the sub-soil of the vaudeville stage, gleaming through its slag and dross in the unmistakably great dramatic gifts of a Bert Williams, a Florence Mills or a Bill Robinson.   Give Bojangles Robinson or George Stamper, pantomimic dancers of genius, a Bakst or an expressionist setting; give Josephine Baker, Eddie Rector, Abbie Mitchell or Ethel Waters a dignified medium, and they would be more than a sensation, they would be artistic revelations.   Pantomime, that most essential and elemental of the dramatic arts, is a natural *forte* of the Negro actor, and the use of the body and voice and facile control of posture and rhythm are almost as noteworthy in the average as in the exceptional artist. When it comes to pure registration of the emotions, I question whether any body of actors, unless it be the Russians, can so completely be fear or joy or nonchalance or grief.

With his uncanny instinct for the theatre, Max Reinhardt saw these possibilities instantly under the tawdry trappings of such musical comedies as *Eliza, Shuffle Along* and *Runnin' Wild,* which were in vogue the season of his first visit to New York.   "It is intriguing, very intriguing," he told me, "these Negro shows that I have seen.   But remember, not as achievements, not as things in themselves artistic, but in their possibilities, their tremendous artistic possibilities.   They are most modern, most American, most expressionistic.   They are highly original in spite of obvious triteness, and artistic in spite of superficial crudeness.   To me they reveal new possibilities of technique in drama, and if I should ever try to do anything American, I would build it on these things."

We didn't enthuse—my friend Charles Johnson of *Opportunity* and myself, who were interviewing Mr. Reinhardt.   What Negro who stands for culture with the hectic stress of a social problem weighing on the minds of an over-serious minority could enthuse. *Eliza, Shuffle Along, Runnin' Wild!* We had come to discuss the possibilities of serious Negro drama, of the art-drama, if you please.   Surely Director Reinhardt was a victim of that distortion of perspective to which one is so liable in a foreign land.   But then, the stage is not a foreign land to Max Reinhardt; he has the instinct of the theatre, the genius that knows what is vital there.   We didn't outwardly protest, but raised a brow already too elevated perhaps and shrugged the shoulder that carries the proverbial racial chip.

Herr Reinhardt read the gestures swiftly.   "Ah, yes—I see.   You view these plays for what they are, and you are right; I view them for what they will become, and I am more than right.   I see their future.   Why?   Well, the drama must turn at every period of fresh creative development to an aspect which has been previously subordinated or neglected, and in this day of ours, we come back to the most primitive and the most basic aspect of drama for a new starting point, a fresh development and revival of the art—and that aspect is pantomime, the use of the body to portray story and emotion.   And your people have that art—it is their special genius.

At present it is prostituted to farce, to trite comedy—but the technique is there, and I have never seen more wonderful possibilities. Yes, I should like to do something with it."

With the New Russian Theatre experimenting with the "dynamic ballet" and Meierhold's improvising or creative actor, with Max Reinhardt's own recently founded International Pantomime Society inaugurated at the last Salzburg festival, with the entire new theatre agog over "mass drama," there is at least some serious significance to the statement that the Negro theatre has great artistic potentialities. What is of utmost importance to drama now is to control the primitive language of the art, and to retrieve some of the basic control which the sophisticated and conventionalized theatre has lost. It is more important to know how to cry, sob and laugh, stare and startle than to learn how to smile, grimace, arch and wink. And more important to know how to move vigorously and with rhythmic sweep than to pirouette and posture. An actor and a folk art controlling the symbolism of the primary emotions has the modern stage as a province ripe for an early and easy conquest. Commenting on the work of the players of the Ethiopian Art Theatre, discerning critics noticed "the freshness and vigor of their emotional responses, their spontaneity and intensity of mood, their freedom from intellectual and artistic obsessions." And almost every review of Paul Robeson's acting speaks of it as beyond the calculated niceties, a force of overwhelming emotional weight and mastery. It is this sense of something dramatic to the core that flows movingly in the blood rather than merely along the veins that we speak of as the racial endowment of the Negro actor. For however few there may be who possess it in high degree, it is racial, and is in a way unique.

Without invoking analogies, we can see in this technical and emotional endowment great resources for the theatre. In terms of the prevalent trend for the serious development of race drama, we may expect these resources to be concentrated and claimed as the working capital of the Negro Theatre. They are. But just as definitely, too, are they the general property and assets of the American Theatre at large, if once the barriers are broken through. These barriers are slowly breaking down both on the legitimate stage and in the popular drama, but the great handicap, as Carl van Vechten so keenly points out in his *Prescription for the Negro Theatre,* is blind imitation and stagnant conventionalism. Negro dramatic art must not only be liberated from the handicaps of external disparagement, but from its self imposed limitations. It must more and more have the courage to be original, to break with established dramatic convention of all sorts. It must have the courage to develop its own idiom, to pour itself into new moulds; in short, to be experimental. From

In a striking series of interpretative designs based on Eugene O'Neill's *Emperor Jones*, the young Negro artist, Aaron Douglas, has recaptured the dynamic quality of that tragedy of terror. There is an arbitrary contrast of black masses and white spaces; and the clash of broken line becomes highly expressive in suggesting the proximate collapse of the Emperor's throne and the fear it inspires.

Photo courtesy of Yale University, New Haven, Conn.

The tropical jungle closing in on the defeated Brutus Jones is here suggested by Aaron Douglas with an utter simplicity of means, yet with no sacrifice of psychological verisimilitude. There is a sharply defined sense of dramatic design—of drama in design. This power is one often missing among men of greater technical skill but less vivid imagination.

Photo courtesy of Yale University, New Haven, Conn.

what quarter this impetus will come we cannot quite predict; it may come from the Negro theatre or from some sudden adoption of the American stage, from the art-theatre or the commercial theatre, from some home source, or first, as so many things seem to have come, from the more liberal patronage and recognition of the European stage. But this much is certain—the material awaits a great exploiting genius.

One can scarcely think of a complete development of Negro dramatic art without some significant artistic reexpression of African life, and the tradition associated with it. It may seem a far cry from the conditions and moods of modern New York and Chicago and the Negro's rapid and feverish assimilation of all things American. But art establishes its contacts in strange ways. The emotional elements of Negro art are choked by the conventions of the contemporary stage; they call for freer, more plastic material. They have no mysterious affinity with African themes or scenes, but they have for any life that is more primitive and poetic in substance. So, if, as seems already apparent, the sophisticated race sense of the Negro should lead back over the trail of the group tradition to an interest in things African, the natural affinities of the material and the art will complete the circuit and they will most electrically combine. Especially with its inherent color and emotionalism, its freedom from body-hampering dress, its odd and tragic and mysterious overtones, African life and themes, apart from any sentimental attachment, offer a wonderfully new field and province for dramatic treatment. Here both the Negro actor and dramatist can move freely in a world of elemental beauty, with all the decorative elements that a poetic emotional temperament could wish. No recent playgoer with the spell of Brutus Jones in the forest underbrush still upon his imagination will need much persuasion about this.

More and more the art of the Negro actor will seek its materials in the rich native soil of Negro life, and not in the threadbare tradition of the Caucasian stage. In the discipline of art playing upon his own material, the Negro has much to gain. Art must serve Negro life as well as Negro talent serve art. And no art is more capable of this service than drama. Indeed the surest sign of a folk renascence seems to be a dramatic flowering. Somehow the release of such self-expression always accompanies or heralds cultural and social maturity. I feel that soon this aspect of the race genius may come to its classic age of expression. Obviously, though, it has not yet come. For our dramatic expression is still too restricted, self-conscious and imitative.

When our serious drama shall become as naïve and spontaneous as our drama of fun and laughter, and that in turn genuinely representative of the folk spirit which it is now forced to travesty, a point of classic development will have been reached. It is fascinating to speculate upon what riotously new and startling may come from this. Dramatic maturings are notably sudden. Usually from the popular sub-soil something shoots up to a rapid artistic flowering. Of course, this does not have to recur with the American Negro. But a peasant folk art pouring out from under a generation-long repression is the likeliest soil known for a dramatic renascence. And the supporters and exponents of Negro drama do not expect their folk temperament to prove the barren exception.

THE DRAMA OF NEGRO LIFE

DESPITE the fact that Negro life is somehow felt to be particularly rich in dramatic values, both as folk experience and as a folk temperament, its actual yield, so far as worth-while drama goes, has been very inconsiderable. There are many reasons behind this paradox; foremost of course the fact that drama is the child of social prosperity and of a degree at least of cultural maturity. Negro life has only recently come to the verge of cultural self-expression, and has scarcely reached such a ripening point. Further than this, the quite melodramatic intensity of the Negro's group experience has defeated its contemporaneous dramatization; when life itself moves dramatically, the vitality of drama is often sapped. But there have been special reasons. Historical controversy and lowering social issues have clouded out the dramatic colors of Negro life into the dull mass contrasts of the Negro problem. Until lately not even good problem drama has been possible, for sentiment has been too partisan for fair dramatic balancing of forces and too serious for either aesthetic interest or artistic detachment. So although intrinsically rich in dramatic episode and substance, Negro life has produced for our stage only a few morally hectic melodramas along with innumerable instances of broad farce and low comedy. Propaganda, pro-Negro as well as anti-Negro, has scotched the dramatic potentialities of the subject. Especially with the few Negro playwrights has the propaganda motive worked havoc. In addition to the handicap of being out of actual touch with the theatre, they have had the dramatic motive deflected at its source. Race drama has appeared to them a matter of race vindication, and pathetically they have pushed forward their moralistic allegories or melodramatic protests as dramatic correctives and antidotes for race prejudice.

A few illuminating plays, beginning with Edward Sheldon's

Threatre Arts Monthly 10 (October 1926): 701–706.

Nigger and culminating for the present in O'Neill's *All God's Chillun Got Wings,* have already thrown into relief the higher possibilities of the Negro problem-play. Similarly, beginning with Ridgeley Torrence's *Three Plays for a Negro Theatre* and culminating in *Emperor Jones* and *The No 'Count Boy,* a realistic study of Negro folk-life and character has been begun, and with it the inauguration of the artistic Negro folk play. The outlook for a vital and characteristic expression of Negro life in drama thus becomes immediate enough for a survey and forecast of its prospects and possibilities. Of course, in the broad sense, this development is merely the opening up of a further vein in the contemporary American drama, another step in the path of the dramatic exploration and working out of the native elements of American life. At the same time, especially in the plan and effort of the Negro dramatist, it becomes a program for the development of the Negro drama as such and of a Negro Theatre. Fortunately this special motive in no way conflicts with the sectional trend and local color emphasis of American drama today with its Wisconsin, Hoosier, Carolina and Oklahoma projects. It is this coincidence of two quite separate interests that has focussed the attention of both white and Negro artists upon the same field, and although we should naturally expect the most intimate revelations to come from the race dramatist, the present situation sustains a most desirable collaboration in the development of this new and fertile province. Indeed the pioneer efforts have not always been those of the Negro playwright and in the list of the more noteworthy recent exponents of Negro drama, Sheldon, Torrence, O'Neill, Howard Culbertson, Paul Green, Burghardt DuBois, Angelina Grimke, and Willis Richardson, only the last three are Negroes.

The development of Negro drama at present owes more to the lure of the general exotic appeal of its material than to the special program of a racial drama. But the motives of race drama are already matured, and just as inevitably as the Irish, Russian and Yiddish drama evolved from the cultural programs of their respective movements, so must the Negro drama emerge from the racial stir and movement of contemporary Negro life. Projects like the Hapgood Players (1917-18), The Horizon Guild (1920), The Howard Players (1921-24), The Ethiopian Art Theatre (1923), The National Ethiopian Art Theatre founded in Harlem last year and The Shadows, a Negro "Little Theatre" just started in Chicago, though short-lived and handicapped for an adequate and competent repertory, are nevertheless unmistakable signs of an emerging Negro drama and the founding of a Negro Theatre.

But the path of this newly awakened impulse is by no means as clear as its goal. Two quite contrary directions compete for the artist's choice. On the one hand is the more obvious drama of social situation, focussing on the clash of the race life with its opposing background; on the other the apparently less dramatic material of the folk life and behind it the faint panorama of an alluring race history and race tradition. The creative impulse is for the moment caught in this dilemma of choice between the drama of discussion and social analysis and the drama of expression and artistic interpretation. But despite the present lure of the problem play, it ought to be apparent that the real future of Negro drama lies with the development of the folk play. Negro drama must grow in its own soil and cultivate its own intrinsic elements; only in this way can it become truly organic, and cease being a rootless derivative.

Of course the possibilities of Negro problem drama are great and immediately appealing. The scheme of color is undoubtedly one of the dominant patterns of society and the entanglement of its skeins in American life one of its most dramatic features. For a long while strong social conventions prevented frank and penetrating analysis, but now that the genius of O'Neill has broken through what has been aptly called "the last taboo," the field stands open. But for the Negro it is futile to expect fine problem drama as an initial stage before the natural development in due course of the capacity for self-criticism. The Negro dramatist's advantage of psychological intimacy is for the present more than offset by the disadvantage of the temptation to counter partisan and propagandist attitudes. The white dramatist can achieve objectivity with relatively greater ease, though as yet he seldom does, and has temporarily an advantage in the handling of this material as drama of social situation. Proper development of these social problem themes will require the objectivity of great art. Even when the crassest conventions are waived at present, character stereotypes and deceptive formulae still linger; only genius of the first order can hope to penetrate to the materials of high tragedy—and, for that matter, high comedy also—that undoubtedly are there. For with the difference that modern society decrees its own fatalisms, the situations of race hold tragedies and ironies as deep and keen as those of the ancient classics. Eventually the Negro dramatist must achieve mastery of a detached, artistic point of view, and reveal the inner stresses and dilemmas of these situations as from the psychological point of view he alone can. The race drama of the future will utilize satire for the necessary psychological distance and perspective, and rely upon irony as a natural corrective for the sentimentalisms of propaganda. The objective attack and style of younger contemporary writers like Jean Toomer, who in *Kabnis* has written a cryptic but powerful monologue, promise this not too distantly.

The folk play, on the other hand, whether of the realistic or the imaginative type, has no such conditioned values. It is the drama of free self-expression and imaginative release, and has no objective but to express beautifully and colorfully the folk life of the race. At present, too, influenced perhaps by the social drama, it finds tentative expression in the realistic genre plays of Paul Green, Willis Richardson and others. Later no doubt, after it learns to beautify the native idioms of our folk life and recovers the ancestral folk tradition, it will express itself in a poetic and symbolic style of drama that will remind us of Synge and the Irish Folk Theatre or Ansky and the Yiddish Theatre. There are many analogies, both of temperament, social condition and cultural reactions, which suggest this. The life which this peasant drama imperfectly reflects is shot through with emotion and potential poetry; and the soggy, somewhat sordid realism of the plays that now portray it does not develop its full possibilities. The drabness of plays like Culbertson's *Jackey* and *Goat Alley* and of *Granny Boling* and *White Dresses* is in great part due to the laborious effort of first acquaintance. They are too studied, too expository. Even in such a whimsical and poetically conceived folk comedy as Paul Green's *No 'Count Boy,* with which the Dallas Little Theatre group won a recent amateur dramatic contest in New York, there is this same defect of an over-studied situation lacking spontaneity and exuberant vitality. It seems logical to think that the requisite touch must come in large measure from the Negro dramatists. It is not a question of race, though, but of intimacy of understanding. Paul Green, for example, is a close student of, almost a specialist in, Negro folk life, with unimpeachable artistic motives, and a dozen or more Negro plays to his credit. But the plays of Willis Richardson, the colored playwright, whose *Chip Woman's Fortune* was the first offering of the Chicago Ethiopian Art Theatre under Raymond O'Neill, are very much in the same vein. Though the dialogue is a bit closer to Negro idiom of thought and speech, compensating somewhat for his greater amateurishness of technique and structure, there still comes the impression that the drama of Negro life has not yet become as racy, as gaily unconscious, as saturated with folk ways and the folk spirit as it could be, as it eventually will be. Decidedly it needs more of that poetic strain whose counterpart makes the Irish folk drama so captivating and irresistible, more of the joy of life even when life flows tragically, and even should one phase of it remain realistic peasant drama, more of the emotional depth of pity and terror. This clarification will surely come as the Negro drama shifts more and more to the purely aesthetic attitudes. With life becoming less a problem and more a vital process for the younger Negro, we shall leave more and more to the dramatist not born to it the dramatization of the race problem and concern ourselves more vitally with expression and interpretation. Others may anatomize and dissect; we must paint and create. And while one of the main reactions of Negro drama must and will be the breaking down of those false stereotypes in terms of which the world still sees us, it is more vital that drama should stimulate the group life culturally and give it the spiritual quickening of a native art.

The finest function, then, of race drama would be to supply an imaginative channel of escape and spiritual release, and by some process of emotional reenforcement to cover life with the illusion of happiness and spiritual freedom. Because of the lack of any tradition or art to which to attach itself, this reaction has never functioned in the life of the American Negro except at the level of the explosive and abortive release of buffoonery and low comedy. Held down by social tyranny to the jester's footstool, the dramatic instincts of the race have had to fawn, crouch and be amusingly vulgar. The fine African tradition of primitive ritual broken, with the inhibitions of Puritanism snuffing out even the spirit of a strong dramatic and mimetic heritage, there has been little prospect for the development of strong native dramatic traits. But the traces linger to flare up spectacularly when the touch of a serious dramatic motive once again touches them. No set purpose can create this, only the spontaneous play of the race spirit over its own heritage and traditions. But the deliberate turning back for dramatic material to the ancestral sources of African life and tradition is a very significant symptom. At present just in the experimental stage, with historical curiosity the dominating motive, it heralds very shortly a definite attempt to poetize the race origins and supply a fine imaginative background for a fresh cultural expression. No one with a sense for dramatic values will underestimate the rich resources of African material in these respects. Not through a literal transposing, but in some adaptations of its folk lore, art-idioms and symbols, African material seems as likely to influence the art of drama as much as or more than it has already influenced some of its sister arts. Certainly the logic of the development of a thoroughly racial drama points independently to its use just as soon as the Negro drama rises to the courage of distinctiveness and achieves creative independence.

ST. JAMES THEATRE

NESCA REALTY CO., INC.

THE · PLAYBILL · PUBLISHED · BY · THE · NEW · YORK · THEATRE · PROGRAM · CORPORATION

Beginning Sunday, March 30, 1941   •   Matinees Wednesday and Saturday

ORSON WELLES and JOHN HOUSEMAN
in association with Bern Bernard
present

A MERCURY PRODUCTION

NATIVE SON

by

PAUL GREEN and RICHARD WRIGHT

(From Mr. Wright's novel of the same name)

PRODUCTION by ORSON WELLES

Settings by James Morcom

with

Canada Lee	Ray Collins	Everett Sloane	Erskine Sanford
Paul Stewart	Anne Burr	Evelyn Ellis	Philip Bourneuf

CAST

(In order of their appearance)

BIGGER THOMAS .... CANADA LEE

HANNAH THOMAS .... EVELYN ELLIS

VERA THOMAS .... HELEN MARTIN

Second page of *Playbill* for *Native Son* by Paul Green and Richard Wright. Courtesy of Moorland–Spingarn Research Center, Howard University, Washington, D.C.

BROADWAY AND
THE NEGRO DRAMA

THERE could be no more convincing indication of the vital place of the drama of Negro life in contemporary American drama than the impressive succession in the last twenty years of plays like *The Emperor Jones, Roseanne, All God's Chillun Got Wings, In Abraham's Bosom, Porgy, Run, Little Chillun, The Green Pastures, Stevedore, Porgy and Bess, Mulatto, Mamba's Daughters,* and in 1941 — *Cabin in the Sky* and *Native Son*. These highlights of the Broadway record are a substantial contribution to our best native drama, and, as such, they stand to Broadway's everlasting credit. But along with a consideration of what Broadway has done must go some critical consideration of what has not, as yet, been done.

Close scrutiny of the panorama of the last two decades reveals, along with precedent-making advances, serious gaps and unexpected shadows. On the quantitative side, after all, the tally of significant Negro plays does not total a distinctive play a season. Qualitatively, the survey is still more disquieting. These peak successes are too isolated and disconnected: Broadway has not built up as yet what is most essential for Negro drama — a plateau of sustained use and support of those Negro materials, human and dramatic, which, from time to time, it has so significantly revealed and so successfully exploited. Sporadic support and intermittent interest have thus wrought havoc with many of the best possibilities. Good, even great actors have gone to seed, and forward-looking precedents have closed in again as timorous lapses have followed some of the boldest innovations. With the courage of its own successes, Broadway could have extended at least a half dozen of the above plays into a sustained tradition of original and typically American drama.

This failure is due in part to general faults of the commercial

Theatre Arts 25, no. 10 (October 1941): 745–750.

theatre. But for a newly developing field of drama, with its inevitable novelties of theme and talents, orthodox and conventional notions are the least profitable of all possible procedures, and the results are bound to be meagre. Many if not most of these Negro successes, though technically to Broadway's credit, were not due to Broadway's own initiative, perspicacity or courage. They were taken over from the more flexible experimentalism and hardier social courage of the tributary theatre. Particularly, as with *The Emperor Jones, Porgy, Native Son*, they were the product of unorthodox direction. Indeed, Broadway would do well to look still more closely, if only for hints and cues, at the materials available in the Negro Little Theatre repertory and its acting groups. The rarer possibilities of Negro drama will never be revealed by the 'big producer's' searchlight hunting in the fixed direction of his past successes or in the arbitrary focus of what he thinks the public wants. Nor will his production methods ever unfold the characteristic talents of the Negro singer, dancer or actor; indeed in too many cases already has this routine treatment taken the spontaneity, vitality and true folkiness out of our Negro artists and left a bizarre hybrid in its place. Sound future development will require instead the patient lantern, carefully exploring the full field, especially the dark corners. There, as often before, will be found the truly fresh novelties which theatrical concoction can never duplicate.

This is not said in carping criticism, but with full appreciation of the progress that has been made, and with the realization that the past Broadway season has given us in *Cabin in the Sky* one of the most genuine expressions of Negro comedy, and in *Native Son* what is incontestably one of the deepest and most unconventional of Negro tragedies. All the more reason, then, to be critical of whatever barriers yet stand between us and the fullest possible development of Negro drama and Negro acting.

As to the Negro actor, there still remains a double handicap: on the one hand, wet-blanketing direction toning down the spontaneous, improvising character of true Negro acting; the same direction exaggerating, on the other hand, the superficially theatrical and supposedly 'typical'. In private, Negro actors complain of this unceasingly, but are too docile — largely because of precarious employment — in accepting before the public the yoke of the Broadway stereotypes. One could name a score of expensive failures due mainly to this short-sighted insistence on acting stereotypes and dramatic clichés. One instructive example may be allowed for illustration — the recent failure of *John Henry*, a sterile hybrid of successes like *Porgy, Green Pastures* and *Show Boat*. Its obvious theatrical tricks not only proved a smothering blanket for the magnetic talents of Paul Robeson, but even more tragically placed in temporary stalemate a dramatic theme destined eventually to produce one of the most characteristic of all Negro-American dramas. It is some consolation to learn of a more genuine folk treatment of the John Henry saga, *Natural Man* by Theodore Browne, a Negro dramatist, promisingly tried out by Harlem amateurs — The American Negro Theatre.

In this matter of Negro acting, managerial Broadway has barely learned the true secret of its effective appeal. Often slyly insinuated between the lines of pat, imposed routines, it is without doubt the subtle and spontaneous interpolations — the equivalents in acting of the rhythmic spontaneity and vitality so familiar now in Negro music — which, we should recall, was similarly stifled by imposed formulas before it broke itself loose. What has been responsible for the recent triumphs of Negro acting has been the partial release of such latent dramatic power by sympathetic and non-routine direction, such as that of James Light, Jasper Deeter, Rouben Mamoulian, Marc Connelly, John Houseman, Orson Welles — to mention the outstanding few. Oddly, but encouragingly enough, the artistic successes have also been the box-office successes. On this point, one need only contrast the reverent, magnetic, completely absorbed impersonation of 'De Lawd' by Richard Harrison, a triumph against the grain of previous Broadway tradition, with the tinsel fustian and superficial theatricality of the movie version of *The Green Pastures*, which followed strictly the most orthodox Broadway-Hollywood tradition. Lest the travesty of the latter be put down too much to the limitations of Rex Ingram's talents rather than to stereotyped direction, let us cite the same actor's effective role of 'Lucifer, Jr.', under better and freer direction, in *Cabin in the Sky*. Putting aside, once for all, the dangerous myth that the Negro is a 'natural born actor', we may conclude that the Negro actor certainly needs direction, and before that training, but both along lines of his own instinctive patterns and idioms of expression.

One of these acting fortes, any close observer can verify, is an unusual mastery of body pantomime, too often crowded out nowadays on both the vaudeville and the legitimate stage by the concern for lines and routine cues. It is significant that stellar actors like Ethel Waters, Dooley Wilson, Georgette Harvey and Canada Lee are veterans of vaudeville, where in a humble but effective way they have acquired mastery of this most basic form of dramatic expression. Personally I would sack many lines of clever script rather than dispense, for example, with the pantomime 'ad-lib-ing' of Ethel Waters and Dooley Wilson in *Cabin in the Sky*. In scene after scene, Miss Waters' gesture-portrayals are priceless, particularly the emotional duel of Petunia's pagan and Christian souls; and so, too, is Dooley

Wilson's kaleidoscopic ebb and flow of sin and virtue under the stress of temptation. In more serious setting, one sees the same skills at the core of Canada Lee's body portrayals of Bigger Thomas' tensions and suppressed desires, registered in restrained but electrically charged postures and gestures. These are the stuff of pure unadulterated drama, and directors, playwrights and critics should know where they come from, and mine the deep ores of latent drama they indicate.

Through ignoring this, even that original Broadway bonanza of Negro musical comedy has been worked out — until someone has the genius to re-work it freshly. Routines, trite slapstick, and stock scenes and situations have about taken all the spontaneity and charm from what was the old vital refreshment of *Shuffle Along*, *Eliza*, *Running Wild*, *Black Rhapsody*, and even the first few versions of *Blackbirds*. Yet a finely naive and whimsical thing like Harry Minturn's *Swing Mikado* — product, let us note, of the freer taste of the Federal Theatre Project — is there to prove that these well-springs are not dried up, but only overlooked and untapped. The expensive, stereotyped *Hot Mikado* — the admitted talent of Bojangles Robinson notwithstanding — told the other side of the story, as the octopus formula reached out and crushed such a promising new thing back into the conventional mould. A real scent for vital novelty should have taken the clue from the earlier production and found a new lode-mine of Negro dance and music in the ballet chorus and the cantata-operetta. Because of its exotic character, it was perhaps pardonable for Broadway to have overlooked the suggestive novelties of *Kykunkor*, the African dance-ballet, but not to have seen in the *Swing Mikado* the new horizons of Negro musical comedy was, it seems to me, unpardonable. The crippling vogue of the stock formulas has even invaded the Negro vaudeville circuits, and less and less of what is novel and spontaneous is to be seen even there.

As to the legitimate stage, it is simply Broadway's loss that the best Negro talent comes so sporadically, and often so tragically late, to its wider, more discriminating audiences. It is simply naive to marvel over the sudden 'discoveries' of such talent when really seasoned actors get their first rare chance on Broadway. Before their Broadway debuts, for example, Charles Gilpin, Evelyn Ellis, Rose McClendon, Leigh Whipper were veterans of the Negro stage, and, further, had been schooled in the exacting versatility of stock repertory. Richard Harrison's forty years in the wilderness of the amateur stage and the elocutionist's recital platform, the consequent fact that De Lawd was his first as well as his last adequate role, was a general loss to the American stage. Gilpin's case was similar: years of obscure Negro stock playing before his one late chance at Broadway and the greater public. And but for the experimentation of the Provincetown Theatre and the insight of Marc Connelly, we might never have had either. Rose McClendon, acknowledged great actress that she was, died without ever having had a fully adequate role, when, in view of her obvious stellar capacities, it would have been the best sort of gamble to have commissioned a play for her. Again, audiences that today are stunned with what seems the sudden emergence of Canada Lee could have been well prepared for his current success from his previous performances in the Harlem unit of the Federal Theatre's *Macbeth* and his admirable playing of Christophe in their *Haiti*. Undoubtedly there in that daring primitive version of *Macbeth* was developed the rapport that made it possible for Orson Welles to co-create in so short a time the colossally difficult title role of Bigger Thomas. To mention one last instance, Katherine Dunham and her brilliant dancing troupe of *Cabin in the Sky* are products of the labor stage and repertory recital encouragement. All of which underscores the point of distributing some of Broadway's Negro dramatic laurels to the tributary theatre and of advising Broadway to cultivate even more closely and considerately these experimental seed-beds of the new and untried in drama.

The choice of Negro plays is, if anything, even less discriminating and courageous than the use of Negro actors. Not quite so reactionary as Hollywood, Broadway is nevertheless decidedly unprogressive on the question of representative Negro drama. Granted that many of the plays of the little theatre groups are amateurish in conception and execution, Broadway can always find means of professionally remodelling the themes it wants. But in the Negro field the tyranny of what the public is supposed to want has stood in the way of the development of some of the most obviously original and significant strains of Negro drama, particularly the social problem play based on one or another aspect of the racial situation. What little exploitation of this theme has been undertaken has been keyed to the defeatist formula which many Broadway magnates insist is the safe outer limit of the general public's tolerance on the subject of Negro drama. Yet *Stevedore* and *Mulatto*, in both metropolitan and road show attractiveness, and now *Native Son* have proved conclusively that this is not true, and that the drama public seems to need only more courageous exposure to themes and situations outside the traditional formulas to grow in responsiveness to sound realism in this field. It is marginal Broadway which has been the real sponsor of the progress that has been made in Negro drama. Financial success has been a reward of many precedent-breaking ventures, and there actually has been a higher percentage of failures among the conservatively produced Negro plays.

Consider, for a moment, the core of these past successes, and you see that the most successful features have been departures from the safe situation and conventional solution. The public has particularly liked what it was predicted 'it wouldn't stand for'. Unconventional situations have been the pivots on which much of the public interest and acclaim has turned: the unfarcical wake scene of *Porgy*, the un-condescending revival scene of *Run, Little Chillun*, the non-defeatist riot scene of *Stevedore*, and the unconventional murder scenes of *Mulatto* and of *Native Son*. These situations have registered favorably primarily because of their essential and undeniable truthfulness to life — the safest long-run criterion of drama, despite other more artificial and arbitrary ones. One of the great practical problems, then, of Negro drama at this critical stage in its development is to overcome these clichés of managerial conservatism and over-ride, not by exception but by general consensus, these handicapping reservations of promotional opinion. The public and the acting talent seem ripe; direction is becoming more and more understanding; the considerable lag in adequate playwriting seems primarily a factor of the uncertain market. It is, of course, no easy task to persuade Broadway at large to treat Negro drama with bold, experimental and liberal policies. Yet in the light of what has already happened even on Broadway itself, it is to be hoped, perhaps expected, that the gradual emancipation of Negro drama will soon quicken its pace.

MUSIC

Locke was an Episcopalian by upbringing, although he was active in the Baha'is of Washington in the 1920s. Locke loved the hymns and choral music of high church service, attending Trinity Church in Boston for its program of Bach toccatas. He may have first realized the possibilities of classical renderings of black folk music when he heard Dvorak's Symphony No. 9 (*From the New World*) in the First Baptist Church of Boston in 1907. Locke's early religious training was far removed from the gospel music of black Americans, and it was not until 1912 that he first heard the spirituals sung at Hampton Institute. Here was the basic tension in Locke's music criticism: his appreciation of folk music, on the one hand, and, on the other, his demand that such music be elevated and transformed into high art.[1]

Locke's nearly annual visits to music concerts in Germany and Austria made it possible for him to report in "Roland Hayes: An Appreciation" (1923) that the black tenor from Georgia had received the acclaim of Europe's most exacting critics. This was more than simply a personal triumph, for recognition by Europe of Hayes, and Hazel Harrison, the black pianist, signified to Locke that blacks were winning universal recognition as classical musicians. Moreover, Hayes, by singing the spirituals on a program of classical choral music, both communicated their ancient religious emotion and elevated them to the level of art songs.

Locke valued the spirituals as folk music, and welcomed research into their African origins in his review, "The Technical Study of the Spirituals" (1925). But Locke also saw the spirituals as part of an evolutionary process of internal development in Afro-American culture. Thus, "the spirituals, ragtime, and jazz" constituted "one continuous sequence of Negro music."[2] In "Toward a Critique of Negro Music" (1934), he argues that this process should eventually produce an American classical music. Locke criticizes the hybrid classical jazz inventions of Gershwin and Copland as unassimilated graftings of European elements onto the Afro-American musical tradition. The true "classical jazz" must come as a further evolution within the tradition itself, signs of which he recognizes in the music of Duke Ellington, and in the South American composers Amateo Roldan and Garcia Cartula.

In the next essay, "Negro Music Goes to Par" (1939), Locke suggests Afro-American music has reached "par" with other national and international music forms, signaled by the growing body of serious literature on the subject. Black musicians were gaining respect, as symbolized by Marian Anderson's triumphant Easter Sunday concert of 1939. Denied permission to sing at Constitution Hall by the D.A.R. because she was black, Miss Anderson not only secured Lincoln Memorial as a replacement but galvanized public opinion against segregation in Washington, D.C. The concert also brought artistic recognition to the "black voice," since Marian Anderson, in Locke's opinion, had "learned early from the spirituals and the atmosphere of that spiritual view of life, how to feel with deep simplicity and reverence, how to project with completely impersonal and absorbed power."

The last essay, "Spirituals" (1940), is transcribed from a presentation Locke made while moderating a program of spirituals sung by the Golden Gate Quartet on December 20, 1940. This evening devoted to Negro folk song was part of a four-day celebration at the Library of Congress of the 75th anniversary of the anti-slavery amendment to the Constitution. Locke was one of the organizers of this symposium, which was a tribute to the Afro-American contribution to American culture.[3] In transcribing his remarks, which were recorded, I have left the text intact with only minor editing of repetitious passages.

In "Spirituals," Locke provides his most compelling discussion of music as the idealization of an oppressed, transplanted African people. As yet, universal appreciation and significance has been attained only by the spirituals, he argues, which have become not only a racial, but a national inheritance—"the cultural tie that binds."

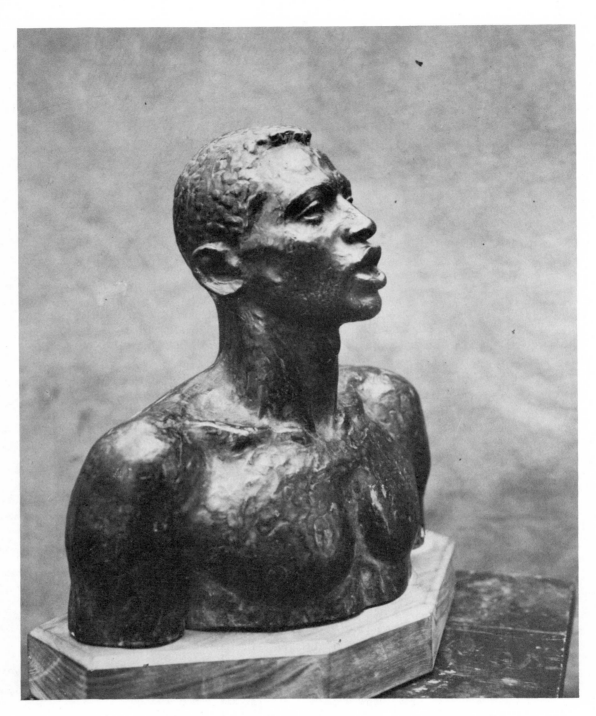

Birth of the Spirituals by Richmond Barthé. Courtesy of Richmond Barthé.

ROLAND HAYES: AN APPRECIATION

ONE of the most accepted of the Viennese musical critics writes in a recent issue of the *Mittag-Zeitung*: "Roland Hayes, heralded before his first concert as a sensation and artistic curiosity because of his color, had already before this last one quite disillusioned the curiosity-seekers and chastened the gossip-mongers. Not as a Negro, but as a great artist, he captured and moved his audience. And our prophecy of April last, that he would always be welcomely heard in Vienna, was fulfilled yesterday. An audience that filled the Konzerthaus to capacity was again enthralled by the magic of his really wonderful mezza voice, was once more astounded by the matchless diction and interpretation of his German songs, and was made to realize the deep religious inspiration and poetic feeling of the Negro spirituals. Indeed, these admirably simple but unfortunately not too happily harmonized songs were among the best that the artist had to offer."

By the time this article is in print, Mr. Hayes will have sung as soloist with the Boston Symphony Orchestra and will be in the midst of a concert tour of America that will be epoch-making with regard to the recognition by the general American public of a Negro singer. As outstanding and commendable as this is as an artistic achievement, it has still more considerable significance—it should serve—it will serve—two timely purposes: it will educate the American public out of one of its worst and most unfair provincialisms (and in this respect, we must remember that the native-born and native-trained artist, white or black, has had great handicaps in America); and then too it will mark a very singular vindication of indisparagable ambition and courage, which would not accept the early rewards of the double standard so often temptingly imposed upon Negro talent by well-meaning but short-sighted admirers of both races. For these reasons, I write this comment—though of course, artistically, racially, and personally I was happy

that the circumstances of travel made me a companion and witness of Mr. Hayes' almost triumphant recent tour of Austria, Hungary, and Tzcheco-Slovakia.

Vienna is the music-capitol of Europe—the Viennese critics are the most exacting and the Viennese public one of the most musically enlightened bodies in the world. The acclaim of Vienna is therefore the ambition of the greatest artists, and the tradition of success here opens all doors; especially that which leads to the historical recognition of posterity. It is perhaps not becoming for a friend to chronicle over-laboriously the details of such a success—I mention as mere suggestions, that the audience cheered about the stage in semi-darkness for quite a half-hour after the regular program; that several critics missed Jeritza's annual leave-taking of the Opera to attend; that Madame Arnoldson Fischoff, the primadonna who has sung with the greatest tenors of two musical generations from Tamango to Bathstini, requested an Italian aria as an encore and declared it "perfectly sung"; that the creator of the role of Parsifal declared very generously that he would have given half his career for such mastery of the mezza-voice; that occasional Americans of the foreign colony spoke with pride of "our American artist" whom until recently they could never have heard without condescension and in some parts of our country, proscription and segregation. How shall we best appraise this triumph—as personal, as artistic, or racially? In each of these respects, it is significant and exceptional.

Personally, it represents the triumph of a particularly high and far-sighted ambition. Just when his admirers in America were on the verge of flattering him into the fatal success of mediocrity, Mr. Hayes began in a fresh field to study and conquer the higher interpretative technique of his art. Indefatigable work, a large part of it is the cultural background so often neglected by musi-

Opportunity 1 (December 1923): 356–358.

cians, has made a seasoned artist out of a gifted, natural-born singer. We have as a group more artistic talent and fewer artists than any other; nature has in music done too much for us—so that in this musical generation we have produced but two artists whose equipment can challenge the international standard—Roland Hayes and Hazel Harrison. There will be many more when the lesson of their careers is sufficiently impressed upon the younger generation of race talent. Race talent in all fields is in the quicksands of the double standard—our own people through short-sighted partisanship and pardonable provincialism, white Americans through sentimental partiality or through haughty disparagement, make it doubly difficult. The turning point of Mr. Hayes' career was when he refused to accept an assured success of this sort, and risked failure for the single standard of musical Europe. Success there has opened doors otherwise closed in America, not only for Mr. Hayes but for all qualified talent in the future. As he himself told me, "I hope to leave open behind me every door that I open—my ultimate intention in coming to Europe, in appealing to European judgment, was eventually to widen opportunity for the Negro artist in America." So an Acropolis has been captured by the shrewd strategy of a flank attack.

Artistically Mr. Hayes, through the very intelligent pedagogy of Mr. Hubbard of Boston and Dr. Lierhammer of London, has cultivated his voice on its own pattern. It is not an imitation of other models, however great; but an intensive cultivation of a voice that had its natural limitations—especially that of medium volume. Through building up the intrinsic resources of the voice, there has been produced a lyric song-tenor of unique quality and flawless technique—a voice that would really be over-refined and two subtle except for the peculiarly fine rhapsodic flow which Mr. Hayes has taken over from the primitive race gift in the art of song. The combination has created a rare medium which satisfies the most critical and sophisticated, without losing the primary universal appeal of simplicity and directly apprehensible beauty. So that a critic can say, "This Negro singer adds a new contribution to the tenor-mystery in producing sensuous effects. It is old traditional culture taken hold of by a new temperament."

Without losing its individuality, the voice adapts itself to every language, to all schools and periods—because of its essential naturalness and freedom. Critical France is satisfied with the interpretation of its best modern music, and the German school with the interpretations of Bach, Schumann, Schubert, Strauss and Wolf, whereas the Italian literature, especially of the older seventeenth and eighteenth centuries, is sung with a flow that qualifies according to the best traditions of *bel canto*. "Perhaps it comes through the deeper naturalness of tone-expression", suggests the same critic—no less than the dean of Viennese critics, Korngold, "that from each phrase, though technically perfectly rendered, a primitive sort of feeling wells up." No better artistic lesson can be taught than that of escaping from the limitations of one school and style of singing by the arduous endeavor to be sincere, genuine, and original—in other words, to be throughout all oneself and wholesomely natural. Refined but unaffected, cultivated but still simple—it is a voice of artistic paradoxes, and for that reason, unique.

Racially? Is there race in art? Mr. Hayes attributes his success to his racial heritage, which fortunately he cannot disown, if he would. Contrary to the general impression, it has not been an easy matter to make musical Europe accept and understand upon an art-plane the Negro spirituals which Mr. Hayes has always insisted upon as part of his program. Accompanists have often failed to interpret them properly, critics have been condescending toward them while nevertheless wholly favorable to other classical numbers, orchestrations have had to be expressly made and orchestral traditions broken to allow them as part of several programs. That which might have been expected to make Mr. Hayes' career easier upon the basis of a novelty has really, to my knowledge, been a difficult crusade, that but for tact and insistence would have failed. The result has been of peculiar value in giving a new cultural conception of the Negro to important circles of European society—a work that has made the artist a sort of ambassador of culture in our behalf. At first they excite only curiosity and the reaction—why does he sing them? Then a few catch the seriousness of the interpretation and eventually the few understand. "Mr. Hayes sang the spirituals with dignity, penetrated by his mission," says one. "We should not forget that of the three wise men who were guided by the star on their quest, one was a Negro, and that the Negro today is able in the cool, peculiar beauty of these spirituals to tell of Him so vividly and touchingly that one might forget much that, had the wise men lived long enough to experience, might bitterly have disappointed them", says another. And not to rest upon the testimony of others, I will venture the opinion that here in this side of Mr. Hayes' work, we have had an artistic missioner of the highest effect and importance—a racial vindication and appraisal that could not have come in any better way, being all the more effective through being expressed through the international speech of melody and insinuated into the mind through the channels of feeling and the heart. The Negro as a group has lived Christianity in a peculiar way and exceptional degree. It has saved him—saved him in this world—saved his heart from corrosion under the acid of persecution, enabled him to survive through optimism and hope when despair and cynicism would have added the last sinking ounce of weight—and in this near future of racial vindication, it is to be one of the most potent mediums of interpretation and vindication.

"The highest tribute we can offer Mr. Hayes is to say that while singing these, he might have been a statue shaped by the hands of his own race through long centuries, for the ultimate purpose of transmitting the soul of the race. It was the soul of his race which sang through him in these childlike yet tragic spirituals; sang of barbarities committed and endured, and of a faith running like a golden thread through the gloomy web of wrongs."* To have elicited such recognition from the stranger is a tribute to interpretative art of the highest character. A similar impression was no doubt made upon the sensitive mind of Mr. Evon Philpot, whose portrait of *Roland Hayes Singing* is more the expression of a race symbol than of an individual— the attempt to translate a spiritual message and give the social rather than the personal note in art. The effect is, in every such instance, reciprocal; the people gain through the art; the art gains in vitality and in spirituality from its background in the people.

Mr. Hayes has given this racial material a balanced background by which it has commanded more respect than when separately and over-exploited as has been the case with many other European presentations of our songs. "I will never sing spirituals without classics, or classics without spirituals, for properly interpreted they are classics,"—this is Mr. Hayes' artistic platform—and he is right and will be eventually justified. From this challenging comparison with other classical song material has come not always an admission of equal value—that could not be expected—but always there has been conceded a seriousness of purpose and mission and loyalty to self that has commanded admiration and respect.

No better instance of the soundness of this procedure can be given than the transfer from these simple folk-songs to Bach, through an affinity of religious feeling, of a religious quality which makes Mr. Hayes' interpretation of Bach songs a delight to all connoisseurs of that great master. And then, finally, their inclusion has demonstrated to the very apprehending the true school of Mr. Hayes' art. It has folk-parentage--it is the mother-art that through intense and sincere and quite religious feeling has given rare capacity in evoking the spirituality which lies back of all great music, but the sense of which comes not so much from the technique and discipline of art, but from the discipline of life itself, and most often from that side of it which we racially have so deeply tasted under the necessities of hardship. To capitalize these spiritual assets, especially in and through art, ought to be one of the main objectives and missions of the younger, more happily circumstanced, generations.

*The *New Age*, May 5, 1921

THE TECHNICAL STUDY OF
THE SPIRITUALS—A REVIEW

WITH three noteworthy book collections, Weldon Johnson's, this and Nathaniel Dett's forthcoming revision of the *Religious Songs of the Negro as Sung at Hampton*, with numerous arrangement collections such as Frey's (Robbins-Engel Co.), William Arms Fisher's (Oliver Ditson Co.) and Hollis Dann's (Birchard Co.), together with numerous recent magazine articles, notably Carl Van Vechten's in *Vanity Fair* and C. L. Adams in the *Charleston Museum Quarterly*, and perhaps most important of all with the concert interpretensions of Roland Hayes, Marian Anderson, Julius Bledsoe and Paul Robeson with Lawrence Brown, Negro folk-music in general, and the Spirituals particularly are having an extraordinary contemporary vogue. Not since their origin have they been so vigorously vital, and never before so artistically potent. With bursting vitality, they seem to have come to the cultural maturity and their artistic prime.

Among all this, Ballanta Taylor's collection, with its scholarly and clairvoyant foreword, is outstanding. For the future of the Spirituals hinges upon their technical study and appreciation and their contribution to the substance of musical art. This with Mr. Ballanta is a matter of particular concern and interest. So while the Viking Press book, with Weldon Johnson's competent essay preface, goes on its dignified, urbane mission of introducing the Spirituals to the wider appreciation and understanding of the amateur, this brochure comes as a find and treasure for the professional student, for whom the technical musical

---

SAINT HELENA ISLAND SPIRITUALS: *Nicholas G. J. Ballanta (Taylor). Schirmer Press for the Penn Normal, Industrial and Agricultural School,* 1925. $1.50.

Opportunity 3 (November 1925): 331–332.

interest is dominant. The two books are thus beautifully supplementary, together giving to contemporary interest just the needed lift and enlightenment—the one the most illuminating social and cultural interpretation since Dr. Du Bois's famous essay on the Sorrow Songs, the other the best scientific study and analysis since Krehbiel. And considering what is accomplished in the compass of this short foreword promises that Ballanta Taylor's full study on completion of his research in the folk music of his native West Africa will turn out to be the definitive technical treatise on the entire subject.

Developing his interesting thesis of "felt" and "pulsed" rhythm as the native and inherited basis of American Negro folk-song, Mr. Ballanta explains the kinship of the Spirituals with African music more convincingly even than Mr. Krehbiel, and further gives the clue that the sophisticated musician with his traditional notion of variant and scanned or divided rhythm lacked. His explanation of the intervallic peculiarities of the scale values of this music is also many steps in advance of any previous analysis. We must approach this great body of music technically if the mechanics of its instinctive art is ever to be understood and utilized. Fortunately, technical though they are, Mr. Ballanta's findings are simple and clarifying: for instance, the notion of syncopation, not, as a displacement of beat, but as a compound beat, introduced from the contrapuntal rhythms of African music, or the theory of cross rhythm and dovetailing harmonic modes below and above the dominant as accounting for the peculiar subtleties and harmonic effects of this music. The conclusions

are perhaps not altogether novel, but it is more
conclusively established than ever that "the
Negro Spiritual is in many respects identical
in the elements of rhythm and melody with
the African conception of those elements," and
that the choral practise of the American Negroes, as might be expected, is a modification
of the African design of solo and chorus refrain by Western choral patterns and form a
sort of "connecting link" between the two.
And certainly all serious students will agree
with Mr. Ballanta that "not until the rhythmic, melodic and other characteristics of the
spiritual are understood, will there arise composers who will bring forth conscious music of
the beauty and inspiration of the Spirituals."

There are in all 103 hitherto unpublished
songs and some interesting variant versions, set
down in plain choral form as still sung by the
Penn Island community. The work was a
research project undertaken under the auspices
of the Penn Island School. It is rather a pity
that for comparison the manuscript arrangements by Carl Diton of some of this same material, collected several years back as the Frogmore Collection of Spirituals, is not available
in print. For these Frogmore melodies are
among the most distinctive Negro songs extant,
and have yet to supply their ore to the art
treasures of American music. After the more
familiar melodies, songs like *King Jedus is muh
only Freu', John saw de Number no man
could number,* and *Mary had de leetle Baby*
are gems both musically and as folk thought.
They merit careful study and attention. For
example, the double or antiphonal choiring
noted (p. 7) of *King Jedus* shows the extreme
musical complexity and technical subtlety of
these apparently simple songs. For the musician, there is more in these unvarnished recordings than in all the reams of figurated arrangements, and rolled chord transcriptions
with which a popular vogue may glut the musical market, threatening genuine musical treasures with their own tawdry counterfeits. Indeed the acclaim of the Spirituals has in it a
distinct element of danger, against which the
serious musician must safeguard the sound maturing and development of Negro folk music.
Mr. Ballanta certainly has performed his share
of this duty and service conscientiously and
skillfully well.

TOWARD A CRITIQUE OF NEGRO MUSIC

PART I

THINGS Negro have been and still are the victims of two vicious extremes,—uncritical praise or calculated disparagement. Seldom, if ever, do they achieve the golden mean and by escaping both over-praise and belittlement receive fair appraisal and true appreciation. Of no field is this more true than Negro music. I have read nearly all that has been written on the subject, and do not hesitate to rate most of it as platitudinous piffle— repetitious bosh; the pounds of praise being, if anything, more hurtful and damning than the ounces of disparagement. For from the enthusiasts about Negro music comes little else than extravagant superlatives and endless variations on certain half-true commonplaces about our inborn racial musicality, our supposed gift of spontaneous harmony, the uniqueness of our musical idioms and the infectious power and glory of our transmuted suffering.

True—or rather half-true as these things undoubtedly are, the fact remains that it does Negro music no constructive service to have them endlessly repeated by dilletante enthusiasts, especially without the sound correctives of their complementary truths. The state of Negro music, and especially the state of mind of Negro musicians needs the bitter tonic of criticism more than unctuous praise and the soothing syrups of flattery. While the Negro musician sleeps on his much-extolled heritage, the commercial musical world, revelling in its prostitution, gets rich by exploiting it popularly, while the serious musical world tries only half-successfully to imitate and develop a fundamentally alien idiom. Nothing of course can stop this but the exhaustion of the vogue upon which it thrives; still the sound progress of our music depends more upon the independent development of its finer and deeper values than upon the curtailing of the popular and spurious output. The real damage of the popular vogue rests in the corruption and misguidance of the few rare talents that might otherwise make heroic and lasting contributions. For their sake and guidance, constructive criticism and discriminating appreciation must raise a standard far above the curb-stone values of the market-place and far more exacting than the easy favor of the multitude.

Indeed for the sound promotion of its future, we must turn from the self-satisfying glorification of the past of Negro music to consider for their salutary effect the present short-comings of Negro music and musicians. It is time to realize that though we may be a musical people, we have produced few if any great musicians,—that though we may have evolved a folk music of power and potentiality, it has not yet been integrated into a musical tradition,—that our creativeness and originality on the folk level has not yet been matched on the level of instrumental mastery or that of

Opportunity 12 (November and December 1934): 328–331; 365–367, 385.

creative composition, — and that with a few exceptions, the masters of Negro musical idiom so far are not Negro. Bitter, disillusioning truths, these: but wholesome if we see them as danger-signs against the popular snares and pitfalls and warnings against corruption and premature decadence. This is why, although sanguine as ever about its possibilities, I entitle my article, *Toward a Critique of Negro Music*.

These shortcomings, however, are not entirely the fault of internal factors; they are due primarily to external influences. Those Negro musicians who are in vital touch with the folk traditions of Negro music are the very ones who are in commercial slavery to Tin Pan Alley and subject to the corruption and tyranny of the ready cash of our dance halls and the vaudeville stage. On the other hand, our musicians with formal training are divorced from the people and their vital inspiration by the cloister-walls of the conservatory and the taboos of musical respectability. Musical criticism for the most part ignores these lamentable conditions, wasting most of its energies in banal praise. Of the four to five thousand pages I have read on the subject of Negro music, four-fifths could be consigned to the flames to the everlasting benefit of the sound appraisal of Negro music and of constructive guidance for the Negro musician. For myself, I would rescue from the bon-fire not much more than these few: W. F. Allen's early comment on the *Slave Songs*, Thomas W. Higginson's essay on them, Krehbiel's definitive treatise on *Afro-American Folk Song*, (still the best after thirty years), the few paragraphs on Negro music in Weldon Johnson's *Anthology*, the essays on Negro music in the *New Negro*, the comments on Negro folk-music by W. C. Handy and Abbe Niles, pertinent commentary on the "blues" by Carl Van Vechten and Langston Hughes, Dorothy Scarborough's *On the Trail of Negro Folk Songs*, Handy's *Beale Street*, certain pages of Isaac Goldberg's *Tin Pan Alley*, R. D. Darrell's essay on Duke Ellington, some of the penetrating and constructive criticisms of Olin Downes, and interpretations of jazz by Irving Schwerké and Robert Goffin—especially the latter's *On The Frontiers of Jazz*. Fifty pages of real value, certainly not more, may have escsaped my memory, but I strongly recommend these few gleanings to the serious reader.

One should also include, of course, what little is said on the subject of Negro music in Henry Cowell's *American Composers on American Music*, a projected review of which was the initial cause of this article. But disappointment at what could have been said in this volume sent me into a turtle-shell of silence and brooding from which the editor of Opportunity, who has patiently prodded me for a year or so, will be surprised to see me emerge. It is not that a good deal of importance on this subject is not said in this volume, but here again it is odd to find the best of it coming from two talented Cuban composers and the rest of it from one or two modernists like Cowell and Theodore Chandler. But it is just as odd to find the best criticism of jazz coming from foreign critics like Schwerké and Goffin. Indeed the whole field is full of paradoxes, for after all the most original and pioneering creative use of Negro musical idioms still goes to the credit of white composers from Dvorak down to Aaron Copeland, Alden Carpenter, George Gershwin, Paul Whiteman, and Sesana.

What does this mean? Primarily that Negro musicians have not been first to realize the most genuine values of Negro music, and that the Negro audience has not pioneered in the recognition and intelligent appreciation of the same. Familiarity has bred contempt and nearness induced a myopia of judgment. With our music thus at the mercy of outside recognition and support, the first flow of Negro creative genius has been unusually subject to commercial control, cheap imitation and easy plagiarism. In fact Negro music, like the seed-sower's in the parable, has chiefly fallen by the wayside and has been picked up by musical scavengers and devoured by the musical birds of the air. But lest we charge all of this to outside factors, let us remember that much has also fallen upon our own stony ground of shallow appreciation or been choked by the hostile thorns of a false and blighting academic tradition. No musical idiom that has arisen from the people can flourish entirely cut off from the ground soil of its origin. Even in the sun of popular favor it is baked to an early death unless it has deep under it roots of vital nourishment. Nor can it be effectively developed by the timid and artificial patronage of arid academicians. Vital musical idioms have not been taken up sufficiently by our trained musicans; most of them have been intimidated by their academic training. Many of them are also aesthetic traitors in their heart of hearts. True, they accept the spirituals and other forms of the folk-tradition in the face of an overwhelming vogue, because they must,—but with half-hearted appreciation, often inner contempt. At the beginning of the vogue, I remember when an urgent appeal had to be sent afield to Coleridge Taylor to transcribe a group of spirituals. In that day our trained musicians disdained the effort. And until quite recently, the Negro composers' treatment of the spirituals has resulted in the most sophisticated and diluted arrangements:—witness a good deal of the work of Burleigh, Rosamond Johnson and Nathaniel Dett. And even those centers which have the avowed purpose of preserving and developing Negro music have ulterior and far from musical motives. To them too often it is a matter of bread-and-butter propaganda, with a fine tradition prostituted to institutional begging and the amusement of philanthropists.

To this must be added the surprising lack of the theoretical study of music beyond conservatory requirements and the resulting paucity of an original vein of composition. This with the tardy development of instrumental virtuosity except in a limited range of instruments, has resulted, despite the efforts of Jim Europe and Marion Cook, in our having almost no orchestral tradition. These facts have blocked the fusion of classical forms with the Negro musical idiom when they have not resulted in an actual watering-down of these idioms by the classical tradition. So except in choral singing,—the one vein of Negro music inherently orchestral, there is yet a deep divide between our folk music and the main stream of formal music.

I ask the reader's patience with these negative but incontestable statements. Encouragingly enough at certain historical stages this same state of affairs has existed with other musical traditions,—with Russian music before Glinka, with Hungarian music before Liszt and Brahms, and with Bohemian music before Dvorak and Smetana.

However, if we would draw consolation from these parallels, we must remember that it took revolutionary originality and native genius to transform the situation, lift the level and break the path to the main-stream for each of these musical traditions. It is inevitable that this should eventually happen with Negro folk-music for it is not only the most vivid and vital and universally appealing body of folk-music in America, there is little in fact that can compete with it. Yet it is far from being much more as yet than the raw material of a racial or national tradition in music in spite of Weldon Johnson's famous statement of its claims. This is, after all a statement of promise, not realization. Mr. W. J. Henderson is right in a recent article, "Why No Great American Music," when he says,—"Where there is no unification of race, as in this country, the folk idiom does not exist except as that of some fraction of the people." He is equally right in saying,—"the potent spell of the Negro spiritual is a deep-rooted, almost desperate grasp of religious belief. It is the song of the Negro soul. It not only interests, but even arouses, the white man because of its innate eloquence," but,—he continues, "the Negro spiritual tells no secret of the wide American soul; it is the creation of black humans crushed under slavery and looking to eternity for their only joy." For the present, this is quite true. But the very remedy that Mr. Henderson prescribes for the creation of a great national music is the same for the proper universalization of the spirituals and other Negro folk-music. What is needed is genius, as he says, and still more genius. That is to say, the same transforming originality that in the instances cited above widened the localisms of Russian, Hungarian and Czech music to a universal language, but in breaking the dialect succeeded in preserving the rare raciness and unique flavor. Certainly the Negro idioms will never become great music nor representative national music over the least common denominators of popular jazz or popular ballads. And perhaps there is more vital originality and power in our secular folk music than even in our religious folk music. It remains for real constructive genius to develop both in the direction which Dvorak clairvoyantly saw.

But the *New World Symphony* stands there a largely unheeded musical sign-post pointing the correct way to Parnassus, while the main procession has followed the lowly but well-paved jazz road. Not that the jazz-road cannot lead to Parnassus; it can and has,—for the persistent few. But the producers of good jazz still produce far too much bad jazz, and the distinction between them is blurred to all but the most discriminating. Jazz must be definitely rid of its shoddy superficiality and its repetitious vulgar gymnastics. Further it must be concentrated nearer to the Negro idioms from which it has been derived. Even good diluted jazz of the sort that is now so much in vogue does a dis-service to the ultimate best development of this great folk tradition. Only true genius and almost consecrated devotion can properly fuse art-music and folk-music. Stimulating and well-intentioned as Gershwin's work has been, I question very seriously the ultimate success of his easy-going formula of superimposing one upon the other. "Jazz," he says, "I regard as an American folk music; not the only one, but a very powerful one which is probably in the blood and feeling of the American people more than any other style of folk-music. I believe that it can be made the basis of serious symphonic works of lasting value in the hands of a composer with talent for both jazz and symphonic music." True,—but out of the union of the two a new style and a new tradition must be forged. Only rare examples of this have appeared as yet, and there is just as much promise of it in Louis Armstrong's and Ellington's best, perhaps more—than in the labored fusions of Carpenter, Gruenberg, Gershwin and Grofe. The late Otto Kahn said, with instinctive intuition: "I look upon modern jazz as a phase, as a transition, not as a completed process." The final jazz will be neither Copeland's bizarre hybrid of European neo-impressionism and jazz rhythms, nor Gruenberg's fusion, however deft, of jazz themes with German and Central European modernisms of style, nor Gershwin's pastiche of American jazz mixed with Liszt, Puccini, Stravinski, and Wagner.

This is not said ungratefully, for each of the above has done yeoman service in the vindication of the higher possibilities of jazz and the education of the popular taste out of the mere ruck of popular song and dance. *Rhapsody in Blue* opened a new era; Alden Carpenter's work brought the first touches of sophistication to jazz, Whiteman and Grofe together broadened the whole instrumental scope of the jazz orchestra; Copeland's *Concerto* carried jazz idiom as far as it could go by sheer intellectual push into the citadel of the classical tradition; Gruenberg has taken jazz to the chamber music level and lately has adapted it more than half-successfully to the dramatic possibilities of opera. However, more remains to be done,—and I hope and expect it from the Negro musician in spite of his present handicaps and comparatively poor showing. Already a newer type of jazz, at one and the same time more intimate to the Negro style and with more originality is coming to the fore, witness Dana Suess's *Jazz Nocturne*, Constant Lambert's *Rio Grande*, and Otto Sesana's brilliant *Negro Heaven*. Unlike the first phase of classical jazz, these are not artificial hybrids but genuine developments from within the intimate idiom of jazz itself. A still further step may be expected from the growing mastery of the Negro jazz composers, who in the last few years have reached a new plane, and also from those brilliant mulatto composers of Latin America who may roughly be called the Afro-Cuban school even though some of them are from Mexico, Central America and Brazil.

Much indeed is to be expected of the two geniuses of the South, Amateo Roldan and Garcia Caturla, who since 1925-26 have been developing a serious school of Negro music out of the Afro-Cuban material. Caturla says: "The so-called Afro-Cuban native music is our most original type of folk song and is a mixture of African primitive music with early Spanish influences. It employs many percussion instruments which have been developed in Cuba and are to be found nowhere else, although they have their origin in African primitive instruments." The manuscript works of these composers for orchestra show greater instrumental originality than has yet appeared in the American school of serious jazz. For its counterpart, we have to go to the unacademic and unwritten but creative jazz technique of our own Negro jazz orchestras.

But with these South Americans, it is a matter of deliberate path-breaking. Roldan expresses his creed by saying "indigenous instruments, both melodic and percussion, should be used not in order to obtain an easy local color, but with the purpose of widening their significance beyond the national boundaries. The sound of a banjo must not always bring jazz to our minds, nor should the rhythm of our guiro always recall a rhumba." Accordingly his *Poema Negro* for string quartet and his *Motivos de Son*, based on native song - motifs with unusual combinations of instruments, and his Afro-Cuban ballet represent, like a good deal of Caturla's work, high points in the serious conquest of a new Negro music.

PART II

With us, however, our music is at a new chrysalis stage: there are stirring signs everywhere of a new promise. But it is as yet uncertain whether the startling new thing will come from the camp of the popular or from that of the formal musicians. Jazz has already prepared us for new things: it may create them. Already it has educated the general musical ear to subtler rhythms, unfinished and closer harmonies, and unusual cadences,—indeed it has been a conquering advance-guard of the modern type of music in general. It has also introduced new principles of harmony, of instrumental technique and instrumental combinations, and promises to lead to a new type of orchestra and orchestration. Yet it must completely break through the shell of folk provincialism as only the spirituals have as yet done, and completely lift itself from the plane of cheap popular music. The academic musicians must look to their laurels.

In conclusion, I would like to discuss what seems to be the most promising possibilities of the contemporary scene. Certainly of the popular musicians, the most consistently developing genius is Duke Ellington, and the white hope of the formal musicians for the moment certainly is Grant Still, especially after the tragic loss of the talented Jenkins. Incidentally, Negro music has had such tragic losses,—the sudden death of Jim Europe, the premature retirement of Marion Cook, the loss of Bob Cole, the death of Jenkins and until recently the sporadic activity of Hall Johnson.

Mr. Still's own declaration in *American Composers* gives little insight into his position: Cowell's estimate gives more. "William Grant Still, Negro," he says, "uses his people's themes and feelings as a base for his music which is otherwise in modern style with some rather vague European influence. Perhaps he possesses the beginnings of a genuine new style." Obviously this vague European influence is that of Varese, the Italian futurist, under whose tuition Still has been. Howard Hanson, who has been responsible for the repeated performance of Still's serious orchestral work, undoubtedly regards him as among the American musicians of promise and originality. This is true in spite of the academic modernism in his work. But there is really an unfortunate schism in Mr. Still's style as in his life work,—for some of his most brilliant orchestral writing has gone into countless anonymous jazz-arrangements for Whiteman, Hollywood and Willard Robeson's orchestra. If this vital substance has been free to flow into his formal composition, they would have been less tainted with stilted sophistication. His *Afro-American Symphony*, not yet completed, promises to outgrow these limitations,— and his colossally elaborate ballet *Sadjhi*, is proof of his mastery of large technical resources. His tardy freedom from musical drudgery on a Guggenheim scholarship this year promises to release a valuable talent. But there are dangers in self-conscious academic racialism; it is no more desirable than self-conscious nationalism; of which sterility we in America have also had too much.

But personally I am not so sure that the development we are looking for may not come from the camp of popular music. The titanic originality of the great Negro orchestras has only to be intellectualized to conquer Parnassus or raise an Olympus of its own, and while there are many practical masters of it from Sam Wooding, Noble Sissle and Fletcher Henderson to the contemporary Don Redman, Baron Lee, Claude Hopkins, Earl Hines, Cab Calloway and Jimmy Lunceford, it seems to me that Duke Ellington is most likely to push through to this development. For Ellington is not only one of the great exponents of jazz, he is the pioneer of super-jazz and the person most likely to create the classical jazz towards which so many are striving. He projects a symphonic suite and an African opera, both of which will prove a test of his ability to carry jazz to this higher level. His style has passed through more phases and developed more maturely than any of his more spectacular competitors and I agree with Robert Goffin in saying that "the technique of jazz production has been rationalized by Ellington" and that "he has gradually placed intuitive music under control." R. D. Darrell's tribute, though rhapsodic, is probably an anticipation of what the future will judge. "The larger works of Gershwin, the experiments of Copeland and other serious composers are attempts with new symphonic forms stemming from jazz but not of it. . . . One can say truthfully that a purely instrumental school of jazz has never gone beyond the embryonic stage. . . . Ellington has emancipated American popular music from text for the first time since Colonial days. . . . Within an Ellington composition there is a similar unity of style of the essential musical qualities of melody, rhythm, harmony, color, and form. Unlike most jazz writers, Ellington never concentrates undue attention on rhythm alone. . . . Delightful and tricky rhythmic effects are never introduced for sheer sensational purposes, rather they are developed and combined with others as logical part and parcel of the whole work. . . . Harmonically Ellington is apt and subtle rather than obvious and striking, and in the exploitation of new tone and coloring, he has proceeded further than any other composer—popular or serious— of today. . . . His one attempt at a larger form, a two-part *Creole Rhapsody,* is not wholly successful, although it does develop and interweave a larger number of themes than usual in his work. It is here that Ellington has most to learn. . . . He may betray his uniqueness for popularity, be brought down to the level of orthodox dance music, lose his secure footing and intellectual grasp in the delusion of grandeur. Most of his commercial work evidences just such lapses. . . . But he has given us, and I am confident will give us again, more than a few moments of the purest, the most sensitive revelations of feeling in music today." It will be to the lasting credit and gain of genuine Negro music if Mr. Ellington or some other of our musicians lives up to this challenge and prophecy.

Negro music should be expected to flower most gloriously and most naturally in the field of vocal music. Here already there is a great tradition, for Negroes sing creatively and orchestrally. But the spirituals that have not been put into the strait-jacket of the barber-shop and stage quartet, have been developed in a line false to their native choral nature. Of course, some superlatively fine music has been made from the treatment of the spirituals for solo voice with instrumental accompaniment, and no one would sensibly dispense with it. But the true vein of this music will never be realized until the spirituals are restored to their primitive choral basis. Herein we have the significance of the newer types of Negro choir that are now beginning to appear or re-appear, among them most significantly, those of Eva Jessye and Hall Johnson. Indeed it is just here that I find the great pioneer significance of Hall Johnson as contrasted with Burleigh, let us say, who served well in his generation, but whose work along with that of his contemporaries represents hybrid versions and a watering-down of the native materials of Negro folk-song. It is Hall Johnson's versions of both the spirituals and the secular songs, that point to the promise of the future, and that alone can realize for Negro choral music the values that have been developed, for example, by the Russian choral composers and singing choirs. This is not a racial matter, although one naturally expects from racial composers and singers the best results. I would, in fact, rather hear the carefully studied and very understanding arrangements of Frank Black for the famous *Revellers* than many missionary circus stunts of quartets and octets from "down home," and there is such competition now in the intimate study of the idioms of Negro singing by white artists that the Negroes in this field will have to look to their laurels and to their heels.

No sounder advice has ever been given us on this point than that of Mr. Olin Downes in his critical comment on the Carnegie concert of the Fisk Choir. He advises us rightly to sing in the Negro idiom and to lift it to the level of formal art. It is easy to turn such good advice aside on the false interpretation of advising Negroes to stick to their own limited province. It is a deeper problem than this; that of developing a great style out of the powerful musical dialect

we have. Eventually choral works of an entirely new sort can and must come from Negro sources —great liturgical forms from the Spirituals— unique choral folk songs as Hall Johnson's arrangement of *"Water Boy"* and *"I'm an Eas'-man"* and perhaps even a technique of chant singing such as was exploited by Gruenberg rather artificially but quite effectively in the operatic version of *The Emperor Jones*.

This brings me to my last observations of a most promising recent development in Negro music—Asadata Dafora Horton's African Dance Opera—*Kykunkor*. Here we have something that starts soundly from the primitive African tradition and not from the exotic grafting on of "native material." The African drum orchestra has been developed into something of vital artistic device—and the dance-motifs have been transposed almost as vitally as Shan-Kar's transposition of Hindu dance forms. This we hope is but the beginning of an entirely new and healthy pioneering in the African tradition after several generations of merely superficial dabbling in its local color and titillating strangeness. With the effective orchestration of Mrs. Upshur, the score proves that the African rhythms can be transposed to the Western scale and Western instruments with some supplementations as one might expect. At any rate *Kykunkor* has given us our first glimpse of the African tradition in a healthy pagan form with primitive cleanliness and vitality instead of the usual degenerate exoticism and fake primitivism to which we have been accustomed.

Out of some negative criticisms, then, we have come to a discernment of truer values and finer possibilities for Negro music in the future. Though he should not confine himself to the limited materials of folk-music, the Negro musician should realize that his deepest hopes and best possibilities are based upon them. For a constructive creed, one could almost paraphrase verbatim the remarks of the Cuban composer, Caturla, reading in Negro where he uses the adjective Cuban. "If composers," he says, "imitate other people's music or already known styles, they are not expressing themselves, nor are they fulfilling their purpose of delivering an inner message to the outer world through music. . . . In order to arrive at genuinely Cuban music, it is necessary to work with the living folk-lore. This should be polished until the crudities and the exterior influences fall away; sane theoretical discipline should be applied, and the music should be condensed into musical forms which shall be especially invented to be suitable, the same as has been done in the case of different

European countries. . . . When these new forms, together with the new musical instruments or orchestral colors derived from them, are woven together into cohesive works which contain a genuine message, this message will represent the fulfillment of Cuban music. . . . When this is done, Cuban music will take its place with the music of the older peoples."

Roldan has a similar Credo—with its striking lesson for the American Negro musician. He says, "My aim is, first of all to attain a production thoroughly American in its substance, entirely apart from the European art; an art that we can call ours, continental, worthy of being universally accepted not on account of its exotic qualities (our music up to now has been accepted in Europe mainly upon the basis of its outlandish flavor that brought something interesting, something queerly new, being received with the accommodating smile with which grown people face a child's mischief, without giving to it any real importance); to produce a music capable of being accepted for its real significance, its intrinsic worth, for its meaning as a contribution of the New World to the universal art."

With such sound principles and high motives, Negro music can confidently and creatively face the future, and achieve rather than betray its birthright.

POSTSCRIPT

THANKS to Leopold Stokowski and William Dawson, the answer to the main challenge of this article has been flung into the arena: the first "Negro Folk Symphony" by a Negro composer has been triumphantly performed in Philadelphia and New York by the Philadelphia Symphony Orchestra. It is not the first symphony of Negro authorship, or the first accredited performance, Howard Hanson and the Rochester Civic Orchestra have played parts of William Still's "Afro-American Symphony"; and Frederick Stock and the Chicago Symphony have played "Florence Bond Price's Symphony" and her Concerto in D Minor for piano and orchestra, all creditable accomplishments. It is the form and character of the Dawson symphony that makes it so significant and promising. It is classic in form but Negro in substance, it shows mastery or near-mastery of the terrific resources of the modern orchestra, it builds on to the classic tradition with enough "modernism" to save it from being purely academic, and with enough originality to save it from the blight of imitation, and more than all else it is unimpeachably Negro.

Negro thematic substance does not alone suffice to make a Negro Symphony. The folk character must enter into the melodic pattern, the instrumentation, the rhythmic line, and if possible the harmonic development. In every one of these respects Mr. Dawson has tried to make his music racial, without at the same time losing touch with the grand speech of the master tradition in music. When one considers how near he has come to success on all these points, it is marvelous as a first symphony. May there be more; not too many; indeed a revised first is in order,—for characteristic as the third movement is in thematic material, it is not particularly distinctive in form. The second movement, in spite of redundance and occasional grandiloquence, is a masterful expression. One can pardon its redundance on racial grounds: the race is artistically rhapsodic. Its greatest grandiloquence is movingly successful, where a duel of pagan melody and rhythm toss wave-high against a Christian spiritual like the meeting of the Gulf Stream and the North Atlantic. It is moments like this that I had in mind in writing that the truly Negro music must reflect the folk spirit and eventually epitomize the race experience. To have done this without too much programistic literalness is an achievement and points as significant a path to the Negro musician as was pointed by Dvorak years ago. In fact it is the same path, only much further down the road to native and indigenous musical expression. Deep appreciation is due Mr. Stokowski for his discerning vision and masterful interpretation, but great praise is due Mr. Dawson for pioneering achievement in the right direction. His future and that of Negro music is brighter because of it.

NEGRO MUSIC GOES TO PAR

THE music season just closing has been one grand crescendo for Negro music, with almost too many events and too wide an up-swing to be adequately chronicled in a single article. In addition, three noteworthy books of serious musical criticism on jazz* have been issued and several notable documentations of Negro folk music made. But the predicament is a pleasant one, since it does vindicate our title as a fair and honest assessment of the musical situation. This year Negro music has really gone to par.

The main reason lies perhaps in this central fact, attested by a number of serious documentary concerts of Negro folk music: that instead of being sentimentalized extravagantly, Negro music is being intellectualized seriously, soberly, and in some cases controversially. Just as the swing era has marked something of a reaction from the dilution and commercialization of the Tin Pan Alley period, so now the faddist interest in Negro music is deepening into technical analysis and criticism. The public taste may still be undiscriminating and fickle, but inner circles, both amateur and professional, are swiftly becoming critical and technically expert. It is, incidentally, high time for the Negro audience to become itself more seriously critical and expertly informed about its own music, which it has tended to take too much for granted all along. And it is more than high time, too, for some of our Negro musicians to have their say.

*"American Jazz Music," by Wilder Hobson—W. W. Norton Co., New York—$2.50.
"Jazz: Hot and Hybrid," by Winthrop Sargeant—Arrow Editions, New York $5.00.
"The Kingdom Of Swing," by Benny Goodman and I. Kolodin—Stackpole Sons, New York—$2.00.

Personally, I am presenting no fanatical racialism on a subject that not only knows no color line, but has proved so convincingly that there is everything to be gained in vital collaboration between all who are seriously interested in the idioms and cause of Negro music. In fact, the testimony to Negro music which I shall review is perhaps all the stronger because it comes from racially outside, but spiritually inside, sources. Aside from the musical fraternalism involved, these enthusiastic white exponents and partisans of Negro music are symbols of the finest and most progressive trends in our present-day culture. They may even be harbingers of a finer future.

WINTHROP Sargeant's *Jazz: Hot And Hybrid* is the best and most scholarly analysis of jazz and Negro folk music to date; all the more welcome because it is objective in attitude and technical in approach. The Negro source influences are freely admitted and correctly traced, the important basic denominators of idioms common to the Negro's religious and secular folk music are clearly seen, the periods of development are competently sketched with the possible exception of the post-Civil War period, where there is little documentation anyway; and most important of all, the musical idioms of modern jazz are carefully analyzed. The nonsense of expecting pure racial idioms is fortunately dispensed with in the frank realization that Negro music is inevitably composite, and should have borrowed, as well as indigenous, elements. The latter are carefully analyzed, with a general conclusion that jazz rhythm is basically Negro, so much so as to be in all prob-

Opportunity 17 (July 1939): 196-200.

ability derivative from Africa; that polyrhythm and group improvisation are its characteristic techniques, that the scalar structure of jazz, on the other hand, is composite and only specifically racial in regard to the tetratonic "blues scale," and that the harmonic structure of American Negro jazz is the least racial of all the elements, although handled with distinctive color and freedom by the best jazz exponents.

Obviously this is a well-tempered analysis, highly illuminating and far from dogmatic since it gives ample musical annotations. I am particularly in agreement with the chapter on the Geography of Jazz Rhythm because it admits characteristic differences between European syncopation and polyrhythm and the dominant African and Afro-American varieties—a sensible solution of a vexatious controversial problem. We are also given profitable hints of differences between African and American Negro rhythm patterns—the one largely in triple measure and the other almost exclusively quadruple—hints which must be followed further in later intensive comparative studies. I suspect that they will definitely confirm my own view of the tango-habanera rhythm as the musical bridge between the Negro's African and American musical expression and perhaps, too, as not only closer to the African idioms but as the missing clue to the persistent three over four polyrhythm back of the purest strains of Negro American folk songs. The absence of these rhythms in the Spirituals I have elsewhere already accounted for as due to the influence of the standard evangelical hymn measures, from which also the alien harmonic influences undoubtedly come.

Although I readily agree that "Jazz does not attempt to sound the profounder depths of human emotion, but gives a meaningful account of some of the shallows," and would equally discount much of the faddist delusions and pretensions of the first decades of symphonic or classical jazz, I do not share Mr. Sargeant's skepticism over the potential contributions of jazz and Negro folk music to music in the larger forms. Jazz does not need to remain, I contend, even "at its most complex" still "a very simple matter of incessantly repeated formulas," or even, as is later hinted "most successful in the looser forms of ballet and opera, where music plays a subsidiary atmospheric role." Mr. Sargeant recants a little when later he says: "The larger forms of jazz, if they are ever evolved, will be more likely to grow out of the jazz idiom itself." Negro folk music, properly maturing, has the capacity to produce new musical forms as well as new musical idioms; that is indeed the task of the trained musician who has the sense and devotion to study seriously the folk music at its purest and deepest sources. To which Mr. Sargeant almost agrees by concluding: "It is meanwhile important to distinguish between jazz in its sophisticated metropolitan form and jazz as a deep-rooted Afro-American social phenomenon. On the one hand," he continues, "we have the chatter and sales-talk of individual jazz artists and their press agents and hysterical admirers; on the other we have a much bigger and profounder thing—a new musical language growing from the cane-brakes and cotton fields of rural America, affecting every stratum of American society, a language certainly capable of expressing deeper matters than those which occupy the world of sophisticated entertainment."

WILDER Hobson's *American Jazz Music* is more of a jazz fan's book, and to that extent less of an objective analysis or survey. However, unlike many of the jazz hobbyists, he is impartial and roots for no particular school. New Orleans, early and late, Chicago, and the various New York varieties of jazz, are given due credit and fair historical treatment, and an important point is made that in each period there was a great divide between the true jazz artists and the commercial exploiters, and that in many cases the real artists started the vogue and then yielded the stage and the dividends to the "organizers" and "stuntists." So that back of many a headline name and reputation stands, as documented in a book like this, some relatively unknown arranger, some hapless troubadour of true inventive genius known to the real cognoscenti of jazz but scarcely to the layman, least of all to the "jitterbugs."

And well documented, too, is the little-realized fact of the ceaseless change of style characterizing some of the greatest of the jazz artists, a sign of their restless creativeness and their skillful versatility. It is the commercial band that has the set style and the patented tricks; the real jazz artists preserve the simplicity and the spontaneity of the folk music which is their basic source and inspiration. Too numerous for exhaustive mention, we are lead through the cavalcade of genuine jazz masters: Scott Joplin, W. C. Handy, Nick La Rocca, King Oliver, Bix Beiderbecke, Jack Teagarden, "Pee Wee" Russell, Bud Freeman, Sidney Bechet, Johnny Dodds, Louis Armstrong, Clarence Williams, Frank Teschmaker, Coleman Hawkins, down to the names known to today's fans:

Fletcher Henderson, Duke Ellington, Don Redman, Benny Carter, Jimmy Lunceford, Earl Hines, Count Basie, the late Chick Webb and many another. Perhaps the best of all of Mr. Hobson's contributions is his annotated list of thirty records spanning the whole range of the jazz age, each a particularly representative sample of a given period or jazz style. As a list of "jazz classics," this is one of the most carefully chosen and broadly representative of the whole lot—in itself a great service to the serious study of jazz and its deep underground connections with various folk music styles. Even a cursory review of it will convince anyone of the phenomenal and almost infinite variety of this music, a good part of which derives not merely from the inventive genius of the jazz composers but from the varied idiom of the folk styles themselves.

Important sociologically is the description of the typical jazz player's life and lot. Behind the glamor of publicity, there is much hardship and injustice: witness the frank statement, "The inequality of opportunity for the Negro is nowhere more clearly marked than in this field where he is often so specially talented," referring of course to the hardships, exploitation and discrimination rampant in the jazz entertainment world. "Commercial opportunities for the Negro musicians are, of course, relatively scarce, and the pay runs consistently below white levels and very often below scale. In this connection it may be noted that despite the large number of brilliant Negro instrumentalists, there are none regularly engaged as radio 'house men' or in the motion picture studio orchestras."

THESE are frank statements of fact; a challenge to all those who truly love this music, for public opinion in the last analysis controls and in too many cases, the public simply does not know the real facts. Much has yet to be done to raise the status of the jazz musician: the dazzling success of an outstanding few must not blind us to the real conditions. As a matter of fact, there is a direct connection between any economic improvement in this field and the artistic quality of the product. In this respect certainly the stock of Negro music is still below par.

It is for this reason that the shifting patronage from the dance hall, vaudeville stage and casual motion picture spot to the concert stage, the non-commercial recording societies, and occasionally government patronage as in the Library of Congress and the Department of the Interior's music recording projects, represents something of great value and promise to the future of Negro folk music and the musicians whose art derives directly from it. They are thereby offered their first real opportunity to play and be heard as "artists." Having survived by sheer luck in spite of commercial exploitation, they should now seize the hand of good management for the next step upwards.

SUCH, then, is the particular significance of the Carnegie Hall concert in December which, under John Hammond's direction, assembled an historical sequence of authentic folk music played by relatively genuine, unspoiled folk musicians. There were slightly contaminating elements of "jitterbug exhibitionism" about this concert, and also of that hieratic snobbery too frequent with faddist patrons of rising causes, but in spite of all that, the concert was a high-water mark in the annals of Negro music. Inspired by it, both the Hot Society Records Club and the Musi-Kraft Company made valuable recordings of most of the artists on the program; followed by the noteworthy album of Lead Belly folk ballads edited by Alan Lomax.

Mr. Sargeant pointed out in his book that only the phonograph could do justice to this music anyway: it represents both the way out for the folk musician to a more serious and discriminating audience, and the only proper medium for the careful perpetuation and comparative study of the rich provincial root sources of the Negro's music. Combined with the increasing trend of field recording by scientific research projects, and with the government's patronage of music record surveys, we may confidently predict that the folk music of the Negro has at last found a safe scientific haven after generations of perilous danger on unruly tides of popular whim and fad.

In my judgment an even more significant step was the Labor Stage concert arranged by Carleton Moss, John Velasco and Simon Rady, at which Negro music was dramatically presented in historical sequence from the far African past to the present, with a very exciting and convincing demonstration of its essential rhythmic unity. Of course, there have been many such "jungle to Harlem" presentations; the outstanding merit of this was its authentic, scholarly background, its carefully restrained artistry, and its welcome freedom from mawkish, sentimental racialism. Folk music needs a dramatic background for its truest appreciation; dance, costume, period setting are essential to its proper understanding. Eventually such a sequence as this must be carefully worked out, film-recorded and preserved in its integral character for posterity.

Notable, too, was the concert of the Mwalimu Festival Chorus, under the direction of Madame Manet Harrison Fowler, now one of the outstanding Negro choral groups in technical proficiency. In their African song cycle they presented a pioneer excursion into the important field of African folk music revived for the concert stage.

Benny Goodman's "Twenty Years of Jazz" concert has not been mentioned in calendar sequence, because, to supplement it, he has a book about his own thirty-odd colorful years as a musician, called *The Kingdom of Swing.* "Pied Piper of Swing" that he is by his own confession, Goodman is nevertheless one of the great constructive forces in the jazz world. With an authentic boyhood apprenticeship in the field of jazz, a consuming love for it, high respect for the often unrecognized master artists in the field, and unprejudiced courage, he has really done as much and more for the artistic advance of this type of music as he has for the "jitterbug" craze. The favorable balance leaves us seriously his debtor.

Though casual and largely biographic, there is much for the student of Negro folk music in this volume; especially the documenting of the constant interchange between Negro and white jazz musicians long before the days of "mixed bands" and open public collaboration. As to the now notorious Carnegie Hall concert, half spoiled by an over-emotional audience, Goodman's intentions were sound and constructive; and his critical praise of Duke Ellington, Count Basie, Johnny Hodges, Harry Carney, "Cootie" Williams, Lester Young, Walter Page—joined with his professional opinion of Teddy Wilson and Lionel Hampton—are authoritative enough for anyone who knows his jazz, or as the modernists will have it, his "swing."

BUT lest, with all this happy behind-scenes friendship and this publicity inspired glamor of the "dukes," "counts" and "earls" of the "swing kingdom," we forget the serious reforms yet needed, I must end this section with a warning that popular music is often the artistic enemy of folk music; and that while good folk music can have popularity, (and should have increasingly), it yet has many bad and shabby imitations to fight and to contend with. The dance hall and the vaudeville stage are still friendly

enemies—all the more dangerous because superficially friendly. An instance in point, it seems to me, was the public preference for the out-and-out caricaturish "Hot Mikado" to the wistfully subtle "Swing Mikado" of Harry Minturn and the Chicago Federal Theatre project. Allowing, as any good critic should, for the semi-amateur basis of the project unit, there was to the real music lover much more charm and artistry in the latter, especially in the interesting contrasts of the regular and the swing choruses and the semi-exotic character of the dances. Too often the public fits the Negro artist into a conventional groove and prefers him there in much the same way as Bourbon Southern prejudice likes the Negro "in his proper place." It is not to the credit of an artist as great as "Bojangles" Robinson is or was, that he so inevitably finds and stays in that sort of groove, and apparently likes it. The majority of the New York critics wanted their Mikado straight or their Mikado piping "hot," but I venture the critical opinion that artistically they went wrong, and that if the music critics had had their say, as they should have had, the verdict would have been reversed.

And now to a brief but important epilogue. In spite of the vitality and importance of folk music, the climax of any musical development is in the art forms and on the formal art level. That is why the real high-water marks of the Negro musical season are the increasing maturity and vogue of William Grant Still and of Marian Anderson. The former, about whom Miss Verna Arvey has done a finely-etched critical biography in the Fischer Bros. Contemporary American Composers series,* is more and more taking his place as one of the most original and outstanding of the younger American composers. As his style matures the folk idiom crops out more and more, tempering his earlier, too intellectualized, ultra-modernistic style. "Rising Tide," the prize World's Fair Theme Song, hardly heard to advantage in the Perisphere against the raucous though celebrated commentator's voice, is really a composition of representative merit and real American flavor. No doubt it will be recorded in a good full version so that music lovers can judge and enjoy it; as far as I can judge, it is in the vein of one of his most inspired and racially typical compositions: the *Lenox Avenue Suite.*

As to Miss Anderson, almost everyone, layman and professional alike, has called up his superlatives, and while I heartily agree, I have no desire to compete. Rather, then, let me re-

* *Studies of Contemporary American Composers: Wm. Grant Still,* by Verna Arvey. J. Fischer & Bros, New York, 1939—25 Cents.

peat, with the vindicating emphasis of time, what I have already said, years back, about her art. It derives in the first instance from the purest strain of Negro folk music; that is to say, she learned early from the Spirituals and the atmosphere of that spiritual view of life, how to feel with deep simplicity and reverence, how to project with completely impersonal and absorbed power. As I see it, she has just carried this great artistic lesson to the world of sophisticated art-forms and the whole tradition of the art song from the early Italian to Sibelius, and the result is something spiritually as well as technically phenomenal.

It is, without detracting credit from her painstaking artistry and technical skill, the open secret of her genius, which makes it appropriate to associate her art as definitely with the traditions of the music of her people as with the great cosmopolitan tradition of the world music which she has also so obviously mastered. That is one reason why, with no jot of change, her art can really move an audience of over seventy thousand, many or most belonging to the musically unsophisticated, as effectively as the most select audience of seasoned and expertly critical music lovers. The memorable Easter Sunday concert of the Lincoln Memorial was, in more than a sociological sense, a triumph of Negro music.

SPIRITUALS

Ladies and gentlemen, nothing quite so subtly or characteristically expresses a people's group character than their folk music, and so tonight we turn to that, to discover if we can sense, the essence of what is Negro, or if we cannot do that, at least to sample the heart of the Negro's racial experience. It is fitting, too, from the musical point of view, that we turn to the folk to render them their just due as the prime sources of our musical and spiritual heritage. I shall speak of the spirituals, and my esteemed friends and colleagues Sterling Brown and Alan Lomax will speak of the even wider problems of the secular folk music, showing you how deep and varied this folk experience has been and how many-sided is the folk character.

But I think we would all agree that the spirituals symbolize, as nothing else can do, our racial past. They are as well the taproot of our folk music. Certainly in terms of the historic occasion which this festival thoughtfully and reverently commemorates, the slave songs have a particular place and significance. It is that dark but rich and worthy side of the people's past which gives at one and the same time the most illuminating background of our present race accomplishment, the true perspective of our future hopes and ambition, and most important of all for us at this moment, the sampling of the mother soil of our creative genius.

For the musical talent that has grown up and flowered so distinctively to the extent that it is original has its basic rootage there. That soil of folk experience it is, which gives the special taste and tang, form and flavor to what we are proud to claim as typically Negro in art and poetry and music. That, too, we must remember, lends its substance by a spiritual chemistry which men cannot curb or control into that other precious and representative cultural product which we are also proud to call American.

The spirituals are [the] taproot of our folk music—stemming generations down from the core of the group experience, in the body and soul suffering slavery and expressing for the race, the nation, for the world, the spiritual fruitage of that hard experience. But they are not merely slave songs or even Negro folk songs. The very elements that make them spiritually expressive of the Negro make them at the same time deeply representative of the soil that produced them. They constitute a great, and now increasingly appreciated, body of regional American folk song and music. As unique spiritual products of American life they've become nationally, as well as racially, characteristic. They also promise to be one of the profitable wellsprings of the native idiom in serious American music. In that sense they belong to a common heritage and, properly appreciated and used, can be, should be, will be part of the cultural tie that binds.

While this is true to a degree of all of our folk music, it is eminently true of the spirituals. For just before and immediately after the Civil War, they were the first Negro folk songs to be discovered and collected. Again, in 1871, through the Fisk Jubilee Singers, they were the first to gain serious musical attention—nationally and internationally. Still again, in 1894, through Dvorak and others, they were the first native folk idioms proposed as the base for a nationally representative American music. We still hear, those of us who were present last night, the beautiful echoes of the Dvorak quartet on American themes, which more convincingly even

This transcription is made from a recording, AFS 6092–6095, available in the Archive of Folk Song at the Library of Congress, Washington, D.C.

than the *New World Symphony* brought them that musical tribute and vindication.* Finally, the spirituals in these glorious times of Roland Hayes, Paul Robeson, Marian Anderson, and Dorothy Maynor, and others have brought our interpretive artists a welcome opportunity, after mastery of the great universal language, to pay their racial homage to the native source of their artistic skill and spiritual strength, and to express their artistic indebtedness to the singing generations behind them and to the peasant geniuses who were, in James Weldon Johnson's apt phrase, "the black and unknown bards" of long ago.

To these humble folk roots we now turn as directly as we can through recordings of contemporary survivals from the Folk Song Archives of the Library of Congress and with the talented assistance of a group of folk singers and musicians close to these roots. They, with their vital and very racial art, give us a comforting assurance that these folk sources are still alive in our generation even though we shall never again hear the spirituals in their original fervor and intensity. Since slavery was their historic setting, we can gladly dispense with that. Even the primitive religion which was their other root is lapsing fast, and both the emotional and musical patterns of so deep a group experience have survived, much to our musical and spiritual gain. Indeed, the contemporary composition of spirituals is still in occasional occurrence as the singers will illustrate in due course, by a rendition of one of their own making. Such, however, is sharply to be distinguished from that modern concoction of artificial, so-called spirituals, with superficial imitations of the folk idioms, that to the trained student of folk music, are misrepresentative caricatures of the deeply sincere and noble tradition. For the spirituals are, even when lively in rhythm and folky in imagination, always religiously serious in mood and conception. That does not even exclude humor of a sort—but the true spiritual is always the voice of a naive, unshaken faith for which the things of the spirit are as real as the things of the flesh.

This naive and spirit-saving acceptance of Christianity is the hallmark of the true spiritual. Other factors have entered in, otherwise we should have merely dialect versions of evangelical Protestant hymns. First and foremost, there is the primary ingredient of a strong peasant soul with its naive faith—a literal believing and soul-saving faith which preserved the emotional sanity of the Negro and kept his spirit somewhat above the fate of his body. Then there was, even out of a mass illiteracy, some great intuitive understanding of his own experience, in terms of a grand and inspiring analogy with the Bible narratives. From which came all those inspiring parallels that kept hope alive, hope and faith alive in even the humblest Negro souls, and formed the basis of the dramatic part of the spirituals. The backbone of their narrative tradition is just such Bible parallels and they were selected on the basis of their closeness to the slaves' experience—own spiritual experience.

There was, too, borne out of the emotional fire of the group, a folk imagination that transposed the already glowing King James texts into real folk poetry. These have given us—and I wish I had more time to illustrate the poetic side of the spirituals—these have given us gems like "I lay in the grave and stretch out my arms, I lay this body down, I go to the judgment in the evening of the day when I lay this body down—when I lay this body down and my soul and your soul meet the day I lay this body down." Or, again, things like that spiritual which Roland Hayes sings so beautifully—"My Lord is so high, you can't get over him. My Lord is so low you can't get under him—you must come in and through the Lamb."

And finally there is the music itself—that great literacy of musical speech towering up over the dialect and the broken, sometimes feeble words to make an instinctive welding of all this into an amalgam of music that shades every meaning and evokes a mood almost independently of the words. This, it seems to me, is that blend of factors which makes the Negro spiritual and makes it so unique.

Now many of them, the purest of them, the oldest of them, it seems to me, must have been pure prayer songs, definitely coming out of the context of a worshiping band with a leader. And, it must have been, of course, somebody as a leader improvising a lead line and a lead idea, but that thing spreading from some kind of contagion that became instinctive as the tradition grew into a song in which finally the lead line and the burden of the refrain merged

*The Budapest Quartet performed the String Quartet in F Major, Op. 96, by Dvorak, as part of the four-day musical program [Editor's note].

with the whole body to make it a great choral improvisation. And it's these things that, though not dated, we can judge by their purity to this tradition, which one might call the core spirituals. And these things, although they have been treated in many ways and have a first- and second- and third-generation attitude toward them, certainly in their origin are among the purest and best examples of religious feeling and emotion, and they communicate that feeling and emotion not just for the participants, but even those who do not share the naive peasant literal beliefs.

Now, these songs have been treated in many ways, but they essentially, of course, call for choral rendition. And their style also calls for, not a set form, but an improvisation of feeling and of singing idiom according as the spirit moves. And they are best represented when they are sung that way, although it's difficult in these days, of course, to even closely imitate the sincere simple conditions out of which these beautiful folk songs sprang. When I hear them as art songs—and they are great as that—I always sort of feel that like that contrast of the Bach cantata, when toward the end after all his great exercise of composition, contrapuntal skill— the great master takes off his hat to what he recognizes as a still greater musical thing and pays that tribute in the simple playing of German choral to the faith of the people and to the folk song from which the whole thing grew.

Now, there was a double meaning in a great deal of spirituals, even to the illiterate Negro, because of this way in which they symbolized their own experience. And we find it even in as old a spiritual as the one that the singers are going to start with, where we think, those of us who look back on it, we see not just merely the feeling of a group of slaves stealing out to worship—for even at that early time worship was something of a . . . [inaudible] . . . from their toil, but that they symbolized in this song also their feeling that there was something ahead of them, most of them thought it was after the grave and after crossing Jordan, but others of them probably thought also that it was over the river toward Canada, toward the North Star, toward the freedom that sometimes so precariously they set out for. The group will sing "Steal Away."

There's a bolder note in some of this music, a note probably that crept in as their enthusiasm rose and as they distanced, in the fervor of their religious excitement, the slave world that they had left behind. And we want to give you shortly, next, one of the instances of this, that expresses the jubilance of the slave in the midst of his religious ecstasy. A good deal of this has a different tone from the prayer song. It verges on the spiritual shout, and it probably, in its original context, had impromptu extemporizations of the sort that we can find half-duplicated probably in some of the cults today.

It has always interested me greatly the frequency of a reference to Jordan. And while I know the importance of that in the Christian tradition and the way in which it would naturally fasten itself on the mind of slave groups, especially that were used to the ritual of baptism, I personally think that there is back of this some of that primitive carry-over of water symbolism of West African religions. But whatever it is, it's something very, very deep that you can immediately feel whenever the mention of Jordan comes in the spirituals or whenever this question of the water ritual comes up. It was symbolic to them, of course, of many things, but particularly of that spiritual purification that they thought was their only salvation within reach, and frequently, again and again, you have it in that reference to Jordan that chose the body but not the soul. The group will sing "Wade in the Water."

Another side of this tradition probably crystallized around the dramatic sermon, which was the illiterate or semiliterate preacher's version—dramatic version of—or expansion of his testament text. But very soon this narrative balladry, which probably was running along concurrently in the secular songs, spread into the field of the spirituals, and we have a whole group of these so-called narrative spirituals retelling dramatically and effectively the Bible stories, the picturesque ones; there are any number of them, but we all, of course, recall "The Walls of Jericho," and "Ezekial in Heaven," and that very dramatic, and I think for the Negro, symbolic one of "David and Goliath," and one that we are later to hear about Moses. But there is one which the singers are to sing that represents another most favorite theme and story of the Negro peasant imagination—the story of Noah where, of course, again, Noah's experience symbolized to them the promise and the fulfillment after hard trials. This particular spiritual is given in a version that originates with the Golden Gate Quartet. It's "Noah."

I surely don't blame the audience, but as the timekeeper I'm afraid we must hurry on. In fact, we are having to telescope the next two numbers, both of which symbolize the mounting confidence and optimism of the Negro as it is nourished on this spiritual food. You find this triumphant note creeping in, in spite of all the suffering and sorrow. It's most inspiring and I'm sure you'll be very glad to listen to a short, joint rendering of the next two spirituals, "I'm So Glad Trouble Don't Last Always" and "We're Climbing Jacob's Ladder."

It's a commonplace that this accommodation of circumstances and this Christian tradition set the slave's and the Negro's eye on the other world, and gave him perhaps an other-worldly, and, in these days, what we call an escapist philosophy. But we must remember that the slave really, always had his eye on freedom of the body, as well as the soul. There was that frequent phenomenon of the slave rebellion, and of the still more frequent phenomenon of the fugitive slave, and I think this escapist tradition of which we complain is perhaps more typical of the Reconstruction than really of the slave period itself. Because during the Reconstruction we had this rather cruel blocking of the hopes of full freedom and the great disappointment that came from that.

Now, of course, the slave didn't get his democracy from the Bill of Rights. He got it from his reading of the moral justice of the Hebrew prophets and his concept of the wrath of God. And, particularly, his mind seized on the experience of the Jews in Egypt and of the figure of Moses, the savior of the people, leading them out from bondage, and, therefore, there is not only no more musically beautiful spiritual, but no more symbolic spiritual than "Go Down Moses."

As freedom came nearer historically, the slave sensed it probably through that great institution of theirs—the grapevine—and their hope for freedom became more pronounced and their songs for freedom really became more triumphant or at least anticipating triumph and release, and the group is now going to sing together two of those, the famous "Freedom, freedom over me, before I be slave I be buried in my grave and go home to my Master, be free" and "Pharoah's Army Got Drowned."

The power of the spiritual looms more and more as they stand the test of time. They outlived the particular generation and the peculiar conditions that produced them; they have survived, in turn, the contempt of the slaveowners, the cold conventionalizations of formal religion, the artistic repressions of puritanism, the cheap corruption of sentimental balladry, the neglect and disdain of second-generation respectability, and now, the tawdry exploitation of Tin Pan Alley and our musical marketplaces. They've escaped the lapsing conditions and fragile vehicle of folk art, and come firmly under the protection of the skillful music folklorists a little late, but not too late to capture some of their fading original beauty. Only classics survive such things.

And now, finally, the quartet will give us one of their own original contemporary spirituals on the theme, a rather characteristic one, that death—that every one has to die—that assertion of a democracy of death which must have meant so much to the Negro peasants in their own thin satisfactions in life. The quartet will close with "Travelin' Shoes."

AFRICAN ART

Locke was a broker and connoisseur of African art. He worked with influential collectors and museums, purchased collections from Europe, and helped found the Harlem Museum of African Art in 1927. He popularized African art with a series of pictorial essays which filled the vacuum in interpretation of this field. Locke believed African art represented a cultural heritage of which black Americans could be proud. Behind this view lay his deep, personal appreciation of African art for its own beauty, something to be admired on its own merits.[1]

Locke introduces African art to a black American audience in "A Note on African Art" (1924), which appeared in a special "African Art Issue" of *Opportunity*. By terming African art "classic," Locke suggests that African art is comparable to 5th-century B.C. Greek art in that both have evolved over hundreds of years to achieve a perfection of form. Since only one percent of the tens of millions of African wood objects have survived, contemporary art historians have not attempted the periodization begun by Paul Guillaume, the Paris art dealer. Similarly, Locke's use of "classic" to describe African art is considered archaic today, although such analogies were common in European literature on the subject in the 1920s.[2]

"Art Lessons from the Congo" (1927) continues to argue that African sculpture exhibits the balance, grace, and sense of proportion which makes it "classic." This essay, and the next, "A Collection of Congo Art" (1927), announce the exhibition of the Blondiau-Theatre Arts Collection, which Locke had suggested to white supporters to purchase in 1926.[3]

In addition to his aesthetic appreciation for African art, Locke also recognized its value as anthropological evidence of the African past. In "A Collection of Congo Art," Locke was one of the first to analyze the function of African masks, cups, and swords in African religious and ceremonial practices.

The last essay, "African Art: Classic Style" (1935), heralds the Museum of Modern Art's exhibition of African art as recognition that African art is "a mature and classic expression." This exhibition was distinguished by its broad and representative selection of the highest quality pieces from several African traditions. Through the gracious permission of the museum, Locke was able to photograph works from the exhibit for this article in the *American Magazine of Art* and further document his claim that African art deserves its own special place in art history.

A NOTE ON AFRICAN ART

THE significance of African art is incontestable; at this stage it needs no *apologia*. Indeed no genuine art ever does, except when it has become incumbered with false interpretations. Having passed, however, through a period of neglect and disesteem during which it was regarded as crude, bizarre, and primitive, African art is now in danger of another sort of misconstruction, that of being taken up as an exotic fad and a fashionable amateurish interest. Its chief need is to be allowed to speak for itself, to be studied and interpreted rather than to be praised or exploited. It is high time that it was understood, and not taken as a matter of oddness and curiosity, or of quaint primitiveness and fantastic charm.

This so-called "primitive" Negro art in the judgment of those who know it best is really a classic expression of its kind, entitled to be considered on a par with all other classic expressions of plastic art. It must be remembered that African art has two aspects which, for the present at least, must be kept rigidly apart. It has an aesthetic meaning and a cultural significance. What it is as a thing of beauty ranges it with the absolute standards of art and makes it a pure art form capable of universal appreciation and comparison; what it is as an expression of African life and thought makes it an equally precious cultural document, perhaps the ultimate key for the interpretation of the African mind. But no confusing of these values as is so prevalent in current discussions will contribute to a finally accurate or correct understanding of either of these. As Guillaume Apollinaire aptly says in *Apropos de l'Arts des Noirs* (*Paris* 1917), "In the present condition of anthropology one cannot without unwarranted temerity advance definite and final assertions, either from the point of view of archeology or that of aesthetics, concerning these African images that have aroused enthusiastic appreciation from their admirers in spite of a lack of definite information as to their origin and use and as to their definite authorship."

It follows that this art must first be evaluated as a pure form of art and in terms of the marked influences upon modern art which it has already exerted, and then that it must be finally interpreted historically to explain its cultural meaning and derivation. What the cubists and postexpressionists have seen in it intuitively must be reinterpreted in scientific terms, for we realize now that the study of exotic art holds for us a serious and important message in aesthetics. Many problems, not only of the origin of art but of the function of art, wait for their final solution on the broad comparative study of the arts of diverse cultures. Comparative aesthetics is in its infancy, but the interpretation of exotic art is its scientific beginning. And we now realize at last that, scientifically speaking, European art can no more be self-explanatory than one organic species intensively known and studied could have evolved in the field of biology the doctrine of evolution.

The most influential exotic art of our era has been the African. The article of M. Paul Guillaume, its ardent pioneer and champion, is in itself sufficient witness and acknowledgment of this. But apart from its stimulating influence on the technique of many acknowledged modern masters, there is another service which it has yet to perform. It is one of the purposes and definite projects of the Barnes Foundation, which contains by far the most selected art-collection of Negro art in the world, to study this art organically, and to correlate it with the general body of human art. Thus African art will serve not merely the purpose of a strange new artistic ferment, but will also have its share in the construction of a new broadly comparative and scientific aesthetics.

Thus the African art object, a half a generation ago the most neglected of curios, has now become

Opportunity 2 (May 1924): 134–138.
Photos in this article courtesy of the Barnes Foundation, Merion, Pa. Photos by Moorland–Spingarn Research Center, Howard University, Washington, D.C.

the corner-stone of a new and more universal aesthetic that has all but revolutionized the theory of art and considerably modified its practice. The movement has a history. Our museums were full of inferior and relatively late native copies of this material before we began to realize its art significance. Dumb, dusty trophies of imperialism, they had been assembled from the colonially exploited corners of Africa, first as curios then as prizes of comparative ethnology. Then suddenly there came to a few sensitive artistic minds realization that here was an art object, intrinsically interesting and fine. The pioneer of this art interest was Paul Guillaume, and there radiated from him into the circles of post-impressionist art in Paris that serious interest which subsequently became an important movement and in the success of which the art of African peoples has taken on fresh significance. This interest was first technical, then substantative, and finally, theoretical. "What formerly appeared meaningless took on meaning in the latest experimental strivings of plastic art. One came to realize that hardly anywhere else had certain problems of form and a certain manner of their technical solution presented itself in greater clarity than in the art of the Negro. It then became apparent that prior judgments about the Negro and his arts characterized the critic more than the object of criticism. The new appreciation developed instantly a new passion, we began to collect Negro art as art, became passionately interested in corrective re-appraisal of it, and made out of the old material a newly evaluated thing."

There is a curious reason why this meeting of the primitive with the most sophisticated has been so stimulating and productive. The discovery of African art happened to come at a time when there was a marked sterility in certain forms of expression in European plastic art, due to generations of the inbreeding of idiom and style. Restless experimentation was dominant. African images had been previously dismissed as crude attempts at realistic representation. Then out of the desperate exhaustion of the exploiting of all the technical possibilities of color by the Impressionists, the problem of form and decorative design became emphasized in one of those natural reactions which occur so repeatedly in art. And suddenly with the substitution in European art of a new emphasis and technical interest, the African representation of form, previously regarded as ridiculously crude, suddenly appeared cunningly sophisticated. Strong stylistic associations had stood between us and its correct interpretation, and their breaking down had the effect of a great discovery, a fresh revelation. Negro art was instantly seen as a "notable instance of plastic representation." . . . "For western art the problem of representation of form had become a secondary and even mishandled problem, sacrificed to the effect of movement. The three-dimensional interpretation of space, the ground basis of all plastic art, was itself a lost art, and when, with

considerable pains, artists began to explore afresh the elements of form perception, fortunately at that time African plastic art was discovered and it was recognized that it had successfully cultivated and mastered the expression of pure plastic form."

It was by such a series of discoveries and revaluations that African art came into its present prominence and significance. Other articles in this issue trace more authoritatively than the present writer can the attested influence of Negro art upon the work of Matisse, Picasso, Modigliani, and Soutine among the French painters, upon Max Pechstein, Elaine Stern among German painters, upon Modigliani, Archipenko, Epstein, Lipschitz and Lembruch among sculptors. This much may be regarded, on the best authority, as incontestable. The less direct influence in music and poetry must be considered separately, for it rests upon a different line both of influence and of evidence. But in plastic art the influence is evident upon direct comparison of the work of these artists with the African sculptures, though in almost everyone of the above mentioned cases there is additionally available information as to a direct contact with Negro art and the acknowledgement of its inspiration.

The verdict of criticism was bound to follow the verdict of the creative artists. A whole literature of comment and interpretation of "exotic art" in general, and Negro art in particular has sprung up, especially in Germany. Most diverse interpretations, from both the ethnographic and the aesthetic points of view, have been given. On good authority much of this is considered premature and fantastic, but this much at least has definitely developed as a result,—that the problems raised by African art are now recognized as at the very core of art theory and art history. Ethnographically the most promising lines of interpretation are those laid down in Joyce and Torday's treatise on the Bushongo and by A. A. Goldenweiser in the chapter on Art in his book entitled "Early Civilization." Aesthetically, the most authentic interpretations are those of Paul Guillaume, who from his long familiarity with this art is selecting the classical examples and working out a tentative stylistic and period classification, and that of the accomplished critic, Roger E. Fry, from whose chapter on Negro Sculpture, (Vision and Design, 1920) the following is quoted: "We have the habit of thinking that the power to create expressive plastic form is one of the greatest of human achievements, and the names of great sculptors are handed down from generation to generation, so that it seems unfair to be forced to admit that certain nameless savages have possessed this power not only in a higher degree than we at this moment, but than we as a nation have ever possessed it. And yet that is where I find myself. I have to admit that some of these things are great sculpture,—greater, I think, than anything we produced even in the Middle Ages. Certainly they have the special qualities of sculpture in a higher degree. They have indeed complete plastic freedom, that is to say, these African artists really can see form in three dimensions. Now this is rare in sculpture. All archaic European sculpture, Greek and Romanesque, for instance—approaches plasticity from the point of view of bas-relief. The statue bears traces of having been conceived as the combination of back, front, and side bas-reliefs. And this continues to make itself felt almost until the final development of the tradition. Complete plastic freedom with us seems only to have come at the end of a long period, when the art has attained a high degree of representational skill and when it is generally already decadent from the point of view of imaginative significance. Now the strange thing about these African sculptures is that they bear, as far as I can see, no trace of this process. . . . So,—far from clinging to two dimensions, as we tend to do, he (the Negro artist) actually underlines, as it were, the three-dimensionalness of his forms. It is in some such way that he manages to give to his forms their disconcerting vitality, the suggestion that they make of being not mere echoes of actual figures, but of possessing an inner life of their own. . . . Besides the logical comprehension of plastic form which the Negro shows, he has also an exquisite taste in his handling of material."

Equally important with this newer aesthetic appreciation is the newer archeological revaluation. Negro art is no longer taken as the expression of a uniformly primitive and prematurely arrested stage of culture. It is now seen as having passed through many diverse phases, as having undergone several classical developments, and as illustrating several divergent types of art evolution. The theory of evolution has put art into a scientific strait-jacket, and African art has had to fit in with its rigid preconceptions. It is most encouraging therefore to see an emancipated type of scientific treatment appearing, with Torday and Joyce's historical interpretation of art in terms of its corresponding culture values, and in Goldenweiser's rejection of the evolutionary formula which would make all African art originate from crude representationalism, that is to say, naive and non-aesthetic realism. For Goldenweiser,* primitive art has in it both the decorative and the realistic motives, and often as not it is the abstract principles of design and aesthetic form which are the determinants of its stylistic technique and conventions. Of course this is only another way of saying that art is after all art, but such scientific vindication of the efficacy of pure art motives in primitive art is welcome, especially as it frees the interpretation of African art from the prevailing scientific formulae. Thus both the latest aesthetic and scientific interpretations agree on a new value and complexity in the art we are considering.

Perhaps the most important effect of interpretations like these is to break down the invidious distinction between art with a capital A for

*See Goldenweiser: Early Civilization, pp. 25, 172-173, 180-183.

Zouenouia—13th Century.

European forms of expression and "exotic" and "primitive" art for the art expressions of other peoples. Technically speaking an art is primitive in any phase before it has mastered its idiom of expression, and classic when it has arrived at maturity and before it has begun to decline. Similarly art is exotic with relation only to its relative incommensurability with other cultures, in influencing them at all vitally it ceases to be exotic. From this we can see what misnomers these terms really are when applied to all phases of African art. Eventually we will come to realize that art is universally organic, and then for the first time scientifically absolute principles of art appreciation will have been achieved.

Meanwhile as a product of African civilization, Negro art is a peculiarly precious thing, not only for the foregoing reasons, but for the additional reason that it is one of the few common elements between such highly divergent types of culture as the African and the European, and offers a rare medium for their fair comparison. Culture and civilization are regarded too synonymously: a high-grade civilization may have a low-grade culture, and a relatively feeble civilization may have disproportionately high culture elements. We should not judge art too rigidly by civilization, or vice versa. Certainly African peoples have had the serious disadvantage of an environment in which the results of civilization do not accumulatively survive, so that their non-material culture elements are in many instances very much more mature and advanced than the material civilization which surrounds them. It follows then that the evidence of such elements ought to be seriously taken as factors for fair and proper interpretation.

Indeed the comparative study of such culture elements as art, folk-lore and language will eventually supply the most reliable clues and tests for African values. And also, we may warrantably claim, for the tracing of historical contacts and influences, since the archeological accuracy of art is admitted. Comparative art and design have much to add therefore in clearing up the riddles of African periods and movements. Although there are at present no reliable conclusions or even hypotheses, one can judge of the possibilities of this method by a glance at studies like Flinders-Petrie's "Africa in Egypt" (Ancient Egypt, 1916) or G. A. Wainwright's "Ancient Survivals in Modern Africa,"—*Bulletin de la Societé de Geographie,* Cairo, 1919-20.) Stated more popularly, but with the intuition of the artist, we have the gist of such important art clues in the statement of Guillaume Apollinaire to the effect that African sculptures "attest through their characteristic style an incontestable relationship to Egyptian art, and contrary to current opinion, it seems rather more true that instead of being a derivative of Egyptian art, they, (*or rather we would prefer to say, their prototypes) have on the contrary exerted on the artists of Egypt an influence which amply justifies the interest with which we today regard them."

But for the present all this is merest conjecture, though we do know that in many cases the tradition of style of these African sculptures is much older than the actual age of the exemplars we possess. Paul Guillaume, who has been the first to attempt period classification of this art, has conjecturally traced an Early Sudan art as far back as the Vth or VIth century, and has placed what seems to be its classic periods of expression as between the XIIth and the XIVth centuries for Gabon and Ivory Coast art, the XIth and XIIth for one phase of Sudan art, with another high period of the same between the XIVth and the

Phrase inserted.

XVth centuries. There are yet many problems to be worked out in this line—more definite period classification, more exact ethnic classification, especially with reference to the grouping of the arts of related tribes, and perhaps most important of all, the determination of their various *genres.*

A new movement in one of the arts in most cases communicates itself to the others, and after the influence in plastic art, the flare for things African began shortly to express itself in poetry and music. * Roughly speaking, one may say that the French have been pioneers in the appreciation of the aesthetic values of African lan-

Modigliani—stone.

Note the striking influence of the conventionalization on the sculpture by Modigliani, one of the foremost of modern artists.

guages, their poetry, idiom and rhythm. Of course the bulk of the scientific and purely philological interpretation is to the credit of German and English scholarship. There were several decades of this, before scholars like Rene Basset and Maurice Delafosse began to point out in addition the subtlety of the expressive technique of these languages. Attracted finally by the appeal of Negro plastic art to the studies of these men, poets like Guillaume Apollinaire and Blaise Cendrars brought the creative mind to the artistic re-expression of African idiom in poetic symbols and verse forms. So that what is a recognized school of modern French poetry professes the inspiration of African sources,—Apollinaire, Reverdy, Salmon, Fargue and others. The bible of this school has been Cendrars' *"Anthologie Negre,"* now in its sixth edition.

The starting point of an aesthetic interest in Negro musical idiom seems to have been H. A. Junod's work,—*"Les Chants et les Contes des Barongas"* (1897). From the double source of African folk-song and the quite serious study of American Negro musical rhythms, many of the leading modernists of French music have derived much inspiration. Berard, Satie, Poulenc, Auric, Honegger, are all in diverse ways affected, but the most explicit influence is upon the work of Derius Milhaud, who is an avowed propagandist of the possibilities of Negro musical idiom. The importance of the absorption of this material by all of the major forms of art, some of them relatively independently of the others, is striking and ought really be considered as a quite unanimous verdict of the creative mind upon the values, actual and potential, in this yet unexhausted reservoir of art material.

Since African art has had such a vitalizing influence in modern European painting, sculpture, poetry and music, it becomes finally a natural and important question as to what artistic and cultural effect it can or will have upon the life of the American Negro. It does not necessarily follow that it should have any such influence. Today even in its own homeland it is a stagnant and decadent tradition, almost a lost art, certainly as far as technical mastery goes. The sensitive artistic minds among us have just begun to be attracted toward it, but with an intimate and ardent concern. Because of our Europeanized conventions, the key to the proper understanding and appreciation of it will in all probability first come from an appreciation of its influence upon contemporary French art, but we must believe that there still slumbers in the blood something which once stirred will react with peculiar emotional intensity toward it. If by nothing more mystical than the sense of being ethnically related, some of us will feel its influence at least as keenly as those who have already made it recognized and famous. Nothing is more galvanizing than the sense of a cultural past. This at least the intelligent presentation of African art will supply to us. Without other more direct influence even, a great cultural impetus would thus be given. But surely also in the struggle for a racial idiom of expression, there would come to some creative minds among us, from a closer knowledge of it, hints of a new technique, enlightening and interpretative revelations of the mysterious substrata of feeling under our characteristically intense emotionality, or at the very least, incentives toward fresher and bolder forms of artistic expression and a lessening of that timid imitativeness which at present hampers all but our very best artists.

ART LESSONS FROM THE CONGO

Except for the few who are familiar with the profound influence of African art on contemporary modernist masters, painters like Matisse, Cezanne, Picasso, sculptors like Lipchitz and Brancusi, art lessons from such a primitive source as this seem ludicrous. But further even than an already mature influence upon the practical technique of modern art, the African craftsmen through their work bring a rich message in fundamental art values and art theory; reenforcement, in fact, for some of our most needed revaluations of art in relation to life. Most of us today will concede the superiority and desirability of an art that is native, healthy, useful as well as ornamental and integral with life, as contrasted with an art that is artificial, borrowed, non-utilitarian, and the exclusive product and possession of cliques and coteries. We have discovered that to capitalize Art, we have robbed it of some of its basic values and devitalized its taproots in the crafts. So, an astonishing demonstration of vital art values from the unexpected source of the folk arts of Congo tribesmen, flowering up from the soil to the plane of beautiful fine art, is not only a thrilling find for the art explorer and museum collector, but a fine text for the art reformer and an inspiration for the new art. In skill of ornamentation and design, in respect for the propriety of materials, in achievement of effect with the utmost simplicity of technique and tools, in directness and power of appeal, this art of the Negroes is exceptional. Ruskin would have [been] delighted to add the force of these examples to the art sermons he drew from the Greek and Gothic; and twentieth-century civilization, though disintegrating it unfortunately in its homeland, can perpetuate it by taking advantage of its open contribution.

The examples of Negro craftsmanship here presented are from the Blondiau-Theatre Arts Collection of primitive Congo art, recently acquired from a Belgian private collector, which is to be exhibited in New York beginning February 7th at the galleries of The New Art Circle. This is a collection representative of Congo work in all the native crafts, especially strong in those of the most artistic of the Bushongo peoples, the Bakuba, Baluba tribes, and the Kasai, brought to America primarily as an educational art project. Beyond the aim of supplementing our none-too-ample museum resources of specimens of this important branch of human art expression, there is the hope of conveying its theoretical but practical art message—the importance of beauty in the ordinary. American art, especially with the current revival of interest in the decorative and craft arts, needs this message, and can profit from it. Then, too, there is the interesting fact that in importing African art to America we are bringing over the cultural baggage of the American Negro that was crowded out of the slave ship.

The finer sides of African life and culture have suffered unduly through having been too long the contraband of the slave trade and the taboo of the misapprehending missionaries. African art for the moment has a very special role to play in the rehabilitation of Africa in general esteem and opinion. More important still it has a very vital mission as a recovered and reinterpreted racial heritage, of stimulating and inspiring the expression of the artistic genius of the American Negro, particularly in the arts of his ancestors. It seems certain that,

This transcription was published in *Survey Graphic* 57 (February 1, 1927): 587–589. (None of the original photographs are reproduced here. See "A Collection of Congo Art," pp. 139–148, for examples.)

at a stage of his development that is noteworthy for the initiation of a cultural program, the Negro of today will accept and benefit from this powerful lesson from his own past. Just as it is also to be hoped that America at large will accept in a fine spirit of reciprocity this and any other cultural lesson from a land where some of the initial steps of human culture were taken, and where, in spite of present backwardness, some significant culture goods have been produced and advanced.

Bakuba Ointment Box.

A COLLECTION OF CONGO ART

INTERMITTENTLY since the De Zayas exhibition of 1916, African art has been called to our attention both as an art object and as an art influence—in ways more calculated, however, to impress us with its importance than its inner significance. For our approach, even in the presence of the primitive originals, has been for the most part secondary, since Negro art has come to our notice principally as an ingredient of contemporary European modernism, and thus has been seen and admired more in the mirror of its influence than valued and understood in the reality of its own intrinsic beauty. To possess African art permanently and not merely as a passing vogue, we shall have to go beyond such reflected values and their exotic appeal and study it in its own context, link it up vitally with its own cultural background, and learn to appreciate it as an organic body of art.

Towards this, the prime pre-requisite is the availability of the original material in collections sufficiently extensive to present a representative unit yet selective enough to make an exclusive appeal as art. This is a combination that is unfortunately rare—rarest of all in America—for there are few collections of African art that do not sacrifice either the scientific interest to the artistic or the artistic to the scientific. In the one case, cultural representativeness is lost in the attempt to cull out the objects of superior beauty and workmanship, with the result that we get a mere exotic hodge-podge of uncorrelated samples, widely separated in type, period and provenance. In the other, in the search for museum completeness, with no rigid principle of artistic selection, this art is allowed to lapse back to the dead level of the ethnographic curiosity, from the dry dust of which the modernists resurrected some of its buried beauty.

The Blondiau collection, now brought to America permanently under the auspices of *Theatre Arts*, and at present on exhibition at the galleries of the New Art Circle in New York, is notable for combining the artistic and the scientific approach to African art. It is a collection drawn from the extensive and varied region of the Belgian Congo, selected over a period of twenty-five years on a rather rigid standard of fine workmanship, yet sufficiently inclusive as to the various types and intensive as to regional representativeness to give a really organic impression of one of the great schools of primitive Negro art. Its acquisition is therefore a valu-

The Arts 11, no. 2 (February 1927): 60–70.
Photos in this article by Simco Custom Photo Lab, Los Angeles, Cal.

able supplementation of our sources for the study and appreciation of this art; for even with the Ward collection of the Smithsonian in Washington, the Barnes Foundation col-

Throne-Stool (Primitive Kasai).

lection at Merion, the University of Pennsylvania Museum collection, and those in New York at the Brooklyn Museum and the Museum of Natural History, our resources are very meagre in comparison with the great special collections of France, Germany, England and Belgium. And

of all these, Belgium, with its concentration on so rich a province as the Congo, and its palatial special government museum of the Congo at Tervueren, has almost uniquely these important combined qualities of scientific completeness and artistic excellence, which on a much smaller scale this distinctive private Belgian collection typically reflects.

The art of the Congo region, despite the conceded craftsmanship of the work of the Bushongo, has yet to come into its proper due of recognition and esteem. In contrast with the art of the coastal regions, which has been seen and appraised in terms of spectacularly beautiful specimens of single outstanding types, Congo art has usually been seen only in its poorer and more rustic examples. Consequently the current reputation of Benin, Ivory Coast, and Guinea Coast art is much higher.

Further, the obvious craft basis of Congo art has led us to judge most of it under what is for us the subordinate category of applied art. In this we fail to see how irrelevant such a distinction is for a culture where fine and decorative art have never been separated out, and where things can be superlatively beautiful and objects of utility at the same time. Indeed it is on this point that African art offers our art its greatest challenge and possible inspiration, as an art that never has been divorced from the vital context of everyday life. Its vindication of one of the soundest and most basic of æsthetic principles—beauty in use—and its distinction in a field where we usually encounter and tolerate the commonplace, entitle it to the most serious consideration and study apart from all its other values, and nowhere do we find more of this vital organic quality than in the arts and crafts of the Congo. Here we have the most intact sample of the old characteristic African culture, work in all possible art media and art forms—large and small scale carving in ivory, horn and wood, forged and decorated work in iron and other metals, metal inlay work, carved and appliqué masks, pottery, woven and decorated textiles, all existing side by side, each in a relatively high state of artistic development.

The additional fact that this level of development has been maintained over the span of three or four centuries at the least, with stability of types and patterns and without percepti-

Throne-Stool (Primitive Badjok).

Bapende Mask.

ble signs of decadence until the recent break-up of the indigenous culture under European influences, gives convincing evidence of a tradition of exceptional richness and vigor. Torday, the Belgian explorer, reports that among the artistic tribes not only has every design *motif* its proper name and association, but also every pattern variant, that there is such a diffusion of art appreciation that the average child is taught to draw the patterns in the sand endlessly, that there is a definite tradition of the introduction of particular crafts in certain dynasties, and that these traditions are so settled that the making of raphia cloth, after three hundred years of use, is still regarded as relatively an innova-

A Kasai Dance Mask. Belgian Congo.

tion.

Incontestably, then, we have here one of the great parent branches of African art, which further comparative study may prove to be one of the main sources, if not the great ancestral reservoir. Many other regions have in single lines more outstanding and distinctive art, but there is no denying Herbert Ward's original impression that the Congo epitomizes Africa, that its culture is one of the oldest and most typical, and that nowhere else do we find an equivalent or more characteristic flowering of the several handicrafts.

The Blondiau-Theatre Arts collection represents all important aspects of Congo art, and though particularly rich in Bakuba and Baluba work—the most developed of the Bushongo schools—includes numerous fine examples of Bangongo, Bayaka, Kasai, Bena Lulua and Azandé specimens, and fine bits of Basonge pottery. Thus both the art of the dominant Bantu and of the subjugated non-Bantu stocks are represented. In several types such as the Bakuba figure cups, the Bushongo decorative bowls and cups, and Azandé lutes and other musical instruments there are interesting series, displaying almost every known variation of type.

Indeed it is from the comparison of such series rather than from the examination of single exceptional specimens that one gets the most convincing proof of a really great art tradition. From the minute variation in the use of highly stereotyped patterns, by the skillful balance between originality and tradition, in the clever transposition of design *motifs* from one medium to another with scrupulous r e g a r d for the limitations and peculiar appropriateness of the material, one can gauge the high artistry of these craftsmen. For instance, a pattern that originated as a woven under-and-over raphia design will be stippled dot and dash on metal, surface-grooved on pottery, surface raised and conventionally broken short at the cross-overs in wood, and in ivory so rigidly stylized as to be scarcely recognizable at first glance. Generations of familiarity with the materials have bred an instinctive feeling for the right thing. None of that naturalistic imitation in alien materials, which a contemporary critic satirizes as "the artiness of withered oak leaves rendered in wrought iron", that is of such painful frequency in our own art; but instead almost always a logical and clean adjustment of motive, design and material. Always too, a quite ingenious observance of surface spacing, gradation of finish to natural texture, and the like—points of artistic value to us so abstract, but to the African artist, so immediate and obvious. Take as an example the group of carved buffalo drinking horns, where the natural curvatures have been arbitrarily set, and observe the striking unity of the added patterns with both surface curvature and outline, and then note in addition, as with almost every bit of African carving, the obvious working out of effective design from every possible visual approach to the object.

But most persons are disposed to concede to African art its characteristic virtuosity of surface ornament and design. That is incontestable. But in the larger plastic technique, and the recognition of its values, there is often hesitancy, especially for Congo works. The high forms of Bushongo art seem to be the sculptural heads combined with ornamental forms, the fetish statuettes, and the semi-portraitistic figurines that are supposed to have reached their artistic acme in the eighteenth century. The two head goblets shown on this page and the next are admittedly exceptional for this or any other general collection. But they show power in the handling of sculptural mass and surface quite of the highest order. Particularly surprising in view of prevalent conceptions, is the subtle, placid tone and smooth flow of surface, and the austere economy of decorative elements. One of the head cups might pass as early Buddhist in its quality of austerity and mystic restraint. Clearly they belong to a seasoned and classic tradition, and could stand almost without commentary as sufficient contradiction of a recent dictum about Congo art that "the vast majority of objects produced here are unimpressive plastically, tending either to extreme crudity of workmanship, to unimaginative naturalism, or to overcrowding with superficial decoration." It is just the exact opposites of these that constitute the

Bakuba Ceremonial Cup.

Bakuba Ceremonial Cup.

special sophisticated strength and conscious power of these particular specimens. Really they exemplify, along with a number of ceremonial objects, scepters, staffs of office and other insignia, jewel-boxes and articles of fine personal adornment, an apparent aristocratic strain in Congo art, with a characteristic refinement and subtlety that marks it, for all the diversity of the objects themselves, as a distinct tradition in itself—a proud art of the ruling and conquering caste.

At the courts of the Bushongo chiefs special artisans are reserved for the chiefs, and the wood-carvers are given precedence over all other craftsmen. This same tradition works itself out in the superfine, almost delicate elaborateness of the ceremonial knives and swords, of which no finer examples exist in all Africa than the Bushongo types.

In marked contrast to this, we have two other quite distinct styles in Congo art, running consistently through the characteristic tribal differences, a bizarre and grotesque strain and another, crudely rustic and realistic. The former as a style dominates most of the strictly religious objects,— the fetish images, the dance and ceremonial masks, and particularly the miniature ivory masks and talismans. These latter, particularly the small circumcision masks of ivory and the body fetishes, are of exquisite workmanship, linking up with the sophisticated court style, but the large masks are for the most part broad and powerful in treatment, and achieve their effect more through emotional than plastic appeal. The Congo seems more likely to become famous for the great variety than for the beauty of its masks; only a few are comparable in stunning originality and artistic effect to those of the Fang, M'Pongwe, Gabun, and Ivory Coast tribes. The plain mask reproduced is rather exceptional in its stark beauty. There are several fine examples of composite masks with elaborate appliqué decoration in beads, cowry shells, and other contrasted ornamentation,—principally of the familiar Kasai, Bapende and Baluba types, but with three rare specimens of unusual Bayaka and Bakette forms.

The Congo masks are in the main more grotesque than beautiful in form, but this is often compensated by unusual decorative values in color and surface contrasts. Strangely enough the accessory articles and accoutrements of the dramatic and ritual ceremonies in which they are used seem to be of greater artistic distinction and beauty. Anklets, collars, rings, pendants, rattles, gongs, whistles, divining-blocks, drums and other musical instruments are so finely conceived and executed that their sheer beauty and abstract decorative appeal lift them quite out of the class of the minor arts. From our point of view they seem almost too fine for practical purposes, yet they are structurally sound and utilize their most essential lines and features as the path of their artistic appeal. Take for example, the drum, lute, and double dance-gong in the collection; they exceed in beauty almost anything of their kind. In bewilderment one wonders why such beauty in accessories with such grotesque starkness and crudity in the masks and costume ensemble. The only explanation plausible is that symbolic requirements and the religious and ceremonial necessity for evoking terror and awe dictate the latter, but that in subordinate details the inhibited instinct for pure beauty seizes upon its only opportunity for free play.

Finally, we come to those crude, heavy, squat and sensuous things which in the popular mind typify the Congo exclusively. As a

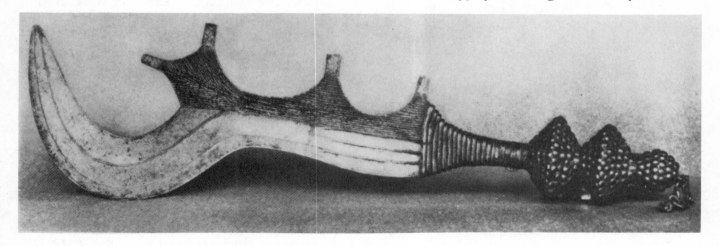

Bakuba Sword.

Plain Pattern Cups.

matter of fact, characteristic as they are, they represent but one strand in Congo art, a rustic and somewhat peasant strain in the culture. These things smack of the jungle, and reflect its crude, primitive realities. And while they doubtless have in them the special idioms of some of the less culturally developed stocks, they know no tribal barriers and exist side by side with the refined and sophisticated work we have already noticed. Here again the best explanation is that of a special controlling tradition, dictating the peculiar style. We find a valuable clue in the fact that this technique of rough bold outline and unfinished masses focuses in particular classes of objects,—the totemic fetishes, the funerary statuettes and the nail and fertility fetishes with their direct practical appeal to sympathetic magic. Can it be that the rationale of the style is after all superstitiously motivated, and that the salient symbolism expressed at the expense of artistic balance and restraint is sensed as making the objects more potent and effective? One cannot be certain of this, of course, until fuller studies of the cultural background of African art become available. Certain it is, however, that many things in this style could have been rendered more expertly, and even as it is, some of them achieve absolute beauty in spite of the first impression which they give of crudity and weirdness.

Oddly enough it is this most primitive strain in the Congo art which is its weakest and least stable tradition. It is the first to yield to the infiltration of European idioms, as is shown by the many examples of this style registering in ludicrous combinations the superimposing of European hats, boots and what-not upon African fundamentals. A few such impossibles have their place in any representative collection, but it is a tragedy to see the easy corruption and degeneracy of the most indigenous and possibly one of the earliest of the African styles. And yet perhaps it is not so certain that this cruder style is the earliest and most basic. That is merely a European assumption. The crude styles may just as well be themselves degenerated strains, or more possibly even, with the criss-crossings of endless tribal warfare, parallel ethnic strands of other tribal traditions, and not the basis from which the fine tradition built itself up.

What is quite certain both by internal and external evidence is that Bushongo and other varieties of African art reached a classic stage of expression very early indeed, and then remained stable over many generations. Certain types have persisted for centuries. Dated both by the registration of early European influences and by the dynastic dates of the Bantu chronicles,—those of the Bushongo record a succession of a hundred and twenty odd chieftains—even the acme of Congo art must be placed back from three to six hundred years. Even when the particular pieces are comparatively recent, since

Kasai Fetish (Slave Carrying
Chief).

We must remember that the enthusiasts of the generation of Matisse who discovered African art and incorporated it into their new æsthetic were by no means in a position to be connoisseurs of African art. To the artistically wise the striking hints of a few examples were sufficient, and the basic characteristics of the African sculpture could be gotten from relatively poor specimens. They but introduced us to its strange values and generalized upon its idioms. But now that the first phase of the technical absorption of the principles of African art has taken place, and the tradition has grown more subtle and complicated in the developments of modern Cubism, Expressionism, and *Sur-realisme*, we are thrown back on a more intensive study of African art in its first principles. We need

Fetish Statuette (Primitive Kasai).

with a stereotyped art like this it is a matter of copying fresh examples over and over, the type forms are exceedingly ancient.

The most important issue about African art is then not that of the dating of the piece itself, but of the dating of the type; it is only in a rapidly evolving culture like ours that copies become so swiftly deteriorations of their originals and lower in creative force. It is possible then in the case of African art to determine roughly the period of the type when it is impossible to determine the age of the particular example, and what is most to be desired in a collection is that it should contain representative examples of standard and classic forms.

to do more than intuite its values and feel its inspiration, we must understand it, and that sufficiently to know how it came to have such an influence.

Modern art in taking up African art into its own substance then has given it a new lease of life, and made it doubly necessary to understand it. Indeed just as the Renaissance rejuvenated and universalized classical antiquity, modernism has permanently revitalized these and all other primitives. It becomes necessary today to understand the arts formerly alien and exotic to our cultural tradition in thoroughness of historical and theoretical grasp, because they are now organically correlated with our own tradition. Seeking only for a Northwest passage in style, the modernists have opened up whole new continental areas of art, and have made it necessary and possible to take the entire range of human art upon the broad basis of its universal factors and underlying common principles.

With this significant instance of the perennial vitality of beauty, how absurd it is to pronounce any art officially dead or lost.

African art is, to be sure, no longer a novelty —its first influences and the faddist flare of interest which it excited have already passed —but neither is it yet fully understood nor have we exhausted its full potentialities. There is one particularly intriguing possi-

bility of further influence which is only beginning to open up, and which gives particular bearing and point to the movement for bringing African art to fuller attention and understanding in America. The importation of representative collections will have a vital effect on our own art apart even from the general modernist trend if, as may reasonably be expected, African art should once more exert a new influence in quickening the artistic development of the American Negro. With the particular appeal of a rediscovered race heritage, it cannot fail to stimulate a generation of artists who are already in the swing of a program to express their racial life and experience in intimate and original ways. Strangely enough until now the artistic development of the American Negro, significant as it has been in music and poetry, has lagged in the field of the plastic and decorative arts, the very forte of his original ancestry. One can of course think of no stronger or more promising stimulus than this which has already influenced contemporary art so notably, but which would have in this particular field of influence such strong additional appeals of intimate force and pull. It is one of the prime motives back of the project that brings the Blondiau-Theatre Arts collection to us, that through this channel especially, African art should be made a vital influence for the creation of fresh sources of beauty in America.

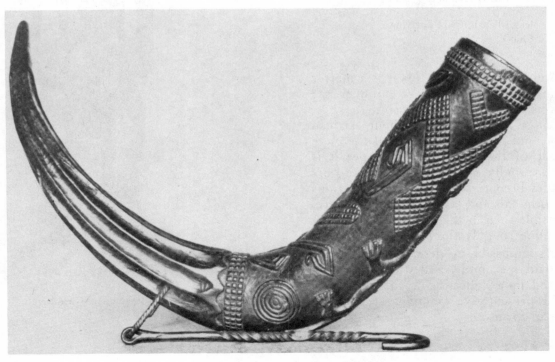

Carved Buffalo Drinking Horn (Bakuba).

AFRICAN ART: CLASSIC STYLE

EVEN to those who have known and appreciated it, African art has been seen through a glass darkly—either as exotic and alien or as the inspiration and source of contemporary modernism. The current exhibition of the Museum of Modern Art, aside from being the finest American showing of African art, reveals it for the first time in its own right as a mature and classic expression. The obvious intent has been to show African art in its own context, and to document its great variety of styles by showing a few pure and classic specimens of each. The whole wide range of extant collections, European as well as American, has been combed for the best examples; of the well-known collections only those of Corail-Stop and the Barnes Foundation are missing, and this wide and highly selective culling has resulted in an exhibit which is a revelation even to the experts. Something like that change in evaluation which was made necessary when the art world first saw the Greek originals of the already familiar Roman copies, or discovered the firm strength and austerity of archaic and pure Greek art in contrast with the subtle delicacy of this art in its period of maturity and approaching decadence, must be the result of a showing such as this. Among other things, our notion of the exceptionally small scale of African sculpture must be abandoned since item after item proves the existence of a "grand style," with corresponding heroic proportion and simplicity. Seventy-two collections have been the vast reservoir from which a selection of six hundred items has been chosen, and these range from small private collections of art amateurs to the great state collections at Leipzig, Munich, Berlin, Tervueren, the Paris Trocadéro Museum and our own collections at Chicago, Brooklyn, the University of Pennsylvania, and even Harlem. Mr. James Johnson Sweeney is the presiding genius who has gleaned this vast territory and pressed out the essence, giving America not only its greatest show of African art among the seven that have been held here since the memorable first one of 1914 at "Gallery 291," but a master lesson in the classic idioms of at least fourteen of the great regional art styles of the African continent. Our title, then, is no exaggeration: this is a definitive exhibition of African classics.

Only such a weeding out could have re-revealed the classical maturity of this native art. As it stands out in a few specimens of pure style rather than the usual jumble of hybrids and second-rate examples, it is only too obvious that, instead of a heightened expression of this plastic idiom, we have in modernist art a dilution of its primitive strength and its classic simplicity. Mr. Sweeney goes further in his preface and argues that the new idiom of modern painting and sculpture was an independent development of European aesthetic that merely happened to be in the direction of the African idioms, and that the adoption of their characteristic Negroid form motives "appears today as having been more in the nature of

American Magazine of Art 28 (May 1935): 270–278.
Photos in this article by Simco Custom Photo Lab, Los Angeles, Cal.

Figure of Man, Baoulé, Ivory Coast. Collection of Charles Ratton, Paris.

of the world."

Having learned the similarities of African art and modernist art, we are at last prepared to see their differences. The secret of this difference would seem to be a simple but seldom recognized fact. The modern artist, as a sophisticate, was always working with the idea of authorship and a technically formal idea of expressing an aesthetic. The native African sculptor, forgetful of self and fully projected into the idea, was always working in a complete fusion with the art object. Sheldon Cheney is exactly right when he says: "These little idols, fetishes and masks are direct expressions of religious emotion. The

Relief with Hunter, Benin, British Nigeria. Collection of Museum für Völkerkunde, Berlin.

attempts at interpretation, or expressions of critical appreciation, than true assimilations." Out of this novel thesis that these two movements—the new appreciation of African art and of the Negro plastic tradition, and the working out of the new aesthetic in European art—were coincidental rather than cause and effect, Mr. Sweeney draws deductions leading to the glorification rather than the belittlement of African art. He believes that African art is best understood directly, and in terms of its own historical development and background, and that it should be recognized in its own idiom and right, rather than in terms of its correlation with modern art or its admitted influence upon modern art. The exhibition vindicates this thesis and the claim that "today the art of Negro Africa has its place of respect among the aesthetic traditions

Terracotta Head, Yoruba, British Nigeria (plaster cast). Original in collection of Forschungs-Institut, Frankfort-am-Main.

Man's Head, Benin, British Nigeria. Collection of Captain A.W.F. Fuller, London.

sculptor approaches his work in humility, always feeling that he is less important than the figure he is carving. His carving is for itself, out of his emotion." Although its vitality, its powerful simplification, "its unerring emphasis on the essential and its timelessness" were appreciated by the European modernist, and were technically and ideally inspiring, few or no modern artists could be at one and the same time naïve and masterful, primitive and mature. And so the enviable combination of naïveté and sophistication, of subtlety and strength could not be reachieved but only echoed. Few may be expected to agree until they have seen the exhibit, but few who have seen it may be expected to dissent.

The basis of the display, correctly enough, is regional. One by one the great regional styles are illustrated. However, the museum

atmosphere is completely abolished by artful spacing and an effect of outdoor setting. In most instances the items can be examined, as they should be, from all points of view. African art, it must be remembered, is a sculptural art basically, and in addition—something which we have almost completely lost—a tactual art. Apart from texture and feel, I fancy there can be little appreciation of it in anything approaching native terms.

The French Sudan, never very well represented in American collections or exhibitions, has been aptly illustrated, principally from

Figure of Young Woman, Pahouin, Border of Spanish Guinea. Collection of Louis Carré Gallery, Paris.

the great French collections; the Carré, Guillaume, Tzara, Chauvet, and Trocadéro collections have furnished the majority of the forty specimens of this little known style. Its rigid angular simplicity and almost inscrutable force show what powerful originality there was in a purely native idiom, for this Sudanese art has few analogies except with the oldest and earliest of Greek archaics by which no one presumes it to have been influenced. Its traditions of ancestor worship and phallic symbolism are stamped deeply upon it but it is just as obviously pure and not applied art.

French Guinea, the Upper Volta, and Sierra Leone are also represented by a few choice examples. Distinctive though they are, they are obviously intermediate between the Sudanese and the French Ivory Coast idioms. They are seldom seen in the pure forms and older styles, as in this case, and are perhaps least familiar to American eyes. On the whole, we have by accident become familiar primarily with the art forms of the Congo—French and Belgian. We do know the Ivory Coast styles, but usually neither in pure form

nor in their rich variety. It was the Barnes Collection that familiarized us with those curiously powerful "Dan" masks, a number of which in this exhibit are included from the collections of Paul Guillaume and Charles Ratton. Beside the more delicate and placid style of the surrounding Ivory Coast types, and the similarly graceful Baoulé style, they suggest some particularly strong ritualistic tradition separate from these. And yet a specimen like No. 101 in the catalogue * illustrates not only that these styles are of the same region, but that they can be combined in something both beautiful and congruous. Here again no finer collection of Ivory Coast specimens has ever been displayed in America, whether of the large-scale carvings or of the inimitable miniature carving for which the Gold and Ivory Coast is famous.

Naturally no exhibition emphasizing classical African styles would be complete without a good showing of Benin—represented here by

*African Negro Art, Edited by James Johnson Sweeney. The Museum of Modern Art, New York, 1935. Price, $2.50.

Head Rest, Urua, Belgian Congo. Courtesy of Kungstgewerbe Museum, Cologne. Collection of Baron von der Heydt, Zandvoort.

well-selected examples of the early and classical bronzes of the non-Europeanized type and period. Side by side are picked specimens of Ifa and Yoruba sculptures; no doubt, to illustrate Mr. Sweeney's challenging and probably correct hypothesis that the Benin art is a derivative of the classical Yoruban, because Ifa has been indicated as the ancestral source of the Benin religion. Surely the striking similarity of the art motifs seems to substantiate this, and the Ifa style is closest to the oldest and purest specimens of the Benin bronzes.

Dahomey, Ashanti, and the Gold Coast are richly represented in wood, ivory and metal media, and in a variety calculated to show the great technical proficiency of this region. Its stylistic relation to classic Benin and Ifa art is that of a later and somewhat decadent version in which technique has been overem-

Four-faced Mask, Mpongwe, French Congo. Collection of Paul Guillaume, Paris.

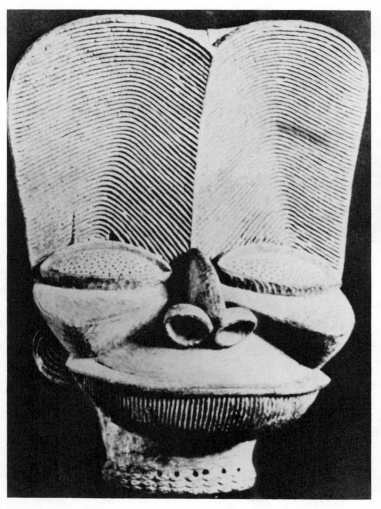

Mask, Grassland Bamendjo, Cameroon. Courtesy of Kunstgewerbe Museum. Collection of Baron von der Heydt, Zandvoort.

phasized with the original significance apparently lapsing. The Ratton Collection has furnished some massive antique Dahomey metal sculptures, one instance a five-foot statue of the "God of War"; but no less striking and certainly more fascinating is the collection of ivory and metal miniatures. Even if we consider the well-known virtuosity of Oriental art in this field, with these Gold Coast miniature gold masks, ivory talismans, and small brass weights of every conceivable variety and technical versatility, Africa enters the lists as a respectable contender in a field that until recently was thought to be an Oriental monopoly.

In the Cameroon section, plastic strength and simplicity have been emphasized rather than the usual grotesqueness or wealth of polychrome surface decoration. One mask (No. 326) from the von der Heydt Collection is exceedingly unusual, and a Cameroon seat with carved pendant figures (No. 336) is particularly fine. This region has been documented in a revealing way.

Similarly, the Gabun, Pahouin, and Mpongwe traditions are splendidly illustrated, the Guillaume Collection carrying most of the burden here. However, one of the most appealing specimens of Bieri (Gabun) head comes from the collection of Madame Helena Rubinstein. There are also three of the rare four-faced moon ritual masks of this district. The art of this region is a mystical art, with a baffling refinement and sophistication which we will not know how to account for until we know more about the religious thought in which it had its roots.

One would naturally expect a heavy representation of the French and Belgian Congo, and we have it in all its dazzling variety from the pure geometric pattern art of the Bakubas—carving and weaving—to the curiously characteristic Congo figure carving. Beautiful specimens of every well-known type have been selected, but attention must be called to such unusual types as Nos. 465 and 452, and the amazingly delicate calabash fetish with carved female figure (No. 489).

Of the rare art of the Angola district (Portuguese East Africa), and of the famous Vatchivokoe figures, there is a respectable display. But not even this extraordinary collection has been able to get the very best specimens. This is an art idiom with which we have as yet very little acquaintance; it is so profound and strange even among the general profundity of African equatorial art that we may suspect one of the ultimate secrets of African art to lie in this tradition.

This exhibit will probably provoke no new furor of decorative mode or faddist wave of imitation as have previous shows. It presents African art as really too great for imitation or superficial transcription. Its result must surely be to engender respect for the native insight and amazement for the native technique. It even explains that trite commonplace about the decadence of native art in

Fetish with Calabash and Shells, Urua, Belgian Congo. Collection of Tristan Tzara, Paris.

Africa; for although the intrusion of Western civilization did break down the life upon which this art flourished, no art can be expected to retain its classic period indefinitely. Even without external influences, a natural decadence would have set in; and the only reason that it was so long avoided was the simplicity of an art that was essentially anonymous and the profundity of a nature-philosophy that could be maintained almost without change for generations. So we have to deal with a phase of African art that has become classic in this final sense. The Museum of Modern Art has thus rendered again a great service to the contemporary understanding of great art.

CONTEMPORARY
NEGRO ART

Locke came from a family of educators: both of his parents were schoolteachers in late nineteenth-century black schools. His family background affected his approach to the visual arts movement in two ways. First, he believed that black art should teach a black sense of beauty, should educate both black and white Americans to admire the black face and form. For Locke, beauty was learned, and constantly needed to be reenforced for blacks in a racist society. Second, as a young child he experienced the negative color consciousness of Afro-Americans. Locke recalled that his grandmother admonished him to stay out of the sun, telling him, "You're black enough already." While Locke loved art for its own sake, he believed that a core responsibility of the Negro visual arts movement was to instill in blacks "a sense of beauty that included our racial own."[1]

In "To Certain of Our Philistines" (1925), Locke defends his choice of Winold Reiss, a white artist who was commissioned to illustrate the landmark "Harlem" issue of *Survey Graphic*. Locke chose Reiss, he says, because other black and white artists were largely ignoring black subjects. Reiss broke sharply with the traditional stylized portrayal of Negro types, and provided bold, clear likenesses of blacks as individuals. Some members of the black elite criticized Reiss's portraits claiming they were "unrepresentative" of the black populace because of the extreme dark skin color and pronounced facial features of the characters depicted.

In the next essays, "The Art of Auguste Mambour" and "More of the Negro in Art," both published in 1925, Locke argues that contemporary black art should follow the European trends toward naturalism, turning to the immediate surroundings of black life for an unstylized rendering of black physiognomy.

Locke's ultimate goal, however, was a black art by Afro-American artists, and by 1931, a group of talented black artists had emerged. In "The American Negro as Artist" (1931), Locke explains why the visual arts are a relatively late blooming flower of the black Renaissance. Locke himself contributed to the maturing of this group, by serving as a go-between for artists, patrons, and foundations. Of particular significance was Locke's work with Mary Beattie Brady, director of the Harmon Foundation, which sponsored exhibits and awards for black artists from 1926 to 1933.[2]

In 1939, Locke was asked to help organize the first exhibit of black American art at the Baltimore Museum of Art. In his Foreword which appeared in the exhibit catalog, Locke links the Negro art movement to the call for cultural democracy under government art patronage in the 1930s.[3]

Locke was upset when a vocal group of black artists objected to being "segregated" by having their work included in a separate international exhibit at the 1939 New York World's Fair. Locke responds to such sentiments in the sharply critical "Advance on the Art Front" (1939).[4]

In "Up Till Now" (1945), Locke hails the eventual absorption of Negro art into American art. Locke's advocacy of a black aesthetic in the visual arts and his optimism for a more democratic, tolerant American art distinguishes him from other critics.

Two Public School Teachers by Winold Reiss. Photo by Moorland–Spingarn Research Center, Howard University, Washington, D.C. (Originally published in the "Harlem" number of *Survey Graphic* 53, no. 11 [March 1, 1925]: 687.)

TO CERTAIN OF OUR PHILISTINES

OF all the arts, painting is most bound by social ideas. And so, in spite of the fact that the Negro offers, in the line of the human subject, the most untouched of all the available fields of portraiture, and the most intriguing, if not indeed the most difficult of technical problems because of the variety of pigmentation and subtlety of values, serious painting in America has all but ignored him. As far as my knowledge and judgment go, the best that has been done by reputable American masters in this line is work like Winslow Homers' "Gulf Stream" or his "A Sunday Morning in Virginia" and the "Pickanniny" of Robert Henri. All of this work is in the vein and mood of the traditional "Study in Brown" — the half-genre, half study-sketch in which so many a master hand has satisfied its artistic curiosity without exerting its full command either of interpretation or expression. Negro artists, themselves victims of the academy-tradition, have had the same attitude, and have shared the blindness of the Caucasian eye. Nothing above the level of a genre study or more penetrating that a Nordicized transcription has been done. Our Negro-American painter of the best academic technique, though in his youth and into his mature period a professed type—realist devoted to the portrayal of Jewish Biblical types, has never maturely touched the portrayal of the Negro subject.

Facts shouldn't be regretted: they should be explained. Social conventions stand closer guard over painting than most of the other arts. It is for that reason that a new school and idiom of Negro portraiture is particularly significant. As might be expected, it began in Europe, and because of the American situation has had to be imported. Portraiture is too controlled by social standards for it to be otherwise. But its really promising and vital development will be American, and, at least we hope, in large part the work of Negro artists. The latter cannot be predicted with as great confidence as the former—for the American Negro mind, in large sections, suffers as yet from repressions which make the idioms of the new school less welcome than the genre-peasant portraiture to which we have become accustomed, and almost as objectionable as the caricature conventions from which our "touchy" reactions have been developed. Too many of us still look to art to compensate the attitudes of prejudice, rather than merely, as is proper, to ignore them. And so, unfortunately for art, the struggle for social justice has put a pessimism upon a playing-up to Caucasian type-ideals, and created too prevalently a half-caste psychology that distorts all true artistic values with the irrelevant social values of "representative" and "unrepresentative," "favorable" and "unfavorable"—and threatens a truly racial art with the psychological bleach of "lily-whitism." This Phillistinism cannot be tolerated. Already on the wane in our social life, after a baneful career, it cannot be allowed this last refuge in art. To rid ourselves of this damaging distortion of art values by color-line, we shall have to draw the culture-line sharply and without compromise, and challenge, without hope or expectation of quarter, our own Phillistines.

Meanwhile, until we can find or create a considerable body of appreciative support for the new art, the painting of the Negro subject will have to rely upon the boldly iconoclastic stand of the convinced and purposefully original artist. The work of Winold Reiss, represented in the Harlem number of the *Survey Graphic,* and more elaborately in the exhibition of the original color pastels at the Harlem Branch of the New York Public Library, was deliberately conceived and executed as a pathbreaker in the inevitable direction of a racially representative type of art. In idiom, technical treatment, and social angle, it was meant to represent a new approach, and constructively to break with the current tradition. In the first place, it breaks as European art has already done, with the limited genre treatment of the Negro subject. Next, it

Opportunity 3 (May 1925): 155–156.

recognizes what is almost a law of development, that a new subject requires a new style, or at least a fresh technique. The Negro physiognomy must be freshly and objectively conceived on its own patterns if it ever is to be seriously and importantly interpreted. Art must discover and reveal the beauty which prejudice and caricature have obscured and overlaid. Finally it must reinforce our art with the dignity of race pride and the truly cultural judgment of art in terms of technical and not sentimental values.

Awed by a name, the Phillistines will accept in a Holbein or a Van Eyck or a Rubens qualities which they bray at in this logical application in contemporary work. All vital art discovers beauty, and opens our eyes to beauty that previously we could not see. And no great art will impose alien canons of beauty upon its subject matter. But it is harder to discover beauty in the familiar—and that may perhaps be why our own Negro artists may be the last to recognize the new potentialities, technical and æsthetic, of our racial types.

Modern art happily has already discovered them: Mr. Reiss is simply a pioneer in the application of this discovery to the American Negro subject. Already Max Slevogt, Pechstein, Elamie Stein, Von Reukteschell, Lucie Costurier, Neville Lewis, F. C. Gadell, and most especially the Belgian, Auguste Mambour, have looked upon the African scene and the African countenance and discovered there a beauty that calls for a distinctive idiom both of color and of modelling. Their work should even now be the inspiration and the guide-posts of a younger school of American Negro artists. Mambour's canvases at the International Art Show at Venice impressed me as standing out among the most pre-eminent work of the entire exhibition, not merely the Belgian section. Not that we would have all our young painters, ultra-modernists of this or that European cult or coterie, but that the lesson of an original and bold approach is just that which must be learned to start any vital art development among us.

We have a right to expect and demand two things of the cultural expression of the Negro, that it should be vital and that it should be contemporary. This isn't the creed of being new-fangled for the sake of being so—let others who have more cause to be decadent and blasè than we, be eccentric and bizarre for the sheer need of new sensations and renewed vigor. But for another more vital and imperative reason the artistic expression of Negro life must break through the stereotypes and flout the conventions—in order that it may be truly expressive at all—and not a timid, conventional, imitative acceptance of the repressions that have been heaped upon us by both social persecution and by previous artistic misrepresentation. Artistically we shall have to fight harder for independence than for recognition, and this we cannot achieve either through slavish imitation, morbid conventionalism, or timid conservatism.

Let us take as a concreet instance, the much criticized Reiss drawing entitled "Two Public School Teachers." It happens to be my particular choice among a group of thirty more or less divergently mannered sketches; and not for the reason that it is one of the most realistic but for the sheer poetry and intense symbolism back of it. It happens to represent my own profession, about which I may be presumed to know something. I am far from contending that there is an orthodox interpretation of any art—many minds, many reactions—but this at least is my reaction. I believe this drawing reflects in addition to good type portraiture of its sort, a professional ideal, that peculiar seriousness, that race redemption spirit, that professional earnestness and even sense of burden which I would be glad to think representative of both my profession and especially its racial aspects in spite of the fact that I am only too well aware of the invasion of our ranks in some few centers by the parasitic, society-loving "flapper." I do not need to appeal to race pride, but only to pride of profession to feel and hope that "The Two School Teachers" in addition to being "good drawing" is finely representative. The young Negro artist, when he comes, will conquer this opposition in his own, unique way; but at any rate, here is the smoothest pebble we can find—ready for David's sling.

THE ART OF AUGUSTE MAMBOUR

OUR main story is about Auguste Mambour and his brilliant contribution to the art expression of Negro types—but the news has just come of the death of Lucie Costurier. We must mix our bay with laurel and grieve as well as praise. Elsewhere in this issue, as is most appropriate, Rene Maran—friend, comrade, fellow-crusader, pays the fuller tribute of which he alone is capable. But it is impossible to speak of the artistic revolution which has invested Negro types with their own inherent beauty and given them their classic tradition and place in art without homage to Lucie Costurier, whose pioneer vision was such a discovering genius in this field. Intimate human understanding, and a universalizing conviction of kinship without reservation or forced doctrinizing gave the author of *Des Inconnues chez Moi* and *Mes Inconnues chez Eux* a moral and spiritual penetration into African life as well as a technical and artistic insight. Madame Costurier was one of the discoverers of the Negro soul—and painting but one of her avenues of approach. But, despite her fervent interest in literature portraiture, she recognized its supreme importance as a channel of revelation for the direct enlightenment of the masses. Certainly this seemed her philosophy of the new social vision for which she so ardently worked and hoped as she arose by a desperate effort of will from her couch that single afternoon when I was privileged to see her, to receive us, Rene Maran, some West Coast students from the Normal College at Bordeaux then on vacation in Paris, and myself. "To see, one must have vision—to understand, one must have more sympathy than curiosity, more understanding than sympathy, more love than understanding." With the peculiar hectic fever of her disease reenforcing the ardour of the adventuresome reformer and traveler, it was a memory-searing scene and experience. That was what made Madame Costurier more than a technical experimenter, or a delver in the exotic: she loved and understood what others have merely used and exploited.

Auguste Mambour's grasp upon the Negro subject is deeper than that of a marvelous technical control, and to that extent he, with many others, is a debtor of one to whom he owes no direct artistic technical debt or influence. Mambour's control is technical, his chief significance is as the painter who of all the many now interested in the portrayal of African types has achieved the most distinctively original idiom of style and color, but back of that lies an intimate sympathy and understanding of his subject. Ed-

Opportunity 3 (August 1925): 240, 241, 252.

From a painting by Auguste Mambour. Photo by Moorland–Spingarn Research Center, Howard University, Washington, D.C.

mond Jaloux in La revue Belge singles out "the striking originality of a man who would go to study in the Congo when others were going to Rome." It is no middle aged quest for fresh fields after the exhaustion of the traditional that brought Mambour to his subject. He is yet counted among the younger generation of Belgian painters. But deeper even than his own strong Walloon tradition, the types of his own Liegeois, is his hold upon African types and scenes. Six of the eight canvases selected to represent him at the International Art Exhibit at Venice were Negro in subject, and Sander Pierron in his review of the Belgian exhibit, also in La revue Belge, credits the Congo with having given him his characteristic atmosphere, — a 'brutally contrasting, almost overwhelming color scheme, weighted down in spite of its brilliance with a heavy, quite tropical melancholy and fatalism.' The reproductions show the forceful stylization of Mambour,—a modelling of masses that is truly sculptural and particularly suited to the broad, massive features of the African countenance—surely mere line and contour treatment can never be the technique for the classical treatment of Negro types—but to this masterful handling of mass and light and shade in bold but subtle planes, there must in imagination be added the striking illumination of the rich browns and vivid greens of a tropical color scheme, and a sense of dripping sunlight from the high-lights of the canvas. It is not to be wondered at, then, that these were among the most startling works of the entire exhibition. Mambour has an originality of technique which he owes largely to his early interest, and his deep study, of things African.

It will take still another article to prove the quite invariable originality of the influence in European painting. The work of Bonnard, Georges Roualt, Klees van Dongen will especially have to be noticed, but Mam-

bour alone even ought to be a revelation to the eye unaccustomed to seeing pure beauty in alien moulds. For the Negro artist, must consider work like this as basic, both from the point of view of technique as well as of interpretation. It is a principle of all art, that each body of material has, so to speak, its own inherent idioms, that are only to be derived through letting the material dictate its own expression. In this sense, Keats' ideal that 'Beauty is Truth, Truth, Beauty' becomes almost a dictum of technique. The spirit of African life is maintained, and not merely the external form and feature. That is what differentiates such work from the merely exotic renderings of so many colonial painters. Mambour is at home with his subject psychologically rather than just physically there. Where others rely on theatrical effect, and draw an attention that they cannot sustain, Mambour's art has an arresting quality that converts curiosity into understanding. A single Mambour may eventually do more for the modern status of African and Negro material than scores of academic studies or reams of critical argument. For, after all, the justification in art is beauty,—nothing more or less, and here is beauty made immediately convincing.

The Marche funebre has appropriately been acquired by the Colonial Museum at Tervueren. But Mambour is still largely in the private collections of his fellow countrymen, and at Liege. His significance however is international, and his influence should be made so. On sheer technical merit, he ranks with the leaders of his nation's art, Jacob Smits, Lucien Rion, Georges Latinis, and almost with the contemporary Belgian masters Laermans and Rik Wouters. M. G. D. Perier, that zealous exponent of the Negro tradition in modern colonial art has used Mambour almost as effectively as text as he has the indigenous native art itself. Belgian criticism is thus almost as actively enlightened in the interest of this important phase of modern art development as France, with its Madame Costurier, its Guillaume Janneau, and its Paul Guillaume. As soon as reproductions are available, it will be interesting to supplement these Mambour illustrations with some of the other material that documents this material as part of a vital art movement rather than shows them as isolated instances of an ephemeral fad. The influence goes beyond the narrow confines of the orignal subject-matter, as was the case also with the influence of the native African art. Indeed in both phases, it has been an influence full of the greatest subtleties — things primitive have had far from a primitive influence and effect in modern art. It was Madame Costurier who said in a symposium upon the value of African art to European art in Le Bulletin de la vie Artistique,—"When our art discovers the real values of Negro art, and our museums open their doors to it, they will find not merely a supplementing addition but will discover their basic common factor." And though Auguste Mambour is the greater artist, it honors his art to be in the context of such ideals of human universality.

MORE OF THE NEGRO IN ART

RESUMING our discussion of the treatment of the Negro subject in contemporary European art, it is perhaps best to start concretely by naming some of the painters who have done distinctive and distinguished work in this field. Beside the Belgian master Mambour,* there is the brilliant Dutch painter Kees van Dongen, the majority of whose canvases with Negro subjects are strict portraiture as opposed to the type sketch or study. Then notable among German painters we have Max Slevogt, Julius Huether, Max Pechstein, Elaine Stern and Walter von Ruckteschell; among English painters, Neville Lewis, F. C. Gadell, Edith Cheesman, John A. Wells and Frank Potter, and among the French, beginning with the well-known Dinet, the later work of Lucie Cousturier, Germaine Casse, Bonnard and Georges Rouault. As might be expected from grouping artists in terms of this one interest, we are for the time being making strange bedfellows of artists of widely different schools and rank, but there is in this very diversity an indirect tribute to the artistic appeal of the subject matter we are discussing.

What characterizes modern work with the Negro is the gradual outgrowing of the casual interest, either of the exotic or the genre sort, and the development of a matured and sustained interest worthy of the resources and difficulties of this special field. Of course when a Rembrandt or a Rubens, or a Gainsborough or Hogarth, with their masterful control, touched even casually the Negro subject, there was a notable reaction. But the effect upon art tradition was negligible, in spite of the occasional brilliant suggestion of canvases like Rembrandt's "Two Negroes" of the Hague Museum, or Rubens' noteworthy "Tetes de Negres" of the Brussel's Gallery, or even later studies like Feuerbach's Negro Sketch of the Hamburg Museum. What we are more interested in, and what is more valuable for

* The Art of Auguste Mambour, Alain Locke in Opportunity, August. 1925.

art is a continuous and sustained treatment of the subject, even though the individual product may not be so outstanding. Perhaps the French Romanticists with their interest in exotic Eastern and North African types prepared the way for this, but not until the full flood of modern realism has the development spread to the true Negro types, which after all offer the greatest novelties and difficulties of technical values and effects.

As a beginning of this particular trend, let us take the Munich Secessionist, Julius Huether. Here we have a front rank artist so enamoured of the Negro subject that it claims nearly a third of his canvases. This interest of Huether's, we learn, was purely technical, long before he was ever able to visit Africa, or see a considerable number of Negro models. His treatment is the approach of a color romanticist, captivated by the new bronze tones and warm browns of his subject. But gradually as his work matures, we see a growing figure interest, a study of type, and eventually a reaching after the most subtle of all the problems in this field, the curiously typical physiognomic expression which may be said to be racial. In his figure work, Huether revels in his new material like a modern Rubens,—indeed allowing for period differences, there are many reminders in his work of the touch of the Flemish master. In interpretative power over the Negro subject, Huether is more modern, and is to be bracketed with van Dongen and von Ruckteschell; others excel them in decorative and atmospheric values, but for type portrayal in this field these artists are preeminent.

Walter von Ruckteschell's drawings are already familiar to readers of Opportunity. They represent careful life studies made in German East Africa, but the point of approach is that warm human interest traditional with the South German school. Half-realist, half romantic, it has given us always painting in which the human interest values were im-

Opportunity 3 (December 1925): 363–366.

mediate and irresistible. In the case of von Ruckte-schell, apart from the beauty of the drawing,* there is a peculiar evocation of what one must call "race soul"; the mellow, sleepy but mystic eye, the sensuous but genial lips, the grotesque, mask-like simplicity of countenance, the velvety tone and texture, the sculptural modelling, common to the many otherwise diverse African types. I do not believe there are many Negroes who understand the underlying race temperament as deeply as the intuitive vision of these artists. When the race awakens consciously to its own spiritual selfhood, such work will be prized beyond measure. It is in fact an artistic forerunner of such an awakening.

Van Dongen is a more mannered artist, inheriting both the Dutch portraitistic skill and the symbolic manner of modern French painting. His portraits are nervous, incisive interpretations of character, more individual than racial. But then, so partial is he to the Negro subject, that an art journal, thinking to exploit this exoticism, asked him to explain his peculiar interest. Van Dongen as artist saw no need for one: his actual reply is worth quoting. It was at the time of Siki's boxing triumph, so he said, in reply to the question of what peculiar interest he found in Negro types, "If you would only ask Georges Carpentier, perhaps he could tell you." Of course back of this clever rebuke, was the main lesson of the whole matter. Why explain, the interest justifies itself; it is a question of art, not sociology. Now van Dongen's work is highly mannered, but only with the general eccentricity of his personal style, the same that produced one of the most striking but debatable interpretations of Anatole France. No connoisseur would put these Negro portraits of van Dongen out of the category of his best and most representative work.

Perhaps it is appropriate at this point to recall again Lucie Cousturier. Madame Cousturier's work represents a painstaking absorption of Negro life. She belongs to that school of artists who believe that Negro types cannot be fully interpreted until their cultural background has been adequately absorbed and reexpressed. For them the African background, and the racial idiom is an essential part of the picture. It requires social as well as artistic vision to approach the subject in this way, and Lucie Cousturier was one of the pioneers of such a broad humanistic view in European art. Artists like Max Slevogt, Max Pechstein, and even Elaine Stern are led to their African subjects by an interest in the exotic; as local colorists, they are the counterparts in painting of the colonial novelists. But the cultural interest which work like Madame Cousturier started has gradually pervaded their work, and raised it to the plane of serious and dignified human interpretation. Slevogt's and Pechstein's paintings are dramatic and in instances only superficially interpretative, but Slevogt's African work would fill a moderate gallery, and in addition to his local color sketches, Max Pechstein carries over into much of his general painting stylistic mannerisms borrowed from African art together with the sharp tropical

tone contrasts and color exuberances of the African scene. Though by no means in the full maturity of her art development, the work of Elaine Stern has a depth and veracity of interpretation that makes her work notably promising. Moreover she has a fine symbolic touch, like some carry over from Gauguin from the South Seas into tropical Africa. Her Madonna of the Tropics, which I saw in Frankfort and of which there was regrettably no reproduction obtainable is one of the first dozen canvases I should purchase for a gallery of Negro pictures. It has the poetry and symbolism that pervades the work of Mambour and that stamps him as the modern master of this subject, representing until the arrival of the great Negro artist interpreter the high water mark for the present in the treatment of Negro types.

We next come to a class of work in which a great number of lesser names could be mentioned, especially if we should include work in black and white mediums and the semi-serious. It is essentially a French tradition. Like the American cartoonist, the French black and white artist has a penchant for the Negro subject, with this difference,—that his treatment is both socially more kind and artistically more decorative. This modern interest in the black rogue—a revival on another level perhaps of the rather erotic Eighteenth Century French interest in the Negro, has been responsible for a considerable amount of work with deft skill and charm. This typical Latin interest and tradition, with its kindly farce in which there is no hint of social offense or disparagement, no matter how broad or caricaturistic the brush, is familiar to us now in the work of Miguel Covarrubias. It may yet be an antidote for that comic art which is so responsible for the hypersensitive feelings of American Negroes and stands between them and the full appreciation of any portrayal of race types. Surely the time has come when we should have our own comic and semi-serious art, and our own Cruikshanks and Max Beerbohms. And perhaps we shall have to go to the French artists for inspiration. At any rate this Quixotic realism, caught up into the texture of great art, characterizes the work of Bonnard and Georges Rouault, with Rouault a sort of French Henry Bellows. Rouault's lumpy canvases reproduce none too well, and it is perhaps just as well for those who are gradually getting over the pathetic fallacies of injured race pride that we are not reproducing pictures like Bonnard's "Sylvestre" or Rouault's "La Negresse" or "Le Boxeur." But in the municipal Museum of Grenoble, where nine of Rouault's works hang, one can forget for hours at a time that the Alps are outdoors. So at least it must be art. And if it is art, why question further?

The sad question is that the Anglo-Saxon mind does. That is, the English and the American, including even the Aframerican. And even the artists, most emancipated of the lot, have to rub their eyes twice, so to speak. Louise Herrick Wall, speaking to von Ruckteschell of "the mask of an unfamiliar physiognomy," quotes him as saying, "Mask! It is

*See page 11 [Editor's note].

we who wear it." I did not intend to chastize English and American artists particularly, but in most of their work, except possibly in work like that of Alfred Wollmark and John Wells, whose beautiful "Star of Bethlehem" has been selected as the cover illustration, there is the obvious effect of a public opinion holding them down to genre limitations. An excuse for painting the subject lurks in the corner of most of the canvases. English art hasn't much of a tradition in this line. There is the single Gainsborough, the single Hogarth, that gorgeously exotic Negro girl in Rossetti's "Beloved.". But we remember that the former were Eighteenth century and that Rossetti was Italian after all.

But English art is outgrowing its limitations in a way. Edith Cheesman had some brilliant studies of Gold Coast life at the Empire Exhibition, particularly striking a Native Court and a Market Scene at Accra. Lewis Neville and F. C. B. Gadell have done some quite competent colonial type studies, but with the impression that what is good material in a colonial setting would never do in London. But it is a different matter with Frank Potter, and Alfred Wollmark and John A. Wells. For them the psychological limitations of the local color school have been discarded, and the subject treated with the fullest resources, imaginative and technical, of the artist. From such treatment comes an interpretative depth that lends an instantly recognizable dignity and universalized meaning to the subject. It is to this level that modern art is gradually rising.

What needs most to be gained is the sense of the complete artistic propriety of the Negro subject. So that neither the slant and squint of social snobbery nor the stare and blink of inordinate curiosity should spoil with a sense of oddness, grotesqueness or triviality the message of the artist. The presentment of the Negro in art may then be in any vein, in any style,—it is for art to choose—with the mannerisms, the distortions even, that go along with individualisms of style, but with a sober technical interest and with appreciation for any serious interpretation of a subject which is difficult because it has not centuries of painting tradition behind it, and important because it does have before it the important significance of yet unexpressed human forms and feeling.

The Old Servant by Edwin A. Harleston.

THE AMERICAN NEGRO AS ARTIST

BETWEEN Africa and America the Negro, artistically speaking, has practically reversed himself. In his homeland, his dominant arts were the decorative and the craft arts—sculpture, metal-working, weaving—and so the characteristic African artistic virtuosities are decoration and design. But in America, the interpretive, emotional arts have been the Negro's chief forte, because his chief artistic expression has been in music, the dance, and folk poetry. One single strand alone has connected the ancestral and the new-world art—the age-old virtuosity in dance and pantomime. Except for this, the American Negro as an artist is completely different from his African prototype.

Why should this be? There is an historical reason. Slavery not only transplanted the Negro, it cut him off sharply from his cultural roots and his ancestral heritage, and reduced him to cultural zero by taking away his patterns and substituting the crudest body labor with only the crudest tools. Thus slavery severed the trunk-nerve of the Negro's primitive skill and robbed him of his great ancestral gift of manual dexterity. Alexandre Jacovleff, the Russian artist whose drawings of African types are to date unsurpassed, has well said of Africa—"A continent of beautiful bodies, but above all of beautiful hands." This fact is really a symbol: with virtuosity of muscle has gone a coördination resulting in great beauty. But the hardships of cotton and rice-field labor, the crudities of the hoe, the axe, and the plow, reduced the typical Negro hand to a gnarled stump, incapable of fine craftsmanship even if materials, patterns, and incentives had been available.

In a compensatory way the artistic urges of the American Negro flowed toward the only channels left open—those of song, movement, and speech, and the body itself became the Negro's prime and only artistic instrument. Greatest of all came the development of the irrepressible art of the voice, which is today the Negro's greatest single artistic asset. Thus the history of generations is back of the present lopsidedness in the Negro's art development, and the basis of his handicap in the graphic, pictorial, and decorative arts explains, as well, his proficiency in the emotional arts. No comment on the contemporary advance of the Negro in the plastic and pictorial arts would be sound without this historical perspective. For in his latest developments in formal fine art, the Negro artist is really trying to recapture ancestral gifts and reinstate lost arts and skill.

Considering this, the early advent of American Negro artists in painting and sculpture was all the more remarkable. As might be expected, however, this early art was of a purely imitative type, but not without technical merit. The two pioneer instances were Edward M. Bannister of Providence, Rhode Island, a landscapist of considerable talent, and founder, oddly enough, of the Providence Art Club; and Edmonia Lewis, our

The American Magazine of Art 23 (September 1931): 210–220.
Photos in this article by Simco Custom Photo Lab, Los Angeles, Cal.

first sculptor, who studied in Rome in the early seventies and executed many very acceptable portrait busts in the current pseudo-classic style. And another pioneer instance is R. S. Duncanson, of Cincinnati, figure painter, landscapist, and historical painter, who achieved considerable recognition between 1863 and 1866 in London and Glasgow. It is characteristic of this period, 1860 to 1890, that the Negro artists were isolated and exceptional individuals, imitative though, judged by contemporary American standards, not mediocre and almost entirely lacking in race consciousness. They were artists primarily and were incidentally Negroes.

The next generation also lived and worked as individuals, but despite their academic connections and ideals, with a sentimental shadow of race hanging over them. The outstanding talents that matured during this period (1895–1915) were Henry O. Tanner, William Edouard Scott, painters; and Meta Warrick Fuller and May Howard Jackson, sculptors. Of these, of course, Mr.

Self-Portrait by Lillian Dorsey.

Tanner is by far the best known and recognized. However varied their talents as artists of this transitional generation, they have much in common. All of them products of the best American academies, their talents were forced into the channels of academic cosmopolitanism not merely by the general trend of their time, but also by the pressure and restrictions of racial prejudice. So they not only matured under French instruction and influence—three of them were products of Julian's Academy—but have received their earliest and widest recognition abroad. Instead of being the challenging influence and special interest that it is for the Negro artist of today, race, by reason of circumstances beyond their control, was for them a ghetto of isolation and neglect from which they must escape if they were to gain artistic freedom and recognition. And so, except for occasional sentimental gestures of loyalty, they avoided it as a motive or theme in their art.

Because of her more completely American experience, May Howard Jackson, the sculptress, was first to break away from academic cosmopolitanism to frank and deliberate racialism. She was followed about 1907 (largely because of her commission to do commemorative Negro historical reliefs for the Jamestown Exposition) by Mrs. Fuller, who has continued since to work in the double vein of her earlier Rodinesque style and a very stylized idealization of Negro types, more exotic and Egyptian than realistically racial. The career of Mr. Tanner, professionally successful as it has been, is in this respect at least typical of the tragedy of this generation of Negro artists. Beginning under the realistic influence of his American teacher, Thomas Eakins, Tanner's early work showed marked interest and skill in painting Negro and Norman and, later, Jewish peasant types. It was the heyday of the regional school and but for his exile and the resentment of race as an imposed limitation, Tanner's undoubted technical genius might have added a significant chapter to the Jules Breton, Joseph Israels school of the half-romantic, half-realistic glorification of peasant life. Instead Tanner's work became more and more academic in treatment and cosmopolitan in theme; while for a treatment of Negro types in the

Meditation by Malvin Gray Johnson.

style of this period we have to rely on sporadic canvases by white American painters like Winslow Homer, Wayman Adams, Robert Henri.

But this generation, Tanner especially, did have, after all, a constructive influence upon the American Negro artist though not in the direction of the development of a special province of Negro art. They were inspiring examples to the younger generation and convincing evidence to a sceptical public opinion of the technical competence and artistic capacity of the Negro artist when given the opportunity of contact with the best traditions and academic training. This is taken for granted now, but largely as a result of their pioneer effort and attainment.

But the younger generation of Negro artists since 1915 have a new social background and another art creed. For the most part, the goal of the Negro artist today projects an art that aims to express the race spirit and background as well as the individual skill and temperament of the artist. Not that all contemporary Negro artists are conscious racialists—far from it. But they all benefit, whether they choose to be racially expressive or not, from the new freedom and dignity that Negro life and materials have attained in the world of contemporary art. And, as might be expected, with the removal of the cultural stigma and burdensome artistic onus of the past, Negro artists are showing an increasing tendency toward their own racial milieu as a special province and in their general work are reflecting more racially distinctive notes and overtones. In 1920, the One Hundred and Thirty-fifth Street Branch, in Harlem, of the New York Public Library began special exhibits of the work of Negro artists, which, having continued to date,

Sonny by William H. Johnson.

Old Snuff-Dipper by Archibald T. Motley.

have given showing to over a hundred young artists. In 1927, public-spirited citizens of Chicago pioneered with a special "Negro in Art Week" series of talks and exhibitions of the work of Negro artists, a programme that has been repeated at centers as far south as Atlanta and Nashville, as far north as Boston and Rochester, and as far west as San Diego and Los Angeles. Most influential of all, the Harmon Foundation has, by a five-year series of prize awards for Negro artists, with an annual New York show and extensive traveling exhibition of a considerable section of the same throughout the country, not only stimulated a new public interest in the Negro artist, but incubated more young talent in these last five years than came to maturity in the last twenty. As has been aptly said, "The public consciousness of Negro art has grown to be nation-wide and practi-

Landscape by Hale Woodruff.

The Wanderers by James Lesesne Wells. Courtesy of Mr. James Lesesne Wells.

cally world-wide in the last decade."

And so, at present, the Negro artist confronts an interested public, and that public faces an interesting array of productive talent. Without undue violence to individualities, these contemporary Negro artists may be grouped in three schools or general trends: the Traditionalists, the Modernists, and the Africanists, or Neo-Primitives, with the latter carrying the burden of the campaign for a so-called "Negro Art." Even among the traditionalists, there is considerable of the racial emphasis in subject matter, but without the complementary adoption of any special stylistic idioms, directly racial or indirectly primitive. But conservatism on this point seems doomed, since the young Negro artist has a double chance of being influenced by Negro idioms, if not as a deliberate racialist or conscious "Africanist," then at least at secondhand through the reflected influence of Negro idioms on general modernist style.

Noteworthy among the traditionalists are William Edouard Scott, of Indianapolis, portrait and mural painter; William Farrow, of Chicago, landscapist and etcher; Laura Wheeler Waring, of Philadelphia, landscapist and type-portraitist of considerable distinction; Palmer Hayden, of New York and Paris, marine painter of talent; Albert A. Smith, of New York; and the late Edwin A. Harleston, of Charleston, South Carolina, whose genre studies of Southern Negro peasant types have competently filled an important niche in Negro painting. His prize canvases of *The Bible Student* and *The Old Servant* are permanent documents by reason of their double artistic and social significance, and it is much to be regretted that his talent expired just at the point of maturity and recognition. The work of four women sculptors, Meta Warrick Fuller, May Howard Jackson, Elizabeth Prophet, and Augusta Savage, despite individual variation in competence and style, would all fall in the conservative category, with a common attitude of heavily idealized and sentimentalized portrayal of racial types and character.

It is this saccharine, romantic quality that has given the younger modernists their foil; they aim at hard realism and verge at times on the grotesque and the

Mother and Daughter by Laura Wheeler Waring.

satirical. The *Old Snuff-Dipper* of Archibald Motley, or the *Self-Portrait* of Lillian Dorsey, or *Meditation* of Malvin Gray Johnson shows these new notes boldly and unmistakably. In this attitude, they have reinforcement from their young modernist contemporaries, but it represents a peculiar psychological reaction and achievement when a persecuted group breaks through the vicious circle of self-pity or compensatory idealization and achieves objectivity. Apart from the artistic merit of the work—which is considerable—the social significance of the recent canvases of William H. Johnson tells an interesting story. Born in Florence, South Carolina, this dock-working night-school student of the National Academy of Design, protegé of Charles Hawthorne and George Luks, disciple of French ultra-modernism with strong influences of Rouault and Soutine, came back from four years in Europe to paint in his home town. The result is a series of landscapes and portrait studies that reek with irony and satire and that probably will not get local appreciation till long after he has put his birthplace on the artistic map. His ironic picture of the town hotel paints the decadence of the old régime, and his quizzical portrait study of *Sonny*, a Negro lad with all the dilemma of the South written in his features, is a thing to ponder over, if one believes that art has anything important to say about life.

The other two modernists of note and promise are Hale Woodruff, of Indianapolis, now painting in France; and James Lesesne Wells, of New York, this year's Harmon award winner. Mr. Woodruff paints landscapes of originality, and his color has a warm beauty that, in spite of abstract formalism, seems characteristically racial. Mr. Wells, on the other hand, has a pronounced mystical lean, which makes his ultra-modern style all the more unusual and attractive. Some of his work has recently been acquired by the Phillips Memorial Gallery, and in terms of accomplishment and promise, Mr. Wells must be rated as one of the most promising of the younger Negro artists.

His work in design and decorative black-and-white media is strong and original. But, as a black-and-white artist, Mr. Wells is a conscious "Africanist." That is, he goes directly to African motives and principles of design for his inspiration. Another of the younger decorative painters, Aaron Douglas, does also; in fact, he has been doing so since 1925 and therefore deserves to be called the pioneer of the African Style among the American Negro artists. His book illustrations have really set a vogue for this style,* and his mural decorations for Club Ebony, New York, the Sherman Hotel, Chicago, and the symbolic murals of the Fisk University Library are things of fine originality. It is in sculpture, though, that the neo-primitivism of an attempted Negro style has to date most clearly expressed itself; in fact it is my opinion that sculp-

ture will lead the way in this direction. So the work of our two younger sculptors, Richmond Barthé and Sargent Johnson, takes on more than individual significance. Both are consciously racial, with no tendency to sentimentalize or over-idealize, and their style emphasizes the primitive. Barthé's *West Indian Girl* has a proud, barbaric beauty that matches Claude McKay's glorification of the primitive in the lines:

"To me she seemed a proudly swaying palm
Grown lovelier for passing through a storm."

Sargent Johnson's bust *Chester* is particularly striking; it has the qualities of the African antique and recalls an old Baoulé mask. It is a long stretch from an isolated Negro sculptor living and working in California to the classic antiques of bygone Africa, but here it is in this captivating, naïve bust for even the untutored eye to see.

Single instances do not make a style, nor can propaganda re-create lost folk-arts, but it is significant that directly in proportion as the younger Negro talent leaves the academic and imitative vein, it becomes stronger; and that the more particularistic and racial it becomes, the wider and more spontaneous is its appeal. And so, the immediate future seems to be with the racialists, both by virtue of their talent and their creed.

However, a truly representative racial style and school of art are as yet only in the making. Reviewing a recent exhibit of the work of Negro artists, Cyril Kay Scott comments on its imitative and derivative character, saying "it is almost purely Parisian and New York art done by Negroes, with almost nothing of the simplicity and directness of folk-art, and little assimilation or use of the African primitive art, which has so profoundly affected the great European modernists." Mr. Scott is right in wishing that some American Negro artists would delve "into the marvelous and beautiful background which is their racial heritage." He is very probably right in thinking that should they do so, "they could make to their age a contribution that would be unique" and which would "surpass the enthusiastic and conscientious efforts of even the great men of our time who have made such splendid use of the inspiration of Negro art."

*See Drama section, pages 83–84 [Editor's note].

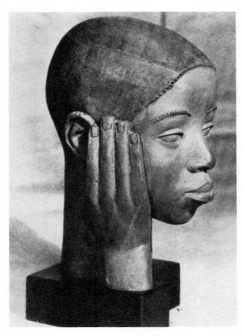

Chester by Sargent Johnson.

Mask of Boy by Richmond Barthé. Courtesy of Mr. Richmond Barthé.

The Breakaway by Richmond Barthé.

West Indian Girl by Richmond Barthé.

But this provocative criticism by the Director of the Denver Museum of Art overlooks one explanatory and extenuating fact: the young American Negro artist must evolve a racial style gradually and naturally. A sophisticated or forced exoticism would be as ridiculous at the one extreme as the all too-prevalent servile imitation is at the other. Moreover, most American Negro artists have not yet been exposed to the influence of African art. Their European contemporaries have been, and likewise the European-trained American artist. As recently as 1927, the first attempt was made to bring the Negro artist and the lay public in direct contact with African art. After an exhibition of the Blondiau-Theatre-Arts Collection of sculpture and metal work from the Belgian Congo, part of this collection was purchased as the permanent and traveling collection of the Harlem Museum of African Art, organized at that time, and has since been housed in the exhibition rooms of the One Hundred and Thirty-Fifth Street Branch of the New York Public Library. The project was organized to preserve and interpret the ancestral arts and crafts of the African Negro, and to make them effective as fresh inspiration for Negro art expression and culture in America. Though yet so recent and meagre a contact, the work of several contemporary Negro artists has begun to reflect African influences. There are marked traces in the motives and design structure of the work of Aaron Douglas; reflected idioms—through European exposure—in the work · of William H. Johnson and Hale Woodruff; and definite suggestions, as we have already noticed in the sculptures of Richmond Barthé and Sargent Johnson.

These are good omens for the development of a distinctively racial school of American Negro art. Naturally not all of our artists will confine their talents to race subjects or even to a racial style. However, the constructive lessons of African art are among the soundest and most needed of art creeds today. They offset with equal force the banalities of sterile, imitative classicism and the empty superficialities of literal realism. They emphasize intellectually significant form, abstract design, formal simplicity, restrained dignity, and the unsentimental approach to the emotions. And more important still, since Africa's art creed is beauty in use, they call for an art vitally rooted in the crafts, uncontaminated with the blight of the machine, and soundly integrated with life.

Surely we should expect the liberating example of such an aesthetic to exert as marked an influence on the work of the contemporary Negro artist as it has already exerted on leading modernists like Picasso, Modigliani, Matisse, Epstein, Lipschitz, Brancusi, and others. Indeed we may expect even more with a group of artists becoming conscious of an historical and racial bond between themselves and African art. For them, rather than just a liberating idiom or an exotic fad, African art should act with all the force of a rediscovered folk-art, and give clues for the repression* of a half-submerged race soul. The younger generation seem to have accepted this challenge to recapture this heritage of creative originality and this former mastery of plastic form and decorative design and are attempting to carry them to distinctive new achievement in a vital and racially expressive art. One of the advances evident in a comparison of the five successful annual shows of the works of Negro artists, sponsored by the Harmon Foundation, along with marked improvement in the average technical quality, has been the steadily increasing emphasis upon racial themes and types in the work submitted. Thus the best available gauge records not only a new vitality and maturity among American Negro artists, but a pronounced trend toward racialism in both style and subject. In this downfall of classic models and Caucasian idols, one may see the passing of the childhood period of American Negro art, and with the growing maturity of the young Negro artist, the advent of a representatively racial school of expression, and an important new contribution, therefore, to the whole body of American art.

*[sic] reexpression [Editor's note].

FOREWORD

ART in a democracy should above all else be democratic, which is to say that it must be truly representative. Step by step, happily sometimes by strides, we are approaching such democracy in American art. We are achieving this desirable goal partly through the broadening of public interest and participation in art, partly through a progressive policy changing the role of the museum from that of a treasure storehouse of the past to that of a clearing house for the contemporary artist; in part also because under the public patronage of the museum and the government more segments of American life are apt to find expression than under the more traditional interests of a private patron class. But most of all, I think, we have the promising prospects of a more democratic and representative art because of our now generally accepted objective to have American art fully document American life and experience, and thus more adequately reflect America.

In this frame of reference an exhibit of the work of contemporary Negro artists takes on a challenging interest. Primarily it may serve to acquaint the general public with what the Negro artist is doing, but more fundamentally it serves as a declaration of principles as to what art should and must be in a democracy and as a gauge of how far in this particular province we have gone and may need to go in the direction of representative native art. As in present-day music, literature and drama, the Negro theme and its development are part and parcel of the movement toward the use of native materials and subject matter.

This fortunately is common ground for both the Negro and the white artist. Indeed from Homer, Wayman Adams, Henri and Bellows of the older generation to James Chapin, Thomas Benton, John Steuart Curry, Reginald Marsh, Samuel Archer, Anne Gold-

Contemporary Negro Art. The Baltimore Museum of Art. Exhibition of February 3–19, 1939, and accompanying catalogue.

thwaite, Julius Bloch—to mention just a notable few of the present generation—the white artist has seized on the Negro subject as a fresh and fascinating province of native materials. Some of them have even pursued the theme beyond the mere portrayal of Negro types to the still more significant interpretation of the social and cultural aspects of Negro life. Only one strand of this is well known as yet, the inevitably popular and often too superficial treatment of the jazz theme, documenting the significant role the Negro has played through song, dance and music as one of the main sources of the American joy of life. But the less-known work of men like Bloch, Cadmus, Orozco, Riviera reveals a school of more serious social interpretation, with challenging renditions of the more sober and somber themes involved in Negro life—religion, labor, lynching, unemployment, and other human or social document subjects.

With legitimately high expectation and consequently some impatience we await the slowly maturing expression of the Negro artist in this province; for first of all perhaps we expect from the Negro artist a vigorous and intimate documentation of Negro life itself. There are reasons, however, why this which seems logically first may actually come last. The Negro artist, doubly sensitive as artist and as oppressed personality, has often shied off from his richest pasture at the slightest suspicion of a Ghetto gate. There can be no question in this freest of all human realms—art—of imposing upon the Negro artist a special, prescribed or limited field: this exhibition, if it shows nothing else, will show how naturally and effectively the Negro artist can range through all the media, provinces and various styles of a common human art. Yet after pardonable and often profitable wanderings afield for experience and freedom's sake, the Negro artist, like all good artists, must and will eventually come home to materials he sees most and understands best. Archibald Motley's provocative and half-Rabelaisian versions of Negro city types and scenes and Malvin Gray Johnson's sympathetic and vibrant pictures of Virginia rural types are cases in point, proving the sanity of coming back and the soundness of doing so with maturity and wide experience as a background. The younger generation seems fortunately to have less of this after-effect of proscription; it plunges naively into the portrayal of Negro life and seems to catch its idioms more characteristically and with less sophistication. Even so, many Negro artists will choose, according to taste and temperament, to concentrate in abstract art, or craft art, on still life, formal composition, marine and landscape painting as the case may be—and have a perfect right to. Few, however, will neglect to contribute their mite to the field of race interpretation, if only by succumbing to that age-old temptation of artists, the self-portrait.

There is a less direct way of revealing race, as also of what we call nationality, in the subtler elements of rhythm, color and atmosphere. Many will anxiously scan this and other group exhibits of the work of Negro artists for clues as to just what characteristic things are cropping out. But to date, they are not too obvious, and who can say just what they will be? We must remember how long it was before American art itself began to exhibit characteristic and distinctive national traits. Then, too, under no condition need we expect the work of the Negro artist to be too different from that of his fellow artists. Product of the same social and cultural soil, it will necessarily be basically American and typically contemporary. This exhibition surely bears that out. If we are looking, therefore, for racial idioms apart from the more obvious ones of subject matter, we must look—or rather listen—for overtones, and that with not too many preconceptions.

Although the Negro artist has been having his occasional say for many generations, sometimes notably, Negro art in the group sense is a comparatively recent development. It dates only from the World War, and a decade later became an important branch of the so-called "New Negro" movement for cultural and racial self-expression. Between 1928 and 1933, five successful shows of the work of Negro artists under the auspices of the Harmon Foundation helped focus public and professional attention on both the need and the accomplishment of Negro artists and gave an impetus through which Negro art has developed a momentum of its own. One-man shows of individual artists, more general participation with other artist groups, a spurt of interest particularly in sculpture, the graphic and the craft arts quickly followed, and finally came significantly the formation of Negro artist groups like The Harlem Artists Guild. Then, in a crisis that would have snuffed out these gains, came the helpful influence of the Federal Art Project, not only underwriting the precarious productivity of the Negro artist but broadening considerably the base of popular art appreciation and use. Recently in strategic places in the South, the same auspices have sponsored public art centers which may serve not only to carry art to the people but to carry the artist, too long isolated from the folk, back to a vital source of his materials. It may be impossible under modern American conditions to revive folk art effectively, but surely a people's art is possible. In this drive toward democracy in art, the Negro artist and the Negro people have an unusual stake, for the very term "Negro art" implies in addition to a blossoming of Negro artists the flowering of an art of folk expression and interpretation.

By good fortune, besides the influence of this modern trend, Negro art has the example of an ancient tradition and legacy—African art. Already as we know, African art has exerted great influence on modern art, being one of the fountain-heads of contemporary modernist style. But the indirect inoculation of African abstraction and simplification may lead, and in some cases has actually led, to slavish imitation and sterile sophistication. But African art, directly approached and sincerely studied, has lessons to teach of precisely opposite effect—lessons of vigorous simplicity and vitality. To mention merely a basic few: on the cultural side. the lesson of art for use, of art for popular appreciation and consumption, of art with a sound rootage in its own cultural soil; on the technical side, the lesson of originality itself, of close adaptation of the medium to the subject, and of subordination of technique to the artistic idea. Surely these are worth-while principles for any group of artists, but doubly so for those who can claim it as a direct legacy of tradition.

So, creditable as is the present attainment of a generation that has given us such painters, sculptors and graphic artists as are represented in this first Baltimore showing of Negro artists, the main significance seems to be the promising prospects indicated for the future development of Negro art. Demonstration of this and of the complete compatibility between the interests of contemporary Negro and contemporary American art is a public service of which any museum can be proud, but of which, none the less, I am sure, both the community and the artists themselves will be deeply appreciative.

The Mother by Richmond Barthé. Courtesy of Mr. Richmond Barthé. Photo by Simco Custom Photo Lab, Los Angeles, Cal.

ADVANCE ON THE ART FRONT

THE recent advances in contemporary Negro art remind me of nothing so much as a courageous cavalry move over difficult ground in the face of obstacles worse than powder and shell—silence and uncertainty. I have only read one book on military strategy, and remember only one or two sentences. But these happen to be appropriate. One said: "It's not the ground you gain but the ground you can hold that counts;" the other: "Even retreat, organized, is safer than disorganized advance." So, sobering though it may be, before we lose our heads and handkerchiefs in hysterical hurrahs for the brave lads who press forward, let us look at the cold strategy of our art situation and ask a few pertinent questions.

After all, we cannot win on the art front with just a thin advance line of pioneering talent or even the occasional sharp salient of genius; we must have behind this talent and this genius the backing of solid infantry and artillery support and the essential life lines of supply and communication. In short, we must have for the most effective use of our art proper public appreciation, adequate financial support, competent and impersonal criticism, and social and cultural representativeness. We must first of all support our artists, or our art will fail—fail outright or what is quite as bad, fail to represent us. We must consolidate our art gains or their accumulative effect will be lost as mere individual and "exceptional" achieve-

Opportunity 17 (May 1939): 132–136.

ment. Finally, we must capitalize our art, for it is, after all, as the most persuasive and incontrovertible type of group propaganda, our best cultural line of defense.

Surely after the recent Marian Anderson case, this is self-evident. But why should we wait upon a mis-maneuver of the enemy or hang precariously on a fumble of the opposition? The essence of strategy is planned action and the tactics of internally organized resources. As illustration, imagine the educative public effect of a permanently organized traveling exhibit of the work of contemporary Negro artists. Or visualize the social dividends on such a representative collection as part of the Golden Gate Exposition or of the New York World's Fair. I heard the subject debated for months pro and con, and in the end, I believe, positive action was impaled on the horns of the usual dilemma. That old dilemma of the persecuted which the successful always dare to ignore! Imagine confronting a Polish artist with the alternative of a national *or* an international showing; if he had as few as two pictures the answer would be "one in each." At the World's Fair practically every nation is reenforcing its share in the international showing with special national collections under its own auspices; and the Union of South Africa, including as a prominent part of its art exhibit the rockdrawings of the prehistoric Hottentots and Bushmen, makes it seem as though consistency was the enforced virtue of the disinherited.

So while we rejoice over a few well-earned inclusions of the works of some of our younger artists in the exhibit of contemporary American art at the Fair, let us frankly lament and take the blame for the lack of a representative unit collection of the best work of contemporary Negro artists. And while we glow over the increasing number of one-man shows by Negro painters and sculptors, let us regret that thus far no comprehensive and representative permanent collection of the work of Negro artists exists.

Too, I have heard Negro artists and critics in some strange befuddlement question the relevance of African art to our cultural tradition. Try to buy, beg, borrow or steal that prehistoric African art from the state collections of the Union of South Africa! Question, if you must quibble on something, the relevance of the African art in the imperial museums and colonial expositions the world over or the often concealed transfusion of African style in contemporary modernist art. Art belongs where it is claimed most or where it functions best.

Bohemian art was in strange and sad succession Bohemian, German, Polish, Austrian, Czecho-Slovakian and now, I daresay will become "German" all over again. Art doesn't die of labels, but only of neglect—for nobody's art is nobody's business.

Negro art is and should be primarily our business, and deserves to be our glory to the extent that it has been our concern. Happily enough, as in the art of Miss Anderson, the more deeply representative it is racially, the broader and more universal it is in appeal and scope, there being for truly great art no essential conflict between racial or national traits and universal human values.

Within the field we are reviewing two illustrations will clinch this point. The intuitive genius of a New York lad, using the Haitian historical materials of the Schomburg Collection in the 135th Street Branch Library, reinterprets in forty-one modernistic tempera panels the life of Toussaint L'Ouverture and the whole course of the Haitian Revolution. It would be hard to decide which cause owed the greater debt to Jacob Lawrence's talents, Haitian national history, Negro historical pride, expressionism as an appropriate idiom for interpreting tropical atmosphere and peasant action and emotion, or contemporary Negro art. As a matter of fact, all scored simultaneously when this brilliant series of sketches was exhibited in a special gallery at the Baltimore Museum of Art's recent showing of Negro artists.

Or again, let us take the *Mother and Son* group exhibited for the first time in the recent one-man show of Richmond Barthé's sculptures at the Arden Gallery in New York, and now to be shown at the World's Fair. Here is a subject racial to the core—a Negro peasant woman kneeling and mournfully cradling in her arms the limp, broken-necked body of her lynched son. But striking enough to be more potent antilynching propaganda than an armful of pamphlets, this statue group is properly, as a work of

Self-Portrait by Malvin Gray Johnson. Courtesy of National Museum of American Art (formerly the National Collection of Fine Arts), Smithsonian Institution, Washington, D.C. Gift of the Harmon Foundation.

the reenforcements of voluntary and sacrificial outside support, such as that of the Harlem Citizen's Sponsors Committee that guarantees rental and materials for the Harlem Community Art Center, or that admirable initiative of the Baltimore Negro Citizens' Art Committee that was back of the Baltimore Municipal Museum of Art's exhibit of *Contemporary Negro Art*, or that pioneer offer of Le Moyne College of quarters for the Federal Art Gallery in Memphis, or the creditable commission of the Armistad murals for the new Savery Library Building of Talladega College. These things, let us hope, are the beginnings of a movement for the popular support of the Negro artist who is beginning to take his place as one of the forceful factors in our cultural advance.

On the artists' part, there have been signs of remarkable activity. In Boston one-man shows of the work of Allan Crite and of Lois Jones have been held recently; in Philadelphia, at the A.C.A. Galleries, Sam Brown exhibited a striking series of water colors—most

art, universalized, and would move with pity a spectator who had never heard of lynching or an art critic merely interested in the problems of sculptural form and tradition that have come down to us from the days of classic sculpture.

What should concern us primarily, then, is how to encourage and support our artists, assuring them that artistic freedom which is their right, but buttressing their creative effort with serious social and cultural appreciation and use so that their powerful influence is widely felt.

As for the present, if it had not been for the Federal Art Project and its direct and indirect support, almost all of our art gains would have been snuffed out in the last few years. More power to this project, but in addition, we need

A Seated Figure, carved in wood by Ronald Moody. Photo by Simco Custom Photo Lab, Los Angeles, Cal.

of them from Nassau, the Bahamas—in a joint show with Hen Jones, who exhibited a new series of oil landscapes and figure studies in a successful modernistic change of style. The same gallery later had an exhibit of the black and whites and lithographs of one of our most skillful technicians in these media, Dox Thrash. In New York, the Labor Club recently held a stimulating exhibit of the work of younger Negro artists, and at the Harlem Art Center under the enterprising direction of Gwendolyn Bennett a whole series of exhibitions has been held, culminating in interest, from our point of view, in the third annual group exhibit of the Harlem Artists Guild. Here in this group we have probably the nucleus of the younger Negro art movement, for in rapid sequence it has brought forward the talents of promising young artists like Georgette Seabrook, Norman Lewis, Sara Murrell, Ernest Crichlow, Vertis Hayes, William Blackburn, Ronald Joseph and Jacob Lawrence.

The New York season has also seen one-man showings of the work of William H. Johnson at the Artists Gallery and of Aaron Douglas at the A.C.A. Gallery. Each of these somewhat older artists has modified his earlier style, Mr. Johnson by moving somewhat extremely to the artistic left of disorganized expressionism and Mr. Douglas by a retreat from his bold earlier style to mild local color impressionism, which though technically competent, gives little distinctively new or forceful either in his Negro type studies or his series of Haitian landscapes.

Then on the general front there have come credible inclusions for Sam Brown and Lois Jones in the Philadelphia Academy Water Color Show, for Florence Purviance, Allan Crite and Lois Jones in the *Corcoran Clarke Biennial*, and for Hale Woodruff and several others in the World's Fair *Contemporary American Show*. Miss Savage's much publicized commission statue, "*Lift Every Voice and Sing*," has back of it a magnificently dramatic idea, and if its execution carries through the force of the conception it will be a notable exhibit and noteworthy representation in a situation which, as we have previously said, the Negro artist and Negro art as such have pitifully inadequate representation.

But certainly the outstanding artistic events of the season thus far have been the Baltimore Museum of Art's well-chosen and brilliantly arranged show and the equally well arranged and unusually comprehensive one-man sculpture show of the work of Richmond Barthé.

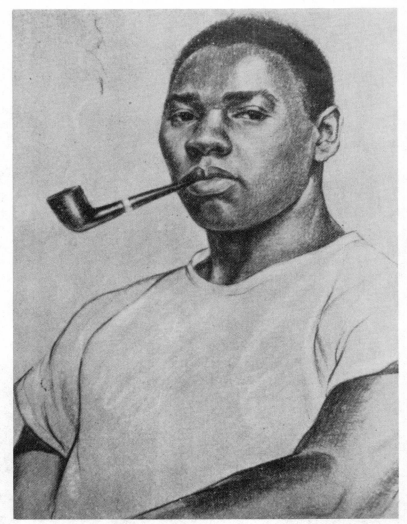

Self-Portrait by Elton Clay Fax. Courtesy of Mr. Elton Clay Fax.

Barthé, by his industrious application, has developed a seasoned technical proficiency: thirty-seven subjects in five media ranging from portrait commission busts to heroic figure compositions like *Mother and Son* and the forty-foot bas reliefs of *Exodus* and *Dance* for the Harlem River Housing Project attest to original talent and steadily maturing artistic stature. Critics, both conservative and modernistic, agreed in their praise because of undeniable proficiency and versatility. This adaptation of style to subject is Barthé's forte. Always seeking for a basic and characteristic rhythm and for a pose with a sense of suspended motion, there is an almost uncanny emphasis, even in his heads, of a symbolic type of line, like the sinuous patterned curves of the Kreutzberg figure, the sensuous ecstatic posture of *The*

African Dancer, the sagging bulbous bulk of *The Stevedore,* the medieval medallion-like faces and figures of the *Green Pastures Exodus* scene, or the lilting lift of Benga, the sophisticated African dancer. Carl Van Vechten is right in his statement that Barthé is actually seeking "the spiritual values inherent in moving figures." This sensitiveness to moods and temperaments makes Barthé an excellent character portraitist, as his portrait busts of John Gielgud, Maurice Evans, Kreutzberg, Jimmie Daniels, and Rose Mc-Clendon show unmistakably. However, it is as a figure sculptor of racial types that his talent, released from surface realism, expresses itself most capably and with greater promise of making a unique contribution to Negro art.

The Baltimore Museum show was in many respects the Negro art event of the year. In the first place, it represented the first regular showing of Negro art in a Southern municipal museum, in which several factors played a role of progressive collaboration: the timely initiative of the Baltimore Negro Citizens' Art Committee under the chairmanship of Mrs. Sarah C. Fernandis, the new liberal policy of the Museum management under the leadership of Mr. Henry Triede, the cooperation of The Harmon Foundation, the pioneer organization in the exhibition of the work of Negro artists; and the selective taste of the Museum's acting director, Mr. R. C. Rogers. As a combined result, there ensued a selective showing of the advance front of Negro art with a decided emphasis on modernism in style and technical maturity. Black and white, oils and sculpture were well-represented, with the emphasis on the graphic media. Among the sculptors, Sargent Johnson, Barthé and Henry Bannarn were well represented, together with the first American showing of a strong newcomer, the Jamaican-born modernist sculptor, Ronald Moody. Moody's work, even though influenced by cosmopolitan expressionism, has a healthy primitivism about it, especially in figures like *Une tete* and *Midonz,* which makes him a welcome adjunct to the growing group of representative Negro sculptors. His talent would undoubtedly benefit from closer contact with racial types, either West Indian or American.

In painting we have already mentioned the sensational series of Jacob Lawrence's Haitian tempera sketches, which attracted favorably both lay and professional attention. Archibald Motley was well represented by a competent series in his later style, Elton Clay Fax had a strong self-portrait and three competent oils, *Coal Hoppers, Steel Worker* and *Lunchtime;*

Palmer Hayden had two vigorously naive racial interpretations, *Midsummer Night in Harlem* and *The Janitor Who Paints;* and Sam Brown, several abstractionist water colors of clever conception and deft execution.

But the chief attraction in the oils section was a most carefully selected group of the work of the late Malvin Gray Johnson that was an object lesson in direct and sincere approach and convincing evidence of what contemporary Negro art lost in the premature death of this young genius. Whether Virginia landscapes or rural Negro types or rural labor themes, all of Gray Johnson's pictures in oil and water color were done with sincerity and power, hinting at that decline among our artists of both imitativeness and derivative exhibitionism which is the main hope for the future of the younger generation

Blanche by Richmond Barthé, and Mr. Barthé. Photo by Simco Custom Photo Lab, Los Angeles, Cal.

of Negro artists. Miss Florence Purviance, a Baltimore artist, made a creditable debut, and in the black and white section James Lesesne Wells, Hale Woodruff, Dox Thrash, Robert Blackburn and most especially Wilmer Jennings gave evidence of maturing powers of technical execution and conceptual grasp. With a request invitation for this show from the Dallas, Texas, Museum, we may justifiably say that Negro art has inaugurated a new phase of public influence and service.

UP TILL NOW

A representative over-view of the work of the contemporary Negro artist, such as this exhibition opportunely offers, achieves, like the proverbial "two birds with one stone," two objectives with a single effort. It documents, in the first place, the quite considerable contribution which the younger Negro is making to contemporary American art. But it also demonstrates, both in its competence and originality as well as by its wide diversity of style, the happy and almost complete integration of the Negro artist with the trends, styles, and standards of present-day American art. The *Albany Institute of History and Art* is to be congratulated upon having assembled, without benefit of special appeal or double standard of values, what is at one and the same time a representative and challenging cross-section of contemporary American art and, additionally, convincing evidence of the Negro's maturing racial and cultural self-expression in painting and sculpture.

Such achievement represents, naturally, a long and arduous struggle against cultural as well economic odds. This has required generations, and a brief panoramic background of the history of the Negro as an artist in this country is necessary for proper perspective and appreciation of the present. Few persons are today aware of how early and noteworthy the pioneer instances are which vindicated the right of the Negro to be an artist. Though not represented in this exhibition, these instances must be cited both for their individual attainment and for their precedent-breaking cultural effect. Naturally, however, much of this early art of Negroes began as did our own colonial art in imitative and derivative European styles. Joshua Johnston (c. 1770-1830) of Baltimore was a practising portraitist of considerable skill and note in the accepted style of his day; so much so that several of his paintings were for years attributed to Rembrandt Peale. Edmonia Lewis (1845-1890) of Boston, pioneer Negro woman sculptor, a protegé of the Storey family, studied and practised her art in Rome, winning prizes at home and abroad for her competent but not overly original neo-classical figures and figure groups. Wm. Bannister* (1828-1901) was a leading and accepted member of the Providence, R. I., art group and a landscapist and marine painter of considerable ability. With even greater talent and success, Robert Duncanson (1821-1871) was similarly an accepted member of the Cincinnati art group in the late 60's and 70's. After study in Edinburg and outstanding success in London art circles, he returned before his death to Cincinnati, there to execute commission portraits and murals for the leading art patrons of that vicinity.

*[sic] Edward M. Bannister [Editor's note].

The Negro Artist Comes of Age: A National Survey of Contemporary American Artists. Albany Institute of History and Art. Exhibition of January 3–February 11, 1945, and accompanying catalogue.

But obviously such exceptional developments by no means established the Negro either as a generally accepted or an integrated artist. Even the next stage of development achieved but one of these desirable goals; and that at the sacrifice of the other. As in so many other artistic fields, owing to the obstacles and discounts of prejudice, the Negro artist was forced to bid first for foreign opportunity and recognition. At that time also, American art generally, by way of outgrowing its early provincialism, was cosmopolitan in focus and outlook. Partly by way of sharing this Parisian orientation, and partly to avoid the handicaps of race, the next generation of Negro artists were divorced both from their own racial backgrounds as well as from the American scene. This went so far with some as an unfortunate but understandable avoidance of racial subject-matter for fear of being insiduously labelled. The outstanding Negro artists of this period accordingly contributed little either to the development of Negro expression in art or to the development of native American art. But they did contribute importantly to the single-standard acceptance of the Negro as artist, first in international recognition and later by national acceptance. This, in addition to their individual contribution, was the significant accomplishment of such outstanding artists as Meta Warrick Fuller, pupil of Rodin in sculpture, and Henry O. Tanner (1859-1937), the internationally-known painter. They and a few lesser lights like Wm. Harper, Wm. E. Scott, May Howard Jackson, demonstrated complete assimiliation of the best academic tradition and style, and beyond that, with Tanner and Mrs. Fuller, creative power and originality.

Trends around 1910, some arising from the external pressures of American realism and others from internal urges for racial self-expression, raised sentimentally at first the basic issue of racial representation in and through art. For a while it divided our artists into two camps of thought, even threatening some with split artistic personalities as they oscillated between the urge to be "racial" and the desire to be "universal" in their art. Not all the landscape, marine and still-life painting of this transitional period was pure preoccupation with form, color and technical problems. Some was escapist, avoiding this ever-recurring issue. Finally in the mid-Twenties the combined weight of realism, Americanism and cultural racialism won dominance and we experienced our first group-conscious school of "Negro art." A few traditionalists as May Howard Jackson, Archibald Motley, Laura Wheeler Waring, yielded to the trend while pioneering talents as Aaron Douglas, Sargent Johnson, Richmond Barthe, Palmer Hayden, Wm. H. Johnson and especially Hale Woodruff, Malvin Gray Johnson, broke through to the avowed acceptance of racial self-portraiture and self-expression as the primary goal of the Negro artist. The Negro artist thus found his place beside the poets and writers of the "New Negro" movement, which in the late Twenties and through the Thirties galvanized Negro talent to strong and freshly creative expression.

All during this critical period the Negro artist had helpful allies. First and foremost was the sustaining example of such non-Negro artists as Thomas Eakins, Robert Henri, George Luks, Henry Bellows, James Chapin, Julius Bloch and others who were raising the Negro subject from the level of trivial or sentimental genre to that of serious type study and socially sympathetic portrayal. Then, too, there was the considerable influence of successful self-expression by Negroes in the kindred arts during this period. Of particular importance and help also were the annual exhibits and prize awards of *The Harmon Foundation* between 1928 and 1935 for the work of Negro artists. Finally there was the culminating lift of the Federal Arts Projects, which greatly multiplied the art contacts and horizons of both this and a younger generation of artistically ambitious Negroes.

By this time fairly coherent groups of young Negro artists were flourishing not only in New York's Harlem, but in Chicago, Cleveland, Boston,

Philadelphia, Hampton, Atlanta. It is this crop, largely, whose work is the core of the present exhibition. Flanked by the figures already mentioned are such talents as Charles Alston, Wm. Artis, Romare Bearden, Henry Bannarn, Wm. Carter, Elizabeth Catlett, Ernest Crichlow, Eldzier Cortor, Fred Flemister, Rex Goreleigh, Jacob Lawrence, Norman Lewis, Edward Loper, Charles Sebree, Charles White, Ellis Wilson, James Lesesne Wells, — to call a partial but significant roll. These, with that exceptional older but modernistically abstract talent of Horace Pippin, constitute what can confidently be described as the Negro's contemporary contribution to American art. For it is a notable contribution both in content and in style.

Important as it is to gauge the extent to which the Negro group experience has ripened and flowered artistically, it is even more important to realize how proper and inevitable it is that this work be viewed and accepted as an integral and representative segment of our native American art. Indeed it runs the gamut of practically every well-known variety of modern art approach and style. It therefore has basic common denominators with the art of our time and has found fruitful fellowship with its fellow American artists. That is to be construed as a happy and necessary coming of age for the Negro artist.

But in spite of such wide divergence of style and art approach, there seem to be many subtle and significant common traits. Some reflect, no doubt, a natural commonality of time and place, — the authentic American flavor and touch. Other overtones suggest, however, common emotional factors of racial life and experience. Certainly among these, one can note to an unusual degree strength and virtuosity of color and rhythm and vivid originality of imagination. This work, too, is on the whole vigorous and vital even when sophisticated: (and a surprising amount of it will be found sophisticated by those who expected a predominant naiveté. Especially in view of the extreme youth of a number of these artists, most of them in their late twenties and early thirties and four under twenty-five, one can confidently anticipate from the young Negro artist in the near future as distinctive creative originality as many have conceded only to the race in music.

Further, the social message of the younger Negro artist is particularly noticeable and noteworthy. Whether treating his theme realistically or symbolically, the artist is obviously keenly alive and sensitive to social documentation and achieves forcefulness in expressing both social sympathy and social protest. These artists have this trait partly of course as products of the depression and latterly the war era, but one feels that they also have drawn on the emotional depths of their racial experience and derived therefrom unusual penetration of social understanding and insight.

Yet the thread of social documentation and commentary is but one strand in this art. There is just as evident a strong decorative interest in design, color and the technicalities of their art, with indications of more than average capacity to find strong and original solutions for the more technical aesthetic problems of painting and sculpture. But what I find most significant, especially in the canvasses of the youngest talents like those of Crichlow, Lawrence, Catlett, Norman Lewis, Charles White and John Wilson, is an ability to blend the somewhat conflicting approaches of a social message with the abstractly aesthetic into a balanced, mutually reenforcing synthesis. This, among others, is a development to be watched for its obvious future promise as these younger artists come to maturity; for exceptional power in these respects in the Negro artist could warrantably be regarded as likely and legitimate dividends from his racial inheritance of group experience.

Such warmly human but piercing social irony is an oft-repeated note in the work of Crichlow, Bearden, William Johnson, Norman Lewis, Charles White, Elizabeth Catlett and others. Particularly characteristic is it of Jacob Lawrence's fertile and powerful talent, more apparent in his *Harriet Tubman*, *John Brown*, *Negro Migration* and *Harlem* series even than in individual subjects. Horace Pippin, especially in his moving *John Brown* series, has the same in his own naively forceful way. There can be no doubt of the increasingly important place of the Negro artist in the social commentary vein that is becoming so characteristic of much recent American art. That with the Negro artist it is expressed with such broad human sympathy and controlled restraint is fortunate for its increased social effectiveness, apart even from its praiseworthy artistic propriety. With great temptation in that direction, the Negro artist is seldom the crude or even overt propagandist.

Much of this work, however, must be judged by absolute standards and abstract criteria; which is only to say again that today the Negro artist is in the first instance an artist and only incidentally Negro. More and more as the present integration spreads will this be the case, and more and more must it become also the general public approach and attitude. By stages, it seems, we are achieving greater democracy in art, — and let us hope, through art.

One phase of this growing democracy in American art has broken the limiting stereotypes through which we traditionally saw Negro life and the Negro. Another has freed the Negro artist alike from the limiting avoidance of Negro subject-matter and later led him to more objective and effective self-portrayal. Still another has brought forward the common denominators of a truly representative native American art, which logically has included the serious interpretation of the Negro elements in the national whole. This democratically shared interest has brought the Negro artist into closer rapport and collaboration with his fellow American artists.

Finally, as a combined result of the new attitude toward the Negro theme and subject and of the increasing maturity of the Negro artist the double standard of performance and judgment is fading out of the national art picture. In the last five years the number of practising Negro artists of accepted merit has about doubled. Their work is appearing increasingly in general exhibitions and recognized galleries, both in mixed and one-man showings: one of the leading New York galleries devoted especially to American art has by choice of its director. and the associated artists two Negro painters in its roster of twenty. The present exhibit, it is to be confidently expected, will have widespread enlightening influence. If the gains of the last five years are matched by the next five, by 1950 we shall have realized almost complete democracy in American art, which will be as significant and valuable an achievement for the national culture as for the Negro.

RETROSPECTIVE
REVIEWS

Although he was fired in 1925 with three other faculty members in a dispute with Howard's last white president, J. Stanley Durkee, Locke returned to full-time teaching of philosophy at Howard University in 1928. About the same time, Locke became dissatisfied with the recent work of several Harlem writers, whom he felt had distorted the socially useful purpose of the Negro Renaissance to profit from the "vogue of the Negro."[1]

When Elmer Carter, the new editor of *Opportunity*, asked Locke to begin a series of annual reviews of Negro literature, he seized on them as a forum in which to clarify the mission of Afro-American art.[2] Published yearly from 1929 to 1942 in *Opportunity* (except in 1930) and later in *Phylon* from 1946 to 1953, these reviews show Locke revising his opinions in the aftermath of the Negro Renaissance and making his most definitive statement as a critic. No longer confined to establishing the credibility of black efforts in any one art field, Locke took a more prescriptive view in these essays, utilizing his philosophical insight into underlying issues and trends in Afro-American life to plot the future course in the arts and the social sciences.

Even before the stock market crash in October 1929, Locke forecasts, in "1928: A Retrospective Review" (1929), the collapse of the "Negro fad." He predicts that "as with many another boom, the water will need to be squeezed out of much inflated stock and many bubbles must burst."

Welcome as a new phase in the movement may have been, the early years of the Depression were difficult for black writers, actors, and artists as publishing contracts, plays, and generous patrons became scarce. In "This Year of Grace" (1931), Locke notes the decline in creative output by blacks. He responds by allotting more comment to the social sciences in "We Turn to Prose" (1932), which praises *The Black Worker* by Sterling Spero and Abram Harris for marking the "beginning of the end of that hitherto endless succession of studies of the Negro *in vacuo*." In "Black Truth and Black Beauty" (1933), Locke follows his own advice by discussing "a score of books that cannot by any stretch be listed as "literature of the Negro."

This broadened Locke's scope as a critic, and allowed him to sit in judgment on the work of black and white authors. Some black writers, however, resented his new, more critical tone. Locke's comments in "The Saving Grace of Realism" (1934) prompted Jessie Fauset to write, "your criticims such as the one I've just read in *Opportunity* point most effectively to the adage that a critic is a self-acknowledged failure as a writer."[3]

Locke was beginning the process of shedding his skin as an apologist for the writers of the Renaissance, and becoming a leader of the more militant, politically charged art of the 1930s. In "The Eleventh Hour of Nordicism" (1935), he shifts his attention from purely cultural issues to the social and economic concerns raised in the literature. In "Deep River: Deeper Sea" (1936), he accepts "proletarian literature" as the next step in the dialectical advance of the Afro-American folk spirit. "God Save Reality!" (1937) repudiates the "wheedling gradualism" of Charles S. Johnson, while offering qualified praise for the class analysis of Abram Harris and Ralph Bunche, two young teachers at Howard University. These and subsequent reviews generally appeared in two installments in consecutive months. In this section (and one other essay in a previous section), they are published together with bibliographical references placed on the first page of each review.[4]

The radical polemics of the 1930s, however, challenged the integrity of older black intellectuals. In the next three essays, Locke responds to criticism of the movement and his leadership.

"Jingo, Counter-Jingo and Us" (1938) parries criticism leveled at the Negro history movement by Bernard Stolberg, a white labor journalist, whose article "Minority Jingo" appeared in the October 23, 1937, issue of *The Nation*. In his review of Benjamin Brawley's *Negro Builders and Heroes*, Stolberg charged that uncritical chronicling of black successes was little more than racial chauvinism, which undermined efforts to build working-class unity and industrial unionism in American life.

Some young black intellectuals claimed that contemporary movements had eclipsed Locke and his older "New Negro" philosophy. In "Blueprint for Negro Writing," Richard Wright argued that the black writer should speak for the black masses, and eschew serving as an "artistic Ambassador" to whites.[5] In "Freedom Through Art: A Review of Negro Art, 1870–1938" (1938), written for *The Crisis* issue honoring the 75th anniversary of the Emancipation Proclamation, Locke responded with his strongest statement of the political ideals of black art.

Later in 1938, John A. Davis, founder of The New Negro Alliance which picketed all-white stores in Washington, D.C., argued in "We Win the Right to Fight for Jobs" that Locke's strategy of improving race relations through art had failed.[6] Locke's "angry temper" shows in "The Negro: 'New' or Newer?" (1939), in which he quotes liberally from earlier writings to chastise these "bright young people."

Locke possessed the remarkable ability to crystallize current issues or debates into a pithy, provocative title, which then became his text for discussing the year's output in literature. "Dry Fields and Green Pastures" (1940) dramatizes the conflict between realism and romanticism in Afro-American literature. Locke defends Richard Wright's portrait of Bigger Thomas in "Of Native Sons: Real or Otherwise" (1941) by questioning why black authors find it difficult to reveal the inner workings of the black mind. In his last retrospective review for *Opportunity*, Locke characterizes the Afro-American tradition in the arts and social sciences as an on-going search for "Who and What is 'Negro'?" (1942).

After Elmer Carter left the editorship of *Opportunity* in 1942, Locke did not publish another "retrospective review" until he was asked to do a new series for *Phylon* by its editor, Ira De Reid. In "Reason and Race" (1947) and "A Critical Retrospect of the Literature of the Negro for 1947" (1948), Locke analyzes the postwar interest in integration. Black participation in World War II, African nations in the United Nations, and the Cold War rhetoric of America as the haven of democracy have made segregation inexpedient internationally for America. Locke hopes that the struggle for the rights of minorities at home and abroad will become the stuff of great literature.

He is gratified in "Dawn Patrol" (1949) by the excellent novels of 1948, especially Alan Paton's *Cry, The Beloved Country*, which symbolizes the growing international literature of race.

In "Wisdom *De Profundis*" (1950), Locke borrows the title of Oscar Wilde's swan song to dispense with the Harlem writers and to welcome a new wave of postwar poets. He also praises recent social scientists like E. Franklin Frazier and John Hope Franklin for taking over the mantle from older black scholars in sociology and history respectively.

"Inventory at Mid-Century" (1951) pays tribute to the special symposium issue of *Phylon* of December 1950, in which several younger critics assess the state of Afro-American literature. In "The High Price of Integration" (1952), Locke renews his argument that such literature will continue to prosper only if it attracts the best talent.

In his final retrospective review, "From *Native Son* to *Invisible Man*" (1953), Locke compares the impact of Ralph Ellison's *Invisible Man* to that of Jean Toomer's *Cane* and Richard Wright's *Native Son*.

These reviews bridged the gap between the decline of the Negro Renaissance in the early 1930s, and the resurgence of black art in the late 1930s and again in the early 1950s. They also crossed boundaries between disciplines in marked contrast to the highly specialized work of critics and scholars who succeeded him. Locke's life as philosopher, teacher, broker-patron, and journalist gave him the ability to temper elements from diverse fields into what became known as "black studies."

1928: A RETROSPECTIVE REVIEW

THE year 1928 represents probably the flood-tide of the present Negrophile movement. More books have been published about Negro life by both white and Negro authors than was the normal output of more than a decade in the past. More aspects of Negro life have been treated than were ever even dreamed of. The proportions show the typical curve of a major American fad, and to a certain extent, this indeed it is. We shall not fully realize it until the inevitable reaction comes; when as the popular interest flags, the movement will lose thousands of supporters who are now under its spell, but who tomorrow would be equally hypnotized by the next craze.

A retrospective view ought to give us some clue as to what to expect and how to interpret it. Criticism should at least forewarn us of what is likely to happen. In this, as with many another boom, the water will need to be squeezed out of much inflated stock and many bubbles must burst. However, those who are interested in the real Negro movement which can be discerned behind the fad, will be glad to see the fad subside. Only then will the truest critical appraisal be possible, as the opportunity comes to discriminate between shoddy and wool, fair - weather friends and true supporters, the stock-brokers and the real productive talents. The real significance and potential power of the Negro renaissance may not reveal itself until after this reaction, and the entire top-soil of contemporary Negro expression may need to be ploughed completely under for a second hardier and richer crop.

To my mind the movement for the vital expression of Negro life can only truly begin as the fad breaks off. There is inevitable distortion under the hectic interest and forcing of the present vogue for Negro idioms. An introspective calm, a spiritually poised approach, a deeply matured understanding are finally necessary. These may not, need not come entirely from the Negro artist; but no true and lasting expression of Negro life can come except from these more firmly established points of view. To get above ground, much forcing has had to be endured; to win a hearing, much exploitation has had to be tolerated. There is as much spiritual bondage in these things as there ever was material bondage in slavery. Certainly the Negro artist must point the way when this significant moment comes, and establish the values by which Negro literature and art are to be permanently gauged after the fluctuating experimentalism of the last few years. Much more could be said on this subject,—but I was requested to write a retrospective review of the outstanding literary and artistic events of 1928 in the field of Negro life.

Opportunity 7 (January 1929): 8–11.

The year has been notable particularly in the field of fiction,—a shift from the prevailing .emphasis in Negro expression upon poetry. In this field there were three really important events.—Claude McKay's *Home to Harlem*, Rudolph Fisher's *Walls of Jericho* and Julia Peterkin's *Scarlet Sister Mary*. An appraisal of the outstanding creative achievement in fiction a year ago would not have given us a majority on the Negro side. That in itself reflects a solid gain, gauged by the standard I have set, — for no movement can be a fad from the inside. Negro fiction may even temporarily lose ground in general interest, but under cover of the present vogue there has been nurtured an important new articulateness in Negro life more significant than mere creativeness in poetry. For creative fiction involves one additional factor of cultural maturity,—the art of social analysis and criticism. If *Home to Harlem* is significant, as it notably is, for descriptive art and its reflection of the vital rhythms of Negro life, *Walls of Jericho* is notable in this other important direction,—the art of social analysis. The ironic detachment of the one is almost as welcome as the emotional saturation of the other; they are in their sveral ways high-water marks in fiction for the Negro artist. Those who read *Home to Harlem* superficially will see only a more authentic "*Nigger Heaven*", posterity will see the peculiar and persistent quality of Negro peasant life transposed to the city and the modern mode, but still vibrant with a clean folkiness of the soil instead of the decadent muck of the city-gutter. Moreover *Home to Harlem* will stand as a challenging answer to a still too prevalent idea that the Negro can only be creatively spontaneous in music and poetry, just as Mr. Fisher's book must stand as the answer to the charge that the Negro artist is not yet ripe for social criticism or balanced in social perspective.

The scene of Harlem is of course more typical of modern Negro life than a South Carolina plantation, but the fact that the year has produced another novel from the South almost equal to *Porgy* is one of outstanding importance. *Scarlet Sister Mary*, by a veteran protagonist of the new school of Southern fiction, represents not only an acme of Mrs. Peterkin's art, but evidence that the new attitude of the literary South toward Negro life is firmly established. To be rooted deep enough for tragedy, layers beneath the usual shallowness and sentimentalism of the older Southern fiction, is of course an achievement for the literature of the South, apart even from the fact that this artistic growth has been achieved in the field of Negro fiction.

Indeed this new attitude of the white writer and artist toward Negro life has now become an accepted attitude, it registers more than the lip service of realism, for it is equally a tribute to the deeper human qualities of black humanity. Dr. Odum's *Rainbow Round My Shoulder* is another case in point. Paul Green's more recent plays and stories reinforce the same motive. Even *Black Sadie* by T. Bowyer Campbell, of the Far South, almost achieves the same respectful approach and the even-handedness of treatment which spells the banishment of propaganda from art.

Of course, it is the problem novel which is the acid test for propaganda. *Dark Princess*, marking the reappearance in fiction of the versatile Dr. DuBois, for all its valuable and competent social portraiture, does not successfully meet this test, but falls an artistic victim to its own propagandist ambushes. This novel by the veteran must on this account cede position in this field to the quite successful thrust of the novice, — Nella Larsen's *Quicksand*. This study of the cultural conflict of mixed ancestry is truly a social document of importance, and as well; a living, moving picture of a type not often in the foreground of Negro fiction, and here treated perhaps for the first time with adequacy. Indeed this whole side of the problem which was once handled exclusively as a grim tragedy of blood and fateful heredity now shows a tendency to shift to another plane of discussion, as the problem of divided social loyalties and the issues of the conflict of cultures. As one would expect, foreign fiction is showing us the way in this, just as it previously did with the "light ironic touch and the sympathetic charm" which is now so accepted an approach to the Negro peasant figure. In the discussion of this social tragedy type, Mrs. Millin has again touched it masterfully this year in *The Coming of the Lord*, it has been too melodramatically stated, though with evident seriousness in *White Nigger*, and rather competently handled by Esther Hyman in *Study in Bronze*.

Even in the literature of the comic approach, sterotypes no longer reign supreme. E. L. C. Adams' *Nigger to Nigger* actually documents the contemporary peasant Negro with real humanity and accuracy; and Roark Bradford's *Ol' Man Adam an' His Chillun* seriously tries to emulate *Uncle Remus*. One of the strange and not too reassuring features of the present situation is the comparative silence of the Negro writers in the field of humor and comic portrayal. There can never be adequate self-portrayal until some considerable section of our own literature rings to the echo with genuine and spontaneous Negro laughter.

After the extraordinary productiveness of the past years in poetry, the subsidence in this field has been inevitable and is wholesome. The gap has been filled in part by the industrious gleanings of the anthology makers; and in another more creative direction in the development of several important literary schools or coteries outside of the central pioneer group in New York. This movement, which I have elsewhere characterized as the spread of beauty to the provinces,* is one of the most potential effects of the Negro cultural revival. Notable instances have been the formation of a literary group in Boston which has sponsored the occasional publication of *The Quill*, the revival of the younger ultra-expressionist group who published *Fire* and who now are publishing *Harlem*, the continued activity of the Philadelphia group that is responsible for the publication of *Black Opals*, the revival of one of the earliest founded of all these producing artistic groups, the *Stylus* group at Howard University, Washington, and the crystalization of several writing dramatic and art groups in Chicago and Indianapolis. This movement of general response to the impulses from the metropolis, has been paralleled by a general quickening of interest in the study of Negro life by white groups over a very wide area, for which two progressive centers have been largely responsible.—Chicago, through the sponsoring of a campaign plan of introducing Negro art and cultural achievement to the general public by a "Negro Art Week" program; and the liberal group at the University of North Carolina, who have been so consistently and effectively pursuing a constructive and valuable program of research and publication with their studies of Negro life and culture, of which the total now is nearly a score of indispensible contributions. In this connection the second issue of *The Carolina Magazine*, devoted to Negro poetry, with the projected third issue on the Negro folk play, must be mentioned as showing a parallel interest and liberal tendency on the part of the younger Southern college generation.

In the field of drama, the Theatre Guild's presentation of *Porgy* has eclipsed everything else, and warrantably. The demonstration of the power and unique effects of Negro ensemble made by this play is a contribution of importance, over and above its intrinsic delightfulness. Broadway is more anxious for Negro plays than ever before; a little too anxious, therefore an unusual list of artistic and commercial failures due primarily to half-baked plays hurried through to exploit the present vogue. Meanwhile the typical musical revue type goes merrily and profitably on, with

*See "Beauty and the Provinces," in Renaissance Apologetics section [Editor's note].

just a crack or two in the banal stereotypes and several laudable attempts at Negro opera,—*Voodoo* and *Deep Harlem*. In the field of the amateur stage, where the hope of Negro drama still focuses, there has been a slight growth in the activity of Negro playing groups, with outstanding achievements centering this year in the work of the Karamu Theatre of the Gilpin Players, at Cleveland, Ohio, and the successful participation of the Dixwell Players in the Yale Theatre Tournament at New Haven. Paul Green has consolidated many of his unpublished or separately published plays in a volume *In the Valley and Other Carolina Plays*, which is almost another contribution to the Negro Theatre, by reason of the fact that a majority of these plays are of Negro subject-matter.

Sociological literature usually if not most technical is ephemeral: this year has exceptionally produced two books of profound interpretative value; Raymond L. Buell's two volume survey of the racial situations of colonial Africa, *The Native Problem in Africa*, and the volume just published on *The American Negro* as the special issue of The Annals of the American Academy of Political and Social Science. This last, for all its authoritativeness, actually succeeds in vitalizing and humanizing the large majority of its subject-matter, and therefore marks a new era in the official sociology of the race problem. A third event of prime importance in this field is the publication of the extensive classified *Bibliography of the Negro*, prepared by the Tuskegee Bureau of Records under the editorship of Monroe Work.

There has been unusual activity in the field of art, stimulated in part by the Harmon Awards in this field and the institution of an annual show of the work of Negro artists. Prior to this, special shows of the work of Negro artists had been inaugurated by the management of the Harlem Branch Public Library, and on a larger scale exhibits of Negro painting, sculpture and decorative art, including exhibits of African art have been held at the Chicago Art Institute, under the auspices of the Chicago Negro in Art Week Committee, at Fisk University, at Howard University, Hampton Institute, Rochester Memorial Gallery, San Diego,

California, and at the exhibit rooms of the new Harlem Museum of African Art in the Harlem Public Library. The increased output of the younger Negro artists is directly attributable to the fresh stimulus of these new channels of public interest and support. An individual fact of more than individual importance was Archibald Motley's one man show at the Ainslee Galleries, New York. Among white artists generally a new interest in Negro types has matured culminating in special exhibitions such as Winold Reiss's Penn Island series of Negro type studies, Captain Perfielieff's series of Haitian sketches, Erick Berry's North African types, Covarrubias's recent African series, Mrs. Laura Knight's studies, and Annette Rosenshine's sculpture studies; to mention only in passing such notable single things as Wayman Adams' *Foster Johnson*, James Chapin's *Negro Boxer* and Epstein's *Paul Robeson*. Indeed the reflection of another interest in the field of the fine arts than that of the casual genre study is one of the most recent and hopeful developments in the whole range of new trends.

I have reserved for brief final treatment what is in my judgment the most significant of all recent developments; the new interest in Negro origins. If there is anything that points to a permanent revaluation of the Negro, it is the thoroughgoing change of attitude which is getting established about Africa and things African. Africa has always been a subject of acute interest; but too largely of the circus variety. A sudden shift from the level of gross curiosity to that of intelligent human comprehension and sympathy is apparent in the current literature about Africa. In their several fields, recent publications like the translation of Blaise Cendrar's anthology of African folk-lore, *The African Saga*, Captain Canot's *Adventures of an African Slaver*, Mrs. Gollock's two informative books—*Lives of Eminent Africans* and *Sons of Africa*, Donald Fraser's *The New Africa* and Milton Staffer's symposium entitled *Thinking with Africa*, the publication of the new quarterly journal of the International Institute of African Languages and Culture called "Africa", and very notably, I think, J. W. Vandercook's *Black Majesty* represent in about the space of a year's time a revolutionary change not only in interest but in point of view and approach. Really this is not to be underestimated, because a revaluation of the Negro without an equivalent restatement of the Negro background could easily sag back to the old points of view. But with so thoroughgoing a transformation of opinion and an approach which implies cultural recognition to the Negro in his own intrinsic rights, no such reaction can reasonably occur; it will encounter the resistance of facts instead of the mere fluid tide of sentiment. Even when the reaction comes that was predicted at the outset of this article, there will be a vast net gain that can be counted upon as a new artistic and cultural foundation for a superstructure which it really is the privilege and task of another generation than ours to rear.

THIS YEAR OF GRACE:
Outstanding Books of the Year in Negro Literature

Fiction

Sweet Man—Gilmore Millen. The Viking Press.

Gulf Stream—Marie Stanley. Coward Mc Cann.

Ol' King David an' the Philistine Boys—Roark Bradford. Harper & Bros.

Black Genesis—Roark Bradford. Harper & Bros.

Not Without Laughter—Langston Hughes. Alfred Knopf, Inc.

Drama

The Green Pastures—Marc Connelly. Farrar & Rinehart.

Scarlet Sister Mary—Julia Peterkin. Bobbs Merrill Co.

Poetry and Belles Lettres

Saint Peter Relates an Incident of Resurrection Day—James Weldon Johnson. The Viking Press.

Shades and Shadows—Randolph Edmonds. Meador Publishing Co.

Black Manhattan—James Weldon Johnson. Alfred Knopf, Inc.

Music

The Green Pastures Spirituals—Hall Johnson. Farrar & Rinehart.

Tin Pan Alley—Isaac Golberg. John Day Co., Inc.

Biography

Aggrey of Africa—Edwin Smith. Richard R. Smith, Inc.

James Hardy Dillard—Benjamin Brawley. Fleming H. Revell Co.

School Acres—Rossa B. Cooley. Yale University Press.

Paul Robeson, Negro — Eslanda Goode Robeson. Harper & Bros.

Folk Lore

The Negro Sings a New Heaven—Mary Grissom. University of North Carolina Press.

Folk Culture on St. Helena's Island—Guy B. Johnson. University of North Carolina Press.

Folk-Say. A Regional Miscellany, 1930. B. A. Botkin. University of Oklahoma Press.

Hebrewisms of West Africa—Jos J. Williams. Lincoln Mac Veagh.

Social Discussion

The Negro Peasant Turns Cityward—Louise V. Kennedy. Columbia University.

The Rural Negro—Carter G. Woodson. The Associated Publishers.

The Negro Wage Earner—Lorenzo Greene and Carter G. Woodson. Associated Publishers.

Black Yeomanry—T. J. Woofter. University of North Carolina Press.

The Negro in American Civilization — Charles S. Johnson. Henry Holt.

The Black Worker—Sterling Spero and Abram Harris. Columbia University Press.

▼ ▼ ▼ ▼ ▼

SINCE it is 1930 that is under retrospective review, there is no need for that superstitious unction which made every year of our Lord a year of grace. The much exploited Negro renaissance was after all a product of the expansive period we are now willing to call the period of inflation and overproduction; perhaps there was much in it that was unsound, and perhaps our aesthetic gods are turning their backs only a little more gracefully than the gods of the market-place. Are we then, in a period of cultural depression, verging on spiritual bankruptcy? Has the afflatus of Negro self-expression died down? Are we outliving the Negro fad? Has the Negro creative artist wandered into the ambush of the pro-

Opportunity 9 (February 1931): 48–51.

fessional exploiters? By some signs and symptoms. Yes. But to anticipate my conclusion, —'Let us rejoice and be exceedingly glad.' The second and truly sound phase of the cultural development of the Negro in American literature and art cannot begin without a collapse of the boom, a change to more responsible and devoted leadership, a revision of basic values, and along with a penitential purgation of spirit, a wholesale expulsion of the money-changers from the temple of art.

I think the main fault of the movement thus far has been the lack of any deep realization of what was truly Negro, and what was merely superficially characteristic. It has been assumed that to be a Negro automatically put one in a position to know; and that any deviation on the part of a white writer from the trite stereotypes was a deeply revealing insight. Few indeed they are who know the folk-spirit whose claims they herald and proclaim. And with all the improvement of fact and attitude, the true Negro is yet to be discovered and the purest values of the Negro spirit yet to be refined out from the alloys of our present cultural currency. It is, therefore, significant that this year has witnessed a waning of creative expression and an increasing trend toward documentation of the Negro subject and objective analysis of the facts. But even after this has been done, there will remain the more difficult problem of spiritual interpretation, so that at last we shall know what we mean when we talk of the Negro folk-spirit, the true Negro character, the typical Negro spirit. At present we do not know, and at last 'it can be told.'

One of the symptoms of progress in the field of fiction is the complete eclipse of the propaganda novel, and the absence of formula and problem even in the novels of white Southern writers. A review of Gilmore Millen's *Sweet Man* says: "The book might have been written by a Negro, so accurate it seems in its details, so eager it seems in sympathy and understanding of the black people." Marie Stanley's *Gulf Stream*, the frank study of the cross-fires of the caste in an Alabama village, may lack the maturity of the best Southern fiction of its subject, but it outdoes them all in sensitive delineation. "You ask those poor blacks," says Berzelia to the Catholic priest, "to worship a simpering white woman with a rosy child in her arms; No, Father, its against reason, and they've got the right idea! We are done with your white God, they say, give us a God of our own who will understand us, who is black like ourselves! But all the same, they hadn't

the courage or the pride or what not to go the whole way. For she's a Madonna with No-Kink on her hair. That's where they failed themselves, Father. They've made her hallowed hair straight; they lacked the courage for the kink. What a pity." When a sensitive mulatto heroines's daughter, near-white herself, swings deliberately back to a black marriage in "poignant opposition" to her mother's ambition for white recognition, you may be sure that the Negro sphinx has come nearer to our literary Thebes. May some real young genius, black or white, go blithely out of the walls to question her.

That almost has happened with the first novel of Langston Hughes,—*Not Without Laughter*. If this book were a trilogy, and carried its young hero, Sandy, through a typical black boy's journey from the cradle to the grave we might perhaps have the all-too-long-prayed for Negro novel. As it is despite immaturity of narrative technique, this novel is one of the high-water marks of the Negro's self depiction in prose. *Not Without Laughter* owes its inspiration to a force far different from the flippant exhibitionism by which some of our younger writers aimed to out-Herod *Nigger Heaven*. Indeed it was born in Mr. Hughes poetry, which aims to evoke the folk temperament truly and reverently; and in its best chapters, *Storm*, *Guitar* and *Dance*, its style palpitates with the real spiritual essences of Negro life. Should its promise be fulfilled, we shall have a Negro novelist to bracket with Julia Peterkin and Du Bose Heyward.

Meanwhile, the Southern tradition flows on in a stream of fiction claiming the virtues of accurate folk-lore. Although many removes from either serious or flippant caricature, it is still fictional enough to be labelled fiction, and treated no more seriously than that implies. Roark Bradford has the gift of genuine low comedy; and low comedy is heavens above the bogs of burlesque and slapstick. *Black Genesis*, *Ol' King David*, and the current *John Henry* are good surface transcriptions of Negro humor and folk idiom. However, if *The Green Pastures* had not been lifted up several levels by the skillful dramaturgy of Marc Connelly and the intuitively reverent acting and singing of a great group of Negro actors, Bradford's *Ol' Man Adam* would never have put off the limitations of Mississippi clay and taken on the imperishable garments of immortality.

Green Pastures is a controversial subject, especially among Negroes. Is it a true version of the Negro's religion? By the warrant of the Spirituals and the characteristic Negro sermons, it is too drably realistic, and not apocalyptic enough. But it is certainly not what some have accused it of being, a white man's version of what he thinks Negro religion ought to be. In spite of a heaven of jaspar walls, golden wings and crowns and harps, the true Negro peasant spirit would stop to tilt a halo and to scratch an itch. As a recent poem of Langston Hughes puts it,

> "Ma Lawd ain't no stuck-up man.
> Ma Lawd, he ain't proud.
> When he goes a 'walkin
> He gives me His hand.
> You ma friend, He 'lowed."

And so *Green Pastures*, in spite of questionable detail and a generous injection of "Black Zionism," achieves spiritual representativeness of the deepest and most moving kind. Incidentally, by one of its typical ironics, the stage has provided a really great play from one of the feeblest of Negro novels; while *Scarlet Sister Mary*, one of the greatest of Negro novels, has fallen far below mediocrity in its dramatized form. Miss Barrymore's fault largely,—but it is a wholesome lesson to the yet only half-convinced American stage that there is some peculiar power in Negro acting. Blackface, let us hope, has received a final setback in its threatened advance on the legitimate stage.

Except for a slender volume by James Weldon Johnson, and some significant magazine verse of Sterling Brown and Langston Hughes, there has been a noticeable lull in the output of the Negro poets. Of course, a good deal of poetizing upon the race question, both by white and Negro sentimentalists, still persists; but that is far from making Negro poetry,—the obsessions of these dilettantes notwithstanding. Indeed, Mr. Johnson's poem, *St. Peter Narrates an Incident of Resurrection Day*, comes itself somewhat under the same criticism, as a half-ironical, half-sentimental bit of propaganda in couplet stanzas.

It is in *Black Manhattan* that James Weldon Johnson makes the literary year his happy debtor. This chronicle of the life of the Negro, knit ingeniously into the general history of New York, decade by decade, is a fine and permanently valuable bit of documentation of the Negro's social and cultural history. No one can read it without surprising enlightenment, or without a subtle appreciation of the forces which have prevented the Negro from being spiritually segregated in the life of America.

One gets the same impression from those chapters of *Tin Pan Alley*, by Dr. Goldberg, that traces the ragtime and jazz elements as they have carried the Negro's contribution through the stream of popular music into the very life-blood of the national life. The climax of the year on the musical side, however, is the publication of the *Green Pastures Spirituals*, arranged by one of the most gifted and genuine of Negro musicians, Hall Johnson. Indeed this publication but makes available a small fraction of the extensive repertory of folk music of the Hall Johnson Negro Choir, which I consider to be the greatest and most typical Negro choral organization we possess.

There have been a number of biographies in the year's list; all most acceptable in substance, but pitiably fettered, with one exception, to the missionary mode, that baneful genre whose conventions have smothered the humanity out of Negro biography since anti-slavery days. The life of Dr. Aggrey chronicles an important chapter and an outstanding pioneer in the modern educational uplift of Africa; *School Acres*, by Miss Rossa Cooley, interestingly tells the story of Penn School and the Penn Island community in its heroic struggle toward economic and spiritual freedom; and Mr. Brawley's life of Dr. Dillard, tells in terms of the life work of this liberal Southern friend and co-worker in the development of mass education for the Negro, the remarkable story of the recent advances in this field. However, from no book of essentially missionary approach can the flesh and blood sense of Negro life be reflected. And yet the life of any beyond average Negro is one of the most fascinating and complicated human documents of this age. Presented in the grand style and the modern manner, it should add a new note even in a period of admitted biographical virtuosity. Sensing this, no doubt, Eslanda Goode Robeson has written a boldly intimate but too worshipful biography of her great and versatile husband. The life of Paul Robeson makes him a symbol; and perspective will make it more and more evident. But welcome as are the facts and details of this intimate chronicle, to me, it rather seems in total effect like a great statue half spoiled by an over-elaborate pedestal. Still this biography stands for the breaking of the confining mould that too long has kept Negro life from the effects of great biography.

Perhaps Negroes as individuals will never come to their latent humanity until the traditional conceptions of the folk itself are revised.

Therein lies the hope and the interest in the increasing number of painstaking and respectful studies of Negro folk life and folk-lore. The activity of the University of North Carolina group, and the prolific output of their press, has been a major factor in this new movement. In time it will have completely revised the stock notions of the Negro, and afford for both the social scientist and the artist a reliable body of folk material, and suitable criteria of what is genuine and truly representative. The article by Professor Guy B. Johnson in the 1930 edition of *Folk Say* on *Folk Values in Recent Literature of the Negro*, indeed the whole section on Negro folk material, ought to be read by any and all interested in the latest trends in the appreciation and development of this important aspect of native American material. The substantial gain of the year has seemed to be a gain in the deeper understanding of the significance of Negro material not in the narrow sense of its peculiarities and differences, but as an integral part of the American tradition and as part of the common cause of all art,—Southern, Northern, Negro, working toward the self-expression of native American culture.

A notable series of sociological studies has reenforced this effort to understand the Negro more scientifically and objectively. The Association for the Study of Negro Life and History has added to its long list of studies the work on *The Rural Negro* and another on the *Negro Wage Earner*; while from the Columbia University Press comes the quite detailed study of the urban migration of the Negro in the last decade. We must add to this Mr. Woofter's study of the rural Negro community at closer range, with some attempt at social interpretation beyond the usual superficial reportorial statistics. However, the tradition of that most inhuman of sociological instruments, statistics, dies hard in this field which, to me, seems to have suffered particularly from its inadequacies. Professor Charles Johnson's very competent *The Negro in American Civilization*, may be either the last stand of statistics on this question or, as I prefer to hope, the watershed of transition from the most arid peaks of the statistical pleateau down into fertile regions of living social interpretation. Just on the eve of this stocktaking comes the economic study of *The Black Worker*, by Sterling Spero and Abram Harris, raising two long denied hopes; that for objective interpretation and integration of the facts of Negro life with general social and economic tenden-

cies. By partially fulfilling these, and its definite consciousness of their absolute desirability, this book may be the turning point in the sociology of the American Negro. One gains from Dr. Johnson's book the impression that the necessary preliminaries of fact-finding have about reached the point of final adequacy and that much, almost too much, awaits critical appraisal and interpretation. From the latter book, comes the definite raising of a new and important point of view. Negro life, considered in isolation, cannot be scientifically interpreted; often its phenomena are but effects of causes located far outside its boundaries, and only in terms of the common factors is any diagnostic view to be obtained.

So, to conclude, the constructive gains of the year have been in the literature of criticism and interpretation rather than in the literature of creative expression. Likewise self-expression has, on the whole, encountered what we hope is only a temporary lag. However, greater objectivity and a soberer viewpoint are good gift-horses to stable, and lest they flee overnight, let us lock the stable-doors. The sober Reformation reenforces and clinches the bouyant Renaissance; at least, so it went once upon a time. I am all for history repeating herself on this point. Certainly we shall not have to wait many years to see; meanwhile, in penance for many who have boasted, let some of us pray.

WE TURN TO PROSE:
A Retrospective Review of the Literature of the Negro for 1931

Historical and Biographic:

Slave Trading in the Old South. Frederic Bancroft. J. H Furst Co. $4.00.

George Washington and the Negro. Walter H. Mazyck. Associated Publishers. $2.00

The Black Napoleon. Percy Waxman. Harcourt, Brace & Co. $3.50.

Negroes of Africa. Maurice Delafosse, translated by Fligel man. Associated Publishers. $3.15.

* * *

Sociological:

Brown America. Edwin R. Embree. The Viking Press. $2.50.

The Negro Wage Earner. L. J. Greene and Carter Woodson. Associated Publishers. $3.25.

The Black Worker. Sterling D. Spero and Abram Harris. Columbia University Press. $4.50.

The Mobility of the Negro. Edward E. Lewis. Columbia University Press. $2 25.

Racial Factors in American Industry. Herman Feldman. Harper & Bros. $4.00

Race Psychology. Thomas Russell Garth. McGraw Hill Co. $2.50.

The Negro in American National Politics. Wm. F. Nowlin. Stratford Co. $2.00.

The Negro Family in Chicago. E. Franklin Frazier. Chicago University Press. $3.00.

* * *

Drama and Folklore:

Brass Ankle. Du Bose Heyward. Farrar & Rinehart. $2.00.

The House of Connelly. Paul Green. Samuel French. $2.50.

Never No More. James Knox Millen. Unpublished.

Cold Blue Moon. Howard W. Odum. Bobbs-Merrill Co. $2.50.

John Henry. Roark Bradford. Harper & Bros. $2.50.

The Negro Sings a New Heaven. Mary Grissom. University of North Carolina Press. $2.50.

Po' Buckra. G. M. Shelby and S. G. Stoney. Macmillan Co. $2.50.

Folk-Say; A Regional Miscellany. Ed. E. A. Botkin. University of Oklahoma Press. $3.00.

The Carolina Low Country. Members of the Society for the Preservation of Spirituals. Macmillan Co. $5.00

Belles Lettres and Criticism:

The Book of American Negro Poetry. Second Edition. Ed. James Weldon Johnson. Harcourt Brace and Co. $2.00.

Outline for the Study of Negro Poetry. Sterling A. Brown. Ibid $.50.

Readings from Negro Authors. Eva Dykes, Otelia Cromwell and Lorenzo D. Turner. Harcourt, Brace & Co., $1.50.

The Negro Author. Vernon Loggins. Columbia University Press. $5.00.

* * *

Poetry:

The Negro Mother and other Dramatic Recitations. Langston Hughes. Golden Stair Press, N. Y. $.25.

Jasbo Brown and Selected Poems. Du Bose Heyward. Farrar & Rinehart. $2.00.

* * *

Fiction:

God Sends Sunday. Arna Bontemps. Harcourt, Brace & Co. $2.00.

Black No More. George Schuyler. The Macauley Co. $2.00.

Not Only War. Victor Daly. Christopher. $1.50.

Zeke. Mary White Ovington. Harcourt, Brace & Co., $2.00.

The Chinaberry Tree. Jessie Fauset. Frederick A. Stokes, $2.00.

* * *

Africana:

Africa View. Julian Huxley. Harper & Bros. $5.00.

Forty Stay In. J. W. Vandercook. Harper & Bros. $2.50.

Fools' Parade. J W. Vandercook. Harper & Bros. $2.50.

Four Handsome Negresses. R. Hernekin Baptist. Jonathan Cape & Harrison Smith. $2.00.

Slaves To-Day. George Schuyler. Brewer, Warren & Putnam. $2.50.

Ivory: Scourge of Africa. Ernest D. Moore. Harper & Bros. $4.00.

Caliban in Africa. Leonard Barnes. J. B. Lippincott & Co. $3.00.

▼ ▼ ▼ ▼ ▼

AS in the world at large, for that increasingly important literary province of Negro life, this has been a year of sober, serious, soul-searching scrutiny and reflection. We have turned from sentiment to thought, from myth to reality, from comedy and farce to tragedy and problem-play, from fiction to folk-lore, from argument to statistics, from dictums to doubts and questions, and even on the creative side from poetry to prose. The Negro can no longer complain about not being taken seriously. Indeed if there is any real ground for complaint, it is now on the other side,—that of being taken too seriously. For though the outlines of the Negro projected by the cold November sun of our day are realistically sharp and clear, at the figure's feet lies an ever-lengthening shadow. The problem has come back to plague both our houses, after an all too brief exile since its brave banishment by the blithe creative spirit of the Negro Renaissance. Negro and white authors alike are obsessed nowadays with the social seriousness of the racial situation, and seem convinced of an imperative need for sober inventory, analysis, and appraisal.

Opportunity 10 (February 1932): 40–44.

And so, we start our yearly review with the sociological end of the spectrum, and can only come gradually through to the upper zone of pure creative literature, of which, indeed there is little,—far too little. But there is consolation in the fact that a new foundation of fundamental truth is being laid down rather rapidly, as a basis, we hope, for a superstructure of later humane and vital interpretation of Negro life. All the minds preoccupied today with the Negro are truth-seeking, even those who do not find it, and more serious revision of the old views and notions has come from the press this year than could have been wildly dreamed of or was ever demanded by those who chafed and smarted under what they called the "conspiracy of misrepresentation." Northern and Southern, Negro and white alike, have come to closer realistic grips with present fact and historic situation and record, and if truth can lead us to higher beauty, the prospect is hopeful.

In the field of historical research, four outstanding revaluations face us with disillusioning force and authority. There is that closely documented, but critically penetrating picture of the slave regime by Bancroft, *Slave Trading in the Old South,*—which finally disposes of the old romantic legend, and sends that subtly seductive tradition to a stony grave. There is great significance in this; not merely from the angle of historic justice. The Negro past holds for both the white and the Negro artist the materials of the greatest American tragedy and the most epical of American themes; but only in the death of the old hypocrisies and sentimental evasions can this material come to artistic life. It is more than a mere historical service, then, which this brave book has done. From a Negro author, we get a supplementary picture,—clear, proportioned and scrupulously just, of the early dilemmas of the race question in colonial times, as they plagued and puzzled the Father of his Country. Caught between his patriarchal tradition as slave-holder and plantation proprietor and the humanitarianism of the period and the abolitionist convictions of Lafayette and Kosciusko, George Washington makes an excellent subject for the new historical realism, and Mr. Mazyck has given an illuminating, carefully documented picture. And in *Black Napoleon,* Mr. Waxman has more nearly approached a full-length historical portrait of a Negro than any other commentator on Toussaint L'Ouverture, or for that matter any other Negro biography. There are a few other Negro figures worthy of the best and most serious historical interpretation;

after this pioneer work, they will most certainly have their proper attention in due course. And of great significance also, is the publication by the Association for the Study of Negro Life and History of the competent primer of Negro African history, written by the scholarly Delafosse, who knew much of the territory of West Africa by first-hand experience and was a competent Arabic scholar to digest the best authorities, the Arabic chronicles and travel sketches that are our only historical sources for these facts.

Then comes a series of sociological treatments, of which it can be said almost without exception that they are objective, scholarly and authoritative. The most popular, Mr. Embree's *Brown America,* leans heavily on the newer findings in anthropology and social research, and though consciously a book for the layman, has the scientific temper and an objective approach. It is challenging in the freshness and fairness of its liberalism, and has the virtue of seeing the Negro as an integral part of democracy and its problems rather than as a special and separate problem. This integration of the Negro problem with the context of American life, economic, industrial, educational, political is the pronounced trend of all the other volumes listed, with the single exception of the study of the Negro in Politics, which has at least the constructive significance of being a ground-breaker in this important field. Especially Spero and Harris' study of the Negro and labor is a work with an important integrating tendency; and may be said to mark the beginning of the end of that hitherto endless succession of studies of the Negro *in vacuo,* which have given all of us the impression that the Negro question is something to be solved by itself, almost without reference to the other more fundamental social, political and economic problems of our day. After the enlightenment, one wonders how we could have fallen victim to such uncommon-sense delusions; however,—such is the actual fact. Feldman's book, *Racial Factors in American Industry,* has the same salutary lesson; and special comment should be given to the careful, critical examination with which Professor Garth breaks down all the pseudo and near-scientific theories of racial superiorities and inferiorities; substituting an individual and environmental explanation of human divergencies and difference. On the whole, no such formidable batch of sociological material has appeared in any five year period as this sober, fact-finding twelve-month has yielded.

Shall we lighten our picture, if we turn to

the drama? Scarcely even there. A reasonably successful Broadway review had a framework of grim melodrama; and three outstanding plays of Negro life, all by white Southern playwrights, have failed or been short-lived because they have been too grim and sobering. *Brass Ankle*,—a study of miscegenation, *The House of Connelly*,—a post-mortem of the decline of the Old Regime in Charleston, and *Never No More*,—a realistic dramatic transcript of a sample lynching, all testifying to the suddenly acquired passion for truth, the bare truth and whole truth, no matter whose ox is gored or whose feelings are harrowed. Well,—the sackcloth has been too harsh and the ashes too gray and choking, but tinsel, paint and whitewash have practically been chased off the legitimate stage as far as serious drama of Negro life or situation is concerned. This, too, is a great service and achievement; may the problem-play, which seems now to be the dominant trend, quicken into real tragic and dramatic life and release its deeply significant possibilities. Du Bose Heyward, Paul Green, and James Millen are steadily moving us toward a tragic Negro drama with light and power and universality.

In my judgment, the pivot of the revaluation of Negro life is and for a long time yet must be the new Negro folk-lore. It was in this field that the white Southern mind made its first significant recanting, after discovering that there was a Negro whom even they didn't know. A good deal of this extensive chronicling of the unwritten Negro saga is still tinctured with the old tradition. Roark Brad-

From the Book Jacket of "Slaves Today"

ford, particularly, still romanticizes overmuch and lays on his local color with too broad and flat a brush; but *John Henry* is closer to real folk-lore than anything he has previously done. Professor Odum continues his careful documentation of the Negro roustabout, whom he often seems to mistake for a true peasant,—perhaps reluctantly, as solace for the almost complete disappearance of the pure soil peasant, whom the Southern fathers had under their very eyes but could not deeply appreciate. So this priceless figure is left either to the sentimental lament of a point of view represented by the elaborate volume, *The Carolina Low Country*,

published by members of the Charleston Society for the Preservation of Spirituals or to the synthetic reconstruction of the regional folklorists who collaborate in *Folk-Say*. The real Negro peasant and his world lie somewhere between these two; and somewhat elude the direct grasp of either. However, it may just be that one view superimposed on the other can in time painstakingly recreate him. This is not said in disparagement; rather in prophecy and to encourage both the scientific and the sentimental reconstruction of the half-lost Negro folk-lore. In the first volume, there is an essay by Robert W. Gordon on the *Negro Spiritual*, which is a substantial contribution to this much-discussed but little understood folk phenomenon; and a hundred pages of the book is given over to recording a number of fine originals and variants, with locale definitely mentioned, — a feature that would be priceless did we have it for the familiar classics among the spirituals.

The significant item in *belles lettres* is undoubtedly the reissue of the *Book of American Negro Poetry*, with inclusions of the younger generation of Negro poets since the date of the first edition,—1922. The most representative tracing of the Negro creative temper that can be obtained comes from his output in poetry; so this anthology extends its already great service to the cause of Negro letters. For this very reason, it is somewhat regrettable that the racial themes are not preferentially stressed, although it is quite possible to make too much of the differences and too little of the common lyric motives of the Negro poets. Sterling Brown's companion, *Outline for the Study of Negro Poetry*, is a syllabus of more than pedagogic importance; it is critically interpretative in a way most helpful even to the mature, general reader. In its critical maturity, slender though it is, it contrasts sharply with the strictly pedagogic approach of the much larger *Readings From Negro Authors*, by Dykes, Cromwell and Turner. This book is, of course, excellent for school use, but has the limitations of that emphasis to what seems to me an unnecessary degree. For after all, the justification of Negro expression, considered separately, lies in the content significance and its representativeness of group thought and feeling,—

and the book is not especially sensitive or discriminating with respect to these values. In *The Negro Author*, Vernon Loggins, carefully exploring the unique resources of the Schomburg Library, has given a very competent and exhaustive historical and critical analysis of Negro authorship from the beginnings up to 1900. So again, in this field, more available material has been brought forward, and the stage set for the commencement of more intensive interpretation and criticism.

The poetry output this year is unusually scant. There is a fine volume of verse in the offing,—Mr. Sterling Brown's *Southern Road*, which will appear in the spring. A small volume by Langston Hughes by no means comes up to the standard of his earlier volumes; and deserts his poetic platform of folk-poetry for the dubious plane of entertainment and propaganda. So the single palm in the field of poetry this year goes to the versatile and genuine Du Bose Heyward, whose *Jasbo Brown* really adds to the sublimated folk-poetry on the Negro theme. But for this really lyric echo, one of the finest strains of the Negro tradition would this year have remained completely silent, unless we count several magazine publications of Sterling Brown's. These verses have authentic flavor, in spite of their metrical competence, and lead us to eager expectancy of fresh creative achievement to the credit of the younger Negro poet.

The year's fiction list holds five novels,—four of them by Negroes. Certainly a year of prose. All the more so, when we consider the style and content of these volumes. *God Sends Sunday* is the only one with anything of the folk flavor or, by any stretch of the imagination, a poetic style. It is probably the last, and one of the best of the low-life novels; this quite moving story of "Little Augie," the gay and hectic jockey of the palmy nineties; for the swing has gone as definitely to the problem novel as it has toward the problem play. Miss Ovington's *Zeke* is frankly a human interest story, attempting to evoke sympathy for the

"other side of the picture." Despite high purpose and true details, in ensemble effect, it scarcely succeeds. *Not Only War*,—Mr. Daly's complicated novelette of the World War similarly fails to move with the conviction necessary to good fiction. However, it does break ground on a field that eventually will yield a great novel. It is certainly to be marvelled that with all the fiction of the war, the paradoxical story of the American Negro fighting a spiritual battle within a physical battle has just now been attempted. Mr. Schuyler's *Black No More* is significant. It has a theme worthy of a great satirist. That it sinks in places to the level of farce and burlesque, and yet succeeds on the whole, is evidence of the novelty and the potential power of the satirical attack on the race problem in fiction. I believe that one of the great new veins of Negro fiction has been opened by this book:— may its tribe increase!

A really mature novel has come from the pen of Miss Jessie Fauset. Her apprenticeship is now definitely over; both in style and theme. *The Chinaberry Tree*, is one of the accomplishments of Negro fiction. The tragedy of mixed blood and the bar sinister leads a half brother and sister to the near tragedy of marriage and the actual tragedy of unmerited expiation of the sins of their father. Like its analogue in classic literature this is one of the great themes of all times; and its Negro peculiarities only tend to give it deeper tragedy and universality. Miss Fauset handles it very competently, with conviction, force and reserve, and at the same time adds materially to the picture of her favorite milieu, — the upper strata of Negro life where responsibility, culture and breeding are the norms. She only requires one or two colleagues to establish what we might call a "Philadelphia" as distinguished from the "Harlem" school of fiction. For this too, there is a place and a time; and after the exploitation of the low-life level that we have had, it would really seem to be the appropriate hour,— provided, of course, we no longer are in danger of returning to the pitfalls of propaganda or the mirages of psychological compensation.

Comment on African literature should

From the Book Jacket of "God Sends Sunday"

constitute an article by itself; for the material is extensive and significant. It must suffice us to show that here, likewise, the truth will out. Even Baptist's extravaganza, *Four Handsome Negresses*, has the effect of showing the relativity of the Nordic and the African norms of life, and leaves us quite puzzled as to which has greater vitality. And all the other books listed dig in to one side or other of the African situation and bring up not a one-sided missionary view, or a partisan certainty and superiority, but tragic conflict, uncertainty and dilemma. Most ironical of all are Mr. Moore's quite frank story of the plunder-motive in "*Ivory: Scourge of Africa*" and Mr. Schuyler's sarcastic account of the slave-trading tyranny of the Americo-Liberian overlords in the little black Republic. These are sad books, that offer little hope, but they do show the factual approach, which is perhaps in itself distantly hopeful. Mr. Vandercook's two books, different as they are in tone, have underneath the primitivism of his well-known formula a frank and realistic approach to the African scene, which at least in its local color aspect leaves nothing to be experienced but the actual physical fatigue and danger of the journey. On the side of human characterization, however, there is much to be desired, if we are not satisfied by bare type portrayal. And certainly the French and German colonial literature has led us far beyond this simple technique, even for African portraiture. The remaining books are new high-water marks in colonial problem literature, because they each recognize the tragic character of the conflict between the European and the African, and by inference suggest the impossibility of resolving it. *Africa View* is especially profound and humane; I should say no finer view was to be gotten on the realistic plane than this which the fine scientific temper of Mr. Huxley has made available for us. Especially as an Englishman's book, it heralds a new spiritual sensitiveness to racial values alien to the English and European standards and conventions,—and such a new orientation might conceivably mark the beginning of a new colonial mind. If one had only time for one recent book about Africa, this is the book he should read. But one doesn't read one book nowadays, either about Africa or about the Negro; there is an interest deeper than superficial curiosity and more universal than mere ethnologic or sociological interest. Science has at least shown us the serious human interest and problem involved. May art in time give us a philosophy of creative interpretation and understanding.

BLACK TRUTH AND BLACK BEAUTY:
A Retrospective Review of the
Literature of the Negro for 1932

FICTION:

Glory, by Nan Bagby Stephens. John Day: New York. $2.50.

Bright Skin, by Julia Peterkin. Bobbs-Merrill Co. $2.50.

Amber Satyr, by Roy Flannagan. Doubleday, Doran. $2.00.

Georgia Nigger, by John L. Spivak. Brewer, Warren & Putnam. $2.50.

* * *

By Negro Authors:

One Way to Heaven, by Countee Cullen. Harper & Bros. $2.00.

Gingertown, by Claude McKay. Harper & Bros. $2.50.

Infants of the Spring, by Wallace Thurman. Macaulay Co. $2.00.

The Conjure Man Dies, by Rudolph Fisher. Covici-Friede. $2.00.

* * *

SOCIOLOGICAL:

The Negro Family in Chicago, by E. F. Frazier. University of Chicago Press. $3.00.

The Free Negro Family, by E. Franklin Frazier. Fisk University Press. $1.00.

Race, Class and Party, by Paul Lewinson. Oxford University Press. $3.75.

The Negro in the Slaughtering and Meat-Packing Industry in Chicago, by Alma Herbst. Houghton, Mifflin Co. $3.00.

The Southern Negro as a Consumer, by Paul K. Edwards. Prentice Hall Co. $3.00.

American Minority Peoples, by Donald Young. Harper & Bros. $3.50.

* * *

DRAMA AND BELLES LETTRES:

Black Souls, by Annie Nathan Meyer. Reynolds Press: New Bedford. $1.50.

POETRY:

The Southern Road, by Sterling Brown. Harcourt, Brace & Co. $2.00.

The Dream Keeper and Other Poems, by Langston Hughes. Alfred Knopf, Inc. $2.00.

Scottsboro, Ltd., by Langston Hughes. The Golden Stair Press. $.50.

* * *

CHILDREN'S BOOKS:

Popo and Fifina, by Arna Bontemps and Langston Hughes. Macmillan & Company. $1.5?.

The Railroad to Freedom, by Hildegarde Hoyte Swift. Harcourt, Brace & Co. $2.50.

* * *

ANTHROPOLOGY:

Sea Island to City, by Clyde V. Kiser. Columbia University Press. $3.50.

Folk Culture on St. Helena Island, by Guy B. Johnson. University of North Carolina Press. $3.00.

A Study of Some Negro-White Families in the U. S., by Caroline Bond Day. Peabody Museum Publication. Harvard University-Cambridge. $2.50.

Voodoos and Obeahs, by Jos. J. Williams, S. J. The Dial Press. $3.00.

* * *

BIOGRAPHY:

Daughters of Africa, by G. A. Gollock. Longmans, Green & Co. $1.25.

Selected Speeches of Booker T. Washington, by E. Davidson Washington. Doubleday, Doran & Co. $2.00.

Woman Builders, by Sadie Daniels. Associated Publishers, Washington, D. C. $2.50.

The English Hymn, by Benjamin G. Brawley. Abingdon Press. $2.00.

IT becomes more obvious as the years go on that in this matter of the portrayal of Negro life in American literature we must pay artistic penance for our social sins, and so must seek the sober, painful truth before we can find the beauty we set out to capture. Except in the rarest instances, in the current literature of the Negro, we continue to find more of the bitter tang and tonic of the Re-formation than the sweetness and light of a Renaissance; and rarely, it seems can truth and beauty be found dwelling, as they should, together. Yet rare instances, gleams here and there, do convince us that in the end we shall achieve the promise that was so inspiring in the first flush of the Negro awakening,—a black beauty that is truth,—a Negro truth that is purely art; even though it may not be all that

Opportunity 11 (January 1933); 14–18.

we need to know. This year one volume gives us special hope, being just that single stroke revelation of both truth and beauty. It is *The Southern Road*, a volume of verse by Sterling Brown; and for that reason I count it the outstanding literary event of the year.

But again, the output of the year is predominantly prose; and not only as last year sober, fact-seeking prose, careful human document study, but this year, in many instances, sharp-edged, surgical prose, drastically probing, boldly cutting down to the quick of the Negro problem. It is as if at last in the process of problem analysis, the scalpels of the scientific and the realistic attitude had suddenly been pushed through the skin and tissues of the problem to the vital viscera in a desperate effort to "kill or cure." Fiction is as bold and revealing as sociology; and at no time have writers, black and white, seemed more willing or more successful in breaking through the polite taboos and the traditional hypocrisies to the bare and naked, and often, tender truth about this or that vital situation of the American race problem. It is a good sign and promiseful omen, even if our nerves do twitch under the shock or wince at the sudden pain. Indeed the scientific approach is revealing the condition of the Negro more and more as just a special phase or segment of the common life, and even as a problem, as but a special symptom of general social ills and maladjustment. The most significant new trend I am able to discover in this year's literature is this growing tendency not to treat the Negro entirely as a separate or special subject, but rather as part of a general situation, be it social, economic, artistic or cultural. A score of books that cannot by any stretch be listed as "literature of the Negro," have important analyses of one aspect or another of Negro life. In "America as Seen by Americans," three of the chapters touch vitally on the Negro, and wise editing has frankly realized it. Again, a book like Ehrlich's masterly study of John Brown,—"God's Angry Man," treats the Negro all the more epically by putting him properly into sane but dramatic perspective. So although books like Donald Young's *American Minority Peoples* or Paul Lewinson's *Race, Class and Party* have enough special relevance to be listed, many of the most important commentaries do not. A recent review of T. S. Stribling's novel of Reconstruction, *The Store*—makes this appropriate statement:—"In this novel, Mr. Stribling shows the consequences to both Negroes and whites by a skilful series of interactions.

Any system inevitably enmeshes all its members equally though diversely." When such a basic fact is fully realized and carried out in literary and sociological practice, we shall be on the last stage of our constantly improving technique in handling the fascinating but difficult theme of Negro life. Except for folk literature and occasional "genre" studies, then, we must expect a return by both white and Negro authors to the common canvas and the large perspective.

In fiction this year, four realists, three of them white southerners, turn to the delineation of the southern scene; each with a certain measure of pioneering success. Miss Stephens, author of the well-known drama *Roseanne*, pictures the same figures, Roseanne and the erring parson, Cicero Brown in full length portraiture in *Glory*. Her novel is most successful in its depiction of a rural Georgia village, with its dual life; and a real advance is scored in the handling of local color material. For Miss Stephen's picture is movingly human and true; it is only with her characterization that she has difficulties, and here only because her motivation is more melodramatic than tragic. Miss Peterkin, more seasoned, ventures forth from her beloved plantation milieu to carry the heroine of *Bright Skin* to Harlem. Here she is less at home, and naturally enough is not completely successful in her portrayal of the mulatto heroine,—Cricket. Yet withal each of these stories is a considerable step toward the triumph of the new southern realism in handling the Negro character and setting sincerely, sympathetically, and truthfully; and both writers have the right idea that Negro life must be treated with a certain amount of poetry, at the same time that sentiment is rigorously excluded. And so, step by step, southern fiction about the Negro approaches great art.

A third novel, *Amber Satyr*, introduces a bold new theme. Roy Flannagan, as a Virginian, breaks the traditional taboos and portrays the love story of Sarah ,a white farmer's wife, and Luther ,the mulatto hired man. It is not just a formula situation or a formula solution; even though the outraged southern gods decree a lynching. *Amber Satyr* is real, moving tragedy; and is a harbinger of what southern fiction will be when it is courageously and truthfully written. No fiction can be great on mere courage and truthfulness, however, and the possibilities of Mr. Flannagan's or Miss Stephens' subjects cannot be judged from these two first novels, any more than their own mature possibilities as writers. But these are particularly significant beginnings. *Georgia Nigger* is the fourth novel in this group. Here is the pure propaganda novel, but with that strange power that propaganda takes on when it flames with righteous indignation. This story of peonage and the southern chain gang and prison labor system is vital fiction for all its biting polemic; it may well be the Uncle Tom's Cabin of this last vestige of the slave-system, even though David Jackson, its black hero, will never become the household idol that Uncle Tom became. Still John Spivak has seized on one of the legitimate uses of fiction, and within the limits of journalistic virtues, has written a powerful and humanly moving novel. It surely is a symptom of a new realism in the air, especially when we place beside it its counterpart, Harrison Kroll's more balanced, but equally revealing story of "poor white" peonage and plantation feudalism, *Cabin in the Cotton*. It is evident that the reform novel is taking on a new lease of life.

Meanwhile, the Negro writer of fiction, as might be expected, leans backward, away from propaganda and problem fiction. But the flight from propaganda does not always bring us safely to art. In fact, when the great Negro writer of fiction comes forward, he will probably steer head-on into what for a lesser talent would be the most obvious and shoddy propaganda and transform it into a triumphant victory for art. For the present, there is only one talent with a masterful touch, and he, less successful with the novel than the short story. But undoubtedly Claude McKay's collection of stories, *Gingertown*, has maturity, skill and the universal touch. His stories run from the tropical Jamaican village to "high Harlem," and then to the river-front of Marseilles, but in all there is real flesh and blood characterization and really human motivation, whether the accent be tragic, comic, or as is favorite with McKay, ironic. Nothing in the whole decade of the "Negro awakening" is to be more regretted than the exile of this great talent from contact with his most promising field of material; for even from memory and at a distance, he draws more powerfully and poignantly than many who study the Harlem scene "from life."

From right within Harlem two novels have come, neither as successful artistically as McKay's fiction. These are Countee Cullen's first novel *One Way to Heaven*, and Wallace Thurman's second novel, *Infants of the Spring*. Both are path-breaking, however, as to theme. *One Way to Heaven*, the story of Sam Lucas,

card gambler but professional penitent at revival meetings, is a story that just barely misses distinction. The duel in Sam's life is unfortunately external; had it been cast as a psychological conflict, there would have been high tragedy and real achievement. Mr. Cullen also ambitiously attempts to weld a low-life and a high society theme into the same story. Desirable as this is, it is a task for the seasoned writer; but as it is, Sam and Mattie's romance and tragedy do not mesh in naturally or effectively with the activities of Constantia Brown, whose maid Mattie is, and Constantia's intellectual set. Mr. Thurman's novel also misses fire, with a capital theme to make the regret all the keener. *Infants of the Spring* is the first picture of the younger Negro intelligentsia, and was conceived in the satiric vein as a criticism of the Negro Renaissance. Here is a wonderful chance for that most needed of all styles and most needed of all attitudes: self-criticism and perspective-restoring humor are indispensable in the long run in the artistic and spiritual development of the Negro. But they are not forthcoming from Mr. Thurman's sophomoric farce and melodrama or the problem-talk that his characters indulge in. The trouble with the set whom he delineates, and with the author's own literary philosophy and outlook, is that the attitudes and foibles of Nordic decadence have been carried into the buds of racial expression, and the healthy elemental simplicity of the Negro folk spirit and its native tradition forgotten or ignored by many who nevertheless have traded on the popularity for Negro art. As the novel of this spiritual failure and perversion, Mr. Thurman's book will have real documentary value, even though it represents only the lost wing of the younger generation movement.

Finally, Rudolph Fisher turns completely away from the serious and the stereotyped to write a Harlem "mystery story," *The Conjure Man Dies*. It is a refreshing *tour de force*, all the more so because one of the flaws of Negro fiction is the failing of taking itself too seriously. But the leaven of humor, and the light touch, will be even more welcome when they come in the context of the serious, literary novel of Negro life by the artist who should know it deepest and best, the young, intellectually emancipated Negro.

This difficult combination of intimacy and detachment is just what distinguishes *The Southern Road* by Sterling Brown. It is no exaggeration to say that this young newcomer among the poets has introduced a new dimension into Negro folk portraiture. A close student of the folk-life, he has caught along with the intimate particularities of Negro thought and feeling, more of the hidden universalities which our other folk-poets have overlooked or been incapable of sounding. The dominant angle of sweet or humane irony has enabled this poet to see a Negro peasant humble but epic, care-free but cynical, sensual but stoical, and as he himself says, "illiterate, but somehow very wise." It is a real discovery, this new figure who escapes both the cliches of the rhetorical propagandist poets and equally those of the "simple peasant" school. Undoubtedly, it is a step in portrayal that would have been impossible without the peasant portraits of Jean Toomer and Langston Hughes, but it is no invidious comparison to point out how much further it goes in the direction of balanced spiritual portraiture.

Meanwhile, as the folk-school tradition deepens, Langston Hughes, formerly its chief exponent, turns more and more in the direction of social protest and propaganda; since *Scottsboro Ltd.* represents his latest moods, although *The Dream Keeper* and *Popo and Fifina* are also recent publications. The latter is a quite flimsy sketch, a local-color story of Haitian child life, done in collaboration with Arna Bontemps, while *The Dream Keeper* is really a collection of the more lyrical of the poems in his first two volumes of verse, supplemented by a few unprinted poems,—all designed to be of special appeal to child readers. The book is a delightful lyrical echo of the older Hughes, who sang of his people as "walkers with the dawn and morning," "loudmouthed laughers in the hands of fate." But the poet of *Scottsboro, Ltd.* is a militant and indignant proletarian reformer, proclaiming:

> "*The voice of the red world*
> *Is our voice, too.*
> *The voice of the red world is you!*
> *With all of the workers,*
> *Black or white,*
> *We'll go forward*
> *Out of the night.*"

And as we turn to the sociological scene, it does seem that the conflicts of Negro life can no longer be kept apart from the general political and economic crises of the contemporary world. Even historical studies like *Race, Class and Party* or Professor Frazier's two competent studies of Negro family life, one the free Negro family and the other, modern family adjustments, as they are taking place in a typical urban center like Chicago, point unmistakeably to the Negro situations as just the symptoms and effects of general conditions and

forces. Similarly a labor study like Miss Herbst's narrative of the struggle of Negro labor to organize in Chicago, or an economic study of economic power like Professor Edward's, both force home the same lesson that the Negro position is a reflex of the dominant forces in the local situation. I have already referred to this trend in several independent lines of investigation. It suggests at least a new attitude of looking beyond the narrow field of Negro life itself for our most significant explanations and more basic causes; and even suggests expecting basic remedies to come from general social movements rather than just the narrow movements of race progress, however helpful or indicative they themselves may be. Possibly the most constructive of all points of view will turn out to be that reflected in Professor Young's *American Minority Peoples.* Here we have the case of the various minorities compared against the common reactions of the dominant majority, and a tracing of common lines through their differences. Two advantages are obvious; one the broader chance of discovering basic reasons, and then also, the possibility of foreseeing the possibilities not only of minority advance, but as Professor Young far-sightedly suggests, minority coalition under the stress of common persecution and suffering. To the conservative thinker or the good-will humanitarian, such alternatives may seem to be unwelcome and unwarranted bogeys, but one of the real services of social science should be a level-headed exploration of all the possibilities in a situation under analysis. And certainly, no one with a scientific-minded or realistic approach could overlook the possibility of such developments. This will be even more apparent as the special research of the Negro question integrates itself more and more with the competent analysis of the common general problems of which the Negro problem is a traditional, but loose and unscientific conglomerate.

In the other fields, the literary output is interesting, but not of outstanding significance. For all their common focus in the rather uniquely primitive life of the St. Helena Island group, Professor Johnson's book, *Folk Culture on St. Helena Island* and Dr. Kiser's study of the break-up and change of pattern between that and migration from there to Harlem, these two studies have only descriptive virtue. Only occasionally do they reveal the mechanisms of the interesting changes or survivals which they chronicle. That deep secret still eludes the anthropologist, and one comes away from these studies only with an impression of the infinite variability and adaptability of the human animal. Decidedly more venturesome is Father Williams' provocative study of *Voodoos and Obeahs* in Haiti. He rightly distinguishes Voodoo as originally a pagan survival, coming from the traditional Ashanti and West Coast cults, driven underground and fusing with black magic or Obeah, which "was originally antagonistic to Myalism or white magic, until the ban of missionarism brought them together in common outlawry." This is a really important suggestion, illustrating more than a mere "description of facts." Controversial as such interpretations must be, eventually our only scientific explanations must come from the analysis of historical roots and causes. Another promising start in true anthropological interpretation is in the volume of family genealogies and anthropometric comparison of direct descendants brought together by Mrs. Day under the auspices of Professor Hooten of Harvard University, who writes the sponsoring foreword. Here we have the very antithesis of bold and highly conjectural tracing of clues, in painstaking and detailed comparisons within limited but exhaustively controlled areas. This is a pioneer and promising approach, put forward undoubtedly more to prove and vindicate a method than to establish as final the very tentative conclusions or suggestions about mulatto trends.

Passing mention must be made of a delightful child's biography of Harriet Tubman in Mrs. Swift's *The Railroad to Freedom*, a continuation of Mrs. Gollock's school biographies of prominent African characters, this time *Daughters of Africa*, companion volume to *Sons of Africa*, and *Women Builders*, a series of life sketches of prominent Negro women, compiled by Miss Sadie Daniels, and published by the press of the Society for the study of Negro Life and History. Professor Brawley has also added to his long list of publications another volume, *The History of the English Hymn*. But generally speaking, the field of biography and *belles lettres* has not been as much to the fore as usual; nor has the field of drama; in which several stage presentations have been at best only partial successes, and the only published play,—*Black Souls* by Mrs. Annie Nathan Meyer, decidedly a propaganda piece, of good intentions and laudable sympathy, but decidedly weak in dramatic conception and execution.

It would seem, then, that the year on the whole had been more notable for path-breaking than accomplishment, with exceptions already noted. It is to the promise of their fulfillment, however, that we look forward to another year and another crop of what still has to be called "Negro Literature."

THE SAVING GRACE OF REALISM:
Retrospective Review of the
Negro Literature of 1933

FICTION AND BIOGRAPHY

Banana Bottom, by Claude McKay. Harper & Bros., N. Y. $2.50.

Comedy, American Style, by Jessie Fauset. Frederick Stokes, N. Y. $2.00.

Kingdom Coming, by Roark Bradford. Harper & Bros., N. Y. $2.50.

Roll, Jordan, Roll, by Julia Peterwin and Doris Ulmann. R. O. Ballou, N. Y. $3.50.

Along This Way—Autobiography of James Weldon Johnson. The Viking Press, N. Y. $3.50.

* * *

HISTORY AND SOCIOLOGY

The Last Slaver, by George S. King. G. P. Putnam, N. Y. $2.00.

A Century of Emancipation, by Sir John Harris. J. M. Dent, London. 5 s.

Slavery in Mississippi, by C. S. Sydnor. Appleton-Century Co., N. Y. $3.50.

Plantation Slavery in Georgia, by R. G. Flanders, University of North Carolina Press. $3.50.

Races and Ethnic Groups in American Life, by T. J. Woofter. McGraw-Hill Co., $2.50.

The Anti-Slavery Impulse, by G. H. Barnes. Appleton-Century Co., N. Y. $3.50.

Liberalism in the South, by Virginius Dabney. University of North Carolina. Chapel Hill. $3.50.

Lynching and the Law, by J. H. Chadbourn. University of North Carolina Press. $2.00.

The Tragedy of Lynching, by A. F. Raper. University of North Carolina Press. $2.50.

The Negro in America, by Alain Locke. American Library Association, Chicago. 25c.

The Mis-Education of the Negro, by Carter G. Woodson. Associated Publishers, Washington, D.C. $2.15.

The Negro's Church, by B. E. Mays and J. W. Nicholson. Institute for Social and Religious Research, New York. $2.00.

* * *

AFRICANA AND EXOTICA

Mandoa, Mandoa, by Winifred Holtby. Macmillan Co. $2.00.

The Adventures of The Black Girl in Her Search for God, by Bernard Shaw. Dodd, Mead and Co., New York. $1.50.

Congo Solo, by Emily Hahn. Bobbs-Merrill, Indianapolis. $2.75.

Chaka—An African Romance, by Thomas Mofolo. trans. by F. H. Dutton. Oxford University Press. $3.00.

At Home with the Savage, by J. H. Driberg. William Morrow & Co., New York. $3.50.

▼ ▼ ▼ ▼ ▼

AS year by year the literature by and about the Negro not only maintains its volume, but deepens and clarifies in quality, there can be no doubt that the Negro theme has become a prominent and permanent strain in contemporary American literature. No mere fad or fashion could have sustained itself for ten or more years with increasing momentum and undiminished appeal and effect. In fact, as the fad subsides, a sounder, more artistic expression of Negro life and character takes its place. What was once prevalent enough almost to be the rule has now become quite the exception; the typical Negro author is no longer propagandist on the one hand or exhibitionist on the other; the average white author is now neither a hectic faddist nor a superficial or commercialized exploiter in his attitude toward Negro subject matter;—and as a result the unexpected has happened, sobriety, poise and dignity are becoming the dominant keynotes of the developing Negro theme.

But fortunately the dignity and sobriety are not the stiff pose and starched trappings of the moralist,—although the Negro artist is still considerably beset by moralizing Puritans, just as the white author is plagued by a babbitized host of Philistines—but instead the

Opportunity 13 (January 1934): 8–11, 30.

simple, unaffected dignity of sympathetic and often poetic realism and the sobriety of the artist who loves and respects his subject-matter. It was one thing to inveigh against the Negro stereotypes in fiction, drama, art and sociology, it was quite another to painfully reconstruct from actual life truer, livelier, more representative substitutes. But just this our contemporary realism has carefully sought and almost completely achieved,—and only realism could have done so, all the contentions of the puritanical idealists to the contrary. Social justice may be the handiwork of the sentimentalists and the idealists, but the only safe and sane poetic justice must spring from sound and understanding realism.

We can trust and encourage a literary philosophy that can sustain the devoted art of a Julia Peterkin, that can evoke from the liberal white South a book like *The Tragedy of Lynching*, that can transform gradually the superficial, caricaturish interest of the early Roark Bradford into the penetrating, carefully studied realism of his latest novel, *Kingdom Coming*. And to the extent that James Weldon Johnson's autobiography represents a new and effective step in Negro biography, it can be attributed to the sober, realistic restraint that dominates it in striking contrast to the flamboyant egotism and sentimentality of much of our previous biographical writing. So we must look to enlightened realism as the present hope of Negro art and literature, not merely because it is desirable for our art to be in step with the prevailing mode and trend of the art and literature of its time,—important though that may be—but because both practical and aesthetic interests dictate truth as the basic desideratum in the portrayal of the Negro,—and truth is the saving grace of realism. As it matures, we may expect this new realism to become more and more humane, and as it mellows to take on cosmopolitan perspective,— perhaps the one new dimension that can carry it beyond the boundaries of national literature to the classic universality of world literature. Readers of *Opportunity* have had a rare foretaste of this humane cosmopolitanism in the observations and attitudes of the well-tempered realism of the accomplished author of *The Good Earth*,—Mrs. Pearl Buck.

Comment on the fiction of the year is comparatively easy when referred to this general trend; in theme or problem no book of the year is out of step with realism, and in style only one,—Miss Fauset's, dissents. In *Banana Bottom*, Claude McKay turns to his native Jamaica, with complete success so far as local color and setting are concerned, and with moderate success in the story of Bita whose life dramatizes a provincial duel between peasant paganism and middle class Puritanism. Real and tragic as the struggle is, one has the feeling that McKay cannot yet handle the problem type story as skillfully as the story of local color, although he has added another important province to Negro fiction. Bita's renunciation of middle-class respectability and her English missionary training in marrying the peasant Jubban might have been made more inevitable, and thus the more moving. McKay's treatment, however, is always stylistically mature and nowhere borders on the amateurish, and his very real characters are far removed from mere types. The same cannot be said for Miss Fauset's latest novel,—*Comedy, American Style*, which though it makes a distinct contribution in its theme, fails to capitalize it fully by forceful style and handling. The one dark child in a family of striving, middle class, prejudice-conditioned Negroes, dominated by an ambitious, lily-white mother, is the setting for one of the really great and original Negro classics, whether it be treated as tragedy or social comedy. This situation Miss Fauset has admirably documented, so that an important segment of Negro life is opened up; but the characterization is too close to type for the deepest conviction, the style is too mid-Victorian for moving power today, and the point of view falls into the sentimental hazard, missing the deep potential tragedy of the situation on the one hand, and its biting satire on the other. Yet Negro fiction would be infinitely poorer without the persevering and slowly maturing art of Miss Fauset, and her almost single-handed championship of upper and middle class Negro life as an important subject for fiction.

Artistically then, the honors still go afield to the more mature fiction of peasant life and the Southern milieu,—for how much longer we dare not predict, but certainly to date. The steady maturing of Roark Bradford's art has already been mentioned. *Kingdom Coming* is masterful fiction, all the more acceptable because the Negro characterization is true and deeply sympathetic. But for a forced and melodramatic ending the novel would have been a masterpiece. As it is, some of the best chapters in all Southern fiction on plantation life have been written, and an important contender has been added to the lists of the liberal Southern realists.

Roll, Jordan, Roll masquerades as non-fiction; but it really is a folk novelist's note book; a workmanlike palette by which one can gauge the technique of Miss Peterkin's intensely studied portraiture of the Southern Negro. It is illuminating to see the actual types from which she has been making up her characters all these years. That they are real Negroes, no one could possibly deny, but the author has the happy but unfortunate illusion that they are the generic Negro,—and that they scarcely are. For one thing, they are too bucolic, too tinted with Miss Peterkin's own Theocritan fancy; and for the other, they are a bit too local and sectional to be generic. This by no means signifies that this careful and sympathetic recording is unwelcome; on the contrary, I would bracket the book with James Weldon Johnson's autobiography as the year's outstanding literary achievement in the Negro field. With Doris Ulmann's superb photographic studies, Negro folk portraiture has been raised to a plane so purely and perfectly artistic that one marvels how realism could have accomplished it. When will the scientific folk-lorists wake up to the possibilities of art as the medium of the truest portrayal of human types?

Along This Way takes its place, too, in this borderland between fact and fiction, where the values of both are happily blended. For although it is the sober narrative of an outstanding individual's experience, the Johnson autobiography is also the history of a class and of a generation. It is the story of the first generation of Negro culture, with all of the struggles, dilemmas and triumphs of the advance guard of the Negro intelligentsia. It could just as well have been the type story of Black Bohemia,—a story that must some day be written, if Weldon Johnson had not been so versatile in adding to his achievements as a musical comedy librettist, song-writer and poet those of the journalist, the diplomat and the race publicist. With the panoramic sweep before him, our author doubtless could not stop for the intimate and careful picture of the Bohemia of Will Marion Cook, Williams and Walker, Cole and Johnson; but what the story lacks in dramatic intensity, it gains in composite variety and representativeness. *Along This Way* is indispensable for the understanding of the upper levels of Negro life. At the same time it is one of the best cross-section pictures of that little known zone of inter-racial cultural collaboration between black and white intellectuals and artists which starting with the vogue of Negro art in New York is spreading gradualy throughout all liberal culture centers of the nation. Mr. Johnson is a

little too close to his scene for daring or thorough appraisal; and he is too much the diplomat to attempt to anticipate posterity's verdict on things he has seen and experienced, with the single and praiseworthy exception of Negro rights,—a subject on which he has always been consistently outspoken and uncompromising. Yet, with it all, one or two more biographies are needed, lest the reading public jump to hasty generalizations about the Negro intellectual and artist in the same unfortunate way in which they have insisted upon generalizing about the peasant Negro.

* * *

Turning now to straight history and sociology, we find a formidable list, which valuable although it is, suggests that Negro life will not be immune from that modern plague called "research." *Slavery in Mississippi* and *Slavery in Georgia* suggest a possible monograph on slavery in every one of the slave states and territories; and there have been three or four contenders for the dubious honor of "*The Last Slaver.*" Personally I would trade one synthetic and interpretative study like Gaines' *The Southern Plantation* for a dozen such detailed historical studies. This is not anti-historical bias, or even lack of recognition that we are just beginning to approach that objective frame of mind from which the real history of slavery can be written. It is rather the contention that what modern social science needs most is an analysis of social forces, attitudes and traditions rather than a rehearsal of facts; even though the record stands badly in need of rewriting. For that very reason, we single out as notable such interpretative studies as Professor Barnes book on *The Anti-Slavery Impulse*, Virginius Dabney's study of the inner conflict of the South in his *Liberalism in the South*, and most of all, Mr. Raper's brilliant and fearless study of lynching. Why in these days of medals and official rewards, have we no way of acknowledging and encouraging such constructive liberalism and scholarship as has centered in Chapel Hill, and sent out through the University of North Carolina Press such a steady and illuminating stream of studies of Negro life and the race question?

It is encouraging to notice that Negro historical scholarship and social analysis keeps pace, more or less, with the increasing general academic interest in the study of the Negro. The list of Negro authorship in this field would be well balanced indeed if it could include Dr. Du Bois's promised publication on *The Negro in the Reconstruction*,—now delayed until spring. But even without this much awaited study, there is no dearth of sound interpretative comment on race history and sociology. The year has seen the first comprehensive study of the Negro church by two competent, young Negro investigators, and with the studies announced and under way, it requires no prophet to predict for next year an unprecedented leap forward of Negro historical and sociological scholarship. This will particularly reveal, if I am not much mistaken, along with such veterans as Dr. Woodson and Dr. Du Bois, an entire younger generation of scholars whose general point of view may be differentiated as a conviction that Negro life needs now to be studied in its inter-relationships with the general life of which it is an integral part. That shift of the modern sociological point of view, from faint beginnings several years back, is now registering almost to the point of becoming the dominant and conceded attitude among all modern-minded students of the race question, whether they be Negro or white. Dr. Woodson alone holds to the counter-thesis of racialist history, and states the case more radically than he has ever stated it in his *Mis-Education of the Negro*. Here, at least, is a challenging defense of propagandist history and an educational emphasis upon race tradition and racial morale. We must ponder this "Black Zionism" carefully, *pro* and *con*—for when the dilemmas of the Negro's position in America are fundamentally intellectualized, this issue that Dr. Woodson so provocatively raises will be found to be the basic and critical question involved. Personally I think the sooner the question is faced the better,—especially since as yet our policies and programs have not quite come to the fork of the road at which a policy of assimilation must part company with a policy of racial self-determination.

Lastly, but not least, comes Africa. This year the travelogues are by no means as numerous,—and we can afford to ignore them in noticing the new genres that are growing into prominence. Inaugurated by such books as Julian Huxley's *Africa View*, the Anglo-Saxon mind is at last achieving a spiritual appreciation of native values. The continental mind, especially the French, but also, it must be said, the German, has long since made this discovery and reflected it in its colonial literature. What they admit directly, the Anglo-Saxon mentality seems to need to admit by indirection, except in an occasional brief and brave passage in men like Llewellyn Powys, E. A. Rattray, Julian Huxley. But in a satiric

allegory, no less a personage than Bernard Shaw suggests to white civilization that it should not be so cock-sure of itself, or so confident that its God sanctions its brutal and egotistical missionarism. Small wonder that he has to conjure up the shade of Voltaire to ward off the racial recoil! But if Mr. Shaw's caution to 'Let Africa alone' is suggestive, how much more so, Miss Holtby's concrete satire,—"*Mandoa, Mandoa*." Here is the real antidote for the virus of missionarism and self-deceptive imperialism. It is an achievement when there is enough of the spirit of self-criticism and relative evaluation to make such a book possible. May its tribe increase!

Of the same new outlook, thought not satirical, is Emily Hahn's *Congo Solo*. Here is a frank, sensitive and uncondescending narrative of equatorial Africa as it is, with no partisanship either for or against the colonial system. Yet as a frank statement of its intimate workings in terms of the life of the governed villages, there can be little doubt that the colonial system would rather have an indignant moralistic diatribe than the subtle indictment of this simple story. Little by little the new respect for native custom and institutions in their own setting is establishing itself, and with the corollary that it is necessary to understand the institutions and traditions of primitive peoples before interfering with their lives. This thesis is more academically carried through in one of the best popular treatises on the life of primitive peoples, Professor Driberg's *At Home with the Savage*. This book is especially competent in its discussion of the legal and political institutions of the Baganda and other East African peoples, and has the virtue of describing their social values in addition to their mere externalities of form and ceremonial.

Then there is that unexpected new thing out of Africa,—a native non-missionary biography, —the narrative of the great Zulu war-lord,— Chaka, by a native scholar who knows and respects the tribal tradition, and yet can evaluate it against its European equivalents. There is much talk in some quarters of a revival of native lore and art as part of the new program of native education. However, if this is to be a missionarized product, it will never rehabilitate native values or soundly integrate the tribal tradition and its sanctions with the necessary admixture of European learning and technique that any modern system of education must also give. The emergence of real native letters is, therefore, something to be heralded with great joy. A sounder and more intelligent interest on the part of the American Negro in the cultural development of Africa could certainly help forward this revival of the suppressed native traditions, and in my opinion, we have more to gain thereby than we have to give.

* * *

To conclude,—a year of material stress and depression has not adversely affected the literature of the Negro, although many a manuscript may have gone unprinted. Indeed it may be that the deepening sobriety and poise of the books that have appeared is in part due to the absence of printing press pressure before and high-pressure salesmanship after the literary event. The natural urge and urgency of the creative impulse, we hope, will suffice for the future, and to aid it the critical and measured appreciation of a public that by now is accustomed to this vein of literary expression. It is to be hoped that Negro authorship will quicken its somewhat lagging pace, and especially reassert its peculiarly intimate medium of poetry. The next field of award for the Du Bois literary prize is poetry, and the wise policy of withholding the award when material of high quality is lacking suggests that the poets, veteran and fledgling, groom themselves. The award for non-fiction prose goes this year to James Weldon Johnson most deservedly; although *Black Manhattan* is crowned rather than *Along This Way* because of calendar limits. Together these two books do certainly represent the most distinguished contribution in non-prose fiction from any Negro author recently. And then, it is sad, but fitting to chronicle against the year's gains a really tragic loss in the early death of Walter H. Mazyck, the most promising of our younger historical writers, whose singular combination of accurate scholarship, clear analytical judgment of men and of issues, and limpid clarity and ease of expository style made him a figure of the greatest promise. His *George Washington and the Negro* was one of the finest bits of historical analysis and writing we have produced; his unfinished biography of Colonel Young will appear, but it grieves me greatly to contemplate the complete loss of his pre-meditated study of Lincoln for which he was deliberately maturing his talents.

THE ELEVENTH HOUR OF NORDICISM:
Retrospective Review of the Literature of the Negro for 1934

PART I
BIBLIOGRAPHY OF LITERATURE OF THE NEGRO: 1934

FICTION

So Red the Rose—Stark Young,
  Charles Scribners Sons, N. Y.—$2.50.
Unfinished Cathedral—T. Stribling,
  Doubleday, Doran, N. Y.—$2.50.
Transient Lady—Octavus R. Cohen,
  Appleton-Century, N. Y.—$2.00.
Let the Band Play Dixie—Roark Bradford,
  Harper Bros, N. Y.—$2.00.
Come in At The Door—William March,
  Harrison Smith & Haas, N. Y.—$2.50.
Candy—L. M. Alexander,
  Dodd, Mead & Co., N. Y.—$2.50.
Portrait of Eden—Margaret Sperry,
  Liveright & Co., N. Y.—$2.50.
Deep River—Clement Wood,
  William Godwin, Inc., N. Y.—$2.00.
Stars Fell on Alabama—Carl Carmer,
  Farrar & Rinehart, N. Y.—$3.00.
The Ways of White Folks—Langston Hughes,
  Alfred Knopf, Inc., N. Y.—$2.50.
Jonah's Gourd Vine—Zora Hurston,
  J. B. Lippincott, Philadelphia—$2.00.
With Naked Foot—Emily Hahn,
  Bobbs-Merrill, Indianapolis—$2.00.
Black God—D. Manners—Sutton,
  Longmans Green, N. Y.—$2.50.

BELLES-LETTRES

Negro, An Anthology—Nancy Cunard,
  Wishart & Co., London, England—
  £2 /$11 plus duty.
Le Noir, A School Anthology—Mercer Cook,
  American Book Co., N. Y.—$1.00.
John Brown, Terrible Saint—David Karsner,
  Dodd, Mead & Co., N. Y.—$3.00.
American Ballads and Folk Songs—John A. and
  Alan Lomax—Macmillan Co., N. Y.—$5.00.
Beale Street, Where the Blues Began—G. W. Lee,
  Robert Ballou, N, Y.—$2.50.

DRAMA

John Brown—Ronald Gow, Mss.
Dance With Your Gods—Perkins, Mss.
Africana—Donald Heywood, Mss.
Roll On, Sweet Chariot—Paul Green,
  Published as "Potters Field"—McBride.

Kykunkor or The Witch Doctor—Asadata Dafora, Mss.
Six Plays for a Negro Theatre—Randolph Edmonds,
  Walter Baker Co., Boston—$.75.
Stevedore—Paul Peters and George Sklar,
  Covici-Friede, N. Y.—$1.50.

HISTORICAL AND SOCIOLOGICAL

Negro White Adjustment—Paul E. Baker,
  Association Press, N. Y.—$2.00.
Life on the Negro Frontier—George R. Arthur,
  Association (Y. M. C. A.) Press, N. Y.—$2.00.
The Negro Professional Man and the Community—
  Carter G. Woodson, Associated Publishers,
  Washington, D. C.—$3.25.
The Shadow of the Plantation—Charles S. Johnson,
  University of Chicago Press—$2.50.
Race Relations—W. D. Weatherford and Charles S.
  Johnson—D. C. Heath & Co., N. Y.—$3.20.
A Guide to Studies in African History—Willis Huggins
  and John G. Jackson—Wyllie Press, N. Y.—$1.25.
Race Consciousness and the American Negro—
  Rebecca C. Barton, Aronld Busck, Copenhagen.
  $2.00.
Negro Americans, What Now?—James Weldon Johnson,
  The Viking Press, N. Y.—$1.25.

EDUCATION

*The Physical and Mental Abilities of the American
  Negro*—Yearbook No. 3—Journal of Negro Educa-
  tion, Howard University, July issue, 1934—$1.50.
The Evolution of The Negro College—Dwight O. W.
  Holmes, Columbia University Press—$2.25.
*The Education of the Negro in the American Social
  Order*—Horace Mann Bond, Prentice-Hall, N. Y.,
  $2.75.

AFRICANA

Liberia Rediscovered—James C. Young,
  Doubleday, Doran, N. Y.—$1.50.
Native Policy in South Africa—Ifor L. Evans,
  The Macmillan Co., N. Y.—$2.00.
Rebel Destiny—Melville and Frances Herskovits,
  McGraw Hill, N. Y.—$3.00.
The Education of Primitive Peoples—Albert D. Helser,
  Fleming Revell Co., N. Y.—$3.00.
The African To-day—D. Westermann,
  Oxford University Press, N. Y.—7s. 6d.

Opportunity 13 (January and February 1935): 8–12; 46–48, 59.

A RETROSPECTIVE review must needs ask the question: what have been the dominant trends in the literature of the year? I make no apology for presenting my conclusions first, although I vouch for their being conclusions and not preconceptions. Only toward the end of a long list of reading was there any semblance of dominant notes and outstanding trends. But in retrospect they were unmistakably clear; each writer somewhere along the road, no matter what his mission, creed or race, had met the Zeitgeist, had been confronted with the same hard riddle, and had not been allowed to pass on without some answer. Even in the variety of answers, the identity of the question is unmistakable. Of course, for almost no one has it been an overt or self-conscious question: the artist is concerned with his own specific theme and knows first-hand only the problems of his own personality. But the Zeitgeist is as inescapable as that goblin of chatter-box days that wormed himself as tape through the key-hole of a bolted door to become a real ogre again as soon as he had twisted through: if the artist bars the front-gate, it slips round to the backdoor, and when he bolts that, up through the trap-door of the sub-conscious or down the chimney of his hearth or in between the windows of his observation of life, the dominant question of the day relentlessly comes in sooner or later. It is the small-souled artist who runs and cringes; the great artist goes out to meet the Zeitgeist.

What is the riddle for 1934? Time was when it was some paradox of art, some secret of Parnassus. To-day, it is a conundrum of the market-place, a puzzle of the cross-roads,—for the literary Sphinx sits there at the crossroads of civilization ceaselessly asking, "Whither, Mankind?" and "Artist, Whither goest thou?" The social question will not down, no matter what the artist's other problems. For the Negro writer, this has been:— Shall I go left or right or take the middle course; for the white writer:—Shall I stick with the Nordics or shall I desert their beleaguered citadel?" It is the eleventh hour of capitalism and the eleventh hour of Nordicism, and all our literature and art are reflecting that. Naturally it is the latter which for the literature of the Negro theme is the matter of chief concern.

One wonders by what strange premonition artists are so suddenly and keenly aware of such crises, until one realizes that they are after all the spiritually sensitive, the barometers of the spirit and the sentinels of change. And now, with striking unanimity they are all agog over Nordicism. Many are for it, passionately, vehemently, but they are just as symptomatic of a present crisis and an impending change as those who are boldly and deliberately recanting it. Dominant ideas behave that way at their critical moments, and before their last relapses always have these hectic fevers and deliriums of violent assertion. Rampant fascism and hectic racialism are in themselves omens of the eleventh hour, as much and more than the rising liberal tide of repudiation and repentance. There is no millenium around the corner, art has little or no solutions, but it is reflecting the decline of a whole ideology and the rise of a new conception of humanity,—as humanity.

Until some evidence is before him, the reader may think this an unwarrantable conclusion from such a provincial segment of contemporary literature as the fiction of Negro life traditionally is. But after glancing at the list of novels on this theme, let him consider that the fiction of Negro life for the year 1934 contains five or six of the best sellers of the year's fiction crop, one prize novel, two choices of the Book-of-the-Month and two of the Literary Guild. The unquestioned prominence and popularity of the theme itself is significant. To that we must add the advance in the treatment that the year has registered. Of course, the old pattern gets itself repeated; Stark Young makes a virtue of a romantic throwback adequately exposed and criticized for *Opportunity* readers in Sterling Brown's recent review. But in the light of many another novel of the South on this same list, who would begrudge the old plantation tradition this beautiful but quavering swan-song? Personally I am not as concerned as some over the persistence of the old tradition, for alongside *So Red the Rose*, and *Transient Lady,* and *Let the Band Play Dixie* there comes also from the same South the corrective antidotes, *Stars Fell on Alabama,* and lest that be cited in spite of its evident close study as a Yankee's novel, then the work of native Southerners like Stribling's *Unfinished Cathedral,* Margaret Sperry's *Portrait of Eden,* William March's *Come in at the Door* and Clement Wood's *Deep River.* It is true no deep vindication comes from the unusual frank realism of these novels of the new school, but for all their present defeatist denouements, they show a South in the throes of a dilemma tragic for both sides and insoluble because of the local traditions. What more can we ask of art; it is only the logic of history that can go further,—and of that such art is a prophet and forerunner.

In *Unfinished Cathedral,* Miltiades Vaiden does take a stand, even though futile, against the lynching mob, and yet fate after forcing him to taste the bitter dilemma of the lynching of his own son, confronts him once again, after the tragedy of his own daughter, with the same situation in the black side of the family escutcheon, and the curtain catches him repudiating even the sacred aristocratic tradition of patronage as he drives off his quadroon half-sister. And in *Stars Fell on Alabama*, Mr. Carmer gets down to the real folk-lore that Joel Chandler Harris coated over, exposes realistically its sordid rootage in the bogs of illiteracy and primitive reversions and boldly suggests that such conditions know no racial boundary. Carl Carmer anatomizes Alabama, and for all his poetic love of the primitive shows the other devastating side of the deep South.

In *Come in at the Door*, William March tells a most unusual story, that of the close psychological relationship between an impressionable white lad, Chester Hurry, and Simon Baptiste, his educated mulatto tutor, whom he unwittingly dooms and from whose spirit, in self-imposed expiation, he can never successfully disentangle his own inner life. Remembering that psychological intimacy is the last taboo, more sacrosant than the admission of sex intimacies, we ought to see the tradition cracking to the core in a book like this, in spite of its poetic diffidence. Then in *Portrait of Eden*, we come under the bold pen of a woman writer to the most unromantic and frank portrayal of the seamy side of the South that I have yet encountered. The hero, Doctor McIntyre, working to reconstruct the almost unreconstructable, has an educated Negro colleague, who is lynched; he himself is murdered by "a cracker imbecile," and in the words of another reviewer, his enemies are "virulent Babbitry, political corruption, barbarous Fundamentalism, primitive superstition and personal feuds." Here is another South, and it is as much the South as that other one of colonels and colonel's ladies, wide porches, rambler roses, juleps and magnolias. For one, I would not deny the South its romanticism; if realism reminds us that it is not the whole story. Even Octavus Roy Cohen in *Transient Lady* has left the banter of black servant's dialogue for the bitter feuds of the townsfolk; and only Mr. Bradford remains in the groove of the old tradition, if we except the apologetic *So Red the Rose*. Bradford's stories cannot be dismissed because of their social philosophy: they are powerful sketches based on acute though narrow vision. If he ever broadens the angle, the South will have another Uncle Remus.

Everyone realizes that *Candy*, Mrs. Alexander's much read novel, is in the Peterkin tradi-

tion, and I suppose will complain that another stereotype is forming. I suppose this is so, but why should the Negro theme be exempt from this general phenomenon of imitation for which we have yet discovered no antidote but the shifting effect of time? The day is fast approaching when no few fixed types can be generalized as portraying the sum-total substance of Negro life and character. Then and then only the invidiousness of certain types will disappear (I admit and deplore their present invidiousness). But the only remedy is the portrayal of the neglected types. And then, too, in the formula of Scarlet Sister Mary and Cricket and Candy, there is one significant strand of the recantation of Nordicism,—the genuine admiration and envy of the primitive and the reaction from Puritanism. No student of the current trend of morals and convention ought to grieve too deeply over the implied slight of the amoralist mores of these South Carolina plantations; the novels of Greenwich Village and Hollywood, except for the setting, reveal the same attitudes and reactions. My complaint is that Mrs. Alexander, for all her studious effort, is no Julia Peterkin, as yet.

Finally, if it is Nordic bear-baiting that the fans call for, no partisan propagandist could have framed a more poetic-justice type of plot than Clement Wood's story of the marriage, quarrel and reunion of a daughter of the South and Elden, the Negro concert singer, even though their private Eden has to be in exile. But *Deep River* is a provocative and not a sincerely artistic or competent novel. One regrets that a theme of such ultimate implications has been reached before the proper maturity of those tendencies we have been discussing; for the present, only irony can make them real or effective with any considerable number of readers.

And just this mechanism has been used in the more successful of the stories of the first Negro writer whose fiction we discuss, Langston Hughes in his much discussed *The Ways of White Folks*. Here is the militant assault on the citadel of Nordicism in full fury, if not in full force. Avowedly propagandist, and motivated by radical social philosophy, we have here the beginnings of the revolutionary school of Negro fiction. But though anti-bourgeois and anti-Nordic, it is not genuinely proletarian. But it is nevertheless a significant beginning, and several stories in the volume, notably *Father and Son* rise far above the general level of rhetorical protest and propagandist reversal, achieving rare irony and real tragedy. But for pure folk quality, even the sort that a proletarian school of Negro fiction must think of achieving, Zora

Hurston's first novel has the genuine strain and the most promising technique. This is not surprising to those who know the careful apprenticeship she has served in the careful study of the South from the inside. John Buddy's folk talk, and later his sermons as "Rev. Pearson" are rare revelations of true Negro idiom of thought and speech, and if the plot and characterization of this novel were up to the level of its dialogue and description, it would be one of the high-water marks of Negro fiction. It is for this reason that I look forward to Miss Hurston's later work with more curiosity and anticipation than to that of any of our younger prose writers. For years we have been saying we wanted to achieve "objectivity" :— here it is. John's first and last encounters with a train are little classics. "You ain't never seed nothin' dangerous lookin' lak dat befo', is yuh?" "Naw suh and hit sho look frightenin'. But hits uh pretty thing do. Whar it gwine?" "Oh eve'y which and whar." The train kicked up its heels and rattled off. John watched it until it had lost itself down its shiny road and the noise of its going was dead. And then the last encounter: "He drove on but half-seeing the railroad from looking inward. The engine struck the car squarely and hurled it about like a toy. John was thrown out and lay perfectly still. Only his foot twitched a little. . . . 'Damned, if I kin see how it happened,' the engineer declared. 'God knows I blowed for him.' . . . And the preacher preached a barbaric requiem poem. So at last the preacher wiped his mouth in the final way and said. 'He wuz uh man, and nobody knowed 'im but God,'—and it was ended in rhythm."

However it is when we turn from the Southern to the African scene that we sense the full force of the anti-Nordic tide that seems to have set in. For here we have the almost unqualified worship and glorification of the primitive, combined with a deep ironic repudiation of the justifying illusions of the "white man's burden." The native now not only dominates the scene, but it is his philosophy that triumphs or at least has the last word. Fatalism and futility brood over the scene like the heat and the fever, and if anything wins, it is nature. Indeed in *Black God*, Miss Manners-Sutton suggests that it is black magic that casts the die: M'Kato waiting for years for vengeance for his maimed hands and the rape of his sister sees a pilgrimage of death overtake trader, missionary, free-booter, government officer, outcast adventurer, and eventually his long awaited enemy. The jungle everywhere exacts its expiating toll for the intrusions of white civilization; a different story from the romantic conquests in the fiction of a decade back. And only the weapon of magic, bribed from the native witch doctor, stops the avenging path of the "Black Master," native agitator and foe of the white man's power, who has undermined the Governor's self-confidence and authority and even become the paramour of his wife. It is a pity to sketch this lurid outline of melodrama, when the real charm and value of the book lies in the ironic etchings of character and description which make the substance of the book so superior to its theme and plot that one quite wishes there were no plot. Nevertheless, the justifications of our main conclusion must be pointed out.

Finally comes Emily Hahn's *With Naked Foot*, a masterpiece of observation, style and conception. Miss Hahn has served a fine apprenticeship in *Congo Solo*,—she knows her terrain and her human subject-matter perfectly. Now she has chosen a daring and a great theme and lifts the last shroud of silence from the tragedy of sex and love as it entangles the white man and the black woman, alien to each other in folkways, but not in basic emotions and common human needs. Mawa has a child by her first master-husband,—Joachim, who throughout the succession of four liasons remains the light and hope of her life. One by one they died or went, and Mawa holds her precarious superiority over her tribesmen as the mistress of the powerful. The Portuguese shop-keeper, the fat trader, the lean, meticulous government officer, and finally the romantic American school teacher with a conscience; they all succumbed to Mawa's charms and the African loneliness. At last it is Adam Kent's conscience that proves her undoing, he hurt her with a kind of love of which she knew nothing and wounded her life to the quick in trying to save her child from the primitive environment to which he only partly belonged. And as he passes out of her life, Mawa or the hull of Mawa sinks back into the chattel marriage she has defied so long to become the headsman's ageing concubine. Here is the compound tragedy of individuals and of the civilizations they represent, told with the swift deft touch and with ironically tempered understanding. This book will be cited years from now as one of the significant atonements for Nordicism: may it and its like provide the catharsis we have awaited so long!

One can afford to linger over the fiction of the year because of the almost complete cessation of poetry. Somehow the poetic strain has dwindled in quantity and quality; the occasional poems of Cullen and Hughes are below the level of their earler work, and only the muse of Sterling Brown seems to mature, and then only with a satirical and somewhat sardonic twist. Evidently it is not the hour for poetry; nor should it be, —this near-noon of a prosaic, trying day. Poets, like birds, sing at dawn and dusk, they are hushed by the heat of propaganda and the din of work and battle, and become vocal only before and after as the heralds or the carolling serenaders. The poetry section of the Cunard *Anthology* for example has for the most part an iron, metallic ring; interesting as it is, it is nevertheless hot rhetoric, clanging emotion. That is indeed the dominant note of this whole remarkable volume; making it one of the really significant signs of these times. There is much of unique informational and critical value in these eight hundred pages which document both the wrongs and the achievements of the black man and capitalize for the first time adequately the race problem as a world problem. But the capital "P" is for propaganda, not poetry, and the book hurls shell, bomb and shrapnel at the citadel of Nordicism. And again we must pause to notice that the daring initiative in so many instances comes from the white woman artist and author: strange, we say until we remember Lucretia Mott and Harriet Beecher Stowe. In passing, we must mention a noteworthy revival of John Brown by David Karsner, to goad the militancy of our day with the tonic of the militancy of our grandfathers' generation.

Still the pealing of the tocsin bell, however timely, cannot completely crowd out the old carefree romanticism and drown out entirely the strum of the guitar and the plunk of the banjo. The Lomax collection of *American Ballads* is with us to recall the immense contribution of the Negro to the balladry of the country, and George Lee's *Beale Street* comes to remind us vividly of the picturesque, swaggering and racy origin of the "Blues." Mr. Lee knows his Beale Street from its respectable end to the river bottoms where "River George" blustered and ruled. Incidentally the story of River George is one of the gems of the book; to my mind he is a better ballad subject than John Henry. In fact I confess to liking the picaresque side of this book; the respectabilities are pitiably pompous by contrast, and one regrets often that the author has chosen to mix his narrative. Yet to leave out the strange incongruities that the ghetto policy creates on Beale Street and elsewhere in Negro life would perhaps be false to the realities of Negro life; Mr. Lee has his justification in fact, if not in the congruities of art.

Turning now to the Negro drama of the year, we find a curious mixture of primitivism and modernism. Perkins' *Dance with Your Gods* and Heywood's *Africana* obviously each tried to exploit the vogue which *Kykunkor* started. To the credit of Broadway be it said that their tawdry tinsel and melodramatic shoddy failed; where the authentic and moving vitality of *Kykunkor* succeeded. Mr. Horton, (Asadata Dafora by original name) has really made a contribution to the drama of the African theme and setting; only its difficult intricacies of dance, pantomime, chant and drum-orchestra technique will prevent its sweeping the Negro stage with cleansing and illuminating fire. The production should by all means have a photo-sound recording; it is a classic of a new genre and will be eventually a turning point in Negro native drama.

The Broadway that is to be commended for thumbing down several specious fakes is to be chided for dooming Paul Green's *Roll On, Sweet Chariot*. Of course it was a cumbersome chariot, too overworked and overlaid with trappings (Mr. Green frequently overloads his plays with ideas and clogs his dramatic machinery), but the theme idea was good and significant. But for the present sound development of Negro drama, anyway, we need the tributary rather than the commercial theatre. It is for such a theatre obviously that Mr. Randolph Edmonds has written his *Six Plays for a Negro Theatre*. Professor Koch is right in his preface when saying: "This, so far as I know, is the first volume of its kind. (He means by a Negro playwright). It suggests new horizons." And Mr. Edmonds is theoretically right when he calls for a few Negro plays that are not defeatist and that are pivoted on the emotions and interests of Negro audiences. But, though they may be considerably redeemed by good acting, these historical and situational melodramas are hardly the stuff of great or highly original Negro drama. But their author has the temperament and the enthusiasm necessary for hardy pioneering, and he has bravely crossed some dramatic Rubicon,—even if the Alps are still ahead.

Finally here is a play that, though it has not scaled the dramatic heights, has burrowed under. Coming into the thick of the race problem by the unusual route of the class struggle and its radical formulae, this vehicle of the Theatre Union has not only made a box-office success but has harnessed the theatre to propaganda more successfully than has been done in this generation. Its clock, so to speak, strikes eleven for capitalism and Nordicism by the same pounding realistic strokes. No matter where one stands on the issues, there is no denying the force and effect of "Stevedore." Only a driving, pertinent theme could carry such amateurish dialogue and technique; but then, *Uncle Tom's Cabin* was one of the worst plays dramatically in the long history of the American stage, but look at its record and its results, in and out of the theatre! Certainly two of the most powerful issues of the contemporary scene have met in *"Stevedore,"* and a synthesis of race and class as a new type of problem drama may just as well be taken for granted. The applause which has greeted this play may well have national and international repercussions, and I do not envy the consternation of Nordic ears.

PART II

WHERE it is a question of Nordicism, sociology might reasonably be expected to be in the vanguard; however it is not so. Sociology, —at least the American brand, is a timid science on general principles and conclusions; fact-finding is its fetich. It particularly side-steps conclusions on the race question, and Negro sociologists, fearing to break with the genteel academic tradition in this respect, have usually been more innocuous than their white confreres,— making a great virtue and parade of inconsequential fact-finding and bland assertions of inter-racialism. That this situation is finally changing after nearly two decades dominated by such attitudes is due to the influence of just a few strong dissenting influences,—the most important of which has come from the militant but unquestionably scientific school of anthropologists captained by Professor Boas. They have dared, in season and out, to challenge false doctrine and conventional myths, and were the first to bring the citadel of Nordicism into range of scientific encirclement and bombardment. An essay in itself could be written on the slow but effective pressure that now has ringed the Nordic doctrines and their advocates round with an ever-tightening scientific blockade. The gradual liberalizing of the American historians and sociologists on the race question has been largely due to the infiltration of the conclusions of cultural anthropology, with its broader perspective and its invalidation of the basic contentions of historical racialism. Yet in the face of this, Negro educators have just made a belated be-

ginning with the study of anthropology and the application of its findings to racial history and the social analysis of contemporary racial situations. At last, however, some beginning has been made.

An item,[1] omitted from our first list, *"Race and Culture Contacts,"* edited from the proceedings of the Twenty-eighth Meeting of the American Sociological Society, aside from interesting papers on *Traditions and Patterns of Negro Family Life* by Professor E. F. Frazier and on *Negro Personality Changes in a Southern Community* by Professor Charles S. Johnson, has important theoretical papers by Professor Robert E. Park on *Race Relations and Certain Frontiers* and Professor W. O. Brown on *Culture Contact and Race Conflict.* In fact for years, Professor Park has been insisting on the application of some general principles of culture contacts to the analysis of the American race problem (our most insidious and unscientific assumption has been and still is that this question is completely *sui generis*). Here in this paper he discusses general phenomena of racial intermixture and through an analysis of mixed blood status tries to get at the basic phenomena of ethnic conflict and change. Professor Brown undertakes more boldly (thank God for a bit of theoretical boldness occasionally) to trace "the process or natural history of race conflict," and tentatively develops a "race conflict sequence through six steps to the ultimate liquidation of conflict in the cultural assimilation and racial fusion of the peoples in contact." I suggest that even with the dangers of hasty generalization, a major interpretative contribution to the fruitful analysis of the race problem has either been made or will grow out of this approach and its comparative technique. Such work lifts the discussion immediately from that futilely academic plane of mere fact-finding upon which our best trained minds, black and white, have been considering the race question for nearly a generation. Though not devoted exclusively to our special subject, I would star this book as the most significant sociological item of the year, in this field of course, because of the promise and significance of this new approach to the scientific discussion of the race question.

---

[1]Race and Culture Contacts, by E. B. Reuter—McGraw Hill Co., New York City.

From such thought-provoking viewpoints, one naturally turns with impatience to the traditional grooves of fact-finding and inter-racial reporting. Under the title of *Negro-White Adjustment*, Paul E. Baker makes a very exhaustive and painstaking summary of inter-racial work and organization, which is redeemed partially from the category of a catalogue by the attempt to analyze the platforms and classify the techniques of inter-racial work in America. Similarly, Mr. George R. Arthur, of the Y. M. C. A. and the Rosenwald Fund, gives an interpretive analysis and history of the welfare work of the twenty-five separate Y. M. C. A.'s in *The Negro Frontier*, with a deserved chronicle of Mr. Julius Rosenwald's contributions and his philosophy of their mission as "frontiers of adjustment in the urbanization of the Negro." It may seem ungrateful to label books of this type as manuals of professional inter-racial work, but they are in the sense that they are committed, unconsciously for the most part, to a definite philosophy of the race question and see the facts of the situation in terms of these commitments. No new light on the nature of the question or of possible new attacks and approaches need be expected under these circumstances, no matter how careful or exhaustive the analysis of the situation. Gradualism and good-will are the dogmatic commitments of this school of social thought,—and that's that.

The Shadow of the Plantation by Professor Charles S. Johnson is a triumph of recording sociology, the general limitations of which we have already discussed. Such detailed description cannot issue, as Dr. Park in his preface seems to think, in interpretative sociology, because the comparative basis and approach are lacking. For example, the conditions described in backward rural Alabama are not merely a relic of slavery and the "belated shadow of the old plantation," but a decidedly different modern deterioration, which though an aftermath of slavery, is actually the product of contemporary exploitation and the demoralization of the rural community life of the South. It is not primarily racial; but a question of a set of conditions as vividly shown by Carl Carmer's *Stars Fell on Alabama*; in this sense a better version of the situation, even in the scientific sense, though a reputed work of fiction. A more interpretative purpose and accomplishment can be credited to Weatherford and Johnson's *Race Relations*,—an elaborate and much belated text-book covering the whole range of the main historical and sociological aspects of the American race problem. The freshest contributions seem to be the discussion of "*Programs Looking Toward Solu-*

tion or Amelioration of Race Relations" and the chapter discussing "*Can There be a Separate Negro Culture?*" Rarely has either topic been put into the frame of full or objective discussion, and it is a distinct service to have done so.

Another wing of Negro scholars have definitely taken the less objective approach and philosophy; and of these Dr. Carter G. Woodson is the pioneer and leader. More and more, this erstwhile factual historian deliberately abandons that point of view and strikes boldly out for corrective criticism and the partisan encouragement of group morale. Dr. Woodson's stock-taking of the *Negro Professional Man and the Community* is weighted as much with trenchant criticism, soundly constructive for the most part, as it is with a factual report of the rise and service of the Negro professional classes. The thesis of the peculiar importance of these groups in Negro life is well sustained and explained, and the diagnosis that today we are seriously suffering from a faulty distribution of our professional group is worth immediate and serious consideration. On the whole, this is a book every Negro professional man or prospective professional should be required to read. Dr. Willis N. Huggins has compiled a useful syllabus outline of references and source materials in *African History* and the wider aspects of the color problem, conceived very much in the same school of semi-propagandist thought that Dr. Woodson is responsible for. An inevitable product of the reaction to Nordic bias, such corrective history and sociology has its definite place and value, even though such a position is difficult to universalize. Until the pseudo-science of the Nordics is completely routed, there will be a grave need for such militant history and for a critical, opinionated sociology.

In *Negro Americans, What Now?*, James Weldon Johnson tries and rather succeeds in striking a happy medium. It is an attempt at pithy, common-sense analysis of the racial situation, its alternatives and of the major objectives of the struggle. It is neither surprising nor discrediting that in the final weighing, the N. A. A. C. P. platform of political and civil rights action should receive very favorable, perhaps preferential emphasis. The value of the analysis lies in the succinct way in which issues usually clouded with partisan bias and emotion are clarified and touched with the wand of common sense; oddly enough an infrequent salt in the problem loaf. One quotation I should like to risk, because it is important: "What we require is a sense of strategy as well as a spirit of determination. . . . I have implied the fact that our policies should include an intelligent opportunism; by which I mean the alertness and ability to seize the advantage from every turn of circumstance whenever it can be done without sacrifice of principle." This is one of my reasons for characterizing this book as 'glorified common-sense on the race question.' It has anticipated its radical critics by saying: "Conservatism and radicalism are relative terms. It is as radical for a black American in Mississippi to claim his full rights under the Constitution as it is for a white American in any state to advocate the overthrow of the existing national government. The black American in many instances puts his life in jeopardy, and anything more radical than that cannot reasonably be required."

Finally, attention must be called to a contribution from the distant perspective of the International Peoples College in Denmark, Rebecca Barton's *Race Consciousness and the American Negro*,—essentially a philosophical study of the psychological complications and complexes of racial consciousness as reflected in Negro literature. This is a painstaking study from a pioneer angle, and only the lack of intimate knowledge of the suppressions that do not get into the literature has prevented its being an interpretation of major and final importance. This book must be taken into consideration in the new social criticism which is just below the horizon.

The field of Negro education is at last in scholastic bloom. To chronicle this is a mild reflection on the profession, but now it can be told. Of course, the obvious handicaps of the profession and the lowered tone of a segregated fraternity have accounted for the lack of productiveness in this field. *The Journal of Negro Education* climaxes a very creditable but young career with a Yearbook on *The Physical and Mental Abilities of the Negro,* a symposium that reflects not only valuable collaboration between white and Negro scholars but the interpretative focussing that only Negro auspices can give to issues that too long have had controversial discussion on uneven terms. The further historical contribution of Professor Dwight O. W. Holmes in his study, *The Evolution of the Negro College* and the analytic study of Professor Horace Mann Bond on *The Education of the Negro in the American Social Order* balance the educational field's contribution in a way that suggests providence since it is not the result of collusion. If the competent discussion of the educational problems and situations of the Negro pick up from this new start, we may anticipate a new phase of development in this numerous but somewhat stagnated and stultified profession. In Dean Holmes' book the dramatic historical role of the Negro college as the pivot of advance

during Reconstruction is importantly documented, and in Dean Bond's book, the present inadequacies and injustices of public provision for Negro education are pointedly briefed and analyzed; to mention only one phase of the constructive contributions of these welcome contributions. In all, there is fortunately reflected a growing tendency not to regard the educational problems of the Negro as different in kind, but only in degree; with a definite trend toward rejoining the mainstream of educational thought after a period of regrettable but inevitable isolation, which has been the heaviest cost of the policy of educational segregation.

In the field of Africana, the contributions this year are not voluminous, but they are significant. In *Liberia Rediscovered* we have little more than a veiled justification of the Firestone policy in that sad tangle of democracy and imperialism, and in Ivor Evans' *Native Policy in South Africa,* we have a faint beginning at objectivity in the discussion of the worst racial situation in the world,—that of the Union of South Africa and adjacent protectorates and mandates. The significant books are those by Helser, Herskovits and Westermann. Dr. Herskovits, this time in collaboration with his wife, resurveys the Suriname cultures of the South American Guinea Negroes after a sojourn in the original home of these cultures, West Africa. He, or rather they, find more evidence than previously for their contention that there are important transplanted survivals of African cultures in the Western hemisphere. Eventually as the outlines of these are retraced, we may be able to reconstruct in rough outline the cultural derivations of various groups of Negroes or various stages in the fading out of these original traits and traditions. In addition to its serious anthropological bearings, *Rebel Destiny* is fascinating reading and proves that sound folk-lore can be as entertaining as pseudo folk-lore.

Helser's book on *"Education of Primitive People"* is primarily an attempt to find a practical technique of missionary education based upon some sensible recognition of the place and worth of the native tradition in such a program. Carried out a little more thoroughly, the study would have constituted a contribution on the part of the practise of social training in primitive society to our own changing system of educational aims and technique. Such a contribution must in time be made, and when it arrives the final reversal on the missionary psychosis of "Greenland's icy mountains and India's coral strand" will have been put into the record. That book will then justify what an over-enthusiastic admirer has said of this one: "A revelation not only of what education among a primitive people may be but of what real education essentially is."

Professor Westermann is co-director of the *International Institute of African Languages and Cultures,* and writes almost pontifically on *"The African of To-Day."* The point of view is that of modified imperialism, naturally,—the benevolent trusteeship conception, the advocacy of the new compromise of indirect rule and the encouragement of integral African traditions with economic but not serious cultural penetration. Of course, it remains to be proved that this reconstructed imperialism is possible; and sound and just, even if possible. However, the brief for it is carefully and humanely advanced by Dr. Westermann, with as much detailed anthropological information as to what is really going on in Africa by reason of the contact and conflict of cultures as is gathered between any two book covers. The study is, therefore, a gift horse that cannot be looked too harshly in the mouth by serious students of the African scene, even though the inspiration is too extra-racial to be a final or a truly representative picture of the African to-day. That picture must, of course, come eventually from the African himself. But in the process that we have been discussing all along, namely the recanting of Nordicism, this book and its dominant point of view represent one long delayed and welcome admission,—namely, that there are elements of permanent value in African cultures and their tradition, and that the complete displacement of these cultures would be an irreparable loss. The idea that they yet have their complementary contribution to make to the cultures of the white man is, of course, below the horizon as yet, but not so far below as not to give some hints of its impending rise.

DEEP RIVER: DEEPER SEA:
Retrospective Review of the Literature of the Negro for 1935

PART I

BIBLIOGRAPHY OF LITERATURE OF THE NEGRO 1935.

FICTION

Kneel to the Rising Sun—Erskine Caldwell,
　　Viking Press, N. Y.—$2.50.
God Shakes Creation—David Cohn,
　　Harper & Bros., N. Y.—$2.50.
Stephen Kent—Hallie F. Dickerman,
　　The Hartney Press, N. Y.—$2.00.
Siesta—Berry Fleming,
　　Harcourt, Brace & Co., N. Y.—$2.50.
Ollie Miss—George Wylie Henderson,
　　Frederick Stokes Co., N. Y.—$2.50.
Mules and Men—Zora Hurston,
　　J. B. Lippincott, Phila.—$3.00.
A Sign for Cain—Grace Lumpkin,
　　Lee Furman, N. Y.—$2.50.
Deep Dark River—Robert Rylee,
　　Farrar & Rinehart, N. Y.—$2.50.
South—Frederick Wight,
　　Farrar & Rinehart, N. Y.—$3.00.

DRAMA

Roll, Sweet Chariot—Paul Green,
　　Samuel French, N. Y.—$1.50.
Porgy & Bess—A Folk Opera,
　　George & Ira Gershwin & Du Bose Heyward,
　　The Theatre Guild, N. Y.
White Man—Samson Raphaelson,
　　Samuel French, N. Y.—$2.00.
Mulatto—Mss.—Langston Hughes,
　　Vanderbilt Theatre, N. Y.
The Two Gifts—Arthur C. Lamb,
　　in Grinnell Plays,
　　Dramatic Publishing Co., Chicago. (one act).

BIOGRAPHY AND BELLES LETTRES

Early Negro American Writers—Benjamin Brawley,
　　University of North Carolina Press—$2.50.
A Saint in the Slave Trade: Peter Claver—Arnold Lunn,
　　Sheed & Ward, Inc., N. Y.—$2.50.
Richard Allen: Apostle of Freedom—Chas. H. Wesley,
　　Associated Publishers, Washington, D. C.—$2.15.

POETRY

The Medea and Some Poems—Countee Cullen,
　　Harper & Bros., N. Y.—$2.00.
Black Man's Verse—Frank Marshall Davis,
　　Black Cat Press, Chicago—$3.00.

Saint Peter Relates an Incident—James Weldon Johnson,
　　Viking Press, N. Y.—$2.00.
The Brown Thrush—An Anthology of Negro Student
　　Verse—
　　Malcolm Roberts Pub. Co., Memphis, Tenn., $1.25.

EDUCATION AND SOCIOLOGY

Negroes in the United States—U. S. Census Publication,
　　Washington—$2.25.
Fundamentals in the Education of Negroes—
　　Bulletin No. 6—Office of Education.
　　Dept. of the Interior—Washington, D. C.—$.10.
The Courts and the Negro Separate School—
　　Journal of Negro Education: July, 1935.
　　Yearbook No. 4—Howard University, Washington,
　　D. C.—$2.00.
Negro Politicians—Harold Gosne'l,
　　University of Chicago Press—$3.50.
The Collapse of Cotton Tenancy—Chas. S. Johnson,
　　Edwin R. Embree, and W. A. Alexander,
　　University of North Caro ina Press, N. C.—$1.00.
90° in the Shade—Clarence Cason,
　　University of North Carolina Press—$2.50.
Black Reconstruction—W. E. B. DuBois,
　　Harcourt, Brace & Co., N. Y.—$4.50.

AFRICANA

In a Province—Laurens van der Post,
　　Coward-McCann, N. Y.—$2.50.
Voodoo Fire in Haiti—Richard Loederer,
　　Doubleday, Doran & Co., N. Y.—$2.75.
A la Belle Flore—Eugene Duliscouet,
　　Editions Delmas—Bordeaux—12 fr.
The Leopard Princess—R. S. Rattray,
　　Appleton-Century Co., N. Y.—$2.00.
The Story of An African Chief—A. K. Nyabongo,
　　Chas. Scribners, N. Y.—$3.00.
Africa Dances—Geoffrey Gorer,
　　Alfred A. Knopf, Inc., N. Y.—$3.50.
Black and White in East Africa—R. C. Thurnwald,
　　Keegan, Paul Co., London—21 s.
Africa: A Social, Economic and Political Geography—
　　Walter Fitzgerald—E. P. Dutton & Co., N. Y.—
　　$5.00.
The Arts of West Africa—Sir Michael Sadler,
　　Oxford University Press—$2.00.
African Negro Art—James J. Sweeney,
　　Museum of Modern Art, N. Y.—$2.50.

Opportunity 14 (January and February 1936): 6–10; 42–43, 61.

237

DEEP river; deeper sea!-even a landlubber knows that! How much water, then, is under our literary keel? Out with the critical plummet! But there's the hitch; in 1934 we felt and announced the shock of the breakwater, we know we are further downstream,— the view has suddenly widened, the sense and tang of the sea are anticipating the actual sight of it, and yet,—the waters are shallower than they were upstream and the current has slackened. Where, then, are we?

If the reader has patience, let us try a simile. A generation back, Negro literature and art were shallow trickles and stagnant puddles in the foothills; in some instance, perhaps, choked sluggish creeks behind rural millponds. Meanwhile, the poets cried out: "Yonder's Parnassus," and the critics blubbered: "We want the sea, nothing will do but the sea." But art had no such magic; water cannot run uphill and doesn't forthright leap dams and ditches. So 'poetic justive,' 'universal values,' 'high life and vindication' were yearned for in vain. Consequently, racial expression had to run inevitably the traditional course; in turns, to trickle in babbling brooks of rhetoric, dally in sentimental shallows and romantic meadows, run headlong and raucously over the sticks and stones of controversy, slow down as it gathered soil and complexion from its native banks and clay bars, chafe in the Negro. Both, incidentally, insist that each must be understood in basic common terms, and that the tragedy of the one is the tragedy of the other. Such developments, coming at this critical time of social reconstruction, have a meaning all too obvious. What is more amazing is the acceptance of these truths in substantial quarters in the South, due somewhat to the irrefutability of the facts, but also in large part to the happy circumstance that most of this writing is "indigenous criticism." Human nature is pretty much like that, everywhere,— and here's a toast to,—and a prayer for, the most desired of all desirables,—indigenous criticism on the part of the creative and articulate Negro himself. Until this shall come, the Negro can really produce no truly universal or even fully representative art. Let the white artist study Negro life objectively and wholly in terms both of itself and its context, as he is showing rapid and wholesome signs of doing; let the Negro artist do so likewise! There is the sea, of which I have spoken.

Some of the younger Negro writers and artists see this situation in terms of what is crystallizing in America and throughout the world as "proletarian literature." What is inevitable is, to that extent at least, right. There will be a quick broadening of the base of Negro art in terms of the literature of class protest and proletarian realism. My disagreement is merely in terms of a long-term view and ultimate values. To my thinking, the approaching proletarian phase is not the hoped-for sea but the inescapable delta. I even grant its practical role as a suddenly looming middle passage, but still these difficult and trying shoals of propagandist realism are not, never can be, the oceanic depths of universal art; even granting that no art is ever groundless or timeless.

But to return briefly to our 1935 crop of Negro fiction. Readers keen on comparative values may wonder why I have not yet mentioned *Deep, Dark River,* Robert Rylee's moving tragedy of Mississippi injustice and persecution. It is more of a novel structurally and more a specific study of Negro character than *Siesta.* But the last few years of fiction have just about illuminated us on the question "What is the South"; the forward turn now is to tackle that more courageous and hopeful analysis; "What makes it like that," in other words the *why* rather than just the *how* of the South. In these terms then, even Frederick Wight's half aesthetic travelogue *South* is more significant, though less powerful, for it tries to explain and is ever conscious of the great dilemmas in southern life by which it is set over against itself. It is important and brave for Mr. Rylee, himself a southerner, to admit, through the mouth of his white Portia, Mary Winston, in talking to Mose, in jail for murder: "You see, Mose, the story you have told me is not a story that can be told in a court room. You are a Negro and Mr. Birney is a white man. A Negro can't tell that a white man was living with his wife or that a white man sent a Negro to kill him. No jury would free you if you made that defense," but it is still more important and profound to say of the eastern Cotton Belt, as Berry Fleming does, "This is the heart of the South; you can't get any farther into the South than this. This is Anglo-Saxon and African, this is the original cotton country . . . and these three states have one-third of all the fertilizer factories in the United States. The fertilizer factory isn't on any of their state seals, but it ought to be . . . the unfertility of the soil makes a hard living. You have to put almost as much money into the ground as you get out." For when Mr. Fleming goes on to say that beauty doesn't grow out of soil like that, he might also have included justice. Diagnosis is better than description; although the day is yet young since frank description came on the horizon, this sort of analysis is still younger.

Mrs. Hallie Dickerman has written an interesting first novel *Stephen Kent,* frank in theme, true enough to fact, but handled with timid sentimentality. Several years ago it would have been an advanced novel because of its frank treatment of miscegenation and the peculiar Southern dilemmas of the "blot on the escutcheon." However, it does not break with the old conventional formula of blood atavism and calmly accepts the rules of caste as framing irrevocable tragedy even for the thoughts of the characters themselves. Thus Stephen Kent's magnanimity in not claiming his white mother actualizes few of the deep potentialities of the plot, and despite a courageous theme, makes a milk and water contrast to the blood, iron and steel of the prevailing trend.

Negro writers of fiction come forward with but two offerings out of the rapidly increasing field. However, both are real contributions to local color and characterization, though unfortunately not in theme or social philosophy. George Wylie Henderson's first novel *Ollie Miss* is a mature and competent study of Negro farm life and its elementals so far as that can take us without any suggestion of its place in the general scheme of things. Just such detached but intimate recording is also done in Miss Hurston's folk-lore collection, *Mules and Men,* which has the effect of novel vignettes because of her great power of evoking atmosphere and character. It has been many years since the patiently against barriers of prejudice, give over much of its substance to alien exploitation before gaining depth and strength enough to overleap the dam of provincialism, spurt forward, dangerously, in a waterfall of deceptive freedom, spin and eddy in self-confusion, labor toward a junction with the mainstream, press along jointly in an ever-deepening channel, though at the cost of the muddy murk of realism and the smelly muck of commercialism, at last, under the accumulated impetus of all this, to meet and challenge,—and lose, to the sea.

The reader has a right to query: "And are we really there?" Even by the simile,—not yet. Just on the threshold of the sea, nature gives us the paradox of the shallow delta with its unproductive mixture of sea sand and river soil and its unpalatable blend of salt and fresh water. And so, in this matter of the literary course of the deep, dark river of Negro literature, here we are at the end of 1935, I think, on the wide brackish waters of the delta, waiting not too comfortably or patiently in the uninviting vestibule of the ocean of great, universalized art. The scenery is monotonous, the air unsavory, the course weed-grown and tricky; half of the literature of the year isn't literature but a strange bitter bracken of commingled propaganda and art. Yet one optimistic factor stands out, in spite of all this, the horizons are wider,—wider than they have ever been: and thus the promise of the sea is assuredly there. Before too very long, the tang, taste, color and rhythm of our art will have changed irreparably from the purely racial to the universal, and those who have cried for the sea will doubtless cry for the loss of their river.

Meanwhile, our art is again turning prosaic, partisan and propagandist, but this time not in behalf of striving, strident racialism, but rather in a protestant and belligerent universalism of social analysis and protest. In a word, our art is going proletarian; if the signs mean anything. Yesterday it was Beauty at all costs and local color with a vengeance; today, it is Truth by all means and social justice at any price. Except for the occasional detached example, those who hope for the eventual golden mean of truth with beauty must wait patiently,—and perhaps, long. Just now, all the slime and hidden secrets of the river are shouldered up on the hard, gritty sand bars and relentlessly exposed to view. Almost overnight, in the fiction and drama of Negro life, generation-old taboos have been completely broken down; in a dozen steely mirrors, miscegenation shows not its intriguing profile but its tragic full face and economic exploitation and social injustice their central tragedy of common guilt and imminent retribution, not just the stock side-show of Negro melodrama. Hollywood still plays with a picture-book version of the old romantic South, but in serious contemporary letters, the work of Erskine Caldwell, though extreme, is typical. Here, the South is on the grill of a merciless realism, administered for the most part by disillusioned and disillusioning white southerners to whom the poor white and the Negro peasant are common victims of a decadent, top-heavy and inhuman system, for which they see no glory and no excuse. This increasing trend has caught the southern defensive completely off-guard because it has made no concessions to its argumentative set; it has just confronted the orators and propagandists with overwhelming and almost photographic reporting. After all, none of us can get away from bare facts in the glare of sun or spotlight; no one can read through Caldwell's *Kneel to the Rising Sun* or Berry Fleming's *Siesta,* or out of the field of fiction, Clarence Cason's *90° in the Shade* and ever be quite the same. Especially important are they for the Negro reader, who suffers acutely from the blindness of familiarity as well as from the blinkered distortion of his own case and problem. As incurable a southern as Edward Larocque Tinker calls *Siesta* "a truthful picture of how the present generation in deep Dixie lives, loves and thinks,"—"an adult novel drawn from true American sources."

I suppose that in this matter of the new radical literature of the American South, there will always be two schools, both for the creators and the consumers, the artists and the critics. Caldwell, of course, represents the social protest approach and Miss Lumpkin's *Sign for Cain* is the most daring and logical expression of that point of view to date, barring, of course, Mr. Caldwell's own brilliant pioneering; Clarence Cason will, I think, more and more come to fame as the brave pioneer of the 'psychographic' analysts, for whom the mind-sets of the South are the keys to the situation rather than the class economics of the Marxian Caldwellites. In which case, it seems to me, Cason, though no novelist, has founded or grounded a school of southern fiction, of which Berry Fleming is, to date, the most brilliant and promising exponent. My own sympathies, temperamentally determined no doubt, are with the psycho-analysts; but I grant the power, integrity and increasing vogue of the Marxians. What is of greater importance than this issue of approach and technique is the overwhelming agreement of both schools on the evidence of fact. They corroborate each other on the facts of the case startlingly; and together they raise up a new plateau both for the artistic and the social understanding of the South and younger Negro writers have had as firm a grip on their material as here indicated; which is so positive a gain that it is probably ungracious to complain of the lack of social perspective and philosophy. While not particularly incumbent on Miss Hurston by reason of the folk-lore objective of her work, there is yet something too Arcadian about hers and Mr. Henderson's work, considering the framework of contemporary American life and fiction. The depression has broken this peasant Arcady even in the few places where it still persisted, and while it is humanly interesting and refreshing enough, it is a critical duty to point out that it is so extinct that our only possible approach to it is the idyllic and retrospective. On the other hand, this same rare native material and local color in the flesh and bone of either the proletarian or the sociological strains of fiction would carry into them the one lacking dimension of great art.

On the dramatic front, however, folk-lore is in the ascendancy with the undoubted and deserved success of *Porgy and Bess*; since in the field of the problem play no real succession to last season's strong play *Stevedore* has come forward in spite of the obvious candidacy of Langston Hughes' current Broadway offering of *Mulatto*. Granting the difficulty of any unpleasant theme on the American stage, it is strange to account for the general lack of success of the serious Negro problem play. Playwrights, black and white, must meet this challenge, for the audience cannot be entirely blamed when one after the other, with the most sympathetic reading, plays in this category smoulder rather than flame. I think it is a problem of craftsmanship primarily, recalling how long the southern realistic novel smouldered before it broke clear and bright. *Porgy* deserves its success, both as a play and as opera, it surges irresistibly with life and is totally convincing. The other themes can do the same, when master craftsmanship appears. Even without master craft a certain flare for the dramatically vital gave real life to *Stevedore*. But *Roll, Sweet Chariot*, though well studied, over-studied perhaps, is cryptic; Raphaelson's *White Man*, with an incandescent theme, sputters and goes feebly defeatist at the end— (though even at that, it is a considerable advance in the treatment of the psychology of inter-marriage over "All God's Chillun Got Wings),—and *Mulatto* merely noses through on the magnificent potentialities of its theme, which for the most part are amateurishly smothered in talk and naive melodrama. Of course, Broadway merely takes a pot chance as yet on serious Negro plays; they are usually hastily rehearsed, poorly staged, and superficially seasoned. But the playwrights themselves must force the issue and above all else let their characters grow up to the full stature of the heroic. Well studied genre or pastiche characters carrying through great themes in only two dimensions will never put over the serious drama of Negro life.

The Negro actor has demonstrated his capacity under great handicaps of inadequate materials; it is tragic, especially in view of her enforced and we hope temporary retirement, to think of the puny roles Rose McClendon has had for the expression of her truly great dramatic genius. Of course, any role in which she would not have been positively mis-cast ought to have been open to her. But she has had to battle not only a limited chance, but even there, half-baked characterization, type roles that ill-befit great dramatic powers. Imagine, for example, to take the case of *Mulatto*, a Cora who really became the Colonel's mistress as the door closed and then shifted suddenly back to the mode of the domestic servant as it opened again to company; it is for such reasons that I place primary blame, not on the audience, the producers and Broadway traditions, but upon the faulty dramaturgy of two-thirds of the plays of Negro life, irrespective of the authorship being professional or amateur, black or white. Negro drama needs full gamut and an open throttle; and not what it has so often had, either skill without courage, or courage without skill.

Turning to *belles lettres*, we witness an obvious revival of biography, and this with the rumors of a projected biographical series of Negro leaders and the promised revival of the plans for an Encyclopedia of the Negro, indicates a decided awakening of the historical impulse. All three of the books in this field extend to the general reading public little known historical material that should be theirs. In the context of a vindication of saintliness and mystical apprehension of the supernatural, Arnold Lunn gives us a vivid biography of *St. Peter Claver*, who labored thirty-eight years during the eighteenth century for the alleviation of the victims of the slave trade. Professor Brawley brings within reach of the general reader biographical and critical material on the least known of our literary fields—the Negro writers of the colonial and early anti-slavery periods, with well-culled selections from their works. Professor Wesley has written the first complete biography of *Richard Allen*, founder of African Methodism and pioneer racialist. All this is more than welcome, even though none of the work is in the contemporary vein of biography. Paucity of material and the Puritan repressions of those who did make the contemporary records of these worthies has undoubtedly crippled their biographers for drawing psychological portraits of their subjects. They will possibly thus remain in the daguerrotype and wood-cut outlines in which they are already familiar to researchers; the gain is that this material is now at the ready disposal of the general reader, competently presented and attractively readable.

Two veteran poets have come to the fore with their medals on, so to speak. In spite of the new material, there are no new notes and no new poetic highs. In general, these two volumes of Countee Cullen and James Weldon Johnson do not advance their poetic reputations. The choruses of Cullen's translated *Medea* are finely turned, with virtuosity in fact, and it is good to have available again the cream of Weldon Johnson's *Fifty Years and other Poems*, now out of print. However, Negro poetry cannot expect in this day of changing styles and viewpoints to live successfully on its past. That is

why I turned most feverishly to the pages of *The Brown Thrush: Anthology of Verse by Negro Students*. Perhaps my present impatience with the elder generation is that I found so many weak and tiring echoes of Dunbar, Johnson, Hughes and Cullen there. Natural enough, no doubt, but if so, why not Whitman, Swinburne, Frost, Millay or Jeffers? In fact, Negro poetry has no excuse today for being imitative at all, and little excuse for being tenuous and trite in substance. For the new notes and the strong virile accents in our poetry today, we must shift from Harlem to Chicago; for there are Willard Wright* whose verse sees the light in the *New Masses* and other radical periodicals and Frank Marshall Davis, who really brings fresh talent and creative imagination to this waning field. Both of these younger poets owe more to the Langston Hughes inspiration than to the academicians, but each in his own individual way has gone deeper into the substance of the folk life, though neither of them so deeply as that other more mature poet, Sterling Brown, who regrettably publishes so little of what he writes. I insist that we shall not know the full flavor and potentialities either of tragic or comic irony as applied to Negro experience until this sturdy, incisive verse of Brown's is fully published. For years we have waited for the sealed vials of irony and satire to open and for their purging and illuminating fire to come down in poetic flashes and chastizing thunderbolts. And for some reason, the gods withhold the boon. The puny thrust that passes for irony, the burlesque smirk that masquerades as satire try one's critical soul, until one remembers illuminatingly that outside antiquity, only the Irish and the French have the gift of it. But it might have been in the gift-box of the Negro, seeing he had such need of it.

*[sic] Richard Wright [Editor's note].

ADDENDA: LITERATURE OF THE NEGRO,—1935
PART II.

NEGRO HISTORY IN THIRTEEN PLAYS: ed. Willis
Richardson and May Miller, Associated Publishers,
Washington, D. C. $3.25.

THE STORY OF THE NEGRO RETOLD: Carter G.
Woodson, Associated Publishers, Washington, D. C.
$2.15.

DANIEL A. PAYNE: Josephus Coan. A. M. E. Book
Concern, Philadelphia, Pa. $1.50.

EVEN in the cold ashes of sociology, some
new fires are burning; like a refiner's fur-
nace in books like Cason's *90° in the
Shade,* like a flaming torch in a book like Dr.
DuBois's *Black Reconstruction.* The subject
needs both heat and light; more light, but in
the impending crisis, heat, too, is salutary. In
the small but searching volume, *The Collapse
of Cotton Tenancy,* even that arch-advocate of
objective sociology, Professor Charles S. Johnson, in the company of Edward R. Embree and
Will A. Alexander, points an accusing finger
and calls for present-day social reconstruction.
This is a healthy symptom of progress in the
artificially isolated and conservative field of
Negro history and sociology.   I take it that
there will not be many more books written in
this field that will ignore the general social and
economic crisis and the necessary and vital linkage of the Negro situation with the general issues. Although not fully repudiated, this handicap and blight of several generations standing
is now definitely on the wane.

Of course, separate discussion of racial issues
and interests is necessary and inevitable, but a
separate and special ideology, especially one
based on outmoded social concepts, never has
been desirable, although until recently it has
been all too frequent. Yet one can scarcely approve in full of Dr. DuBois's passionate leap to
close the gap and throw the discussion of the
Negro problem to the forefront battle-line of
Marxian economics, even though *Black Reconstruction* is one of the most challenging worth-
while books of the year. This merely because it
is more difficult to apply the Marxian formula
to the past decades of Negro history, and that
inaccurately done, really detracts considerably
from the main purpose and accomplishment of
the work,—viz. a crashing counter-interpreta-
tion of the Reconstruction period and a justifiable impeachment of its American historians.

Ultimately,—soon perhaps, we shall have the
other problem realized in a scientifically economic interpretation of the Negro's status in
American life and history; meanwhile we grate-

fully salute Dr. DuBois's spirited and successful
historical challenge.

A useful publication, purely factual and statistical, comes from the government press, compiling the figures of the 1930 U. S. Census as
they relate to the *Negroes in the United States.*
For the first time, this appears under the acknowledged editorial supervision of Charles E.
Hall, veteran Negro statistician of the Census
department.   Under the editorial supervision of
Dr. Ambrose Caliver, and the imprint of the
U. S. Department of Education, comes a small
but pithy publication,—*Fundamentals in Negro
Education,* collating the findings of last year's
conference on Negro education. The pamphlet
gives the best statement available of the state
of Negro education in terms of the present crisis.

The Year Book issue of the *Journal of Negro
Education* brings forward, similarly, a most opportune subject, in fact the crucial one of the
separate Negro school. Although the pattern of
previous volumes is followed, and thus the symposium issues are well balanced, *pro* and *con,*
the trend of the argument is decidedly against
the principle and practise of educational segregation, and forecasts a militant reaction against
it. Most of the disputants advocate challenging
its legality before the courts, such as has been
recently done in the University of Maryland
case, so successfully prosecuted under N.A.A.
C.P. auspices by the young Washington attor-
ney, Charles H. Houston. The symposium and
its conclusions anticipated the case, it should be
noted, in estimating its significance as a gauge
of educational opinion among Negroes.

As has been hinted, *The Collapse of Cotton
Tenancy,* although not completely militant,
turns its back definitely upon palliative measures
in the problems of the rural South. It pictures
vividly the present plight of the cotton tenant
farmer, and though interested in the Negro
particularly, uses the more scientific concept of
the share-cropper, be he black or white. The
authors conclude that the present crisis in southern agriculture is the final stage of the generation-old breakdown of the plantation system,
that this system must be radically changed, and
that there is no solution short of converting the
share-tenant into an owner tenant with whatever
legal and governmental aids are necessary. So,
whichever way we turn, from the economic,
historical or psychological angle, a more radical
and challenging point of view confronts us.
One warns, another challenges, still another, as
with Cason, almost vivisects; but none condone,
placate or play hopeful Pollyana. We ought,

at least know where we are and not be victims of time-old illusions.

As one might expect, the field of Africana is a baffling mixture of tinsel and gold; this year's yield has some of the profoundest and some of the most superficial interpretations yet made of primitive life and custom. Surely one of the worst is Loederer's *Voodoo Fire in Haiti*, where again the unhappy isle is distorted by the flippant sensation monger, looking for cheap, glamorous exotic primitivism. The verdict of competent scholarship is that the Haiti of Seabrook, Craige and Loederer simply does not exist except in the hectic imagination of these journalist-adventurers. They see largely what they preconceive, superficially document it, and are off with their wares to the eager but misguided devotees of the cult of the jungle. Those who know the jungle life more expertly come out with sober and radically different interpretations.

An instance, and an encouraging contrast is Captain Rattray's novel of a primitive African cult, *The Leopard Priestess*. It is a novel, and should perhaps have been listed with our fiction, but for the fact that its folk-lore and background are too important. The author knows his Africa from years of study and intensive experience. Authentic mystery, accurate primitive magic and ceremonial, appropriate tropic situations follow the fate of the guilty lovers; they are enmeshed in an even more typical African guilt than the lovers of Batouala, and the stark simplicity of their fate convinces us that a real African romance has been written. Had it the stylistic excellence of Batouala, it would be the undisputed classic that the latter still is.

Another competent and illuminating record of African custom and thought is the story of a native African chieftain's son, told by Akiki Nyabongo, himself an educated native of Uganda. Mr. Nyabongo has little need of a dubious veil of fiction to decorate his narrative, unless it be to save some embarrassment in this nearly autobiographical story of the conflict between native and European mores in the youth and adolescence of little Prince Ati. In some respects, this is the first book to bring out from the inside the dilemmas of the intelligent African involved in education at the hands of missionaries and tutelage from the self-appointed trustees of their civilization. Time and again the ignorant disdain of native custom is clearly and cleverly illustrated, and more than once, the native tradition comes off best. One cannot refrain from repeating the refreshing incident of the young prince reading to his father and his assembled wives, after the year-long diatribes

of the Reverend Mr. Hubert on polygamy, of the passages from the Holy Bible detailing the story of King Solomon with his seven hundred wives and three hundred concubines. A gale of laughter is sometimes more effective than a blast of polemics.

In a Province, a problem novel of South Africa, reports for the first time effectively the main outlines of the class struggle and the industrial dilemmas of that quarter of the globe. Laurens van der Post is a painstaking artist as well as a competent reporter,—and the book betokens a new breath of artistic liberalism from the stagnant conservatism of its traditional background.

Professor Fitzgerald's social and economic geography of Africa is a path-breaking analysis that ought to be the base of whatever prescribed studies of Africa are given in our colleges. The arts and antiquities of Africa are important for the true understanding of African life, and nothing is less known and more misunderstood by the average American Negro) but without a scientific, objective basis such as this study of the great continent affords, they are a deceptive veneer. That is why, with an interest of long standing in such subjects as Professor Sadler's book on *The Arts of West Africa*, Mr. James Sweeney's admirable essay and catalogue on African art prepared for the Museum of Modern Art's remarkable spring show, or even Monsiuer Carré's fine preface on the Benin civilization and its art prepared for the recent Knoedler Gallery show, I still insist that a fundamental knowledge of African geography and the economics of the colonial situation are indispensable in any sound and comprehending knowledge of the land of our forefathers.

Those who need the short-cut of an interpretation combining several of these factors into a single book will, therefore, welcome and praise Geoffrey Gorer's *Africa Dances*, to my thinking, the book of the year. Starting out as an aesthetic caravan, studying the African dance, the magic key of taking Feral Benga, the talented Sengalese dancer, as devoted and respected travel companion, opened for Mr. Gorer, though a novice in Africa, doors closed to missionaries, traders, government agents and even canny anthropologists. And so, natives, chiefs, fetish priests, colonial society, high, low and middle-rank, townsmen, coastmen, hinterlanders all flit graphically across Mr. Gorer's diary pages with a life-like vividness and candid reality. Of course, all praise to Mr. Gorer's own temperamental equipment, sensitiveness, amazing candor, freedom from prejudice of civilization and color

(many who have immunity from one of these
are chronic victims of the other), and a contagious power of description; but with all these,
he could have forgotten the magic open sesame
of an African friend and sponsor. He magna-
nimously admits this, so there is little virtue in
calling attention to it, except to praise the book,
which I do in everything but its pessimistic conclusions,—and this only because Africa has survived so much that it seems likely that she will
survive even the modern plagues of imperialistic
exploitation.

GOD SAVE REALITY!
Retrospective Review of the
Literature of the Negro: 1936

PART I.

BIBLIOGRAPHY OF LITERATURE OF THE NEGRO: 1936

FICTION:

Death Is a Little Man—Minnie H. Moody, Julian Messner, N. Y.—$2.50.
Big Blow—Theodore Pratt, Little Brown & Co., Boston, —$2.50.
Courthouse Square—Hamilton Basso, Scribner & Sons, N. Y.—$2.50.
A White Man and A Black Man In the Deep South—James Saxon Childers—Farrar & Rinehart, N. Y.—$2.50.
The sub-plots of
Gone With the Wind—Margaret Mitchell, Macmillan, N. Y.—$3.00.
Absolom, Absolom—Wm. Faulkner, Random House Press, N. Y.—$2.50.

* * *

Under the Sun—Grace Flandrau, Chas. Scribner's, N. Y. —$2.50.
African Witch—Joyce Cary—Wm. Morrow, N. Y.— $2.50.

* * *

POETRY and BELLES LETTRES:

April Grasses—Marion Cuthbert, The Woman's Press, N. Y.—75 cents.
No Alabaster Box and Other Poems, "Eve Lynn"—Alpress, Phila.—$1.50.
We Lift Our Voices and Other Poems—Mae V. Cowdery Alpress, Phila.—$1.50.
Poems in *The American Caravan: 1936*—Willard Wright —Wm. Morrow & Co., N. Y.—$3.95.
We Sing America: An Anthology—Marion Cuthbert—Friendship Press, N. Y.—$1.00.

* * *

Belles Images—Rene Maran, Editions Delmas, Paris—8 fr.
Poems, Prose and Plays by Alexander Pushkin—trans. by Yarmolinsky and Deutsch—Random Press, N. Y.—$3.00.

* * *

DRAMA:

White Man—Samson Raphaelson, National Theatre, N. Y.
One Way to Heaven—Mss. Countee Cullen and Arna Bontemps—Hedgerow Theatre, Moylan, Pa.

When the Jack Hollers—Mss. Langston Hughes and Arna Bontemps—Gilpin Players, Cleveland.
New Theatre League Plays: N. Y.—25 cents each:
1. *Trouble with the Angels*—Bernard Schoenfeld.
2. *Mighty Wind a Blowin'*—Alice H. Ware.[1]
3. *Angelo Herndon Jones*—Langston Hughes.
Federal Theatre Project—Negro Unit—Lafayette Theatre, N. Y.
   Walk Together Chillun—Frank Wilson.
   The Conjure Man Dies—Rudolph Fisher.
   Turpentine—J. A. Smith and Peter Morell.
   Obey's *Noah*—dramatized by Carlton Moss.
   Shakespeare: *Macbeth*—dramatized in Negro style by Orson Welles.
   Bassa Moona—African Dance Drama by Momodu Johnson and Norman Coker.

* * *

NEGRO MUSIC AND ART:

Negro Musicians and Their Music—Maud Cuney Hare—Associated Publishers, Washington, D. C.—$3.15.

The Negro and His Music—Alain Locke, Associates in Negro Folk Education, Washington, D. C.—25 cents.

Hot Jazz—Hughes Panassié—N. Witmark & Co., N. Y.—$5.00.

Swing That Music—Louis Armstrong—Longmans, Green & Co., N. Y.—$2.50.

Negro Folk Songs—John and Allan Lomax—Macmillan Co., N. Y.—$3.00.

Folk Songs of Mississippi—Arthur Hudson, University of North Carolina Press—$5.00.

Rolling Along in Song—ed. by Rosamond Johnson—Viking Press, N. Y.—$3.50.

Negro Art: Past and Present—Alain Locke, Associates in Negro Folk Education, Washington, D. C.—25 cents.

* * *

SOCIOLOGY, BIOGRAPHY & RACE RELATIONS:

Alien Americans—B. Schrieke—Viking Press, N. Y.—$2.50.

A Preface to Racial Understanding—Charles S. Johnson—Friendship Press, $1.00.

Preface to Peasantry—Arthur Raper—University of North Carolina Press—$3.50.

The Story of the American Negro—Corinne Brown—Friendship Press—$1.00.

Twelve Negro Americans—Mary Jenness — Friendship Press—$1.00—paper—60 cents.

Paul Laurence Dunbar—Benjamin G. Brawley—University of North Carolina Press—$1.00.

Opportunity 15 (January and February 1937): 8-13; 40-44.

From Harlem to the Rhine: Story of New York's Colored Volunteers—Arthur W. Little—Covici-Friede, N. Y.—$3.00.

The French Quarter—Herbert Asbury—Alfred Knopf, Inc., N. Y.—$3.50.

My Great Wide Beautiful World—Juanita Harrison—Macmillan Co., N. Y.—$2.50.

God in a Rolls Royce—John Horsher—Hilman-Curl, N. Y.—$2.50.

* * *

ECONOMICS, POLITICS and COLONIAL
PROBLEMS:

The Negro As Capitalist—Abram Harris, American Academy of Political and Social Science, Phila.—$3.00.

The Negro Labor Unionist of New York—Charles Franklin—University of Columbia Press, N. Y.—$3.75.

The Negro Question in the United States—J. S. Allen—International Publishers, N. Y.—$2.00.

A World View of Race—Ralph J. Bunche—Associates in Negro Folk Education, Washington, D. C.—25 cents.

Out of Africa—Emory Ross—Friendship Press, N. Y.—$1.00.

How Britain Rules Africa—George Padmore, Lathrop-Lee & Shepard, N. Y.—$3.50.

Haiti and Her Problems—Dantes Bellegarde—University of Porto Rico Press.

Negroes and the Law—Fitzhugh Styles — Christopher Press, Boston—$3.50.

Pro-Slavery Thought of the Old South—William Sumner Jenkins—University of North Carolina Press—$2.50.

The Negro School Curriculum: A Symposium — July issue—Journal of Negro Education, Washington, D. C.

Adult Education Among Negroes—Ira DeA. Reid—Associates in Negro Folk Education—25 cents.

* * *

AFRICANA:

The Gentle Savage—Richard Wyndham—Wm. Morrow & Co., N. Y.—$2.75.

Journey Without Maps—Graham Greene.

Civilizations of the Negro: Part III, of Murchison's *Handbook of Social Psychology* — Clark University Press, $6.00.

TRUTH may be stranger than fiction, but fiction is certainly more confusing than reality. And especially so, the modern fiction of the South, which means, in large part, the fiction of Negro life; since the Negro is almost the pet obsession of the Southern novelist. Once, however, it was a solid South, fictionally speaking, and a stereotyped Negro. Now the pendulum has swung to another bad extreme: one is bewildered by the contradictions of the divergent interpretations and must agonize over the problem "Which South" and "What Negro"! Every author almost has his "private South," and in desperation, one is forced to say: "God save Reality!", since the writers can't.

The publishers' blurb for Minnie Hite Moody's *Death Is a Little Man* says: "you will not find here the depraved South of *God's Little Acre* or *Tobacco Road;* not the soft, aristocratic South of *So Red the Rose,* nor the labor-troubled South of *A Sign for Cain.* Neither the mumbo-jumbo of *Stars Fell on Alabama* nor the sinister mob-rule of *Deep Dark River*

have been set down here for your entertainment. This is just a tender, heartfelt story of simple people!" All of which is more than half true. But it is not true, as they continue to assure, that its reading "will do no more than make you glad you've read it"; and not from any defect of the book, which is a carefully observed, convincingly told story, but from the fact that again the South is a burning issue, and there are only two ways of reacting to it. There are the novels that condone and those that condemn; emotional neutrality is almost impossible.

There are, of course, degrees of attitude on both sides. *Death Is a Little Man* condones subtly, perhaps regretfully,—but condones just the same. But it should be read; it is far from being a mere white man's picture of the Negro. Ernie's life in the typical Shantytown "Bottoms" is vividly pictured; her trials, marital and otherwise, are well portrayed, we aver, her husband's temptations and persecutions are carefully documented; the moods are correct; considering the level of life the book reports, it is a true document of the outward action of Negro life and of its articulate speech, all that an outsider can hear. But of the private thought, and even Mrs. Moody's Negroes have it,—half of it subconscious and the rest slyly suppressed beneath their conventional servility,—of that, not a word. But where is the blame? With not a single sustained serious piece of fiction by a Negro author in this year's list, I think it is too easy a way out to blame white authorship for not reporting what it does not, cannot hear. Mrs. Moody guesses at some of it intuitively, but she catches only swaggering fatalism for the men, Christian resignation for the women;—which again is the half truth or a fraction over. But the rest! That part of the question is up to the Negro novelist in a day when the Negro cannot complain that he is a victim of literary neglect. We strain our ears and wait.

Moreover, although the trend in contemporary Southern fiction is to admit the inextricable tangle of white and black lives in the Southern scheme, it is not to be expected, either on moral or literary grounds, that the Negro character should always receive specialized attention. For this reason I have not listed as fiction of the Negro the year's two most sensational Southern novels: Margaret Mitchell's *Gone With the Wind* or William Faulkner's *Absolom, Absolom,* for all their importance, sectional as well as racial. Mammy is far from a stock or minor character in this best seller of Secession apologetics; and the half-wit mulatto son of Faulkner's Quixotic hero, Colonel Sutpen, is after all the living symbol of Faulkner's morbid and satirical obituary of the "Old Regime." The one manages her mistress by the age-old Negro subtlety of flattering servility; the other stands as the futile indictment of miscegenation. But after all, the tragedy is on both sides and for the general reading public, it is the South, not the Negro that matters. However, how is that public divided: hundreds of thousands of copies for the sentimental, nostalgic resurrection of historical ghosts; and only thousands for the revealing, but tedious surgery of Faulkner's post-mortem. However no amount of romancing will conceal the fact that the old South is dead; and whoever must know why it died, must have read *Sanctuary*, *Light in August* and now *Absolom, Absolom*.

The popular verdict may be with the condoning apologists (and this classification does not impugn motives, in fact admits that much which affects the public this way originates less harmfully as escapist day-dreaming), but the literary verdict, and this year's weight of numbers, is for those who criticize and by implication condemn. We can take them in order of degree. Theodore Pratt's *Big Blow* is a melodrama of love and social antagonisms in Florida. Its real achievement is the fearless realism of its portrayal of white "cracker" low-life, showing its common denominators with the black peasant life surrounding it, Holy Roller revivals, barbecues and all. But Wade Barrett's love of Celie brings him into the snares of the community's prejudice, and the symbolic "Big Blow" is a hurricane that pens Wade, Celie and the fear-stricken Negro they have saved from a lynching party in a shack with a social as well as an atmospheric storm over their heads. This story is good melodrama, good sociology, and entertaining prose.

Better still, in literary and social values is Hamilton Basso's *Courthouse Square*. It too is a drama of the chronic feud of race in Southern life; with a white victim (as is frequent now in contemporary Southern fiction). The third generation of Southern liberals, David Barondess seeks a haven after a disillusioning life in the North in his ancestral and typical Southern town. He and his father espouse the cause of an enterprising Negro physician struggling to found a hospital sanitorium for his people. The antagonisms of property owners, politicians and a newspaper editor kindle the "poor whites" to mob action, the Negro section is attacked, the hospital burned and, in saving the Negro physician from their fury, David is felled, seriously beaten and wounded, in Macedon's Courthouse Square. This is really a contribution to Southern fiction, not because it pleads the Negro cause, but because it turns an accurately focussed wide-angle lens on the contemporary Southern scene. Incidentally, it is beautifully written.

Duplicating another native Alabamian's feat (Clement Wood's precedent-breaking novel of fifteen years ago), James Saxon Childers writes *"A Novel about a White Man and a Black Man in the Deep South."* It is a breathtaking title, and a breathtaking story: if just a little less tense and didactic, it would be a classic. But that is pardonable, if one considers what Southern Medes and Persians this story defies. Gordon Nicholson of a prominent Birmingham family becomes the college friend of Dave Gordon, Negro fellow student, at a Northern college. After interludes typical of their generation, the World War in France for one, Harlem professional life for the other, they meet again in Birmingham, and continue their friendship on the plane of what the orthodox South calls "social equality," but what is to them and a few understanding liberals, common interests. One is avocationally an author, the other a composer; after workaday journalism and college teaching they exchange confidences and aspirations in stimulating companionship. Whisperings, mutterings, threats, then violence spell out the rising crescendo of reactionary Birmingham's indignation, but they fight out their hazardous friendship, to the costly tune of Gordon's social connections, Anne, his sister's broken engagement, Dave's narrow escape through Gordon and a liberal lawyer friend's loyalty from a framed up charge of arson. Finally, at the point of moral victory, fate steps in with the suicide of Anne, too weak to stand the community pressure. They stick out this tragic Southern Ophelia's funeral, write each other consoling letters, but at the end the shadow of it all accumulatively falls between them and they stoically realize the cost and drift apart. This sounds defeatist, but the reactions of the main characters, especially Gordon's frequent rhetorical challenges and protests, puts the moral defeat elsewhere, and where, most readers will agree, it belongs. Falling just short of being a classic of style, Mr. Childers' novel is a classic of human insight and courageous social analysis. It is unmistakeable evidence of the new leaven in the old Southern lump.

Turning from the fiction of the "Black Belt" to that of the "Dark Continent," we find two significant indictments. Grace Flandrau goes back to her familiar Congo for nine psychological studies of white men's lives in Central Africa; and the upshot of all the tragic complications registers a moral verdict: defeat for political and economic and human exploitation, success for scientific research and truly humanitarian effort. Miss Flandrau never set out to defend such a thesis, which makes her reporting all the more convincing; but the colonial administrators, adventurers and other parasites of the colonial system do come to naught (truth telling observers have said so since the days of Joesph Conrad), and in that sense the jungle conquers and has the last laugh. Her explorers and medical research characters, however, finally "come through" to the mutual gain of black and white. It is indeed strange the way in which, even in fiction, the truth will out. Finally, Joyce Cary, veteran of the British Nigerian civil service, but Irish by birth, tells an amazing true story of witchcraft in *"The African Witch."* For seeing beneath the surface of African life, Mr. Cary has at last understood witchcraft as Africa's system of mass control, and chronicles the shrewd, vindictive victory of the juju priestess, Elizabeth Aladai over the white colony, her Caucasian loving brother, who had been to Oxford, the intriguing courtiers of the Emir who would not have her brother for the chieftain's successor, and the people themselves whose force she ruthlessly used. I stressed Mr. Cary's ancestry; nothing short of Irish intuition could have discovered what has escaped so many British eyes and ears, and only Irish irony could tolerate Africa's last laugh at all, for Aladai comes in between Colonel Rackham and Jude, his fiancee, between Louis Aladai and his ambition to mix white and black civilization, and even between Elizabeth and her own ambition to make her brother rule. Not that futility is the last word about Africa; but that the beginning in important African fiction must be honesty and penetration; and that Mr. Cary eminently has.

Turning to poetry, once the Negro literary stronghold, we find most of our poets versifying; and that in these days means the condoning school of thought or its near neighbor, the escapist mode of compensation. Miss Marion Cuthbert, who atones somewhat later by a well edited and readable racial anthology for young people, *We Sing America,* in her volume of original poems, *April Grasses* is as typically in the vein of minor lyricism as the title suggests. A just critic, without being too arbitrary, would have to insist on one of two turns for these versifiers, either that they should put more of the honest-to-goodness substance of life into their work or write and rewrite until their lyrics become tech-

nically mature. The same applies to another fragile, anaemic volume of verse *No Alabaster Box and Other Poems* by "Eve Lynn." Her sponsor boasts "that not once does she refer to the peculiar problems of her own group" (she does in one or two places, just the same)—but adds that "hers is a heart that transcends the narrow bonds of race and seeks to encompass that mysterious realm of "love ye one another," by which I infer, he means "the universal." Downright fine, if the poet in question does succeed in reaching the universal. But to escape the narrow bonds of race and shoal on the flats of minor poetry, that is the thrice repeated tragedy of this school of Negro literary escapism. One wonders when some tide of actuality will rise high enough to sweep some of these poets across their Tennysonian sand-bars.

Stanley Braithwaite is a happier sponsor of Mae Cowdery's *"Lift Our Voices,"* although some of her poetry, too, is tangled in not too congruous or vital imagery and merely precipitates personal love lyricism when the poetic fish come to market. Garden pools, spring clouds, and summer clover are all too frequent. But Miss Cowdery, who has always had real poetic possibilities, gathers her talents to a real focus in places, especially her title poem with its:

> "Beat out the brazen brass of the sun
> Give us sharp pointed stars
> To cleanse our hands of your cowardly
>   clay,
> Shut out the brazen music of patriot
>   bands,
> Give us the soft humming of rain
> To soothe our weary ears. . . .
> O Liberty, you have been a vow too
>   long! . . . .
>   * * *
> We cannot build our dreams
> Into strong towers of reality
> On your faltering foundations—
> We cannot let our thoughts run free
> In a sluggish pool of prejudice!
>   * * *
> We must clear this humid air
> Of vows and promises never kept,
> Of fear and false confidence,
> That we may fill the lungs
> Of our young with the cold wind,
> The clear pure wind of courage!
>   * * *
> O audience
> So unaware of our music,
> We are a symphony reaching the final

movement,—
Fortissimo!"

The fortissimo Miss Cowdery heralds, comes thundering in, gusty, lusty and not too clear throated in the poetry of a so-called proletarian poet like Willard Wright, whose poems in *The American Caravan* are doubly significant:—of a new strain in Negro poetry and a slow maturing of one of our really vital poetic talents. Willard Wright faces crude reality and dares to try to render it poetically, which is the contemporary poet's real job; in time it will ring more clearly and artistically.

Across the water, and a literary generation removed, Rene Maran, still faithful to his poetic master, Henri de Regnier, brings out his fourth,—a slender volume of poems, *Belles Images*. Not exactly happy images, but crystal clear in their observation of life and sharpened by a skillful style to a poetic focus. For one who has come to grips with reality in a masterful way as in *Batouala* and *The Book of the Jungle*, these diversions are warrantable, and our ambitious stylists should be sentenced to read them. In fact —(to continue this year's curtain-lecture mood), what seems to me primarily wrong with our younger poets is that they haven't read enough of the great poetry that has preceded them. It would silence some, and reform others. One book that they—and all others should read, now that it is cheaply available in English, is the collected work of Alexander Pushkin. In spite of the fault finding with the translation by those more competent than I to judge, it is a great satisfaction, human and racial, to have this master's work handily available. There is no other way, at second hand, to realize what this literary colossus meant to Russian literature and what, today, at his centenary, he means to world literature. No one expects another Pushkin to rise soon, here or elsewhere, but he has a message for today's writers; one of penetrating insight into life, realistic courage, love and understanding of folk materials, ability to criticize without hate, power to reduce a mood to potent symbols.

Drama we must treat impressionistically, mainly because less than half of the increasing activity in the drama of Negro life is available to the reader in printed form. But without its consideration, a picture of contemporary culture as it relates to racial interests would be impossible. Outstanding above all else is the great momentum that the Federal Art and Drama projects have given to Negro talent, both in the field of interpretation and creative writing. Freedom from box-office risks and anticipated indifference, the development for the first time of sound group organization promise a chance for Negro art and artists such as they have never before enjoyed. Next outstanding is the anxious and for the moment not too productive attempt of the radical or revolutionary Theatre to follow up its strike hit of *Stevedore* with Negro plays of social analysis and criticism. They have made a good beginning under the auspices of the New Theatre League, but even they would scarcely claim it to be more than a beginning. Intimate technical acquaintance with the theatre has been the Negro playwright's chief handicap and the Federal projects in New York and many other centers promise to remedy that.

The Gilpin players have presented *When the Jack Hollers,* a pioneering attempt at satire and farce by Langston Hughes and Arna Bontemps, and the Hedgerow Theatre has made another beginning in middle class drama of Negro life in presenting *One Way to Heaven* dramatized from Countee Cullen's novel by the author and Mr. Bontemps as collaborator. The New Theatre League prize plays are nest eggs of the radical theatre. No one doubts their ultimate purpose or the desirability of turning the Negro problem play to vital account. But they hardly more than lay a foundation for this vital dramatic future. Mrs. Ware's ground breaking of the share-cropper situation is welcome though not smashingly dramatic; *Trouble With the Angels,* the revolt of the Green Pastures' cast, is too anecdotal to fully develop its implications, and *Angelo Jones* is too obviously dramatized propaganda. Yet, these are good beginnings. Far beyond that stage, though yet short of maturity, has been the considerable repertory of the *Lafayette Theatre Federal Drama Unit.* Next to their phenomenal *Macbeth,* which was a revelation of what fresh and daring adaptation can do, when supported by such acting as Eric Burroughs in Hecate and the general ensemble gave, must be rated *Turpentine,* a labor drama of the Carolina log camps. More than any play of the New Theatre group, this drama brought the thesis of labor and class struggle dramatically to life. *Walk Together Chillun,* in spite of one or two vital characters, was not sufficiently convincing of its theme; the feud of religious and secular leadership in the Negro community; and the W.P.A. version of *Noah* was little more than an experiment in staging and mechanical stage effects; a good apprenticeship experience, however. On Broadway, Sam Byrd's stage presentation of *White Man,* (reviewed last year), proved this reviewer's contention as to the unconvincing character of its denouement. Finally, with tremendous significance, *Bassa Moona,* first project of the *African Dance Unit*, follows the promising trail of *Kykunkor*—with an African plot, setting, chants, dances and special drum orchestra music. *Macbeth* and *Bassa Moona* point the lesson of success by the pathway of originality and raciness as over against the dead hand of imitation, propaganda and the set formula.

The literary phenomenon of the year is the sudden simultaneous appearance of seven publications on Negro music. Negro music has been rising to spectacular dominance in American and world music;—that we have known for a long time. But suddenly we seem to have become aware of the need for a critical stock-taking. Fortunately most of these critical and historical appraisals are the careful work of experts. Maud Cuney Hare, who devoted a lifetime to the defense of serious Negro music by lecture recitals with Theodore Richardson, gathered industriously a remarkable volume of information, critical and historical, about Negro music and musicians. She lived to see the manuscript on its way to publication, and it was completed, with an appendix on African music, by Dr. Woodson, her publisher. The book is indispensable to the serious student of Negro music. It is written, however, with a pronounced bias against jazz and popular music in general, and with what the writer believes a false conception of an antithesis between folk forms and art forms in music. From the opposite point of view, I have written, in the new series of *Bronze Booklets*, sponsored by the *Associates in Negro Folk Education*, of Washington, D. C., a critical analysis of Negro music, about which it is only appropriate to say that it was independently written. The two schools of thought on this question thus come forward simultaneously to the benefit—or confusion, of the interested reader.

The folkists and folk-lorists in this field seem to have conspired; four studies of Negro popular music surge at the reader. Hughes Panassie's monumental analysis of jazz, known for several years to specialists who have followed the serious European literature of the subject, has at last been adequately translated—a hard task: since like other European critics, Panassie takes his jazz as seriously and critically as one traditionally takes Bach. For the layman, there is the infinitely easier but authoritatively competent narrative of Louis Armstrong; who justifies his admirers by a remarkable demonstration of modest simplicity and sanity in his story of "how he grew up with jazz" and how jazz "went wrong" on Tin Pan Alley before the vogue of "Swing" and pure Negro idiom brought it back to its original folk spontaneity. His geuss is that

"swing is America's second big bid to bring forth a worthwhile music of its own." Let us hope Louis is as good a prophet as he is a musician!

On the trail of American folk songs, the Lomax brothers have been the most indefatigable and successful hunters. This time they have found a folk bard, by the not too encouraging name of "Lead Belly" and have documented the living reality, music, words, commentary and all. Such research should have been made before the older generation died off; but since it wasn't, we must be grateful to the Lomaxes. Professor Hudson, not to be outdone found a certain "Two-time Tommy" in a Mississippi penitentiary, and got another bonanza; as far as folk ballads go, unfortunately without the most vital part,—the music. Recently a Marxian critic has taken the professional folk-lorists to task, saying "the professional collector of Negro folklore simply capitalizes upon the artificial peculiarities of a group kept in systematic impoverishment and ignorance. Minstrelsy was originally a definite expression of the Southern land-owners, who defended slavery by adorning it with the mellifluous phrases of Stephen Foster and Daniel Emmett." I presume that he would not altogether approve either of "Lead Belly" or "Two-Time Tommy," and many readers will agree, most of the latter without reading these three and five dollar volumes. However with Soviet Russia spending millions of roubles on folk-song and folk-lore collection for its many minorities, one anxiousy awaits the opening of the Marxian counter-offensive in folklore: Mr. Gellert made a good start a year or so ago. Only one thing is certain: folk-life is basic and precious, and no good Marxian can deny that. A comprehensive anthology of Negro songs of all types has been announced by the Viking Press, edited by the quite experienced hand of Rosamond Johnson. A companion volume to *The Negro and His Music, Negro Art: Past and Present* has been written for the Bronze Booklet series by the writer.

We began with the cry: God Save Reality! In the confusion of the critics and the partisanships of the artistic creeds and camps, perhaps we should have said, in the 18th Century phrase: "God save the Gentle Reader."

ADDENDA TO BIBLIOGRAPHY OF LITERATURE OF THE NEGRO: 1936

Minty Alley—A Novel—C. L. R. James, Martin, Secker & Warburg, London, 7/6.

Toussaint Louverture—A Play—in Life and Letters Today, London.

The Black Laws of Virginia—June P. Guild, Whittet & & Shepperson, Richmond, Va.

The Negro in the Philadelphia Press—George E. Simpson, University of Pennsylvania Press, $2.00.

Opportunities for Medical Education of Negroes— E. H. L. Corwin & G. E. Strugees. Charles Scribners, N. Y., $1.50.

The Moveable School Comes to The Negro Farmer— T. M. Campbell, Tuskegee Press, Ala.

THE layman will doubtless not have expected reality from the novelist, poet and dramatist, but will expect it of the economist and sociologist. But I, for my part, would rather take my chance with the fraternity of recreative insight and imagination than with the professedly objective analysts and reporters. For they, like philosophers, idolize their "isms" while pretending to worship "fact"—(only,— philosophers don't always pretend), and at their worst, are like downright social theologians, peddling their pet panaceas for society's final and everlasting salvation. A critic's job, as I see it, with this increasingly controversial and competitive situation, is to tag and label as properly and fairly as he can and let the public buy and eat, each to his own pocketbook and taste. And so, by their schools, we shall know them.

Speaking of schools of economics and sociology, however, it is pathetically interesting to note how many otherwise intelligent people approach the Negro question with hopelessly antiquated categories. They only half realize that Booker T. Washington is long since dead, and would undoubtedly have changed tactics in the shifting issues of our times, as his professed followers have not, and do not seem to comprehend that Dr. Du Bois has left a deftly moulted skin occupying his traditional position and is nesting in quite another. And to me, it seems their primary motivation is their own mental comfort,—for the changes are too obvious for open eyes to overlook. Fortunately—(or unfortunately for the "comfortables-at-all-costs"), we have today not only an amazing gamut of positions, a rich variety of schools of interpretation but, most important of all, ever lessening of the old fallacy of trying to have a special yardstick for the Negro problem and a separate formulae for its solution apart from the basic general problems of our contemporary society. Even for those who reject it—(or them, since

the Marxist positions are so sub-divided), the class theory must be credited at least with this fundamental gain,—that it carries through a 'sauce for the goose, sauce for the gander' analysis and links the Negro question into the general scheme and condition of society. But this year's literature of the social aspects of Negro life ranges through almost the whole spectrum of possible views; strict Communist interpretations, the Communist opposition, a revised Marxist interpretation, several non-Marxist but modernistic economic and anthropological analyses, two schools of economics,—the traditional and the institutionalist, studies of the race question from the labor unionist angle, Y.W.C.A. and Methodist church humanitarian liberalism, orthodox and liberal imperialism, and the now professionalized gradualism of the missionaristic-philanthropic approach, which is the contemporary survival of the Hampton-Tuskegee school of thought. Hardly a notch is missing, unless it be the C.I.O. craft-union labor philosophy, which has its important conception of the industrial and economic problems of the black laborer. Here, then, they string themselves out for the wisely critical reader to window-shop through the whole display or for the impatiently practical to get the right-size sociological hat or an economic shoe to fit, with perhaps an aesthetic tie and kerchief to match.

Alien Americans, by an eminent and experienced Dutch colonial administrator who studied the American race question under the auspices of the Rosenwald Fund, has the advantage of perspective and urbane detachment. It is a good precedent to set,—to discuss American minority problems and attitudes over a common denominator, and Dr. Shrieke discusses the Chinese and the Japanese in the West, the Mexicans in the South and Mid-West, the American Indians, the Filipino and then the bulk of the Negro problem. His conclusion, however, that, even though the product of a traditional and common American policy, there is a progressive slackening of prejudice with education and enlightenment toward the other groups, but a "petrification" of the attitudes toward the Negro, really contradicts, if true, his original assumption that they are the same social phenomenon, only different in degree. Likewise, his essentially economic solution, claiming that "a systematic effort must be made to free the South from its colonial economy" and proposing the "development of a free peasant economy in the rural South" is not in exact alignment with the author's differential diagnosis; nor the statement:—"For anyone who studies southern problems objectively, it is evident that there is an identity of black and white interests. Up till now the plantation legend has impeded the realization of this fact. Will it be otherwise in the future?" In spite of such inconsistencies and its frankly pessimistic turn, Dr. Schrieke's book should be widely read; his graphic and incisive description of the American patterns of racial discrimination has seldom, if ever, been equalled. His account of what he calls the "Great Southern Legend," of the concrete inconsistencies of southern ways and morals, his pointed suggestion that "the black spectre rules the South" all register a high score for the descriptive and analytical side of a most stimulating study. It is perhaps too much to expect, especially from a foreign visitor, equal excellence of diagnosis and proposed remedy.

Under the auspices of the Friendship Press, in a well-intentioned and valuable project of the study of the race question by Methodist church groups, Professor Charles S. Johnson contributes *A Preface to Racial Understanding*. That this book is obviously a primer for the great unenlightened does not excuse Dr. Johnson's equally obvious lapse from the advanced position of last year's book,—*The Collapse of Cotton Tenancy,* to the "coaxing school" of moralistic gradualism and sentimental missionary appeal, especially since these concessions are almost entirely absent from another book in the same series;—Corinne Brown's *Story of the American Negro,* which states the Negro's case with its moral challenges unblunted and its sociological warnings clear. The constructive effect of much painstaking and competent exposition is thus regrettably off-set by such evasive and wheedling gradualism; as reflected in statements like:—"In the field of race relations, it is not so important that there should be envisaged exact solutions, for there will inevitably be differences of opinion . . . it is important that there should be principles guiding these relationships, and that these principles should be high. . . . A sound principle of action, thus could well be: "Respect thy neighbor as thyself, even if thou canst not love him, and do not permit that he or thyself be treated with disrespect." A primer may warrantably be elementary, but it need not slur fundamentals.

Arthur Raper, Field and Research Secretary for the Commission on Interracial Cooperation, gives us a convincing statement of fundamentals in his *Preface to Peasantry,* and with it perhaps a hint as to what Dr. Schrieke specifically meant by his "creation of a free peasant economy in the South." For Mr. Raper, after an intensive survey of typical plantation farm areas, concludes: "With no reasonable hope that an adequate civilization for the majority of the rural dwellers will come either with the rejuvenation or with the collapse of the cotton plantation system, the reclamation of Greene and Macon counties and of much of the cotton South awaits a constructive land policy" . . . a policy enabling "the poorest farmers to build up the soil, to own livestock, to raise vegetables and fruits for their own tables, to cooperate with their fellows in making their purchases and in producing and marketing crops—in short, if it enables landless farmers to attain ownership and self-direction on an adequate plane. Comfortable homes, more doctors, better schools, and wholesome human relations can be maintained only through such basic economic advances. These are not simple matters, and their accomplishment will require the investment of large sums of public money and an administrative personnel with scientific training and a bold faith in the common man." With such thoroughgoing and almost revolutionary specifications, "a free peasant economy" does have a constructive connotation and an attractive challenge as a proposed solution. Mr. Raper's trenchant report of the ways in which the New Deal's agricultural relief measures were thwarted by the traditions and practises of the old regime calls for timely consideration of stringent safeguards for the next steps in the government's agricultural program for the South. Here is a vital book with a modern message; giving added evidence of the way in which the basic and realistic approach to race questions is gaining ground.

Turning aside, however, for a while from the mass aspects of things, we encounter a considerable batch of biography in the literature of the year, with an interesting human sample array of personalities. *Twelve Negro Americans,* by Mary Jenness, is also a Friendship Press book, taking a cross-section view of the Negro social pyramid at an unusual level,—that of social work and uplift projects, calculated to appeal particularly to the missionary aim of the series. These life stories of a leading liberal pastor, a pioneer organizer of cooperatives, a Jeanes school supervisor, the organizer of the Tuskegee farm extension service, several social workers and student and young peoples leaders show both the trends and the typical personalities of an important segment of race leadership. On this level of human interest and appeal, the humanitarian and moralistic notes are not out of place; indeed, have their proper usefulness provided the palliatives of social work and uplift movements are not posed as "ways of solving the race problem," which they are not and cannot be. It is only this implication that detracts from this readable collection of human interest and "success" stories.

Professor Brawley gives us this year a much needed biography of *Paul Laurence Dunbar;* so needed that it may seem ungrateful to mention its limitations. However, it is far more successful as an extended essay of literary criticism than as biography. For a Victorian biography of an only semi-Victorian poet and an entirely un-Victorian personality misses the most vital of all biographical objectives, — the re-creation of a personality. A sugar-coated Dunbar, like a sugar-coated Bobby Burns, may even go further than taking the flavor out of biography, since the dilemmas of the personality had connection with the leading motives in the poetry, it may also take a vital dimension out of the critical analysis and literary interpretation. And for this reason the first biography of Dunbar, welcome though it is, can never take rank as the definitive one.

In *From Harlem to the Rhine,* Colonel Arthur Little elaborately documents the epic story of the New York 15th Regiment in the World War. It is written with candor and obvious devotion, and only misses being a great tribute by the narrow margin of bad dialect reporting and little realization of the irony of the whole venture. As it is, with its concrete vindication of the black soldier and its remarkable tribute to Jim Europe, an important gap in Negro history has been filled in, from an undisputable eye-witness. It is good reading for Negroes, but should be prescribed reading for whites, for it is as ironic comment on American democracy as ever has been or could be written. Another missing chapter of American social history comes clear in Herbert Asbury's. history of the New Orleans underworld,—*The French Quarter.* It is racially important in many respects, not merely for the reports of the "Quadroon balls," the voodoo cults of Marie Laveau et al, and the levities of Basin Street: for the whole social history of the South is laid bare in epitome, even though in perhaps its extremest example. And now for two other not too edifying but significant exposures: John Horsher's journalistic expose of George Baker, "Father Divine, styled *"God in a Rolls Royce"* and the naive, self-expose of Juanita Harrison, in her autobiographic travelogue of a trip round the world, called *My Great Wide Beautiful World,* which should be sub-titled The World Through a Mental Chink. Here certainly is biography with the important modern dimension of human psychology, baffling though it is. Page 80 of the biography of Harlem's self-styled "God" quotes a Negro high school graduate with two years' training at Boston University declaring on the court witness stand that "he believes Father Divine is God" and a white stenographer employed by the Board of Child Welfare testifying to the same effect; two instances, we should say, of seriously deluded thousands. But follow the phenomenon to its root in human suffering and social maladjustment, and the secret of these crowd hypnotists is an open one. Follow even the other line of causation to the social trauma that created the powerful over-compensations of these megalomaniacs, and realize that it was a bad day for society when Garvey was snubbed in his Jamaica boyhood for his dark complexion, and likewise, when, as Horsher reports, in his boyhood town of Savannah, George Baker confronted a socially false Christianity in the guise of a Jim Crow church and Sunday School, which he refused to attend, and later when he "was sent to jail for sixty days for riding in that part of a trolley car reserved exclusively for whites."

From such psychological acorns, with strong personalities, powerful movements grow, dangerously irrational in their creed, but dynamically righteous in their spirit and conviction. So what Mr. Horsher reports as a farce conceals a deep human and social tragedy. As to *My Great Wide Beautiful World,* the significance fortunately is only individual: an illiterate carried round the world is at the end of the trip, and in the volume that reports it, an illiterate still. And is so, whether a moronic millionaire or a moronic menial. The latter is more unusual, however: Barnum after all may have been the best American sociologist.

Now to more important subjects:—economics, politics and colonial questions. Professor Abram Harris has added an incisive study, *The Negro as Capitalist,* to his important project of a survey of the economic history of the Negro. Begun in *The Black Worker* as a partial study of the role of Negro labor in the development of modern industrialism, and specifically as "the role of the Negro industrial worker from the end of the Civil War to 1929," Dr. Harris now covers the history of the Negro as capitalist and investor from pre-Civil War days to the early years of the present depression. Taking advantage, however, of his well-known thesis about the plight and prospects of a "black bourgeoisie," which he has always viewed as a helplessly handicapped "effort to gain economic status and social respectability by erecting within the larger framework of capitalism a small world of Negro business enterprise, hoping thereby to develop his own capitalist-employer class and to create employment opportunities for an increasing number of Negroes in the white collar occupations," our author extends his economic study into definite sociological implications. From the comparative failure of Negro banking, which beside Negro insurance, has been the largest scale capitalistic effort of Negroes, he argues the improbability of any successful economic petty capitalism as a secure foundation for a Negro middle class; not so much on grounds of inexperience or incompetency (although plenty of that is revealed by the detailed history of Negro business enterprise and particularly Negro banking), but on the grounds that the large-scale capitalistic organization of American business today makes the success of any small-scale capitalist enterprise difficult and highly improbable. So, though its primary significance is as a very thoroughgoing technical economic study, there are practical and sociological corollaries to Dr. Harris's work that must be given serious consideration. His concluding chapter on the "Plight of the Negro Middle Class" would probably be borne out by an equally competent analysis of Negro insurance and retail store enterprise, but caution requires the statement that these conclusions are based mainly on an analysis of Negro banking, taken, however, as a sample.

Charles L. Franklin has written on the crucial subject of the labor front a clear factual analysis and history of the Negro worker of New York City in relation to labor union membership and organization. In spite of substantial improvement in the total numbers of Negroes in labor union affiliation, Dr. Franklin's figures show that Negro membership in unions of the highly skilled workers is negligible and that Negroes constitute a higher proportion in the membership of independent unions than in affiliates of the American Federation of Labor. He finds also that in Manhattan a pre- and post-N.R.A. survey reveals sudden increase in the disposition of Negro labor to organize, as between 3.8 per cent before 1928 and 9.3 per cent with a total unionization quota of 39,574 at present estimate; showing some creditable and significant gains for this period. Such a study needs either to be duplicated for other important industrial centers or made on a national scale, in which case the industrial profile of the Negro can be determined on this all important question of differential occupations labor union affiliation, with opportunity then to compare the policies of the craft and the industrial unions, and labor trends.

In *The Negro Question* by J. S. Allen, we have the most rigid but at the same time most rigorous Marxian analysis of the American Negro's situation yet written. It redefines the Black Belt in close but commendably lucid statistics and proves the persistence of the plantation system in a large area of the United States which includes millions of blacks and whites in what it justly calls "semi-feudal conditions of semi-slavery," since under the prevailing conditions of farm tenancy and share cropping not only is there a sub-American standard of living but the system of wage labor has never there become the basis of the economic structure of the region. A South thus X-rayed to its economic bones is a startling and challenging revelation: no polemic dust in the air can long obscure such facts. Mr. Allen then applies the Communist formula to this situation with results equally startling and challenging; with his greatest dilemma, of course, the issue between the economic common denominator theory of the proletariat and the politico-cultural formula of self-determination and cultural autonomy for oppressed minorities or in this case, the "oppressed majority"—(50.3 being the latest census figure of the ratio of the Negro population of this Black Belt area and it being 40 per cent of the total Negro population or roughly five millions). He decides for the latter, not without careful consideration of the arguments for and against; especially the Norman Thomas criticism that self-determination is impossible under capitalism and unnecessary under socialism. Anti-Communists should read *The Negro Question*, not so much to agree or be converted, as to realize what alternatives social medicine must experimentally face and try before conceding the desperate measures of social surgery. That the plantation system is economic cancer is something that all can afford to learn and agree upon.

In the international perspectives of the race question, there is also increasing realism of analysis and here and there, increasing radicalism of suggested remedy. Emory Ross paints a sober picture in *Out of Africa*, which never could have come out of the missionary movement a decade ago; it is tantamount to an admission of an unholy alliance of the church with imperialism and a warning of the complete incompatability of the two programs. Similarly, but much more radically, George Padmore presents a detailed indictment and expose of the procedures and techniques of contemporary imperialistic exploitation in *"How Britain Rules Africa,"* ending with the realistic conclusion that "the British and the French empires are colored empires, since Africans, Arabs, Egyptians, Indo-Chinese, Hindus, etc., form the overwhelming majority of their populations . . . and neither England nor France can face another European crisis without the military and economic support of the colonial peoples." In a more dispassionate and urbane vein, Dantes Bellegarde, the esteemed former Haitian Minister to this country, discusses in four lectures delivered at the University of Porto Rico, *Haiti and Her Problems,* indeed in the concluding lecture, the whole frame-work of Latin American relations. His formula, as might be expected, is international liberalism, trade agreements and honest diplomacy. Finally, Professor Bunche has written for the Negro Folk Education series a very readable digest of the latest scientific and political theories of race, relating them to the issues of modern imperialism and the racial aspects of colonial policy. It is Dr. Bunche's contention, however, that the primary objectives of imperialism are economic consequences of capitalistic expansion, and that race policies and attitudes are their *ex post facto* rationalizations. For the same series, Professor Ira Reid has written a manual of adult education principles and techniques for the use of adult education group executives and teachers, stating the specific objectives and experience to date of the adult education movement among Negroes.

Especially because there is a considerable list of *Addenda,* space scarcely permits further detailed mention, except of the thought provoking issue of the *Journal of Negro Education* on the *Negro School Curriculum* and the most competent and enlightening section on *West African Civilization of the Negro* by Professor Melville Herskovits. The additions reveal a West Indian novelist and playwright of considerable power and much promise, C.L.R. James, author of *Minty Alley,* a realistic novel of Jamaica city life and a full length *Toussaint Louverture,* scheduled for performance by the London Stage Society. In Part I, Richard Wright was inadvertently referred to as Willard Wright and John and Allan Lomax, father and son, as the "Lomax brothers."

JINGO, COUNTER-JINGO AND US.
Retrospective Review of the
Literature of the Negro: 1937

PART I

FICTION:

Us Three Women—Roger Wiley & Helen Wood, Penn Publishing Co., $2.00

Jordanstown—Josephine Johnson, Simon & Schuster, N. Y., $2.00

Night at Hogwallow—Theodore Strauss, Little, Brown & Co., Boston, $1.25

Children of Strangers—Lyle Saxon, Houghton Mifflin Co., Boston, $2.50

River George—George W. Lee, Macaulay Co., N. Y., $2.00

Sad Faced Boy—Arna Bontemps, Houghton Mifflin Co., Boston, $2.00

Their Eyes Were Watching God—Zora Neale Hurston, J. B. Lippincott, Philadelphia, $2.00

These Low Grounds—Waters Edward Turpin, Harper & Bros., N. Y., $2.50

Big Boy Leaves Home—Richard Wright, in 1936 New Caravan: W. W. Norton, N. Y. $3.95

The Ethics of Living Jim Crow—Richard Wright in *American Stuff*, Viking Press, N. Y., $2.00

* * *

POETRY AND BELLES LETTRES:

I Am the American Negro—Frank Marshall Davis, Black Cat Publishing Co., Chicago, $1.50

Sterling Brown, Claude McKay and others in *American Stuff*—edited by Henry Alsberg.

Anthology of Negro Poetry—B. Wormley & C. Carter, New Jersey WPA Project.

From the Deep South—edited by Marcus B. Christian, Privately printed, New Orleans.

The Negro Genius—Benjamin Brawley, Dodd, Mead & Co., N. Y., $2.50

Negro Poetry and Drama—Sterling Brown, Bronze Booklet No. 7—Associates in Negro Folk Education, Washington, D. C., 25c.

The Negro in American Fiction—Sterling Brown, Bronze Booklet No. 6, 25c.

Ro'ling Along in Song—J. Rosamond Johnson, Viking Press, N. Y., $3.50

BIOGRAPHY:

A Long Way From Home—Claude McKay, Lee Furman, Inc., N. Y., $3.00

Let Me Live — Angelo Herndon, Random House, N. Y., $2.50

Pushkin—Ernest J. Simmons, Harvard University Press, $4.00

Negro Builders and Heroes — Benjamin Brawley, University of North Carolina Press, $2.50

The Incredible Messiah—Robert Allerton Parker, Little, Brown & Co., Boston, $2.50

DRAMA:

How Come Lawd—Donald Heywood, The Negro Theatre Guild, N. Y.

The Case of Philip Lawrence—adapted by Gus Smith Federal Theatre Project, New York

The Trial of Dr. Beck—Hughes Allison, Federal Theatre Project, Newark, New Jersey

Jute—Kathleen Critherspoon, Morgan College Players.

* * *

SOCIOLOGY AND RACE RELATIONS:

Half-Caste—Cedric Dover, Martin Secker & Warburg, London—10s 6d.

Our Racial and National Minorities—Brown & Roucek, Prentice-Hall, Inc., N. Y., $5.00

Caste and Class in a Southern Town, John Dollard, Yale University Press, $3.50

The Etiquette of Race Relations in the South—Bertram Wilbur Doyle, University of Chicago Press, $2.50

The Negro's Struggle for Survival—S. J. Holmes, University of California Press, $3.00

Interracial Justice—John LaFarge, America Press, N. Y., $2.00

The Negroes in a Soviet America—J. W. Ford & J. S. Allen, Workers' Library, N. Y.

Reconstruction—James S. Allen, International Publishers, N. Y., $2.00

The Negro in Washington in "Washington: American Guide Series." Federal Writers Project. $3.00

Opportunity 16 (January and February 1938): 7-11, 27; 39-42.

The Negro and Economic Reconstruction—T. Arnold
Hill. Bronze Booklet No. 5. 25c.

Negro History in Outline—Arthur A. Schomburg,
Bronze Booklet No. 8. Associates in Negro Folk Education, Washington, D. C. 25c.

Negro Year Book—edited by Monroe N. Work. Tuskegee Institute Press. $2.00

* * *

ANTHROPOLOGY AND AFRICANA:

Life in a Haitian Valley—Melville J. Herskovits,
Alfred A. Knopf, Inc., N. Y., $4.00

Suriname Folk Lore—Melville J. and Frances Herskovits, Columbia University Press. $5.00

Introduction to African Civilizations—Willis N. Huggins and John G. Jackson, Avon House, N. Y.,
$2.50

The Savage Hits Back—Julius Lips, Yale University
Press, $5.00

Africa Answers Back—Akiki Nyabongo, Routledge &
Sons, London—7s 6d

Stone Age Africa—L. S. B. Leakey, Oxford University
Press, London, $2.75

Prehistoric Rock Pictures in Europe and Africa—
Leo Frobenius and Douglas Fox, Museum of Modern Art, N. Y., $2.00

Reaction to Conquest—Monica Hunter, Oxford University Press, $10.00

Race Attitudes in South Africa—I. D. MacCrone,
Oxford University Press, $4.25

Out of Africa—F. G. Carnochan and H. C. Adams,
Dodge Publishing Co., $2.75

THE literature of the year, both by Negro
and white authors, still continues to be
racially tinged, some of it pro, some of it
anti, little or none of it objective enough to be
called "neutral." And yet some of it, for all
that, is healthy and sane and true enough to be
called art rather than propaganda and science
rather than polemic or partisan jingo. Jingo is
a touchy word since the caustic but stimulating
article of Mr. Benjamin Stolberg on "Minority
Jingo" in the *Nation*, (October 23). Nevertheless let's consider, by way of an aperitif, jingo,
counter-jingo and "us"; us meaning Negro.

Like Mr. Stolberg, I also say: "Good Lord,
deliver us from jingo!"—But unlike him, yet
like a philosopher, I must begin with the beginning. And 'minority jingo' isn't the beginning,
and so, not the root of the evil, evil though it
may be. Minority-jingo is counter-jingo; the
real jingo is majority jingo and there lies the
original sin. Minority jingo is the defensive reaction, sadly inevitable as an antidote, and even
science has had to learn to fight poison with
poison. However, for cure or compensation, it
must be the right poison and in the right
amount. And just as sure as revolution is successful treason and treason is unsuccessful revolution, minority jingo is good when it succeeds
in offsetting either the effects or the habits of
majority jingo and bad when it re-infects the

minority with the majority disease. Similarly,
while we are on fundamentals, good art is sound
and honest propaganda, while obvious and dis-
honest propaganda are bad art. Thus, I think,
we must not load all the onus (and ridicule)
upon the pathetic compensations of the har-
rassed minority, though I grant it is a real dis-
service not to chastise both unsound and ineffective counter-argument. The Negro has a
right to state his side of the case (or even to
have it stated for him), as for example in Professor Lips' *The Savage Hits Back* and Melville
Hershkovits' *Life in a Haitian Valley*, antidotal
to reams of falsification like Seabrook's *Magic
Island*, or Erskine Caldwell's *You Have Seen
Their Faces* poking out its realistic tongue at
Gone With the Wind and *So Red the Rose*. But
some of these counter-arguments have the racial
angle and are interested in the group particularities, (notice I didn't say peculiarities) while
another has the class angle and significantly
includes the Negro material relevant to that.
We must not praise or condemn either because
of its point of view but rather because of its accomplishment in terms of its point of view. It
happens that in each of these cases there is
sound science and good art on the side of the
opposition, and much majority jingo is de-
bunked accordingly. The minority is entitled
to its racial point of view provided it is soundly
and successfully carried through. However, we
shall have to take account of volumes a little
later,—and some of them by Negro authors,
that deserve every inch of Mr. Stolberg's birch.

As I see it, then, there is the chaff and there
is the wheat. A Negro, or anyone, who writes
African history inaccurately or in distorted perspective should be scorned as a "black chau-
vinist," but he can also be scotched as a tyro.
A minority apologist who overcompensates or
turns to quackish demagogery should be exposed, but the front trench of controversy which
he allowed to become a dangerous salient must
be re-manned with sturdier stuff and saner
strategy. Or the racialist to whom group egotism is more precious than truth or who parades
in the tawdry trappings of adolescent exhibitionism is, likewise to be silenced and laughed
off stage; but that does not invalidate all racialism. There are, in short, sound degrees and
varieties of these things, which their extremisms
discount and discredit but cannot completely
invalidate. I am not defending fanaticism, Nordic or Negro or condoning chauvinism, black or
white; nor even calling "stalemate" because the
same rot can be discovered in both the majority and the minority baskets.

I merely want to point out that minority expression has its healthy as well as its unhealthy growths, and that the same garden of which jingo and counter-jingo are the vexatious and even dangerous weeds has its wholesome grains and vegetables, its precious fruits and flowers. Selective cultivation, then, rather than wholesale plowing-under or burning over should be the sane order of the day. Transposing back to our main theme, which is literary, this would mean corrective criticism rather than general excommunication, intelligent refereeing instead of ex-cathedra outlawing. For there can be proletarian jingo as well as bourgeois and capitalist jingo and class jingoism as well as the credal and racial varieties.

As for the Negro cause in literature there is a double concern,—we are threatened both by the plague of bad art and the blight of false jingo. And jingo is more deceptive with the gloss of art and more subtly effective with the assumed innocence and disinterest of art. By all means let us be on our guard against both. Mr. Stolberg was performing a much needed critical service, then, in giving a forceful warning against any double standard in criticism, against any soft tolerance of the fallacies and opiates of internal minority chauvinism at the very time when we were making a point of the exposure and discrediting of majority jingoism. It is a matter of keen regret that much of the cultural racialism of the "New Negro" movement was choked in shallow cultural soil by the cheap weeds of group flattery, vainglory and escapist emotionalism. To that extent it was neither sound racialism nor effective and lasting counter-assertion. The first generation of these artists, (1917-1934), were primarily handicapped by having no internal racial support for their art, and as the movement became a fad the taint of exhibitionism and demagogery inevitably crept in. They are not to be excused entirely for having prostituted their wares and their artistic integrity. But a sounder cultural racialism would have avoided these pitfalls, would have aimed at folk realism and the discovery of basic human and social denominators to be thrown under the numerators of racial particularities for a balanced and factorable view of our group life, and in my judgment a second generation of Negro writers and artists, along with their white collaborators, are well on the way toward such a development. Some of them are writers like Langston Hughes, Zora Hurston, Arna Bontemps, Sterling Brown, whose life bridges both generations, while others, like Richard Wright, Waters Turpin, Hughes Allison, Frank Davis belong entirely to the younger generation. Their more penetrating, even-

handed and less-illusioned portrayal of Negro life is realizing more deeply the original aims of what was too poetically and glibly styled "The Negro Renaissance." Although in self-extenuation, may I say that as early as 1927 I said:—(Ebony and Topaz: "Our Little Renaissance")—'Remember, the Renaissance was followed by the Reformation.' Another quotation,—if I may:—"The Negro Renaissance must be an integral phase of contemporary American art and literature; more and more we must divorce it in our minds from propaganda and politics . . . the self-expression of the New Negro, if conditions in the South were more conducive to the development of Negro culture without transplanting, would spring up as just one branch of the new literature of the South, and as one additional phase of its cultural reawakening."

This is just what has happened or is happening. Josephine Johnson's *Jordanstown* is in the strict sense not a novel of Negro life, but a novel of the tragedy of labor organization in the sharecropper South; but it is notable for its rare and penetrating perception of the basis of the race problem and the Negro's position in the small town rural areas and for its daring analysis of the integration of Negro and white lives. Similarly Theodore Strauss's *Night at Hogwallow,* which details not only the lynching of an innocent Negro by a labor gang of mixed southerners and northerners but gives a more detailed account of the crowd psychology of the mob than I recall having ever read. It is both good art and good sociology; all the more notable and promising because it is Mr. Strauss's first publication. Mrs. Johnson is a Pulitzer Prize veteran which gives weight and occasionally edge to her laurels. Her sociology, too, is indisputable; she goes as far as balanced realism can go, and gives a vital sense of tragedy over and above the documentation. Incidentally, it is to be noted that most socialistic novels refuse to consider themselves defeatist in the tragic death of their main characters, as in this case of the martyrdom of Adam, the militant labor leader. Why should they? Yet why should tragedy in other contexts invariably raise the hue and cry of "defeatism"?

Defeatism in art is where the issues are unfairly joined, and where the implications, social or psychological, are vicious or mis-representative. Both bad art and poor sociology alike can lead to that. In sinister conjunction they lead to falsity in a novel like *Us Three Women,* for all its profession of detailed documentation of the lives of three Negro women and their southern friends. The book is a deceptive survival of the old Plantation Tradition, which still thrives perniciously and unabashed in Hollywood plots, children's stories and popular romance fiction very generally. However, one is meeting it less and less on the level of serious realistic writing: *Us Three Women* being one of these exceptions.

Two novels, one by a white and the other by a Negro author, although unevenly matched in artistry, go a long way toward proving that the return to the plantation need not be trite or reactionary. Lyle Saxon's *Children of Strangers,* has some sentimental tourists looking on at the crucial scene in Famie's tragic life, taking snap-shots in the assurance that she looks "so typical" and that they are the "happiest people —not a care in the world." This after a lifetime of struggle after her early seduction, her ostracism by her proud Creole relatives, her vain and pathetic sacrifices for her illegitimate son, and the final breach of the law of her land-owning clan that spells her final sacrifice. Even with the romantic touch and the charm of the old tradition, Saxon sacrifices neither truth nor social perspective; and this novel will only seem defeatist to local color tourists on the one hand and fanatical proletarians on the other. With far less artistic power, George Lee's *River George* is yet noteworthy. The flaw probably lies in the too concocted expansion of the legend of River George, so dramatically told in the author's *Beale Street*, who was just a John Henry "bad man" of the slums, into a race-defiant protagonist of the oppressed sharecroppers. So, as other critics have noted, the first half or more of the story runs convincingly and the second not at all. Arty dialogue and sophomoric interlardings contribute to this; but the attempt to over-modernize material out of its tradition is risky. But the Negro novelist, though he needs criticism, needs to be read. He is definitely on his way somewhere. And the average Negro should know what is being written about him; he needs that analytical dimension in his life. Otherwise, his life is the cultural equivalent of living in a house without a mirror.

Part of the Negro novelist's dilemma is his obviously divided public. Few have the courage to write straight across the stereotypes of the whites and the hyper-sensitive susceptibilities of the blacks. And yet in no other way can great writing or a great master emerge. As good an author as Arna Bontemps, for example, writing belligerent and heroic *Black Thunder* (Macmillan—1936),—which by the way was inadvertently and regrettably omitted from our 1936 list, this year writes a children's story which

barely escapes from the melon-patch stereotypes. Wistful here and there, in a revamped setting of three little black southern adventurers in Harlem, there is still an unfortunate reversion to type even after all allowances are made for the unrealistic tradition of the child story. Whereas *Black Thunder* was historical fiction of considerable power and decided promise. Even though a highly fictionalized version of an historic slave insurrection, it documented Negro character and motivation in unconventional and all but convention-breaking ways.

And now, Zora Hurston and her magical title: *Their Eyes Were Watching God.* Janie's story should not be re-told; it must be read. But as always thus far with this talented writer, setting and surprising flashes of contemporary folk lore are the main point. Her gift for poetic phrase, for rare dialect and folk humor keep her flashing on the surface of her community and her characters and from diving down deep, either to the inner psychology of characterization or to sharp analysis of the social background. It is folklore fiction at its best, which we gratefully accept as an overdue replacement for so much faulty local color fiction about Negroes. But when will the Negro novelist of maturity who knows how to tell a story convincingly,—which is Miss Hurston's cradle-gift, come to grips with motive fiction and social document fiction? Progressive southern fiction has already banished the legend of these entertaining pseudo-primitives whom the reading public still loves to laugh with, weep over and envy. Having gotten rid of condescension, let us now get over over-simplification!

Just this Waters Turpin attempts in *These Low Grounds,*—and for a first novel more than half succeeds in accomplishing. A saga sweep of four generations of a family is daring for a fledgling writer, but the attempt is significant, not merely in breadth of canvas but in the conception that the Negro social tragedy is accumulative and the fight with the environment, dramatic or melodramatic for the individual is heroic and epical for the race. So from pre-Civil War Virginia to Baltimore, Philadelphia, New York and the contemporary Eastern Shore Maryland of the Salisbury lynching (Shrewsbury is the fictional name of the town), Turpin doggedly carries his story and the succession of parents, children and grandchildren. The modern scene, especially rural Maryland, is well painted, and the futility of the odds of prejudice dramatically shown. It is in the dating of the generations—a task for a scholarly writer of historical fiction, and the characterization of his central figures that one finds it necessary to speak of the high promise rather than the finished attainment of this book. As it should be, it is a moving tale of courageous matriarchy, closer to Heywood's *Mamba's Daughters* than anything else in the fiction of Negro life unless still further back we recall, as we oftener should, Clement Wood's *Nigger*.

In *American Stuff*, under the editorship of Henry Alsberg, the Federal Writers Project presents its cross-section miscellany, with a reasonably representative participation of Negro writers and poets. Of the prose, Richard Wright's thumb-nail sketches of prejudice,—*The Ethics of Living Jim Crow*, is by far the most powerful and thought-provoking. However, one is left wondering whether cold steel rather than hot steel would not have been better as an etching tool; but it is encouraging to see Negro writers turning to irony on their way to the maturer mastery of satire. Incidentally, gleams of the latter are in Sterling Brown's poetic contribution to this volume,—*All Are Gay*. To me the growing significance of Richard Wright still pivots on his last year's performance of 1936 in "The New Caravan,"—*Big Boy Leaves Home*, the second serious omission of my last year's chronicle. It must be mentioned even after this delay because it is the strongest note yet struck by one of our own writers in the staccato protest realism of the rising school of 'proletarian fiction'. There is a legend that the spring really begins in some surprising after-midnight March clash of lightning and thunder. To my ears and with reference to the new generation note, *Big Boy Leaves Home* sounds like an opener similarly significant to Jean Toomer's startling and prophetic *Cane*. Lusty crude realism though it is, it has its salty peasant tang and poetic glint, two things that one likes to think necessary for Negro folk portraiture rather than drab, reportorial realism, no matter how often tried.

Poetry proper still lags, as indeed for the last four years. A creditable anthology of Negro poets for popular use has come from the Newark, New Jersey, WPA project and a slender volume of original verse has been printed in New Orleans under the guidance of Marcus B. Christian, himself a rising poet of some distinction. His *Southern Sharecropper* in July OPPORTUNITY excels anything in this small volume, however. Frank Davis's *I Am The American Negro* becomes thus the outstanding verse effort of the year. Yet the book has too many echoes of the author's first volume and overworks its mechanism of rhapsodic apostrophes flung out in flamboyant Whitmanesque prose poetry. The mannerism dulls the edge of his social protest

and again suggests hot untempered steel. Alone it would be notable, but it is not a crescendo in the light of the achievement and promise of the author's initial volume. In occasional publication there is also another Chicagoan poet, Robert Davis, with much the same ideology, but a more restrained style. Indeed until the recent publication of the *New Challenge* under the sponsorship of a New York group, it began to look as though the center of the literary scene was shifting from Harlem out to the Mid-West, and even with that promising recovery, Harlem must still look to its literary laurels.

In the Bronze Booklet series, Sterling Brown has outlined in carefully documented sequence and penetrating interpretation the course of the Negro theme in American poetry and drama in *Negro Poetry and Drama* and of the Negro theme in American fiction in *The Negro in American Fiction*. It is not too much to say that this is a greatly needed critical service, especially since the dimension of social interpretation has been brilliantly stressed. On the contrary, in *The Negro Genius*, Professor Brawley, enlarging and bringing up to date his *The Negro in Literature and Art*, has stuck to his previous method of mere chronicle narrative with trite praise and blame evaluations. Apart from the lack of social interpretation, this is not analytical criticism of the kind it models itself after,—Arnold, Lowell and Gates. But more of that later. Concluding our *belles-lettres*, Rosamond Johnson has a creditable anthology of Negro folk-song, in which he has achieved considerable perspective and corrected in a simpler style of arrangement the over-ornate style of arrangement that somewhat marred his volumes on the Spirituals.

Proportionately, it seems, as poetry has withered away, biography has waxed strong, following a dominant trend in contemporary letters. Negro biography is a province of potential importance; if ever the anomalies of the race problem are caught between the cross-fire of close grained fiction and well-defined biography, we shall at last know something about its intriguing dilemmas and paradoxes. But Negro biography has yet to grow up either to the grand manner or the expertness of contemporary biography and autobiography. The single figure in the grand manner is a figure of purely historical interest and only sentimentally connected,—Pushkin. The extent to which his mixed ancestry influenced either his career or his personality are highly debatable; he was Russian among the Russians, and stands clearly only as a striking example of cultural assimilation and the timeless and spaceless universality of first-water genius, over and above cultural and national traits. But while I would not loud pedal Pushkin's ancestry, I also see no point in ignoring it, and some point in giving it a sustained pedal for a bar or so for the color-deaf ears of the prejudiced.

Coming nearer to our time and locality, the other biographies stack up interestingly, but to no Alpine heights. Curiously in contrast, McKay's autobiography exploits a personality while Angelo Herndon's exploits a cause. Balanced biography can come from neither over-emphasis. Yet an important chapter of the younger generation Negro life has been documented and oddly enough both trails lead to Moscow, one in terms of cosmopolitan vagabondage and the pursuit of experience for experience's sake, the other in the hard rut of labor struggle and the proletarian movement in the deep South. The clash of individualism and collectivism, of aestheticism versus reform, of the contemporary dilemmas of race and class could not be better illustrated if these books had been pre-arranged and their respective authors' lives accordingly. Because of its live issues and heroic attitude *Let Me Live* has no apologies to offer even in juxtaposition with the clever style and picaresque charm of *A Long Way From Home.*

It was Professor Brawley's *Negro Builders and Heroes* that precipitated the Stolberg article and that had to sustain the full force of that blast against compensatory racialism. Exhibit A sociology, as I have said before, has bred a vicious double standard; the American success story (a majority pathology, by the way) has added its shabby psychology of Pollyanna optimism and sentimentalism, and the combination, I agree, although still the meat and bread of many professional inter-racialists and well-intentioned inter-racial movements, is stale cake on the contemporary table. Not so indigestible, once you acquire a taste for it, its chronic use induces, if I may keep up the metaphor, two serious symptoms of acute indigestion, cultural vertigo and split or dislocated social vision. Inevitable a generation ago, tolerable a half generation back, it is today not only outmoded but for the younger generation, dangerously misleading. Irrespective of personalities, then, it is time to call a halt on it.

The Incredible Messiah, from the other side of the racial fence points the same moral: its readers and its author forget the characteristic American phenomenon from Barnum to Billy Sunday, and regard the black "Father Divine" as peculiar and racially characteristic. That's

what racialism at its worst does for us; and after that, it is a hardy soul that elects not to abandon the racialist point of view altogether. Yet we cannot even if we would, and should not, as I said in the beginning, just because many cannot be sane and fair and honest about it. After all, cultural racialism has better odds on long futures than nationalism, which incidentally has similarly fallen into the hands of the emotional extremists until some reaction of sanity comes to its rescue,—if it can.

Unless the sanity index of the literary discussion of race rises more rapidly, although I think it is slowly rising, we shall perhaps have to turn to other arts for our truest view of the social scene. Two books, in each of which the Negro is incidental but perhaps all the more significant, Caldwell and Margaret Bourke-White's *You Have Seen Their Faces* and Thomas Benton's *The Artist in America* tell more of life than chapters of biography and reams of fiction.

PART II

DRAMA, as far as propaganda is concerned, is the broncho of the arts; most playwrights who venture dramatic jingo finish in the dust while a riderless horse makes a hasty and disorderly exit. It takes genius to balance a problem in the dramatic saddle; yet if ever a problem gets itself effectively dramatized, nothing in the whole run of art can be as spectacular or compelling. But the many-phased Negro problem still awaits its Ibsen or even its Bernard Shaw. *Stevedore, Turpentine, Run, Little Chillun,* and *Mulatto* are still the best we have to show, and with each the dramatist finishes out of control and nearly unhorsed. As for the 1937 drama field, only in combination do they register any noteworthy placing; as single performances they scarcely rate as successes. Donald Heywood's *How Come, Lawd,* on which the promising Negro Theatre Guild unwisely gambled away its future, was a flat failure. It attempted to raise the previously successful formulae of *Stevedore* and *Turpentine* to a melodramatic folk-play, but instead of generating the conviction of persecution or the premonition of class war, *How Come Lawd* hatched a Deadwood Dick welter of corpses. Leaning on an already successful play for support, Gus Smith of the Lafayette Federal Theatre project, more than half successfully dramatized *The Case of Philip Lawrence.* Here was the set-up for a great Negro play,—the ghetto drag-down of a successful college athlete whose family and friends had no boot straps to lift themselves by, and little helpful conception of the success he yearned for. But a gangster racket and infatuation bring him down with a melodramatically contrived "framing" for murder, from which he escapes at the end only by a hair's breadth capture of the racket boss. Had social fate rather than a jealous, revengeful gangster been Philip Lawrence's downfall, real tragedy might have ensued instead of a Hollywood finish. Dramatically the strongest of the crop, *The Trial of Dr. Beck* revealed a promising newcomer to the thin ranks of Negro playwrights, Hughes Allison. His play, a success of the Newark Federal Theatre project, enjoyed a brief but effective Broadway showing at the Maxine Elliott. But here again a vital racial theme was overlaid with the trappings of an Oppenheimer crime story and two acts of well-documented but melodramatic court scenes. Though there is much talk of color complexes and considerable arraignment of the paradoxes of prejudice,—all to the good as among the first effective dramatization of these issues, both Dr. Beck's lily-whitism and his sister's-in-law counter color hate are far from being what they should be, the real protagonists of the play. Instead, Pinkertonian detective tactics and an over-idealized lawyer are the short-circuiting artifices by which Mr. Allison gets justice done and his moral put over. Still the talent of Hughes Allison, more mature in dramatic technique and depth of characterization than any Negro playwright to date, warrants hopeful watching and encouragement. The Morgan College Players are responsible for presenting the one creditable work of the white dramatist in Negro drama for 1937. Various professional concoctions of Broadway producers, two of them by George Abbott, have fortunately been as short-lived as they were mercenary and misrepresentative. At least this negative gain seems to have come about, —that except in the movies and on the vaudeville stage, the Broadway stage formula for a successful Negro play has obviously worn itself out. *Jute*, on the other hand, is the very antithesis of the Broadway play, but probably for that very reason a portent of what Broadway must come around to. Its strong bitter social realism, smacking of *Tobacco Road* on the one hand and *Stevedore* and *Waiting for Lefty* on the other, is the much needed antidote to too much *Black Boy, Sweet River* and *Brown Sugar*. In social content, Phillistine Negro protests notwithstanding, *Jute* is significant and promising for the social content of vital Negro drama.

In the ever important field of social analysis and criticism, one general change is increasingly obvious; "race sociology" is growing up. It is less frequently nowadays a puny missionary foundling or the awkward patronized protege of the interracial sentimentalists. Here and there it is sociology of full strength and maturity. And even where it is not, the pretension to scientific accuracy and objectivity is a significant omen.

Certainly one of the best and most illuminating of this year's race studies is Cedric Dover's *Half Caste*. With a panoramic swoop of world perspective on the race question, the book achieves a unique coordination of the phenomena of race. With eagle-like penetration of vision, international imperialism and fascist nationalism are seen to have common denominators of repressive, self-righteous racialism. Relentlessly the biological and cultural stalking horses of race prejudice are unmasked and the politico-economic objectives of race policies exposed. This is deftly done because the problem is tackled in terms of its crucial dilemma, the half caste, who as Mr. Dover senses, is the Dalmatian sword over the heads of all racialists: For the factualities of the human hybrids contradict either the theories or the practises of racialism; which then stands biologically contradicted or morally condemned. No other survey to date has given so wide a perspective on human hybridization or such a realization of its common factors, the similarity of situations and policies, the uniformity of its social dilemmas, and perhaps most important of all, the preponderant numbers of the mixed bloods. In the chapter on the American Negro, *God's Own Chillun*, the author achieves an illuminating analysis of the general situation, with pardonable lapses of proportion in the detailed statements of Negro achievement in which he has followed several uncritical and provincial sources. But the general soundness of his main thesis saves serious distortion, and it will be salutary for all who lack objective perspective on the American race question, Negro chauvinists included, to review the situation in this unusual and broad scientific frame of reference.

In *Our Racial and National Minorities*, under the editorship of Professors Brown and Roucek, the polyglot character of America is documented by some thirty spokesmen for national and racial sub-groups of our population. James Weldon Johnson has a double inning on Negro American achievement history and *The Negro and Racial Conflicts*. The approach of the whole study is too superficial for any sound interpretation of the interaction of minorities or the cultural problems involved in dual loyalties. Cultural pluralism and its educational objectives are, however, rather convincingly presented. The special degrees of isolation and differential treatment involved in the cases of the Negro, Indian, Mexican and Oriental minorities are dangerously minimized in the interest of the general thesis that we are all cultural hyphenates and that cultural reciprocity is our soundest, most progressive type of Americanism. Professor Johnson in keying his chapters in with this platform has not glossed over the particular injustices and inconsistencies of the Negro's position, but he has not sufficiently stressed the unusual cultural assimilation of the American Negro as compared with other minorities or the special inconsistencies of majority behaviour toward the Negro.

With *Caste and Class in a Southern Town* and *The Etiquette of Race Relations in the South*, we pass to sociological anatomy of the most scientific and painstaking sort. And yet what we get eventually in both cases is not any enlightenment as to social causes but only elaborations of the mechanisms of caste control and majority dominance. Can it be that this descriptive analytic point of view is hopelessly undiagnostic and therefore just so much academic "busy work?" Both works agree that caste rather than class describes the racial cleavage, and that its outlines are only correctly traced by examining in detail custom patterns in the social mores. But neither gives any very clear understanding of what economic interests and political policies all these elaborate mechanisms serve. In short, the vital question, it seems to me, is not the *how* but the *why* of these social differences and differentials.

In *The Negro's Struggle for Survival*, subtitled "a study in human ecology," Professor Holmes of the University of California assembles the Negro's biological statistics elaborately and tries to trace trends and prospects. In most of these balancings, our author finds Negro survival outdistancing or off-setting its handicaps, whether directly biological like the birthrate or socio-economic like the influence of poverty, migration and hybridization. However, toward the conclusion the banished bugaboo of race ascendancy comes back to threaten serious issues should the Negro rate of population increase decidedly to disturb the present balance. The author then predicts "population control" as the probable outcome. Even with the pseudo-scientific coating of "eugenics," this is the abandonment of the plane of science for that of politics and is a disappointing conclusion for an otherwise factual and objective book.

On the sound platform that "the essential human rights of Negroes do not appertain to them as Negroes, but simply as members of the human family" and that "modern Catholic sociologists see in the tendency to subordinate all considerations of the dignity of the human person to the unbridled quest of material gain the primary source of interracial, as well as of economic, industrial and international injustice," Father La Farge works out a program of really radical equalitarianism differing only in its sanctions and reform machinery from the economic radicals. In spite of this wide difference of proposed remedy, it is interesting to note this startling agreement in diagnosis. "Cheap labor," says Reverend La Farge, "brings cheap lives. And from cheap lives follow customs and maxims sanctioning the cheapening of lives."

In *The Negro in a Soviet America*, J. W. Ford and J. S. Allen expound the now familiar Communist formula for revolutionary socialism and minority self-determination. It has become too much of a formula perhaps, but that does not remove its realistic thrust as a contending alternative to the yet unsuccessful reformism of moral appeal and legislative guarantees. *Reconstruction* by J. S. Allen gives a much less doctrinaire analysis of the relation of the Negro to the political and economic interests of the nation and the South. Particularly revealing are documentary evidences of Negro statesmanship in realistic political and labor programs from 1865 to 1879 that were frustrated by the tacit alliance of Northern industrialists and Southern Bourbons not to insist on thoroughgoing reconstruction or political power for the Negro in the South. This picture of American history after 1878 as a counter-revolution to the Civil War is an important and plausible interpretation; it culminated not merely in the setback to Negro advance but in the stultification of the labor movement for several decades and of the full functioning of democratic machinery even up to the present. A few close students of history have known this all along, but it is important that the layman should know it as well.

T. Arnold Hill's *The Negro and Economic Reconstruction* in the Bronze Booklet series also presents an indispensable layman's manual on the connection of the Negro question with past and present labor issues and programs. Volume No. 8 of the same series presents a readable and well-proportioned outline of *Negro History*, by the well-known bibliographer and source collector, Arthur A. Schomburg. But also in social history, which has been so neglected in Negro historical effort, most promising beginnings have now been made in various guide books of the Federal Writers Project. With Virginia, Louisiana and New York documentary chronicles in preparation, the project leads off very auspiciously with a revealing account, edited by

Sterling Brown, of *The Negro in Washington* in the Washington : American Guide Series.

In *Life in a Haitian Valley,* Professor Herskovits vindicates even more brilliantly than in his previous books his thesis of acculturation. Studying the Haitian peasant rituals, he discovers not only substantial traces of African religions, especially the Dahomean Vodun cults, but clearly demonstrates the prevailing Haitian popular religion to be an amalgam of this, Catholicism and local superstition. This points to a completely general human pattern of acculturation, with none of the specious doctrines of innate racial primitivism or mysterious blood survivals, the favorite formulae of the culture-mongers who thrive on fashionable exoticism and bad anthropology. Cut free from such false implications, the search for African survivals is merely an excursion into social history. There is cold comfort for Nordicism or any other racial condescension in any such results, and for this service the Haitian cause in particular and the Negro cause in general have much to be grateful for in such studies as this and the previous volume of *Suriname Folk Lore,* documenting even more extensively striking survivals and parallels in the folk lore of the Negroes of Dutch Guiana. Nigerian and Dahomean patterns, both of behavior and thought, are found strikingly perpetuated.

But while we are shutting doors to Nordic jingoists, we should not be opening them to Negro jingoism. And such we must frankly label *Introduction to African Civilizations* by Huggins and Jackson. On a brittle thread of sentimental interest in Negro blood admixture, pre-historic Cromagnons, semi-Semetic Mediterraneans, Egyptians, Ethiopians, ancient and modern, South and West African peoples of diverse stocks are all hodge-podged into an amateurish hash of the black man's vindication. Such facts and conjectures are warrantable offsets to rampant and hysterical Nordicism provided they escape the same fallacies they challenge. But when they commit the same errors of over-generalization, assumption of fixed racial character and instinctive heredities, and worse than all, the ignoring of distinct culture groupings, the results must be repudiated as just as pseudo-scientific as the conclusions and prejudices they try to counteract. A much more intelligent and effective statement of the counter-case comes from an African author, Akiki Nyabongo, whose *Africa Answers Back* continues the pointed critique he began with his *Story of an African Prince.*

With a most laudatory preface by Malinowski, and a thrilling and trenchant account of his own liberal stand against German Nazi oppression and censorship, Professor Lips launches out in his *The Savage Hits Back* into an extensive documentation of the manner in which primitive peoples have represented the white man,— ruler, trader, missionary and colonial administrator. It is sufficient indictment of fascism that so indirect a criticism of colonial exploitation should seem dangerous enough to persecute and exile a scholar for daring to compile it. But this is neither the first nor the most impressive vindication of the primitive or even the African as artist. In fact most of the representations treated betray the native art in a bastard genre both with respect to style and subject matter, and necessarily we must discount its artistic and allow principally its sociological or cultural importance. Most of this work is therefore in the minor category of genre and even caricature; though of course it is interesting documentary proof that the native both sees and sees through the white overlords and takes due recourse to shrewd and half-concealed ridicule. Only rarely, however, do the European forms and accoutrements blend harmoniously with the native styles of expression, so that there is much more that must be labelled curiosa than can be called art proper. Nevertheless Professor Lips has documented very unmistakably the colored world's reaction to cultural jingoism and the loss of prestige which is taking place under the surface of professed respect. For exposing this significant symptom he merits our gratitude, even though we may not entirely grant his prophesy of a "future collision of the white and colored worlds" and his contention that "it is not class cohesion that will be the decisive factor in such a collision but the sense of race unity."

A joy to the scientific type of mind is the way in which both anthropology and the analysis of culture contacts are slowly disengaging themselves from the fog of prejudice and preconceived racialisms. Whether one grants the thesis of Frobenius that the similarities of prehistoric art indicate wide diffusion into Europe of African peoples or whether one holds with Leakey that parallel or roughly similar culture sequences worked themselves out both in Europe and different areas of the African continent, it is only too obvious in either case that the net conclusion is one of the basic similarity and parity of the human species. No sounder antidote for false racial pride or propagandist history could be found than in the cultural anthropology which is giving us increasing evidence along these new lines of the antiquity and the versatility of primitive man.

To the same collaborated authorship, as *Prehistoric Rock Pictures*, we owe the illuminating collection of African fables and creation myths in *African Genesis* (Stackpole Sons, N. Y.—$3.00). Berber, Fulbe, Soudanese, Rhodesian,—these tales are of wide range and diverse cultural quality, but they are all indicative of a more seasoned folk-lore and a higher level of literary form than other collections reveal, even the celebrated Cendrars *Anthologie Negré*. Interestingly enough, in some of them Frobenius believes he has discovered common symbols and rituals to early Egyptian mythology.

The really authoritative studies of African colonial contacts as they effect changes and breakdowns and fusions of cultures bear out the same liberal relativism of values. Notable among such are Monica Hunter's *Reaction to Conquest* and MacCrone's *Race Attitudes in South Africa*, each of which in a very different way illustrates the principle that one civilization more often demoralizes a different culture than it civilizes or improves it. In brief, according to the more recent scientific accounts, the white man makes his own burden and then has to carry it, not to mention the disproportionate profit he makes on the other side of the imperialistic ledger.

Although unnecessarily fictional for so detailed and painstaking a narrative of native folk ways, Carnochan and Adams' *Out of Africa* is a remarkably sympathetic biography of Kalola, chief of the Nyamwesi serpent cult. Nowhere has a better analysis of such ritual fetishism been drawn, with the balance carefully kept between black and white magic, conjure and tribal medicine, superstition and sound institutional tradition. In such books as we have reviewed, the African counter-statement is just beginning to gather momentum, but it certainly will have its day of assertion. However, let us hope that it will be a scientific, sanely directed counter-statement, and not another deluge of bigotry, hysteria and counter-prejudice. Not for moral reasons, but for effectiveness, let us be saner than our opponents. And let us welcome as champions only those who are scientifically convinced and convincing.

FREEDOM THROUGH ART:
A REVIEW OF NEGRO ART, 1870–1938

EVERY oppressed group is under the necessity, both after and before its physical emancipation from the shackles of slavery,—be that slavery chattel or wage—of establishing a spiritual freedom of the mind and spirit. This cultural emancipation must needs be self-emancipation and is the proper and peculiar function of a minority literature and art. It gives unusual social significance to all forms of art expression among minorities, often shading them unduly with propaganda or semi-propaganda and for whole periods inflicting them also with an unusual degree of self-consciousness and self-vindication, even to the point of cultural exhibitionism and belligerency. But for these faults and dangers we have compensation in the more vital role and more representative character of artistic self-expression among "the disinherited;" they cannot afford the luxury, or shall we say the vice, of a literature and art of pure entertainment.

The literature and art of the Negro, and to an extent all serious literature and art about the Negro, have had almost universally this quality of moral seriousness and social significance. That has not been an unmixed blessing, since the arts of the Negro have had to struggle through to some degree of artistic freedom from these fetters of polemics and didacticism. The Negro artist has worn mental chains, and his achievements are all the more creditable. He has always faced two dilemmas;—how to speak for himself as an individual at the same time that he was being considered a racial spokesman; how to galvanize inert propaganda and racial doctrines with the electric and moving qualities of art. His present achieve-

ment of recognized contribution to universally significant and nationally representative art is thus a double achievement; in the first instance a mastery over the inherent difficulties of his art, in the second instance, a victory over the artificial odds of cultural stigma and persecution. In this double aspect we must review briefly the career of Negro art and literature from Emancipation till now.

It is hard to realize that at the beginning of the brief period of 75 years which this issue of The Crisis is retrospecting, the Negro artist was a cultural freak of circus proportions in the North and proscribed cultural contraband in the South. The characteristic Negro author was then a runaway slave with an Abolitionist amanuensis or a natural born orator who had only become literate as an adult. There were exceptions, but this was the rule. But the astonishing thing was the way in which these slave-born narrators, poets and orators mastered the art of powerful and influential expression, conspicuously challenging their more advantaged freeborn contemporaries, white and black. There was the poetic power of Horton and Albery Whitman for example, quite excelling the early literate Ellen Harper and Madison Bell; there was the dominance of Douglass, Pennington, and William Wells Brown, slave-born, over the university-trained McCune Smith, Highland Garnet, Daniel Payne, and Samuel Ward. Indeed the fervor of the anti-slavery movement and the rare cultural comradeship of that cause seem to have raised Negro literary expression on all sides to a high level in the 1850's and 60's from which it actually receded in the dull early Recon-

The Crisis 45 (July 1938): 227–229.

struction decades.

The '70s and '80s Dull

Anti-slavery controversy and the hope of freedom brought poetry and fire to the Negro tongue and pen; whereas the setbacks and strained ambitions of Reconstruction brought forth, in the main, leaden rhetoric and alloyed pedantry. Thus the 70's and the 80's were the awkward age in our artistic development. They were the period of prosaic self-justification and painful apprenticeship to formal culture. Yet these years saw the creditable beginnings of Negro historical and sociological scholarship, even at the expense of an endless elaboration of problem discussion themes, and saw also an adolescent attack on the more formal arts of the novel, the drama, formal music, painting and sculpture. Before this almost all of our artistic expression had flowed in the narrow channels of the sermon, the oration, the slave narrative and didactic poetry.

But in spite of their talents and labors, authors like Highland Garnet, Alexander Crummell, George Williams, the historian, Martin Delaney, and even Frederick Douglass in these later days had a restricted audience, much narrower than the wide national and international stage of anti-slavery times. There was, instead of the glamor of the crusade against the slave power, the dull grind of the unexpected fight against reaction. The larger audience and a more positive mood were not recaptured until the mid-nineties, when strangely enough a clustered group of significant events came together, any one of which would have been notable. In 1895, Booker Washington caught national attention with his Atlanta Exposition speech; in 1896 Paul Laurence Dunbar rode into fame and popular favor; in the same year the first Negro musical comedy took Broadway; in '98 and '99, Chestnut, the novelist, came to the fore; in '95 Burleigh was helping Dvorak with the Negro folk themes of the "New World Symphony" and at the same time making his first entry to the New York concert world; in '98 Will Marion Cook launched serious syncopated music with "Clorindy;" '96 was the year of Tanner's first substantial Paris recognition; and in '98 Coleridge Taylor came to maturity and fame in the first part of the Hiawatha Trilogy. The only other stellar artistic event of this period for which we have to wait is the appearance in 1903 of Dr. Du Bois's "Souls of Black Folk." Quite obviously there was a sudden

change of trend as this blaze of talent ushered in a new era of racial expression. It was more than a mere accession of new talent; it was the discovery of a new racial attitude. The leading motive of Reconstruction thought was assimilation and political equality; following the cry for physical freedom there had been the fight for the larger freedom of status and the right to be the same and equal. But the leading motive of the new era (1895-1910) seems to have been racialism and its new dynamic of self-help and self-assertion. Even the motivations of Du Bois's equal rights crusade were militantly self-conscious and racial; in fact, race consciousness was now definitely in the saddle striving to re-direct the stalled logic of the assimilation program and revive the balked hopes of the thwarted equal rights struggle. The formula of special gifts and particular paths had been discovered, and became the dominant rationalization of the period. The leading conception of freedom now was the right to be oneself and different. Thus the groundwork was laid for the cultural racialism of the "Negro Renaissance" movement which, however, was not to appear definitely till the mid-twenties and the next literary generation. In its first phase this racialism was naive, emotional and almost provincial; later under the influence of the World War principles of self-determination and the rise of other cultural nationalisms, it was to become sophisticated and historically grounded in Africanism and the philosophy of cultural revivals.

Reaction from Racialism

Of course, no such formula held undisputed sway, either in the first or second decade of the new century. Nor were most writers or artists formal converts to it. But historically it is characteristic just the same, and helps us in retrospect to symbolize and understand the composite mind of this generation. Race pride, self respect, race solidarity, the folk-spirit are to anyone who has lived through these decades slogans vibrating vitally with the thought of the time. The art of these decades keynoted them; they were its spiritual dynamic. And that is all the more apparent as this phase of our cultural life begins to pass with the new issues and ideology of the present crisis and its struggle for economic freedom and social reform. For new viewpoints and values, geared in with these social forces, are again changing the whole cast and direction of Negro expression in literature and art. Thus the latest generation thought was veered away from racialism and sharply repudiated historical romanticism, and while still continuing some of the folk interests of cultural racialism, it is definitely realistic, socialistic, and proletarian. Its ideals and objectives, like those of the anti-slavery epoch, are radical and broadly humanitarian and its slogans of economic equality, freedom and justice are not distinctly racial.

The reader may wonder what this has to do with a brief review of Negro artistic achievements. The answer is that except from the point of view of these shifts in Negro thought as cultural tactics veering to the changing drift of social forces, there is no sane and significant account of our art expression, especially in panoramic perspective. Every quickening of the pulse and change in the flow of our art has represented some intensification of social forces, the peak of some social movement. In 1914-17, when the sensitive minds of the group faced the growing dilemmas of democracy and the World War from the racial angle, they could not share its enthusiasms, and a whole school of challenge and ironic protest sprang up keyed to Fenton Johnson's "We are tired of building up somebody-else's civilization," James Weldon Johnson's challenging "To America" and the social protest verse of Claude McKay. Then with the urban migration and its accompaniments came the more positively toned movement of cultural racialism and solidarity, coupled with a fresh interest in the peasant folk life. One wing of this movement was caught up and diverted in the neurotic jazz age with its freakish aesthetics and its irresponsible individualism while another linked on to a realistic rediscovery of the folk; both over the common denominator of racialism. Finally with the depression and the second disillusionment of the elite came the reformist and socialistic reaction of the present day, which we have already described. Personalities and individual achievements may stand out, do stand out on close inspection, but this is the general path and, we think, the major significance.

In the main, each generation, with a shift of tactic almost each decade, has been seeking cultural freedom through art; at one time with a moralistic goal, at another through aestheticism; in one phase in terms of a social program, in another, highly individualistically; its motivation now racialistic, now socialistic; for a while dominated by disillusionment and protest, at another by optimistic forecast and crusading reform. The tempers of each phase are clearly discernible as, with few exceptions, the art follows the social trends. Of course, if aestheticism, realism, regionalism or proletarianism are the general cultural vogue, Negro art reflects it, but always caught up in the texture of a racially determined phase, as might also be expected. There is no possibility of a separate account of the course of the Negro's art, but there is great point to a special secondary line following the fluctuations of racial situation and attitude.

Road Map of Progress

And now let us turn finally from generalities to specific cases. I shall venture the risky job of an annotated road map of this artistic progress; risky because subject to the double hazard of personal opinion and the greater danger of accidental oversight:

"My Life and Times" by Frederick Douglass (1882); George Williams "History of the Negro in America" (1883); Albery Whitman's long epic poem, "The Rape of Florida" (1884); Payne's "Recollections of Seventy Years" (1888); Edward Blyden's "Africa, Christianity and Islam" (1888); Alexander Crummel's "Africa and Christianity" (1891); Dunbar's "Lyrics of Lowly Life" (1896); the founding of the Negro academy (1897); Chestnut's "Wife of His Youth" and "The Conjure Woman" (1899); Coleridge Taylor's oratorio "Hiawatha" (1898); Booker Washington's "Up From Slavery" (1901); Marion Cook's "In Dahomey" (1902); Burleigh's "Plantation Melodies" (1901); William Stanley Braithwaite's "Lyrics of Life and Love" (1904); Kelly Miller's "Race Adjustment" (1909); W. C. Handy's "Memphis Blues" in 1910 and "St. Louis Blues" in 1912; James Weldon Johnson's "Autobiography of an Ex-Colored Man" (1912); the founding of THE CRISIS (1910); Stanley Braithwait's first "American Anthology" (1913); Fenton Johnson's "Songs of the Soil" (1916); James Weldon Johnson's "Fifty Years and After" (1917); The Hapgood Players (1917); the founding of the "Journal of Negro History" (1916); Georgia Douglass Johnson's "The Heart of a Woman and Other Poems" (1918); the founding of "Opportunity" magazine (1923); Gilpin's debut in the "Emperor Jones" (1920); Roland Hayes's first London concert (1920); The Gilpin Players, Cleveland (1920); The Howard Players, Washington (1921); Brawley's "Social History of the American Negro" (1921); Claude McKay's "Harlem Shadows" (1922); Carter Woodson's "The Negro in Our History" (1923); "The Book of American Negro Poetry" (1922); Jean Toomer's "Cane" (1923); Walter White's "Fire in the Flint" (1924); Jesse Fauset's "There is Confusion" (1924); Roland Hayes's American debut (1924); Harlem Number of

"The Survey Graphic" (1925); "The New Negro" (1925); Countee Cullen's "Color" (1925); Langston Hughes' "The Weary Blues" (1925); "The First Book of American Spirituals" (1925); Dett's "Religious Folk Songs of the Negro" (1925); Claude McKay's "Home to Harlem" (1926); Rose McClendon's debut (1926); "God's Trombones" (1927); the Negro cast in "Porgy" (1927); The Harmon shows for the "Works of American Negro Artists" (1928); Rudolph Fisher's "The Walls of Jericho" (1928); Archibald Motley's one-man show (New Gallery) (1928); Aaron Douglas's show of 1930 (Caz Delbos); Paul Robeson's "Othello" (1930); Langston Hughes' "Not Without Laughter" (1930); the debut of Richard Harrison in "The Green Pastures" (1930); Richmond Barthe's show (Caz Delbos) (1931); William Grant Still's "Afro-American Symphony" (1931); Cullen's "One Way to Heaven" (1932); Sterling Brown's "The Southern Road" (1932); Lesesne Well's shows Delphic and Brooklyn Museum, 1933 and 1934; Hall Johnson's "Run Little Children" (1933); Langston Hughes' "The Ways of White Folk" (1934); William Dawson's "Symphony on Folk Themes" (1934); George Wylie Henderson's novel "Ollie Miss" (1935); Marian Anderson's major debut of 1935; Frank Marshall Davis's "Black Man's Verse" (1935); Arna Bontemp's "Black Thunder" (1936); the founding of the Harlem Artists Guild (1936); Dett's oratorio "The Ordering of Moses" (1936); Edward Turpin's novel "These Low Grounds" (1937); Angelo Herndon's "Let Me Live" (1937); Richard Wright's "Uncle Tom's Children" (1938).

These at least and more! A significant list.—but more significant even the ever broadening base of the cultural advance as poetry, historical scholarship, fiction, drama, musical composition, painting, sculpture, criticism come successively under mature control and as the advance integrates more and more with the mainstream trends of American literature and art. For racial expression is after all a forced mode in our cultural life, and artistic creativeness and even national representativeness are really more vital. As long as this dubious bookkeeping lasts, however, we must take stock and claim credit in these separatist terms, but it should always be remembered that every contribution to Negro art is also a contribution to the general stock of American culture and that every Negro achievement is, *ipso facto,* a human achievement.

THE NEGRO: "NEW" OR NEWER:
A Retrospective Review of the
Literature of the Negro for 1938

PART I.

IT is now fifteen years, nearly a half a generation, since the literary advent of the "New Negro." In such an interval a new generation of creative talent should have come to the fore and presumably those talents who in 1924-25 were young and new should today be approaching maturity or have arrived at it. Normally too, at the rate of contemporary cultural advance, a new ideology with a changed world outlook and social orientation should have evolved. And the question back of all this needs to be raised, has it so developed or hasn't it, and do we confront today on the cultural front another Negro, either a newer Negro or a maturer "New Negro?"

A critic's business is not solely with the single file reviewing-stand view of endless squads of books in momentary dress parade but with the route and leadership of cultural advance, in short, with the march of ideas. There is no doubt in the panoramic retrospect of the years 1924 to 1938 about certain positive achievements:— a wider range of Negro self-expression in more of the arts, an increasing maturity and objectivity of approach on the part of the Negro artist to his subject-matter, a greater diversity of styles and artistic creeds, a healthier and firmer trend toward self-criticism, and perhaps most important of all, a deepening channel toward the mainstream of American literature and art as white and Negro artists share in ever-increasing collaboration the growing interest in Negro life and subject-matter. These are encouraging and praiseworthy gains, all of which were confidently predicted under the convenient but dangerous caption of "The New Negro."

But a caption's convenience is part of its danger; so is its brevity. In addition, in the case in question, there was inevitable indefiniteness as to what was meant by the "New Negro." Just that question must be answered, however, before we can judge whether today's Negro represents a matured phase of the movement of the 20's or is, as many of the youngest Negroes think and contend, a counter-movement, for which incidentally they have a feeling but no name. These "bright young people" to the contrary, it is my conviction that the former is true and that the "New Negro" movement is just coming

●

Fiction

The Dead Go Overside—Arthur D. Howden Smith, Greystone Press, N. Y., $2.50.

Tommy Lee Feathers—Ed Bell, Farrar & Rinehart, N. Y., $2.50.

How Sleeps the Beast—Don Tracy, M. S. Mill Co., N. Y., $2.00.

The Back Door—Julian R. Meade, Longmans, Green & Co., N. Y., $2.50.

Point Noir—Clelie Benton Huggins, Houghton Mifflin Co., Boston, $2.50.

Aunt Sara's Wooden God—Mercedes Gilbert, Christopher Publishing House, Boston, $2.00.

Uncle Tom's Children—Richard Wright, Harper & Bros., N. Y., $2.50.

Love at the Mission—R. Hernekin Baptist, Little Brown & Co., Boston, $2.50.

What Hath a Man—Sarah Gertrude Millin, Harper & Bros., N. Y., $2.50.

into its own after a frothy adolescence and a first-generation course which was more like a careen than a career. Using the nautical figure to drive home the metaphor, we may say that

Opportunity 17 (January and February 1939): 4–10; 36–42

there was at first too little ballast in the boat for the heavy head of sail that was set. Moreover, the talents of that period (and some of them still) were far from skillful mariners; artistically and sociologically they sailed many a crooked course, mistaking their directions for the lack of steadying common-sense and true group loyalty as a compass. But all that was inevitable in part; and was, as we shall later see, anticipated and predicted.

But the primary source of confusion perhaps was due to a deliberate decision not to define the "New Negro" dogmatically, but only to characterize his general traits and attitudes. And so, partly because of this indefiniteness, the phrase became a slogan for cheap race demagogues who wouldn't know a "cultural movement" if they could see one, a handy megaphone for petty exhibitionists who were only posing as "racialists" when in fact they were the rankest kind of egotists, and a gilded fetish for race idolaters who at heart were still sentimentalists seeking consolation for inferiority. But even as it was, certain greater evils were avoided—a growing race consciousness was not cramped down to a formula, and a movement with a popular ground swell and a folk significance was not tied to a partisan art creed or any one phase of culture politics.

THE most deliberate aspect of the New Negro formulation—and it is to be hoped, its crowning wisdom—was just this repudiation of any and all one-formula solutions of the race question, (its own immediate emphases included), and the proposed substitution of a solidarity of group feeling for unity within a variety of artistic creeds and social programs. To quote: "The Negro today wishes to be known for what he is, even in his faults and shortcomings, and scorns a craven and precarious survival at the price of seeming to be what he is not. He thus resents being spoken of as a social ward or minor, even by his own, and to being regarded a chronic patient for the sociological clinic, the sick man of American Democracy. For the same reasons, *he himself is through with those social nostrums and panaceas, the so-called 'solutions' of his 'problem', with which he and the country have been so liberally dosed in the past. Religion, freedom, education, money—in turn he has ardently hoped for and peculiarly trusted these things; he still believes in them, but not in blind trust that they alone will solve his life-problem."* *

How then even the *enfants terribles* of today's youth movement could see "cultural expression" as a substitute formula proposed by the "New

Negro" credo I cannot understand, except on the ground that they did not read carefully what had been carefully written. Nor would a careful reading have been auspicious for their own one-formula diagnosis of "economic exploitation" and solution by "class action." Not only was there no foolish illusion that "racial prejudice would soon disappear before the altars of truth, art and intellectual achievement,"[†] as has been asserted, but a philosophy of cultural isolation from the folk ("masses") and of cultural separatism were expressly repudiated. It was the bright young talents of the 20's who themselves went cosmopolite when they were advised to go racial, who went exhibitionist instead of going documentarian, who got jazz-mad and cabaret-crazy instead of getting folk-wise and sociologically sober. Lest this, too, seem sheer rationalizing hind-sight, let a few direct quotations from *The New Negro* testify to the contrary. Even more, the same excerpts will show that a social Reformation was called for as the sequel and proper goal of a cultural Renaissance, and that the present trends of second generation "New Negro" literature which we are now passing in review were predicted and reasonably anticipated. For reasons of space, quotations must be broken and for reasons of emphasis, some are italicized:

"A transformed and transforming psychology permeates the masses. . . . In a real sense it is the rank and file who are leading, and the leaders who are following. . . . It does not follow that if the Negro were better known, he would be better liked or better treated. (p. 10) . . . Not all the new art is in the field of pure art values. There is poetry of sturdy social protest and fiction of calm dispassionate social analysis. But reason and realism have cured us of sentimentality: instead of the wail and appeal, there is challenge and indictment. Satire is just beneath the surface of our latest prose and tonic irony has come into our poetic wells. These are good medicines for the common mind, for us they are the necessary antidotes against social poison. Their influence means that *at least for us* the worst symptoms of the social distemper are passing. And so the social promise of our recent art is as great as the artistic. (p. 52) . . . Each generation, however, will have its creed, and *that of the present* is the belief in the efficacy of collective effort, in race cooperation. This deep feeling of race is *at present* the mainspring of Negro life. . . . It is radical in tone, but not in purpose and only the most stupid forms of opposition, misunderstanding or persecution could make it otherwise. Of course, the thinking Negro has shifted a little toward the left with the world trend, and there is an increasing group who affiliate with radical and liberal movements. But fundamentally *for the present* the Negro is radical on race matters, conservative on others, in other words a "forced radical," a social protestant rather than a genuine radical. Yet under further pressure and injustice iconoclastic thought and motives will inevitably increase. Harlem's quixotic radicalisms call for their ounce of democracy today lest tomorrow they be beyond cure. (p. 11).

*"Enter the New Negro," p. 9 [Editor's note].

†John A. Davis, "We Win the Right to Fight for Jobs," *Opportunity* 16 (August 1938): 232 [Editor's Note].

IT is important, finally, to sum up the social aspect of the New Negro front with clarity because today's literature and art, an art of searching social documentation and criticism, thus becomes a consistent development and matured expression of the trends that were seen and analyzed in 1925.

"The Negro mind reaches out as yet to nothing but American wants, American ideas. But this forced attempt to build his Americanism on race values *is a unique social experiment,* and its ultimate success *is impossible except through the fullest sharing of American culture and institutions. There should be no delusion about this.* American nerves in sections unstrung with race hysteria are often fed the opiate that the trend of Negro advance is wholly separatist, and that the effect of its operation will be to encyst the Negro as a benign foreign body in the body politic. This cannot be--even if it were desirable. The racialism of the Negro is no limitation or reservation with respect to American life; it is only a constructive effort to build the obstructions in the stream of his progress into an efficient dam of social energy and power. Democracy itself is obstructed and stagnated to the extent that any of its channels are closed. Indeed they cannot be selectively closed. So the choice is not between one way for the Negro and another for the rest, but between American institutions frustrated on the one hand and American ideals progressively fulfilled and realized on the other." (p. 12).

The generation of the late 30's is nearer such a cultural course and closer to such social insight than the tangential generation of the late 20's. Artistic exploitation is just as possible from the inside as from the outside, and if our writers and artists are becoming sounder in their conception of the social role of themselves and their art, as indeed they are, it is all the more welcome after considerable delay and error. If, also, they no longer see cultural racialism as cultural separatism, which it never was or was meant to be, then, too, an illusory dilemma has lost its paralyzing spell. And so, we have only to march forward instead of to counter-march; only to broaden the phalanx and flatten out the opposition salients that threaten divided ranks. Today we pivot on a sociological front with our novelists, dramatists and social analysts in deployed formation. But for vision and morale we have to thank the spiritual surge and aesthetic inspiration of the first generation artists of the renaissance decade.

And now, to the literature of this year of reformation, stir, and strife.

In fiction, two novels by white authors remind us of the background use of Negro materials that used to be so universal. Many such have been ignored as not basically "Negro literature" at all. However these two, Clelie Benton Huggins' *Point Noir* and Arthur Smith's *The Dead Go Overside,* do exhibit significant if limited use of Negro historical and local color materials. The latter particularly, documenting intensively New England's part in the slave traffic, weaves a melodramatic love story and sea rescue over the sombre details of a New Bedford fishing schooner's conversion into a slave raider and a sturdy personality deteriorating as it passes from codfishing to the more prosperous job of manhunting. Also picaresque is Ed Bell's *Tommy Lee Feathers,* a local color novel of Marrowtown, a Tennessee Negro community. Reasonably well studied local color and characterization are seldom met with in the rustic humor school of Negro fiction, so *Tommy Lee Feathers* registers progress even in its broad stroke characterizations of the exploits of the town's "Black Angels," Tommy's football team, and the more conscious angels of Sister Feather's "Sanctified Church." One does not, of course, expect serious social commentary under this idiom. But too much "safe" entertainment of this sort has laid the groundwork for bad sociology.

However, it is noteworthy how much serious social commentary there really is in this year's crop of fiction, from both the white and the Negro authors. Already we are used to the semidoctrinal criticism of the Erskine Caldwell school, which by the way he continues with usual unsparing and unrelieved realism in his latest volume of stories, *Southways,* but there are other and as I think more effective brands of realism. Certainly one of the most convincing and moving bits of documentary fiction on the racial situation is Don Tracy's reportorial but beautifully restrained *How Sleeps the Beast.* More even than the famous movie *Fury,* this novel gives the physiology of American lynching; not just its horror and bestialities, but its moods and its social mechanisms. Vince, who starts out by saying to his girl, "I ain't goin', I got no truck with lynchin's" eventually goes under her taunts; Al Purvis, whose life poor Jim had saved, starts out to rescue him but succumbs to social cowardice and mob hysteria; the Sheriff is jostled from official indifference to sectional hate at the sign of a "Yankee meddler," and a newspaper reporter hunted by the mob for fear of exposure barely escapes the same fate by sleeping the night through in the "malodorous room marked 'Ladies'," after having been ordered out the back-door of the local Eastern Maryland Shore hotel while the mob pickets the entrance. In realism charged with terror, but tempered with pity and understanding, Don Tracy has written in the Steinbeckian vein the best version yet of this great American tragedy and of the social obsessions that make it happen.

More notable still, because about a more normal social subject, is Julian Meade's saga of Mary Lou Payton, the most fully characterized domestic Negro servant in all the tedious range of Negro servitors in American fiction. *The Back Door* is a book of truthful, artistically-balanced human documentation. Mary Lou's always precarious hold on the good things in life, on both domestic job and self-respect, on her amiable tobacco-worker lover beset by the wiles of looser women on the one hand and unemployment and occupational disease on the other, on her cherished but socially unrewarded respectability that every other week or so confronts the dreaded advances of Frank Anderson, the philandering white rent-collector, on even the job itself, are all portrayed with pity and sympathetic irony. *The Back Door* is as much a step above *Porgy* as *Porgy* was above its predecessors. Its deftly true touches—the wedding ring bought on installments and eventually confiscated, the lay-off that enables Jim to half conquer his consumptive cough, the juvenile blackmail of "Mr. Willie's" retort, "I know durn well *you* hook a plenty on the sly" as reply to Mary's frantic, "Mr. Willie, please don't bother them sandwiches," even the unwitting irony of the waiting ladies' missionary hymn,

> *"Can we whose souls are lighted*
> *With wisdom from on high,*
> *Can we to men benighted*
> *The lamp of life deny?"*

are all triumphs of the school of delicate realism well contrasted with the bludgeoning effects of the school of rough-shod realism. To the small sum of Southern classics must be added this tender saga of Stoke Alley and Chinch Row.

TO the fine achievements just mentioned, two Negro writers make this year a sizeable contribution. In the first, Mercedes Gilbert's *Aunt Sara's Wooden God*, the theme of the story is more important than its literary execution. Despite a too lenient introduction by Langston Hughes, this first novel is no masterpiece, not even a companion for *Ollie Miss* or *Jonah's Gourd Vine* with which it is bracketed; but it is promising and in subject matter significant. William Gordon, the illegitimate son, is the favored but profligate brother, Aunt Sara's "Wooden God." From the beginning a martyr to his mother's blind partiality, Jim, the darker brother, takes from start to finish the brunt of the situation the childhood taunts, the lesser chance, the lion's share of the farm work while William is in school or frittering away time in Macon, then the loss of his sweetheart, Ruth, through the machinations of William, and finally imprisonment for William's crime. Amateurish overloading, as well as the anecdotal style of developing the episodes of the story, robs the book of its full tragic possibilities. William's eventual return to a death-bed reconciliation and Aunt Sara's pious blessings is only relieved by his attempted confession and Jim's heroic resolve not to disillusion Aunt Sara. Our novelists must learn to master the medium before attacking the heavier themes; a smaller canvas dimensionally done is better than a thin epic or a melodramatic saga. Here is a great and typical theme only half developed, which someone—perhaps the author herself—must some day do with narrative power and character insight.

IN contrast, Richard Wright in *Uncle Tom's Children* uses the novella with the sweep and power of epic tragedy. Last year the first of these four gripping tales, *Big Boy Leaves Home*, was hailed as the most significant Negro prose since Toomer's *Cane*. Since then it has won the *Story Magazine* award for the national WPA's Writers' Project contest, and a second story, *Fire and Cloud*, has won second prize in the O. Henry awards. This is a well-merited literary launching for what must be watched as a major literary career. Mr. Wright's full-length novel is eagerly awaited; perhaps in the longer form the nemesis of race injustice which stalks the fate of every chief character in the four stories will stalk with a more natural stride. One often feels in the shorter form that the nemesis makes forced marches. This is not a nerve-wrecked reader's cry for mercy; for we grant the author the terrible truth of his situations, but merely a plea for posterity that judges finally on the note of universality and artistry. By this criterion *Big Boy* and *Long Black Song* will last longer for their poignant beauty than *Down By the Riverside*, certainly, and perhaps also, *Fire and Cloud*. Yet as social indictments, the one of white oppression and ingratitude and the other of black cowardice and gullibility, these very two have the most documentary significance. The force of Wright's versions of Negro tragedy in the South lies in the correct reading of the trivialities that in that hate-charged atmosphere precipitate these frightful climaxes of death and persecution; an innocent

Juvenile

Shuttered Windows—Florence C. Means, Houghton Mifflin Co., Boston, $2.00.

Araminta's Goat—Eva Knox Evans, G. P. Putnam's Sons, N. Y., $2.00.

Country Life Stories—Elizabeth Perry Cannon and Helen Adele Whiting, E. P. Dutton & Co., Inc., N. Y., 65c.

Bantu Tales Retold—Pattee Price, E. P. Dutton & Co., Inc., N. Y., $1.50.

Negro Folk Tales—Helen Adele Whiting, Associated Publishers, Washington, D. C., $1.10.

Negro Art, Music and Rhyme—Helen Adele Whiting, Associated Publishers, Washington, D. C., $1.10.

The Child's Story of the Negro—Jane D. Shackelford, Associated Publishers, Washington, D. C., $1.40.

●

boy's swimming prank in *Big Boy*, a man's desperate need for a boat to rescue his pregnant wife during a Mississippi flood, a white salesman's casual infatuation while trying to sell a prosperous black farmer's wife a gramophone, a relatively tame-hearted demonstration for food relief in the other three stories. And so, by this simple but profound discovery, Richard Wright has found a key to mass interpretation through symbolic individual instances which many have been fumbling for this long while. With this, our Negro fiction of social interpretation comes of age.

Love at the Mission is Mr. R. Hernekin Baptist's sternly tense story of the frustrations of three daughters of Pastor Oguey, a South African missionary. Hedged about by the double barriers of race and Puritanism, Hortense, the eldest, becomes involved in morbid jealousy of her younger sister's love affair, plots to poison her father, the symbol of this isolation, blames it after the fashion of the country on the African serving boy. But finally she has to stand for her intended crime and wither jealously in prison. Fani, the African nurse and housekeeper, is the counter-symbol of black paganism tolerant of this intruding Puritanism but never quite corrupted by it. Indeed the novel is really a pictorialized analysis of the futility of missionarism, and is of considerable significance because of its frank and carefully-studied approach to the clash of native and Nordic *mores*. In key so far as conclusions go, Sarah Gertrude Millin, with greater maturity, has analyzed the South African paradox from the point of view of an English civil servant with a tender conscience. Henry Ormandy, the hero of *What Hath a Man*, is outwardly successful as an individual but is haunted to the end of his career by his realization of the futility of the white man's self-imposed mission of imperialism. Mrs. Millin has woven into the earlier part of the story, when Ormandy encounters Cecil Rhodes just after the raid of Matabeleland, remarkable documentary evidence that Rhodes himself had a troubled conscience and paused once in his ruthlessness. But the very brevity of such a gesture in a cold-blooded game keynotes Mrs. Millin's indirect but quite effective indictment of imperialism as does also Henry's lonely, terrorful death. This too, although on the surface a novel of character study, is a novel of social protest; another David's pebble against our modern Goliath. The cause of social justice has been well served this year by the novelists.

A PROMISING symptom is the rapid growth of serious and sympathetic juvenile books on the Negro theme. Mrs. Florence Means in *Shuttered Windows* has written a story of an educated girl from the North, Harriet Freeman, and her struggle for the enlightenment of the illiterate South Carolina Island folk. Eva Knox Evans adds to her already well-known Jerome Anthony series of Negro child stories a sympathetic and quizzical tale of *Araminta's Goat*. Two gifted Negro teachers have collaborated to bring out a laudable public school reader series, beginning with *Country Life Stories*, a book that deserves wide circulation. Mrs. Helen Adele Whiting, Miss Cannon's collaborator in the foregoing, has independently brought out through the Associated Publishers two attractively bound and illustrated child's books, *Negro Folk Tales* and *Negro Art, Music and Rhyme*; the first much more successful in diction than the latter, but both only laudable pathbreakers in the important direction of introducing African legends and simplified race history to children. Dutton has also brought out Pattee Price's rhymed versions of *Bantu Tales*, genuinely true to folk idiom, which is all to their credit, but not too successfully adapted to the average child mind. All this is symptomatic of an important trend, of as much significance for general social education as for mere child entertainment. The crowning achievement in this field, however, is *The Child's Story of the Negro*, written by Miss Jane Shackelford. Here in fascinating style the riches of race history are minted down in sound coin for juvenile consumption and inspiration. More attractive format would make this real contribution a child's classic, and it is to be hoped that a second edition will make this advantageous addition.

Poetry

Exile—Leslie M. Collins, Privately printed, Fort Valley, Ga.

Pigments—L. G. Damas, La Pleiade Press, Paris.

Poems in All Moods—Alfred Cruickshank, Port of Spain, Trinidad, $1.00.

Negro Voices—Edited by Beatrice M. Murphy, Henry Harrison, N. Y., $1.50.

Through Sepia Eyes—Frank Marshall Davis, Black Cat Press, Chicago, 50c.

A New Song—Langston Hughes, International Workers Order, N. Y., 15c.

●

Returning to the adult plane, the situation of poetry must claim our attention briefly. Time was when poetry was one of the main considerations of the Negro renaissance. But obviously our verse output has shrunk, if not in quantity, certainly in quality, and for obvious reasons. Poetry of social analysis requires maturity and group contacts, while the poetry of personal lyricism finds it hard to thrive anywhere in our day. Especially so with the Negro poet whose cultural isolation is marked; to me it seems that this strain of expression is dying a natural death of spiritual suffocation, Beatrice Murphy's anthology of fledgling poets, *Negro Voices,* to the contrary. Here and there in this volume one hears a promising note; almost invariably, however, it is a poem of social analysis and reaction rather than one of personal lyricism. To the one or two veterans, like Hughes, Frank Davis, Louis Alexander, a small bevy can be added as discoveries of this meritorious but not too successful volume: Katherine Beverly, Iola Brister, Conrad Chittick, Marcus Christian, Randolph Edmonds, Leona Lyons and Helen Johnson. However it is clear that the imitation of successful poets will never give us anything but feeble echoes, whether these models be the classical masters or the outstanding poets of the Negro renaissance, Cullen, McKay and Hughes. If our poets are to serve well this generation they must go deeper and more courageously into the heart of real Negro experience. The postponement of Sterling Brown's expected volume *No Hidin' Place* thus leaves a lean poetic year of which the best garnerings, uneven at that, are Frank Marshall Davis's *Through Sepia Eyes* and Langston Hughes's *A New Song.* Both of these writers are vehemently poets of social protest now; so much so indeed that they have twangy lyres,

except for moments of clear vibrancy such as Hughes's *Ballad of Ozzie Powell* and *Song of Spain* and Davis's *Chicago Skyscrapers,* the latter seemingly the master poem of the year in a not too golden or plentiful poetic harvest. On the foreign horizon the appearance of the young Martiniquian poet, L. G. Damas, is significant;

Drama

Big White Fog—Mss., Theodore Ward, Chicago Federal Theater.

Haiti—Mss., William Du Bois, New York Federal Theater.

The Divine Comedy—Mss., Owen Dodson, Yale University Experimental Theater.

Don't You Want to be Free?—Langston Hughes, One Act Play Magazine, Nov., 1938.

●

otherwise the foreign output, like the domestic, is plaintive and derivative.

Whereas poetry languishes, drama seems to flourish. The honors are about evenly divided between the experimental theatres and the Federal Theatre Project. The latter, with several successful revivals, *Run Little Chillun* among them, had as new hits Theodore Ward's *Big White Fog* and William Du Bois's moving though melodramatic *Haiti* to its credit. On the other hand, the experimental theatre has given two Negro playwrights a chance for experimentation both in form and substance that may eventually lead somewhere. Dodson's *The Divine Comedy,* the Yale Theatre's contribution, is a somewhat over-ambitious expressionistic rendition of Negro cult religion that shows promise of a new writing talent, while the Harlem Suitcase Theatre's *Don't You Want to Be Free?* has vindicated the possibilities of a new dramatic approach. Both are to be watched hopefully, but especially the latter, because a people's theatre with an intimate reaction of the audience to materials familiar to it is one of the sound new items of a cultural program that in some of the arts, drama particularly, has stalled unnecessarily. This theatre and the Richmond Peoples' Theatre, under the auspices of the Southern Youth Congress and the direction of Thomas Richardson, supply even better laboratory facilities than the drama groups of the Negro colleges, laudable as their Intercollegiate Dramatic Association is. It is to be hoped that real folk portraiture in drama may soon issue from these experiments. In the dramatized "Blues Episodes" of *Don't You Want to Be Free?,* and in the promising satirical sketches that the same theatre has recently begun, I see potentialities such as I have previously discussed at length. I am not only anxious to see them develop but anxious for some further confirmation of the predicted role of the drama in the Negro movement of self-expression in the arts. Not that an individual critic needs to be sustained, but since the course was plotted by close comparative study of other cultural movements, some national and some racial, rather that the history of this phase of our cultural development should demonstrate the wholesome principle that the Negro is no exception to the human rule. For after all, it is the lesson of history that a cultural revival has been both the symptom and initiating cause of most people's awakenings.

PART II.

AS we turn now to the biographic, historical and sociological literature of the year, we find the treatment of the Negro, almost without exception, maturing significantly. There is, on the whole, less shoddy in the material, less warping in the weaving, and even what is propaganda has at least the virtue of frank, honest labeling. The historical cloth particularly is of more expert manufacture and only here and there exhibits the frousy irregularities of amateur homespun. General social criticism reaches a record yardage; and so far as I can see, only the patient needle-point of self-criticism has lagged in a year of unusual, perhaps forced production. Forced, because undoubtedly and obviously the pressure behind much of this prose of social interpretation is that of the serious contemporary economic and political crisis. But fortunately also, a considerable part of this literature is for that very reason, deliberately integrated with the general issues and the competing philosophies of that crisis.

Before inspecting the varied stock of the year, a brief retrospective word is needed. Committed to no one cult of aesthetics (and least of all to the creed of "art for art's sake," since it tried to focus the Negro creative writer upon the task of "folk interpretation"), *The New Negro* movement did have a rather definite set of objectives for its historical and sociological literature. These were a non-apologetic sort of biography; a boldly racial but not narrowly sectarian history; an objective, unsentimental sociology; an independent cultural anthropology that did not accept Nordic values as necessarily final; and a social critique that used the same yardstick for both external and internal criti-

cism. A long order—which it is no marvel to see take shape gradually and by difficult stages. Again to satisfy the skeptical, let quotations from *The Negro Digs Up His Past* attest:

"The American Negro must remake his past in order to make his future. Though it is orthodox to think of America as the one country where it is unnecessary to have a past, what is a luxury for the nation as a whole becomes a prime social necessity for the Negro. For him, a group tradition must supply compensation for persecution and pride of race the antidote for prejudice. History must restore what slavery took away, for it is the social damage of slavery that the present generation must repair and offset." *

But this call for a reconstructed group tradition was not necessarily pitched to the key of chauvinism, though there is some inevitable chauvinism in its train. Chauvinism is, however, the mark and brand of the tyro, the unskilled and unscientific amateur in this line, and we have had, still have and maybe always will have our brash amateurs who rush on where scientists pause and hesitate. However, this was recognized, and warned against, and was spoken of as the mark of the old, not of the newer generation. It was said:

"This sort of thing (chauvinistic biography and history) was on the whole pathetically over-corrective, ridiculously over-laudatory; it was apologetics turned into biography. But today, *even if for the ultimate purpose of group justification,* history has become less a matter of argument and more a matter of record. There is the definite desire and determination to have a history, well documented, widely known at least within race circles, and administered as a stimulating and inspiring tradition for the coming generations. But gradually as the study of the Negro's past has come out of the vagaries of rhetoric and propaganda and become systematic and scientific, three outstanding conclusions have been established:

"First, that the Negro has been throughout the centuries of controversy an active collaborator, and often a pioneer, in the struggle for his own freedom and advancement. This is true to a degree which makes it the more surprising that it has not been recognized earlier.

"Second, that by virtue of their being regarded as something 'exceptional,' even by friends and well-wishers, Negroes of attainment and genius have been unfairly disassociated from the group, and group credit lost accordingly.

"Third, that the remote racial origins of the Negro, far from being what the race and the world have been given to understand, offer a record of creditable group achievement when scientifically viewed, and more important still, that they are of vital *general* interest be-

*Arthur Schomburg, "The Negro Digs Up His Past," in *The New Negro,* ed. Alain Locke, 1925 [Editor's note].

cause of their bearing upon the beginnings and early development of culture.

"With such crucial truths to document and establish, an ounce of fact is worth a pound of controversy. So the Negro historian today digs under the spot where his predecessor stood and argued."*

THE mere re-statement of this historical credo of the New Negro (1925) shows clearly that not only has it not been superseded, but that it has yet to be fully realized. Indeed it was maintained at that time that the proper use of such materials as were available or could be unearthed by research was "not only for the first true writing of Negro history, but for *the rewriting of many important paragraphs of our common American history.*" One only needs an obvious ditto for sociology, anthropology, economics, and social criticism to get the lineaments of a point of view as progressive, as valid, and as incontestable in 1939 as fifteen years ago.

Indeed we may well and warrantably take this as a yardstick for the literature which we now have to review. Professor Brawley has excellently edited the *Best Prose of Paul Laurence Dunbar;* a service as much to social as to literary criticism. For by including with the short stories excerpts from his novels, Dunbar's pioneer attempts at the social documentation of Negro life are brought clearly to attention. Less artistic than his verse, Dunbar's prose becomes nevertheless more significant with the years; here for the most part he redeems the superficial and too stereotyped social portraiture of his poetry and shakes off the minstrel's motley for truer even if less attractive garb. Robinson's volume of stories, *Out of Bondage,* is, on the other hand, such thinly fictionalized history as to have little literary value and only to be of antiquarian interest. It is hard, no doubt, to galvanize history either in fiction or biography, but Arthur Huff Fauset's crisp and vivid *Sojourner Truth* proves that it can be done. This—beyond doubt the prize biography of the year and one of the best Negro biographies ever done—takes the fragile legend of Sojourner and reconstructs an historical portrait of illuminating value and charm. It lacks only a larger canvas giving the social background of the anti-slavery movement to be of as much historical as biographic value; and even this is from time to time hinted back of the vigorous etching of this black peasant crusader.

Just this galvanic touch is missed in the scholarly and painstaking biography, historical critique, and translation of the poems of *Juan Latino,* by Professor Valaurez Spratlin. Thus this detailed documentation of the ex-slave Humanist, the best Latinist of Spain in the reign of Philip V and incumbent of the chair of Poetry at the University of Granada, rises only momentarily above the level of purely historical and antiquarian interest. In the verses of Latino there was more poetics than poetry, but the *Austriad* faithfully reflected the florid Neoclassicism of Spain of the 1570's; the biography could and should have shed a portraitistic light, if not on the man, then at least on his times, for concerning them there is plenty of material.

The Life of George Washington Carver, under the slushy caption of *From Captivity to Fame,* is a good example of what race biography once was, and today should not be. Purely anecdotal, with an incongruous mixture of petty detail and sententious moralisms, it not only does not do the subject justice, but makes Dr. Carver a "race exhibit" rather than a real human interest life and character. One is indeed impressed with the antithesis between the sentimental, philanthropic, moralistic approach and the historico-social and psychological approaches of modern-day biography. They are perhaps ir-

Biography and Belles Lettres :

The Best Short Stories of Paul Laurence Dunbar—Edited by Benjamin Brawley, Dodd, Mead & Co., N. Y., $2.75.

Out of Bondage and Other Stories—Rowland E. Robinson, Charles E. Tuttle Co., Rutland, Vermont, $2.50.

From Captivity to Fame, The Life of George Washington Carver—Raleigh H. Merritt, Meador Publishing Co., Boston, $2.00.

Black Dynamite—Nat Fleischer, Ring Publishing Co., Madison Square Garden, N. Y., $1.50.

Sojourner Truth—Arthur Huff Fauset, University of N. C. Press, $1.00.

William Alpheus Hunton—Addie W. Hunton, Association Press, N. Y., $2.00.

Against the Tide—A. Clayton Powell, Sr., Richard R. Smith & Co., N. Y., $2.00.

The Black Jacobins—C. L. R. James, The Dial Press N. Y., $3.75.

Tell My Horse—Zora Neale Hurston, J. B. Lippincott Co., Philadelphia, $2.00.

Linea de Color—I. Pereda Valdez, Editions Ercilla, Santiago y Chile.

El Negro Rio-Platense y otros Ensayos—I. Pereda Valdez, Editions Garcia, Montevideo, Uraguay.

Juan Latino: Slave and Humanist—Edited by V. B. Spratlin, Spinner Press, Inc., N. Y., $2.00.

Negro and African Proverbs in *Racial Proverbs*—S. G. Champion, Geo. Routledge & Sons, London, $10.00.

●

*Ibid. [Editor's note].

reconcilable. Mrs. Addie Hunton's biography of her well-known husband, William Alpheus Hunton, pioneer leader of the Y.M.C.A. work among Negroes, is an example and case in point. A point of view that spots a career only by its idealistic highlights, that is committed to making a life symbolic, whether of an ideal or a movement, that necessarily omits social criticism and psychological realism, scarcely can yield us what the modern age calls biography. It is more apt to be the apologia of a "cause." In spite of such limitations, the Hunton biography is a record worth reading just as the life behind it was thoroughly worth living, but neither a moralistic allegory nor a thrilling success story like Pastor Clayton Powell's creditable autobiography will give us the objective social or human portraiture which the present generation needs and for the most part, desires.

The Black Jacobins by the talented C. L. R. James is, on the other hand, individual and social analysis of high order and deep penetration. Had it been written in a tone in harmony with its careful historical research into the background of French Jacobinism, this story of the great Haitian rebel, Toussaint Louverture, and his compatriots Christophe and Dessalines, would be the definitive study in this field. However, the issues of today are pushed too passionately back to their historic parallels—which is not to discount by any means the economic interpretation of colonial slavery in the Caribbean, but only a caution to read the ideology of each age more accurately and to have historical heroes motivated by their own contemporary idiom of thought and ideas. There is more correctness in the historical materials, therefore, than in the psychological interpretation of these truly great and fascinating figures of Negro history.

UNLESS it be characterized as the breezy biography of a cult, Zora Neale Hurston's story of voodoo life in Haiti and Jamaica is more folklore and *belles lettres* than true human or social documentation. Scientific folk-lore, it surely is not, being too shot through with personal reactions and the piquant thrills of a travelogue. Recently another study has given Voodooism a more scientifically functional interpretation and defense, and Voodooism certainly merits an analysis going deeper than a playful description of it as "a harmless pagan cult that sacrifices domestic animals at its worst." Too much of *Tell My Horse* is anthropological gossip in spite of many unforgettable word pictures; and by the way, the fine photographic illustrations are in

themselves worth the price of the book. The social and political criticism, especially of the upper-class Haitians, is thought-provoking; and caustic as it is, seems no doubt deserved in part at least. One priceless epigram just must be quoted: "Gods always behave like the people who make them."

Contrasting in thoroughness and sobriety with these excursions into *Caribbeana* are the two works of the Uraguayan race scholar, Ildefonso Pereda Valdes. Through the studies of Fernando Ortiz, the learned scholar of Afro-Cubana, and the work in Afro-Braziliana by Dr. Arthur Ramos, shortly to be published in abridged translation by the Association for the Study of Negro Life and History, the field of the Negro elements in Latin American culture is at last being opened up to the scientific world generally, and to the North American reader in particular. Not yet translated, Senor Valdes's studies are an important extension of this most important field. In *Linea de Color,* he largely interprets the contemporary culture of the American and Cuban Negro while in *El Negro Rio Platense,* he documents the Negro and African elements in the history, folklore and culture of Brazil, the Argentine and Uraguay, and traces Negro influences from Brazil right down into furthermost South America. Important studies of Negro idioms in the popular music of Brazil, of African festivals and superstitions in Uraguay and the valley of the Rio de la Plata open up a fresh vein of research in the history and influence of the Negro in the Americas. In *Linea de Color* are to be found pithy urbane essays on Nicholas Guillen, the Afro-Cuban poet, the mulatto Brazilian poet, Cruz E Souza, and on African dances in Brazil. In the other volume, more academic essays on the Negro as seen by the great Spanish writers of the Golden Age in Spain and several other cosmopolitan themes attest to the wide scholarship of Senor Valdes. It is refreshing and significant to discover in far South America an independently motivated analogue of the New Negro cultural movement. *Linea de Color* reciprocates gracefully by giving a rather detailed account of the North American Negro renaissance in terms of its chief contemporary exponents, cultural and political. It has been an unusual year for Negro biography and folk-lore, the latter capped academically by the exhaustive collation of African and Negro American proverbs in Champion's monumental *Racial Proverbs.*

AS is to be expected, the documentation of Negro life in the Federal Writers' Project, *The American Guide Series,* is varied, uneven and ranges through history to folklore and from mere opinion to sociology. But on the whole the yield is sound and representative, due in considerable measure to the careful direction of these projects from the Federal editorial office. *New York Panorama,* however, in its sections on the Negro, misses its chances in spite of the collation of much new and striking material. Moderately successful in treating early New York, it fails to interpret contemporary Harlem soundly or deeply. Indeed it vacillates between superficial flippancy and hectic propagandist expose, seldom touching the golden mean of sober interpretation. In *The New Orleans City Guide* the Negro items are progressively integrated into the several topics of art, music, architecture, folk lore and civic history in a positively refreshing way. This exceeds the usual play-up of the Creole tradition at the expense of the Negro, and for once in the Creole account the Negro element is given reasonable mention. The *Mississippi Guide* is casual, notable for its omissions in its treatment of the Negro; and savors as much of the reactionary tradition of the Old South as the New Orleans Guide does of the liberal New South that we all prefer to hold with and believe in. The Old South is an undeniable part of the historical past; but as a mirror for the present it is out of place and pernicious.

Thus liberal studies like *A Southerner Discovers the South* by Jonathan Daniels and Frank Shay's *Judge Lynch: His First Hundred Years* become the really important guides to social understanding and action. They, with most of the solid literature of the New South—which someone has said is the necessary complement of the New Negro—keep accumulatively verifying these basic truths: that the history of the South itself is the history of the slave regime, that the sociology of the South is its aftermath and retribution, and that the reconstruction of the entire South is its dilemma and only possible solution. Whatever common denominator solution can be found is the problem of the present generation. Thus for Mr. Shay, lynching is rightly not just the plight of the Negro but the disease of law and public opinion; while for Mr. Daniels the Negro is not so much a problem as a symptom. This realistic third dimension now being projected into the consideration of the race problem is the best hope of the whole situation, and should never be lost sight of by any observer, black or white, who wishes today to get credence or give enlightenment.

For this reason, Professor Stephenson's study of *Isaac Franklin: Slave Trader and Planter of the Old South* is as social history of the newer, realistic type as much a document of Negro history as it is of the socio-economic story of the plantation regime. Factual almost to a fault, it is a model of careful objective statement; no one can accuse this author of seeing history through colored spectacles of opinions. Only slightly less objective, and even more revealing is Professor Bell Wiley's study of *Southern Negroes: 1861-1865.* But a decade ago so frank and fair an account of the Negroes during the crisis of the Civil War would have been very unlikely from the pen of a Southern professor of history and certainly unthinkable as a prize award of the United Daughters of the Confederacy. Southern abolitionism, Negro unrest and military service to both sides, the dilemmas of Southern policy and strategy, are not at all glossed over in a work of most creditable historical honesty. Almost a companion volume, by chance has come Professor Wesley's penetrating study entitled *The Collapse of the Confederacy.* Here surely is a fascinating division of labor—

Historical and Sociological:

Chapters on the Negro in *The American Guide Series*—Federal Writers Project—*The Mississippi Guide,* Viking Press, Inc., N. Y., $2.50; *The New Orleans City Guide,* Houghton Mifflin Co., Boston, $2.50; *New York Panorama,* Random House, Inc., N. Y., $2.50.

Isaac Franklin, Slave Trader and Planter of the Old South—Wendell Holmes Stephenson, Louisiana State University Press, $2.00.

The Negro in Louisiana—Charles B. Roussève, Xavier University Press, New Orleans, $2.00.

The Collapse of the Confederacy—Charles H. Wesley, Associated Publishers, Inc., Washington, D. C., $2.15.

Southern Negroes: 1861-1865—Bell Irvin Wiley, Yale University Press, New Haven, $3.00.

Judge Lynch: His First 100 Years—Frank Shay, Ives Washburn, Inc., N. Y., $2.50.

A Southerner Discovers the South—Jonathan Daniels, The MacMillan Co., N. Y., $3.00.

The Black Man in White America—John G. Van Deusen, Associated Publishers, Washington, D. C., $3.25.

The Negro and the Democratic Front—James W. Ford, International Publishers, N. Y., $2.00.

Howard University Studies in Social Science, Vol. I.—Edited by Abram L. Harris.

The 1938 Year Book: Journal of Negro Education: Relation of the Federal Government to Negro Education, $2.00.

The Negro College Graduate—Charles S. Johnson, University of N. C. Press, $3.00.

American Caste and the Negro College—Buell G. Gallagher, Columbia University Press, $2.50.

an analysis of the policy of the Confederacy by a Negro historian and of the status and behavior of the Negro population during the same period by a white historian. Dr. Wesley carefully and incisively documents the economic breakdown of the Confederate economy, showing its military defeat as merely its sequel. He is also insistent on the too often forgotten facts of the Confederacy's last frantic dilemma about military emancipation and the proposed use of Negro soldiers to bolster its shattered man-power. Thus both the historical and the contemporary Southern scene have this year had significant, almost definitive interpretations.

The fascinating subject of *The Negro in Louisiana* has unfortunately not had anything approaching definitive treatment at the hands of Professor Rousseve; for his volume, a creditable ground-breaker, has too much sketchiness and far too little social interpretation to match worthily the rapidly rising level of Southern historical studies.

Turning from the regional to the national front, we find the discussion of the race problem gains by the wider angle of vision and attack. We find also one great virtue in the economic approach, apart from its specific hypotheses—an insistence on basic and common factors in the social equation. The economic interpretation of the race question is definitely gaining ground and favor among students of the situation. Both studies in the long anticipated Volume I of the *Howard University Studies in Social Science* have this emphasis, the one explicitly, the other by implication. Wilson E. Williams'* dissertation on *Africa and the Rise of Capitalism* breaks pioneer ground on the importance of the slave trade in the development of European commerce and industry in the 16th, 17th and 18th centuries and establishes the thesis that it was a "very important factor in the development of the capitalist economy in England"—one might warrantably add, of Western capitalism. The second essay, by Robert E. Martin, skillfully analyzes *Negro Disfranchisement in Virginia,* not in the traditional historical way, but by documenting the shifts of political policy and the mechanisms of majority-minority interaction, thus bringing to the surface conflicts of interest and motives too often unnoticed or ignored. Apart from such clarifying information these studies, reflecting the trend of the graduate instruction of which they are products, seem to predict a new approach in this field with broad implications and deep potentialities.

*Eric Williams [Editor's note].

IN contrast to this critical economic attack, J. W. Ford's *The Negro and the Democratic Front* hews rather dogmatically to the official Marxist line, but with frank and zealous insistence. Its frankness is a virtue to be praised; as is also the value of having a clear, simply-put statement of the Communist interpretation of major national and world issues from the angle of the Negro's position. Though largely a compendium of Mr. Ford's addresses, it does focus for the layman a unified picture of radical thought and programs of action. Quite to the opposite, John G. Van Deusen in *The Black Man in White America* has taken up the cudgels for gradualism, gratuitously and with feeble effect. To a book seven-eighths full of patiently assembled and well-organized facts about every important phase of Negro life, Professor Van Deusen adds the banalities of philanthropic platitudes and dubious advice. He counsels "patience," expects "education and understanding" and in another paragraph "that universal solvent: Time" to solve the Negro problem, yet admits that "the greatest part of the work of conciliation remains to be accomplished." If there were some automatic strainer to separate fact from advice and opinion, this book would be a boon to the average reader, for there are regrettably few up-to-date compendiums of the facts about Negro life.

In education, there are three books of note this year. The Yearbook of the *Journal of Negro Education,* in keeping with the high standard of all its five annual year-book issues, documents exhaustively and in many regards critically *The Relation of the Federal Government to Negro Education.* Similarly exhaustive, with elaborate deduction of trends but little or no overt social criticism, Professor Charles Johnson's study of *The Negro College Graduate* offers for the first time since DuBois's *Atlanta Studies* an objective and composite picture of the college-bred Negro. Significant conclusions are the relatively low economic standard of the Negro in professional service and the serious displacement of trained Negro leadership from the areas of greatest mass need. It may be plead that an objective survey study should only diagnose and must not judge or blame. But just such vital correlation with social policy and criticism of majority attitudes is boldly attempted in President Buell Gallagher's book, *American Caste and the Negro College.* Instead of just describing the Negro college, Dr. Gallagher spends seven of his fourteen chapters analyzing the social setting and frame of reference of the Negro college, namely the American system of color caste with its taboos and techniques of majority domination and minority repression. Then he illuminatingly decides that in addition to its regular function as a college, a Negro college has imposed upon it the function of transforming and transcending caste, or to quote: "the segregated college has a special set of responsibilities connected first, with the problem of transforming the caste system" and second, "with the success of the individual member of the minority group in maintaining his own personal integrity in the face of defeat, or of partial achievement." If for no other reason, such keen analysis of the social function of Negro education would make this an outstanding contribution; but in addition, the diagnosis is sound, the prescriptions liberal and suggestive, and the style charming. Indeed a noteworthy contribution!

AFRICAN life has a disproportionately voluminous literature, since any European who has been there over six weeks may write a book about it. It is safe to say that over half of this literature is false both as to fact and values, that more than half of what is true to fact is false in interpretation, and that more than half of that minimal residue is falsely generalized— for Africa is a continent of hundreds of different cultures. So, the best of all possible interpreters is the intelligent native who also knows, without having become de-racialized, the civilization of the West. Next best is the scientific interpreter who uses the native informer as the open sesame to African social values. The virtue of Rene Maran's *Livingstone* is that he himself knows by long acquaintance that same equatorial Africa which was Livingstone's country. Jose Saco speaking of slavery in Brazil, Dantes Bellegarde speaking for Haiti and, with some reservation for amateurishness, J. A. Jarvis speaking for the Virgin Islands make their respective books welcome and trustworthy as native opinion upon native materials. The same should have been true for Nnamdi Azikiwe's *Renascent Africa* but for the almost adolescent indignation distorting the outlines of a statement of native West African conditions, grievances and programs. Even so, an expression of native opinion is valuable at any price. Just as radical, in fact more so in spite of its cool reasoning, is George Padmore's *Africa and World Peace*. In addition to being one of the sharpest critiques of imperialism in a decade of increasing anti-imperialist attack, this book vividly expounds the close connection between fascism and imperialism, on the one hand, and fascism and African interests and issues on the other.

Turning to the less controversial, we have from Professor Herskovits a monumental and definitive two-volume study of the Dahomean

●

Africana:

Livingstone et L'Exploration de L'Afrique—Rene Maran, Nouvelle Revue Francaise, Paris, 25 fr.

Renascent Africa—Nnamdi Azikiwe, Zik Press, Lagos, 12s. 6d.

Africa and World Peace—George Padmore, Secker & Warburg, London, 7s. 6d.

Historia de la Esclavitur de la Raza Africana en el Nuevo Mundo—Jose A. Saco, La Habana Press.

Le Nation Haitienne—Dantes Bellegarde, J. de Gigourd, Paris, 25 fr.

Brief History of the Virgin Islands—J. Antonio Jarvis, The Art Shop, St. Thomas, V. I., $3.00.

Dahomey, An Ancient West African Kingdom, 2 Vols. —Melville J. Herskovits, J. J. Augustin, N. Y., $12.00.

Black and Beautiful—Marius Fortie, Bobbs-Merrill Co., Indianapolis, $3.50.

Out of Africa—Isak Dinesen, Random House, Inc., N. Y., $2.75.

African Mirage—Hoyningen Huene, Charles Scribner's Sons, N. Y., $3.75.

Kings and Knaves in the Cameroons—Andre Mikhelson, G. P. Putnam's Sons, N. Y., $3.00.

culture. A careful historical and functional approach yields a sympathetic view of a much misunderstood people, and both illustrates and fortifies a growing trend toward the independent interpretation of African life not in terms of Nordic *mores* and standards but of its own.

So conceded is this point of view becoming that even the best travel literature is now being keyed to it. *Black and Beautiful* is one such, not just by wishful thinking in its title but by virtue of twenty-five years of "going native" by the author, Marius Fortie. His natives are individuals, not types; several of them were his "wives" and sons, and he speaks passionately for and in behalf of his "adopted people," a far cry indeed from the supercilious traveler, missionary or civil servant. Even Andre Mikhelson's *Kings and Knaves in the Cameroons*, mock-heroic and ironic, is a cynical fable castigating "so-called

European civilization"; while Isak Dinesen's *Out of Africa* gives a delicately sensitive and respectful account of Kenya native life and the Kikuyu, the Somali and the Masai. The approach is human rather than anthropological and we have that to thank for a general impression that these peoples have a future and not merely a tragic present and an irretrievable primitive past. An impassioned defense of pagan primitivism is the subtle theme uniting the impressionistic diary pictures of *African Mirage,* by Hoyningen-Huene, by considerable odds one of the most understandingly observed and beautifully written volumes in the whole range of this literature. Even with all of our scientific revaluation, all our "New Negro" compensations, all our anti-Nordic polemics, a certain disrespect for Africa still persists widely. There is only one sure remedy—an annointing of the eyes. *African Mirage* seems to me almost a miraculous cure for cultural color-blindness. Such normality of social vision is surely one of the prerequisites also for effective history, sociology and econmics; no scientific lens is better except mechanically than the eye that looks through it. Let us above all else pray for clear-minded interpreters.

DRY FIELDS AND GREEN PASTURES

PART I

THERE are two traditions in the portrayal of Negro life and character, the realistic and the romantic, and it seems that they are coming into sharper contrast and conflict. This is more than the usual aesthetic controversy between realism and romanticism, for that is an issue of the past which realism has won decidedly, at least as far as seriously creative literature is concerned. But as relating to Negro materials, either the battle has to be fought all over again, belatedly; or else there is something more to the issue in this field—and the latter, I think, is the case. A minority literature is likely to suffer the orphan's fate of being forced always to wear hand-me-down, ill-fitting clothes. And even minority artistic spokesmen are apt to revel in these tatters of the past, especially if they once have been "elegant." This accounts for some of the shoddy, second-hand romanticism that perenially pervades the Negro literature of this or any typical year. But, as has already been said, I think there is even more to it than that.

What can it be—this additional something? Well, it is surely obvious to all but Hollywood and the Southern obscurantists that there are several sorts of Negroes, in addition to those that never were except in the imagination and tradition of the school of official Southern romance. Even the progressive and creatively original Southern writers have abandoned these stereotypes, but for all that, they are still very much alive and unbelievably popular. We should stop to consider this, for not all of it is Southern obscurantism and regional propaganda. There is a legitimate appetite for the picturesque, the naive, the zestful and the ex- uberantly imaginative, and even in their baneful social misrepresentativeness, these traditional Negro types do have a deep human appeal that in some measure accounts for their wide vogue. They were, for example, the charm of "Green Pastures," and against them realistically drab and drear characters, even though sociologically sound, have little chance in competition for general favor and interest. Putting it in a phrase, folk life, as poetically picturesque, enjoys a more than ten-to-one advantage over folk life as prosaically pictorial. A small section of reformists, a disillusioned intelligentsia, will accept sociological realism, and an occasional wider hearing may come to it as in the recent vogue of *Grapes of Wrath*, but on the whole and in the long run, romantic versions of life, especially minority life, are bound to have greater currency and popularity.

Personally in spite of the charm and the diversion I vote for the realistic art of the "dry fields," even the parched meadows and the scorched earth of our contemporary social crises, as against the romantic art of the "green pastures." We need more informative and less escapist literature and art. But that is not to ignore the general human inclination to lie down, mentally and emotionally, in the cool green shade beside pleasantly running waters So it remains a very practical question for us partisans of truth in art to figure out what can and must be done about it. Here I think the literature of the year gives us a clue, and to those of us who have special interests in Negro materials and subject-matter, gives also a new hope.

One form of realism can shorten the long

Opportunity 18 (January and February 1940): 4–10, 28; 41–46, 53.

odds against it, and that is poetic realism; for that, without making concessions to the truth, still manages somehow to lift the drab sordidness of the prosaic varieties of realism and give instead the warm human touch, the throbbing rhythm, the vital balance of contrast so necessary to an art that would make us see and feel and move rather than merely sit and stare and listen. Certainly here and there touches of a particularly successful poetic realism are to be detected in Negro literature—amid, I admit, a terrific amount of realistic slag and romantic dross, but worth all the hard prospecting that it takes to find it and all the patient refining and careful vouching that may be necessary to get it into accepted and profitable circulation.

Such art combines beauty with truth, and reconciles the dilemma of having to have one at the expense of the other. For some time now I have had the conviction that not only the Negro writer, but whatever artist worked long and hard and deeply with Negro materials would find, by virtue of some things deeply characteristic of Negro life, the rare formula of poetic realism. And where it does crop out, we have, I am sure, the best of this or any year's production.

Fiction, especially with this rare combination, should not be expected of the average writer, nor of a period like ours which is so inevitably commercial. Yet it is to be marveled at that unconventional fiction is so much the order of the day. New types and new backgrounds are fairly frequent these days. Arna Bontemps, after a fine apprenticeship in the unromantic historical novel, follows his *Black Thunder* of several years back with a novelette of the Haitian revolution, *Drums at Dusk*. He has a grand theme, the young aristocrat intrigued by the impending slave revolt and dabbling back and forth between the moribund world of the Breda estate and the rising black Haiti of the peasants. But for all the broad canvas and the carefully studied historical and local color, *Drums at Dusk* fails to be either thrilling romance or moving realism. It is, however, a competent second novel in a field that promises a great deal.

The Negro historical novel is still in the making, but we can begin to glimpse what it will be in its full stature, with the homely epic character and unusually dramatic incident, in this book. In pioneering quality, *Drums at Dusk* is most significant, but it falls between the old and the new traditions.

So does another ambitious historical novel by two white writers, Roland Barker and William

Doerflinger, a semi-realistic romance of the slave trade entitled *The Middle Passage*. So divided are the two parts of the canvas, and so different their brush-strokes, that one can almost imagine that it was a divided assignment.

Some commendable research has dug up vivid and true details of the slave trade, particularly about the African slave raids, the trading compounds on the Guinea coast, and the ruthless inter-tribal wars that fed the slave markets. Against this admirably realistic background, however, a melodramatic romance acts itself through, in too swashbuckling a fashion to be either convincing or in key. Stephen Bishop's blighted romance, his desperate resort to slave trading, his gradual conformation to type, his bitter feuds with his ship companions and trade rivals, and his final disappointment when, on his return for his last cargo, he finds his Emilia married to the Spanish trader, Esperanza, all move on another stage, and not until the ironic escape from capture by the British brig tracking down the outlawed slavers does the main plot mesh in effectively with the sub-plot. Again, then, a good beginning in an important new vein of historical material; or better than a mere beginning if we recall last year's slave melodrama, *The Dead Go Overboard*, for in *Middle Passage* the local color is genuine.

We now come to an interesting but painful contrast, with some of the worst and best of Southern fiction on our hands. In fact we have, interestingly enough, four literary traditions represented in four books. Two of them are traditional and stereotyped; two, modern and pioneering. There is, on the one side, the sentimental paternalism of the old Southern school, the carefully studied indifference of the Neo-Confederates, for whom Negroes are but so much necessary background and local color; and on the other, the modern humanist tradition, folk-lore-ing the Negro with careful but not too-well-integrated realism, and the school of sociological realism integrating him with increasing skill and success. *It Will Be Daybreak Soon* typifies the first; *Journey Proud*, the second; *Star Spangled Virgin*, the third; and *Some Like Them Short*, the last. Here one really has the full gamut of Negro characterization exemplified.

Archibald Rutledge is an old and honorable name; undoubtedly *It Will Be Daybreak Soon* is well-intentioned. But the practical upshot of this moribund paternalism is mawkish sentimentality, unconvincing moralism, condescension, and worse than these from the literary

Fiction

Drums at Dusk—Arna Bontemps, Macmillan Co., New York, $2.50.

The Middle Passage—Roland Barker and William Doerflinger, Macmillan Co., New York, $2.50.

Some Like Them Short—William March, Little, Brown & Co., Boston, $2.50.

Journey Proud—Thomasine McGehee, Macmillan Co., New York, $2.50.

It Will Be Daybreak Soon—Archibald Rutledge, Fleming H. Revell Co., New York, $1.25.

Star Spangled Virgin—DuBose Heyward, Farrar & Rinehart, New York, $2.00.

O Canaan!—Waters E. Turpin, Doubleday, Doran & Co., New York, $2.50.

Moses: Man of the Mountain—Zora Neale Hurston, J. B. Lippincott Co., Philadelphia, $3.00.

Let Me Breathe Thunder—William Attaway, Doubleday, Doran & Co., New York, $2.00.

Negro Narratives in *These Are Our Lives,* Federal Writers' Project, edited by W. T. Couch, University of North Carolina Press, $2.00.

Bright Morning Star—Richard Wright, in O'Brien Anthology, 1939.

●

point of view, bad characterization.

"Lifelong and affectionate association with the plantation Negro, who is, I think, the Negro at his very best," has produced a classic of the old-school attitude; a palpable misreading of fact and character in spite of the author's statement: "I frequently feel inferior to these humble and beloved people; inferior in the most important thing in life, in matters pertaining to the human spirit, both here and hereafter." One can understand, after reading this, why the Old South turned to Romance; it dared not face reality.

Journey Proud, by Thomasine McGehee, is, on the other hand, modernized ancient tradition. It passes for realism, and is realism in part. The Old South of Virginia from 1845 to 1879 is carefully resurrected, and the lives of the Mackays and the Wyatts are lovingly documented from ante-bellum ease and prosperity, through the shattering storm of Harpers Ferry and Wilderness, Cold Harbor and Petersburg, to post-bellum decadence and proud maintenance of tradition. But, if possible, more pride cometh after than went before the fall: this is a tradition glossed over, steadily romanticized and only superficially representative.

Not only are the Negro characters stereotyped, but many human sides of Southern life are as carefully omitted as in any prudish Victorian novel. In fact, Victorianism still survives in the Southern aristocratic tradition although elsewhere it is outmoded. With no apparent conception of their own society, these figures move on in pasteboard serenity. Ellen asks her husband if the man who is to buy the estate "expected to take the Negroes," and Thomas says: "Of course! My Lord, what could he do without 'em!"

It must not be overlooked, however, that the Southern tradition has been undone by enlightened Southern writers, and among them none has a more honorable record than DuBose Heyward, the author of *Star Spangled Virgin.* This time he has gone to the Virgin Islands for his background, and pens as usual a well-studied story. But this ironic idyll of the New Deal regime in the Islands, for all its careful technique, is not a moving portrait and it will not make a trilogy with *Porgy* and *Mamba's Daughters.* Perhaps it is not intended so seriously, but Rhoda, star-spangled virgin with five children, and her primitivisms may pass with many readers for serious social portraiture. Mr. Heyward seems to be falling too much into the exotic formula of a child-like Negro, which is the pitfall of the South Carolina school.

In contrast, it is important to see what William March does with a more enlightened and penetrating realism. There are twenty stories in *Some Like Them Short,* and only two are about Negroes. But some years back I said, apropos of Mr. March's *Come In at the Door,* here is the beginning of a new tradition in Southern fiction. The great stars of that day were William Faulkner, Erskine Caldwell and Thomas Wolfe. I felt then that the first was too doctrinaire and insistent; the second too morbid and introspective; and the third too inchoate and kaleidoscopic. Truly great art has clarity, perspective, balance, sanity, and the human touch. March's two stories of Negro character, *Runagate Niggers* and *The Funeral,* are the most significant bits of Southern fiction in this regard that I have ever read. Here is poetic realism at its best: and oddly enough, for all the brevity and naturalness, there is more effective social indictment and protest, more anatomizing of the Southern regime, than in reams of Faulkner and Caldwell.

Lafe Rockett's share tenants complain and sink deeper into debt; they try to run away to Chicago, are intercepted by the sheriff, and are on their way back to Lafe's farm when a Northern newspaper woman hears the story from the modern slave catchers, reports the case to Washington, and Lafe is indicted for peonage by Federal agents. Six stacatto pages end with the ironic complaint of one of Lafe's friends: "For two cents I'd move out of this country and go to some place where people still enjoy liberty. That's how disgusted I am with this here country, and I don't much keer who knows it, either!"

The Funeral is even more tragic, but with greater poetic depth. Reba, the cook's little mistreated child, is whipped for spying on the little white girl's funeral. Her mother, in the thwarted role of the domestic, sees the child's behavior only in the light of the white folk's command and pleasure, which to her are the laws of life itself. When she turns to the backyard after the busy spells of kitchen duty on the funeral supper, it is to find Reba hanging from the backyard tree, for she too wanted kind words, a great to-do over her, a magnificent funeral. Here, too, the force of the social indictment flows naturally and justly from the mere description of scene and character; this is art, not a tract, tragedy rather than diatribes or dialectic. And when a reader finishes with the feeling, *"this is the truth, the whole truth,"* realism has really triumphed.

In ineffectual contrast is a novel like *Boss Man* true enough in detail, but packed so overfull with harrowing incidents that it fails both of conviction and social understanding. Such raw-document literature has its place, and has served a social purpose, but it has one great failing: it isn't literature. When this is fully realized we shall prefer tracts that are not fictionalized and fiction that is not tractarian.

Four Negro writers conclude the year's fiction, with increasing collective power and penetration, but not in every case with completely successful literary grasp and style. Zora Neale Hurston's *Moses: Man of the Mountain* might have escaped the category of fiction had her characterization and dialogue been less sustained. And it would have been better so, for after all this is cleverly-adapted *Green Pastures* in conception, point of view, and execution. Genuine folk portraiture it is not; and, lacking the vital dramatization that superb acting gave to *Green Pastures*, it sinks back to the level of the original Roark Bradford. What if the stereotyping is benign instead of sinister, warmly intimate instead of cynical or condescending? It is still caricature instead of portraiture. Gay anecdotes there are aplenty, but somehow black

Moses is neither reverent nor epic, two things I should think that any Moses, Hebrew, Negroid or Nordic, ought to be.

Waters E. Turpin's second novel has a great epical theme, the saga of a family living in Chicago after a successful transplantation from the deep South. The Benson family introduces, from intimate Negro portrayal, a new milieu into our current fiction, and essays for the first time on any grand scale the migration theme. But somehow there is lacking the increased maturity one should expect of a second novel after so good a first as *These Low Grounds*. *O, Canaan!* is needle-point realism, too detailed and close focused for epic sweep or deep social perspective. More than one reviewer has therefore had to regard the book as a groundbreaker of merit rather than a definitive treatment of a novel and important theme. *O, Canaan*, too, could have gained by treating its theme less prosaically and with something of the fire of poetry and swift dramatic movement.

Just that lilt which is missing in so much realism comes into the style of William Attaway's first novel, *Let Me Breathe Thunder*. The title says so, and the narrative bears it out. Much ado has been made over the fact that this is not a novel of Negro character and situation. I thought that old Ghetto question was long since buried, but if it isn't, let this novel heap the last spadeful. What is significant, beyond some excellent local color and picaresque narration, is the strong naturalness of characterization and the subtly conceived human trio of Step, Ed and Hi Boy. The little Mexican waif is almost a symbol, yet very much alive. I call this the second triumph of the poetic kind of realism, and it marks Attaway's career as promiseful. And should he never write of Negro life—which is just as inconceivable as that he or any other free artist should write only of Negroes—there will still be something Negro in the equation. By that I do not refer to race or complexion, but to a brand of homely, folky imagination which I regard as characteristically Negro. *Let Me Breathe Thunder* has that rare quality in the overtones of its prose-poetic style.

Richard Wright, who has that quality too, was to have published his first novel this year, but it has been delayed. *Bright Morning Star*, regarded by many as his best short story, reappears, after its first publication in the *New Masses*, in the Valhalla of O'Brien's *Best American Short Stories*. It deserves this place, although personally I think it misses superlative greatness by an over-insistence on its theme and a redundancy that still betrays a young artist, albeit perhaps a young genius. The Caldwell influence has done much harm to many young writers, who pack it on too thick for credence and crisp flowing outline. An overdocumented or over-insistent realism is too prosy even for good prose. One can readily see the temptation to overdo and overstress, for Stribling, Caldwell and Faulkner had to tilt a risky tournament against the plumed Knights of the Confederacy —Dixon, Page, Cohen, Roark Bradford, and Stark Young. But the best Southern fiction will come neither from the glamor boys nor from the calamity boys, but from the non-partisans to whom truth is dearer than either Marx or Caesar.

Juvenile fiction continues to improve, as it should but as for a long time it didn't. Publishers and authors are beginning to awaken to the possibilities of this neglected market. *Tobe*, by Stella Sharpe, is a beautifully pictorialized story for small children, and comes near to being the long-awaited antidote for the "pickaninny" tradition. It has been tried before, but *Tobe* achieves it, more than half by virtue of its beautiful photographs.

Junior, A Colored Boy of Charleston, by Eleanor F. Lattimore, a book for older children, has much of the same charm and inspirational lift. It has even touches, here and there, of social implications, as for instance in the appeal of the children for their unemployed seniors. William C. White's *Mouseknees* reverts to the comic tradition, but sympathetically so. It is a good West Indian picnic story, artistically carried through. *Lion Boy*, by Alden G. Stevens, goes to East Africa and presents well-documented tribal folk-lore. It, too, follows in the pioneer footsteps of the better fiction and like Erick Berry's work, offers American children for the first time a sane and fair idea of Africa. The importance of that, to the Negro child particularly, cannot be over-estimated.

Turning next to poetry, the yield is still meagre. One can scarcely believe that verse-making has so suddenly ceased, and I have

Juvenile Fiction

Junior, A Colored Boy of Charleston—Ella Lattimore, Harcourt, Brace & Co., New York, $2.00.

Mouseknees—William C. White, Random House, New York, $1.75.

Tobe—Stella Gentry Sharpe, University of North Carolina Press, $1.00.

Lion Boy—Alden G. Stevens, Frederick A. Stokes Co., New York, $1.75.

●

much reason, from manuscript experience, to know that it has not. The financial depression has clipped Melpomene's wings: poetry seldom paid, nowadays it bankrupts. A. S. Cripps, an English missionary, has succeeded in having the Oxford Press bring out a volume of serious but over-sophisticated verse, a great deal of it of African locale or inspiration. Here and there are important notes of insight and revaluation, as in *The Dirge for Dead Porters;* and in *A Mashona Husbandman*:

"You find him listless, of but little worth
To drudge for you, and dull to understand?
Come watch him hoe his own rain-mellowed land:
See how the man outbulks his body's girth!"

Gwendolyn Bennett has resumed writing in periodicals, and exhibits a maturing of a talent that always was promising. Her *Threnody for Spain*, in extended ode form, bears the quotation of two sample stanzas of considerable beauty and competence:

"The lovely names of Spain are hushed today—
Their music, whispering with a muted tone,
Caresses softly mounds of restless clay
Where urgent seeds of liberty were sown. . . .

And from your soil and from the bones beneath,
For those who quest anew a Golden Fleece,
A sword will rise, undaunted from its sheath,
To cleave a path for universal peace!"

In the significant anthology, *This Generation*, edited by George Anderson and Eda Lou Walton, Sterling Brown is represented by seven poems of his later "social criticism" vein, *Transfer, Old Lem, Conjured, Colloquy of a Black and White Worker, Bitter Fruit of the Tree, Slim in Hell, Break of Day,* and *Glory, Glory.* Here, too, is successful poetic realism, all the more so when the turn of thought is ironic and farcical than when it is socially indignant. The satire of *Slim in Hell* is effective social indictment and protest, perhaps more so than verse like *Old Lem* and *Colloquy*. However, we need more of both from one of the strongest of our younger poets. For there is Negro grief and tragedy that needs forceful telling; the grief, for example, of Mame, waiting for her murdered Big Jess, waylaid fireman on the Alabama Central:

> *"Sweet Mame sits rocking, waiting for the whistle*
> *Long past due, babe, long past due.*
> *The grits are cold, and the coffee's boiled over,*
> *But Jess done gone, baby; he done gone."*

and there is Negro desperation also, on many minds though fewer tongues, as in this from *Transfer*:

> *"But this is the wrong line we been ridin',*
> *This route doan git us where we got to go.*
> *Got to git transferred to a new direction.*
> *We can stand so much, then doan stand no mo.' "*

For the most effective social discussion and the most potent realism we must in the end, I think, turn to the drama. Yet here it seems to come so slowly; on the issue of the effective portrayal of Negro life, drama is still in the hands of the enemy; and of late in the hands of that difficult variety, the friendly enemy. The commercial theatre has increased the Negro vogue but has not capitulated yet either to complete truth or sincere art. *Mamba's Daughters*, for instance, although it offered Ethel Waters a chance for a spectacular role, took a great deal of the balanced social documentation out of the original novel, and concentrated on a pitiful and almost moronic primitivism in Hagar —good theatre but not necessarily good drama. Then along comes the new *John Henry*, with the potentialities of a moving folk epic, but throttled down to melodramatic pageantry and musical-comedy triteness in many of its big scenes. It is still doubtful whether Paul Robeson's talent and fine singing presence can make a success of this pastiche of the John Henry saga, that as a libretto has cast too green an eye toward *Show Boat*, *Porgy* and *Green Pastures* and as a musical score has set gems of genuine folk-song in too stylized a matrix. The success curse of the stereotype was also on *Swingin' The Dream*, where only the truly genuine Negro things like the dancers and the inset jazz, were moving. The rest was farce, and of the vaudeville variety at that, but with *The Hot Mikado* still in circulation, it would appear that we are

Poetry and Drama

Africa: Verses—A. S. Cripps, Oxford University Press, New York, $2.00.

Seven Poems: Sterling Brown, in *This Generation*: Anthology edited by Anderson & Walton; Scott, Foresman & Co., Chicago, $3.00.

Mamba's Daughters—Dorothy and DuBose Heyward, Farrar & Rinehart, New York, $2.00.

The Garden of Time—Mss.—Owen Dodson, produced by Yale University Theatre.

Joy Exceeding Glory—Mss.—George Norford, produced by McClendon Players, New York.

John Henry: A Play with Music—Mss.—Roark Bradford and Jacques Wolfe, produced by Sam Byrd.

Front Porch—Mss.—Langston Hughes, produced by Gilpin Players, Cleveland.

Swingin' the Dream—Mss.—Erik Charrell and Gilbert Seldes, produced by Erik Charrell and Jean Rodney, New York.

Music

Haiti Singing—Harold Courlander, University of North Carolina Press, $3.50.

The Voice of Haiti—Laura Bowman and Leroy Antoine, Clarence Williams Music Publishing Co., New York, $2.00.

American Jazz Music—Wilder Hobson, W. W. Norton Co., New York, $2.50.

Jazz: Hot and Hybrid—Winthrop Sargeant, Arrow Editions, New York, $5.00.

Jazzmen: Edited by Frederic Ramsey, Jr. and Charles Edward Smith; Harcourt, Brace & Co., New York, $2.75.

in for plenty of it. The Negro *Macbeth,* a fine thing in itself, has had a fearful progeny—all of them black sheep, in my opinion, except *The Swing Mikado.*

In more serious drama, the little-theatre groups are experimenting feverishly, but not as yet with great success. The Karamu Theatre produced Langston Hughes' three-act drama of labor, *The Front Porch.* It proved to be not as strong as either *Mulatto* or *Don't You Want To Be Free.* The Rose McClendon Players of New York presented several novelties, most promising among them George Norford's "*Joy Exceeding Glory.*" The Yale University Theatre presented Owen Dodson's *The Garden of Time.* This second play of the talented author of *The Divine Comedy* is the most competent piece of playwriting that any of our young authors has yet turned out. Very skillfully it dramatizes, in beautiful prose poetry, the story of Jason and Medea, first in its ancient Greek setting and then, breaking over to a Southern analogue, the clandestine inter-racial romance of John and Miranda. With the good acting and superb setting which it received at New Haven, this was a powerful and challenging play despite its occasional expressionistic mannerisms. In its big scenes—Medea's seduction, Medea's appeal to Jason, and Blue Boy's comforting of Miranda—*The Garden of Time* achieved exceptional but restrained dramatic effect. Dodson's is a career to be watched. We badly need a dramatist who knows his theatre and who is not too lazy to polish his lines. Serious Negro drama must shake off the blight of the amateur just as the regular drama must shake off the curse of the "surefire success" and the box-office.

Negro music has done extraordinarily well this year. The University of North Carolina Press is bringing out Harold Courlander's carefully annotated anthology of Haitian folk-lore, melodies, drum-rhythms and dances; and the Clarence Williams Music Publishing Company has issued the excellent *Voice of Haiti,* another annotated collection of Haitian folk-songs by Laura Bowman and LeRoy Antoine. The year has also brought an array of careful and technically competent analyses of jazz, all three studies notable for the absence of that flippant and fashionable faddism so associated with this all-too-popular subject.

Wilder Hobson's study, *American Jazz Music,* traces the origins of the various jazz styles with important new sidelights on the "musical underground" that has been going on for twenty-five years between the white and the Negro exponents of popular American music. This documents all the more the Negro's claim to the origination of this musical material, without in any way detracting from the genuine talent and artistic democracy of the white musicians. On the whole, they have behaved well; it has been public opinion largely that has been responsible for the clandestine character of the close association: Negro music was bootlegged in the "bootleg era."

Winthrop Sargeant's *Jazz: Hot and Hybrid* is the best and most scholarly analysis of jazz and Negro secular folk music to date, and *Jazz-*

men, by Frederick Ramsey and Charles E. Smith—a careful and zestful pilgrimage to the home sources of jazz, recounting first-hand reminiscences of the 'old masters' which were about to die out—has performed an inestimable service to present and future students of this important musical tradition. It has also done belated justice to many an humble unknown who deserves the credit and should have had his share of Tin Pan Alley's millions. In the December issue of *Esquire,* Elmer Simms Campbell has a well-documented article on *The Blues: The Negro's Lament,* with very fortunate authoritative material given by Charles C. Cooke and Clarence Williams.

Interestingly enough, the streams of realism and romance, the traditions of dry fields and green pastures, meet and mingle gloriously in Negro folk music and above all, in Negro jazz.

PART II

THERE is a "Green Pastures" tradition in the sociological and economic interpretation of Negro life and history as well as in the fictional. Once it dominated its field about as definitely as the lush and sentimentally romantic tradition dominated the literary and artistic treatment of the race life. However it, too, is now on the defensive, and at points it is in disorganized retreat. The "dry fields" view of objective and factualist versions of the racial situation has the backing of the new scholarship, both of the white and Negro scholars who concern themselves with the American minority scene. Once the sociologists wrote with one eye on the scene and another on some forecast solution of the "race problem," and there was many a fine talent and intention led astray by the ideological mirage. For the real opponents of Negro interests this was a boon, for under cover of race formulas, they were deadly realistic in sinister ways of repression, exploitation and unrelenting persecution. The panaceas and the millenial hopes of the Negroes and their advocates covered up their antagonists' animosity and social rascality, and the glowing treatises, and prolonged oratorical sessions and interracial meetings served, often unwittingly enough, as smoke-screens and alibis for the white opposition. That situation seems to have changed materially and, let us hope, permanently, and the sociological literature of 1939 definitely shows it. Most encouraging of all is the growth of younger Negro social scholars, demonstrating an ability to handle social analysis of situations in which they are themselves deeply involved, with competence and objectivity, and an ability, also, to interpret and indict in an impartial fashion as well as to describe scientifically.

There are this year a half dozen books on the American racial situation that are outstanding, three of them by Negro scholars, with notable race participation in one of the others. That is a record, though I am not enough in favor of "race statistics" to mention it except for its objective significance, which is qualitative. It is the quality of these studies that counts.

Nominally in another field, in fact entitled *Negro Education in Alabama*, Horace Mann Bond's book is actually a thorough and incisive socio-economic analysis of the Southern scene. He connects up, almost for the first time, the trends of education with the economic policy and issues of a significant region. Alabama is significant in this sense, not only in being representative of the lower South, but of having in it two economies—the lowland cotton economy, and the mining industrial economy around Birmingham. Bond traces the fight between them, and then the alliance with Northern industrialism in this region, and probably gives us our best account, to date, of why it was (and is) that the Southern policy toward the Negro has had such tacit support from Northern industrial forces, in spite of the traditional Northern espousal of the Negro's cause. Bond definitely suggests that the improvement of Negro education in the South is contingent on the social reconstruction of the South as such. The information on educational history and trends is also thoroughly competent and clearly interpreted.

Dr. Hortense Powdermaker has provided another top flight analysis in her semi-anthropological survey of a Delta town, alias "Cottonville," to save the inhabitants embarrassment. This is the same community investigated a short while back by Dr. Dollard of Yale, as the basis of his book, *Caste and Class in a Southern Town*. In *After Freedom*, which she sub-titles *A Cultural Study in the Deep South*, Miss Powdermaker investigated the background, attitudes and class structure of this typical Southern bi-racial community. Her notable results are her tracing of the roots of the Southern code not to tradition alone but to a continuance of a system of economic exploitation; her documentation of the class structure of the Negro group, with its differential values and attitudes; and her report of the increasing acculturation of the Negro, even in an unprogressive community. She also reports the growing spirit of resentment and incipient revolt which that entails, and gives a rather vivid picture of the inner workings of the Southern bi-racial code, with all its inconsistencies anatomized. Such a study could not have been made without other pioneer work such as Dollard, Guy Johnson, Odum, Raper

Historical and Biographical

Black Folk, Then and Now—W. E. Burghardt DuBois, Henry Holt & Co., New York, $3.50.

The Slavery Controversy—Arthur Y. Lloyd, University of North Carolina Press, $3.00.

The Controversy Over the Distribution of Abolition Literature 1830-1860—W. Sherman Savage, Associates for the Study of Negro Life and History, Washington, D. C., $2.10.

Thaddeus Stevens—Alphonse B. Miller, Harper & Bros., New York, $4.00.

Five North Carolina Negro Educators—Edited by N. C. Newbold, University of North Carolina Press, $1.00.

Haiti, The Calvary Of A Soldier—Col. D. P. Calixte, Wendell Mallict & Co., New York, $1.25.

Palestine and Saints in Caesar's Household—A. Clayton Powell, Sr.; Richard R. Smith, New York, $1.50.

Living With Others—J. Irving E. Scott, Meador Publishing Co., Boston, $1.50.

The Negro in Sports—Edwin B. Henderson, Associated Publishers, Washington, D. C.

●

and Gallagher did in previous years. Books like *The Tragedy of Lynching*, *Black Yeomanry*, *The Collapse of Cotton Tenancy*, and *American Caste and the Negro College* have directly led up to it by laying down a basis of frank, realistic social analysis for the Southern social scene. That movement has now matured, and is bringing powerful scientific criticism of the Southern regime; the sort upon which social reconstruction can be based whenever there is sufficient courage and practical incentive.

After Freedom is particularly good in revealing the interaction of majority and minority life, and in locating a large part of the trouble in the general economic predicament of the

Sociological and Economic

Negro Education in Alabama—Horace Mann Bond.

After Freedom—Hortense Powdermaker, The Viking Press, New York, $3.00.

These Are Our Lives—Federal Writers' Project, edited by W. T. Couch, University of North Carolina Press, $2.00.

The Negro Family in the United States—E. Franklin Frazier, University of Chicago Press, $4.00.

Black Workers and the New Unions—Horace R. Cayton and George S. Mitchell, University of North Carolina Press, $4.00.

The Race Problem and Race Relations—Edgar T. Thompson.

The Negro Immigrant: His Background, Characteristics and Social Adjustment, 1899-1937—Ira DeA. Reid, Columbia University Press, New York, $3.50.

Journal of Negro Education, 1939 Yearbook on *The Position of the Negro in the American Social Order*, Howard University, Washington, D. C.

South, black and white. A penetrating analysis of the Negro church as an agency of palliative and escapist influence is another of its important contributions.

What the Powdermaker volume does for one community and for one rather static segment of the racial scene, the Negro sections of the North Carolina, Tennessee and Georgia Federal Writers' Project publication, *These Are Our Lives,* does for a wider and more changing field and over both rural, small-town and industrial centers. It is not too much to say that this self-portraiture of the lower and lower-middle classes in terms of typical life histories is a new and promising procedure in sociological analysis. It vindicates both the project and its editorship, and gives us a vital and humanized understanding of social conditions instead of merely objective scientific reporting. The Negro sharecropper, cash-renter, independent farm owner, unskilled worker, freight handler, odd-job worker, bootblack, housemaid and dentist—all have their respective say, and tell a revealing story in their substantial parallels with white lives on the same levels. What is striking, in spite of the differentials of race prejudice and proscription, is the basic similarity of the social situations and reactions; telling the progressive-minded reader what is basically wrong with Southern society, irrespective of racial discrimination. Here is a great supplementary human document on the "Number one economic problem."

PROFESSOR Burgess calls E. Franklin Frazier's study of *The Negro Family in the United States* the most valuable contribution to the literature of the family since the publication, twenty years ago, of Znaniecki's *The Polish Peasant in Europe and America,* and with considerable warrant. For Professor Frazier's exhaustive study, with an historical background unusual for the average sociological study, gives both a cross-section and an evolutionary view of Negro life and the social forces that have played upon it, by using the Negro family as a frame of reference. As a study of progressive acculturation, under great odds, it is important beyond the narrow field of Negro social data and history. It traces the original adaptations during slavery, the development of the Negro class structure, the readaptations after slavery in the Reconstruction, and most important of all, the more recent changes of urbanization, which in the author's opinion are gradually but surely integrating the Negro minority with the working classes and the contemporary economic order.

No superficial optimism, but a careful analysis of current social forces and their trends yields these conclusions, illustrating what was said at the beginning about the growing value of an interpretive rather than a purely descriptive brand of sociology.

Of almost equal importance is Horace Cayton and George Mitchell's study of the relation of Negro and white labor in their *Black Workers and the New Unions.* The very process which Professor Frazier found most significant — urbanization with gradual industrial integration —is here traced and analyzed both with respect to its factors of progress and factors of retardation. A differential between the C. I. O. and the A. F. of L. policies of unionization permits an illuminating picture of both, although it is obvious from the data reported that the more liberal C.I.O. program has put indirect pressure on the American Federation of Labor and is beginning to affect its attitude toward the wider unionization of Negro labor. Not only the more liberal policy, but also the fact that the bulk of Negro workers are in the relatively more unorganized sections of labor, puts the C.I.O. in a vital relationship to Negro industrial interests.

The volume traces the story of the Negro in the iron and steel industries, the meat packing firms, railroad car shops, and the mines and factories of the Birmingham district. These latter are most important, for successful bi-racial unionization is taking place in this Southern center and its importance is being recognized increasingly by the white workers. This means, if a relatively successful nation-wide extension can follow, conscious industrial cooperation between large sections of the white and the Negro masses; something having potentialities for the removal or modification of race prejudice on a realistic basis and in terms of self-interest such as could not have been imagined ten years ago. "A movement for the single purpose of integrating Negroes into the trade union movement" is seen by the authors as one of the needs of the hour, and one of the greatest prospects on the contemporary social horizon.

Under the editorship of Edgar T. Thompson, Duke University Press has published a notable study with a traditional title but an untraditional approach, *The Race Problem and Race Relations*. The novelty of the book—another milestone in advancing Southern sociological scholarship—is the more generalized approach to the race question as neither local nor national solely, but as an instance of a minority situation and its adjustment. With an introduction by Professor Robert E. Park validating this point of view, ten other scholars, two of them colored, discuss various aspects of changing race relations. Edward B. Reuter discusses what he calls the racial division of labor; Guy B. Johnson, patterns of race conflict; Lloyd Warner and Allison Davis, a comparative study of the class and caste cleavages in the South, or the way racial caste modifies the class structure; and Edgar Thompson, the plantation tradition as a basic pattern for Southern life. Particularly notable, it seems to me, are Copeland's article on the *"Negro as a Contrast Conception,"* showing the origin and basis in the socio-economic order of the false stereotypes of the whites about the Negro and their role in facilitating and rationalizing prejudice and social discrimination; Stonequist's study of the mulatto, which, in addition to an historical review of the status of the mulatto in the United States, makes an excellent comparison of the mulatto status under the Latin and South American pattern of society; and Charles S. Johnson's admirable study on *Race Relations and Social Change,* in which he goes over unequivocally, for perhaps the first time, to large-scale interpretive conclusions. There were suggestions of this trend in Professor Johnson's cotton tenancy study, but here he definitely declares for the economic factors as basically determining race conflict issues, as the factors in terms of which he thinks the dominant trends of minority-majority relations can be forecast, and as revealing the common denominators between the race problem and other issues of social conflict and reconstruction. Quite evidently, then, this is an important book with a progressive and objective outlook on the racial situation.

PROFESSOR Ira Reid's doctoral study on *The Negro Immigrant* opens up the important new field of the investigation of the West Indian Negro in the United States. This is a contingent of about a hundred thousand persons, not by any means all concentrated in New York, who have had a disproportionate influence on Negro life generally, so much so that it is rather to be regretted that the study does not run back to the migrations before 1899, the opening date of the book. The study shows that even in this later period of mass migration, the West Indian Negro has taken important leadership in the fight against racial discrimination. In the period prior, this was also importantly true. This seems due to the galvanizing experience of migration and reaction to new social conditions.

Dr. Reid also shows the initial hostile reactions of the native-born Negroes, both in their aspect of economic competition and in their less pardonable aspect of nativist prejudice, but shows how the common situation of proscription has gradually forged a solidarity of interest and cooperation, beginning at about the period of the Garvey movement, but continuing with appreciable momentum since. A few typical life histories are given, as are statistical tables of much interest and value for the further study of the transplanted Negro West Indian.

The 1939 Year Book of the *Journal of Negro Education,* on *The Position of the Negro in the American Social Order,* is, among its many outstanding previous issues, easily the most comprehensive and provocative. Every aspect of the minority group life is analyzed critically by an expert, generally with reference to current trends. A critical forecast section is added to insure more than mere analysis as the outcome of this elaborately collaborated study.

The recent volume by Dr. DuBois, *Black Folk, Then and Now,* immediately challenges attention in the historical field because of its tremendous scope: it is a vivid sketch of the world history of the Negro. Partly for that very reason, but also due, no doubt, to the strong dramatic strain in Dr. DuBois's outlook and style, there is considerable of what I have called "Green Pastures" romanticising in this book, particularly in the earlier sections on the pre-history of the Negro, where, after all, there is unfortunately more opinion than fact available. Readers familiar with the author's *The Negro,* of which the present book is something of a modernized version, will remember with gratitude that brilliant, effective defense and apologia of the darker peoples. In its day it rendered great service in widening the historical perspective on the Negro and in challenging Nordic versions of world history. However, scientific scholarship now needs no such challenge and merits no such indictment on the whole. The general public still needs the facts, perhaps, written as Dr. DuBois can write them, but from the scientific point of view no extended historic polemic is now necessary. Consequently, the reviewer finds other parts of the present book more worthwhile, especially the section on *Black*

Europe—a vivid picture of the colonial scene and the alignments of the black-white world under imperialism. Here the book will serve to break through the provincialism of the average American reader, black or white, and open out to him color as a world situation and problem. Dr. Du Bois's interpretation here is, briefly, that of the incompatability of real democracy and economic empire, and the common interests, hardly yet realized; of the economic emancipation of the white European masses; and of the black and yellow masses in the colonies and protectorates, exploited by the same machinery of ruthlessly expansive and competitive capitalism. This is undoubtedly the stronger section of the book, for which its too-racially-conceived earlier history can be forgiven.

The difficulty with historical apologetics is the fact that the other side always has its inning, and from that point of view, one is doomed to a relay of heated statements in partisan succession. Such a book, from the other side, is Arthur Lloyd's *The Slavery Controversy*, which really blames the war on the provocative tactics of the extreme Garrisonian Abolitionists. The thesis is that the North was precipitated into challenging the South by propagandized over-statements indicting the slave system, which, as the controversy progressed, entered into the political issues of the time. This construction of the "sectional struggle" is far from new, Dr. Lloyd's evidence is factually interesting, and some readers may be convinced by its interpretation. The old formula of states' rights and the confederation concept of the Union is really the pivot of the author's argument, and according as one takes sides on this, he will agree or disagree with the conclusions.

Admitting, too, the important influence of the abolitionist controversy, W. Sherman Savage documents rather competently the controversy from 1816 to 1860 in terms of the quarrel over the distribution of the movement's literature. Here, undoubtedly, was one of the earliest and greatest propaganda movements in our national history, and even as Lloyd claims, the public opinion it crystallized did finally flow into political channels. But the point Lloyd overlooks is the formidable counter-movement of Southern pro-slavery controversy and propaganda that also had its day and chance, and lost. So that to blame the issue on the provocative tactics of one side merely, and to represent the South's economy as a misunderstood sectional system or a martyred minority cause has little or no historical warrant. Indirectly, by showing the frantic tactics of Southern statesmen, particu-

larly Calhoun and Jackson, the Savage book restores historical impartiality to the record.

A POWERFUL book, particularly well-documented, is Joseph Carroll's sketch of *Slave Insurrections in the United States*. The theme has become popular of late, and is an important restoration of a glossed-over chapter in the Negro's social history. This is one of the most extensive of the studies from the point of view of documentation, although the pioneer work of Aptheker, barely mentioned by this author, must not be forgotten. The study lacks much mention of the social conditions behind these insurrections, although the Wilberforce historian lists some 78 slave conspiracies.

Professor Ralph V. Harlow of Syracuse adds to the growing historical literature of the abolition movement a competent biography of Gerrit Smith, a narrative that might have gained in social importance had it discussed at greater length the abolitionist conception of the Negro's possibilities and future as it figured so largely in Smith's controversies with his contemporaries. Professor Harlow has almost the Lloyd thesis about the provocative effect of the uncompromising wing of the Abolitionists, and rather blames them for precipitating a Civil War that could have been avoided by compromise. Closer to Negro life and interests therefore, is Alphonse Miller's thoroughly vital biography of *Thaddeus Stevens*, whom he styles the "Sinister Patriot," referring to his complex for stubborn, tactless,

Belles Lettres

To Make A Poet Black—J. Saunders Redding, University of North Carolina Press, $1.50.

The Negro Character in the Southern Novel, Louisiana State University Abstracts, Baton Rooge, La.

Moorland Collection, Catalogue of Books by and on the Negro, Howard University, Washington, D. C.

Orbita de la Poesia Afro-Cubana, 1928-1937—edited by Ramon Guirao.

The Negro in Brazil—Arthur Ramos, translated by Richard Pattee, Associated Publishers, Washington, D. C., $2.15.

L'Homme de Couleur—Cardinal Verdier, Jacques Roumain, Leopold Senghor and others, Paris, Plon, 1939.

Know This Of Race—Cedric Dover; Martin, Secker & Warburg, London, 2s. 6d.

Anti-Semitism, The Struggle For Democracy and the Negro People—James W. Ford, Workers Library, New York, $.03.

but brave opposition to both convention and tyranny. Fortunately for the veracity of the portrait, none of Steven's life is glossed over, including his close associations with Negroes; so here is the definitive biography of this most belligerent of the Negro's advocates.

A slight but interesting contribution to the biographic field is *Five North Carolina Negro Educators,* edited by N. C. Newbold and written by persons acquainted with the lives of Simon Atkins, J. B. Dudley, Annie Holland, Peter W. Moore and Ezekiel E. Smith, all pioneers of public school education in North Carolina. The significance of their cooperative contribution toward developing the first progressive policy of state education in the South is not without its social significance.

An autobiography of Colonel D. P. Calixte, former commandant of the Haitian army, detailing his disagreement with the Vincent regime and consequent exile, is an interesting contemporary document, far too much a personal apologia to be good biography, but perhaps of considerable historical value on the none-too-liberal administration of the first nominally Haitian government after the withdrawal of the American occupation. Mainly of personal interest is the volume supplementing his autobiography of last year, Rev. A. Clayton Powell's travel sketches from the Holy Land, and decidedly more ephemeral, even, is J. Irving Scott's homiletic guidance and pedagogic manual, *Living With Others,* based on his personal teaching experience.

A book that might easily have been just as ephemeral, *The Negro in Sports,* has been saved from that fate by careful documentation and a sound educational perspective on a popular subject, the Negro's athletic achievements. Not enough of the social history and influence of the sports is given, however, for here we could have had a discussion of the interaction of racial discrimination upon the players and upon the standards of American collegiate competition. In this sense the book could have been a side-treatise on the paradoxes of American public opinion on the race issue, and not just a primer of athletic prowess and success.

Heading the list in *belles lettres* is an opinionated critique of the Negro author in relation to his public, or rather what the author considers his "two opposed publics." J. Saunders Redding's *To Make a Poet Black* is groundbreaking, in a very important field, the psychological conditioning of the Negro author throughout the various periods of Negro literary

Africana

African Majesty, By F. Clement Egerton, Charles Scribner's Sons, New York, $3.75.

The Southern Bantu, L. Marquard and T. G. Standing, Oxford University Press, New York, $2.50.

An African Survey, Lord Hailey—African Research Survey of the Royal Institute for International Affairs, Oxford University Press, New York, $7.00.

African Notebook, By Albert Schweitzer, Henry Holt & Co., New York, $2.00.

●

expression; but Mr. Redding is too insistent on his pet thesis, mentioned above, to do justice to many of the writers and movements he surveys. It is questionable that the dilemma of trying to please two audiences is the root of the Negro author's trouble. An academic but competent study of the development of the *Negro Character in The Southern Novel* has been published in the Louisiana State University abstracts.

Compiled under the supervision of Mrs. Dorothy Porter, the catalogue of the Howard University *Moorland Collection* of books by and on the Negro has appeared, and is an invaluable addition to Negro bibliography.

In another province of *belles lettres* in spite of its appearance in 1938, attention must be called to a brilliant anthology of Afro-Cuban poetry, *Orbita de la Poesia Afro-Cubana,* 1928-1937, edited by Ramon Guirao, for it introduces an important new province of Negro creative talent. The work of these Cuban poets of mixed blood is of superior talent, both technically and in social interpretation. It almost appears that the declining stream of fresh creative effort in poetry has shifted South.

Along the same line, Richard Pattee's welcome but unfortunately abridged translation of Arthur Ramos's *The Negro in Brazil,* has appeared under the Associated Publishers' imprint. This is a cultural history primarily, giving particular attention to Negro influences on the music, folklore and the arts in Brazil.

More sociological, but discussing the cultural issues of the world problem of color, comes an important French publication, under Catholic auspices, *L'Homme de Couleur.* It ranges from Indo-China, Japan and Polynesia to the contacts of white civilization and cultural policies as they affect the Negro in East, West and South Africa, in the United States, the West

Indies and the Phillipines. The frame of reference is the new and highly significant campaign for racial and social justice being emphasized in Roman Catholic circles today, which, launched by certain liberal circles in the church, has lately achieved, under the new Pontificate, special emphasis and the status of an official policy.

In criticism from a more realistic angle, Cedric Dover's book, *Know This of Race,* covers the same ground of the world problems of racialism, with the author's usual trenchant and broadly informed criticism of contemporary prejudice—Nazi, British, American and colonial. James W. Ford's *Anti-Semitism, The Struggle for Democracy and the Negro People* covers the same ground from the angle of Marxist social criticism and solutions of class structure reform. All in all, the consideration of race on the world and cultural fronts is steadily increasing, and the American race problem is gaining in perspective thereby.

Even in the African literature there seems this year, to be more science than romance. The only significant sentimental document is F. Clement Egerton's spicy narrative of a personal journey to the Cameroons, *African Majesty.* It is one of the more penetrating travelogues, with sympathetic and valuable data on the Bangante people and their social customs. Quite factual in approach, on the other hand, and almost too non-committal, is the simply written but authoritative account of *The Southern Bantu* by L. Marquard and T. G. Standing. This becomes now the best available handbook on the race situation of the Union of South Africa: it is only mildly liberal in viewpoint, but is unimpeachable as to its factual information on a segment of the race question which should be better known, especially to Negro Americans.

Stupendously comprehensive and official is the publication of the African Research Survey of the Royal Institute for International Affairs, Lord Hailey's *An African Survey.* It is a digest of the whole area of colonial black Africa south of the Sahara, and especially from the side of political administration and policy, it states exhaustively the latest details on imperialism in Africa. Indispensable to the student, it cannot be expected to give the general reader any clear picture, despite its wealth of detail. From such official, documentary literature, it is a relief, then, to turn to penetrating insight into native life and social problems in the African scene. This one gets from the simple but revealing narratives of the veteran scholar-missionary, Albert Schweitzer, in his *African Notebook.*

Schweitzer knows his Africans not as problems but as human beings, and etches indelibly aspects of their lives and character. It might almost be characterized by paraphrasing the North Carolina project title, *These Are Their Lives.* In such a tradition and spirit, the lives and the folklore of the African peoples must someday be presented: it will eventually take the educated native, and not the detribalized half-educated native, to do it authoritatively and adequately. Signs are not wanting of such native authorship, although this year no titles of native writings, beyond some linguistic primers, have come this way.

OF NATIVE SONS: REAL AND OTHERWISE

Part I

MINORITIES have their artistic troubles as well as their social and economic ones, and one of them is to secure proper imaginative representation, particularly in fiction and drama. For here the warped social perspective induces a twisted artistic one. In these arts characterization must be abstract enough to be typical, individual enough to be convincingly human. The delicate balance between the type and the concrete individual can be struck more easily where social groups, on the one hand, have not been made supersensitive and morbid by caste and persecution, or on the other, where majority prejudice does not encourage hasty and fallacious generalization. An artist is then free to create with a single eye to his own artistic vision. Under such circumstances, Macbeth's deed does not make all Scotchmen treacherous hosts, nor Emma Bovary's infidelity blot the escutcheon of all French bourgeois spouses. Nana and Magda represent their type, and not their respective nations, and *An American Tragedy* scarcely becomes a national libel. But it is often a different matter with Shylock, and oftener still with Uncle Tom or Porgy, and for that matter, too, with the denizens of *Tobacco Road,* or even Southern colonels, if too realistically portrayed. All of which is apropos of the Negro literary phenomenon of 1940, Bigger Thomas. What about Bigger? Is he typical, or as some hotly contest, misrepresentative? And whose "native son" is he, anyway?

These questions, as I see them, cannot be answered by reference to Negro life and art alone. That indeed is the fallacy of much of the popular and critical argument about this masterwork. Only in the context of contemporary American literature, its viewpoints and trends, is it possible to get a sound and objective appraisal of *Native Son.* For all its great daring and originality, it is significant because it is in step with the advance-guard of contemporary American fiction, and has dared to go a half step farther. Year by year, we have been noticing the rising tide of realism, with its accompanying boon of social honesty and artistic integrity. Gradually it has transformed both the fiction of the American South and of the Negro. The movement by which Stribling, Caldwell and Faulkner have released us from the banal stereotypes—where all Southern ladies were irreproachable and all Southern colonels paragons of honor and chivalry—has simply meant, eventually, as a natural corollary, another sort of Negro hero and heroine. It is to Richard Wright's everlasting credit to have hung the portrait of Bigger Thomas alongside in this gallery of stark contemporary realism. There was artistic courage and integrity of the first order in his decision to ignore both the squeamishness of the Negro minority and the deprecating bias of the prejudiced majority, full knowing that one side would like to ignore the fact that there are any Negroes like Bigger and the other like to think that Bigger is the prototype of all. Eventually, of course, this must involve the clarifying recognition that there is no one type of Negro, and that Bigger's type has the right to its day in the literary calendar, not only for what it might add in his own right to Negro portraiture, but for what it could say about America. In fact Wright's portrait of Bigger Thomas says more about America than it does

Opportunity 19 (January and February 1941): 4–9; 48–52.

about the Negro, for he is the native son of the black city ghetto, with its tensions, frustrations and resentments. The brunt of the action and the tragedy involves social forces rather than persons; it is in the first instance a Zolaesque *J'Accuse* pointing to the danger symptoms of a self-frustrating democracy. Warping prejudice, short-sighted exploitation, impotent philanthropy, aggravating sympathy, inconsistent human relations, doctrinaire reform, equally impotent punishment stand behind the figures of Bigger, the Daltons, Mary, Jan and Max, as the real protagonists of the conflict. This is timely and incisive analysis of the core dilemmas of the situation of race and American democracy. Indeed in the present crisis, the social import of *Native Son,* with its bold warnings and its clear lessons, temporarily overshadows its artistic significance. Its vivid and vital revelations should be a considerable factor in awakening a social sense and conscience willing at last, after much evasion and self-deception, to face the basic issues realistically and constructively. No sociological treatise or economic analysis has proved half so well just where the crucial problems lie or what common interests are at stake: America cannot any more afford to ignore the issues presented in this book than she could in 1853, when *Uncle Tom's Cabin* anticipated Lincoln's insight in saying: "This land cannot long continue to exist half-slave and half-free." And as before, it is not just a plea for the Negro, but a challenge to the nation and its own enlightened self-interest.

Just to make this clear, let me quote briefly from Wright's brilliant critical postscript, *"How Bigger Was Born."* Says he:

"I felt that Bigger, an American product, a native son of this land, carried within him the potentialities of either Communism or Fascism. I don't mean to say that the Negro boy I depicted in *Native Son* is either a Communist or a Fascist. He is not either. But he is a product of a dislocated society; he is a dispossessed and disinherited man; he is all of this, and he lives amid the greatest possible plenty on earth and he is looking and feeling for a way out. Whether he'll follow some gaudy, hysterical leader who'll promise rashly to fill the void in him, or whether he'll come to an understanding with the millions of his kindred fellow workers under trade-union or revolutionary guidance depends upon the future drift of events in America. But, granting the emotional state, the tensity,

the fear, the hate, the impatience, the sense of exclusion, the ache for violent action, the emotional and cultural hunger, Bigger Thomas, conditioned as his organism is, will not become an ardent, or even a lukewarm, supporter of the status quo."

This is why I call *Native Son* Zolaesque, and insist that it is an important book for these times, and that it has done a great national service in making this acute diagnosis and putting American democracy, if it will act intelligently, on the defensive.

Native Son has brilliant and imposing collaboration from other novelists of the American scene. It seems as though our writers had all resolved to tear chapters out of Zola and probe society's wounds and ulcers. They have little need for the old-fashioned romantic imagination that was once the novelist's chief stock-in-trade. They do, however, need the realist's imagination to set both the social and the psychological perspectives so that we have another and more enlightening experience than from reading the notations in a psychiatrist's or a social case worker's notebook.

Fiction

Native Son—Richard Wright, Harper & Bros., N. Y., $2.50.

Light Over Ruby Street—Edward H. Heth, Smith & Durrell, N. Y., $2.00.

Follow the Drinking Gourd—Frances Gaither, Macmillan Co., N. Y., $2.50.

This Side of Glory—Gwen Bristow, Thomas Y. Crowell Co., N. Y., $2.50.

God Rides a Gale—James R. Peery, Harper & Bros., N. Y., $2.50.

The Keepers of the House—Harry H. Kroll, Bobbs; Merrill Co., Indianapolis, $2.50.

Trouble in July—Erskine Caldwell, Duell, Sloane & Pearce, N. Y. $2.50.

Weevil in the Cotton—Samuel M. Elam, Frederick Stokes, N. Y., $2.00.

Sapphira and the Slave Girl—Willa Cather, Alfred A. Knopf, N. Y., $2.50.

The Caballero—Harold Courlander, Farrar & Rinehart, N. Y., $2.50.

●

Edward Heth, for example, anatomizes Ruby Street, a marginal city community of white pleasure-seekers and semi-impoverished Negroes, demoralized into parasitic living as merchants of gaiety and joy. This border-line situation, the sex analogue of Wright's laboring class ghetto—and an equally sinister and explosive by-product of the half-insulated lives of the two races—is drawn with bold, ironic skill by Heth, and with evident understanding of its basic factors of thwarted opportunity and easy victimization. It is Aggie's chief ambition that her daughter Julee escape the physical and moral barriers of Ruby Street, but environment tragically conquers and Julee chooses to remain and follow the precarious path that, unfortunately, is one way in our pattern of life, liberty and the pursuit of happiness.

The Southern scene takes its turn, too, before the same unrelenting literary analysis. Erskine Caldwell, veteran of this fiction of actualities, has come back with an analysis of the Southern small town and its modern lower-middle class hatreds and racial problems. An hysterical woman vents her spleen against Negroes in a false rumor, and Sonny Clark pays the penalty as a Saturday crowd of townsmen and sharecroppers track him down for a race riot and lynching bee in *Trouble in July*. Unpleasant reading, it is nevertheless part of the bitter medicine we must take to find a true diagnosis and cure for a sick democracy. Less macabre, but just as diagnostic, are his many Negro situation vignettes in the newly-issued volume of collected stories, *Jackpot*, where we meet again such challenging sketches as *Blue Boy, Daughter, Runaway* and *Yellow Girl*. All these incidents have the stamp of unimpeachable truth, and what is significant now is not so much that they could have happened, as that nowadays they can be told, and by a native son of the white South. With something of his own individual brand of irony, Caldwell says in the epilogue to one of these stories:

"Does it make any difference, after all, whether an event actually happened or whether it might have happened?" Well, except as the South can see itself in the literary mirror that the new realism is burnishing, there is no hope; for, as has happened before in history, it is easier to stand the fact than its portrayal.

Gwen Bristow completes her trilogy of the Southern plantation with *This Side of Glory*, showing the double clash of the poor white and the lapsing aristocratic traditions and the economy of the old plantation and tenant sharecropping. The title is itself a text, for she finds the glory gone and a new order the only hope of survival from mortgages, boll-weevil and restive workers. Samuel Elam's *Weevil in the Cotton* is even more revealing, because he pictures the corrupt political machinery which is in the Southern saddle, and rides the tottering system through its last decades. Somewhat too melodramatic and not the artistic equal of these other novels, it still has something important to add to the new realistic tale of the South.

Follow the Drinking Gourd reverts a little to the romantic tradition, with a story of an Alabama plantation. However even here, there is a Banquo at the romantic feast—absentee ownership—and the estate finally winds up in bankruptcy and a foreclosed mortgage. In *The Keepers of the House*, Harrison Kroll actually comes to grips with the plantation cycle and almost writes its obituary in terms of Bart Dowell's losing struggle with fertile soil but a declining market and a disintegrating social order. *God Rides A Gale* also has Mississippi for a locale, and includes more of a class study of the interactions of tradesmen, landlords, sharecroppers, black and white, than his first novel, *Stark Summer*. It is not strictly a novel of the Negro's situation, but has significance as a relatively new use of the Negro as background material.

FINALLY, Willa Cather breaks a long silence and many precedents in her story of *Sapphira and the Slave Girl*, pivoting this novel of her native Virginia on the jealousy of Sapphira for the mulatto slave girl whom she suspects of being her husband's mistress. Here is the frank admission and analysis by one of the master novelists of our generation of the canker at the heart of the plantation rose, even in its heyday of bloom and prosperity—a significant note in the contemporary reconstruction of Southern fiction.

In *The Caballero*, Harold Courlander evidently fictionalizes on his observations in Haiti to paint the drama of the clash of the mulatto and the black, the patois and the peasant culture in the Caribbean. Romantically seasoned by the story of the rise of a native dictator, the story, for all its mythical location in the island of Puerta Negra, is sufficiently realistic as to have some thinly veiled analogies with the American occupation of Haiti and the rise of Trujillo in Santo Domingo. Here too, in the guise of fiction, we get an important analysis of present-day social forces in the West Indies.

Our year's fiction is so factual that one turns to the biography with a positive thirst for adventure. Langston Hughes provides it—perhaps too much of it—in his biographic memoir, *The Big Sea*. Too much by way of contrast certainly, for the broad areas of his life's wide wanderings—Europe, Africa and America from east to west coast—are not plumbed to any depth of analysis or understanding, with the possible exception of Washington society. If, as in this case, righteous anger is the mainspring of an interest in social analysis with Langston Hughes, one wishes that more of life had irked him. For time and again important things are glossed over in anecdotal fashion, entertainingly but superficially, without giving us any clear idea as to what a really important participant in the events of the last two decades thinks about the issues and trends of his generation and the Negro's relationship to them. Occasional hints of attitudes on such matters argue for an awareness of their existence, and seem to call for a more penetrating analysis, even if it should sober down the irresponsible charm of the present narrative.

Of such things Dr. Du Bois does speak at considerable length in his *Dusk of Dawn* autobiography, projected, as one might expect, through an experienced and observant personality. This might easily have been one of the important biographic memoirs of the generation had there been greater psychological perspective on the issues and events. But an egocentric predicament involves the author all too frequently, so that his judgments of men and issues, warrantably personal in a biography, are not stated as that, but are promulgated dogmatically as though by an historian who had objectively examined all sides of the evidence. Valuable then only as the chronicle of an important career, *Dusk of Dawn* scarcely justifies the promise of its sub-title to give us reliably the outlines of race programs and race thinking over the five active decades of the author's eventful and useful life.

Two entirely anecdotal publications document interestingly the careers of five pioneer Negro educators in North Carolina, and John Paynter's fifty years of government service in Washington. It is of considerable importance to have more of such memoir materials appear in print, for the sake of a fuller documentation of Negro experience and accomplishment. These are, however, but the raw material of adequate social history, which in most cases comes a generation or so after the event and the first-hand publication of the factual evidence.

In a more ambitious mold, Mrs. Mary Church Terrell has published her memoirs, under the title of *A Colored Woman in a White World,* prefaced by what to this reviewer seems an unnecessarily patronizing introduction by H. G. Wells, for all his well-intentioned moralizing on the analogies of racial and class prejudice. Essentially Mrs. Terrell's story is that of the generation when the so-called "talented tenth" were struggling for recognition, and were

confronting, with considerable embarrassment, the paradoxes of the educated mulatto. It is to Mrs. Terrell's great credit that she overcame most of these, and rendered public service with some considerable recognition of what race leadership involves as to responsibilities. Too many of her generation thought of it merely in terms of special personal honors and privileges. This is a valuable factual chronicle of that particular over-lapping generation of Reconstruction, one that will be even more helpful as it recedes into history. However, it must pale to relative insignificance in comparison with the reissue by the Douglass Literary and Cultural League of the *Life and Times of Frederick Douglass;* a

Biography

The Big Sea— Langston Hughes, Alfred A. Knopf, N. Y., $3.00.

Dusk of Dawn—W. E. B. DuBois, Harcourt, Brace & Co., N. Y., $3.00.

Five North Carolina Negro Educators, edited by N. C. Newbold, University of North Carolina Press, $1.00.

Fifty Years After——Jno. H. Paynter, Marfent Press, N. Y., $2.00.

A Colored Woman in a White World—Ronald, Inc., Washington, D. C., $2.50.

much needed new access to this classic among Negro biographies.

One of the outstanding items of belles lettres has already been quoted from: it is Richard Wright's *How Bigger Was Born*—the critical account of the literary genesis of his novel. From it we learn that Bigger Thomas was really a synthetic character of five individuals observed in different years and places, and we get an insight seldom given by an author into the crucible of his art and experience. This is a great critical document, noteworthy for that very objectivity of self-analysis which we have complained of as lacking in the two outstanding biographies of the year. Perhaps it is saner to rejoice over its attainment here than its absence there, for a sensitive and intelligent Negro has to compensate mightily if he is ever to achieve poise and detachment on situations in which he is personally and socially involved. Wright is clearly conscious of the basic issues involved both in the Negro artist's relation to himself and to contemporary society.

Another important analysis of the social position of the Negro artist and writer is to be found in *Fighting Words,* in the symposium on the subject by Langston Hughes, Melville Herskovits and Alain Locke, reprinted from the proceedings of the League of American Writers. Langston Hughes is also represented in a critical study of his work and social philosophy by Rene Piquion, in which his social slant is too definitely platformed, for though it is emotionally radical, it is not as Piquion claims, overtly Marxist.

The music field is richer this year by a one-volume reissue of the still-popular James Weldon and Rosamond Johnson *American Negro Spirituals*, and the addition to Laurence Gellert's valuable collecting of contemporary Negro work-songs of new numbers, *Me and My Captain*. In the art field, Alain Locke has edited, as illustrative sequel to his *Negro Art: Past and Present*, the first comprehensive illustrated portfolio of the *Negro in Art*; embracing both the work of Negro artists and the treatment and development by artists generally of the Negro subject as an art theme.

In poetry the yield is slenter, and but for Countee Cullen's cleverly conceived and executed poetic fable would be negligible. *The Lost Zoo*, with its fascinating color illustrations by the gifted young artist Charles Sebree, is bound to be one of the notable specimens of its genre; at least it belongs on the same shelf with *Alice in Wonderland*. The posthumous volume of David Cannon's poems, *Black Labor Chant*, can only be condoned as a sentimental tribute to a very amateur talent. Cullen, however, shows in a new vein of epigrammatic comedy a rare quaint imagination and all the old knack of clever versifying.

●

Poetry and Belles Lettres

The Lost Zoo—Countee Cullen and Christopher Cat, Harper & Bros., N. Y., $2.50.
Black Labor Chant—David W. Cannon, Jr., Association Press, N. Y., $1.00.
Fighting Words—"The Negro Troops"—edited by Donald Ogden Stewart, Harcourt, Brace & Co., N. Y., $1.50.
How Bigger Was Born—Richard Wright, Harper & Bros., N. Y., $.25.
Un Chant Nouveau—Langston Hughes & Rene Piquion, Imprimerie de L'Etat, Port-au-Prince, Haiti.
Me and My Captain—edited by Lawrence Gellert, Hours Press, N. Y.
American Negro Spirituals—New Edition by James Weldon Johnson and J. Rosamond Johnson, Viking Press, N. Y., $2.95.
The Negro in Art—Alain Locke, Associates in Negro Folk Education, Washington, D. C., $4.00.
The Negro and The Drama—Frederick W. Bond, Associated Publishers, Washington, D. C., $2.00.

In *The Negro and the Drama*, Frederick Bond had the chance to bring the analysis of this field up to date and with some critical finality. But he is historically not as inclusive nor critically as sound as either the prefaces to *Plays of Negro Life* or the three short but pithy chapters of Sterling Brown's *Negro Poetry and Drama* (1937).

Indeed, drama is still but a half-conquered province for us as yet, both critically and creatively. The year's drama offerings were considerably disappointing. In the first place there was Paul Robeson's regrettable decision to create the flimsy role of *John Henry*, which is even more obviously threadbare in published print than in the acted presentation. Only one

Drama

John Henry—Roark Bradford, Harper & Bros., N. Y. $2.50.
Cabin in the Sky—Mss. by Lynn Root. Martin Beck Theatre, N. Y.
Place: America—Thomas Richardson, N. A. A. C. P., N. Y., $.25.
Big White Fog—Mss. by Theodore Ward, Negro Playwrights Group, N. Y.
Booker T. Washington—Mss. by William Ashby, Rose McClendon Players, N. Y.

●

Broadway production to date on the Negro theme registers favorably, and that excites as much through marvelous acting on the part of Ethel Waters as through its whimsical but not overly-profound script. However, the play, *Cabin in the Sky,* does convey an authentic and characteristic Negro feeling, which for Broadway is quite a commendable accomplishment. Its comedy is inoffensive, particularly as so deftly portrayed by Dooley Wilson, and its tempo and emotional tone are set true to real folk values, thanks again especially to the great talent of Miss Waters.

In the non-commercial theatre, where we had great promise and hopes for the year, there have been considerable disappointments. The blame must be divided between the actors and their public. In the first place, Harlem can support both financially and artistically one good repertory company and theatre, and only in pooling all possible resources there can success be optimistically anticipated. Then, too, the serious vehicles lack, through over-seriousness, sufficient theatre to be compelling, a fault to be found in all three of the major new efforts by Negro playwrights that this season has brought forth. *Big White Fog,* by Theodore Ward, as re-set for the Negro Playwrights Group, was competently staged and acted. It holds a situation with first-class dramatic possibilities. But instead of holding to its excellently posed character conflicts, over money and race loyalty, Americanism and Garveyism, it swerves to a solution by way of radical social action for its denouement. Harlem is to be blamed at that, for not taking sufficient interest in one of the few meaty, serious plays it has had a chance to support, but the Playwrights Group should have had a more balanced repertory to offer before it ventured so boldly with a regularly leased theatre. The McClendon Players have continued their policy of plays by Negro authorship, but have as yet this season only found one play of even moderate merit, William Ashby's *Booker T. Washington*—and that a revived play from their previous repertoire. We still await the much needed drama revival.

Part II, and a Postscript on Poetry.

NINETEEN hundred and forty ends one decade and begins another. In some minds, with the world crisis in view, it portentously looms through the mist like the threshhold of an epoch. One is tempted, therefore, to take this sense of crisis and critical change as the touchstone of an author's real significance and vitality. More than ever we want either the truth and nothing but the truth, or what we feel is the writer's humanly best effort to get at it. Yesterday's charm and irresponsibility we now think reprehensible, and do not lightly forgive whoever writes with his tongue in his cheek or prissily *à la mode* or with conscious reservations. In the light of the times, we have the right to ask this honest integrity of the novelist, the playwright, even of the poet, —and some we have seen live up to this expectation.

All the more necessary and obligatory, then, is this criterion for the historian, the economist and the sociologist. For, born of the crisis, we have the wish to know what in the crisis of illness we tritely call "the worst," but what we really mean as the truth without reservation.

Now factual literature, historical, sociological and economic, has been for generations notorious for its conventions and its formulae, and these, from the very nature of the case, have been traditional deceptions and conventional lies. They haven't all been sinister; most indeed have been placatory and polite. Discussions of race and class have been almost as discreet and polite—and therefore as superficial—as discussions of religion and morals. Basic realism in social science has been relatively rare and in many cases, from the point of view of the tradition-breakers, costly. And so with that in mind as a fair and now imperative criterion, we glance at the social literature of the year as it relates to our subject of special interest, the Negro.

Although threadbare in treatment from the conventional point of view, slavery and anti-slavery analysis has an important bearing on our social attitudes in contemporary race relations. In fact, we get our cues for the present from the past, and when we do change in contemporary alignments, we are apt to reorganize our history. The changed views, or rather perspectives, on slavery are thus indicative of to-day's changing attitudes and *mores.* Though of late 1939 vintage, here is a significant book, Dumond's *Anti-Slavery Origins of the Civil War.* It is neither pro nor anti-slavery, and is probably the most objective analysis of slavery ever offered in so small a compass. Thus it should be prescribed reading, particularly for Negroes, who, on the whole, do not understand the historical issues involved, and to that extent have only a sentimental grasp on the basic factors of race and class status in America. Dumond has done a great service in trying to focus historical evidence on the explanation of a situation rather than to vindicate either personalities, regional sections, or even schools of historical opinion. Particularly does he bring out the importance of the mid-West and the Southwest and their economic interests and political opinions in complicating and finally balancing the traditional rivalry between the North and the South.

Coleman's *Slavery Times in Kentucky* is similarly a far cry from the usual documentary local history: for it presents factual evidence primarily, and leaves evaluations to the reader. One of the main lines of this evidence shows what is now conceded by modern historians of the institution, the complete interdependence of the master and slave and their common deterioration in both human and economic fortunes as the economy matures. In Kentucky, as the narrative shows, black and white were, at first, mutually helpful frontier pioneers and retained much of that independence and vigor in sections of the state which did not embrace the cotton economy. Mangum's exhaustive treatise on the *Legal Status of the Negro,* on the other hand, merely perpetuates a lapsing tradition of scholarship. Even in bringing its subject up to date, it performs no very useful historical service, for in its ultra-legalistic approach, the important connection between law and public opinion is relatively overlooked. Hence the fluctuations of degrees of civic privilege and disability are merely chronicled, carefully it is true, but unexplained.

The Negro in Congress, however, is a serious and fairly successful attempt at interpretation. Stemming from the liberal traditions of Chapel Hill, this is as successful as a ground-breaking treatise could hope to be, and strikes a rather happy mid-ground between the violent detractions of the Negro reconstruction politicians and equally partisan vindications. The wide diversity of these Negro legislators is wisely emphasized, and some of them are shown to have been men of considerable acumen and statesmanship. The study is really, it seems to me, a challenge to Negro historians to supplement the picture from documentary evidence likely to be more accessible in the correspondence of some of these men, or if not available, then from the closest scrutiny of their legislative records. Our historical scholarship is, as yet, strangely weak on the biographical side.

Mabry's analysis of *The Negro in North Carolina Reconstruction Politics* adds little beyond mere detail to the repeated studies of the sad aftermath of slavery: in all the Southern states practically the same forces were in operation, and North Carolina history only makes a little more clear the role of the poor white faction in the drama of reaction. Obstruction was the real character of the Reconstruction period, postponing to our day the real reconstruction problems. In this basic interpretation Herbert Aptheker is right in regarding both the Civil War as a postponed act of the original American struggle for human rights, and today's reconstruction efforts as the further development of an abortive emancipation of the Negro. However sound this reading of American history is, Aptheker pushes his thesis too hard and dogmatically either for general conviction or for an unforced interpretation of the historical facts. Insinuated into the history of the *Negro in the American Revolution,* the conclusions fall out suspiciously. More overtly Marxist, Elizabeth Lawson's intelligently consistent study outline of *Negro History* commands attention and respect, even where one does not agree with its emphases. It has the virtues of a frank economic and labor interpretation of the issues, and of less dogmatic statement than most readings of this school of historical thought.

It is to be regretted that Mr. Newcomb's study of *Henri Christophe* is cast in so romantic a vein; for its length and apparent intent promise what should have been a definitive life of this important historical character. Haitian history, except in French treatises, has generally run to the popularized and superficial type, with the exception of James' still unsurpassed *Black Jacobins.* Consonant with the growing interest in the Caribbean, we do have two competent diplomatic histories of Haiti, which oddly enough almost parallel each other. Mr. Montague's work looks very comprehensive and final until one compares it closely with the Logan book, which has much more extensive bibliographic sources. With contemporary hemispheric politics tending toward the same objectives, the celebrated affair of the coaling base at Mole St. Nicholas takes on a revived interest, and throws a dimension of statesmanship into what many have regarded a mere political incident. Frederick Douglass' connection with this affair and his dilemma between racial and national patriotism are definitively treated in Professor Logan's book, and that along with closer regard for Haitian sources and interests stamps this as the more objective and permanently valuable contribution to the subject.

Mr. Van Voorhis has assembled a much too partisan and unobjective narrative of *Negro Masonry*; the earlier history of Prince Saun-

Historical

Anti-Slavery Origins of the Civil War in the United States—Dwight L. Dumond, University of Michigan Press, $2.00.

Slavery Times in Kentucky—J. W. Coleman, Jr., University of North Carolina Press, $3.00.

The Legal Status of the Negro—Charles S. Mangum, Jr., University of North Carolina Press, $5.00.

The Negro in Congress, 1870-1901—Samuel Denny Smith, University of North Carolina Press, $2.50.

The Negro in North Carolina Politics Since Reconstruction—William A. Mabry, Duke University Press, $1.00.

The Negro in the American Revolution—Herbert Aptheker, International Publishers Co., N. Y., $.15.

History of the American Negro People, 1619-1918—Elizabeth Lawson, Workers Bookshop, N. Y., $.40.

Negro Masonry in the United States—H. Van Buren Voorhis, Henry Emmerson, N. Y., $2.50.

The First Negro Medical Society (Medico-Chirurgical Society of the District of Columbia 1884-1939), W. Montague Cobb, Associated Publishers, Washington, D. C., $2.00.

Black Fire: A Story of Henri Christophe—Covelle Newcomb, Longmans, Green & Co., N. Y., $2.50.

Haiti and the United States—Ludwell L. Montague, Duke University Press, N. C., $3.00.

The Diplomatic Relations of the United States with Haiti—Rayford W. Logan, University of North Carolina Press, $5.00.

ders, though out of print, still remains by all odds the more acceptable historical source. Dr. Cobb has documented an interesting chapter in Negro professional history in his study of the first *Negro Medical Society of the District of Columbia;* it has more than memoir significance since it recounts also the early history of the first fight of Negro professional men for recognized professional standing and association—a fight not yet won as far as the National Medical Association membership is concerned.

Dr. Murphy, in his *Analysis of the Attitudes of American Catholics Toward the Immigrant and the Negro,* traces very objectively the gradual liberalization of Catholic thought on matters of race, linking reactionary Americanism somewhat too superficially with the attitudes toward the immigrant, since, after all, race prejudice is many degrees more violent and often of more traditional derivation.

M. S. Stuart's book on *Negro Life Insurance* has ironically chosen its own obituary in its title: at best a flimsy Who's Who of Negro insurance, it itself makes a wide economic detour around the basic problems and trends of Negro business enterprise. So the studies of Professor Harris remain almost our sole reliable guide in this crucially vital field; much needed, however, is bringing such objective and competent analyses up to date through the later years of the depression crisis.

Turning to sociology proper, we have a number of creditable documentations both of Negro history and present-day conditions in the various state guides, among others the Pennsylvania and the Nebraska guides. Two state WPA projects have extensive special studies—the Georgia project in *Drums and Shadows* and the Virginia project in *The Negro in Virginia.* The former focuses on the coastal communities and undoubtedly has gathered the crude materials of several further anthropological studies. In their present shape they suggest a little too strongly the thesis of straight African survivals, and need to be gone over carefully from the acculturation angle as composite folkways and folk-lore, which in the main they seem to represent.

The Negro in Virginia, on the other hand, is much more than a compendium of raw materials; it is a well-balanced and illuminating historical and social analysis, one of the best over-all accomplishments of the Writers' Project in toto.

Able editing has integrated into it a panoramic review of the Negro experience, which since Virginia is the oldest site, save Florida, of Negro settlement, makes it a readable and enlightening epitome of the Negro's history.

Especially the slave narratives have rescued important material that in another decade would have lapsed completely, and much new light is thrown both on the domestic pattern of slavery and on the slave insurrections.

Two contrasted community studies also challenge comparison, this time to the disparagement of the more elaborate volume. For Crum Mason's simple, straightforward description of the *Gullahs* has merit of a factual sort, while Claude McKay's more pretentious analysis of *Harlem* is disappointingly shallow and misleading. Coming from the inside and from a well-known participant in a good deal of the movements considered, this is particularly inexcusable.

Quite clearly there have been two abortive motivations behind McKay's work—the desire on the one hand to be journalistically spectacular, and on the other to be personally vindicating. There is accordingly a double distortion, of facts out of true proportion and of movements and personalities seen askew. McKay outdoes *The Big Sea* for superficiality and lack of serious evaluation, and the DuBois biography, which is professedly historical also, in personalisms of under-and over-emphasis—according, of course, to personal whim. In all frankness this is what I meant in my prefatory remarks. If ever warrantable, this flippancy and egocentrism is not to be condoned in a time like this. Which doesn't mean that we insist at all times on documentary treatises and case studies, but rather upon a more sober regard for factuality and fair play. Sufi and Garvey in parallel panels, the Harlem literary movement and the numbers racket bracketed, are examples in point: they hardly spell good journalism, certainly not representative social analysis.

Great strides in such analysis have nevertheless been made, some from the point of view of enlarged scope in the papers published under the caption of *The Negro in the Americas,* where the subject benefits considerably from the contrast consideration of the Caribbean and the South American Negro; but still greater strides in the group of American Youth Commission studies which are the climax of the social literature of the year. Perhaps even they would be challenged in modernity and thoroughness by the yet unpublished and extensive monograph studies of the staff of the Carnegie Myrdal collaborative research, tentatively styled, *The Negro in America.* But the published and announced Youth Commission analyses of contemporary Negro life—five in all—represent highwater marks of the younger generation scholarship.

Ira Reid's volume is a readable and graphic epitome of the Negro's situation in America, useful for beginners and for a panoramic review of the situation. Professor Frazier's volume covers youth in the borderline states, Professor Charles Johnson's is to cover youth in the rural South, while the Davis-Dollard study covers the Southern cities.

Each in its way is committed to combining psychological with sociological findings, to going beyond statistics to trends and if possible beyond trends to attitudes and other causal factors of explanation. Each also tries to resolve the overgeneralizations so conventional previously, and to take account of class position and economic background as variants in the social experience.

FRAZIER's conclusions show the variation of class status to be quite as important as sectional differences, and also reveal considerable difference in reaction according to the personality patterns of the individual. However, they also show in the main how appallingly oppressive the minority predicament is, and suggest it as one of the grave unsolved problems both of education and of social reform.

A comparison with other minority groups undoubtedly would throw up such common denominators, in varying degree of course, as

Sociological

An Economic Detour: A History of Insurance in the Lives of American Negroes—M. S. Stuart, Malliett & Co., N. Y., $3.00.

Drums and Shadows—Georgia Writers' Project, W.P.A., University of Georgia Press.

The Negro in Virginia—Virginia Writers' Project, W.P.A., edited by Roscoe Lewis, Hastings House, N. Y., $2.50.

An Analysis of the Attitudes of American Catholics Toward the Immigrant and the Negro, 1825-1925—John C. Murphy, Catholic University Press, Washington, D. C.

Gullah: Negro Life in the Carolina Sea Islands—Crum Mason, Duke University Press, N. C.

Harlem: Negro Metropolis—Claude McKay, E. P. Dutton & Co., N. Y., $3.00.

In A Minor Key—Ira De A. Reid, American Council on Education, Washington, D. C., $1.25.

Children of Bondage—Allison Davis and John Dollard, American Council on Education, Washington, D. C., $2.25.

Negro Youth at the Crossways—E. Franklin Frazier, American Council on Education, Washington, D. C., $2.25.

The Negro in the Americas—edited by Charles Wesley, Howard University Division of the Social Sciences, Washington, D. C., $1.50.

to suggest entirely new approaches both to the study and the remedial treatment of the so-called racial problem. This indeed seems to be the final upshot of what is perhaps the most provocative study of them all, the progressive Davis-Dollard book with the unprogressive title, *Children of Bondage*. Here, by a promising attack on the situations of class and race psychoanalytically, a general contribution to social analysis seems on the verge of realization. It is to the effect that social conditions operate through their action upon the psyche of the individual, which gives education a diagnostic and possibly corrective approach to these problems both of class and race. The study also shows the roots of the considerable variation within the same community of the individual reactions and the individual aspects of the problem, and fortunately, too, shows them to have common denominators with the general human situations of frustration and limited opportunity. This, it seems to me, even at the price of a too doctrinaire theory of caste and class, is a contribution of general significance in addition to being an advance step in the concrete and realistic study of racial situations.

The war clouds have almost grounded the scholarly flights of African studies, despite the increasingly crucial relation of African situations to world politics. A revised reissue of Seligman's *Races of Africa* is more than welcome, as one of the few anthropological analyses both readable and reliable at the same time. C. K. Meek's *Europe and West Africa*, probably written before recent developments of the African campaigns, clearly admits and documents the vital stakes of the imperialistic system in the colonial markets and sources of raw products.

Yet few scholars have the courage to press the obvious corollaries as to the imperative need for colonial fair play and reform. Professor Hoernlé alone seems willing to go to the moral

Africana

Europe and West Africa—C. K. Meek, Oxford University Press.

Races of Africa—C. G. Seligman, Thornton Butterworth, London, 2s. 6d.

South African Native Policy—R. A. F. Hoernlé, Phelps Stokes Lecture, University of Capetown, S. A.

●

roots of the imperialistic dilemmas between democracy's creed and its practises. Says he:

"There have been many champions of liberty. . . . But they have all been content to re-state the ideal of liberty on traditional

lines against attacks upon it, and denials
of it, by 'totalitarian' thinkers, whether belonging to the Communist or the Fascist
'ideologies'. What none has done is to re-
examine, in the light of a multi-racial society, like South Africa, what liberty
means and how, if at all, it can be realized
in that sort of society. Yet, if 'liberty' as
the Balfour Declaration has it, 'is the life-
blood of the British Commonwealth,' then,
so long as the Commonwealth includes
multi-racial societies, the realization of
liberty for all races is the most urgent and
important problem, both in theory and
practise, which the members of the Commonwealth have to solve."

Where "natives" are outcasts, as in colonial
South Africa, or native sons are sub-citizens
and "children of bondage" as in the United
States, society is manifestly in the throes of paradox and crisis: the literature that calls these
facts and dilemmas to our attention may not
be so pleasant or entertaining, but certainly it
is sound and potentially constructive. More of
it, let us hope, in 1941!

I must append a poetry postscript, for two
volumes of verse have come to hand since Part
I was written: Nick Aaron Ford's *Songs From
the Dark* and Robert Hayden's *Heart-Shape in
the Dust*. Mr. Ford is a competent versifier of
the academic sort, and his emphasis is racial
rhetoric in the main; a variant, in short, on the
formula of the last decade. Though some of
Mr. Hayden's poems are also in this vein, his
obvious bent and stronger talent is the direction
of social poetry, of contemporary mood, and he
can occasionally speak with an accent of real
power and promise, as in the lines on *Coleman,
Negro Veteran murdered by the Black Legion*:

"In the tolerated weeds of murder,
Coleman lies. . . .
Blood is the color of this season's flower,
Fires, blood-colored, consume our days. . . .

They leave him bleeding there,
Believing that his death
Can prove their superior aliveness,
Loosen the vises of defeat.

(Coleman, all had been saved,
Had we forestalled your lonely martyrdom)

O cancelled face that stares
Into the desolate windows of our long night,
Tell us it is not yet too late;

Tell us the blood seeps down
To give rich suck unto the roots
Of yet another season."

WHO AND WHAT IS "NEGRO"?

Part I

A JANUS-FACED question, "who and what is Negro"—sits like a perennial sphinx at the door of every critic who considers the literature or the art of the Negro. One may appease it, as many do, with literary honey-cakes and poppy-seed, but hackneyed clichés and non-committal concepts only postpone the challenge. Sooner or later the critic must face the basic issues involved in his use of risky and perhaps untenable terms like "Negro art" and "Negro literature," and answer the much-evaded question unequivocally, — who and what is Negro?

This year our sphinx, so to speak, sits in the very vestibule with almost no passing space; for several of the most important books of 1941 pose this issue unavoidably. It is useless to throw the question back at the sociologist or the anthropologist, for they scarcely know themselves, having twin sphinxes in their own bailiwicks. Indeed it is a pertinent question in its own right whether the racial concept has any legitimate business in our account of art. Granted even that folks are interested in "Negro art" and "Negro literature," and that some creative artists consciously accept such a platform of artistic expression, it is warrantable to ask whether they should and whether it should be so. After all, mayn't we be just the victims of an ancient curse of prejudice in these matters and so, unwittingly blind partisans of culture politics and its traditional factionalisms?

Let us take first the question "Who is Negro," provocatively posed by the challenging foreword of Richard Wright's *12 Million Black Voices.* "This text," he says, "while purporting to render a broad picture of the processes of Negro life in the United States, intentionally does not include in its considerations those areas of Negro life which comprise the so-called 'Talented Tenth,' or the isolated islands of mulatto leadership which are still to be found in many parts of the South, or the growing middle-class professional and business men of the North who have, in the past thirty years or more, formed a certain liason corps between the whites and the blacks. Their exclusion from these pages does not imply any invidious judgment, nor does it stem from any desire to underestimate their progress and contributions; they are omitted in an effort to simplify a depiction of a complex movement of debased feudal folk toward a twentieth-century urbanization. This text assumes that those few Negroes who have lifted themselves, through personal strength, talent or luck, above the lives of their fellow-blacks—like single fishes that leap and flash for a split second above the surface of the sea—are but fleeting exceptions to that vast tragic school that swims below in the depths, against the current, silently and heavily, struggling against the waves of vicissitudes that spell a common fate. It is not, however, to celebrate or exalt the plight of the humble folk who swim in the depths that I select the conditions of their lives as examples of normality, but rather to seize upon that which is qualitatively and abiding in Negro experience, to place within full and constant view the collective humanity whose triumphs and defeats are shared by the majority, whose gains in security mark an advance in the level of consciousness attained by the broad masses in their costly and tortuous upstream journey."

Here is a clear and bravely worded challenge.

Opportunity 20 (February and March 1942): 36–41; 83–87.

Who is the real Negro? Well, not only the mass Negro as over against both the culturally "representative" elite or "talented tenth" and the "exceptional" or "untypical" few of the bourgeoisie, but that "mass Negro" who in spite of the phrase about what is "qualitative and abiding in Negro experience," is common denominator proletarian rather than racially distinctive. For all its local and racial color, then, this approach practically scraps the racial factor as inconsequential and liquidates that element culturally as well as sociologically.

As I shall say later, this is an important book, a valuable social analysis, dramatically exposed and simplified, more than that,—a sound working hypothesis for the proletarian artist who has a right to his artistic *Weltanschauung*. But a school of thought or art or social theory that lays claim to totalitarian rectitude must, I think, be challenged. The fallacy of the "new" as of the "older" thinking is that there is a type Negro who, either qualitatively or quantitatively, is the type symbol of the entire group. To break arbitrary stereotypes it is necessary perhaps to bring forward counter-stereotypes, but none are adequate substitutes for the whole truth. There is, in brief, no *"The Negro."* More and more, even as we stress the right of the mass Negro to his important place in the picture, artistically and sociologically, we must become aware of the class structure of the Negro population, and expect to see, hear and understand the intellectual elite, the black bourgeoisie as well as the black masses. To this common stratification is added in the Negro's case internal splits resulting from differential response to particular racial stresses and strains, divergent loyalties which, in my judgment, constitute racial distinctiveness, not by some magic of inheritance but through some very obvious environmental conditionings. For just as we have, for comparative example, the orthodox and the assimilate, the Zionist and anti-Zionist Jew, so in Negro life we have on practically all of these levels, the conformist and the non-conformist strains,— the conformist elite and the racialist elite, the lily-white and the race-patriotic bourgeois, the folk and the ghetto peasant and the emerging Negro proletarian. Each is a significant segment of Negro life, and as they severally come to articulate expression, it will be increasingly apparent that each is a representative facet of Negro life and experience. For a given decade one or the other may seem more significant or "representative," chiefly as it may succeed to the historical spotlight or assume a protagonist role in group expression or group movement. However, as our historical perspective lengthens and our social insight deepens, we should no longer be victims of the still all-too-prevalent formula psychology. Common denominator regional and national traits are there to be taken into account, as are also, more and more as overtones, the factors of group and racial distinctiveness. In cultural and creative expression, the flavor of idiom seems to count especially, which to me seems a valid reason for not scraping the racialist emphasis, provided of course, it does not proceed to the isolationist extreme of ghetto compartmentalization. But more important even than this emphasis is the necessity of an objective but corrective insistence on the variety of Negro types and their social and cultural milieu.

Turning to the other basic question,—what is Negro, we may ask ourselves what makes a work of art Negro, if indeed any such nomenclature is proper,—its authorship, its theme or its idiom? Different schools of criticism are obviously divided on these criteria. Each has had its inning, and probably no one regrets the comparative obsolescence of the artificial separatist criterion of Negro authorship. Only in the hectic early striving for credit and recognition could it be forgotten that the logical goal of such a viewpoint is an artistic Ghetto of "Negro art" and "Negro literature," isolated from the common cultural heritage and the vital and necessary fraternalisms of school and generation tendencies. The editors of the brilliantly panoramic anthology, *The Negro Caravan,* pose the issue this way: "In spite of such unifying bonds as a common rejection of the popular stereotypes and a common racial cause, writings by Negroes do not seem to the editors to fall into a unique cultural pattern. Negro writers have adopted the literary traditions that seemed useful for their purposes. They have therefore been influenced by Puritan didacticism, sentimental humanitarianism, local color, regionalism, realism, naturalism, and experimentalism. . . . The editors do not believe that the expression "Negro literature" is an accurate one, and in spite of its convenient brevity, they have avoided using it. "Negro literature" has no application if it means structural peculiarity, or a Negro school of writing. The Negro writes in the forms evolved in English and American literature. A "Negro novel," "a Negro play" are ambiguous terms. If they mean a novel or play by Negroes, then such works as *Porgy* and *The Green Pastures* are left out. If they mean works about Negro life, they include more works by white authors than by Negro, and these works have been most influential upon the American mind. The editors consider Negro writers to be American writers, and literature by American Negroes to be a segment of American literature." . . . "The chief cause for objection to the term is that Negro literature is too easily placed by certain critics, white and Negro, in an alcove apart. The next step is a double standard of judgment, which is dangerous for the future of Negro writers."

Again, these are brave and necessary words. But there is a trace in them of corrective counter-emphasis, and the objective truth lies probably somewhere between, as indeed the dual significance of the anthology itself evidences. Simultaneously, a segment of American literature and a special chapter of racial expression and reaction, most of the materials in this same anthology have a double character as well as a double significance. The logical

Poetry and Belles Lettres

The Negro Caravan—Sterling Brown, Arthur P. Davis, and Ulysses Lee. New York: The Dryden Press. $4.25.

Golden Slippers—Edited by Arna Bontemps. New York: Harper & Bros. $2.50.

Harlem—Al Hirschfeld and William Saroyan. New York: The Hyperion Press. $12.50.

Send Me Down—Henry Steig. New York: Alfred A. Knopf, Inc. $2.50.

Dunbar Critically Examined—Victor Lawson. Washington, D. C.: The Associated Publishers. $2.00.

●

predicament is in not seeing the complete compatibility between nationally and racially distinctive elements, arising from our over-simplified and chauvinistic conception of culture. Neither national nor racial cultural elements are so distinctive as to be mutually exclusive. It is the general composite character of culture which is disregarded by such over-simplifications. By that logic, a typical American character could never have been expected as a modification of English artistic and institutional culture, but there it is, after some generations of divergence, characteristically Anglo-Saxon and American at the same time. Strictly speaking, we should consistently cite this composite character in our culture with hyphenate descriptions, but more practically, we stress the dominant flavor of the blend. It is only in this same limited sense that anything is legitimately styled

"Negro"; actually it is Afro- or Negro-American, a hybrid product of Negro reaction to American cultural forms and patterns. And when, as with many of our Negro cultural products, it is shared in the common cultural life, —our jazz music, as a conspicuous example,— it becomes progressively even more composite and hybridized, sometimes for the better, sometimes not. For we must abandon the idea of cultural purism as a criterion under the circumstances just as we have abandoned the idea of a pure race under the more scientific and objective scrutiny of the facts of history.

Thus the interpenetration of national and racial characteristics, once properly understood, resolves the traditional dilemma of the racialists and on the cultural level puts an essential parity on racial, national and regional idioms. As the point of view matures, perhaps we shall regard all three as different dimensions of cultural variation, interchangeably blended in specific art forms and combinations. Such reciprocity actually exists, and would have been recognized but for our politically minded notions of culture, which flatter majority strains in our culture and minimize minority culture elements. As a matter of fact, the racial evolves by special emphasis from the general cultural heritage and in turn flows back into the common culture. With neither claiming more than its proper due, no such invidious and peculiar character accrues to the racial, and, on such a basis, it should not be necessary to play down the racial contribution in order to prove the essential cultural solidarity of Negro creative effort with American art and letters. The position leads, if soundly developed, not to cultural separatism but to cultural pluralism. To be "Negro" in the cultural sense, then, is not to be radically different, but only to be distinctively composite and idiomatic, though basically American, as is to be expected, in the first instance.

According to such criteria, the critic has, like the chemist, the analytical job of breaking down compounds into their constituent culture elements. So far as characterization goes, this involves the task of assessing the accent of representativeness among the varying regional, racial and national elements. Theme and idiom would bulk more significantly than source of authorship, and important expressions of Negro material and idiom by white authors would belong as legitimately in a Negro as in a general anthology.

Turning to the novels of the year, the most publicized of them all, Mrs. Weaton's *Mr. George's Joint*, Jefferson Prize Award winner, turns out by my analysis as Negro in theme only but unrepresentative in idiom, despite its laboriously studied local color and dialect. It is

●

Fiction

Mr. George's Joint—Elizabeth Lee Wheaton. New York: E. P. Dutton & Co. $2.50.

Cottonmouth—Julian L. Rayford. New York: Charles Scribner's Sons. $2.75.

Royal Road—Arthur Kuhl. New York: Sheed & Ward. $1.75.

Blood on the Forge—William Attaway. New York: Doubleday, Doran & Co. $2.00.

The Sun Is My Undoing—Marguerite Steen. New York: The Viking Press. $3.00.

The Unquiet Field—Beatrice Kean Seymour. New York: The Macmillan Co. $2.50.

comforting to learn that since the decision, the editor of the *Virginia Quarterly Review* has disavowed further responsibility for the award series. Far too often, as in this case, meticulous photographic reporting passes in these days of realism for vital interpretation. At best a second-rate regional novel of small-town Texan life, there is nothing deeply interpretative of Negro life in the book; there is more insight in single short stories of Faulkner or Caldwell, who know how to find the human significance of the sordid and otherwise trivial.

Julian Rayford's *Cottonmouth*, however, for all its slight sketchiness, has much of the genuine feel and tempo of the deep South, and an emotional insight into Negro-white relationships. The regional Southern novel has not had a particularly good yield: only Idwal Jones' *Black Bayou* and the late William Percy's *Lanterns on the Levee* approach any close companionship with the previous high levels in this genre. In initiating a new approach, Arthur Kuhl's *Royal Road* is significant, but it is scarcely a full realization of its potentialities at that. A melodrama with dimensions of moral symbolism, it fails to convince either in the realistic vein or in its symbolic overtone. And so the tragedy of Jesse Stewart, born of Mary and Joseph in Bethlehem, Pa., scarcely warrants the atonement motive insinuated into a sad story of persecution, false witness and miscarriage of judicial procedure. The social forces responsible are not sufficiently delineated; so that Jesse's electrocution seems more a bizarre accident

than a racial tragedy.

William Attaway's *Blood on the Forge*, however, fully evokes its milieu and also most of its characters. The story of the three Morse brothers, temperamentally so different, tragically caught in the slum-ghetto of a Pennsylvania steel-mill town, fighting rather blindly the tides of labor feuds just as they had previously struggled with the tragic precariousness of their Kentucky sharecropper farm is a contribution to the still small stock of Negro social analysis fiction.

The stock of slave-trade fiction, with its romantic appeal is, on the contrary, overfull. As these lurid historical canvasses multiply, one marvels at the general state of the reading public that apparently so avidly consumes them. *The Sun Is My Undoing* promises to become another *Gone With the Wind* sensation. Interspersed with its romance and adventure is some rather unorthodox truth about the slave trade's social complications, its intrigue, concubinage and miscegenation, but the endless rehearsing of these particular chapters of history seems worse than gratuitous. *The Unquiet Field* is a much more sober and integrated account of the same materials, but it will in all likelihood be much less popular than its glamorous competitor.

With the postponement of Langston Hughes's *Shakespeare in Harlem*, the poetry output dwindles to almost negligible proportions. Several books of verse in the category of children's verse

Drama

Native Son—Paul Green and Richard. Wright. New York: Harper & Bros. $2.00.

Dust to Earth—Shirley Graham. New Haven, Conn.: Yale University Theatre, Jan., 1941.

On Strivers Row—Abram Hill. New York: Harlem Peoples Theatre, March, 1941.

●

will be considered later; and even Arna Bontemps' *Golden Slippers* anthology is gauged for youthful readers, with emphasis on the lighter lyric vein. He has nevertheless had the taste to include principally the better poets, so that the book becomes an acceptable anthology of the lighter genre apart from age limitations. Surely the poetic lull must have some other explanation than a creative drought; probably the disinclination of publishers to venture verse publication for "fledgling" poets, but just possibly also the distraction and disillusionment prevailing in the ranks of Negro youth.

One of the major contributions of the year thus becomes the very comprehensive and much needed anthology of Negro authors in all the literary forms which Sterling Brown, Arthur Davis and Ulysses Lee have collated in *The Negro Caravan.* Here is definitive editing of the highest order, combined with authoritative historical and critical annotation. For years to come it will be the indispensable handbook for the study of the Negro's contribution to the literature of the Negro. In the critical introductions to the various literary types, brief mention is wisely added to give some notion of the important correlation of Negro creative effort with that of white authors treating Negro themes; which somewhat offsets the inconsistency of the anthology's non-racialist critical platform and its actual restriction to Negro authorship.

Steig's *Send Me Down* is a very authentic and penetrating analysis of Negro jazz and jazz-makers, proving that in competent hands even the picturesque side of Negro life can be instructively presented. In blatant contrast is the elaborate but superficial *Harlem* of Saroyan and Albert Hirschfeld. The flippancy, both literary and artistic, is condescending, and though the types have changed in the decade that has elapsed, Miguel Covarrubias's *Negro Drawings* still remain the unchallenged superior version of Harlem types and atmospheres. Hirschfeld has caught only surface values, with little psychological or social penetration; clever as caricatures, his drawings only occasionally apt as type portraiture.

Victor Lawson's maiden critical effort is a very competent analysis of Dunbar as man and poet; the one from a not too insistent or enlightening psycho-analytic approach and the other from a rather illuminating analysis of the strains of sentimental romanticism from which his literary pedigree derives. The study quite outdistances the only other extant critical study and biography of this poet, and should supercede it with students of Dunbar or his period of race poetry.

In the field of drama, the joint version of *Native Son* by Richard Wright and Paul Green is the highpoint of the dramatic crop. Oddly enough the climaxes of the drama toward the close die down to dramatic monologues and tableau, while earlier scenes are electric with the best of both drama and melodrama. This only accentuates in some ways the faults of the novel itself, which is more skillfully contrived in its earlier chapters. But no dimuendo of values in the sequence can stifle the power and veracity of the material, which after all is one of the most incisive versions of contemporary Negro life and its social implications. The success of the drama with audiences of all types has already demonstrated the importance of such frank veracity and such uncompromising vitality.

Shirley Graham's full length drama of the West Virginia coal mines, *Dust to Earth,* was elaborately presented by the Yale University Theatre group. Its social background reporting is unfortunately overlaid by a melodramatic plot interest which does not gain force by the defeatist sacrifice of the hero, a denouement which decidedly takes the edge off a play that could have been a pioneering essay in Negro labor tragedy. Our dramatists have on the whole not yet shaken off the timidity which once so banefully beset our novelists. In *On Strivers Row,* Abram Hill has written a good ground-breaking excursion into social comedy. It still remains to be seen what success this type of play will have with Negro audiences, who have yet to become conditioned to dramatic self-criticism. It is to be hoped that the Harlem Peoples Theater will have eventual success in so obvious a need of the Negro drama.

Part II

NEITHER history nor sociology nor even anthropology have as yet any definitive answer to our eternal question. But they are steadily though not directly approaching that goal. Progress toward such an objective, it seems, cannot follow the bee-line, but must go, like the sailboat, on a tactical course, now overshooting the mark and tacking back on a counter zig-zag in the other direction. Out of successive emphases and from the polemical clash of differing interpretations, we are finally getting where the objective truth about the Negro can be pieced together and put into a clear and meaningful perspective.

In what is one of the richest seasons of sociological yield, we have in the factual literature of 1941 several cases in point,—as an important historical example, the corrective counter-statements of Buckmaster's unconventional history of the anti-slavery movement, *Let My People Go;* or in the sociological field, the unorthodox approaches and conclusions of the current American Youth Commission studies of Negro youth; or again, in the case of anthropology, the provocative counter-statements of Herskovits' *The Myth of the Negro Past.* The older commonplaces about the Negro are being challenged on every hand, and the last phase,—let us hope, of the generation-long polemics of race theory is coming to a head. As I have already stated, there is often over-emphasis and over-simplification in these new provocative counter-statements; and they, too, in many cases lack the full objectivity and final equilibrium of the ultimate truth. However, they are far more objective and realistic than the points of view and theories which they challenge and threaten to displace or modify, and unlike them, are not grounded either in majority bias or minority apologetics. Two very vital requisites for scientific objectivity and final truth are rapidly establishing themselves,—race scholarship is shedding its protective sentimentalities and apologetic bias, while white scholarship, on the other hand, both by more sympathetic penetration and through wise interracial collaboration, is getting almost for the first time an "inside" view of Negro life. Such collaboration, in fact, is becoming the order of the day, as will be even more apparent when the full series of the Carnegie-Myrdal monographs becomes published. The American Youth Commission series is another notable example of this warrantable and fruitful type of collaborative study.

As such scholarship matures, scientific integration removes more and more the isolation and the "peculiar" uniqueness of the Negro's situation and its problems. Common denominator forces and factors are increasingly used to explain and interpret Negro life. The *en bloc* conceptions of the Negro are breaking down gradually into proper and realistic recognition of the diversifications as circumstances and environment vary from place to place, or from generation to generation. Both sociologists and anthropologists are beginning to recognize the complementary effect of the Negro on whites as well as the effects of the white on the Negro; class stratification among Negroes is at last being taken into serious account, and general economic and social factors are coming to the fore as transcending in influence the traditionally "racial." A book like *Color and Human Nature*, as last year's *Children of Bondage*, introduces the welcome novelty of the case study approach and psycho-analytic interpretation, as well as the diversification of individuality alongside those of class stratification and type of community environment. *Thus Be Their Destiny* specifically stresses community structure and the part it plays in racial and interracial reactions. *Color, Class and Personality* not only takes into account all these vital variables, but poses the basic problems of Negro youth over the common denominator of the cognate issues in the life of American youth generally. Community studies of the Negro, like that on the *New Haven Negroes*, wisely styled a "social history," take on increasingly what the Chicago school calls an "ecological" approach, that is, revealing the influence on the Negro of the immediate environment and its socio-economic forces. Indeed some of them treat the Negro condition as one of the significant indices of these common community factors. Even Professor Herskovits' study, in spite of its emphasis, (indeed, I would say, its overemphasis) on the hypothesis of African culture survivals, uses the Negro as a base for the study of general sociological and cultural phenomena, and thus makes the analysis yield something beyond the mere explanation of the Negro's own situation in terms of insight into the general nature of social forces and cultural process. The positive side of *The Myth of The Negro Past* thus becomes its analysis of the interplay of the forces of cultural survival and assimilation and its evidence about the general character of acculturation. A book like *When Peoples Meet*, sub-titled "A Study in Race and Culture Contacts," generalizes even further, and places the so-called race question in a universal context of culture contacts and conflicts, emphasizing the common features and forces involved in majority and minority relations and their interaction on a world scale. In a period of world crisis, precipitated by a global war, it is particularly significant and promising when the study of race and interracial problems broadens out into an integrated analysis, on the one hand, of basic problems of human group relations and on the other, of wide-scale comparative study of universal forces in group interaction.

Henrietta Buckmasters' well documented story of the "Underground Railroad" and the Abolition movement, in addition to being the most outspoken evaluation of the part played by the Negro himself in the struggle for freedom, rightly stresses the sustained and widespread collaboration of the white and Negro anti-slavery forces. Historically authoritative, the narrative is lifted from the level of dead history to its proper plane of a great national crusade. Even more than in the previous studies of slave revolts and insurrections, the figure of the militant Negro is strikingly documented and vindicated in his all too underestimated role of co-author of his own freedom; the Negro abolitionists, Purvis, Forten, Redmond, Lenox, Wells Brown, Delancy, Douglass and Harriet Tubman are properly paired with their white sponsors and collaborators,—Garrison, Tappan,

Coffin, Parker, Burney and John Brown. Carrying the same heroic story, with less documentation and somewhat less accurate perspective, Anna Curtis' *Stories of the Underground Railroad* performs a similar service for the less sophisticated reader.

In a more traditional historical vein, A. A. Taylor continues his reconstruction period studies with a factual but not too interpretive nar-

History and Biography

Let My People Go. Henrietta Buckmaster. New York: Harper & Bros. $3.50.
Stories of the Underground Railroad—Anna L. Curtis. New York: Island Workshop Co-op. Press, Inc. $1.75.
The Negro in Tennessee, 1865-1880—A. A. Taylor. Washington, D. C.: The Associated Publishers. $3.00.
New Haven Negroes—Robert Austin Warner. New Haven, Conn.: Yale University Press. $3.50.
A History of Wilberforce University—F. A. McGinnis, Wilberforce, Ohio: Wilberforce Press. $2.50.
Howard University: A History, 1867-1940—Walter Dyson. Washington, D. C.: Howard University Press. $4.00.
12 Million Black Voices—Richard Wright. Photo-direction by Edwin Rosskam. New York: The Viking Press. $3.00.
Life and Times of Frederick Douglass. New York: The Pathway Press. $5.00.
Father of the Blues: An Autobiography—W. C. Handy. New York: The Macmillan Co. $3.00.
Marian Anderson—Kosti Vehanen. New York: Whittlesey House. $2.50.
Amber Gold—Arnold H. Maloney. New York: Wendell Malliet & Co.

●

rative of *The Negro in Tennessee;* important principally for its documentation of the Negro factors in the politics of a border state. Of decidedly different scope and interpretative power is the social history already mentioned of *New Haven Negroes* by Robert A. Warner. Here, with the aid of obviously competent Negro research assistance, the life story of a Northern Negro community has been illuminatingly told from colonial times to the present day. This is a type of story sorely needed despite the somewhat discouraging revelation in this instance of a group tragedy of economic displacement downward to marginal and less skilled labor, typical, we fear, of the older Northern centers of the Negro population and especially of New England. More and more Negro studies will need, as in this case, to be put on an intensive regional or local basis, both for historical and sociological accuracy and for the correct evaluation of interracial reactions.

Two pioneer chronicles of the history of Wilberforce and Howard Universities open up the lagging field of institutional history. Each garners the materials needed for the definitive his-

tories that must eventually be written of these institutions, which in that case, must discuss them more penetratingly in terms of their contemporary social conditions and educational policies. The Howard narrative, product of a lifetime's avocational interest on the part of Professor Walter Dyson, though cast in the reminiscent "alumni mould," more nearly approaches a generally useful and interesting public chronicle of one of our most important educational centers. In a documentary way, it has performed a very necessary service.

But history has long since outgrown the traditional job of factual chronicling; the modern brand stands or falls by interpretation. In a less traditional, in fact in a provocatively unorthodox vein, Richard Wright has attempted in *Twelve Million Black Voices* a folk history of the Negro. His identification of the mass Negro with the whole historical Negro cause has already been discussed; with the qualified reservation that however over-generalized, a neglected segment of our problem and an important economic analysis of our disadvantaged minority status is not to be ignored. But although such a gift horse is not to be looked at too much askance, from the point of view of a complete and objective historical story the work has to be challenged and taken with the reservations necessary to polemical and *partis pris* interpretations. Frankly stated as a thesis at the outset, the reader knows, however, precisely what assent or discount to apply; certainly Mr. Wright cannot be accused of sailing or riding under false colors.

*   *   *

In the field of biography a wide gamut is covered by a minimum of publications; at least they do not overlap in type. One of the most significant is the timely re-publication by the Pathway Press of one of the few classics of Negro autobiography,—Frederick Douglass's *Life and Times.* Here, of course, we not only have this heroic past and its still pertinent example, but the field of statesmanship and public movements. At the other pole of achievement, we have an intimate and first-hand account of Marian Anderson's mid-career by her friend and accompanist, Kosti Vehanen. This authentic record of her phenomenal and rather sudden international success after years of painstaking preparation becomes a rare item of Negro biography in the field of formal music, and preserves the record in undisputed inside documentation. It also gives us inspiring glimpses of the imperturbable personality around which the exciting drama seems to revolve without considerable change or effect; to the extent that the symbolic element rather than the human eventually dominates the book, particularly with that historically symbolic climax with which the narrative ends,—the Easter Sunday Lincoln Memorial concert.

Quite more earthly and human in its appeal is the chatty, almost garrulous narrative of W. C. Handy, the *Father of the Blues*. Here is the inning of the Negro folk element and its Cinderella story of early persecution and disdain and eventual fame and glory. The riches of that bonanza of jazz and ragtime were not vouchsafed to Mr. Handy, but at least from an authoritative source the Negro credit for the original contribution that Tin Pan Alley and the commercial music trust have all too glibly claimed is set down beyond all dispute and gainsaying. To have accomplished this culminating task of a lifetime of loyal music pioneering is probably one of Mr. Handy's deepest satisfactions as it will also be one of his most appreciated racial services. In quite another field, that of research science, Dr. Maloney contributes the autobiography of a pioneering pharmacologist. Aside from its personal significance, this book will undoubtedly have inspirational value in documenting the possibilities of Negro success in a field that, as a matter of fact, has had considerable achievement, like that of Delany, Turner, Carver, Hinton, Imes, Julian, and Just, but far too little biographical chronicling.

●

Education and Sociology

Gullah—Mason Crum. Durham, N. C.: Duke University Press. $3.50.
Drums and Shadows—Georgia Writers' Project. Athens, Ga.: University of Georgia Press. $3.00.
Sharecroppers All—Arthur Raper and Ira De A. Reid. Chapel Hill, N. C.: University of N. C. Press. $3.00.
Growing Up in the Black Belt—Charles S. Johnson. Washington, D. C.: American Council on Education. $2.25.
Deep South—Allison Davis, Burleigh G. Gardner and Mary R. Gardner. Chicago, Ill.: University of Chicago Press. $4.50.
Thus Be Their Destiny—J. Howell Atwood, Donald W. Wyatt, Vincent J. Davis and Ira D. Walker. Washington, D. C.: American Council on Education. $.75.
Color and Human Nature—W. Lloyd Warner, Buford N. Junker and Walter A. Adams. Washington, D. C.: American Council on Education. $2.25.
The Negro Federal Government Worker—J. W. Hayes. Washington, D. C.: Howard University Press. $1.50.
When Peoples Meet—Alain Locke and Bernhard J. Stern. New York: Progressive Education Assn. $3.50.
The Myth of the Negro Past—Melville J. Herskovits. New York: Harper & Bros. $4.00.

In the historical chapters of the various state guides sponsored by the Federal and now the State Writers' Projects, from time to time the honorable precedent set at the outset of including the Negro has taken firm root and flourished. With variable interpretative power, but almost without exception, such chapters or passing mention have been a creditable feature of this mounting list of publications that now includes almost every state in the union. Two specialized studies of Negro life, both of folklore and folkways, have also appeared this year, —Mason Crum's *Gullah* and the Georgia Project's *Drums and Shadows*. They are both acceptable contributions to the documentation of our folk-lore, though in each case, I think they are too naively primitivist in their interpretation of the materials. They do the invaluable service, whatever reservations will ultimately be placed on the commentary, of collating this material before it vanishes completely. But they reveal the South and the Negro that are vanishing.

The South that is still very much with us, and that remains one of the basic concerns of national reconstruction is presented by another series of books, three of which are definitive studies of prime sociological importance. *Sharecroppers All,* the joint work of Ira Reid and Arthur Raper, in addition to being a sound economic and sociological diagnosis of the breakdown of the Southern rural economy, provides a basis of constructive remedy not merely for the economic nub of the "race problem" but of the much needed economic rehabilitation of the entire South. It finds common factors behind the regional as well as the racial differentials, furnishing scientific confirmation of Booker Washington's instinctive common-sense which expressed itself in the epigrammatic—"You can't hold a man down in the ditch without staying down there with him." The book's bold analysis is matched by its brave prophecy, for on the one hand it frankly says: "The representative of the new South knows that the region is less handicapped by the sharecroppers than by the heritage of the plantation system, less by outside opposition than by inside complacency, less by the presence of the Negro than by the white man's attitude toward him, less by the spectre of class uprisings and Negro domination than by the fear of them" and then concludes that "the South, by integrating national and community efforts may be able to pay the bills of yesterday's exploitation of land and man, may be able to conserve and use her natural resources and so restore the region to its rightful place in the nation."

With usual statistical thoroughness, but with the implementation of case studies and personality profiles, Dr. Charles S. Johnson adds to his impressive series of studies the latest,— *Growing Up in The Black Belt.* His picture gains an important human dimension thereby, and to the usual analysis of the Southern rural economy is added a picture of a restive, changing though bewildered younger generation. No one reading the analysis can overlook the imminence of momentous psychological change in spite of all the expected provincialisms and inferiority depressions: the almost frightening paradox of a changing Negro in a recalcitrant South that either refuses to change or to recognize change.

The Deep South takes a more academic turn in a painstaking analysis of the structure of what a group of researchers have chosen as the "typical Southern society." As a general thesis the authors emphasize the rigid dominance of the bi-racial "caste system," but in spite of its almost endless documentation have to report from time to time such numerous anomalies and exceptions as almost to invalidate the practical usefulness of this much-mooted "caste theory" for a practical understanding of Southern social code and practise. Both sex and business relations have always had their devious ways of bridging the "great social divide," and the Old South, never any too consistent in its actual practise of race relations, except on the basis of anything pragmatically conducive to dominance and exploitation, should not have been taken so seriously according to the letter of its stock rationalizations. The longer one resides in the South the more conscious one becomes of its inconsistencies and exceptions. Not only more notice should have been taken of these, but also of the forces of insecurity and challenge which the South now faces. Scant attention has been paid, however, to the insecure economic structure of the entire society or to the increasing conflict of economic interests with the traditional social values both among the whites and Negroes. For lack of this, the study is on the whole academic, sterile and retrospective, whereas with emphasis on such economic factors, it could so easily have been enlighteningly diagnostic and practically helpful.

Color and Human Nature, the parallel story of Negro life in an urban industrial center, furnishes, in marked contrast, a vital, dynamic account of what it means to be a Negro in America of today. The basic forces and reactions to which it calls attention are common even to the rural Southern situation which *The Deep South* so dully anatomizes, but in addition, the peculiar stresses of urban competition, of wider class differentiation and of economic and cultural advancement are illuminatingly reported. Nor are the findings too highly generalized, for case reports emphasize both the successful and the unsuccessful accommodations which circumstance and personality introduce into the racial equation. The reader gets the impression that there are important variables of color, class, economic and educational status, and even of sex and personality which defy any mass or even any regional formula, and make of each individual life a rather unpredictable drama of personality development and adjustment in spite of the handicaps of prejudice. Superimposed, one gets, of course, the other side of the picture, a clear knowledge of the group predicament and its resistant, reactionary traditions and limitations. The net result is a balanced sane perspective.

The Myth of the Negro Past, culminating years of painstaking comparative study of the Negro in Africa, North, Central and South America, is inevitably an important book. In line with the progressive wing of anthropological scholarship, it attempts considerable and vindicating revision of traditional conceptions of the Negro. Over against the stereotype of the Negro's childlike, docile character, it documents the little known facts of considerable social and cultural resistance to slave subordination. Against conventional notions of low-grade African stock and of "inferior," negligible culture background, it advances and justifies the facts of biological hardihood, seasoned social discipline and considerable cultural development in the African racial background. It is argued that a knowledge of this cultural background will lessen prejudice and rehabilitate the Negro considerably in American public opinion,—a strangely moralistic corollary, arguing well for the author's humanity but scarcely realistic enough to justify this moralistic departure from scientific objectivity. What is of most value in the book is neither this cultural vindication, salutary as it is for the lay public, black and white, nor this moral reformism, but the broadly gauged analysis of the African background and its widespread linkages with all parts of the American continent through the dispersion of the slave trade. This, as has already been said, is a story of reciprocal cultural interchange and influence, of Negro on white, and white on Negro, and constitutes a pioneer contribution to the ground problems of acculturation as it has affected the African peoples and their Western descendants. In this area, the study is as valuable for the lines of prospective research it forecasts as for those it tentatively summarizes.

But here again, a reformist zeal overremphasizes the thesis of African survivals, transforming it from a profitable working hypothesis into a dogmatic obsession, claiming arbitrary interpretations of customs and folkways which in all common-sense could easily have alternative or even compound explanations. Instead of suggesting the African mores and dispositions as conducive factors along with other more immediate environmental ones, the whole force of the explanation, in many instances, pivots on Africanisms and their sturdy, stubborn survival. The extreme logic of such a position might, as a matter of fact, lead to the very opposite of Dr. Herskovits' liberal conclusions, and damn the Negro as more basically peculiar and unassimilable than he actually is or has proved himself to be. As elsewhere, the truth would seem

Africana

Mumbo Jumbo, Esquire—James Saxon Childers. New
    York: D. Appleton-Century Co. $5.00.
Focus on Africa—Richard U. Light. Washington, D. C.:
    American Geographic Society. $5.00.
Native African Medicine—George Way Harley, M.D.
    Cambridge, Mass.: Harvard University Press. $3.50.
The Customs of the Baganda—Sir Apolo Kagwa. Edited
    by G. Kalibala. New York: Oxford University Press.
    $4.00.
Married Life in an African Tribe—I. Schapera. New
    York: Sheridan House, $3.50.
The Colour Bar in East Africa—Norman Leys. London: Hogarth Press. 7s. 6d.
The Economic History of Liberia—George W. Brown.
    Washington, D. C.: The Associated Publishers. $3.00.

to be in between either extreme of interpretation, either that of the Negro as the empty-handed, parasitic imitator or that of the incurably atavistic nativist. In fact, because of his forced dispersion and his enforced miscegenation, the Negro must eventually be recognized as a cultural composite of more than ethnic complexity and cultural potentiality.

James Saxon Childers in *Mumbo Jumbo Esquire* recognizes the same growing complexity in the African. Of Africa today he says: "Any book that limits itself to either the primitive or the modern in Africa is unfair; such a book does not tell the whole story. A reporter must leave the city and go into the jungle, leave the jungle and return to the city; he must travel over paved highways in automobiles and over the desert on camels." Sketchy but highly suggestive, and what is more important, openminded, this enlightened and enlightening travelogue represents a new symptom of broadened interracial and intercultural understanding. Dr. George Brown's competent *Economic History of Liberia* is particularly gratifying, as an American Negro's evaluation of this offshoot of American Negro colonization. The Oxford

Press reprint of the Baganda scholar's study of his own people's customary law is equally symptomatic; as is also Professor Schapera's comprehensive study of *Married Life in An African Tribe*, a study of constructive modifications of Kgatla tribal customs after the initial forced changes and disruption of colonial South African contact. Such studies are no longer exotica; they are at the heart of our contemporary problems of world crisis and world reconstruction. Though sentimentally interested as Negroes, we should more and more become interested in these issues as world citizens. The international significance and import of Africa today may very well add another dimension to the experience of being Negro, and lead even to the renovation and enrichment of the all too confused and limited current concept of who and what is Negro.

REASON AND RACE:
A Review of the Literature of the Negro for 1946

FICTION

JULE, George Wylie Henderson, Creative Age, N. Y. $2.50.

MRS. PALMER'S HONEY, Fannie Cook, Doubleday & Co., N. Y. $2.50.

A STAR POINTED NORTH, Edmund Fuller, Harper & Bros., N. Y. $2.75.

THE FOXES OF HARROW, Frank Yerby, The Dial Press, N. Y. $2.75.

LIGHTS OUT, Baynard Kendrick, Wm. Morrow & Co., N. Y. (Late 1945). $2.50.

THE STREET, Ann Petry, Houghton Mifflin Co., Boston. $2.50.

POETRY and BELLES LETTRES

POWERFUL LONG LADDER, Owen Dodson, Farrar, Straus & Co., N. Y. $2.50.

AMERICAN DAUGHTER, Era Bell Thompson, University of Chicago Press. $3.

JOURNEY TO ACCOMPONG, Katherine Dunham, Henry Holt & Co., N. Y. $2.50.

SHINING TRUMPETS—A History of Jazz, Rudi Blesh, Alfred A. Knopf, N. Y. $5.

TO MASTER, A LONG GOODNIGHT, Brion Gysin, Creative Age Press, N. Y. $3.

SOCIAL SCIENCE . . . .

A NEGRO'S FAITH IN AMERICA, Spencer Logan, Macmillan Co., N. Y. $1.75.

COLOR BLIND: A White Woman Looks at the Negro, Margaret Halsey, Simon & Schuster, N. Y. $2.

WHITE MAN'S BURDEN, Ruth Smith, The Vanguard Press, N. Y. $2.

SOUTHERN EXPOSURE, Stetson Kennedy, Doubleday & Co., N. Y. $3.

ANATOMY OF RACIAL INTOLERANCE, ed. Geo. B. de Huszar, H. W. Wilson Co., N. Y. $1.25.

THIS WAY TO UNITY, ed. Arnold Herrick and Herbert Askwith, Oxford Book Co., N. Y. $2.

MINORITY PROBLEMS IN THE SCHOOLS, Theodore Brameld, Harper & Bros., N. Y. $2.50.

THE 14TH AMENDMENT AND THE NEGRO SINCE 1920, Bernard Nelson, Catholic Univ. Press, Washington, D. C. $2.

THE BROTHERHOOD OF SLEEPING CAR PORTERS, B. R. Brazeal, Harper & Bros., N. Y. $3.

NEGRO LABOR: A National Problem, Robert C. Weaver, Harcourt, Brace & Co., N. Y. $3.

COLOR AND CONSCIENCE, Buell G. Gallagher, Harper & Bros., N. Y. $2.50.

The literature of the Negro theme in 1946 has been solid and sober, and on the whole, constructively progressive —a creditable crop for the first post-war year. Even the creative literature, with a notable exception or two, has been cast in a socially serious vein and a crusading mood; while, as might have been expected, the sociological crop, under the pressure of war issues and experiences, has almost completely abandoned orthodox academic objectivity and has concentrated almost surgically on the social pathology and hygiene of race.

Unfortunately in being so sober and searching, the current yield will satisfy the reformer rather than astonish the aesthete. But from the practical point of view, that is good warrant to be enthusiastic about it: it is good medicine for the social mind and strong tonic for our social will.

Phylon 8 (First Quarter 1947): 17–27.

Indeed, if we experience several successive years of such intellectual fare and diet, an intellectual crusade for social health and sanity will be in full swing, and our writers and artists will have paralleled our physical victory over fascism with a psychological conquest of racism, prejudice and cultural intolerance.

Like many another recent development, the war will seem primarily responsible. But that is not the full truth of the matter. What the war influence has performed is a precipitation and acceleration of issues that had previously been joined: for more than a decade a great social enlightenment has been in the making. But the war and its aftermath has stirred the mass mind from apathy to some real degree of receptivity and, more important still, has emboldened our critical and creative minds to more outspoken advocacy of social sanity and truth. Reason has taken up the challenge of unreason on the issue of race.

A word on audience receptivity is important: indeed in some respects this is the more significant phenomenon, and probably the one for which we have the galvanizing shocks of war to thank. Books, plays and social studies which the publishers and public pulse-takers have thought too "strong" for public acceptance have been accepted to the unmistakable degree of best sellers and season's 'hits.' *Native Son, Strange Fruit, Black Boy, Freedom Road, Deep Are the Roots,* the Myrdal Studies, especially the extraordinary circulation of the summary volumes,—*An American Dilemma,* fully attest to this. The psychological ceiling has appreciably lifted, and some of the publications and productions of 1946 promise to raise or pierce it—Ann Petry's novel, *The Street,* Gallagher's *Color and Conscience,* Stetson Kennedy's *Southern Exposure,* Margaret Halsey's *Color Blind,* and especially, I think—if I can trespass a little on the field of drama—the southern satire scenes of the new play, *Finian's Rainbow.* Such receptivity challenges our writers, Negro and white, to their utmost of truth-telling and plain-saying: there is no longer that old excuse,—'the public will not listen.' They have, and they will, and before long the effects will be felt.

As to the writers, they are hardly equal for the moment, with exceptions of course, to the new and unexpected opportunities. It remains to be seen what 1947 and 1948 will give us; for, after all, the situation has to most observers developed suddenly. But we must not forget that our present assignment is the literature of 1946.

The Crop in Fiction

George Wylie Henderson, who some years back with his first novel, *Ollie Miss,* raised expectations of a promising talent in the southern regional school, has not shown appropriate maturity in his recent novel, *Jule* (Creative Age). Jule's progress from peasant boyhood in Alabama to half-awakened manhood in Harlem, his dilemmas of adjustment, social and economic, and his eventual defeatist retreat to the South and his first love, Bertha Mae, are not told with sufficient insight and projection either to make Jule completely real or his fate sufficiently moving. Too colorless in narrative style and too superficial in characterization, this character study barely rises above the plane of melodrama or breaks the shell of formula, thereby proving an important point for the future work both of Mr. Henderson and all others,—that the mere novelty feature of Negro subject-matter has about vanished with the present-day audience, and only skillful characterization and projection can hope to succeed. Except for the printers' union and the interracial friendship episodes, this novel scarcely enlarges a formula already threadbare,—the race novel of vain struggle against odds. When, incidentally, will our novelists realize that countless Negroes successfully meet these same odds? Not that we call for non-defeatist novels *per se*, but must insist that both in life and fiction, character counts.

But just as character must play a vital role in the interaction with environment, it should not, on the other extreme, play a seemingly improbable, wishful role; and that is the defect of another type of weakly conceived race novel, represented by *Mrs. Palmer's Honey* (Doubleday). This race Cinderella who blossoms from model servant to social reformer is another wishful version of life. Not that it couldn't happen; but countless writers, especially those on both sides of the color-line, intent on moralizing in fiction, forget the basic essentials of good and effective art discovered and rediscovered by all incisive aestheticians since Aristotle,—that in a work of fiction, the truth must be more than possible or even probable, it must seem inevitable. The best sociological intentions often make the worst dramas and novels.

Just for the record, three other relatively weak novels must be mentioned, all of which too feebly challenge the more or less trite formulae of their respective plots,—Edward Kimbrough's *Night Fire* (Rinehart); Cid Roberts Sumner's *Quality* (Bobbs-Merrill); and John Henry Hewlett's *Cross on the Moon* (Whittlesey House). Of the three, the last, analyzing as it does the psychological perplexities of a sensitive white child in the pettinesses of a small Georgia town, is the least trite and accordingly the most successful. Here again, the racial situation is not enough by itself; if vivid essential humanity is lacking, no amount of race drama will bring a character or story to life.

Edmund Fuller's novel of Frederick Douglass' epic career, *A Star Pointed North* (Harper), although a part-failure, is of different caliber. Here is a pathbreaker, having historical verity and sincere character conception, and for that very reason, it is significantly worth while. It would be difficult to find a more carefully studied piece of historical narration; in fact, over-meticulous regard for fact may be the cause of its loss of the full force of fiction. Somehow the vividness, brighter in the earlier chapters of Fred's boyhood, youth and dramatic escape, fades out into wanly dramatized history in the later episodes of Douglass with John Brown, Lincoln and Andrew Johnson. But even so, two positive contributions are to Mr. Fuller's credit—a permanently valuable period documentation of the all too sketchy outlines of Douglass' own autobiography and a vindication of the potentialities of the historic novel of heroic Negro achievement. It is not without significance, in this connection, that the Julius Messner Award went to Shirley Graham for a yet to be published dramatic narrative on the life of Douglass, *There Once Was a Slave*. Both a great American play and a great American novel lie dormant in the life-story of this symbolically great man.

On grander, more colorful but less socially significant canvas, Frank Yerby has written *The Foxes of Harrow* (Dial)—a romantic historical best-seller. Superior to most novels of this genre in his carefully drawn historical background of early 19th century New Orleans, Yerby's smooth romancing accomplishes an interesting tour de force, giving him the right to a vast audience and a deeper influence when and if he should later choose to write more seriously realistic fiction, whether of Negro life or American life in general. Surely that is any writer's privilege, and it is significant to see a Negro author shake free of the conventional confinement to racial themes and strictly serious social objectives. Even the cliches of *The Foxes* are racially harmless, which is more than can be said for most other southern period romances, and its popular success will be an enfranchising encouragement to other Negro writers who may aspire to the neutral but rewarding field of entertainment fiction. When, moreover, the separate but intertwined strands of white and Negro life do cross in Yerby's book, they are held in firm and honest balance, strictly true to fact, and occasionally even in ironic contrast as in the episode of the white women watching their menfolk at the Quadroon Ball from the curtained ambush of the family carriage drawn up outside. And if, as is announced, his next novel is to be of Reconstruction instead of patrician ante-bellum New Orleans, it is not at all unlikely that Mr. Yerby will have a significant say on the more serious side of black-white relations.

The one novel that could not have been written before the last war, *Lights Out* (Morrow), though not great, is also a pathbreaking revelation of what we may eventually expect when that experience matures in the minds of the younger generation. The blinded soldier who forms a close friendship with a Negro ward-mate, only to discover long after by accident that his friend Joe Morgan is Negro, more than conveys an individual dilemma: the whole irrationality of prejudice is epitomized in the simple but poignant situations of their psychological predicament. And great praise to Baynard Kendrick's true conception of art, not all of the predicament is located in the white southerner, Larry Nevins' mind: Joe has his difficulties as well as his hurts. If a fine matured French hand, master of psychological depiction, could have handled this situation, a 20th century classic could have emerged. As it is, the courageous readjustment on both sides, the war-born psychological reconstruction of an honest but traditionally prejudiced mind, and the projection of that on his insistence in including his fiancee and his circle of friends is a real subject-matter contribution to the fiction of the race question. The force of fiction in social reform is much underestimated and little utilized, far too little, and yet it is most effective when it is furthest from deliberate propaganda, as indeed it is, in this case.

The artistic success of the year is, of course, Ann Petry's *The Street* (Houghton Mifflin). It is in the first place a novel without ulterior good intentions, other than the best of artistic intentions to tell the truth vividly, honestly, objectively. Lutie's struggle on her own behalf and that of her son against the disintegrating influences of a slum neighborhood, even though full of the minutest and most well-observed local color of Harlem, is universally human, and to that it owes its great human appeal. Of course, it is deftly embroidered with the particularisms of Negro life, but not in "this is another world" style of so many "Harlem stories." Local color carries only its share of the story; the main burden is borne by probably the deftest characterization skill of any Negro novelist to date; for Mrs. Petry's characters, etched out vignette fashion at first and then etched over in later episodes, eventually stand out fully and intimately known. From the inner logic of their personalities as well as from the environmental forces that bear down upon them the story flows with a sense of conviction and inevitability, even down to its tragic end. Some critics have felt Lutie's tragedy as slayer of her lover and the unsolved life problem of the son are defeatist: to me they are the cleverest kind of social indictment, — Zolaesque, if that be not too superlative as praise. More than half the characters, Jones; his bedraggled wife, — Min Jones; the "super"; Mrs. Hedges — the unforgettable Mrs. Hedges, are Hogarth characters. They symbolize the environment which made them, and in realism, that is the height of art. Not only should we await with high anticipation the further work of this talented novelist and story-teller, we should hail this quiet, courageous, unsentimental realism as a substantial contribution to the true and effective novel of race.

Poetry and Belles Lettres

Poetry, once the crown of Negro creative output, has grown so withered that it may seem ungrateful to question critically any respectable volume of verse. Owen Dodson's *Powerful Long Ladder* (Farrar, Straus) is certainly that, and would be more but for the unsatisfied expectation that by this time so promiseful a talent would have come to maturity. But competent as most of it is, and distinctive as some poems are, the total impression of the volume is still that of a poet in search of a style. True enough, for those who belong to a transitional generation, there is always the inescapable dilemma of being caught between two contrary-minded aesthetics; still, one has ultimately to choose, if for no other reason than to achieve proper fusion of style and integration of feeling. Whereas to remain in doubt as whether to be racial or generic, introspective or expressionist, symbolic or realistic, mystic or socially oriented, is to hover rather ineffectually in a poetic void, with only the cold comfort of facility in rhythm, words and phrases.

Last year was rather rich in biography; this year is unusually lean. Era Bell Thompson's autobiographic *American Daughter* (Chicago) is the chief offering. The childhood and youth spent in the rural Northwest, with its comparative absence of race bias or even race consciousness, give this honest, good-humored, almost naive life story a touch of real novelty; her late discovery of race in Chicago and the East makes it a wholly worthwhile social document. In the background of Iowa, the Dakotas and Minnesota, she was just plain, middle-class American, full of the natural democracy of the plains. In Chicago, she becomes an advantaged and charmingly quizzical reporter of the complexities and inconsistencies of the American mind on race. Particularly because the level of experience is middle-class, the book will be revealing to any reader who wants a plain, unvarnished but at the same time truly inside account of what race looks like from the viewpoint of an intelligent and psychologically well-compensated Negro woman. Between the lines, she preaches a plain American creed of just being human, — where and when you can.

In its second publication — *To Master, A Long Goodnight* — the Creative Age Press has made a real contribution to the year's literature of race, just as has the author to historical research and sociological criticism. Mr. Gysin in his biographical study of Josiah Henson, prototype of Uncle Tom in Mrs. Stowe's novel, very cleverly passes over from an historical account of the original character to an analysis of the tradition which converted this melodramatic and sympathy-evoking abolitionist stereotype into the reactionary stereotype of the contented slave and cringing servitor. Recalling that the original Uncle Tom was a fugitive slave and active collaborator in the anti-slavery movement instead of a contented retainer is, of course, most salutary, and it becomes a sharp reminder that yesterday's liberalisms too often become today's conservatisms. Nothing perhaps more vividly points up the changed psychological climate of race today than such a contrast, for in its original context Mrs. Stowe's characterization was beneficent and helpful, even though it was a highly fictionalized and one-sided version of Henson. But it is not only the shifted emphasis of Mrs. Stowe's characterization which makes today's difference; it is due even more to the psychological transformation that two generations have effected both within the Negro himself and upon what society sees in the Negro. It is as reflecting this that *To Master, A Long Goodnight* is most significant

Katherine Dunham's *Journey to Accompong* (Holt), dressed up as a rather casual narrative of a month's visit to the mountain village of the Maroons in the highlands of Jamaica, is really an important contribution to the study of surviving African folklore. With the tradition crumbling, Miss Dunham was able to arrive just in time to rescue the remaining few of their old instruments, and by way of winning their confidence, finally not only to witness their oldest, most traditional dances but to secure initiation into the Obeah rites as a parting favor. Both on historical and internal evidence, the older customs of this mountain-fastness community are direct survivals from ancestral Africa, and it is of great value to have them even sketchily recorded. Already they are layers deep beneath later acquired customs, but they finally came to the surface as Miss Dunham won the confidence of several of the oldest inhabitants. One thing should be stressed, that in addition to the tact and the anthropological experience which helped open the way, her passport of color was an important, perhaps a decisive factor. Anthropological research has time and again ignored this fact and has lost much by disdaining the use of the Negro investigator. Of course, the researcher must be properly trained, and skillful in the arts of personal approach, but no reader of the remarkable results accomplished by this sojourn of a month can doubt the effectiveness of color as an open sesame.

One anticipates eagerly the incorporation in Miss Dunham's choreography of some of the Koromantee dance materials which she collected; all the more eagerly because the synthetic tinsel of Broadway has begun to overdo and cover up her original folk-materials. It is to be hoped that the journey to Accompong will revivify her art, and make it even more racially true and representative. The social survivals are quite as interesting as the musical and dance forms; so the few remaining reservoirs of African survivals on this continent should be speedily and competently investigated.

Another incisive bit of folklore research and analysis is Rudi Blesh's *Shining Trumpets: A History of Jazz* (Knopf). Mr. Blesh brings to his task the triple qualifications of an ardent jazz fan, a skilled musicologist, and a careful folklorist. To date, this is the definitive analysis of jazz and its derivations, even though I find myself in disagreement with such obiter dicta as his disparagement of Handy in favor of Jelly Roll Morton re the early history of the "blues." Granted that Morton was nearer the original sources, Handy's role and services should not be minimized. At that stage, around 1910, only a diluted and partly synthetic blues could have captured the public ear, and but for that original vogue the history of jazz might well have been the sad story of another one of those folk idioms that died out at the folk level. The popular vogue of jazz, just like that of the spirituals, functioned to preserve a precious legacy for posterity. Musical scholarship can today lead us back to the pure folk-roots, mainly because the plant has flourished instead of withering. The documentation of *Shining Trumpets*, historical, photographic, in musical analysis as well as in the discography, is most painstaking, competent and complete. Students as well as lovers of jazz will be long indebted to Rudi Blesh.

Historical and Sociological Works

Into what is now an arena of gladiatorial struggle, the champions of democracy seem to have come at last to close quarter combat with their opponents. Not since the era of abolitionism have the issues been so tightly and uncompromisingly drawn. Race really is a dominant issue of our thinking about democracy; and the stage of academic discussion being almost past, pragmatic action is being advocated more and more.

For that very reason, it is unfortunate that the Macmillan Centenary Award went to an unrepresentative book, *A Negro's Faith in America* (Macmillan) — unrepresentative on two counts, first, that it does not represent the present militant temper of our younger generation, nor the similar attitudes of our liberal friends, including, happily, many reconstructed southerners. Together they agree on seeing this issue as crucial both for the country at large and the Negro, and would prefer defeat to compromise. Not that all of Spencer Logan's points are unsustained; he himself in his chapter "The Harlems of America" says: "The Negro of the city is caught in the web of the struggle to survive at its worst" and later, — "certain changes in our economic life will be a matter of national expediency." It then is, even in Mr. Logan's own analysis, a situation of crisis, which ill comports with his general overall attitude of faith and promise. His enthusiastic acceptance of many merely palliative programs and agencies as still significant and potential today shows superficiality of social insight and experience; in short the book is a sophomoric version of the contemporary racial situation.

Deeply different is Margaret Halsey's courageous and incisive *Color Blind* (Simon Schuster), perhaps the prize book of the year in spite of all its unpretentiousness. Out of the experience of the bravely democratic Stage Door Army Canteen, Miss Halsey experienced a front-line initiation into the color-line frontier of race. Out of that experience has come one of the most clarifying analyses of race relations ever written. Candor and courage were her passports to the inner psychological recesses of the question, taboo with so many other analysts. Sex, intermarriage, the color-line within the color-line, class reactions among Negroes, racial hypersensitiveness, — all are faced unblinkingly and accordingly with great profit of clarified understanding. Felicity of phrase goes hand in hand with virtuosity of insight; Miss Halsey speaks "of the 'Solid South' and the 'Frozen North,' of the fact that practical steps toward racial democracy do not increase the prejudice of prejudiced people: they only make it more articulate." She clearly sees that "the economic and the sexual aspects of race relationships in the United States are inextricably intertwined. By this expedient of concealing an economic motive with sexual red herrings, many well-meaning white people are confused." One could go on endlessly — but for a final sample, — "The pragmatist — with his eye on the main objective of minimizing prejudice — has not one, but two reactions to prejudiced Southerners. The wish of these Southerners to corrupt American democracy cannot be allowed to go unchallenged. No amount of terror gives them the right to lower the ethical standards of the country and to cause those standards to fall into disrepute. But the pragmatist also understands that terror-stricken people are not pretty and do not behave well, and that the way to make them pretty and well conducted is to attack, not what they do, but the hallucinations which are responsible for what they do." Here pragmatic action and commonsense put a keen cutting edge on the lessons of sociology, anthropology, social psychology, and it is only in that way that reason will be to any very practical degree a solvent of the difficult American traditions and mores of race.

Proof that the realistic and enlightened approach will convert southerner, northerner, Negro and white alike is to be found in such forthright volumes as Ruth Smith's *White Man's Burden* (Vanguard), and Stetson Kennedy's *Southern Exposure* (Doubleday), the latter being particularly objective and outspoken. Kennedy speaks of "that subversion of democracy in the South by the poll-tax, white primary, antiunionism and race prejudice," clearly exposing the subtle combination most responsible. How wise, too, is Mr. Kennedy in saying: "there is an unfortunate propensity on the part of many Southerners, white and Negro, to regard prejudice as the *sine qua non* of race relations, and to overemphasize the role of education in combating it." "So long as white supremacy remains an economic and political reality, no amount of education or agitation or mental therapy can bring about the abolition of segregation in the South by the South . . . The Southern Negro must be emancipated economically and politically before he can be emancipated socially. This means he must first join democratic labor unions and beat a democratic path to the polls. Once those two things have been accomplished — gains in one will facilitate gains in the other — the abolition of Jim Crow will be as inevitable as the abolition of chattel slavery after the Civil War broke out. Once the political and economic functions of Jim Crow have been negated, its social aspect will vanish as the subterfuge that it is." Again, forthright words, and they are a southerner's words.

In spite of such reservations about the power of educative measures, one of the main fronts of the new struggle for race equality is the educational. Huszar's resourceful anthology, — *Anatomy of Racial Intolerance* (Wilson), Herrick and Askwith's *This Way to Unity* (Oxford), are welcome new storehouses of the scientific and educational ammunition for this fight. More important still is *Minority Problems in the Schools* (Harper), Brameld's account of actual school procedures by which teachers in many city centers are marshalling their professional energies and resources in an organized campaign for teaching American youth the principles and the attitudes of democracy. At least for youth, not yet indoctrinated and routinated in the ways of prejudice, this approach is promising and, in all likelihood, effective. We simply cannot afford to minimize or neglect any of the possible fronts of the democratic struggle, whatever our opinions as to the key salient or the most rewarding strategy. That the issue is being joined on so many fronts simultaneously is the real new hope in the present-day situation.

Turning briefly to the historical material, we note two welcome additions, — Bernard Nelson's doctoral thesis on *The 14th Amendment and the Negro since* 1920 (Catholic University), documenting the swing back to its original civil rights objectives under recent decisions of the U. S. Supreme Court, and another doctoral study, — Brailsford Brazeal's careful account of the early struggles for labor unionization by the Brotherhood of Sleeping Car Porters and their subsequently successful history as the first Negro labor union.

But with Robert Weaver's *Negro Labor: A National Problem* (Harcourt, Brace), we are back on the level of applied scholarship, which with no loss of academic competence, adds the important dimension of social guidance. From a rich background of war-agency experience, Mr. Weaver fully justifies his diagnosis of the Negro's status in industry as a national problem. While not staking the whole issue on governmental control and protection, the author evidently regards the New Deal concepts and mechanisms of legislation against racial discrimination in industry and overall planning for sustained if not full employment as the sanest and surest roads to economic justice and peace. The recently improved general position of the Negro worker is, therefore, still insecure and highly dependent on the trends of reconversion. This, in addition to its valuable data on the recent labor history of the Negro in wartime, is the clear and momentous warning of an important, penetrating analysis.

Buell Gallagher sub-titles his brave and forthright book, — *Color and Conscience* (Harper), "The Irrepressible Conflict." He is right in harking back to the days of abolitionism, both for historical parallels and for the proper moral frame of reference. However, it is his realistic contemporaneity, which added to the historical analysis, gives his book its unique place among the moral and religious discussions of the race question. Gallagher, an ardent believer in social Christianity, admits no disjunction between theory and practice, a position which happily many churchmen are returning to after years, almost generations, of temporizing and compromise. Says he: "We know what we ought to do. If we try . . ., and fail, we shall at least have made the effort. . . . If we fail to try, we are then exposed as the hypocrites we shall have become, permitting moralizing to take the place of moral action. If we try, and succeed, we bring the whole family of God within the circle of brotherhood. That is where we belong." Nor does Dr. Gallagher ignore the secular arguments; on the contrary he stresses them, particularly the fact that the contemporary world situation clearly indicates that social democracy is the only safe choice for the survival of Western and Christian civilization.

It is because religious liberals are beginning to think and act in such realistic but at the same time logical fashion that there is renewed hope for some early progress toward racial and social and cultural democracy. The identification of one with the other is itself manifest evidence of a new age of reason on the subject of race. One cannot, of course, expect social enlightenment automatically to convert itself into social reform, but one is a necessary preface to the other, and throughout history they have never been far apart. We have reached our century's cross-roads point on the crucial matter of race.

A CRITICAL RETROSPECT OF THE LITERATURE OF THE NEGRO FOR 1947

THERE can be little doubt that we have entered an era of crisis literature and crisis art, when even our fiction reflects, like a sorcerer's mirror, instead of the face of society, the crucial inner conflict and anxiety of society itself. Our artists increasingly become social critics and reformers as our novelists are fast becoming strident sociologists and castigating prophets. One has to go back a long while to discover an analogous age, and even then, we miss today the wit and satire of a literature of urbane social criticism, for our artists feel too co-guilty with their fellows and seem to wince before the terror of some impending doomsday.

In the better fiction certainly, and surprisingly enough in much of the popular fiction, sociology is at a premium, often at the expense of style. Race as a symbol of social misunderstanding has become fully recognized as the great tragedy of our time, both nationally and internationally. And as surely as in a previous decade, art was in the saddle, now it is sociology that sits, for better or worse. Too often, from the point of view of art, it is for the worse, but not always, as some of the rare combinations of talent show how possible it is to reconcile good sociology with good art. By the span of less than a month an admirable example escapes the calendar classification of a 1947 book, but Alan Paton's *Cry, The Beloved Country* must nevertheless be mentioned as just such an outstanding instance. Yet among the books of 1947, several approach this ideal balance, among them, Jacques Roumain's *Masters of the Dew*, Wilfred Hambly's *Jamba* and in a more limited way, Willard Motley's *Knock On Any Door*. But we still have no twentieth century Zola, *Kingsblood Royal* nothwithstanding. We are, it seems, on the way. However, in less than no time, that conjunction of art and sociology will recur, and I predict it will be the novel of race which achieves it, and maybe a Negro writer. If so, we will then have produced our first Negro-American novelist or short story writer of first magnitude.

Indeed, no white or Negro fictionist seems as yet to have fully realized how much art it takes to hold in smooth suspension the heavy sociology of racial issues and interracial tensions. It cannot be easy when a veteran novelist like Sinclair Lewis all but fails and has to

Phylon 9 (First Quarter 1948): 3–12

resort to periodic dashes of satire and in the end, inconclusive melo-drama to keep his story vital and moving. Eventually, though, all practised exponents of the "race novel" will learn never to rely primarily on the inherent drama and tragedy of their material, but to put their trust in style, which alone can make these narratives soar and sing. Since Jean Toomer's *Cane* in 1923 I can recall few passages that really made the fictional projection of race come to life as great fiction, but this year another novel of fragile proportions does so. It is Jacques Roumain's *Masters of the Dew,* an incandescent work of art for all its deep and heavy sociological implications. But that credit must go to the Haitian rather than the North American account. Our nearest recent approach to masterful presentation seems to be Willard Motley's *Knock On Any Door,* which does have epic surge and scope and downright narrative power. However, this is only a race novel by implication. As a challenging sociological novel and the work of a newcomer in the ranks of Negro fiction writers, *Knock On Any Door* must be rated a singularly successful welding of good sociology and good art, with Zolaesque power and promise. If Mr. Motley's subsequent output keeps this pace and level, he will outdistance the competitor talents of Richard Wright, Chester Himes and Ann Petry.

It is interesting to observe the shifting fortunes of our Negro novelists. Several do not maintain altitude, so to speak, after having gotten relatively high on the wing. Only increasing competition and the most zealous cultivation of maturity of style will assure them of secure status and permanently significant stature. Since they are all sociological realists, let them all re-read Zola.

That this is a common predicament in this particular field of contemporary letters and no special handicap of the Negro "race novel", however, is clearly shown by analogous weaknesses in Laura Hobson's novel of anti-Semitism, *Gentleman's Agreement,* of Gwenthalyn Graham's *Earth and High Heaven,* of Arthur Miller's *Focus,* of even Arthur Koestler's *Thieves in the Night.* All these, successes of content and conception are considerably less than unqualified successes of literary execution and style. But the encouraging side to all this is the increasing lure of the subject, not only for novelists, but for the general reading public. With last year's persistence of these titles on the best sellers' lists, the theme of interracial tension and intolerance may become a beaten path to today's big audience. Such a vogue will in due course produce its one or more great masters, and should also pivot revolutionary changes of public thought and social behavior. "Ideas of the times" usually do.

In *Kingsblood Royal,* with careful and conscientious documentation both of white middle-class prejudice and Negro middle-class living, Sinclair Lewis pries open for the general reader two closed precincts of American life. That in itself is a great service toward breaking down or through the psychological walls of American pride and prejudice. Neil Kingsblood, who begins with seeing the Negro only through the orthodox peep-hole of his colored servant, finds himself exploring the middle-class Negro life of his community, after discovering by chance that he, too, has Negro ancestry and is in the traditional code of race a "Negro". His increasing identification breeds resentment of the prejudices he once espoused, and in a heated argument at his club, he owns up to his mixed ancestry. Here at the very point when a great artist would have focussed the confusion and dilemma of the white mind, Sinclair Lewis, hound-bent on taking the reader across the "color line", plumps Neil, a too swift and too willing ex-white man, into the heart of the life and struggles of his 'black brethren' on the Negro side of his home town. Ostracism, the loss of his bank job, the complete espousal of his Negro friends and their lot, the mob raid on his home that he is asked to vacate because of a restrictive covenant, all logical enough in the sequence of American race prejudice, turn somehow to strained melodrama and incessant sheet-lightning of satire instead of becoming the terrifying crash and thunder of the high tragedy potentially there. This is not ingratitude for a social service sincerely and gallantly rendered, but rather critical grief over a worthy objective only half-fulfilled.

Worth Tuttle Hedden's *The Other Room* similarly states a novel approach and an unusually deep projection into the psychological heart of the race question. This time, it is the dilemma of a liberal white woman, bewildered, sympathetic but only half-accepted as a faculty member of a Southern Negro school. The barriers of suspicion and counter-prejudice work both ways, and Nina Lathem's love affair with Leon Warwick, a Negro colleague, is only paper tragedy, not for lack of courage in statement of the situation but by reason of inability to make the reader feel its impact. A Zola would have vitalized the dilemma of the South by contrasting the ease of a mixed romance between a white man and a Negro woman with this unorthodox situation of the white woman and a Negro man. Again, a high tragedy or searing problem novel would have ensued instead of a well-intentioned parable. Once more, no ingratitude. Each time a little wider angle and a longer focus atone for the deficiencies in ultimate, definitive social portraiture, and the average reader can have sounder sociology to read and, if he will, better social insight and understanding. That consists, in *The Other Room*, of a competent portrayal, for the first time, of interacting white and Negro characters on a professional level in the sustained associations of a mixed faculty of a Negro missionary college.

The stereoscopic realism which the two foregoing novels have lacked an English novelist has achieved in a fine war novel of racial intolerance. By a double panel portrayal of a Negro G I's love for an English girl and an English soldier friend's subsequent courtship and marriage of a native Burmese girl, Nevil Shute broadens and deepens the treatment of the basic theme. Since each romance confronts, as is the usual case, the opposition of some friends and the approval of others, the balance of social forces is honestly analyzed and this novel, taking advantage of its World War background, reasonably achieves fair statement of the issues and a challenging answer subtly suggestive of the "oneness of mankind". Leslie Walker's *Show Me the Way* is a more melodramatic but less competent version of the same problem. Wally Blanchard is a heartening portrait of younger generation liberalism, forged by the experiences of soldiering in our armed forces. It documents both the anti-Jewish and the anti-Negro prejudices in concrete action and honest proportions, and in Weaver, the Negro GI, a significant aspect of the American dilemma has been presented, not as a mere incident but as the internal drama of the white mind that it really is.

In *Lonely Crusade,* Chester Himes portrays in Lee Gordon a psychological, almost psycho-pathological study of a Negro, half defeated by prejudice but fighting vicariously as a convinced but almost hysterical labor organizer. His personal involvements in the cross currents and animosities of working class life in wartime Los Angeles document, also for the first time extensively, the inner dilemmas of this milieu. Yet the net result is weak art and over-tinctured sociology. In a criticism in *Opportunity* Philip Butcher spots the likely seat of the weakness in what he aptly styles Himes' "unilluminating concern with violence", which of course in *Lonely Crusade* smolders and fumes rather than flames and purges.

Brand Millen's *Albert Sears* demonstrates again how fast the stereotypes and the stock situations are going into the discard. His setting is the invasion line of the disintegrating white residence area and the expanding black ghetto in Jersey City, and it is not only well delineated but brings new interracial contacts to public view. Sears, a stubborn white character, decides to stay in the mixed neighborhood, where he has an illegitimate son, Al, as well as a more orthodox family. He befriends the Mannhursts, a border-line Negro family, who in turn become his friends. Around them swirl the divided forces of society, depicted with quiet but courageous veracity by the author. This twilight zone where the more typical race contacts of the contemporary generation really are taking place is to become, no doubt, one of the classic mileus of the new liberal fiction of race. *Albert Sears* not only pioneers this significantly, but suggests that class and caste have common denominators.

What *Albert Sears* suggests, Motley's *Knock On Any Door* explicitly states. Though superficially incorrect to claim this book as race fiction, at heart it really is. For not only has it been referred to aptly as another *Native Son,* since Nick Romano, its Italian hero is under the skin another Bigger Thomas, but it carries the Wright thesis several dramatic steps forward. As in *Native Son,* society is the protagonist, but Motley broadens the Zolaesque indictment to a common denominator of class and environment rather than mere race and environment. This is a net gain, both artistically and sociologically. In this book Motley joins the challenging company of Farrell and Wright, and should he turn to the race novel may create its *Studs Lonnigan.*

Alden Bland's *Behold A Cry* is a novel of the personal triangle of wife, mistress and desertion as well as of the economic triangle of labor, capital and race, set in World War I, Chicago. Ed Tyler's final desertion and the unsolved dilemma of his wife and children, beyond introducing a promising new Negro writer, adds little to the fundamental documentation of current Negro life. Whereas Phyllis Whitney's *Willow Hill,* though not too strong artistically, does freshly document a new milieu in the race novel, that of adolescent youth in the mixed society of a Chicago high school. For that as well as for its optimistic democracy, it deserves attention.

One surely need not worry over the sociological scope and accuracy of today's fiction of Negro life. The chief concern from now on must be its artistic power of penetration and its force of artistic projection. We can even spare, with only a twinge of regret, the loss of such capable narrative talent as that of Frank Yerby, who with his second best-seller, *The Vixens,* deserts seriously intentioned fiction for the pot-boiler market.

Yerby's only distinction now dwindles to his pathbreaking invasion of the field of general fiction in his successful first novel, *The Foxes of Harrow.* We now have more and better examples in Motley and in Ann

Petry's second novel, *Country Place*. But the latter, for all its needle-point competence, has neither the surge nor the social significance of her first novel, *The Street*. Ann Petry has deeply studied and carefully documented her setting, and it has the distinction of being an authentic cross section of New England town life instead of a vignetted Harlem ghetto. Yet it says nothing of grand importance and, while neatly re-flecting social atmosphere, has, if anything, less power of character delineation than the memorable characters of 116th Street. This is not said to advocate our writers confining themselves to the racial milieu as one into which they have inevitable emotional projection, but only to warn that as they move out to mainstream, they must look to their literary keels and be capable of breasting the ocean swells of single standard comparison and competition.

Negro fiction beyond the domestic scene seems suddenly to have burst into creative bloom and maturity. We have already mentioned the 1948 sensation of Paton's *Cry, The Beloved Country;* now comes the even more welcome appearance of a strong novel by a South African native, Peter Abraham's *The Path of Thunder*. One cannot doubt that these are not the offshoots of the world ferment of color and the har-bingers of a new important province of racial fiction. But already in 1947 there was work of considerable significance, which must be re-viewed all too briefly. Kurt Sachs has a good novel of culture conflict in *Black Anger*, his story of a Johannesburg medicine man, John Chava-fambira. Within the old pagan tradition, it would be hard to find a more sympathetic and artistic a portrait of African tribal life than Wilfred Hambly's beautifully conceived *Jamba*. And of course, *Masters of the Dew* is brilliantly successful on three scores, as sociology of the small native village life of Haiti, as a tensely vital proletarian novel, and first and last as a prose poem of poetic fiction with dialogue, characterization and atmosphere all masterfully delineated. On the level of folklore, Courlander and Hertzog also have brought us authentic and exhili-rating African folk-tale and imagination in the *Cow-Tail Switch* volume.

Poetry and Belles Lettres

Sadly enough, the significant poetry volume of 1947 is a valedictory rather than the hailing of new talent. Countee Cullen's *On These I Stand* is only a self-culled anthology with six fragile unpublished poems added. They sadly tell the story of a dimmed talent, and its cause, which was not the decline of technical power but a personal retreat from the world of significant outer experience without any compensa-tory opening up of a world of internal experience. This narrowing of social vision and immersion in the mere charm and magic of words whis-pered its way out to lines of sentimental deftness, like "Goodnight, dear friends and gentle hearts", while yet capable of such magnificent bursts as these from his translation of Baudelaire's "Death to the Poor" "Ec-static sleep/ In easier beds than those we had before/ Death is the face of God." Ironically Cullen's widest social vision was in his youth; there it was based on a sensitive heart and a passionate love of race. No in-tellectual maturing replaced it when it lost its youthful ardor, Cullen shrank from reality, perhaps, because it wore the frightening mask of prejudice. Even our poets of the virile school, Langston Hughes, Sterling Brown and Waring Cuney speak only intermittently at present. These are fallow years for Negro poetry.

Historically reminiscent, but hopefully and encouragingly so, is Mrs. Edith Isaac's critical review of the Negro actor and his place in the American Theatre. *The Negro in the American Theatre* is all the more important because told in the overall context of the development of the drama of American life, on which Mrs. Isaacs, as the godmother through *Theatre Arts* of serious American drama, speaks with authority and intimate insight. The story of the Negro's part in all this and of his progressive integration with it profits greatly through being told as an integral part of the general story. That is the great virtue of a book which adds to a well documented and beautifully illustrated panorama of Negro drama and the Negro actor this unique contribution of a humane, universal and uncondescending approach. For that very reason, though generally optimistic, Mrs. Isaacs' gentle but penetrating criticisms should be well heeded by Negro actors and playwrights, for for nearly three decades Negro drama has had no more consistent and constructive a friend.

Shirley Graham's dynamic biography of Frederick Douglass, *There Once Was A Slave*, added to its intrinsic worth the acclaim of the Messner Prize Award. Within the modest specifications of a popular biography, it perfoms a much needed service. It is not definitive biography, however, which is gratuitous to mention doubtless, since it does not claim to be. Whereas Mary White Ovington's autobiography, *The Walls Came Tumbling Down*, being a first-hand narrative, might have been expected to be more definitive a history of the NAACP than it really turns out to be. Anecdotal and personalistic, it adds interesting facets of the equal rights movement since 1909, but hardly gives the depth or perspective to be rated as an official inside story of the movement, Miss Ovington's official and inside connection notwithstanding.

Mbonu Ojike's second book of experiences, *I Have Two Countries*, lacks the firm narrative skill of his narration of his African youth and childhood. But it is an important documentation of the attitudes and struggles of an important segment of our group leadership — those American trained Africans who are trying to build bridges of understanding between us and our African confreres. We must not only share their experiences but more and more must help ourselves by helping them and their cause.

Selden Rodman and The Quadrangle Press have paid the definitive tribute to the late Horace Pippin in a beautiful portfolio listing and reproducing all of his work. Its thoroughness assures that this phenomenal talent is safely embalmed for future study and reference. In addition the critical analysis is a splendid, even though provocative interpretation. It, too, because of the regard for first hand source materials on Pippin, will stand for a long while as the definitive interpretation of his work. Those who think they know the Negro artist merely by knowing Tanner have much to learn of Negro art today by the knowledge of Pippin which now becomes possible by means of this monograph.

History and Sociology

Good social science, though its main virtues are those of scientific truth, needs at least the reenforcement of good style to be influential. That virtue John Hope Franklin's definitive history of the "Negro Peoples", *From Slavery to Freedom*, has to a unique and most laudable degree. Here once more the main gain is in careful integration of the

Negro minority's history with the overall majority history of which it has been a part. Too much Negro history writing in the past has either ignored this or executed it feebly. By adding to this a panoramic comprehensiveness not previously attempted for the Negro in Africa, the Caribbean, Canada and South America is included in the scope of the volume, and by weaving in the important strands of economic and cultural history, Dr. Franklin has brought forth for the general reader of this decade what may likely be the definitive one-volume history of the Negro.

The Liberian Centenary has appropriately called forth two books of Liberian history; one for the general reader, the other, obviously for the historical archives. Dr. Huberich, legal adviser to the Liberian government, has compiled an exhaustive two-volume legislative and official record to which the interpretative historians will later go for factual data. Charles Wilson's book is so keyed to the layman's interests that it is in large part descriptive journalism rather than proper history. It fills a need, however, and makes intelligible both the progress and the lack of progress in this potentially important country. Fully justified in his criticism of Americo-Liberian leadership, Mr. Wilson would have been in better balance to have added more facts on the neglect of Liberia until very recently by her logical sponsor and tutor, the United States.

In the field of applied sociology, Dr. Charles S. Johnson, in each case with staff collaboration, has given us useful summarization of the trends in two important areas. *Into the Main Stream* chronicles the recent projects and policies of interracial adjustment in the South, and paints, incidentally, a reassuring picture of progressive trends in this region; while *People vs. Property* gives a useful summary of the restrictive covenant situation and the struggle against the black residential ghetto. Another approach to the same issues comes from Bucklin Moon's *The High Cost of Prejudice,* which in a most realistic and provocative way takes stock of the social losses of American prejudice. Mr. Moon's titles tell his argument pointedly, "Unions Within Unions", "Are Two Armies Better Than One", "Representatives Who Represent Nobody", "What Doesn't Show" (the education record), "Sales Resistance Abroad". Any careful reader will have to admit that Mr. Moon proves his case; the great question is what dent can be made in the public mind by using this type of ammunition. For it is Mr. Moon's thesis that a price appraisal of prejudice will strike at the crucial focus of American thinking. That remains to be seen, but the attempt is worth inaugurating. Of course, if so, professional publicity must be put behind such a campaign. Dr. Richardson has undertaken a far less extensive debit analysis on the Negro rural church in *Dark Glory.* Here, too, the little known facts are staggering in their report of wasted opportunity and general social losses.

Dr. DuBois in *The World and Africa* has put the general reader deeply in debt, for he has written a comprehensive analysis of the place of Africa in the modern world in a most unusual combination of readability and competence, of scholarship and sound popularization. Perhaps one should say, dramatization, for that is one of Dr. DuBois's native gifts of style. To have done this for the contemporary importance of Africa and at the same time to give it an historical dimension in a panorama of African history is a feat for any mind, but a marvel from a writer approaching his eightieth birthday. The cumulative force of Dr. DuBois's scholarship and points of view is increasingly being felt and appreciated. Some day a more definitive outline of African history will, of course, have to be written, but until then no one book on Africa will hold as much for the lay reader as this one.

What DuBois has been saying for decades now about the crucial and strategic importance of Africa should in the context of today's world be self-evident. Yet there is still a state approaching apathy on the part of too many American Negroes on this, to them, most vital of all subjects. *Presence Africaine*, a new journal devoted to the intellectual promotion of the Pan-African viewpoint and specifically aiming at linking American Negro intellectuals with their French confreres is worthy both of attention and support. Volume I derives the bulk of its articles from translations of American Negro scholarship and letters. We should not only be interested; we should actively collaborate. If even our race fiction has acquired an international dimension, surely our social and cultural thought must follow through. It really should have pioneered the movement, and among our intellectuals there have been a few, perhaps a half dozen such pioneers. However, it is now high time for a redirection as well as a regalvanizing of our group thinking, for race has now international scope and meaning.

FICTION

Albert Sears, Millen Brand, Simon & Schuster, N. Y. $2.75.

Behold a Cry, Alden Bland, Charles Scribner's Sons, N. Y. $2.50.

Black Anger, Wulf Sachs, Little, Brown, Boston. $3.00.

Chequer Board, The, Nevil Shute, Morrow & Co., N. Y. $2.75.

Country Place, Ann Petry, Houghton, Mifflin, Boston, $2.75.

Cow-Tail Switch, The, and Other African Stories, Courtlander & Hertzog, Holt & Co., N. Y. $2.50.

Jamba, Wilfred Hambly, Pellegrini & Cudahy, Chicago. $2.75.

Kingsblood Royal, Sinclair Lewis, Random House, N. Y. $3.00.

Knock on Any Door, Willard Motley, D. Appleton-Century, N. Y. $3.00.

Lonely Crusade, Chester Himes, Alfred Knopf, N. Y. $3.00.

Masters of the Dew, Jacques Roumain, Reynal & Hitchcock, N. Y. $2.50.

Other Room, The, Worth Tuttle Hedden, Crown Publishers, N. Y. $2.75.

Show Me the Way, Leslie Waller, Viking Press, N. Y. $3.00.

Willow Hill, Phillis Whitney, Reynal & Hitchcock, N. Y. $2.50.

Vixens, The, Frank Yerby, Dial Press, N. Y. $2.75.

BIOGRAPHY, POETRY & BELLES LETTRES

I Have Two Countries, Mbonu Ojike, John Day Co., N. Y. $2.75.

Negro in the American Theatre, The, Edith J. R. Isaacs, Theatre Arts, Inc., N. Y. $3.50.

On These I Stand, Countee Cullen, Harper & Bros., N. Y. $2.50.

There Was Once a Slave, Shirley Graham, Julius Messner, Inc., N. Y. $3.00.

Walls Came Tumbling Down, The, Mary White Ovington, Harcourt, Brace, N. Y. $3.00.

HISTORY & SOCIAL SCIENCE

Clarion, Call, The Negro Peoples Convention Movement, Bella Gross, Private Publisher, N. Y. $0.50.

Dark Glory, Harry V. Richardson, Friendship Press, N. Y. $2.00.

From Slavery to Freedom, John Hope Franklin, Alfred Knopf, N. Y. $5.00.

High Cost of Prejudice, The, Bucklin Moon, Julian Messner, Inc., N. Y. $2.50.

Horace Pippin, Selden Rodman, The Quadrangle Press, N. Y. $12.00.

Into the Mainstream, Charles Johnson & Associates, University of North Carolina Press, Chapel Hill. $3.50.

Liberia 1847-1947, Charles Morrow Wilson, Wm. Sloan Associates, N. Y. $3.75.

Negro Business and Business Education, Joseph A. Pierce, Harper & Bros., N. Y. $4.00.

Negro Handbook, The, ed. by Florence Murray, Current Books, Inc., N. Y. $5.00.

People vs. Property, Herman Long & Charles S. Johnson, Fisk University Press, Nashville. $1.00.

Political and Legislative History of Liberia, The, Charles H. Huberich, Central Book Company, N. Y. $30.00 2 vols.

Presence Africaine—Vol. I: 1947, Paris, Dakar. 80 fr.

World and Africa, The, W. E. B. DuBois, Viking Press, N. Y. $3.00.

DAWN PATROL:
A Review of the Literature of the Negro for 1948

PART I

NEAR the turn of the century, in 1903, Dr. DuBois said prophetically in *Souls of Black Folk*: "The problem of the Twentieth Century is the problem of the color-line." Readers, then and since, even those few who have pondered the deeper meaning of the forecast, could not have possibly foreseen the global significance and proportions of the race question today. But with two World Wars and the threat of a third, with a resurgent Asia and a renascent Africa, the race question has become number one problem of the world. In almost every particular, its issues have transcended their old boundaries and limitations; once domestic and national, they have now become international in scope and influence; previously matters primarily of minority grief and concern, they are becoming even more situations of majority handicap and predicament. Traditionally closet phenomena, covered up with the strongest tabus of the mores, they are now the talk of the hour, the preoccupation of the laboratory, the classroom, the council chamber and the marketplace. As we approach 1950, we come to the realization that behind our economic and political problems, and in large part controlling them, are the more fundamental psychological and cultural dilemmas of human group relations, and that our attitudes and reactions toward them may well determine whether the mid-century decade shall witness the downfall of Western civilization or a dawn of newly integrated cultures. Many of us are deeply concerned to discover whether we are a death-watch or a dawn patrol.

In addition to reflecting this crisis, our contemporary literature, art and drama have promising portents, optimistic hints of new sensitivities of social conscience, of radically enlarged outlooks of human understanding. If they spread, these trends may be crucially reconstructive. Let us be cautious and realistic, for they are as yet only indications. Yet there are recurring signs of many wholesome tendencies; a decided waning of the formerly unquestioned assumption of cultural superiority, a relaxing, at least among the intelligent, of the tensions and fears of race, class and cultural differences, a marked trend toward facing the full facts involved in racial situations, as especially indicated by a fresh curiosity and non-committal neutrality toward intermarriage.

Phylon 10 (First and Second Quarters 1949): 5–14; 167–172.

Sartré, for example, writes with surgical penetration *The Respectful Prostitute,* a drama that skillfully lays bare the sex phobias of American race prejudice in the South. He aptly calls it a "disclosure" rather than an exposé, and it is all the more effective and revealing because it is neither pro-Negro nor anti-Southern by virtue of being pro-fact. A liberal English clergyman, Alan Paton, writes *Cry The Beloved Country* — an unsentimental, but for that very reason a moving novel of the race situation in South Africa, a portrayal unsurpassed for deep and uncondescending identification with the predicaments of the South African native, but as ironic and detached as a fine Greek tragedy. It is not without significance that while meriting the accolade of discerning critics as "the greatest novel of the year," it has brought out the dilemmas and injustices of colonialism to tens of thousands of readers uniquely and probably with incalculable effect. It has almost equal significance that out of South Africa (by way of London, where he now lives safely) should have come from the pen of Peter Abraham, a South African mulatto, *The Path of Thunder,* in my judgment the strongest and most objective portrayal we have yet had of love transcending the color line. *Cry The Beloved Country* and *The Path of Thunder,* one of white, the other of Negro authorship, coming in the same year out of the darkest sector of race and culture conflict, have, I believe, epochal significance. They are beacon signs of clear social vision and uncompromising social courage, and above the darkest murk of prejudice, hate and conflict, they forecast an eventual liberating enlightenment.

This is not sentimental optimism, ignoring the realistic facts of the increasing acuteness of racial issues the world over. The hope that is raised arises not from the situation but from profound change in our attitude toward it. Such books, piercing irrevocably curtains of silence and hypocrisy, have revolutionary significance, and set in motion great reformative influences primarily by forcing us to confront the facts as they are. For then, our minds can no longer harbor conventional illusion and indifference and our consciences cannot plead their customary alibis.

Paton's hero in *Cry The Beloved Country* is the Zulu pastor, Rev. Stephen Kumalo, whose tragic Odyssey from his hillside village church into the Shanty Town ghetto of Johannesburg in search of his errant son and lost sister, mirrors the whole tragedy and injustice of colonial exploitation. His quest ends in factual, but significantly enough, not in spiritual defeat. Yet he discovers the sister a penitent and pregnant prostitute and the son the recently arrested murderer of a white benefactor, whose goodwill interest in the natives has made him the scapegoat victim of the general racial hate and misunderstanding. On the morn of his son's execution, Kumalo, back home, stands on a hilltop back of his village facing a mountain-country dawn. He has brought back the black Magdalen and has resigned himself to the technical justice of the white man's civilization, but not to the tragic general injustice of the colonial crime. Says Paton symbolically, with almost Greek irony as he concludes the novel:

> The sun tips with light the mountains of Ingeli and East Griqualand. The great valley of Umzimkulu is still in darkness, but the light will come there. Ndotsheni is still in darkness, but the light will come there also. For it is the dawn that has come, as it has for a thousand centuries, never failing. But when that dawn will come, of our emancipation, from the fear of bondage and the bondage of fear, why, that is a secret.

It is Paton's insight into this double bondage — the material one of the blacks and the spiritual one of the whites — and his ability to communicate this in moving, human drama, that lifts this novel to the plane of great social vision, and, simultaneously, to the plane of great art. It is a contemporary classic, and promises to remain one. That it is to be dramatized for *The Playwrights Company* by Maxwell Anderson and also to be filmed by Korda is appropriate to its worth and an earnest of its moral potential.

Peter Abraham's *Path of Thunder* gives us vividly and convincingly the psychological tragedy at the core of the same situation, for his is the story of Lanny Schwarz, an educated Cape Town mulatto and Sarie, a white girl, who against the implacable mores of South African race prejudice dares to love him and aspire to be his wife. Their plot to escape from the veldt village to Cape Town and from there presumably to England or Europe is discovered or rather, betrayed, and they end in a battle-royal of death behind the farmhouse barricade after an intercepted flight. Slight and melodramatic as the story outline is, the telling is an intimate and well-balanced revelation of all the inter and intra-racial tensions and hatreds of the South African, or for that matter, any typical race situation. Even their courage is taken from them in the news account of the happening, for Sarie is made the victim of her native lover and their betrayer a martyr to an educated Negro run amok. Unfortunately there is no comparable fictional version of the American analogue, neither in narrative frankness and boldness, nor in artistic power and psychological insight. But when art approaches greatness — and with all its signs of youthful immaturity — this novel does approach greatness, it becomes universal in relevance and appeal. Harpers have shown wisdom in putting this work in the special promotion category of their "Harper Finds," and in my judgment have had the distinction of launching one of the great Negro writers of our generation.

Speaking of distinction, it is an indefinable, and certainly cannot be gauged by bulk or even technical maturity. I list, therefore, with critical confidence a short story by an American newcomer, James Baldwin, *Previous Condition*, which Elliott Cohen, the discerning editor of *Commentary* magazine, has chosen to print. In so doing, he, too, has launched in all probability a significant young Negro writer. This account of the psychological shocks of prejudice of a sensitive and adolescent Negro artist, with excellent revelation of the ironic complications of his being neither "fish nor fowl" between the social ambiguities of Harlem and Greenwich Village, shows new dimensions of literacy and psychological power, particularly because of being told so frankly and objectively. There are reaches of artistic achievement, our young writers should realize, that are only to be attained through psychological frankness requiring great courage and daring. It is the lack of these that so often dims the power and reach of much contemporary Negro artistic expression.

William Gardner Smith's war novel, *The Last of the Conquerers*, for example, though a creditable journalistic version of the life of a typical group of Negro occupation troops, first in the American sector of Berlin and then in a Jim Crow dominated village post in the Bemburg area, lacks the psychological penetration and daring which could have transformed it from an interesting historical document into a great and moving exposé of the inconsistences and dilemmas of exported race prejudice. The personal love romance of the hero, Hayes Dawkins, and Ilse, the German army-post clerk, is told with journalistic competence; so are the rather crude but typical behavior and reactions of American soldiers in the face of German friendliness and army discrimination. But the full irony of the acceptance as an equal by Germans and rejection as inferior by fellow-citizens and comrades in arms is somehow lost either in the immaturity of a first novel or in the caution of psychological timidity. It is, of course, of importance that this much of the story has been documented, but the full artistic impact of the theme has not been realized. Other work, either of Mr. Smith or other G. I.'s must eventually do this, with what is doubtless the fictional dynamite of our decade, the Negro soldier's World War II's experiences.

Though also a first novel, Dorothy West's *The Living Is Easy* has more power of boldness. It is the story of Cleo, mulatto and Southern-born, who relentlessly pursues respectability and fashion in Boston on the business fortunes of a proletarian banana merchant, whom she never fully respects or understands because of her color and society complexes Overloading his resources with her own ambitions and those of her married sisters, whom she imports disastrously in each case to Boston, gives Miss West good chances of characterization, which she adroitly uses as well as ample opportunity for the satirical exposure of intra-race prejudice and snobbery. As a relatively new field, this is welcome subject-matter, materially extending the range of social documentation and intimate inside self delineation of Negro class structure. But satirical portrayal often glosses over too superficially the real pathetic import of these drives, for the conflict of value loyalties in the middle-class Negro are matters of real and pathetic significance. This, too, is therefore only ground-breaking effort, though its pioneering is much to be applauded, because it takes emotional courage to be as "racy" and intimate as Miss West has been in her narrative.

From the side of the white writer, Irwin Stark has been just as courageous. But on the whole, though a careful and unique documentation of all elements, black and white, in the Harlem community, *The Invisible Island,* suffers the faults of its virtues in over-documentation. Matthew Stratton, well-intentioned liberal and potential reformer, finds himself a white schoolteacher in a Harlem public school. He is resolved to get on the inside, and does even at the price of embarrassment and disillusionment. Good social realism compels the author to register this negative net result, but it is wisely traced to the community irreconcilables of cross-hates and cross-loyalties. In some respects this may be regarded as a fictional documentation of group prejudice in its urban aspects, for Gentile-Jewish, Protestant-Catholic, radical-conservative, middle-class and proletarian antipathies are just as vital in the situations as color prejudice. Stratton's re-dedication to a teaching-social service career in Harlem, even after the disillusionments of the failure of Johnny Boston, his test protegé, gives a moral twist to the sad story that is far from defeatist, but the best that this novel offers the reading public is an unglamorous and well-rounded inside look at Harlem, or for that matter, any typical northern urban Negro community.

John Hewlett's *Harlem Story* is concocted of the very opposite stuff; it is a melodramatic pot-pourri of stereotypes, misrepresentative, not because they do not exist but because they are not typical. A melodramatic variant on the intermarriage theme makes Flutie, a fair-skinned social climber, marry a songwriter whom she thought was white, only to discover eventually that he, too, was of mixed blood. Intragroup jealousy and exploitation are rather too sketchily presented to be convincing; so this merely stakes out a milieu that someday must be more carefully and sympathetically portrayed. *The Well of Compassion* by David Alman is another essay in interracial marriage, a notably swelling theme in race fiction, it appears. Here again, the narrative only superficially delineates its situations, probably from having conceived them first as problems and then secondarily as human character reactions. Both Lock Sharon, the Negro painter and Jo, the white Bohemian, have compensatory motivations, and so unlike Abraham's novel, one has only a problem situation on one's hands, which, when it fails, brings no vital sense of tragedy and no unusual social enlightenment. The novel, however, is not condescendingly written, which was not typical of the earlier treatment of this theme, even O'Neill's *All God's Children*.

There is at least that much substantive gain.

If all gains are to be thankfully received, and I suppose they are, the comparatively non-artistic best-seller benefits (and profits) of Frank Yerby's *Golden Hawk* must be put into the inventory. For it does vindicate the right to cater to that numerous and rewarding reading public that wants fiction for fiction's sake, and likes a good, rollicking story, entertainingly told. But from the viewpoint of the socially and artistically significant literature that is our criterion, *The Golden Hawk* can be written off, even in spite of its West Indian background, as blank and neutral on our scoreboard.

Southern fiction on the Negro used to be equally deductible. But much of it is no longer so. This year's crop is exceptionally serious and represents sober effort at realistic portrayal. *South Wind Blows* is a carefully studied and obviously Freud-inspired analysis of a small Mississippi community, seething with race hate and tension. The story of Abe Lacey's lynching is a sober but not too inspired saga of share-cropping, its inequities and institutional animosities, and the inevitable violence and hate below the drab surface of its uneasy living. Clark Porteus has more merit, however, for frankness than for artistry, either in style or characterization. On the other hand, David Westheimer's *Summer on the Water* has distinction in both, as well as documentary frankness. As a drama of undercover jealousy between Mrs. Carably and her Negro maid, Mathilde, whom she gradually comes to suspect as the paramour of her husband, this Texas novel has a real story to tell. Convinced more by the resemblances and ways of Jay, Mathilde's eight-year old son, Mrs. Carably sets about her revenge of spite treatment of Mathilde, who is eventually driven to the one excluded possibility in the white Texas mind (for Negroes) — suicide. Westheimer ranges himself clearly in the new school of Southern liberalism, for his book ends with the poetic justice of Aunt M'Lou's insistence on adopting Jay, the forlorn orphan symbol of the sad, tangled dilemmas of miscegenation. An inner penetration of both sympathy and understanding lifts this novel to an unusual plane, and for the work of a young Southerner of thirty, it promises strong reenforcements of liberal Southern fiction.

Zora Hurston'. *Seraph on the Sewanee*, however, for all its preoccupation with the heroine, Arvay Meserve's, character development, remains in the class of local color fiction. It is a fascinating but not too purposeful study of the transformation of wayward passion into understanding love. Arvay, though married to Jim Meserve, is doubtful of him, and in turn, only faithful to him in her easy-going fashion. Gradually her respect for

his ambition and its eventual success in what, for the region, is a profitable fishing enterprise with status creates a loyal wife out of the wayward strumpet, and the book ends on a belated honeymoon of mutual
understanding. But Arvay and the main incidents of the story are far
from seraphic, and one feels at times that the glorification of instinct is
more of an objective than the documentation of Arvay's rehabilitation.
Certainly, as with all of Miss Hurston's books, the folklore and the background rather than the story or the characterization are the redeeming
features. For a seasoned story-teller, and one of the best, it is not reassuring to observe the almost completely anecdotal character of this latest
novel. Pardonable in the Bohemian phase of the Negro renaissance, there
is too much of serious social import to be said today for mere story-spin-
ning to be regarded as worthy of such indisputable talent.

With a folk life as skillfully observed, but with infinitely more depth of
social vision, John W. Wilson, another liberated Texan, gives us in *High
John The Conqueror* a poignant portrayal of present-day life in the South.
In a blameless and manly struggle against the traditional economic and
moral odds, Cleveland Webster, although inheriting a small farm from
his grandfather, is shown slipping back into the economic quicksands of
tenantry. His is a double-cross of bondage — hopeless debt and moral
crucifixion under the clandestine but increasingly obvious trysts of John
Chaney, their white overlord, with Ruby, his wife. Just on the verge of
complete peonage and degradation, floodwaters come as a blessing in
disaster, for with the last bitter courage of desperate folk, they sell the
land back to the ever-greedy Chaney and embark on the trek to the mill
and the city, at best a risky half-chance but still eventual hope of freedom. Few novels have caught as has this one the full tragedy of the system, and almost none have shown the moral victory in outward defeat
that characterizes this simply but ironically told saga of poverty and
prejudice. At last, even in Southern fiction the discerning distinction between outer and inner defeat: instead of being defeatist, such writing
evokes the dark and awesome victory of Job.

POETRY AND BELLES LETTRES

The poetic yield of the year is meagre in quantity, but not qualitatively. In W. Stanley Braithwaite's *Selected Poems*, we have the veteran poetry critic's own gleaning of what he considers the best essence of
his lifelong poetry output from 1907 to 1947. Formed on the taste of his
youth — mystical romanticism — this work over the four decades reflects
a maturing of style but no essential change of aesthetics. It has bravely
followed its chosen path, despite the vogue of the earthy schools of folk
realism. That reign, too, it seems is about to close, and what is to take
its place is not too apparent in spite of the confident clarion of some of the
youngest poets. Two of these, Robert Hayden and Myron O'Higgins, have
issued what at first blast sounds like a poetic manifesto ushering in a new
dawn in Negro poetry. In *The Lion and the Lamb* they proudly proclaim
the permanent emancipation of the Negro poet from the shackles of racial
verse. If on no other ground, the Braithwaite publication is justified by
showing us that this literary freedom, never contested by the wiser advocates of racial representation in poetry, has always had exponents
among the Negro poets, and so is not as new or revolutionary as this recent proclamation. A significant new swing of the poetic pendulum may
be and probably is due. However, it can hardly be fully representative

or effective either as a poetry of the esoteric mood or as an utterance in cryptic style and symbol, and this, rather unfortunately, much of the writing in *The Lion and the Lamb* most obviously is, even while showing genuine poetic gifts in both the older and the younger author. They are thus more praiseworthy in their experimental drive than in their present accomplishment. Indeed both authors have clearer insight and accent in some of their older selections in the recent and admirable Hughes and Bontemps anthology — *The Poetry of the Negro*.

Carruthers and Hughes' translation of a sheaf of the best-known folk poems of Nicholas Guillen, *Cuba Libré* serves to give an introductory taste to English readers of one who is undoubtedly a great Cuban poet. However, except for a few of these translations like Sensemaya, the subtle rhythm and elusive overtones of Guillen's verse escapes. Only his great devotion to the folk and their songs and his great social indignation at their oppression and exploitation persist to give the English reader some idea of what he misses by not knowing them in the original versions.

Hugh M. Gloster's *Negro Voices in American Fiction* is most welcome, if for on other reason than the paucity of critical literature by Negroes. This book is a competent, near academic resumé of the treatment of the Negro in American fiction until recent years. Its main lack is in not carrying the critical scalpel further below the surface of an essentially descriptive account of the ever-growing material treating Negro life fictionally. Although superficially a chapter of American literature, it is also a cross-section of the development of the American social mind, and a more penetrating critical analysis could and should reveal it as such. We must meanwhile be grateful, however, for a clear and accurate compendium of this important sub-field of American letters.

It is just the attempt at deeper penetration than a narrative account which gives merit to Sidney Finkelstein's *Jazz: A People's Music*. Not only is this a readable and not too technical history and analysis of the varieties of jazz from "rag" to "Be-bop," but the story of the Negro's music is meaningfully connected at all points with the Negro's social history. This is great gain, for it is precisely in the social interpretation of our music that most significance is to be found. We have heard, for the most part previously, from the jazz musicologist; now we can welcome a competent jazz historian. Similar social insight and correlation are to be found in Earl Leach's study of the folk music of the Caribbean. His *Isles of Rhythm* takes up where Harold Courlander's pathbreaking *Haiti Singing* left off. and has the advantage of being broadly comparative of the various mixed strains and idioms of the whole region.

Selden Rodman's sumptuously illustrated account of the recent rise of a school of folk painting in Haiti — *Renaissance in Haiti* documents competently and sympathetically one of the rare and encouraging cultural phenomena of this decade. Rooted in an unfortunate and stifling tradition of imitation, painting in Haiti was languishing. The provocative influence of DeWitt Peters, a visiting American artist and Inter-American exchange teacher, has in the short space of five years stimulated a native school of painting based on the folk life and its way of seeing life. Although he founded a Centre D'Art, it was merely a workship where relatively untrained artists were encouraged to paint as they saw and felt without benefit of formal teaching and an academic tradition. The result has been a brilliant vindication of the theory, for some five or six of these folk artists have come through with great originality and creative power; — Rigaud Benoit, Philome Obin, Hector Hyppolite, a voodoo priest who went to the native cult for his main inspiration, Dieudonne Cedor, Fernand Pierre and Louverture Poisson, to mention the outstanding talents at the moment. What is even more notable is the probable influence of this development upon the spirit of the Haitians, who will find themselves fully justifying the motto of a "renaissance" if they succeed, as appears likely, in rejuvenating the folk spirit and its strongly creative originalities. Ultimately such a movement will spread its influence to the other arts, and a New Haitian art, music and letters may be anticipated which will be both a true racial expression and a proud national symbol.

Although of primary interest to the technical students of African art, Carl Kjersmeier's *African Negro Sculpture* is an indispensable handbook of the subject. For it is a graphic and authoritative analysis of the important tribal styles, and only an appreciation of African art well-grounded in a sense of tribal idioms is permanently profitable. All else is sentimental amateurism, and like the fads it consistently follows, it is a shallow as well as a fading fashion. If our knowledge of things African is to be sound and profitable, it must be based on an interest and a scholarship which has accuracy and authority beyond all challenge.

FICTION

CRY THE BELOVED COUNTRY, Alan Paton, Charles Scribner's Sons, N. Y. $3.00.

THE PATH OF THUNDER, Peter Abrahams Harper & Bros., N. Y. $2.75.

SOUTH WIND BLOWS, Clark Porteus, A. A. Wyn, Inc., N. Y. $2.50.

SUMMER ON THE WATER, David Westheimer, Macmillan Co., N. Y. $3.00.

SERAPH ON THE SEWANEE, Zora Hurston, Charles Scribner's Sons, N. Y. $3.00.

THE WELL OF COMPASSION, David Alman, Simon & Schuster, N. Y. $3.00.

HARLEM STORY, John Hewlett, Prentice-Hall, N. Y. $2.50.

THE INVISIBLE ISLAND, Irwin Stark, Viking Press, N. Y. $3.00.

THE LIVING IS EASY, Dorothy West, Houghton Mifflin Co., Boston. $3.50.

THE GOLDEN HAWK, Frank Yerby, Dial Press, N. Y. $3.00.

THE LAST OF THE CONQUERORS, William G. Smith, Farrar & Straus, N. Y. $2.75.

PREVIOUS CONDITION, James Baldwin, in October, Commentary.

POETRY and BELLES LETTERS

SELECTED POEMS, William Stanley Braithwaite, Coward McCann, Inc., N. Y. $2.50.

THE LION AND THE ARCHER, Robert Hayden and Myron O'Higgins, Counterpoise Press, Nashville, Tenn. $1.00.

CUBA LIBRE, Nicholas Guillen, Trans. by Langston Hughes & Ben Carruthers, Ward Richie Press, Los Angeles. $3.50.

NEGRO VOICES IN AMERICAN FICTION, Hugh M. Gloster, University of North Carolina Press, N. C. $3.50.

JAZZ — A PEOPLE'S MUSIC, S. Finkelstein, Citadel Press, N. Y. $3.50.

ISLES OF RHYTHM, Earl Leaf, A. S. Barnes & Co., N. Y. $5.00.

RENAISSANCE IN HAITI, Selden Rodman, Pellegrini & Cudahy, N. Y. $4.50.

BIOGRAPHY

WITNESS FOR FREEDOM, Rebecca C. Barton, Harper & Bros., N. Y. $3.50.

FREDERICK DOUGLASS, Benjamin Quarles, Associated Publishers, Washington, D. C. $4.00.

BOOKER T. WASHINGTON, Basil Mathews, Harvard University Press, Cambridge, $4.75.

THE STORY OF JOHN HOPE, Ridgely Torrence, The Macmillan Co. N. Y. $5.00.

A MAN CALLED WHITE, Walter White, Viking Press, N. Y. $3.75.

HISTORY AND SOCIOLOGY

THE STORY OF THE NEGRO, Arna Bontemps, Alfred A. Knopf, N. Y. $3.00.

BLACK ODYSSEY, Roi Ottley, Charles

Scribner's Sons, N. Y. $3.50

THE NEGRO IN AMERICA, Arnold
Rose, Harper & Bros., N. Y. $3.75.

THE NEGRO GHETTO, Robert Weaver,
Harcourt, Brace & Co., N. Y. $3.75.

THE NEGRO FAMILY IN THE
UNITED STATES, E. Franklin Frazier, Dryden Press, N. Y. $3.75.

CASTE, CLASS AND RACE, Oliver C.
Cox, Doubleday & Co., N. Y. $7.50.

BALANCE OF POWER, Henry Lee
Moon, Doubleday & Co., N. Y. $3.00.

THE CHRISTIAN WAY IN RACE RE-
LATIONS, Ed. William Stuart Nelson, Harper & Bros., N. Y. $2.50.

NEGRO HIGHER AND PROFESSION-
AL EDUCATION, 17th Yearbook,
Journal of Negro Education. Wash-
ington, D. C. $2.00.

THE NEGRO YEARBOOK, 10th Edition, Tuskegee Institute Press, Alabama. $4.50.

AFRICANA

NEW SONG IN A STRANGE LAND.
Esther Warner, Houghton, Mifflin Co.,
Boston. $3.50.

ZULU WOMAN, Rebecca Reyher,
Columbia University Press, N. Y.
$3.00.

THE AFRICA OF ALBERT SCHWEIT-
ZER, Charles Roy & Melvin Arnold,
Harper & Bros., N. Y. $3.75.

JEUNE AFRIQUE, No. 4, Elizabethville.
Belgian Congo. 30fr.

PRELUDIOS ETNICOS DE LA MU-
SICA AFRO-CUBANA, Fernando
Ortiz, Revista Bimestre Cubana, No.
LIX & LX, Havanna.

AFRICAN NEGRO SCULPTURE, Carl
Kjersmeier, Schultz, Inc., N. Y. $5.50.

PART II

BIOGRAPHY is the flourishing category in this year's literary crop: both
in quantity and quality, it is exceptional. Foremost in my judgment
is a study in comparative biography — Mrs. Rebecca C. Barton's *Witnesses for Freedom*, which critically epitomizes and compares twenty-
three Negro autobiographies from Frederick Douglass and Booker T.
Washington to Langston Hughes and Richard Wright. By exhibiting between the covers of one book so many differing varieties of personality,
such divergent types of social and racial philosophy, so radically contrasted views of the proper "solution" of the race question, Mrs. Barton
has realistically and effectively de-stereotyped the Negro. This achievement would alone justify the work, but additionally there is sensitive
correlation of the individual's temperament and philosophy with his or
her social environment and life experience, documenting all but psychoanalytically the importance of these factors. Indeed the psychoanalytic
job has only to be done along the line of these hints and intuitive insights
to yield us our first really modern, scientifically grounded type of Negro
biography. Strange indeed it is, that almost no psychoanalytic biographies have been written about Negro figures, excepting of course, the
obviously psychotic Garvey and Father Divine. The antidote to the overdone emphasis on the Negro as a problem, must be more critical analysis
and comparison of the Negro as man and individual. Negroes, hostile to
stereotyping, nevertheless are too prone to over-generalize themselves on
the egocentric pattern of their own experience. For this reason, the
reading of *Witnesses for Freedom* will be as salutary and enlightening
for the Negro reader as for any non-Negro who may take the time to
learn that *The Negro* is a mythical entity.

Benjamin Quarles' biography of *Frederick Douglass* is the most comprehensive and objective account of this increasingly important figure
to date. It is still short of the definitive biography, yet so superior in accuracy of fact and perspective that it must be gratefully received. At last
the full facts, including the often hush-hushed involvements of his second
marriage, are accurately stated and adequately documented; and here
and there some sound psychological insights are available. Indeed the
work needs only a less pedestrian style and fuller painting of the historical

background canvas to give us the real Douglass in the outstanding stature of his personality and his time.

The biography of *Booker T. Washington* by Basil Mathews, though also a welcome document, is far from the claim and dimensions of a definitive biography. But the lack here is from another quarter; the definitive biography of Washington, in addition to detailing the great components of his own career and personality, must show him in interaction with those forces and interests of the white world of the South and of Northern industry which he both manipulated and by whom, in turn, he was manipulated. As a character sketch of Washington, the present work is illuminating; and nowhere more so than when utilizing Washington's unpublished correspondence. Witness such priceless insights as "I find markets more instructive than museums . . . I have never been greatly interested in the past, for the past is something that you cannot change. I like the new, the unfinished and the problematic." One new additional sidelight to be credited to this volume is the documentation of Mr. Washington's keen and influential insight into the colonial problem, in which he was skillfully and realistically interested.

Ridgely Torrence's more mature and penetrating biographical treatise on *The Story of John Hope* is an even better balance between man and background. Sensitive both to the curious combination of the aristocrat and the missionary in the man, and the educational anachronism of higher education on a shoestring, Torrence presents the triumph of a sturdy, quietly steady personality who constructively resolves this dual dilemma. It will be a long while before a Negro personality of John Hope's caliber receives such reverent and understanding treatment. Obviously the unusual combination of projected sympathy and objective portrayal stems from Ridgley Torrence's own spiritual penetration of the color-line by artistic identification — an achievement relatively rare even among the many white artists who have conscientiously sought to explore the world of Negro experience. Many of John Hope's objectives for education are as yet unachieved, in spite of the tremendous accomplishments of present-day Atlanta University — his strategy-built monument. Among them is his quiet but daring concept of the Negro college as the vantage point for "some technique for the minority." Today, I think, we should have to say "some techniques," and make them both intellectual and social, for the short generation in which the Negro college will still remain an existent institution. In spite of his services to it, no man of his generation, not excepting DuBois, was more conscious than Hope of its tragic self-contradiction and irony.

Of the autobiography of Walter White, vaingloriously inept in both its title, *A Man Called White,* and its melodramatic emphasis on a color identification not exactly voluntary for any Negro born and bred in the deep South, this much can be said: it adds some valuable and important details to the biography of the N.A.A.C.P. This is not said to belittle but to restore the correct emphasis after the unfortunate misemphasis of many overenthusiastic but mis-cued reviewers. Even so, however, one must gratefully acknowledge the debt for a more representative insight into this most important of all Negro defense organizations than the moralistic and somewhat superficial account of last year, Miss Ovington's *The Walls Came Tumbling Down.* The progressive development of Negro militancy is the real protagonist in this story, without, of course, any undue discount or credit of persistently militant leadership. It is perhaps too early yet for a non-tractate account of the N.A.A.C.P. or any of its leading personalities.

Turning to history or near-history. we come to two useful and probably widely circulated books, Arna Bontemps' *The Story of the Negro* and Roi Ottley's *Black Odyssey,* the former journalistic in a good, the latter in a bad sense. For the Bontemps volume relates in simple, readable and entertaining sequence for school-age readers the "story of the Negro." It is a welcome addition to the few narratives that do attempt this important educational and educative job. On a quite more ambitious plane, and erring considerably both on the score of fact and competent interpretation, the Ottley book has many of the virtues but most of the faults of journalism and journalese. In a context of the work of Carter Woodson, John Hope Franklin and Franklin Frazier, such work is gratuitous and inexcusable.

On the contrary, *The Negro in America,* by Arnold Rose, a readable and proportioned condensation of much of the materials in Myrdal's *An American Dilemma,* does supply the general reader with valuable in-between understanding, ampler than a school text but easier of comprehension than the learned treatise. Material of this level is greatly needed in a day of expanding curiosity and tolerance; and the more the better. This is a good one, of unchallenged competence. Similarly competent and enlightening is Robert Weaver's study of *The Negro Ghetto,* outlining the causes, trends, economic costs and social injustices and dilemmas of residential segregation. Especially forceful in its exposure of the fallacies in the economic arguments for the ghetto, Dr. Weaver's book introduces a new realistic attack on the problem, and predicts some probabilities of improvement from the added legal leverage of outlawed restrictive covenants. Henry Lee Moon's study of the increasingly strategic distribution of the Negro vote in border states and large urban communities fully vindicates his title, *Balance of Power*: The Negro Vote. A pre-election analysis, it accurately predicted some of the effects of the Negro vote in pivotal key areas in the last presidential elections, and is another of an increasing number of laudably objective analyses of race situations, political. social and economic, by a creditably reliable younger generation of Negro students of the social scene. The enlarged and revised edition of Franklin Frazier's exhaustive study, *The Negro Family in the United States,* makes available again one of the pioneering works of this caliber: it is difficult, re-reading it, to recall how recently it was a rarity for such objective analysis to come from a Negro scholar. Today, it is the average expectancy.

This remark gives point and background for a reservation and regret apropos of another work of the highest competence in social scholarship. Professor Oliver C. Cox's prodigious volume *Caste, Class and Race.* For seven-eighths of a lengthy historical and analytical treatment of class, caste and race distinctions, Dr. Cox is commendably scholarly, objective and illuminating. He then, for some strange and to this reviewer unnecessary reason, leaves the academic chair for the propaganda podium, some would say, the sidewalk soapbox. Even should the Marxist tenets coincide with his scholarly conclusions, and many of them are tightly reasoned and objective enough to be acceptably so, it seems an error to risk the suspicion of any precommittments for conclusions which the reader must thereafter critically review for warrant and cogency. Any reader, having done so, however, will likely reach the conclusion that Professor Cox is one of our ablest sociological thinkers, especially in theoretical analysis, and that this book is one of the high-water marks of erudition in the theoretical field of social group distinctions, their process development and their operational enforcement and rationalization.

For those who are interested in the American race question on the increasingly active plane of social Christianity, the symposium of the Howard University Institute of Religion, edited by Dean William Stuart Nelson, will prove an enlightening and challenging set of arguments for morally motivated social justice, equality and fraternity. The reactivation of both the Protestant and the Catholic Churches in the matter of race relations is a significant and hopeful sign of the last decade or so; and more power to it and the books and works that support what should long ago have been a vital and crusading church policy and program.

In my opinion, it is the realistic exposure of actual church practises such as are factually detailed in Frank Loescher's *The Protestant Church and the Negro* that will needle the conservative elements in the church to reform, because of the devastating negative evidence of discrimination and inconsistency.

It is gratifying to chronicle in the 10th edition of *The Negro Yearbook* a much more systematic and scholarly competent a compilation than the issues of previous years. There is always competence in the yearbooks of *The Journal of Negro Education;* and this year's issue is devoted to a very timely issue — Negro Higher and Professional Education The crucial current issues of the decisions against inequalities of segregated state systems and the countermeasures proposed are accurately reported and submitted to forthright constructive criticism.

Books about Africa are never-ending; but happily their quality improves. Correct projection and its correlated proper understanding are gradually becoming the rule rather than the exception. And even more important and impressive there are increasing signs, as we shall see, of native self-expression and interpretation.

Rebecca Reyher's *Zulu Woman*, a fictionalized biography of Christina, first wife of Solomon, one of the great Zulu kings, dramatizes the struggle of monogamous love and traditional polygamy in the royal household. It is a sensitive portrait both of an individual and a transitional stage in acculturation in contemporary South Africa. The force of it as a particularized and authentic story obtained by direct interview, in no way diminishes its anthropological significance, indeed enhances it. The conquest of changing values and ideals is the real road of influence between cultures, not the forced imposition of colonial reform, which, oftener than not, detribalizes, disintegrates the mores and alienates the two racial groups even while making them more alike in thought and behavior. This same lesson is the insight and evidence of Esther Warner's account of cultural change in the West African hinterland, *New Song in a Strange Land*. For its unique combination of lyric sympathy and realistic description, the work of Mrs. Warner is indeed a rare accomplishment, and further evidence of the trend under discussion.

Of course, the grand pioneer of this change of values in the European mind is Albert Schweitzer and it is symptomatic that so many volumes keep appearing about him and his transforming mission. The present small volume by Joy and Arnold is frank journalism, but charming as well as competent for all that. A concluding essay on his interpretation of the need for constructive assimilation of the advanced techniques of civilization as more important than the need for self-government and political independence must be given respectful attention as the mature opinion of a well-intentioned expert, however one may wish to differ. One may, indeed, differ even then, since progress is notably slow under official tutelage, and considerable areas of Africa are manifestly ripe for self-government and the right to learn by making one's own mistakes.

Two interesting and impressive native publications are the 6th issue of *Presence Africaine*, edited in Paris with notable native collaboration of high literary and academic excellence and an important anthology of poetry by Negro French Africans and colonials, edited by Leopold Sedár-Senghor, *Anthologie de La Nouvelle Poesie Negre et Malagache*, published by the University Press of France. Like the output of the Afro-Cuban poets, the verse of these French Negro poets is slender in volume but of exquisite literary skill and taste. Such figures as Léon Damas of French Guiana, Gilbert Gratiant Etienne Lero and Aimé Césaire of Martinique, Guy Tirolien and Paul Niger of Guadeloupe, Birago Diop, Sedár-Senghor and David Diop of French Africa, and Ranaivo and Rabearivelo of Madagascar need to be known and being known admired. Of the poets in this anthology only Léon Laleau and Jacques Roumain of Haiti are known to any considerable number of American litterateurs. And the Haitian Jean Briere and Rene Belance are still unknown to most of us. Yet when it comes to poetic skill and maturity hardly any Negro American poet can match a considerable number of these.

When the two magazine monographs of Fernando Ortiz on *Afro-Cuban Folk Music* are expanded to book form, as is imminent, they will form not only a definitive study of that important phase of Cuban culture, but I can think of no comparable study of the African elements in North American musical idiom since Ballanta's work of years ago — and that, though highly suggestive, was fragmentary. American Negro interest in Africa on the level of scholarship is on the whole laggard and where it does exist is, for the most part, sentimental and puerile. Having seen so much change for the better, one hopes to live to see even change in this — a cultural desideratum of the greatest significance as a sign of cultural balance and maturity.

WISDOM *DE PROFUNDIS*:
The Literature of the Negro, 1949

PART I

FICTION

YEAR BY YEAR, it seems, the delving goes deeper, and as might be expected, out of the depths come greater insight and wisdom, as from even deeper wells, one sees not only the moon but the stars. The sociological literature — to be reviewed in the next issue — is likewise more penetrating, but the creative literature of 1949 dealing with Negro life and its problems is especially enlightening, at the inevitable cost, though, of being quite sobering and disquieting. The tragic pall of social injustice, the heavy costs and confusions of prejudice, the dilemmas and frustrations of miscegenation, the innner conflicts and bewilderment of a divided Negro mind — these are the sad, sober but necessary themes as white and Negro writers try to get down to the marrow of varying situations, past and contemporary, involving race and its social pathology. Superficiality and melodrama, having become so generally outmoded, give a sense of shock when they crop up occasionally. This makes for hard and bitter reading, equally so, praise God, for Negro and for white readers. But now that the general conscience is astir and racial hypersensitivity slowly passing, it is sound and salutary that we are all more willing and able to face the facts.

Let us document our credo of wisdom *de profundis*. Somewhat over a year ago, out of darkest South Africa came that sheet-lightning revelation of Alan Paton's *Cry, the Beloved Country*. Unpredictably that vision seems to have caught and captured the public eye. Even in the somewhat diluted brilliance of *Lost in the Stars* it still radiates pity and terror on Broadway. A starker, more nativized version might easily make it a twentieth century *Uncle Tom's Cabin*, though, on second thought, we must remember how shallow and melodramatic the stage *Uncle Tom's Cabin* really was. But it wrought miracles nonetheless with public opinion. This year similar enlightenment emanates from darkest Mississippi, focussed by the seer-like genius of William Faulkner. Strange coincidence, too, is the fact that this gloomy, high-brow novel, *Intruder in the Dust*, should so quickly become a Metro-Goldwyn-Mayer film, beaming, without too much Hollywood distortion, Faulkner's insight and message to the mass millions who

Phylon 11 (First and Second Quarters 1950): 5–14; 171–175.

never will read the book. Happily portentous stars have hung over the murk and confusions of Johannesburg and Oxford, Mississippi, when such objective vision and illuminating understanding emerge from these dark cores of racial intolerance and conflict. That they have is the very essence and vindication of art and genius.

Faulkner, who has been patiently brooding over the Southern scene these many years now seems in his seventeenth volume to thunder out the doomsday of racial injustice by the simple device of holding up, quietly but unflinchingly, a relentless mirror before the face of the characteristic South. This time one look is enough and convincing: both sermonizing and apologia instantly become superfluous. In a quarrel over cheating in their sawmill partnership, one of the Gowries has murdered another. Lucas Beauchamp, a proud and independent Negro, as an early morning witness of the incident, has fallen into the fatal net of circumstance and as the scapegoat suspect is "good as dead" in the hands of an irate community. His lynch mob is led by the real murderer, who has a double score to exact, his vengeful hate of the Negro who will not take off his hat to a white man and his fear of exposure. Against this almost certain doom, to which Beauchamp himself is almost stoically resigned, there stands only the deep-seated gratitude of a half-grown white lad whom he had befriended in a hunting accident some four years previously when the boy was at the impressionable age of twelve.

From that small seed of humanity and justice proceeds a web of triumphant vindication that frees Beauchamp and at least harries the dormant conscience of the community. The one clue, whispered by Beauchamp to Chick: "My pistol is a fawty-one Colt and Vinson Gowrie wasn't shot with no fawty-one Colt" is followed by a macabre series of events — Chick's resolve to exhume the body, a chance involvement of the elderly Miss Habersham in the eerie graveyard quest, the discovery of an empty coffin and rival marauders, for the murderer had hastily rifled the grave and thrown the body in nearby quicksands, Chick and Miss Habersham's slow convincing of the sheriff, the official recovery not only of Vinson's corpse but that of a murdered accomplice, killed to scotch all tell-tale of the unburying, Miss Habersham's strange use of Southern chivalry toward white women by a rocking-chair blockade of the lynch mob, mending in the jail hallway, and finally Beauchamp's release despite his stolid nonchalance and Southern reluctance to displace a Negro by a white man in the criminal dock. In skeletal outlining, a plot for a mediocre but soundly moralistic melodrama; in Faulkner's expert hands. an overwhelming evocation of the tragic dilemmas of the Southern mores of race, to my thinking, the greatest novel of the South yet written

Considerably behind in artistry and power of character and regional delineation, but with skill and equal staunchness to reveal the whole truth about Southern life, Bucklin Moon's novel, *Without Magnolias*, holds and will hold a place of importance. Its chief distinction is its wide gamut of type portrayal, from the Negro president of a Florida state college on down through his temperamentally variegated family to the humble folk of the town. This is possibly the most successful literary invasion to date of the Negro bourgeoisie; rather devastating, I would say, but all too true, with its most redeeming feature the generation contrast between the Mathews, father and son, the father truckling and hypocritical, the son rebellious and sullenly discontent, the mother, snobbish and ambivalent. Mr. Moon's honest coverage, his full-scale canvas of the basic types and levels of Negro circles will do great service for

the average reader. For the Negro reader it will undermine the protective
and compensatory stereotypes that have grown up to counter the traditional derogatory ones; for the white reader these will be the targets
exploded. Important, too, is the author's convincing exposure of the
shortcomings of gradualism and reliance on white Southern "liberalism"
and his documentation of the fact that "speaking out" by a Negro college
professor can be nearly as fatal as "sass," "rape" or riot on the proletarian
level. Sanely enough, however, *Without Magnolias* has neither a fatal nor
a defeatist ending.

More in the groove of tradition, but not yet fully in its ruts, come next
two novels by Southern-born women trying to fathom the old situations
with new skill and insight. Neither quite succeeds, for no matter how
delicate the psychological projection or sympathetic the telling, the en-
tanglements of miscegenation, however tragic, are rooted in unenlight-
ening stereotypes of character and situation. Basically these are tragedies
only because of the traditional acceptance of false premises. Everything
hinges on the impossibility of publicly admitting what everybody knows
to be true. Until a talent like Faulkner stresses this basic angle, all mixed-
blood tragedies will have this shallow melodramatic motivation. Frances
Gaither's *Double Muscadine*, carefully documented from the trial records
of a mulatto slave-girl's trial for poisoning, even though it culminates in
a conscience suicide of her seducer-master and her faint-hearted ac-
quittal, has these inescapable limitations. Similarly the semi-romantic
counterpart in Cid Ricketts Sumner's *But the Morning Will Come*, with
its threatened and narrowly avoided separation of a happy couple by
reason of the whispered dark blot on the escutcheon. This is not said to
minimize either the seriousness, the growing courage of human detail
or the level-handed sympathy of character portrayal in two readable and
plausible novels of the Southern scene. It is solely to say that the best
southern fiction today must go deeper under to the roots from which such
situations spring.

Two other novels do go deeper, one by a Negro, the other by a
Southern white author. Each is a study of mulatto ambivalence and both
trail their chief characters through various stages of acceptance, denial
and reacceptance of race. In Barbara Anderson's *Southbound*, Amanda
Crane is reared in mid-west Ohio far from her Alabama origin by a doting
grandmother, Laura, lily-white to the core, and her darker great-grand-
mother, Perse, who cannot comprehend the virtues of transplantation and
"passing." Bereft of a patron and finally of both her guardians, Amanda
goes to Paris with a small legacy and large ambitions. Posing as Cuban,
she runs the gamut of love and music study, with disillusionments that
might befall any such girl but which are augmented by the tangled
loyalties of color. Miss Anderson obviously means her repatriation to
America in the wake of war to be a symbolic solution, but admirable as
that may be, it would require another novel to indicate the social logic.
And what is too often missed, there is no generalized solution: what is
wrong for Amanda may not be wrong for another — the subterfuge of
concealment, as it aptly has been called, is no more intrinsically wrong
than the wisdom of acceptance is universally right. Even the most sympathetic fiction can overgeneralize, and often does, sometimes explicitly,
sometimes by implication. In this case, the author is pretty explicit.

In *Alien Land*, a highly creditable first novel, Willard Savoy has his
main character, Kern Roberts, run the full gamut. Told as an inside story
by a Negro author who undoubtedly has shared some of his hero's dual

experiences, *Alien Land* arouses high expectations of being a definitive novel on the psychological conflict of race loyalties. This, unfortunately, it is not, partly because of a lack of sufficient maturity to turn the melodrama of this cycle of successive acceptances and rejections of race into full tragedy and resolution. It does, however, bring fresh materials on the dilemmas of "passing," and especially on the great variety of motivations back of the same behavior. It is, therefore, welcome news that the book is to have a wider audience through a New American Library reprint edition.

Kern Roberts, in short, is too beset with the dilemmas of race to be typically significant. In his Washington boyhood, he is a double victim of intra-group and intergroup prejudice, having testified in court against the Negro murderer of his white mother. With warrantable relief, he "passes" as white in a New England college, only to be discovered and denounced by a white Southern classmate. That sent him back to Washington with a chastened Negro loyalty, culminated by voluntary missionary enlistment at Valley View, a Negro college. Here in Alabama, he is again shaken, not only by the restrictions of ghetto-living, but by the violent death of his Negro aunt and uncle. Back again in white circles in New York, an expedient denial of race leads to a romance with Marianne and the temptation to "pass" permanently. On its verge, he decides to tell her of his mixed racial origins, is initially rejected but finally accepted. There one good novel ends where, however, a still maturer and more difficult novel really should begin. For, after all, little known as these situations are to the general reader, their mere documenting is not the main point; nor even the hortatory indictment of the mores which create them, of which there is far too much also in this pyramided story. Kern's chequered "ins and outs" are not as important as what happens inside his character and personality: it is Kern's final decision to tell that really frees him, and a maturer hand would have made more of that point and what led up to it. Throughout his vignettes are well observed and depicted; but like too many young writers, Willard Savoy has emptied too many notebooks into his first novel, leaving less room for character interpretation.

In a maturer way, James Gould Couzzens has made the same mistakes in *Guard of Honor*, primarily a full canvas of a wartime air base in Florida, secondarily a full-fledged and courageous documentation of race prejudice in the U.S. Army. His saving grace, however, is knowing how to explode melodrama into real conflict and irony, as when a personal encounter sets the racial powder keg on fire, or when the simultaneous arrival of citations for a general and a Negro airpilot nearly explodes the same tinder. Apart from a ruthless exposé of official double-dealing and its precarious equilibrium, Couzzens does state the basic problem with clarity and an implied but positive prediction of the impossibility of indefinitely prolonging double-standard democracy. To achieve this without preaching makes for a notable novel, though not all notable novels are inevitably great. Faulkner is great; Couzzens is notable.

Guard of Honor reminds us of how little has come out of the important milieu of the Negro soldier and World War II. Fortunately Gardner Smith's *Last of the Conquerors* has enjoyed wide interest because it did treat realistically and interestingly some of the experiences of the Negro soldiers in the last war. A Library reprint has sold extensively, and opens up prospects of a mass audience for the young Negro writer. To date, however, I have to vote for *Walk in Darkness* by a German-American, Hans Habe, as the best book yet on the Negro soldier's war experience. Not that it can be taken as typical; God forbid, since it descends through the underworld of the black market to a court-martial sentence for murder. But it is nevertheless a masterly analysis of the psychological inter-reactions of American race prejudice and war situations in the European theatre. Washington Roach's discharge from the army returns him to an unsatisfactory lower-class niche in Harlem. In a mid-town bar he resents the insult of a prejudiced white patron, assaults him and receives a minor jail sentence. On his way up Broadway from the Tombs, he relives in gaudy shipping posters the freedom possibilities of Europe, and finding further disillusionment from family and employer in Harlem, impulsively reenlists for the occupation forces in Germany. There in Bavaria he passes through casual fatherhood to real romance and contemplated marriage with Eva, a German girl, but the official ban on the marriage despite the good offices of a liberal Catholic priest lead to further involvement in black-marketing, a murder, kidnapping of his own daughter, and finally a capture which ends in a Munich court-martial and return to New York for execution. These sad happenings are but the outer shell of a deeper inner tragedy, and it is this portrayal of situational tragedy which raises this novel to the plane of Faulkner — that is, of human fate conditioned on the racial and human levels simultaneously, and thus both racial and universal. For Washington Roach is seen as the combined victim of prejudice, war and the aftermath of war, dying in the end more as the scapegoat of our social sins than as the guilty criminal. Again I question whether a greater book will be written in this segment of the Negro experience.

The motley procession of fiction ends quietly, almost idyllically with V. S. Reid's fictionized narrative of Jamaican history, reflected in the story of the Campbell family. From the Morant Bay Rebellion of 1865 to the installation of a constitution in 1944, the slow but dogged progress of proud peasants toward freedom is graphically chronicled, in Jamaican dialect, which for idiomatic charm can only be surpassed by the choicest of Irish English. *New Day* marks the discovery of new material and a new talent; V. S. Reid is a fiction-writer of high caliber.

DRAMA AND FILM

More significant perhaps than this fine crop of fiction is the increasing extent to which movie and stage are reflecting it out to the larger public, and in the most convincing of all art forms, visual action. We must pay the price of distortion that stage and screen exact, if only it be not too exorbitant. As it is, *Lost in the Stars* loses less than was feared, although Harlem cabaret idiom for a Johannesburg dive, a down-stage pulpit for a mission church, and not too African Negroes in prominent roles transpose Broadway assets into African liabilities. Yet on the whole, here is a moving reincarnation of *Cry, the Beloved Country*, with a reverent script and capable music to sustain a finely reenforcing atmosphere.

Similarly, but with too sophisticated music, Langston Hughes' *Mulatto* has undergone a successful third transmutation into an opera, *The Barrier*, successfully put on by the Columbia University Workshop.

I have already spoken of the movie version of *Intruder in the Dust*, but too much cannot be said for it, either about the script, the brave and inspired direction by Clarence Brown, using the town and townsfolk of Oxford for accurate documentary, and the carefully restrained acting of all the principal roles, including a stellar performance of Juan Hernandez as Lucas Beauchamp But then in the year's Broadway film crop we have additionally *Home of the Brave, Lost Boundaries, Pinky* and *The Quiet One,* a bevy of popular and artistic successes. Three have figured in the best ten on various honor listings, and certainly *Intruder in the Dust* and *The Quiet One,* for documentaries, promise to outrank all contenders. That they simultaneously register new seriousness and dignity in Negro characterization and new moral dimensions in theme makes for unprecedented progress, and joy over its attainment. With the further promise of *Never No More,* a Twentieth Century Fox problem movie on the story of a Negro interne, it may be that suddenly and unexpectedly Hollywood has been converted, and the American film brought nearer to moral and artistic maturity.

POETRY AND BELLES LETTRES

In scope and selection and critical competence, *The Poetry of the Negro* by Langston Hughes and Arna Bontemps is definitive. Aiming to be broadly representative, it could not possibly be a *Golden Treasury;* but it is nonetheless a sterling compendium. One must particularly commend the inclusion of "tributary" verse by white poets, a sound procedure calculated to exorcize any hint or suspicion of black chauvinism or of racism in the arts. Similar praise is merited for the interesting inclusion of the mixed-blood poets of the Caribbean. I personally find the greatest interest in the variety and growing strength of the contemporary younger poets, Margaret Walker, Gwendolyn Brooks, Robert Hayden, Myron O'Higgins and M. Carl Holman particularly. Poetic creativeness seems on a slow upswing after a serious decline from the heyday of Cullen, Hughes, McKay and Sterling Brown. Now, with a difference, it may be on the march again, and the significant difference is the rise of the universalized theme supplementing but not completely displacing the poetry of racial mood and substance. This, too, is sound in principle, morally as well as artistically. The Negro poet is of course basically a modern poet and an American poet. But conversely, too, he must be at the proper time and in the proper way a Negro poet, a spokesman for his innermost experiences.

Such instances of successfully universalized expression as *Birth in a Narrow Room* by Gwendolyn Brooks, Helen Johnson Collins' *To An Avenue Sport,* and *Two Lean Cats* by Myron O'Higgins amply attest to this. With basic human denominators of experience discovered, the racial overtones are all the more poignant and meaningful through being left implicit. Bruce McWright's *Journey to a Parallel,* even though merely ironic in mood, stands out as a distinctive statement of the younger generation's war experience. *Sunset Horn,* by Myron O'Higgins, does so even more. Though uneven in execution, it is a notably sincere and courageous war poem, and reflects a talent of such quiet, unrhetorical strength and a vision of such perceptive depth that the best commentary is a quotation of some of its strongest passages:

> Block the cannon; let no trumpets sound!
> Our power is manifest in other glory;
> Our flesh in this contested slope of ground.
>
> In thin silences we lie, pale strangers to the corn-gold morning,
> Repeating what the fathers told . . . the promised legacy of tall sons;
> The hushed sibilants of peace; and the far tomorrow on the hills.
>
> O, we went quickly or a little longer
> And for a space saw caste and categories, creeds and race
> Evaporate into the flue of common circumstance.
> We sought transcendent meaning for our struggle,

And in that rocking hour, each minute, each narrow second
Fell upon us like a rain of knives,
We grappled here an instant, then singly, or in twos or tens, or by
    bewildered hundreds,
Were pulverized . . . reduced . . . wiped out —
Made uniform and equal!

            *   *   *   *   *

Raise no vain monuments; bury us down!
Our power is manifest in other glory;
Our flesh in this contested slope of ground.
There is no more but these, a legacy, a grim prediction. . .
One day the rest of you will know the meaning of annihilation
And the hills will rock with voltage;
And the forests burn like a flaming broom;
And the stars explode and drop like cinders on the land.
And these steel cities where no love is —
. . . O in that day
When the tongues confound, and breath is total in the horn
Your judas eyes, seeking truth at last, will search for us
And borrow ransom from this bowel of violence!

Of Countee Cullen's *On These I Stand,* suffice it to say that most of the six new poems are not of the best, though it is good to have samples of his latest vintage. The rest is representative enough of a high but prematurely dimmed and now regrettably lost talent. Whereas in *One Way Ticket,* Langston Hughes seems merely to have turned out, on a now overworked formula, glibly synthetic, one-dimensional folk vignettes, reflecting varied shrewdly observed facets of the present scene. Facility, undisturbed by fresh vision and new insight can dim and tarnish almost any talent of whatever potential magnitude. Especially with the field of seriously experimental young contenders, Mr. Hughes, should he persist in his facile superficiality, will have to surrender his erstwhile cloak and laurels.

In a special Negro Poets edition of *Voices,* he has rendered constructive service to true poetry. For this considerable sheaf of new poems has both merit and promise. O'Higgins' "Death of Bessie Smith" is a real folk poem; Robert Hayden's "Noel, Noel" is gem-like, even though a bit too precious; M. Carl Holman's "Dawn Like a Hunting Hawk" is both competent and original. There are, of course, others of merit, but any group of poems as varied and underivative as most of these raise hope for the near future.

There remains among the poetry items Gwendolyn Brooks' latest book of verse, *Annie Allen.* Here is distinctively original and professionally competent poetry. One sees the striving, too, to discover the universal in the particulars of a modern woman's experiences of love, motherhood, struggle, frustration. However, much remains turgid and overanxious. These poems that at their best fuse class and race experience into a sardonic yet vibrant comment on modern living represent, one hopes, a transition stage, for surely Gwendolyn Brooks is en route to a style and idiom of her own and an unhackneyed, perhaps shocking message of her own. But at the present stage, she too often smolders where, at a few more puffs of inspiration, she might break into flame. "The Children of the Poor," for instance, verges close to this, as does "The Rites for Cousin Vit," while in a lighter, lilting mood, there is scarcely anyone equal to finer rhythm than

        The men and women long ago
        In Africa, in Africa,
        Knew all there was of joy to know.

In sunny Africa
The spices flew from tree to tree
The spices trifled in the air
That carelessly
Fondled the twisted hair.

The men and women richly sang
In land of gold and green and red
The bells of merriment richly rang.

But richness is long dead,
Old laughter chilled, old music done
In bright bewildered Africa

The bamboo and the cinnamon
Are sad in Africa.

Earl Leaf's superbly appreciative and excellently documented study of Caribbean folk traditions and dances, *Isles of Rhythm*, is fortunately available in an inexpensive reprint, including the wonderful photographs. That is good news, for I know no similar book better fitted for generating that sadly lacking respect for the ancestral heritage and the pagan folk background.

FICTION

Intruder in the Dust, William Faulkner, Random House, N. Y. $3.00.

Without Magnolias, Bucklin Moon, Doubleday and Company, Inc., N. Y. $3 00

Alien Land, Willard Savoy, E. P. Dutton and Company, Inc., N. Y. $3.00.

Last of the Conquerors, William Gardner Smith, Farrar, Straus and Company, N. Y. $2.75.

Double Muscadine, Frances Gaither, The Macmillan Company, N. Y. $3.50.

But the Morning Will Come, Cid Ricketts Sumner, The Bobbs-Merrill Company, Inc., Indianapolis. $3.00.

Guard of Honor, James Gould Couzzens, Harcourt, Brace and Company, N. Y. $3.50.

Walk in Darkness, Hans Habe, Trans. by Richard Hanser, G. P. Putnam's Sons, N. Y. $3.00.

New Day, V. S. Reid, Alfred A. Knopf, Inc., N. Y. $3.00.

POETRY AND BELLES LETTRES

The Poetry of the Negro, (ed.) Langston Hughes and Arna Bontemps, Doubleday and Company, Inc., N. Y. $5.00.

On These I Stand, Countee Cullen, Harper and Brothers, N. Y. $2.50.

Voices, (ed.) Langston Hughes, Winter Issue, 75¢.

Annie Allen, Gwendolyn Brooks, Harper and Brothers, N. Y. $2.50.

Isles of Rhythm, Earl Leaf, A. S. Barnes and Company, N. Y. $5.00.

One Way Ticket, Langston Hughes, Illustrated by Jacob Lawrence, Alfred A. Knopf, Inc., N. Y. $2.75.

PART II — THE SOCIAL LITERATURE

SINCE MYRDAL, the consideration of the Negro as a group phenomenon has veered toward the consideration of the Negro in the framework of American society at large, with accent on developmental trends and on the shortcomings and potentialities of democratic society. To have definitely established this frame of reference is the main contribution of *The American Dilemma*, although the approach was advocated vigorously and cogently by several earlier studies, among them *The New Negro*, it may now be said twenty-five years after. The core of this interpretation is the tracing of a double line of interacting majority-minority influences, reciprocally determining and modifying one another. With the entrance of this theme, racial polemics and chauvinism died, or should have, on both sides, and sociological objectivity became possible. Against this norm, the progressive and constructive work in the historical and the sociological fields can and should be measured. Increasingly year by year, the social literature of the Negro measures up to this norm.

Professor Maurice R. Davie in *Negroes in American Society* carries through very comprehensively and explicitly this point of view. Not just history but trends, change as correlated with socio-economic and socio-cultural factors supply the basis of interpretation so welcome and so necessary to an understanding of the facts by giving reasons for the facts. It is only on such a basis that social intelligence can be developed in both groups, to the ultimate effect, it must be hoped, of some really operative and effectual social understanding and sanity. Primarily in the mould of an enlightened text-book, this volume has significance for the general reader. Shrewdly moderate and practical, it has the faults of its virtues, but it is full of pithy and enlightening observations. A typical one is worth quoting: "The most promising line of attack, as Professor MacIver emphasizes in his book *The More Perfect Union,* is not on the prejudicial attitudes but on discrimination. Whereas prejudice is a way of feeling and uncontrollable as such, discrimination is a way of behaving and in its public aspects at least is amenable to control." Although, thank God, there are the inter-culturalists whose special care and concern is the moulding and reconstruction of attitudes.

More ponderous, and inevitably so, Professor Franklin Frazier's *The Negro in the United States* is a definitive compendium of contemporary historical, sociological and cultural scholarship on the American Negro. Its prime usefulness, accordingly, must be for the serious scholar, in spite of its laudable clarity and readability. Comprehensive coverage has necessitated these limitations. As might be expected, particular attention is given to institutional history and organization, the church, the school and the family receiving particularly objective and illuminating treatment. Dr. Frazier's volume is not only based squarely on the frame of reference we have just discussed, but thoroughly vindicates it as an effective mode of interpretation. Enlarging previous lines of emphasis, the book gives fresh and adequate coverage to literature and art among Negroes and to the role and trends and limitations of Negro leadership. A particularly important set of observations documents the emergence of "functional leadership" as developed in specialized fields like labor unions, specific technical and scholarly activities, with the parallel lapsing of contact and spokesmanship leadership so peculiar to segregated minorities. As a symptom of integration, these facts have great significance and should be especially emphasized in the training of the younger generation.

It is pertinent at this point to call attention to other inevitable consequences of increasing integration, since as a consequence both leadership and participation must take on radically different techniques and objectives. We are probably confronting the last half-generation of race or symbolic leadership in the scholarly, creative and professional fields as well. To note, by way of high tribute and deep solicitude, the passing of Dr. Carter Woodson and for the first time in a quarter of a century the absence of books from his pen or press, it is nevertheless appropriate to say that, with his passing, the day of Negro history as such very probably also ends. For the inevitable price of integration must sooner or later be paid, and the history and sociology of the Negro become quite different in the changed context of scholarly collaboration and integration. But the militant pioneers of recognition and acceptance such as Du Bois and Woodson have played an important role, and they richly deserve their due of honor and gratitude.

If one wants the best facts about the Negro, as objective and well-interwoven as modern scholarship permits, Davie and Frazier are basic and essential, as was, in a more explicit frame of history, John Hope Franklin's *From Slavery to Freedom* of several years back. If, however, one wants the human essence and the psychological implications of the "American dilemma," one must go to Lillian Smith's *Killers of the Dream*. Here, at least in three of her more notable chapters, "When I was a Child," "Southern Waste," and "Man Against the Past," is to be found some of the most incisive and poignant analysis ever given the tragi-drama of American race relations. In other chapters, the theme seems too closely identified with Miss Smith's own personal philosophy of history, civilization and progress. But, being her own story, it must be told in her own way to have the integrity and conviction which it so preeminently has. Nonetheless, *Killers of the Dream* is a sound parable of race prejudice and its killing effects upon both black and white as well as of its present-day ominous threat to world peace and world understanding. Its strongest single contribution is its quiet but effective use of the principles of psychoanalytics to give the ordinary layman insight into the roots and results of prejudice.

Without benefit of psychiatry, or for that matter much else sophisticated, Ray Sprigle in *In the Land of Jim Crow* narrates with forceful and convincing realism the detail of contemporary Jim Crow in the South. Added to this is the realistic irony that Mr. Sprigle is a white journalist who merely had a voluntary "assignment sentence" as a white man masquerading as a Negro. This, I think, compared with the life-sentence of the born Negro dramatizes the story all too meaningfully. As shock enlightenment for average readers nothing could be more wholesome. Experts, of both the inside and outside variety, will have much to cavil at as well as much to restore to correct proportion. Yet it would be difficult to get from the most exhaustive scholarship anything more accurate or practical than Mr. Sprigle's "This sharecropping in the South is grand larceny on a grand scale" or his epigram "separate and equal just isn't equal."

An important pioneer study in its field is Professor Arnold Rose's book on *The Negro's Morale*. Over and above very illuminating and well-documented tracings of the rise of race pride and solidarity as reactions to persecution and prejudice, fortunately with an objective regard for this as a common minority phenomenon, Dr. Rose goes into the further problem of the growing negative effects of racialism when, as chauvinism, it confronts the present-day situations of growing recognition and integration. The author rightly considers this the internal dilemma of the Negro minority and its leadership and issues a timely warning about its puzzling and dangerous implications. In further service to this relatively new field, there is a challenging list of yet unsolved research problems which opens new vistas of profit for such relatively new techniques as socio-metrics, psycho-dynamics and plain social psychology.

America Divided: Minority Group Relations in the U. S. by Dr. Rose in collaboration with Carolina Rose, mainly a war-time study of the changing tensions toward minority groups, does not make the same impression of scholarship as a guide to social progress and understanding. For one thing, the authors, probably under the depressing shadow of the setback reactions from recent war gains in minority relations, seem to be full of cautious reservations. They are perhaps justified, especially in the light of obviously increased religious intolerance both between Jews and Christians and Protestants and Catholics. It is by no means clear as yet that we are not observing a shift rather than an overall decline in group tensions and animus. However, more space should have been given, if not to the documentation of recent gains, certainly to the newer techniques of education, public relations and mass media propaganda now available for a crusade for democracy, if we have the general will to pursue it. The evaluation that we have, along with marked reduction of overt "strong prejudice," heavy, perhaps heavier retention of "gentlemanly" or secondary prejudice is challengeable. However, not being subject to statistical examination, we must regard this as almost wholly within the realm of opinion.

In error on the other side of over-optimism is Ina Corinne Brown's quite useful and constructive brief for progress and increase of tolerance, *Race Relations in a Democracy*. Addressed primarily to educational circles and thus to childhood and youth, its optimism is well-founded. At the preventive level lies whatever grand-scale hope there is, but the correlated problem of infection and reinfection from parents and community mores has yet to be fully estimated and objectively diagnosed. This, however, was not Miss Brown's primary assignment; her own she has carried out most persuasively. Under the auspices of the National Board of the Y.W.C.A., Dorothy Sabiston and Margaret Hiller have in collaboration edited a praiseworthy and eminently practical report of actual procedures and gains in interracial reconstruction — *Toward Better Race Relations*. A joint adult-youth effort, it has definitely proved real accomplishment in organizational associations.

Noteworthy, too, particularly in view of the dissolution of the Fund and the even more recent demise of Mr. Embree himself, we must note the useful and informative history of the Rosenwald benefaction — *Investment in People*. In the context of this article the fellowship program, especially in the creative arts for so much Negro and Southern white talent which has already made its constructive contribution, must be praised and tentatively evaluated. Full realization of its effect must come later, since a large portion of this talent is still potential. The shrew foresight of stimulating Southern liberalism and underwriting constructive collaborators such as Ralph McGill, Rupert Vance, Liston Pope, Lillian Smith and others is one of the chief points to be noted. But here again, in its way, the closed Rosenwald chapter marks the close of an era. Today it is the Guggenheim Award, and the like, gained in open single standard competition which has significance for the future. Particularly a propos is recent word of a National Institute of Arts and Letters grant to Shirley Graham for further studies in biography and the merited and significant Pulitzer Poetry Prize to Gwendolyn Brooks.

Shirley Graham's *The Story of Phyllis Wheatley* and of Benjamin Banneker in *Your Humble Servant* are both of a familiar and worthy genre, which she has made peculiarly her own. It is a combination of vividly dialogued facts that fits particularly such subjects as the two most recently treated. Confronted with slim, sketchy documentation, such figures do need such filling out and benefit from a treatment which, in the reviewer's judgment is inappropriate for figures of the stature of later historical characters. The shortcomings, therefore, of Miss Graham's biographies of Carver and Douglass become virtues in her Phylis Wheatley and Banneker. These are in their way vignettes of skill and informative impact. Definitive biographies of either are doubtless beyond available sources of research; in their place these warm and moving, though naive, tributes have force and meaning.

For all its initial limitations of appeal as a research monograph, Professor Lorenzo Turner's *Africanisms in the Gullah Dialect* is a volume of high general significance. On the vaguer grounds of superstition and folklore the argument about African survivals in American Negro life has reached a prolonged stalemate. Only on the Brazilian and Caribbean fronts has it turned in any considerable way in favor of the "survivalist" school of thinking. Here on the linguistic front and with respect to definite North American areas, the case for large intact survivals has certainly been clinched. And if for verbal vestiges, why not, then, others, especially since customs and thought-ways lie deeper even than language? With twenty-five native African informants, Dr. Turner has assembled a convincing array of close parallelisms of words, phrases, syntactical idioms and folk-lore imagery. Tribally documented, they are not only convincing evidence of survivalisms, but, I dare say, can later be of enlightening use in historical tracing of traits and origins. Musical and anthropological collaboration should have been available to follow through these important clues.

Although for a long time now, I have urged African studies and comparative research, there still seems to be little lay or professional interest in it. Negro college centers, partly through lack of financial resources, but also, let us confess, by reason of unfortunate mental alienation and disinterest, have done very little; and worse yet, Negro students have rarely gone in for anthropological study, either linguistic, anthropometric or cultural at other well-equipped and thriving centers, such as Yale, Chicago and Northwestern, the latter a highly specialized center of African research. When it comes to the literary representation of African life, we accept the most meretricious and unrepresentative and often ignore the really competent interpretations. In the stereotyping of Africa and Africans, we repeat and reflect the stereotypes of racial and religious prejudice, and are, in the main, as pot-kettle black as our worst detractors.

INVENTORY AT MID-CENTURY:
A Review of the Literature of the Negro for 1950

Part I

FICTION

IN A REAL and deserving sense the title of this annual review article could more appropriately have been the caption of the entire last issue of *Phylon*. For there, carried through collaboratively and most commendably, was the full critical inventory of this most significant half century of the literature of the American Negro. Both as stock-taking and appraisal — the two most basic functions of criticism — the net result was constructively encouraging. From its careful perusal anyone should know where we are on the literary highway, and approximately where we are heading. As a thorough account of our literary accomplishment and an incisive analysis of our objectives, the issue merits listing as an outstanding achievement of the year.

Yet in the perspective of such objective criticism the Negro writer as artist has several Rubicons yet to cross and many more provinces to try to conquer. In the context of the 1920's, very obviously poetry and music were the advancing salients of our creative effort: today, it is just as inevitably fiction, drama and criticism. Drama still lags, but fiction seems on the march. In most instances still qualitatively immature, at least there is both quantitative gain in volume and more importantly still, in spread of theme. Negro authors particuarly are invading the fie'd, for paradoxically, they have yet to take over the establisted lead of the white fictionists. Any gain here, we may presume, is a gain, in which case one can cite in passing, but only in passing, the case of Frank Yerby, whose mass production of best sellers (a combined circulation of over five million to date) denotes the conquest of the general market and of the general theme, for whatever that may be worth. We are, I suppose, entitled to our share of Harold Bell Wrights and Elinor Glynns. With seasoned narrative craftsmanship and leisure based on financial independence, Mr. Yerby may yet return to the plane of the literary novel and the fold of the serious fictionists of Negro life and experience.

In view of the distant date of its regular analysis (as an early 1951 publication), I take the liberty of another passing mention — to call

Phylon 12 (First and Second Quarters 1951): 5–12; 185–190.

attention to the literary and subject-matter significance of Owen Dodson's first novel, *Boy at the Window*. This sensitive study of Negro adolescence in Brooklyn adds valuably to Negro portraiture in several ways: Coin Foreman's story presents the Northern urban neighborhood background which has been so rarely treated in fiction, and when it has, so unconvincingly treated, especially in its interracial and intercredal aspects. Here in Dodson's book, it is convincingly portrayed and taken for granted as indeed it should be, since it is becoming increasingly typical and characteristic of American youth experience. Yet, despite this, the special emotional overtones of Negro family and church life are adroitly superimposed, and the book's poetic prose, with its deliberate luxuriance of sensuous imagery, gives, I think, a characteristic and almost elemental Negro quality. There are, of course, the expected immaturities of a novice in the form, at times too great lushness of language, inappropriate sophistication in spots, unevenness of character portrayal, but none of these obscures the refreshing achievement of a notable and perhaps path-breaking book. One further point: in the final chapters, Coin's Washington visit presents Southern prejudice from the mind-set of a northern-bred boy, adding a significant and illuminating angle, hinted at years ago by Countee Cullen's poem of the first encounter with prejudice called "Incident."

J. Saunders Redding's novel, *Stranger and Alone*, as foreshadowed in several chapters of his earlier *No Day of Triumph*, opens up his promised exposé of Negro education in the South, its jim-crow inequities and its internal psychological frustrations. As a pioneer exploration, the evidence and the courage of its presentation are to be welcomed and applauded. Mr. Redding, however, is so obsessed with moral indignation at the disloyalties and self-contradictions of go-between "race leadership," that in his portraits of Shelton Howden and President Wimbush, his two type educators, he often misses the master accent of realistic fiction, credability. For he evokes more horror than sympathy and rouses more indignation than understanding. His detailed documentation of the typical Negro missionary college of Howden's college years and of the hypocrisy and sycophancy of the Southern system of segregated education is, in the main, incontestable. But though true to fact, these characters are not projected sympathetically enough to throw any blame on the environment itself, where it mainly belongs. Redding's 'J'accuse' points too exclusively to them, and the society which imposes such a hard price for survival and such extortionate character costs for success escapes the main force of the author's just thunderbolts. With more evenly distributed blame and with subtler nuances in degrees of race treason, for, as in the Bible, some deny, some disown and few only actually betray, there could have emerged a more definitive portrayal of this hitherto closed and signally important phase of Negro and Southern life. So, with all due appreciation for painstaking and courageous pioneering, *Stranger and Alone* must be put down as a greater achievement in theme and subject-matter than in character portrayal and narrative artistry. This is not a limitation of style, for Mr. Redding writes well, but of psychological approach and conception. Surely there are maturer works in store when the author's anger and moroseness temper down into compassion or sharpen into satire or irony. One leaves the book, however, with revealing insights into the milieu of the Negro college, the segregated school system and its paradoxes, the confusions of intra-race prejudice, and of the little-known dilemmas of middle-class status in Negro communities.

Beetlecreek, by the third of these Negro novelists, William Demby, is noteworthy despite immaturities both of conception and technical execution. For it reverses with interest and profit the usual focus of portraiture and tells the life of a white recluse, living marginally and precariously on the fringe of a Negro community. Making friendly overtures at last to the Negroes, particularly the children, he makes a near-convert in one sensitive lad, Johnny Johnson, who is too much under the pressure of his Negro group and their suspicion and counter-hatred to carry through. Old Bill Trapp is thus eventually and ironically the victim of his own attempts to be human, and the fog of prejudice closes down in an unusual way on this strange segment of a West Virginia community. Psychologically, this is a grand theme, fresh and promising, for the potentialities of prejudice are all too human, and provincialism plays out its sinister role on both sides. But Mr. Demby does not meet the challenge of his theme forthrightly, one suspects for lack of power rather than of courage or conviction. Yet he, too, has struck, if not blazed a trail. Bill Trapp mobbed by suspicious and misunderstanding Negroes is a sad and chastening symbol.

Finally, for the current fiction by Negro writers we come to a second novel by William Gardner Smith, *Anger at Innocence.* It is a story of low life in slum areas of Philadelphia, and the author has had the advantage of long home-town familiarity. This and the fitful power of his previous novel, *The Last of the Conquerors,* raises high expectations, doomed, however, to severe disappointment. For this book is largely journeyman reporting, with all the faults of melodrama, superficial stock characterization, banality and cliché situation. Mr. Smith's situations have real tragic potential; Rhodina's affair with Theodore, a married weakling, who still clings to his former wife, and the double triangle rivalries of a venal ex-boy friend and a psychotic Mexican admirer packed together in explosive closeness in the same slum lodging house could make a powerful proletarian story. But neither fate nor environment pull the strings of the action; in writing that is psychologically naive and sociologically superficial, the drama unrolls in tabloid newspaper fashion, with little to commend it to serious readers anxious to explore the Negro "lower depths" to which the author invites them. This end result is all the more disappointing when we recall how few Negro novelists have had courage to attempt low-life portraiture (incidentally, two chapters of Dodson's Washington gin-mill delineation are worth a novel-full prosaically and superficially described). It is all the more so because in the previous issue of *Phylon,* Mr. Smith showed such perspicacity and perspective in discussing the Negro writer's proper attitudes toward his own "race" materials.

Turning now to a series of novels, mostly of the Negro in the Southern scene, by white writers — and we must pause to stress the merely casual import of the ethnic identification — we come to a courageous and powerful study of the psychological aftermath of lynching, Arthur Gordon's *Reprisal.* In a fictional Georgia town he calls Hainesville, the author projects a vivid and pitiless description of the murder and lynching details of the famous Monroe case. The town becomes a tinder box of hatred, suspicion, uneasy conscience and terror of new outbreaks of violence. But contrary to the usual over-simplifications of the Southern school of fiction writing on this subject, the town is not divided racially but temperamentally. Most whites are partisan, but a few are outraged; the majority of the Negroes, too, are terrorized, but Yancey Brown, leading Negro citizen, is in underground revolt and connives at outside aid from the NAACP. The white liberals, headed by Unity Cantrell, the local minister's daughter, pin their hopes on the F.B.I.

Neither group reckons on the unexpected factor of deliberate Negro revenge. But Nathan Hamilton has heard, in Harlem, of the tragic murder of his wife, one of the mob's victims. He returns to Hainesville, hides out in his mother's quarters in the Cantrell garage, and from that vantage point ferrets out the identity of the Aycock brothers, the leading assailants. Later the town is racked by the mysterious murder and fatal stabbing of Neal and Bubber Aycock, whom most folk know to have been the guilty culprits. The sequel is starkly though melodramatically tragic: Nathan is by chance clue discovered, makes a final desperate but unsuccessful effort to escape, dying by his own hand in glum but unflinching satisfaction over his blood reprisal. The story compounds no moral, other than that violence begets violence, and only ironically skirts the issue of proper justice. It is, however, a terrifying exposé of the real conditions, and as an even-handed description of the situation as it actually is, must be chalked up as a hit for a sort of ruthless neutral realism which actually does accuse by indirection. As a native Georgian, Arthur Gordon has had a brave and challenging session with the social truth, and has spared neither his readers nor his native South and its tragically unjust mores.

Excelling *Reprisal* in human as well as social documentation, we next encounter *A Wind Is Rising* by William Russell. He, too, is native born to the milieu he depicts, in this case, the Mississippi Delta. Overshadowing the content truth of these recent novels is the significance of such outspoken and objective delineation by native white authors. Both Gordon and Russell are strong re-enforcements for the Caldwell-Faulkner school of fearless Southern fiction. In *A Wind Is Rising*, the story also shuttles between North and South in the mechanics of the plot; in fact, the cleverly juxtaposed experiences of Beal Jackson as a repressed Delta sharecropper and as a dazed but welcomed visitor to New York contain some of the socially significant material of the book. The purpose of his visit, however, is to find aid for his brother, caught by the intrigue of Ashley King, the planter's ne'er-do-well son, in circumstantial suspicion of the murder of the local sheriff, of which he himself is guilty. After the failure of his appeals for help, Beal returns single handed to intervene in behalf of his brother. His plotted jail rescue breaks down because of the stupid apathy of Brother, and Beal then finds himself on the day of execution himself the victim of a second manhunt engineered by Ashley. Circumstance and the boldness of desperation contrive to give him the satisfatcion of a last man to man confrontal of Ashley King with its chance to accuse him face to face and the good luck of an unusual ending — an escape from the pursuing posse through the conscience-stricken mercy of one of them.

Here, also, the starkness of the story and its conventional outlines have only secondary significance. The real message is in the picture of the decaying feudal structure of the old agrarian South, the moral disintegration of the mores, the trap-like vice of the old tradition, the dilemma of the dual morality, and the rising factors of challenge in the thinking and action of occasionally non-conforming whites and Negroes.

By contrast such traditional novels as Mrs. Coker's *Daughter of Strangers* seem like faded wax-flowers of the dead past. And even they have, here and there, signs of faint change in the stock stereotypes: Mrs. Coker, for example, gives quite an adequate picture of the ante-bellum Charleston free Negroes. But in spite of its hold on a certain section of the reading public, there is ample evidence that the traditional Southern novel is moribund.

In quite another vein, Loren Wahl's *The Invisible Glass* attempts, only half-successfully, the portrayal of Negro troops in Italy, suffering at first under the injustice of a prejudiced Southern captain, only half-relieved under the regime of a liberal and unprejudiced white lieutenant, and perplexed by their genial but curiously misunderstanding reception by the Italian townsfolk. A more skillful treatment of this situation would perhaps have given us the much to be desired and the long-awaited Negro war novel. This one merely pins down the theme for later development.

POETRY

However one may judge or catergorize it eventually, Melvin Tolson's long poem "Libretto for the Republic of Liberia," commissioned for the Liberian Centennial and printed in July *Poetry,* and to be published by The Decker Press, is challenging and significant. Modelled on the ultra-modernistic idiom, including the language echoes of the Eliot-Pound tradition, this is a heavy heave against trite traditionalism, of which indeed we have had and still have too much. In the *Poetry* issue, it evoked a laudatory prose preface by Allen Tate, who calls to attention the necessity for Negro poets not to "limit themselves to a provincial mediocrity in which one's feelings about one's difficulties become more important than poetry itself." Sound advice, as well as the remark that by assuming this "the assumption has made Mr. Tolson not less but more intensely Negro in his apprehension of the world." Witness such strong lines as

> the ferris wheel
> of race, of caste, of class
> dumped and alped cadavers till the ground
> fogged the Pleiades with Gila rot.

It is to be hoped Mr. Tolson will have the hardihood to wrestle with this heady muse until he piles up a poetic accomplishment of worth and note.

In pallid contrast with such meaty poetry is the traditional and watered lyricism of such publications as Oliver LaGrone's *Footfalls,* Robert H. Brown's *Wine of Youth,* and Andrew N. Aheart's *Figures of Fantasy.* One wonders from time to time at the decline of virility and originality in so much contemporary Negro verse production. What forces are responsible? Against this serious overall decline, the rugged creativeness of Gwendolyn Brooks and Melvin Tolson must be measured and doubly cherished, for surely, modern poetry in general has not declined either technically or in conception.

BELLES-LETTRES

Professor Herman Dreer of St. Louis has compiled another anthology of *American Literature by Negro Authors.* Though it includes all the important figures of the past and the present, and in practically all of the major prose and poetic forms, this compendium is too narrow gauged even for the "text-book" that it frankly claims to be. By the excision of difficult passages, an over-elementary simplification has resulted, not to mention an obvious toning down also to Puritanical standards for the exclusion of content materials. When we consider that even high school students are necessarily exposed to Shakespeare, such procedure seems unnecessary and gratuitously demeaning to the Negro materials in their original texts. I do not say the book will not be useful, but it is difficult to conceive by what logic the editor thinks such simplification is in the sound interests of effective education.

In *The Bewitched Parsonage,* William Stanley Braithwaite has skillfully and fluently retold the story of the Brontes. Turning his back deliberately to the vogue of psychiatric literary biography, our elder critic has kept his narrative in the groove of old-style literary biography. Except as carried through with the seasoned charm of an appropriate style, there would be little prospect of wide vogue or acceptance. Within its frame of reference, however, this is skillful and rewarding narrative.

In the field of music criticism three definitive studies have appeared: Alan Lomax's technical and authoritative analysis of Jelly-Roll Morton and his pioneering contribution to jazz music; Rudi Blesh and Harriet Janis's equally competent *They All Played Ragtime,* and Fernando Ortiz's monumental study of the folk idioms and Afro-Cuban backgrounds of Cuban and Antillean music. These three works round out the materials on Negro music in the Americas to the point where we can definitely say that the amateurist phase of commentary on Negro music has at last closed. One can now speak confidently of a reliable musicology for Negro music, for with a few gaps, the works of the last five years have now about rounded out the territory. There is one fly in this ointment, the comparative scarcity of work by Negro musicians and analysts in their own special field. There are, of course, some exceptions, but they are relatively and embarrassingly few.

In drama, though there is little to chronicle, that little is significant. Chief of all, perhaps, the subtle and uncondescending creation of Berenice as really the central character in *Member of the Wedding* has not only given Ethel Waters her lifetime's chance at a truly stellar role but stated more sympathetically and precisely the psychological dominance of the Negro servant in the old-type Southern family. A play by Paul Peters on *Nat Turner* and a revival in opera form of Langston Hughes' *Mulatto,* under the caption of *The Barrier,* comprise the only other serious dramatic offerings of the season. Moderate success was achieved by the latter two, but as yet no great new beacon has loomed on the Broadway stage. *No Way Out* proved to be a sincere but not too adroit statement of its important theme; indeed, its documentary truth got somehow, in spite of good intentions, pretty well smothered under in melodrama. Sidney Poitier played the role of the Negro interne convincingly, but not with the distinction of his teammates, Richard Widmark and Linda Darnell. Obviously it is difficult to make really tense drama out of race riot materials; yet, neither dramatists nor librettists can afford to assume it cannot be done. Whenever they do, they should recall *Intruder in the Dust.*

FICTION

Boy at the Window, Owen Dodson, Farrar, Straus & Young, N. Y. $2.75.

Stranger and Alone, J. Saunders Redding, Harcourt, Brace & Co., N. Y. $3.00.

Beetlecreek, William Demby, Rinehart & Co., N. Y. $2.50.

Anger at Innocence, William Gardner Smith, Farrar, Strauss & Young, N. Y. $3.00.

Reprisal, Arthur Gordon, Simon & Schuster, N. Y. $3.00.

A Wind Is Rising, William Russell, Scribner's Sons, N. Y. $3.00.

Daughter of Strangers, Elizabeth Coker, E. P. Dutton & Co. $3.00.

The Invisible Glass, Loren Wahl, Greenberg Publishers, N. Y. $2.75.

POETRY AND BELLES LETTRES

"Libretto for the Republic of Liberia," Melvin B. Tolson, *Poetry,* July, 1950.

Footfalls, Oliver LaGrone, Darell Press, Detroit. $1.50.

Wine of Youth, Robert H. Brown, Exposition Press, N. Y. $2.00.

Figures of Fantasy, Andrew N. Aheart, Exposition Press, N. Y. $2.00.

American Literature by Negro Authors, (ed.) Herman Dreer, Macmillan, N. Y. $3.20.

The Bewitched Parsonage, William Stanley Braithwaite, Coward-McCann, N. Y. $3.50.

Mr. Jelly Roll, Alan Lomax, Duell, Sloane & Pearce, N. Y. $3.50.

They All Played Ragtime, Rudi Blesh and Harriet Janis, Alfred A. Knopf, N. Y. $4.00.

La Africania de la Musica Folklorica de Cuba, Fernando Ortiz, Publication of the Ministry of Education, Havana, Cuba.

PART II

HISTORY

IN THE social science fields, the mid-century has brought us, rather suddenly, to crucial and puzzling crossroads. So-called "Negro history" and the early sociology by Negro writers on the "race problem" began quite inevitably as protest operations. Their main objectives were corrective and compensatory. It was necessary to rectify the unjust omissions of biased and uninformed majority historians, to offset their defective and often derogatory interpretations, historical and sociological, and also to provide compensatory morale and group pride for educated Negroes in terms of an adequate knowledge of their own accomplishments, past and present. Such motivations, legitimate enough, were, however, damaging to balance and objectivity, even in the most competent writers and additionally brought a plague of pseudo-scholars and amateurs from which we are not yet fully rid.

Two generations of Negro historians and sociologists of repute and valor have struggled with these difficult tasks, many of them with unimpeachable success and academic integrity. This year marked the passing of the most valiant and indefatigable of these, Carter G. Woodson. His constructive work both in research history in his own major writings and the monumental *Journal of Negro History* and in the popularization efforts of his school and textbook publications and the "Negro History Week" crusade cannot be denied or minimized. It was an heroic and constructive accomplishment not merely to the Negro cause but to American history as such. His best work will continue to have influence and in able hands *The Journal of Negro History* has an important specialized usefulness. But with Dr. Woodson's death, the transitional era of "Negro history" has really and appropriately ended. In fact, several years back a new phase of fully integrated historical writing began with John Hope Franklin's *From Slavery to Freedom,* successfully weaving together, as it does, the double strands of majority and minority group happenings and presenting them in their mutually conditioning interaction. From now on, this must be the single norm and the common expectation from both white and Negro historians and sociologists, and it is gratifying to observe rather rapid progress of this sort on both sides of the racial fence. Ultimately, of course, the fence itself must come down. Not immediately perhaps, because documentation from the Negro side is still far from complete, and some degree of "inside interpretation" is still needed. Nevertheless the demise of "Negro history" will usher in a new era of Negro historiography and sociology.

Although written in a minority studies series, *The Peoples of America, They Came in Chains: Americans From Africa*, by J. Saunders Redding, qualifies by the new criterion. It really presents the story of the Negro as part of the growth and maturing of America, doing justice at the same time to some neglected phases of minority reaction, particularly the quite neglected significance of the many slave revolts and the little treated divisions of leadership opinion among Negroes during the anti-slavery and the reconstruction periods. In fact the historical interpretation is nicely balanced between the influence of socio-economic forces and those on the ideological side. This wise eclecticism added to a very vivid and readable narrative style qualify *They Came in Chains* as one of the best available layman's history of the Negro. And because of the author's own literary predilections, intellectual and cultural events and reactions are aptly and significantly woven into the overall interpretation.

BIOGRAPHY

To Philip S. Foner we are indebted for what is to date the definitive edition of the writings of Frederick Douglass, to be completed in four volumes, the first two of which, dealing with *The Early Years* 1817-1850 and *The Pre-Civil War Decade* have just appeared. Extensive search and judicious culling from Douglass's papers, letters and speeches have resulted in a well-rounded panorama both of his public life and his inner growth. Skillfully combined with running commentary and interpretative transitions, there emerges a well-studied but somewhat less objective biography of the man. The critical reader may, of course, discriminate for himself between the historical record and the interpretations. For the larger number of instances, these interpretations seem to the present reviewer to be well-sustained. There are intimations however of a somewhat monolithic conception of Douglass's character, due to a tendency to equate Douglass's contemporary ideology and motivation of humanitarian liberalism with that of the present-day Marxist class struggle. One must for final judgment on this point await the concluding two volumes, for it was in that later period of his life that the ambivalent rationale of Douglass manifested itself most clearly, although it has already shown itself in his break with Henry Highland Garnett's advocacy of slave revolts and his reservations about John Brown's attack. Despite this shortcoming, Dr. Foner's work, evident outcome of great labor and love, is a monumental piece of historical scholarship, contributing as much to vital aspects of American history as to the documentary portraiture of the nineteenth century's greatest American Negro.

Another informative biography on a far different level of life is the story of Haywood Patterson, *Scottsboro Boy*, told in peasant and prison lingo with the enthusiastic assistance of Earl Conrad. The reader can at least realistically retrace almost any line of the tragic Scottsboro story, for it is partwise an exposé of the chain-gang, prison-farm milieu which makes its own chronic criminals and partwise a telling description of the medieval institution of contemporary Southern "justice" with its own triple crime of race hate, licensed sadism and brutalizing terrorism. Earl Conrad's social conscience and warrantable indignation spell out between the lines a convincing indictment of the sinister combination of antiquated penology and tradition-sanctioned race prejudice. Though the subject is obviously himself a criminal type, this story has all the more force because as retold his and his companions' innocence of the Scottsboro accusations appears circumstantially very probable.

We encounter what purports to be a character-sketch biography of the "ordinary, average Negro," reacting to life as it passes in bar-room banter and street-corner chatter, with special emphasis on prejudice as it says: "Stay in your place" or "Thou shalt not pass." In *Simple Speaks His Mind,* Langston Hughes has chosen a novel and promising line of approach, but seems to this reviewer to have miscalculated the responsibilities of such portrayal and the possibility of a general reader's misinterpretations. It is, of course, too late a date to saddle an author, Negro or white, with the impossible task of group portrayal through type characters. But for all its alibis against seriousness, Hughes does undertake signficant group portraiture. And as such, the general effect of the book comes dangerously close to the empty over-simplifications of caricature. At times a serious moral or satirical slap is administered, and there may be a large group of readers for whom the most effective treatment is just such neutralizing of the sting of social criticism with the clownish blandishments of humor. But even so, these folk characters should have been better studied; in many of their reactions, though staged in Harlem, they sound like small-town types of a decade ago. Indeed in farce and slapstick superficiality, Mr. Hughes in too many places gets by with psychological incompetence in drawing his characters and sociological irresponsibility in stating their reactions. So broadly drawn are many situations that, if they had been the product of a white humorist, a chorus of protests would have swamped both author and publisher.

I may be taking Simple over-seriously, but I am afraid too many readers will also. I grant that most of the folk-attitudes are generically correct, though not deeply observed, but even this synthetic Simple does not speak his full mind.

It is time for rejoicing, at least for the advocates of realism, when even the autobiography of American Negro clergymen breaks free from the pious platitudes and moralistic clichés that for generations have been their stock in trade. In *Road Without Turning,* Rev. James H. Robinson has performed this precedent-breaking feat. A few excerpts will graphically demonstrate. Told in his student days by a leading pastor that "A Negro minister is a king to his people. You can be king," Mr. Robinson's comments are: "Leaving Dr. Walker's study, I thought that he had not understood my purpose. I wanted not to be a king, but a servant to the people." That this was not an illusion of pious youth or rhetorical sophistry, the story of Rev. Robinson's ministry at the Church of the Master in Harlem substantiates as it cites such episodes as participation in controversial campaigns in city politics, a blind-fold visit to the vice overlord of the neighborhood in a gamblers' clearinghouse for the numbers racket, struggle for the introduction of courses in African history in the Lincoln University curriculum, and for the appointment of qualified Negro teachers in New York's municipal colleges. As might be expected, such ministry comes up with verdicts and techniques similar to those of the scientific social worker and, one hopes, with comparable realistic results.

Finally, one has to take quick inventory of a considerable crop of popular Negro biographies which is now beginning to broaden out the typical success story genre, basic to a deep-rooted American interest. Beginning with the popular jazz musicians a decade or so back, it has now reached such public figures as Jackie Robinson in a run-of-the-mill biography by Bill Roeder, with obviously careful collaboration by the subject himself, and a most interesting and withal modest biography of Lena

Horne, *In Person:* "as told to Helen Listern and Carlton Moss," culminating just beyond the calendar date line in Ethel Waters' sensational and much discussed *His Eye Is on the Sparrow.* I am glad to have the respite of a year for a fuller and more considered analysis of this book, whose success is inevitable considering its ingredients. However, as with *Simple,* the main problem in such matters seems to me to be the important question of keeping stereotypes and the individual separate and apart, and facing the atypical with all the necessary sangfroid of an unbiased, non-generalizing mind. In the end, we shall just have to fill out the full gamut of portraiture by telling all about all instead of just all about some.

SOCIOLOGY

In a collaborated volume, *Studies in Leadership,* Dr. Oliver C. Cox has a penetrating analysis of the periods and schools of Negro leadership that for perspicacity and objectivity can hardly be excelled. His terse account is worth twice the volume of Julius Adams on *Negro Leadership,* which in addition to its subjective confusions, shows the hand of the sociological novice. No more important subject can be thought of, however, especially in these crucial days, so that the reading of either or both is much to be recommended.

Of prime significance and effectiveness, too, is Father John LaFarge's renewed and forceful argument for the elimination of racial discrimination and segregation in American political, civic and social practice. *No Postponement,* as its title indicates, marshals all the possible arguments, those of practical expediency and of international strategy as well as the expected ones of traditional Christian morals and creed. It provides another bastion for the commendable Catholic crusade against prejudice and puts Protestant churchmen and churches on their mettle.

On the economic front, a really notable contribution has been made by Robert Kinzer and Edward Sagarin in their doctoral study, *The Negro in American Business.* With the exception of an early study by Abram Harris, previous studies in this field have been narrowgauged and superficial. They have taken the limited view of business unconnected with other social factors in the society. These authors, however, by treating it as "the conflict between separatism and integration," have seen the situation in vital and illuminating perspective. They have traced the fluctuations both of Negro business activity and of its policy rationalizations from its earliest beginnings to the present. They are particularly informative about the failure of the Freedmen's Bank, about the role of the benevolent insurance companies in reviving faith in business enterprise. They also objectively discuss the separatist business philosophy of Booker Washington, and while giving it credit for its pump-priming influence, expose its blind alleys and self-contradictions. They conclude with a careful analysis of present trends toward integration with an account of the slow inclusion of the Negro in investment enterprise, with large scale manufacture and merchandising and finance management largely below the horizon as yet. They conclude that, while separatism still has followers, it can today find few if any overt defenders.

The 1949-50 edition of *The Negro Handbook,* edited by Florence Murray, this time with the wise collaboration of special experts for many of the several fields, shows growth in scope and accuracy, sufficient to make it now the definitive ready reference book in its field.

AFRICANA

Of the considerable volume of Africana, we shall only have space for three of the most significant. Martin Flavin's *Black and White in Africa* is conspicuous for its frank reporting of the paradoxes and inequities of the contemporary African scene. On the reserves as well as in the towns and work compounds, he finds the same intensification of the contradictions of colonialism. Similarly, but in a far more documented way, Henry Gibbs furnishes in *Twilight in South Africa* an alarming report of the most crucial area of race tension in the world. Written just before the current climax of the Malan government segregation laws, Mr. Gibbs saw the inevitable logic of the situation and predicted the tragic impasse of the present moment. He is brave enough, however, to quote a native journalist, Jordan K. Ngubane, who says: "Without being very much aware of it, the Nationalist government might organize Africa's 150,000,000 people in one solid anti-European bloc and in that way seal the fate of the white man in Africa." Considering the potential involvements of the present policies in Asiatic politics, through the inclusion of the Hindus in South Africa, this alarming prediction may be, in the long run, a not so exaggerated forecast, and, should history confirm it, will furnish another instance of the old maxim: "Whom the gods would destroy, they first make mad."

In calmer waters, Professor Wingert's *The Sculptures of Negro Africa* is the most comprehensive and comprehending layman's book on the subject. Combining the approaches of cultural anthropology and art analysis, it gives a truly stereoscopic view of the native arts, in the setting of their own native cultures and in the more universal framework of a classic achievement in the field of human art.

BIBLIOGRAPHY

They Came in Chains, J. Saunders Redding, J. B. Lippincott, Philadelphia. $3.50.

The Life and Writings of Frederick Douglass, Philip S. Foner, International Publishers, N. Y.
　Vol. I., *The Early Years*, $4.50;
　Vol. II., *The Pre-Civil War Decade*, $5.00.

Scottsboro Boy, Haywood Patterson and Earl Conrad, Doubleday & Co., N. Y. $3.00.

Simple Speaks His Mind, Langston Hughes, Simon & Schuster, N. Y. $3.00. Paper Ed. $1.00.

Road Without Turning: An Autobiography, James H. Robinson, Farrar, Straus & Co., N. Y. $3.00.

Jackie Robinson, Bill Roeder, Barnes, N. Y. $2.50.

In Person: Lena Horne, As Told to Helen Listern & Carleton Moss, Greenberg, N. Y. $3.00. Paper Ed. $1.50.

No Postponement, John LaFarge, Longmans, Green & Co., N. Y. $3.00.

Negro Leadership, Oliver C. Cox in *Studies in Leadership*, Harpers & Bros., N. Y. $5.00.

Negro Leadership, Julius Adams, Wendell Malliett, N. Y. $2.75.

The Negro Handbook, Florence Murray, ed., Macmillan Co., N. Y. $5.00.

Twilight in South Africa, Henry Gibbs, Philosophical Library, N. Y. $4.50.

The Sculptures of Negro Africa, Paul S. Wingert, Columbia University Press, N. Y. $4.75.

Black and White in Africa, Martin Flavin, Harper & Bros., N. Y. $4.00.

THE HIGH PRICE OF INTEGRATION:
A Review of the Literature of the Negro for 1951

YEAR BY YEAR, our cultural bookkeeping becomes more difficult; not primarily because of increased volume of production, but because of added complications in the computing of net gains or losses. We are now confronted by a more elaborate system of double-entry accounting appropriate to these times. For the Negro author is moving over more and more into the field of general authorship, while at the same time, the white author is moving ever more boldly and competently into the delineation of Negro life. Each of these trends is in itself as desirable as it was inevitable, but for the moment they raise between them considerable confusion, best considered, no doubt, as the temporary stresses and shortages involved in liquidating the double literary standard and the cultural color-line.

For the time being, however, and for some time to come, we must calmly face in our literary economy a situation already quite familiar in our monetary affairs, double taxes. The high cost of prejudice, to which we had all but become accommodated, is now being compounded by the high price of integration. Together they add up to a capital levy, and strain to the utmost our artistic resources and our intellectual morale.

But like taxes, these exactions must be paid, and it is not easy to make reliable appraisals, let alone forecasts, with both balances and shortages turning up in the wrong column and the most unexpected places. Certainly no general gain for American letters at large can be sensibly reckoned as a loss for the special literary interests of the Negro, whether Negro authorship or subject-matter is involved. And yet what, for instance, is the correct estimate of a situation like that of Frank Yerby, who year after year on the second-class level of popular fiction continues his voluminously successful output of sentimental historical and period fiction? Obviously he is the most seasoned story-teller we now have. Granted that there is no obligation on Mr. Yerby's part to touch the relatively rich and untapped resources of the Negro theme in the historical field, the tragic dilemma remains that in turning to such subject materials he could not possibly persist in being as slickly superficial as in *The Golden Hawk* or *A Woman Called Fancy*. Assured now of both an income and an audience, it would obviously be sheer prudence to be giving thought to a position in American letters rather than merely on the best-

Phylon 13 (1952): 7–18.

seller lists. Certainly Mr. Yerby puts himself on record for impeccable literary standards and high seriousness when in choosing the "best fiction of the year" he selected Thomas Mann's *The Holy Sinner*, Faulkner's *Requiem for a Nun* and William Styron's *Lie Down in Darkness*.

My motives are not to presume to be critical on prerogatives that have long since lapsed, but principally to report a new sort of situation where considerable contemporary gains must still be reckoned as net losses, and for all concerned. Is this to become a trend? Here we also have Willard Motley, who in *Knock On Any Door* wisely exploited a mixed milieu, the marginal Chicago between the South and the North sides that he knows so intimately, but who now in his second novel, *We Fished All Night*, an obvious bid for success in the novel of social criticism, shows evidence of a studied avoidance of the Negro factors at hand. Beyond question, Motley's proper niche is in the Chicago school of ultrarealism; but *We Fished All Night* as an analysis of contemporary frustration fails to give the impress of vital conviction which alone can transform reportorial realism into real art. Except for the passages dealing with war and its after-effects, Motley's closely studied transcripts of life read more like a reporter's notebook sketches for a novel than the finished novel itself. This is no runner-up performance to James Farrell, or Cain or James Jones, and certainly not to Richard Wright, to whose mantle Motley, with more concern for the necessary illusion even of realism, could reasonably aspire. In actual writing this second novel overlaps the composition of *Knock On Any Door*, which may account for the fact that it is not an encouraging or expected advance in artistic maturity over its promising predecessor.

The high price of integration exacts a double toll; in the general field, the competition is keen, the pace swift and the odds of success proportionately greater, while the same has become true for the special field of both the fiction and social analysis of Negro life due to the exceptionally penetrating recent performances of white writers in these areas. We are for the moment on the red side of the ledger, temporarily, let us hope; one reason being this inevitable but transitory deflection of some of our strongest talent into the general field. Eventually the challenge must be met. No Negro author has yet delivered a strong novel of the Negro's war experience, while in succession such significant fiction has been produced as Hans Habe's *Walk in Darkness*, James Gould Couzzens' *Guard of Honor* and Lorenzo Wahl's *The Invisible Glass*. In the social analysis field, Abram Kardiner and Lionel Ovesey have in *The Mark of Oppression* pioneered in the important new field of psycho-social dynamics, where the safeguards of inside interpretation could have profitably been utilized, while in the studies by Arnold Rose and Wilson Record a challenging virtuosity has developed that must put Negro sociologists and historians on their utmost guard and mettle. For both the latter, in addition to impeccable thoroughness and objectivity, have in addition such virtue of penetration that no argument about the necessity for inside minority insight is relevant or justifiable. The situation has clearly resolved itself into a free-for-all contest in an open tournament of artistry, skill and scholarship, with the hard but fair task of absorbing the costs of integration in this Ghetto-clearance development, now well under way in American culture.

*   *   *   *

FICTION

Motley's social seriousness is beyond challenge; he has both a serious theme and perhaps an over-serious approach. However, as a novel of frustration, *We Fished All Night* is itself artistically frustrated, partly because of an almost pathological concentration on the "lost generation" components in all three of the main characters, but also because it is hard to fuse a set of case studies into either a vivid social indictment or a convincing novel. Yet, one of the great contemporary American novels must one day be written on this very theme of the confusion of values in which present-day American youth finds itself involved, particularly of the lower middle class milieu of his main characters, and with more matured skill of characterization and a firmer hand in social analysis. Mr. Motley still remains one of the most promising contenders in this field. But whoever writes it will do well to remember that the value dilemmas of a Don Lockwood, born a Chet Kosinski, of Aaron Levin, torn between orthodox Jewish traditions and a Gentile group of associates, of a Jim Norris, labor leader with upper-class ambitions is paralleled by the younger generation Negro paradox of belonging in one sense and not belonging in another.

Every Man His Sword, on the contrary, is a well focussed and convincing social novel, this time incisive surgery of the racial dilemmas of the South. It depicts from obviously intimate observation the helpless subservience of the Negro community and its preacher "leader" in the hands of the sadistic whites in political power, and also gives an unusually realistic portrayal of the feuds and jealousies within the white community itself. It is a story of three lynchings and one near-lynching, two of them Negro and two white. The sheriff, trying to find a scapegoat for a real lynch murder in the Negro community, deliberately frames an innocent Negro, but is so involved in a feud with a rival for the affections of his wife that he himself is murdered. only to have his cover-up lynching tracked down in the end to a melodramatic finish of a mistrial of the Negro suspect and the eventual discovery and lynching of the white perpetrator of the crime. In spite of the melodrama and the hopeless stalemate of the community's utter disregard for legal process and authority, this book does not have the typical moral imbalance of most Southern novels on this theme, nor the social fatalism so aggravatingly associated with it. Quite the opposite, *Every Man His Sword* is written in the vein of militant exposure and a convincing diagnosis of a fatally sick and discordant society, systematically infecting itself like a progressive social cancer. This is one of the notable contemporary novels of the South, morally more militant even, in my opinion, than the considerably outstanding performance last year of Arthur Gordon's *The Reprisal*.

Lloyd Brown's *Iron City*, a story of a "framed" Negro prisoner in the death row of a mid-Western penitentiary and the heroic efforts in his behalf by an underground "cell" of Communist fellow-prisoners, has strong but unrealized potential both in theme and setting. The latter as well as the characterization are realized with fair competence, but the plot and theme badly miscarry by virtue of obvious propagandist handling. In this respect, *Iron City* is a typical failure of the special pleading approach, failing to galvanize the basic human components of a story to artistic effect and conviction. As a result, a potentially good plot turns into an obvious tract peopled with ideological puppets and marionettes. If readers want a concrete example — (page 113) the capitalists, who "threw Joseph into jail and Samson into jail and the Apostle Paul too, and when all the jails got filled up the only thing they could do was to throw them to the lions."

Cloud on the Land and *Intrigue in Baltimore* are both carefully, almost painfully, studied historical novels, each involving the slavery-antislavery controversy, the one in Virginia of 1822 and the other Baltimore of 1860. However, for all of the abolitionist slant of their rather melodramatic plots, they are second-rate in skill and conception. They are mainly significant as part of a trend nowadays to resurrect the era of abolitionist struggle after what surely has been a long eclipse of both moral and artistic interest. The period is an unworked mine of fictional possibilities; so great that one regrets the steady continuity of well-written but narrowly conceived novels like *The Fortune Tellers,* with its stereotyped crusading Yankee journalist, its victimized but supine Negro scapegoats and its fanatical and successful Southern reactionaries. For the Literary Guild to give prestige and vogue to such trite formula fiction is regrettable, for competent characterization is just another dimension in fiction of good writing, and without it, however fluent and plausible, a novel is, in the truest sense of the word, badly written.

In contrast, both unhackneyed and more finely observed situations are crowded, with real artistry however, into Thomas Hal Phillips' *The Golden Lie.* Both the account of the contrasted temperaments of the white farm proprietor Walter Lloyd and his religious wife, Savanna, and of Roy, the Negro sharecropper, are real, unstereotyped and their unconventional relationships made plausible and humanly significant. Phillips is evidently one of the younger Southern novelists to be hopefully watched, just as the even more obviously talented Lonnie Coleman, whose *Clara* is tantalizingly over the calendar boundary of our 1951 listings.

*   *   *   *

POETRY and BELLES LETTRES

There is another volume of verse from Langston Hughes, *Montage of a Dream Deferred,* a golden title and a potential bonanza of the Negro's urban frustration moods. Here is a subject and a poet made for each other, and here and there are occasional glints of this gifted poet's golden talent — as in "Night Funeral in Harlem."

> When it was all over
> And the lid shut on his head
> and the organ had done played
> and the last prayers been said
> and six pallbearers
> Carried him out for dead
> And off down Lenox Avenue
> That long black hearse done sped.
>   The street light
>   At his corner
>   Shined just like a tear —
> That boy that they was mournin'
> Was so dear, so dear
> To them folks that brought the flowers,
> To that girl who paid the preacher-man —

It was all their tears that made
That poor boy's
Funeral grand.

But then one finds the flip doggerel and an uneveness of artistic conception which careful self-criticism could easily have avoided. Surely if, as the publisher's blurb says, "a poet laureate of the Negro folk," then a carelessly tipsy laureate who wears his laurel askew and sometimes with the cap-backward antics of sandlot baseball. For the skeptical reader, just let me cite two:

Daddy,
don't let your dog
curb you!

and

I don't give a damn
for Alabam'
Even if it is my home.

A competent but fragilely traditional volume of verse comes from the pen of J. Alpheus Butler, but on the whole the poetic harvest this year has reverted to the minor mood and minor caliber.

A first-rate historical study of the Cincinnati-born Negro romantic painter, Robert S. Duncanson, amply illustrated and exhaustively documented, has been written by James A. Porter, and has been published as a special supplement of *Art In America*. The competence of the study adds to Professor Porter's increasing stature as an art critic, as does also his discerning article in the Winter issue of *The Mid-West Journal* on "Expressionist Trends in Afro-Cuban Painting."

Professor Wingert of Columbia has written what is probably the best general or layman's analysis of African Negro sculpture, a most serviceable contribution since so much of the literature on this important subject is either amateurish twaddle or much too technical and recherché for the average reader. This work will probably remain the best single source in English for the reader seeking both competent artistic and cultural interpretation of the arts of Negro Africa, although for the expert, a forthcoming work of Ladislas Segy on African Negro sculpture is awaited with keen and hopeful interest.

John J. Daly has earned the gratitude of friends of Negro music by reconstructing carefully and sympathetically the life of James Bland, the neglected Negro analogue of Stephen Foster and really in retrospect a comparable figure in the hey-day of American minstrelsy. The record, including the tardy but most commendable tribute of the State of Virginia to the author of their theme song, "Carry Me Back to Ole Virginny," is a story everyone should read. On the other hand, the familiar story of the Fisk Jubilee Singers, as retold in Arna Bontemps' *Chariot in the Sky*, except for the plausible excuse of a special narrative within the mindscope of the juvenile reader, has sparse justification. Even as a juvenile, more mature interpretation of the social background of Reconstruction would have been both useful and enhancing. Shirley Graham in her synthetic reconstructions of significant Negro historical characters strikes a better and more effective balance, and has set a standard in this field that other writers must take into account.

Stella Brewer Brooks' study of Joel Chandler Harris is a noteworthy contribution to the relatively small body of literary criticism by Negro authors. It is a matter of astonishment how few works of competent

literary criticism have come as yet from Negro teachers and students of
language and letters. Mrs. Brooks' approach is that of the student of folk-
lore rather than the literary critic; however, in this case her commentary
has added point and propriety, for the moot question is how accurate was
Harris as a folklorist? Until recently, hardly anyone has dared join issue
on this question.

BIOGRAPHY and AUTOBIOGRAPHY

The moot book of the year is, of course, Ethel Waters' autobiography,
His Eye Is on the Sparrow. I was prepared not to like it, knowing how
many unfavorable stereotypes it might confirm. However, the big question involved here is what a minority person should do about stereotypes
that not only exist but persist regardless of what one does about them.
Given a set of stereotypes, the realistic commonsense attitude is to meet
them head-on and stare them out of countenance. By that, I mean, not
being unrealistically thrown off balance by them into shame and confusion, but by what I take it has intuitively been Miss Waters' shrewd
technique of not being too concerned about them. Like derogatory nick-
names, stereotypes can be confounded by not taking them overseriously
and certainly the worst of all strategies is to be hypersensitive over them.
I was finally won over by her robust disregard of what people may think;
for after all, the bogey of mock respectability has too often made cowards
of us all. Miss Waters has at least not committed the unpardonable
artistic sin of hypocrisy; and in many incidents, even when skirting the
perils of confirming silly, over-generalized stereotypes, has disarmed them
and even put them to rout in the mind of the careful reader by revealing
their social roots and causes.

His Eye Is on the Sparrow seems to me, accordingly, to be on the plus
side of the ledger on three counts: as a uniquely lively and candid autobiography relating with considerable courage and consistency a life story
worth telling but that many others with conventional inhibitions would
have glossed over or suppressed; as a valuable, comparatively rare document on the life of the Negro entertainer and vaudevillian during a crucial
period of his evolution; and finally, as what should be taken by any intelligent reader as a generic documentary on the life of the slum child rather
than one specifically related to race, in spite of its added features of racial
handicaps of which there are enough to make it valuable also on that
particular score. In the latter regard, note the poignant narrative of her
auto accident in the deep South that came so near to having the same
tragic end as that of Bessie Smith. The saving graces are, of course, Miss
Waters' candor and unextinguishable sense of humor, with the expected
complementary shortcomings of incurable naivete and unabashed sentimentality.

J. Saunders Redding's *On Being Negro in America*, although nominally
an essay in social interpretation, is really more an autobiography than
appears on the surface. It is best apprehended as such, for its major shortcoming, in spite of its initial warning, "This is personal," will undoubtedly
be that it will be taken as a more general account of the Negro intellectual
than it actually is. This book, too, has a commendable candor and earnest
integrity that cannot be too highly praised or appreciated. However, it
has an undertow of righteous resentment, indignation and self-pity, which
so far as I can judge is not as basically generic with the Negro intelligentsia as the average reader will take it to be. In addition to speaking for
himself, and very eloquently, Mr. Redding speaks for thousands whose re-

actions he makes articulate. Indeed, this articulation is very timely and useful, provided it is not over-generalized to be the typical or predominant reaction of the Negro intellectual as such. They may even be statistically a minority, but there are more robust spirits for whom Claude McKay, whom incidentally Redding much admires, spoke when he said:

> Although she feeds me bread of bitterness
> And sinks into my throat her tiger's tooth,
> Stealing my breath of life, I will confess
> I love this cultured hell that tests my youth.

I am not making the superficial and unwarranted insinuation of any supineness of spirit, but merely calling to attention the existence in considerable numbers of what William James would have called the "tough-minded" rather than the "tender-minded" among the Negro intellectuals, who at least typically would never have wound up with a more Christian America as the overall solution of our national race question. With the caution to the reader to heed constantly the author's own reservation of the personal character of the reactions, here is a franker than usual documentation of Negro experience at a level rarely made available to the general reading public. In fact, all that is needed for even greater effect is to have other Negroes at this level to take the public into their confidence, on the ever more warrantable assumption that they are open-mindedly and seriously interested in knowing what goes on in the educated Negro's mind and heart. Once that trend develops momentum, we shall not be guilty as a class in compounding the "American dilemma" by continuing to make the Negro mind a dark enigma for those who may wish to know what goes on inside. In the nearly fifty years since Dr. Du Bois wrote *The Souls of Black Folk,* there have not been a half-dozen books following this courageous precedent of saying how and what the intellectual Negro feels and thinks. Bravo, then, for Mr. Redding's significant initiative: may his tribe increase!

HISTORY and SOCIOLOGY

On the modest level of good journalism, Roi Ottley's impressions of the attitudes of European countries toward their sparse Negro populations as reported in *No Green Pastures* is a creditable, readable and informative, even provocative account. Unfortunately, however, either Mr. Ottley has sold his publishers or they have sold him a too pretentious bill of goods, with the net result of making his relatively superficial and amateurish generalizations ridiculous in their claim to sociological and cultural competence. Years of European experience, intimate knowledge of the languages and cultural traditions of at least the major four of these countries, entree to circles of scholarship would be a requisite for any such conclusiveness, and it is unfortunate that Mr. Ottley has exposed himself to any such broadsides as can and will be aimed at many of his conclusions from those possessing such seasoned experience and entree. At the cabaret night-club, tourist level of experience, no such profound insight is possible, and basically that is the level of Mr. Ottley's observation, dinners with René Maran and interviews with Pope Pius XII notwithstanding. It is to be regretted, then, that these quite interesting impressions were not presented more modestly as what they are — good journalism, reporting, by the way, the not quite normal atmosphere of Europe during and after a catastrophic war. For the general reader, without such misleading claims to finality, they make interesting, informative reading entertainingly pitched between the level of travel letters and journalistic versions of popularized history. Incidentally, one of the best written chapters is the one on Italy, and the account of the Papal interview is a fine bit of reporting, but even here, for instance, to over-generalize from Neapolitans and a popular summer outdoor audience in Rome to characteristic analogies between Negroes and Italians temperamentally is a flagrant example of the amateurish superficiality of which I have spoken: Milan, Turin or even other more representative circles in Rome would register another story.

In the revised edition of *Brothers Under the Skin,* Carey McWilliams has in a very limited scope given an astonishingly comprehensive panoramic view of the Negro in relation to American history and the basic issues of democracy and civil liberties. The background benefit of a comparative discussion of other minorities, of course, largely makes this possible although the author's own forthright liberalism and perspicacity also add their share.

Similar enlightenment flows even more systematically from one of the best books yet published in this area of comparative minority studies, *Race Prejudice and Discrimination,* edited by Arnold Rose, chief editorial collaborator in Gunnar Myrdal's *An American Dilemma.* Although lavishly endorsed by high authorities, Brewton Berry's *Race Relations* is not to be compared. This comparative approach, inaugurated just a decade ago by *When Peoples Meet,* has increasingly established itself in the scholarship of the race question and by transforming its context has really transformed its whole intellectual perspective.

The historical and sociological literature of the year is most uneven, as is perhaps to be expected, but with the plethora of books on the subject, authors must be prepared for embarrassing comparisons. Dean Reppy's authoritative study on *Civil Rights in the United States* is certainly one of those to be heartily welcomed. As also is the competent study of Helen Edmonds, *The Negro and Fusion Politics in North Carolina.* For that very reason, then, one cannot much longer be indulgently patient with such hodgepodge and amateurish efforts as Elbert Tatum's *The Changed Political Thought of the Negro* or the well-intentioned but completely journalistic compendium of Dees and Hadley in *Jim Crow.* More and more a seasoned, growing public is calling for well-documented facts and less and less propaganda, having acquired gradually the knack of wanting to make up its own mind.

In the category of historical antiquaria, there are two valuable additions to the literature, Melvin Kennedy's carefully edited and revealing letters of Lafayette on the subject of slavery, and the extensive Journal of William Johnson, a successful free Negro pioneer, on conditions in pre-Civil War Natchez.

Three other items are important enough for comment. Allan Chalmers' detailed inside account of the Scottsboro case comes late, but is an indispensable batch of first-hand evidence on that case, which in historical perspective looms as one of the turning points in civil rights protest. Wilson Record's *The Negro and the Communist Party* is a fine example of an objectively factual study which at the same time shows unusual skill of inside projection into the subtleties of minority politics. In fact, besides being a fair account of communist plans, tactics and results in the period 1919 to 1950, this book, in the absence of the publication of Dr. Bunche's monographs on Negro leadership done for the Myrdal study, gives perhaps the most incisive account of the main trends and strategy of Negro leadership organizations for the period covered.

Finally, we have in Kardiner and Ovesey's *The Mark of Oppression,* a significant ground-breaker in the field of racial psycho-dynamics. This is independent of the actual conclusions, which seem to rest on too few case studies, twenty-five psycho-analyses, but which nevertheless show the important bearing on specific individual life histories of the traumatic psychological effects of prejudice. Undoubtedly too weighted on the negative side of decompensation, since only psychotic cases came to the researcher's attention, there is quite sufficient evidence to document both the individual frustrations and the social costs of what they aptly refer to as "The Mark of Oppression." Further emphasis on such avoidable maladjustment and damage may lead to a new attack and approach to the amelioration of minority persecution and oppression, not merely Negro but minority discrimination in general.

Because of space, a small number of listings — self-explanatory as entries for readers with special interests in their respective fields — have been made without extended comment. René Maran's biography of Savorgnan de Brazza, the French analogue of Stanley and pioneer of the French Congo and the interesting project of publisher Seghers in Paris in promoting contemporary poetry by French Africans, call at least for passing mention.

BIBLIOGRAPHY

FICTION

We Fished All Night, Willard Motley, Appleton Century, Crofts, New York. $3.75.

A Woman Called Fancy, Frank Yerby, Dial Press, New York. $3.00.

Every Man His Sword, Irving Schwartz, Doubleday & Co., New York. $3.00.

Iron City, Lloyd Brown, *Masses & Mainstream,* New York. $3.00.

Cloud on the Land, Julie Davis, Rinehart & Co., New York. $3.00.

The Fortune Tellers, Berry Fleming, J. B. Lippincott Co., Philadelphia. $3.75.

Intrigue in Baltimore, Janet Whitney, Little Brown & Co., Boston. $3.00.

The Golden Lie, Thomas Hal Phillips, Rinehart & Co., New York. $3.00.

POETRY & BELLES LETTRES

Montage of a Dream Deferred, Langston Hughes, Henry Holt & Co., New York. $2.00.

Philosopher and Saint, J. Alpheus Butler, Exposition Press, New York. $2.00.

Robert S. Duncanson, James A. Porter, *Art in America,* Vol. 39. New York. $1.50.

The Sculpture of Negro Africa, Paul S. Wingert, Columbia University Press, New York. $4.50.

A Song in His Heart; Life of James Bland, John J. Daly, John C. Winston Co., Philadelphia. $3.00.

Chariot in the Sky, Arna Bontemps, John C. Winston Co., Philadelphia. $2.50.

BIOGRAPHY-AUTOBIOGRAPHY

His Eye Is on the Sparrow, Ethel Waters and Charles Samuels, Doubleday & Co., New York. $3.00.

Joel Chandler Harris — Folklorist, Stella Brewer Brooks, University of Georgia Press, Athens. $4.00.

Mary McLeod Bethune, Catherine O. Peare, Vanguard Press, New York. $2.75.

Amos Fortune: Free Man, Elizabeth Yates, Aladdin Books, New York. $2.50.

On Being Black in America, J. Saunders Redding, Bobbs-Merrill, New York. $3.00.

HISTORY AND SOCIOLOGY

No Green Pastures, Roi Ottley, Charles Scribners Sons, New York. $3.00.

The Negro and the Communist Party, Wilson Record, University of North Carolina Press, Chapel Hill. $3.50.

Brothers Under the Skin, Carey McWilliams, Rev. Ed. Little Brown & Co., Boston. $3.50.

The Mark of Oppression, Abram Kardiner and L. Ovesey, W. W. Norton & Co., New York. $5.00.

Race Prejudice and Discrimination, Ed. Arnold M. Rose, Alfred A. Knopf, Inc., New York. $4.50.

Civil Rights in the United States, Alison Reppy, Central Book Co., New York. $4.50.

The Integration of the Negro into the United States Navy, Lt. Dennis D. Nelson, Farrar, Straus & Young, New York. $4.00.

Lafayette and Slavery, Melvin D. Kennedy, American Friends of Lafayette, Easton, Pennsylvania. $1.00.

The Negro and Fusion Politics in North Carolina, Helen G. Edmonds, University of North Carolina Press. Chapel Hill. $3.00.

William Johnson's Natchez, Ed. W. R. Hogans and E. N. Davis, University of Louisiana Press, Baton Rouge. $10.00.

They Shall be Free, Allan K. Chalmers, Doubleday & Co. New York. $3.00.

Interracial Housing Morton Deutsch and M. S. Collins, University of Minnesota Press, Minneapolis. $3.00.

Race Relations, Brewton Berry, Houghton Mifflin, Boston. $4.75.

Jim Crow, J. Walter Dees and James Hadley, Ann Arbor Publishers, Michigan. $2.50.

Say Amen, Brother, William H. Pipes, Williams Frederick Press, New York. $4.00.

Unesco Pamphlets, *Race and Culture*, Michel Leiris; *Race and Biology*, L. C. Dunn; *Racial Myths*, Columbia University Press, 25 cents each.

AFRICANA

Africa: Continent of the Future, George E. Haynes, Association Press, New York. $3.50.

The Mango and the Mango Tree, David Mathers, Alfred Knopf, New York. $3.00.

Savorgnan de Brazza, René Maran, Editions du Dauphin, Paris. 450 fr.

Chants pour Naett, Leopold S. Senghor, Pierre Seghers, Paris. 100 fr.

Poemes Africains, Keita Fodeba, Pierre Seghers, Paris. 100 fr.

FROM *NATIVE SON* TO *INVISIBLE MAN*:
A Review of the Literature of the
Negro for 1952

I N THE thirty years' span of my active reviewing experience, there have
been in my judgment three points of peak development in Negro fiction by Negro writers. In 1923 from a relatively low plateau of previous
problem fiction, Jean Toomer's *Cane* rose to unprecedented artistic
heights. Not only in style but in conception it raised a new summit, as it
soared above the plane of propaganda and apologetics to a self-sufficient
presentation of Negro life in its own idiom and gave it proud and self-
revealing evaluation. More than that, the emotional essences of the Southland were hauntingly evoked in an impressionistic poetic sort of realism;
it captured as well some of the more distinctive tone and color of Negro
living. Its only shortcomings were that it was a series of character
sketches rather than a full length canvas: a succession of vignettes rather
than an entire landscape — and that its author chose not to continue. In
1940, Richard Wright's skillful sociological realism turned a hard but
brilliant searchlight on Negro urban life in Chicago and outlined the
somber tragedy of Bigger Thomas in a well-studied setting of Northside
wealth and Southside poverty. Artistically not the equal of the more
masterful series of short stories, *Uncle Tom's Children*, that preceded it,
Native Son's narrative was masterful and its character delineation as
skillful as any work of Dreiser's or Farrell's. The book was marred only
by Wright's overreliance on the communist ideology with which he
encumbered his powerful indictment of society for Bigger, the double
pariah of the slum and the color-line. Wright was essentially sound in
his alignment of the social forces involved but erred artistically in the
doctrinally propagandist tone which crept into his novel chapter by chapter until the angry, ineffective end. The greater pity it was — and is —
that later he disavowed this ideological commitment that cheated him of
an all-time classic of American fiction. Despite this, *Native Son* has remained all these intervening years the Negro novelist's strongest bid for
fiction of the first magnitude.

But 1952 is the significant year of Ellison's *Invisible Man,* a great novel,
although also not without its artistic flaws, sad to say. Ralph Ellison is a
protege of Wright, who predicted for him a bright literary future. Written
in a style of great force and originality, although its talent is literally
smothered with verbosity and hyperbole, *Invisible Man* is both in style

Phylon 14 (1953): 34-44.

and conception a new height of literary achievement. The life story of its hero, obviously semi-autobiographic, ranges from the typical South of a few years back to the metropolitan North of New York and vicinity. Conceptually it runs also almost the whole gamut of class in American society and is interracial at all stages even in the deep South from the benefactor patron of the college visiting for Founders Day to the sinister "crackers" of the rural backwoods. It is in fact one of the best integrated accounts of interaction between whites and Negroes in American society that has yet been presented, with all characters portrayed in the same balance and perspective. Ellison's philosophy of characterization, incisive, realistic, unsparing of physical and psychological detail — all his major characters are stripped bare to the skin and bone, so to speak — is close to the best European realism in that it is so three-dimensional. We see a grand caravan of types, all registered first person on the sensitive but rather cynical retina of the young Negro protagonist. In the South, the patronizing but well-intentioned school trustee, the piously hypocritical Negro school principal, the gauche, naive but not too honest students, the disillusioned, institutionalized war veterans, the townsfolk, the peasants of the countryside, white and black, and most particularly the unforgettable earthy peasant character of Jim Trueblood. In the North, the pageant resumes with all sorts and manner of men and women: the financiers of Wall Street and their decadent jazz-loving sons, factory workers, pro and anti-union varieties, the urban peasants and their homely oddities, parlor-pinks and hard inner-core communists, race leaders, educated and illiterate, each after his kind — and the Harlem community generally displayed finally at frenetic tension in its one big authentic riot. Stylistically all this unrolls in a volcanic flow of vivid, sometimes livid imagery, a tour de force of psychological realism. A double symbolic meaning piled on top of this realism gives the book its distinctive and most original tone and flavor. *Invisible Man* is actually a surrealistic novel because of this, and but for its lack of restraint would rank among the very best of the genre. But the unrestrained bravado of treatment, riding loose rein at full gallop most of the time and the overprecious bravura of phrase and diction weight it down where otherwise it would soar in well-controlled virtuosity. Many readers will be shocked at Ellison's daring franknesses and dazed by his emotional intensity but these are an integral part of the book's great merit. For once, too, here is a Negro writer capable of real and sustained irony. *Invisible Man*, evidently years in the making, must not be Ralph Ellison's last novel.

Lonnie Coleman's *Clara* is uniquely different, but it deserves placement in the same high bracket of fiction of the first magnitude. Within a four- or five-year period it is the top product of the fiction of Negro life by white southern novelists. Coleman, Georgia-born and Alabama-bred, needs no authentication as truly of the South; his easygoing intimate knowledge of southern ways, Negro included, testifies sufficiently to that. No southern novel has gone further, also, in that ultimate candor of insight and outspoken courage toward which the younger generation of southern writers seems to be moving. In handling the interracial triangle of his plot from the woman's side and by putting the narrative first person in the words of Lillian Sayre, the white wife, Coleman approaches his subject the steep, bold way, but he succeeds. Lillian, marrying largely for convenience, finds herself not quite mistress of the Sayre household, already routined by her husband's recently deceased mother under the competent management of Clara, the Negro housekeeper, who, with her mulatto son, Petie, lives in a small cabin behind the house. Rivalry begins instantly between the two women and mounts as it is goaded on by Clara's more seasoned knowledge of the husband's ways. Particularly is this so as with the passing years Sayre relapses into chronic alcoholism, partly in frustration from Lillian's frigidity. Clara stands out more and more in her bossy dignity as the pillar of the household, while Lillian appeases her unhappiness in doting on her godchild, Randall, her sister's son, who becomes the inseparable playmate of Clara's Pete. Soon Lillian's suspicions are aroused, and by bold accusation she learns from Clara that Petie is Sayre's child. Clara is forced to leave and that night her cabin burns to the ground. In Pluma, Alabama, Lillian is automatically above suspicion, so she has her moment of triumph.

But the household caves in after Clara's departure, and shortly Clara must come back to manage and to hold the roof up over an increasingly drunken Carl; Lillian's steadily declining maiden Aunt Aster; the growing exigencies of Randall and Pete, still bosom friends; and Lillian's own frustrated dependence. Tragic events, mutually endured, gradually alter the tensions — Carl's death, Randall killed in war, Pete successfully installed on Aunt Aster's farm, married to Lutie and happy father of a son, "Randy," after Randall. But Pete, disliked both for his success and his progressive farming, marked as "an uppity nigger," is in that community already doomed. The trigger incident finally happens — Toll Cannon, white reactionary with whom he has been feuding, is murdered; in Pluma's eyes "no one but Pete could have done it," and with similarly anonymous bullets, Pete himself is lynched. Lillian, resolutely matured by now, gathers up the remnants, and the triangle that began with prejudice, jealousy and hate resolves into a strange household trio for that community; Lutie, Clara and Lillian, protectively focussed in Lillian's house as mother, grandmother, foster-mother around Randy, Petie's child. In the bare telling the story of *Clara* seems melodramatic, but in full length reading it is a moving and convincing drama of character transformation. It has balanced, consistent characterization, three-dimensional, not type treatment for all, and makes Clara, who plays the title role, the most wholesome and dignified member of the cast.

Earl Conrad's *Rock Bottom* is the South documented well but too laboriously to register vitally. It, too, is told in the first person, by Leeha, the heroine who is supposed to move us as she moves from one vicissitude to another, from one sordid environment to the next. But all the way from Mississippi to Harlem, even in the bogs of Florida's muck swamps, she is a pasteboard pillar for propagandist indictments of society. Not that this is untrue, but all the more pity if it does not move to pity and terror. Why, we ask ourselves, knowing the earnest intentions of these tractarian authors? The answer is an old one; excess is never good art. *Rock Bottom* accordingly misses its target by shooting it, so to speak, to shreds. Thirty years of unrelieved sordidness and oppression are quite possible in life, unfortunately, but only a Gorky could have brought this sort of story out of its overdone effect.

With *Strangers and Afraid* and *Trespass,* we come to another overdone subject, the Harlem interracial, which threatens to become the Waterloo of so many serious but over-ambitious junior authors. There is a field here, but no one has quite mastered it. Of course, one of the first difficulties is to realize that life and character and circumstances are pretty much the same everywhere. There is no magic in the Harlem setting that will rectify a poor plot or vivify shallow characterization or evoke a philosophy of life when an author has none. But such things have to be there in any work of art, and color, skin color or local color, cannot compensate for the lack of them. Though obviously most seriously intentioned, Eugene Brown's story is merely an excursion into Harlem, and really should end with the discovery that Harlem and Flatbush are very much alike after all. And why not? Far too many think it should not be so, and go stubbornly on to proclaim the difference. Particularly on this moot subject of mixed marriage, all novelists should be instructed that it is an old human phenomenon; sometimes successful, in other cases not, but always for specific, never general reasons. The prejudices which with one couple would wreck a marriage would be cementing pressures in another instance: in telling a story, to be successful one must tell a specific story. A stock situation documented to death will never bring a real situation to literary life. The notebooks, yes, but when it comes to the crucial point of writing, young authors must have the courage to throw away the notebooks.

There is much more of moment and substance in *Strangers and Afraid* and yet it, too, is not successful. Here the two protagonists are too much of a polarity: Lyle Bishop, the reformer, and Maccabee David, the perfect foil. The die is cast from the beginning, and once again the plausibility is gone. This novel is wrecked on the shoals of formula character, a little more interestingly than the average Harlem adventure, but wrecked just the same without the sense of a profitable struggle. I think sometimes that there persists, especially with the racially "enlightened," one damaging vestige of the corporate prejudice from which they think they have detached themselves completely, and that is the notion that the Negro character is foredoomed to a defeatist end. The very essence of tragedy is the chance of evading defeat, which in good tragedy is indeterminate until near the end, or even when destined is fought out to the very end. This is not a novel of moving tragedy in spite of all its tragic happenings, and it well may stem from some such attitude, conscious or more likely sub-conscious.

Truman Nelson has novelized the Boston anti-slavery story of a celebrated fugitive case, that of Anthony Burns, espoused by Theodore Parker, Wendell Phillips and the Ward Howes. He has done a colossal amount of research on this celebrated case, and used much, perhaps most of it in his novel, *The Sin of the Prophet*. It can never be asserted against it that it is not authentic; but even in the historical novel authenticity is but the beginning. And for all the dialogue, and the direct quotation of sermon, court pleas and conversations, this is hardly a genuine novel, but a case history. It is true, an important case history for the times and for the antislavery cause, as well as for the revelation of the inner niceties of difference of opinion among both abolitionists and their proslavery opponents, most of all for a portrait of a Boston divided deeply enough on the issue to cause violence and intrigue normally alien to its cold-blooded ways; but I will be much surprised if the novelization adds much to either the circulation or the comprehension of the facts. *The Case of Anthony Burns* could well have been the title, and the nonhistorically minded would have been forewarned.

Laughing to Keep from Crying is typical Langston Hughes. That means many things, among them uneven writing, flashes of genius, epigrammatic insight, tantalizing lack of follow-through, dish water — and then suddenly crystal springs. Fortunately, this is a motley of anecdotal scenes and stories, scattered from his own cosmopolitan experience — Africa, Hong Kong, Frisco, Paris and the like, but all pointing up to Harlem and its theme of color. The title story, a very good one, has the dominant key and clue: "Who's Passing for Who?" It pokes ironic fun at the color line, as for example also does "Something in Common" — the encounter of a white Kentuckian and a color-weary Negro in a Hong Kong bar, where after failing out violently over the color question and being ejected by the bartender, they stagger back together to fight for their rights, presumably including the right to fight over the color question. This is a fair sample; as thumb nail sketches both are well observed and in that sense anecdotally good; one, however, is well told, the other, just an anecdote. And so it goes, not alternately as in this case, but spotty to the end. "Saratoga Rain," a two-page cameo of incisive etching, suggests that this type of thing is Hughes' forte, and that sustained development is not, whether it be plot or character. Why complain? Simply because from the point of evoking it, Langston Hughes knows Harlem so much more surely than all the rest that his vignettes are, with all their faults, worth dozens of so-called "Harlem novels," and with just a little more art, Hughes could be Harlem's Daumier, or to change to the right figure, its Maupassant. How true what W. C. Handy says of another book of his, "Read it for yourself and have a laugh on Harlem, not at it." There's the difference — and the right approach for all writing about this province of Negro life: to see, feel and show not its difference but its different way of being human.

The review of the year's fiction should include mention of Frank Yerby's most recent best-seller achievement, *Saracen Blade*, one of his best and most elaborate historical romances. In this, Mr. Yerby vindicates once more the right of the Negro as artist to any theme and province he chooses as a freeman of the world of letters. This particular work shows cumulative maturity in his chosen field, and its success with the general public will be an incentive to younger Negro writers that may spread our creative production over wider subject-matter fields than usual.

Poetry and Belles-Lettres

Langston Hughes as poet has received this year the recognition of a translation of a volume of selected poems in Spanish, doubly appropriate because of a long standing constructive interest of his in Cuban, Haitian and other Latin American poets and writers. The quite neglected field of literary criticism comes in for welcome mention at last: serious sustained work in straight criticism, Dr. Nathan A. Scott's *Rehearsals of Discomposure* and Helen Chesnutt's biography of her father, which has a valuable dimension of literary criticism because of the light it sheds on his literary philosophy and on his relations with his publishers and literary contemporaries.

Dr. Scott's scholarly and thought-provoking contribution is a series of essays in philosophical criticism dealing with four great literary figures of contemporary culture, Franz Kafka, D. H. Lawrence, Ignazio Silone and T. S. Eliot. What he is interested in is the twentieth century concept of man, what he calls "the human predicament" as it presents itself to these representative modern thinkers. After chastising formal academic philosophy for its evasion of this urgent problem, Dr. Scott goes on with an acute, enlightening analysis of what he considers the common denominator problem of these more sensitive artist-thinkers, who do attempt to resolve the confusions of our contemporary culture. Dissatisfied with what he regards a superficial diagnosis of their reaction as "disillusionment," Dr. Scott suggests viewing it as "spiritual withdrawal" or "cosmic isolation and exile," connecting it with existentialism as a parallel phenomenon. With a conviction that the common question is more significant as "the modern intellectual's dilemma" than any individual answer, he then compares the several specific solutions, and concludes that the grand overall objective of creative thinking in our time is the quest for the rediscovery of inner, life-sustaining values. Whether we agree or not with Dr. Scott's suggestion that a rethinking of Christianity along more mystic but more humane lines is the goal of the search, all serious readers can agree on the indisputable value of his incisive comparative analysis of some of the most significant trends in contemporary thought.

The Chesnutt item is drawn from the family treasury of Charles Waddell Chesnutt's private correspondence as well as from the memories of an objectively intelligent daughter. It gives us definitive light on the personality background of a man who, with time, looms more and more as the important literary Negro of his generation. His stature should be considerably helped by this revelation of high seriousness on the race question, for his group loyalty was really deeper than that of many of his more vociferous contemporaries. Or at least, it was based on more intelligent courage, the resolution to tell the full objective truth about Negro-white relations as he saw them in his day. This was disinterested truth telling, since it is evident from the account of his family life and of his interracial circle of admiring friends in Cleveland, that as a personal problem, race discrimination was already satisfactorily solved for him. This justifies quite meaningfully Miss Chesnutt's subtitle, calling him a "pioneer of the color line."

Both the history and the analysis of Negro music enjoy unusual contributions this year. Rex Harris' small but scholarly booklet, *Jazz*, is illuminating both for the layman and the expert, and treats jazz as a world phenomenon, with adequate documentation of its European developments; while Barry Ulanov's work is restricted by title to the history of jazz in America. It, too, brings the common sense and the expert approaches together fruitfully. Particularly sane is Mr. Ulanov's rejection of "the legend of African origins," confirming, as he says, "the average man's impression of the Negro as a jungle-formed primitive whose basic expression is inevitably savage." Jazz, for him, is correctly an American social development, and his close analysis of its various schools and idioms is a valuable contribution to the subject. In addition to an enlightening discussion of the various locales and what they have contributed to jazz idiomatically, Ulanov gives us an almost complete genealogy of the outstanding jazz musicians, Negro and white. These biographical details are in themselves a priceless contribution; and his discussion of these player-composers by instrument groups adds greatly to our understanding of jazz style development. Harris, on the other hand, is a special devotee of the New Orlean's school, and though he therefore exhibits definite partiality to New Orleans and St. Louis, in return he has given us one of the best documentations of the early roots of jazz in these two seedbed centers. With the voluminous literature of the last decade or so, there is little more now to be said on the subject.

Historical and Sociological

In the third volume of *Life and Writings of Frederick Douglass*, Dr. Foner brings his monumental edition and biography of Douglass through the critical period of the Civil War. Admirably edited and documented, and for the most part objectively interpreted, this is indispensable reading for whomever would really understand the intricate issues of slavery, emancipation, the inner politics of the abolition movement, and the fateful vicissitudes of the Civil War. How near this or that historic decision came to disaster, including the Emancipation Proclamation, is a lesson all need to learn, as also how to admire and evaluate the resourceful strategy which combined with Douglass' fixed convictions to make him so powerful an advocate of freedom's cause. He emerges from the record of these five years, 1860-65, in the full stature of a statesman, and this account, documented point by point, establishes it as has no previous study.

Similar recognition and gratitude are due Herbert Aptheker for another arduous editorial task, the compiling from tons of old records, most of them nearly inaccessible to any but the research historian, of *A Documentary History of the Negro People*. With a pardonable stress on the rebel traits and reactions — and it is indeed noteworthy to see how continuous this strain is in Negro leadership, especially in the earlier years, 1790-1860, there has been gathered together from all sides an amazing mass of evidence showing how much a collaborator the Negro was in the fight for his own freedom. The full gamut of Negro cultural activity is also well represented from church and politics to labor, social welfare and artistic and literary expression, again a rather unusual coverage. Along with the full time span of the Negro's whole articulate life in this country, this, then, is a unique offering. It is good to remember, though, that it was Carter Woodson who laid down the model for all this sort of work, especially in his little known *The Mind of the Negro as Reflected in Letters Written During the Crisis, 1800-1860* (1926). *The Negro Freedman*, a contribution of Dr. Henderson H. Donald, is a welcome but somewhat superficial sketch of the conditions of the Negro in the early emancipation period. Of course, the evidence itself is patchy for this period, and biased pro or con; but still there ought to be enough indirect documentary evidence to check by — sufficient, for example, to avoid accepting obvious bias and hearsay for fact as well as to safeguard against over-inclusive generalization. These occur more than occasionally, particularly in the sections on religious and social customs and "on social classes and traits." *The Romance of African Methodism* by George A. Singleton has somewhat similar flaws, in this case more faults of perspective and overheroic interpretation than of incompleteness of historical facts.

We come finally, in this group, to a brief discussion of a significant and probably very influential book, Carl Rowan's *South of Freedom*. *South of Freedom* represents effective and skillful journalism, detailing the positive as well as the negative challenges of a changing South. Its great virtue and special service, it seems to me, is his presentation of the situation as still a challenging touch-and-go between the forces of reaction and the forces of progress. One comes away with the feeling that the American South is an open battleground in a current war for political, economic and cultural democracy — this time involving Negro reactionaries, the vested interests of segregation as well as the white die-hards on the one side and the liberal white South, the "New South" of the younger generation for the most part, and the progressive Negroes on the other. As

Mr. Rowan vividly documents it here and there over a wide area of the South, deep, middle and southwest, a reader gets a dramatic account of a struggle, the scope and import of which few actually realize — even those who are engaged and involved in it. But in Rowan's sharp, graphic account it reads like a war correspondent's journal of a tour crisscross the South along six thousand miles of American democracy's internal battle-front.

Exotica and Africana

Liberia by R. Earle Anderson, which he correctly subtitles "America's African Friend," recognizing her past and future usefulness as a keystone base of our transcontinental military air routes, is a realistic but appreciative analysis of a country in transition. It forecasts for Liberia both a great economic and cultural development, which is all the more certain now because of the new development plans for the adjacent Gold Coast and Nigeria. The author is unusually fair in his appraisal of the Liberian government and of native life and customs, giving more justice to both than probably any previous study. The reading public, for example, needs to know that tribal bride-buying is a family contract of amends for the loss of a family worker, subject even to repayment if the wife is "divorced," and that the ancient custom of women trekking behind, carrying heavy burdens on their heads, stems from the time when the man was traditionally kept unburdened to be ready to fight or protect from any hazards of the journey. Liberia, or any other country, seen through such understanding lenses, is well served by its foreign observers. In this case, the situation seems full of promise, especially as the tragic rift between Americo-Liberians and the natives seems, at last, on the constructive mend.

Of the increasing number of books on South Africa, the most incisive seems to be Dvorin's *Racial Separation in South Africa.* By any account, it is an appalling story, this fantastic outbreak of hysterical racism. But it must be faced, as in this study, with realistic intelligence. Obviously liberal, Dvorin makes sure not to be partisan in his factual statements, and although warrantably apprehensive, does see some possibility, with a divided white opinion, of some eventual solution.

Strange Altars by Marcus Bach adds still another item to the unending bibliography of Haitian voodoo "research," research in quotation marks. Without condemning either the motive or the genuine interest of many of these books, this one included, one must at last realize that no amount of dramatic description adds up to what is now needed on this subject of Haitian voodoo: detailed study of the rites and symbolic interpretation of the rituals, a job for professional anthropologists only. Neither Mr. Bach, nor his worthy sponsor, the ex-marine Doc Reser, for all their special entree and kindly interest, is capable of that.

The literature of Negro African art, hitherto scant, has grown to an all-time high. After last year's competent treatise by Professor Wingert, *The Sculptures of Negro Africa,* now come two studies of equal competence but superior de luxe format. The Ladislas Segy and Paul Radin volumes are among the most beautiful art books produced in America in the last quarter century; the former, *African Sculpture Speaks,* is exclusively devoted to African sculpture and a stylistic study of its tribal varieties while the latter, *African Folk Tales,* written with the collaboration of Elinore Marvel and James Johnson Sweeney, is a superb collection of African folk tales paralleled by equally superb reproductions (165 folio plates) of African sculpture tribally arranged. The higher levels of African culture, as known already to the present-day cultural anthropologist, are now graphically available to the lay reader, who cannot — if he has a grain of artistic and literary sensibility—ignore or misinterpret them. These tales, many of them cosmological myths of deep symbolic significance, and these plastic creations are indisputable evidence of qualities and culture traits comparable to the better known culture traditions of the whole human race. One yearns for the time when such knowledge and its transforming evaluations will percolate down to the level of generally educated men and women. That they are not yet so disseminated, even among educated American Negroes, is just to be put down to contemporary medievalism or cultural lag. Consider the evidence objectively, especially since the Greeks and the Teutons were "pagan" and the Jews non- or at least pre-Christian: some African creation myths are as "good" or meaningful as any, Genesis included, and some African fables are, even in their moral values, equal to the parables of the New Testament. Considering the billions of dollars worth of psychological damage missionary and racist misconceptions of Africa and the African have wrought, on both countless Negro and Caucasian minds, books such as these, though relatively expensive, are cheap and welcome antidotes — good medicine for the mind diseased.

BIBLIOGRAPHY

FICTION

INVISIBLE MAN — Ralph Ellison, Random House, N. Y. — $3.50.

CLARA — Lonnie Coleman, E. P. Dutton & Co., N. Y. — $3.00.

ROCK BOTTOM — Earl Conrad, Doubleday & Co., N. Y. — $3.75.

STRANGERS AND AFRAID — Thomas Sterling, Simon & Schuster, N. Y. — $3.00.

TRESPASS — Eugene Brown, Doubleday & Co., N. Y. — $2.25.

THE SIN OF THE PROPHET — Truman Nelson, Little, Brown & Co., Boston — $4.00.

LAUGHING TO KEEP FROM CRYING — Langston Hughes, Henry Holt, N. Y. — $2.75.

SARACEN BLADE — Frank Yerby, Dial Press — $3.50.

POETRY AND BELLES-LETTRES

POEMS — Langston Hughes, Trans. by Julio Galer, Editorial Lautero.

CHARLES WADDELL CHESNUTT — Helen M. Chesnutt, University of North Carolina Press — $5.00.

REHEARSALS OF DISCOMPOSURE — Nathan Scott, Columbia University Press — $4.00.

JAZZ — Rex Harris, Penguin Books — London.

A HISTORY OF JAZZ IN AMERICA — Barry Ulanov, Viking Press, N. Y. — $5.00.

HISTORICAL AND SOCIOLOGICAL

LIFE AND WRITINGS OF FREDERICK DOUGLASS — Vol. III. Ed. by Philip Foner. International Publishers, N. Y. — $4.50.

A DOCUMENTARY HISTORY OF THE NEGRO PEOPLE — Ed. by Herbert Aptheker, Citadel Press, N. Y. — $7.50.

THE NEGRO FREEDMAN — Henderson H. Donald, Henry Schuman, N. Y. — $4.00.

SOUTH OF FREEDOM — Carl T. Rowan, Alfred A. Knopf, N. Y. — $3.50.

THE ROMANCE OF AFRICAN METHODISM — George A. Singleton, Exposition Press, N. Y. — $4.00.

SOLDIER GROUPS AND NEGRO SOLDIERS — David G. Mandelbaum, University of California Press, Berkeley — $2.75.

FAREWELL TO THE PUBLIC SCHOOLS — Lena B. Morton, Meador Press, Boston — $2.50.

EXOTICA AND AFRICANA

LIBERIA AMERICA'S AFRICAN FRIEND — R. Earle Anderson, University of North Carolina Press — $5.00.

RACIAL SEPARATION IN SOUTH AFRICA — Eugene P. Dvorin, University of Chicago Press — $4.50.

STRANGE ALTARS — Marcus Bach, Bobbs-Merrill, Indianapolis — $3.00.

AFRICAN SCULPTURE SPEAKS — Ladislas Segy, A. Wyn & Co., N. Y. — $7.50.

AFRICAN FOLK TALES & SCULPTURE — Ed. by Paul Radin, Elinore Marvel and James Sweeney, Pantheon Books, N. Y. — $8.50.

RACE AND CULTURE

Locke was a philosopher, who studied under Josiah Royce, George Herbert Palmer, and Ralph Barton Perry, and immersed himself in the writings of William James. He received a Ph.D. in philosophy from Harvard University in 1918. His dissertation asserted, among other things, that our aesthetic and ethical values emerge from the sociohistorical context of our lives. Our valuations of ourselves and others are learned from our culture, which itself is constantly evolving and changing. While Locke taught philosophy for over thirty years, attended conferences and wrote papers on value theory, he used his theory of value, along with his thorough grounding in contemporary anthropological theories of race and culture, to fashion a philosophy of culture that was the foundation of his social views of art.[1]

In "The American Temperament" (1911), Locke utilized the notion of a distinct American character to explore the question of why America lacked a national high culture. This essay is valuable for showing Locke's early bias against popular forms of art and culture, and his belief that the function of art is to liberate man from provincialism.

Although Locke believed in distinctive racial temperaments, he did not believe they had a biological basis, but instead, were "traceable invariably, however, to historical economic and social causes." That was the message of the next essay, "Race Contacts and Inter-Racial Relations" (1916), a privately published syllabus of a series of five public lectures Locke gave under the auspices of the NAACP on the Howard campus. Originally proposed as a formal course on "inter-racial relations" at Howard, Locke's proposal was rejected by Howard's Board of Trustees which discouraged courses on race relations.

While these lectures were attended primarily by a small group of black and white educators at the time, the real significance of this syllabus is that it outlines Locke's concept of race and his cultural strategy of race advancement in American life. The syllabus is reproduced here with minor changes of punctuation and spelling.

Whereas this syllabus explored the anthropological meaning of culture from a black perspective, the next essay, an address to Howard's freshman class of 1922–23, provides us with another sense of Locke's definition of culture, as refined sensitivity to aesthetic values. "The Ethics of Culture" (1923) is a remarkable self-portrait of Locke as an aesthete, and shows his role as a bearer of high cultural values to blacks.

"The Concept of Race as Applied to Social Culture" (1924) expands on Locke's argument in "Race Contacts and Inter-Racial Relations" that race is not a fixed biological category, but a social myth with important psychological value.

"American Literary Tradition and the Negro" (1926) pioneered the American studies technique of using American literature to gauge social attitudes of the past. Locke's research confirms that white attitudes toward blacks are not monolithic, but "have changed radically and often, with dramatic turns and with a curious reversal of role between the North and the South according to the class consciousness and interests dominant at any given time."

Believing that the image of blacks held by both whites and blacks shaped racial interaction, Locke sought in the "New Negro" art movement to redefine blacks as America's quintessential folk artists, who promised to become America's premier formal artists as well. In "The Negro's Contribution to American Art and Literature" (1928), Locke focuses attention on the folk influences in American popular culture. By arguing that American culture developed out of a process of interaction between Afro-American and other culture groups, Locke critiques the notion that America is the "white man's civilization."

By 1939, some blacks rejected identification as a separate racial group and argued that their contribution to American culture was no more distinctive than any other group's. In "The Negro's Contribution to American Culture" (1939), Locke answered critics who believed that the concept of race should be dropped from cultural studies. "Like rum in the punch," he wrote, "that although far from being the bulk ingredient, still dominates the mixture, the Negro elements have in most instances very typical and dominating flavors, so to speak."

Locke provides a comparative overview of such mixtures in the Caribbean and in North and South America in "The Negro in the Three Americas" (1944). This reprint of Locke's concluding lecture as an Exchange Professor to Haiti in 1943 moves the discussion into the rich atmosphere of the diverse African presence in the Western Hemisphere.

In the final essay, "The Negro in the Arts" (1953), Locke argues that it is through the mirror of the arts that blacks have gained a positive self-image. He also acknowledges that the cycle of assimilation and racialism has come full circle in the 1950s, as "the sense of integration has taken strong hold on many of our younger artists. . . ." Yet in this essay, which appeared a year before his death on June 9, 1954, Locke remains optimistic that "in time the return to native materials will occur in a context free of provincialism or propaganda; and the Negro artist will then find full and proper recognition and fraternal acceptance as a creative participant in the arts of America."

THE AMERICAN TEMPERAMENT

It is a curious but inevitable irony that the American temperament, so notorious for its overweening confidence and self-esteem, should be of all temperaments least reflective, and for all its self-consciousness, should know itself so ill. When criticised, it is either perplexed or amused; when challenged, apologetically boastful, and seemingly delights in misconception and misrepresentation. A striking instance of this singular trait is the way Americans abroad exaggerate their native mannerisms and become veritable caricatures of themselves in good-natured mimicry of the national type. In its extreme form the tendency might be characterized as living up to a libel to save the trouble and expense of legal proceedings. Whether this be due to a sort of mistaken chivalry or to mere childish irresponsibility is as hard to determine as it is unnecessary;—either is reprehensible. There is in this dependence upon foreign opinion something of a native shrewdness for judging others by their opinion of oneself, but much more is to be attributed to an instinctive aversion from the pangs of introspection and a childish capacity for using other people as mirrors. No other nation, perhaps, has played so sensational a rôle, but no other nation has stood so in need of its audience. The histrionic demeanor of Americans abroad, at times so very like the behavior of actors off the stage, exacting calcium-light duty of the sun, is a real clue to the national temperament. If only by the reactions of others do we achieve any definite notion of what we ourselves are, it is small wonder that we have cultivated the actor's manner and practise his arts, only it is a strange art for an otherwise inartistic nation, a curious dependence for a free people.

That a people by theory and instinct so individualistic should believe at all in a national character and should be so obviously content with a composite portrait is, indeed, marvellous. With its history and traditions, America might quite logically have repudiated any such thing as a national

North American Review 1914 (August 1911): 262–270.

temperament and have rid itself of this inveterate superstition of the journalist and the patriotic orator. The dema-
gogue picks his following from the worshippers of this idol
of the tribe; and the early republican fathers, who were
philosophical Democrats, feared and detested both. It is
due to their heroic efforts that the idea has still so little
content and so few traditions to take root in, but America
of the present day insists on the national type: it has cultivated it most successfully and believes in it most instinctively and whole-heartedly.

Society is quite at the mercy of the class that paints its
portrait, and it has been no credit to us that ours has been
the hasty evocation of journalists and cartoonists in league
with the publicist, rather than the careful creation of novelists and artists in their hereditary conspiracy to make the
best representative. With us, as with other industrial civilizations, the national loyalties grow out of individual prosperity and success, and the bond between the individual and
the impersonal or corporate interests is very strong and
immediate. But the same ideal loyalty to a national character and belief in a national will and destiny, which promote the industrial arts, promote, under favorable circumstances, the reflective and representative arts, and make
for that sense of institutions, which, beginning in jingo
patriotism, ends in sound traditions. And as containing the
promise of all this, the current idea of the American temperament is worthy of some serious analysis and deliberate
propaganda.

The democratic and individualistic tone of modern living
will no longer allow a class product to be foisted on it as
an expression of the national life and ideal as has so often
before been the case. America is wise, after all, in pre-
ferring to remain artless and unenlightened rather than
accept contemporary art as a serious expression of itself.
Drawn by detached and almost expatriated æsthetes at the
commands of the most disinterested class of art patrons
ever in existence, it has no real claims except upon the curiosity of the people. To force an art first to digest its civilization in all its crude lumpiness is, after all, a good and
sound procedure, and it is safe to prophesy that in America
either the result will be representative and unique or that
there will emerge no national art at all.

America, indeed, in the construction of the American temperament, is producing her first immaterial or art product.
One only wishes there was more conscious art in the process.
At all events, there has developed a national character so
unique that it is the despair of critics, and yet so simple
and available that to acquire it one only need live in America. Even the English and Chinese ambassadors assume it
for a while, and what is more significant, the emigrant,
Slavic, Teutonic, Irish or of the Romance stocks, acquires
it and becomes an American spiritually before he has re-
sided long enough to be naturalized. And in certain instances he becomes so even in retaining strong hereditary

national and racial characteristics. His children are " born Americans." Against many foreign critics it must be maintained that this is something more than the assumption of a certain commercial-mindedness and personal self-assertiveness everywhere recognized as American. Certain temperaments quite without these traits, notably the American negro participate to a remarkable degree in the American temperament. In last analysis, it is a mental atmosphere as unavoidable and free as air, and this, to my thinking, characterizes it as something spiritual, as being free, accessible, contagious. On festival days we are tempted to think of it as something political, and to make it a matter of the Constitution and the Declaration of Rights. Oftener still do we think of it as a sense of social partnership and corporate prosperity of a commercial type or industrial, at least, in its manifestations. But it is really a very limited and simple system of conventional ideas, associated with certain very contagious but superficial mannerisms whose only justification is that as a light but strong social harness it works so well. How shallow and contentless it is as an idea or how indefensible and inadequate as a code, fortunately only philosophical historians realize. At present the pragmatic verdict must prevail; it works quickly, effectively, as a bond between men and, under the circumstances, seems to them less tyrannous than a convention of forms, permitting of the almost unhindered exercise of that personal initiative and freedom which an American calls his individuality.

It is a unique thing,—this American sort of individualism, perhaps even a transitory thing, and one feels that it alone is the cause of such theoretical antinomies working in actual practice. An American's idea of himself, though highly personal, is not fixed; it is really Protean and even puerile. How it claims everything and yet refuses to identify itself permanently with anything. Criticise the American for any trait intimately personal or nationally characteristic, and he will evade the thrust by insisting that you have not touched a vital spot, though perhaps mortally wounded. It is like rebuking a child for one of his moods; he changes it, and you cannot hold him to account for the submerged personality, the discarded rôle. The American temperament is histrionic as the healthy child; its naïve individuality is unquestionable, and because it is so plastic it knows no self-contradiction.

But to portray Americans as heroic children will seem unwarranted to those who know the drawn-faced and tense-lipped features of our fellow countrymen: surely these people do not look young or irresponsible. America's superb boyishness does threaten to succumb to the undue responsibilities it has taken upon itself in overconfidence. But that overconfidence is youthful, youthful to a fault.

It must be remembered that America, though an amalgam of peoples, is of the Anglo-Saxon stock in mental characteristics, and that it has taken upon itself what may be the final experiment in the Anglo-Saxon type of civilization. More reflective and calculating peoples are inclined to count the costs and experiment by proxy. Among these people a leisure class arises and paints a national character at its leisure, an ideal portrait that men cherish retrospectively and read into the whole life of the people who supported the leisure class. Individualism and a certain self-willed energy has possessed us, and that with fury in the American temperament, and the modern demand for material progress is the result. If we are to credit this tendency with an ultimate goal, it must aim at securing a final and restful mastery over the means of life. In this experiment America is at present engrossed, and the result is likely to justify or repudiate the whole idea;—at least in the eyes of others who are following more cautiously and with less conviction. One sometimes fears that in event of failure, the American temperament will become the scapegoat of many nations and bear the blame of a second Babel. The true American disposition is, however, careless of the end; it neither wants nor anticipates leisure, and cheerfully and without sense of loss waives what the forefathers thought a primary right of man, the pursuit of happiness as an end in itself. It is even a question whether American opinion will tolerate for any considerable time a leisure class devoted to this end, or a leisure class of any sort, so prepared is the American temperament to dispense with the reflective arts and all those posthumous satisfactions, dear to past civilizations, of leaving behind it adequate records and imposing traditions.

Indeed, the real uses of leisure still seem to be below our mental horizon. The second generation succeeds the first and seems intent on discovering whether or not the pursuit of material progress is really endless. This is quite to be expected of a people who have not as yet made any real distinction between work and play, and who have acquired no interests for impersonal pursuits. Most of all do we dislike the person who has aged prematurely through contact with older traditions, the impersonal observer, the onlooker who merely comments; we contrive to eliminate or ignore him as children do grown-ups. One can see why we should, for introspection and reflection are the arch enemies of our dearest illusions. To them our politicians are irresponsible demagogues, our captains of industry merely capricious experimenters, our teachers intellectual sophists, our legislators social extemporizers, our clergymen moral improvisers, and our writers adroit apologists. And so they may, indeed, appear to us later; but now the make-believe is upon us and for us they are not. It is to be hoped that when they come to be matters of history, they will be found to have harmed their contemporaries most, and to have committed fewer crimes against the future than any other active generation of men.

The greatest anomaly of the American temperament is its evasiveness. No one knows what organ it inhabits or can define " the people of the United States " in whose name so much is perpetrated. An astute Frenchman, coming from a country that really possesses a social mind if any country does, accuses America of not having that organic sense called " public opinion." " I hardly discern a national consciousness," he says, " only everywhere a national self-consciousness." Our journalism is a sad witness of this fact; public opinion is too plastic to mould; it runs in rivers and tidal eddies. To record its variations and predict it for short periods is the barometric function of our whole press.

Yet there is on any great occasion, and there issues from any real crisis, political or social, a well-formulated public opinion, terse, simple, emphatic, often already patched into catch-words and phrases, which run from mouth to mouth and are on everybody's tongue at once. We act almost automatically and, consequently, spasmodically as well. There is at the time such unanimity of opinion that no one, parties with traditional policies, institutions with hereditary traditions, even men with fixed principles—none—will think of denying the popular will. Public opinion in America asserts itself violently, impulsively, and more often than in any other country perhaps, accomplishes its immediate aims and demands, owing to the plastic and tentative nature of our institutions and ideas. But once asserted, it does not maintain itself, or if it must maintain itself, does so grudgingly, with a sense of restraint and handicap. This is the price of our amenability to reform.

Peculiarly characteristic in this respect is the national will in any moral issue. Only at times of the greatest tension is the popular mind in sight of principles: the Civil War and its reactions are incontrovertible witnesses of this. So forgetful, except at rare moments, is the national consciousness that it cannot understand or sanction its own actions when involved in the inevitable reaction. Historical-mindedness and patience while the natural equilibrium is re-establishing itself are two traits, most lacking and most needed, in the American temperament.

America is certainly, of all countries, least politically minded. Its politics are a professional game played by professionals,—in all senses of the word it is to be deplored,—for the amateurish amusement and approval of the public. Exactly to what this is due is a very great puzzle. Perhaps it is an American trust and belief in experts, a trait which in our whole life exacts from us more unquestioning reverence for authority and greater faith in delegated power than we are given credit for. The autocratic possibilities of our nominally democratic institutions are only lately beginning to reveal this essential and deeply lodged strain in the American character. A country that worships power, respects the autocrat, and may even come to tolerate the tyrant. Indeed, the analogies between the republican temper of Rome and that of America may well worry those who believe that history repeats itself. Recent attempts against the capitalist have proved that such a type is too representative of the ideals of the common ordinary man to be attacked without a sense of self-contradiction and injury.

Such facts bring us within range of the important discovery that American democracy is not a political theory, but a social instinct. As patriotism, it is sheer rhetoric, bombastic and effusive; as a deep conviction, it is almost religious in its intensity and individual hold upon every citizen. It differs from other continental forms of patriotism in being so associated with the personal and individual well-being of each man, and in having slight reference either to a national past or future. There is little of reflective pride, that grave and historic achievement of the English temperament, and strangely little of a definite notion about the national purpose and destiny. America is too engrossed with the present to have anything but empty and boastful claims upon the future. The sense of power and prosperity, the sense of aggregate power and prosperity, quite opposite to the selfish and individual satisfactions so often charged to the American temperament, is at the very bottom of the national character and is the root of its patriotism.

One can account for the presence of this corporate feeling in closely knit and socially compact groups, or in the country where one racial stock or predominant institution supplies a coercive feeling of kinship and unity. But in America, a land of startling divergencies and instinctive antipathies, it is difficult to explain. Neither as a carelessness or indifference to these contrasts, nor as democratic tolerance, nor even as theoretical or practical humanitarianism, can one account for the American sense of fellowship. It is due to an acute responsiveness, an intellectual sensitiveness, that are born of insatiable curiosity and a surplus of individual energy.

To such a temperament nothing is really trivial, and the points of contact between things are almost infinite. As soon as one examines this trait on an intellectual plane, one sees what curious laws of association govern the American mind. Its superb eclecticism, its voraciousness, its collector's instinct for facts and details, and its joyous disregard for proportion and an artificial order are still in need of adequate exposition. They impose so many handicaps from an artistic point of view that as yet no literary genius except Whitman has found it possible to accept them all. The temperament is, however, extensively catered for: the informational press is its creature. To instruct pleasantly and with the minimum of effort is the debased aim of present-day art; a wide-spread and ever-growing disease of taste of which America produced the germ. The informational short-story, the character sketch, the photographic novel, the popular encyclopædia, the unscientific travel study, and the whole pictorialization of literature and art can be traced to American initiation and patronage. A strange survival of Puritanism,—for the American temperament is still profoundly Puritan,—this idea of art and letters as the handmaids of knowledge, serving in bond to the insatiable curiosity of men. A Republican and utilitarian art, however, is generally short-lived, though we may expect a longer vogue for the contemporary information-monger than that enjoyed by his predecessor, the political pamphleteer. There are even now in America signs of reaction against an impersonal art, and a return to the lyric and dramatic motives. At present the reaction is, unfortunately, at the same time a revulsion from the national idea and temperament.

Thus the only justification America has yet had comes direct from the self-satisfaction of the individual American. His satisfaction, however, is both unmistakable and voluble. He is content, though the competition becomes daily more severe and evident. He is beginning to realize now that many are handicapped at the very outset, that the struggle is prolonged by the stronger for the sheer joy of conquest, and even that a good third of the energy expended is consumed in piling up success on the top of victory. Yet a cheerful acceptance of the situation is the price of his individuality, his optimism, and his chance of winning out, and he pays it ungrudgingly. There is a greater measure of content and less of a sense of environmental injustice in America than anywhere else in the world to-day. And the principles of conduct and social relationships, though elemental, are like the rules of a game, there is an immediate appeal to public censure or approval, and little discrepancy between theory and practice. Naturally our theories suffer when compared with idealistic and more divorced codes. Where every man is supposed to consider his own interests, no social blame is imputed, and no one, except for initial handicaps, has an excuse. That is not, on the whole, an unenviable state of affairs: the American temperament only approximates it. As an instinctive theory, this is what it believes in.

Yet with us, with every man theoretically for himself, public spiritedness prevails to a marked and unusual degree. For every man drives a frank bargain with the community; there is a competitive and open market for altruistic wares. Consider for a moment that phenomenon of our civilization, the millionaire philanthropist. Is he an enigma, this person who has seemed to change character and tactics under our very eyes? By no means: if Americans worship money, they worship it as power, as cornered energy and not in an intrinsic and miserly way. The time comes when the force he has been collecting threatens to vanish in latent inertia as it were, and the millionaire can only release it again by giving. The process of accumulation, becoming automatic, discharges him; he takes to his new vocation of giving, but as far as the muscular reactions are concerned there is very little difference between shovelling in and shovelling out. The community in giving social rewards of a very specious sort in exchange seems quite to have the better of the bargain. But it should not be deluded into thinking that the millionaire has really changed character, and that it is fostering altruistic pursuits.

Somehow, in the end, the American temperament exacts what it needs most, the attitude of suspended judgment. But self-analysis is not necessarily fatal, and if it is too early to make up our minds as to what we are, or, better, what we intend to be, surely it is time to rid ourselves of the delusion that we already know both. As long as the American temperament remains its own sole excuse for being, one cannot expect it to be humble and unassertive, but one may point to the need for self-analysis and expression. The materials at hand are, it is true, a stupendous handicap, so unsuitable that at times one fears that nothing can be produced so wholly vital and unique and interesting as the national character itself.

RACE CONTACTS AND INTER-RACIAL RELATIONS:
A Study in the Theory and Practice of Race

I

The Theoretical and Scientific Conceptions of Race

Race theory of recent development (de Gobineau, 1854)—scientific in data and method, pseudoscientific in postulates and conclusions—invariably the philosophy of the dominant groups—propagandist in the interests of the prevailing civilization types: anthropological and ethnological evidence inconclusive, sociological and dynamic theories prevailing—false expectations of ethnopsychology—race theory essentially committed to the historical bias,. awaits correlation of biological and sociological science for its final conclusions—meanwhile useful only in the study of primitive social levels and origins, or as a guide to the relative value of hereditary and environmental influences upon social groups.

Racial differences and race inequalities undeniable, traceable invariably, however, to historical economic and social causes: no static factors of race, even anthropological factors variable, and pseudoscientific except for purposes of descriptive classification—race prejudice an instinctive aberration in favor of these factors erected into social distinctions—need for evolutionary and dynamic factors expressing divergent culture stages and civilization types; the real scientific criteria of race to be found in language, customs, habits, social adaptability, and survival—the true theory of race a theory of culture stages and social evolution.

Modern races "ethnic fictions," the biological meaning of race lapsing—its sociological and cultural significance growing—social perpetuation of race legitimate, but in need of rationalization.

Race is at present favorable or unfavorable social inheritance falsely ascribed to anthropological differences: race prejudice, a social paradox, and as prejudicial to science as to practical social organization and progress. Race contacts increasingly inevitable: modern civilization, dependent upon their successful maintenance and extension demands race reciprocity—false conceptions of race therefore an obstacle to progress and a menace to civilization.

References

Scholes, T.E. Glimpses of the Ages. London: John Long, 1905. Vol. I, chaps. II, IV, VIII, IX, pp. 1–172.

Finot, Jean. Race Prejudice, trans. Dutton, 1907, pp. 3–125 and 178–218.

de Gobineau, Count. Essai sur l'inegalité des races humains. Paris, 1854.

Proceedings Universal Races Congress. Ed. Spiller. London: King, 1911.
a. von Luschan: The Anthropological Conception of Race.
b. Fouillée. The Sociological Conception of Race.

Royce, J. Race Questions and other American Problems, Macmillan, 1908, pp. 1–53.

Hertz. Moderne Rassenprobleme.

Syllabus of an Extension Course of Lectures given in the Spring semesters of 1915 and 1916 under the auspices of the Howard Chapter of the NAACP and the Social Sciences Club.

Boaz, F. The Mind of Primitive Man. Macmillan, 1911. Chaps. I, II, III, VI, VII.

Boaz. The Instability of Racial Types. Universal Races Congress Proceedings.

II
Practical and Political Conceptions of Race

The political and social practice of race world-old, only the theory modern. The sense of race born of its political practice: the race or kinship bond a traditional and important factor in all forms of group organization from the tribe to the nation—civilization as "ethnic competition"—dominance breeds the "political" races; conquest, and the consequent political and economic subordination, determine the "subject" races—"superior" and "inferior" or even the relatively more scientific contrast of "advanced" or "backward" races, a reference in the last analysis to the political fortunes of race groups—for this reason much false race theory is orthodox history—as well as the apologia of prevailing practice: being more vicious, however, in the latter case than in the former.

Imperialism essentially a "practice of race"—ancient imperialism: modern imperialism— the Roman example of race assimilation and culture absorption superceded. Instead of one civilization superimposed upon another, modern imperialism attempts the substitution of its own for the subjected civilization—economic factors the controlling ones in this characteristic modern aim, growing out of the competitive and industrial basis of modern imperialism. Missionarism, the corollary and important moral sanction of modern imperialism, often a pernicious reenforcement of the creed of race superiority—such conceptions, however idealized, complicated by the racial approach, result in implications of a status of dependence and inferiority, and dominance justifies itself as tutelage.

A study of imperialistic practices important because over half of the colored races live within their direct sphere of operation, and the rest indirectly, since the creed and practice of dominant classes is derived from that of dominant states; no such doctrine survives without the substantiation of successful political practice. Anglo-Saxon superiority a trademark of modern empire—literature of Anglo-Saxonism confessedly racial—fundamental European agreement with English theory and policy of empire—the most liberal and enlightened statesmanship (Cromer, Morley, Bryce, Beaulieu, Clemenceau, Zimmermann, Dernberg) insists upon racial ascendancy as the keystone of empire. Adoption of this policy independent of the practice of Empire: the United States a participant and ally in Anglo-Saxon dominance. We confront in this the common factor of modern race problems: The phenomenon of the color line encircling the globe really the result of commercial imperialism, linking up dominant groups on the one hand, and dominated groups on the other. To be subjected to economic subordination and social prejudice similar under modern conditions to being subject to political domination and commercial exploitation. Present-day civilization of a type calculated to stress the ethnic basis (Giddings), and characterized by "ethnic concentrations," or federations (Finot)—Anglo Saxonism, the Pan-Slavic, Pan-Germanic, and Pan-Anglian movements, and the Pan-Islamic, Pan-Asiatic, and Pan-Ethiopian countermovements. These as tendencies uniquely characteristic of modern civilization need careful study—perhaps peculiar to the expansive types of civilization, or traceable to unusual and not necessarily permanent factors in modern life. This world situation and problem presents great possibilities, if favorably solved—at present it intensifies all specific race contacts and issues, making inter-racial relations the "problem of the twentieth century."

References

Pearson, C.H. National Life and Character. London: Macmillan, 1894.

Cromer, Lord. Ancient and Modern Imperialism. Murray, 1910, pp. 77–127.

Leroy, Beaulieu, P.P. De la colonisation chez les peuples modernes. Paris, 1898.

Thierry, C. de. Imperialism (trans.). Duckworth, 1898.

Reintsch, P.S. Colonial Administration. Macmillan, 1895.

Scholes. Glimpses of the Ages. Vol. I., chaps. 25–28.

Scholes. The British Empire and Alliances. Britain's Duty to her Colonies and Subject Races. London, 1899.

Desmoulins. Anglo-Saxon Superiority (trans.). 1898.

Kennedy, J. The Pan-Angles. Longman's Green, 1913.

Bryce, Lord. The Relations of the Advanced and Backward Races of Mankind. Romanes Lectures. 1902.

Blyden, E.W. Christianity, Islam and the Negro Race. London, 1887.

Giddings, F.J. Democracy and Empire.

Proceedings of the Fifth Session, Universal Races Congress. Papers by Adler, Bruce, and Caldecott.

Johnston, Sir H. The Negro in the New World. Methuen, 1910.

III
Phenomena and Laws of Race Contacts

A study of race contacts the only scientific basis for the comprehension of race relations—yet the history of race contacts is needless, inconclusive, and tantamount to rewriting history: the scientific approach is the sociological, which studies not how the racial contacts have come about, but how society, confronting them, readjusts its life, and works out a modus vivendi—the relations between social conditions and the social code or program constitute the vital phenomena of race contacts.

Danger of erecting phenomena into laws, and of construing race contacts as wholly automatic or wholly deliberate. Race problems, like class problems, originate in the practical issues involved in the relations of mass groups, most often between those that must live together under the same system. The scrupulous regulation of social relationships by race and class codes inveterate, yet no purely ethnic distinction exists apart from underlying political, social, or economic disparities: the tragedy of social forms being that even the necessary recognition in law and custom of these disparities tends to perpetuate them. Complete absorption and wholesale adoption not impossible, and perhaps not infrequent, though it must always seem the exception for historical reasons. Civilization itself a "counter-tendency," so the conscious checking of "social osmosis" or natural assimilation seems, like self-preservation, the "first law of human society." Still the social inequalities of race, rather than their equality, invariably provide the conditions conducive to blood intermixture and physical assimilation.

Restricted status the clue to broad racial relations in society—legal distinctions, though conservative and subject to variation through custom, nevertheless the most reliable clues. The older practices of economic, political, and legal disability—as slavery, position of serf, helot, and metic. Modern disabilities characteristically different, though only slavery, of all the many forms of social disability, is inoperative under modern conditions. Peonage and helotage still exist. Reservation with communal or private tenure still a governmental policy in dealing with intractable groups—the Kraal and the legalized ghetto in dealing with groups whose economic cooperation is necessary, and all forms of partially restricted political participation between delegate representation and full political participation, and on the social side from absolute social exclusion to the full recognition of a "mezito" or a representative class, prevail. Much political practice of race is obsolescent, yet much still remains to be eradicated.

Legal disabilities, except under benevolent colonial systems, repellent to the modern conscience. Social distinctions more typically modern—operative in the absence of political and legal restrictions, and intensifying with their sudden removal. Periodicity of race antagonism not yet clearly established, but the necessity of legislative adjustment of group status sufficient in itself to establish waves of moral reform, and of inevitable social reaction. Variability itself, however, provides a margin of social control, and establishes the moral responsibility of society in these matters. Racial antipathy, though instinctive in appeal and operation, cultivated and not spontaneous—as shown by its comparative absence in periods of slavery. A second, subtler phase of race antagonism only develops with emancipation and subsequent rivalries—violent intensification as race contacts pass from one stage or level to another—especially from an automatic to a voluntary basis, becoming acute on issues arousing a sense of social jeopardy. One variety of racial antipathy decreases, and another increases as the unlike race approaches more the level of the civilization type. Native British, French, and Russian racial feeling of the former type; colonial British, Australian, and American sentiment of the latter type. Though yet unexplained, a possible sociological clue to these differences is the distinction between "primary" and "secondary" groups (Cooley).

Color or other cardinal race differences complicate, but do not cause these issues, for they are as intense in southern Europe. It is a problem of social conformation, becoming acute with peculiarly assimilative peoples, of whom the Negro is admittedly the most imitative. Unlike class issues, which within common culture interests are issues of practical and immediate social ends (Schmoller), race struggles project their issues to the ultimate purposes of society, and awake more fundamental antagonisms. They generate a vortex in society until broken up into class issues.

Race feeling has an undetermined relation to population, intensifying with marked changes in its relative proportions, as well as a definite relation to economic condition, varying inversely with economic differentiation, or any condition that permits of the race group's being thought of *en masse*. Economic and political disabilities require legislative change and legal control—political equality or participation must either wait upon practical conditions, or tolerate apparent discrepancies, the latter preferable under democratic institutions. Social prejudice indicative of a secondary stage in race relations. The mixed blood the first class to become representative and recognized—an inevitable reaction against this class from without and later from within as soon as prejudice has passed into the social and cultural phases of life. Social problems and relations only remotely touched by legislation—their solution the final stage of any race situation.

References

Bryce, Lord. Studies in History and Jurisprudence.

Stephenson, G.T. Race Distinctions in American Law. Appleton, 1910.

Zollschan, Ignaz. Das Rassenprobleme. Vienna, 1912.

Lapouge, G. Vacher. Les Selections sociales. Paris, 1897.

Tarde, G. The Laws of Imitation (trans.). Holt, 1903, pp. 213–243 and 310–322.

Mecklin, J.M. Democracy and Race Friction. Macmillan, 1914. Chaps. I and V, pp. 1–18; 357–81.

American Journal of Sociology, 1914–1915.
a. Vol. 20, No. 4. Schmoller on Class Conflicts.
b. Vol. 19, Park, R.E. Racial Assimilation in Secondary Groups.

Stone, A.H. Studies in the American Race Problem. 1908.

Murphy. The Basis of Ascendancy.

IV

Modern Race Creeds and Their Fallacies

Race creeds control social and even political policies, especially under modern conditions—

an account of this factor important. Cromer suggests a distinction between ancient and modern society on this point of the psychological complication of race creeds, regarding color prejudice as distinctively modern. Color prejudice and race prejudice not quite the same—its historical factors; its social factors. The psychological factors still undetermined, their study valuable for general social psychology—rooted in the deepest and most indispensable social instincts, like the consciousness of kind—inhibitive in the highest degree, yet of necessity to be regarded as eradicable and to be eradicated. Race prejudice a Moloch of the Baconian "idols," yet essentially in its recent phases an "idola theatri"—the feature of indoctrination making modern race creeds more pernicious than their practices—evidence in the spread of anti-Semitism in Europe and the second crop of race prejudice in America.

A scientific study of race prejudice awaits the further development of social psychology—closest analogies in class problems involving a sentimental issue—a comparison with class issues imperative. Recent observers frankly admit the irrational element in color prejudice—but these factors remain to be explained: being perhaps the most important, as nearest to the origin of race antipathy in individual and group instincts. Its enigmatical nature as a peculiar phenomenon in democratic societies, and in its relation to social solidarity not to be minimized.

Practically, race prejudice is what it is psychologically, a false standard or tendency of social judgment: the social standards of its exponents and opponents alike paradoxical. The mere verbal transfers among the many meanings of the conceptions of race a real contributing factor. The most fundamental fallacy is the standard used to justify race superiority—this ideal root of the evil disproved (Zollschan), chiefly by pointing out the false identification of race in the ethnological and biological sense with race in the historical and social sense. The derivations of this doctrine in 19th-century scholarship (Aryan superiority and Indo-Germanic accounts of civilization) explain why science has reenforced with theoretical race creeds and political race theory the unfavorable social practices of race. A rational or a purely scientific theory of social culture the great desideratum.

The Biological Fallacy—since physical race integrity is contradicted in practice through miscegenation, race purity is irretrievable and its maintenance as a social fetish and fiction unwarrantable. The Fallacy of the Masses—the estimation of peoples in terms of aggregates untrustworthy, and not our best attitude even in history, which treats representative groups and factors: wherever inevitable, a strict comparison of equivalents must be attained. The Fallacy of the Permanency of Race Types—no race or class maintains its social role or relative social position long, and further the race types change under environmental adaptation: instances among both the Semitic and the Negro peoples. The Fallacy of Race Ascendancy—a bi-racial organization or a dual code socially unstable, generating the very issues that accelerate social changes toward their termination. The Fallacy of Automatic Adjustment—race distinctions partly deliberate; it is a mistake to regard them as automatic in operation and not subject to remedial measures. All these fallacies involve false social standards as well as false habits of judgment. "Social kind" not necessarily "racial kind"—establishing and maintaining a "social kind" is the vital business of civilization.

Civilization committed practically to some kind of adjustment of various races under the same civilization and polity, the bi-racial organization of such societies a typical modern solution, essentially a transitional form—its immediate advantages often cause its adoption even by the group discriminated against—Booker Washington's acceptance of it notable—as a means to an ultimate end it has appealed to many statesmen having to deal with race problems acutely affecting large groups. Society will not make large concessions simultaneously in the economic and the social fields, even in class issues. The only successful contradiction to invidious race creeds is that of social practice; social theory being invariably conservative, and not lapsing until the customs supporting it have lapsed.

References

Cromer, Lord. Ancient and Modern Imperialism. Appendix A.

Mecklin. Democracy and Race Friction. Chaps. V, pp. 123–156; VII; and IX.

Jastrow, J. Character and Temperament: The Psychology of Group Traits. Chap. VII.

Annals of the American Academy of Social and Political Science, 1901.

America's Race Problems—
a. Winston. Relations of the Whites to the Negroes.
b. Du Bois. The Relations of the Negroes to the Whites.
c. Ross. The Causes of Race Superiority.

Chamberlain, H.S. Foundations of the 19th Century (trans.).

Journal of Race Development—
a. Vol. 5, No. 3. Ellis, G.W. Psychology of American Race Prejudice.
b. Vol. 5, No. 4. Odum, H.W. Standards of Measurement in Race Development.

Boaz. The Mind of Primitive Man. Chap. X.

Finot. Race Prejudice. Part V, pp. 283–320.

Zollschan, Ignaz. Das Rassenprobleme; Bloch, The Jewish Question.

Finch, Earl. The Effects of Racial Intermixture. Universal Races Congress Proceedings.

Adler, F. The Fundamental Principle of Inter-racial Morality. Universal Races Congress Proceedings. 1911.

V
Racial Progress and Race Adjustment

Race as a unit of social thought is of growing importance and necessity—it is not to be superceded except by some revised version of itself—the history of ideas of this kind the history of a succession of meanings—what conception of race is to dominate in enlightened social thought and practice is the present problem. The sociological conception of race as representing phases and stages and groupings in social culture repudiates the older biological and historical doctrines of race as working formulae in social practice, though it does not wholly supercede them in their scientific uses. Physical race or "pure race" is a scientific fiction—biologically, it is irretrievable, if ever possessed—historically, it is an anachronism, being attributed to national not racial groups, and then only to justify the historical group sense—politically, it is a mere policy or subterfuge of empire—it is socially extinct under a competitive industrial order, as its oldest origin as caste was really economic, and required artificial economic limitation for its perpetuation. Social race, or "civilization-type" and "kind," the only thoroughly rational meaning of race.

Every civilization tends to create or mold its own racial type (Tarde); and if civilization is conformity to civilization-type, races must inevitably follow their social affiliations and contacts according to the social environment. Assimilation, limited on the physical side by climatic adaptability, but involving also the capacities to absorb social culture, is the final racial test under modern conditions. Physical assimilation immaterial, but conducive to more rapid assimilation of social culture wherever prevalent. Social assimilation necessitated by modern political and social organization—and necessary also for progress, since all modern civilizations are "assimilative" and not "spontaneous" cultures.

This process is a real collaboration of races—the alien race has its influence, though not invariably unfavorable as LaPouge asserts. His formula, "It is the lower race that prevails," an unscientific generalization. Contacts may be in the control of the stronger groups—assimilation or amalgamation depends more upon the attitude of the alien group—if it desires to annihilate itself in merging, no reaction on the part of the other group can stem it. Instances: the Negro and the Japanese both biologically adaptable, and socially imitative; the Japanese in their contact with western civilization have made a reservation in favor of their own racial tradition, and have adopted for the most part only the "utilities" of modern civilization; the Negro, being denied this through slavery, makes in America no reservation, and is on the way to complete culture assimilation. Modern civilization is approximating a common utility civilization (Santayana), but after this has been accomplished, a more stable and diversified culture grouping may reappear.

Anglo-Saxon race contacts unprecedented in extent, and in degree of divergence between the groups—social integration difficult—rapidity of assimilation under democratic institutions develops countercurrents or reactions. Afro-Americans confront the most paradoxical situation, one that involves the ultimate race issue, if not the ultimate solution. Mere social "imitation" useless—it arouses antagonisms and reactions; while social assimilation is in progress, the steadying and apparently contradictory counterdoctrine of racial solidarity and culture seems necessary. This secondary race-consciousness stimulates group action through race pride; it is the social equivalent of self-respect in the individual moral life; it is a feature of national revivals (Celtic, Provençal, Polish, etc.) in European politics and in modern art; it prevents the representative classes as they develop being dissipated in the larger groups, harnesses them in the service of the submerged group, and gradually as social stigma and taboo pass into social respect and recognition, eliminates itself as the race antagonisms subside. This is not a doctrine of race isolation, or so-called "race-integrity," but a theory of social conservation, which in practice conserves the best in each group, and promotes the development of social solidarity out of heterogeneous elements.

Culture-citizenship is not acquired through assimilation merely, but in terms of a racial contribution to what becomes a joint civilization. With the development and education of a higher type of social consciousness the "race-type" blends into the "civilization-type." Race progress and racial adjustment must achieve this end, and whatever theory and practice makes toward it is sound; whatever opposes or retards is false.

References

Mecklin, J.F. Democracy and Race Friction. Chap. VII.

Boaz, F. The Mind of Primitive Man. Chaps. V; VII, pp. 244–250.

Miller, Kelly. Race Adjustment. Neale, 1912. An Appeal to Reason in the Race Problem, pp. 88–108.

Washington, Booker T., Du Bois, and others. The Future of the American Negro. Small-Maynard, 1908.

Sinclair, W.A. The Aftermath of Slavery. Small-Maynard, 1905.

Santayana, G. Reason in Society. Scribner's, 1908.

King, Irving. The Influence of Social Change upon the Emotional Life of a People. American Journal of Sociology, Vol. 9:124–135.

Cook, C. Comparative Study of the Negro Problem. Proceedings, American Negro Academy, 99.

Wallis, W.D. Moral and Racial Prejudice. Journal of Race Development, Vol. 5, No. 3.

Proceedings Universal Races Congress, 1911. Articles, Baron de Constant, 7th Session. Prof. MacKenzie, Final Session.

Miller, H.A. The Race Problem and Psycho-Physics. Doctoral Thesis, Harvard, 1905.

Locke, A.L. The Negro and a Race Tradition. A.M.E. Quarterly Review (April 1911).

Royce, J. War and Insurance. Macmillan, 1914.

Harris, G. Inequality and Progress. Houghton Mifflin Co., 1897.

Carver, T.N. Essays in Social Justice. 1916.

THE ETHICS OF CULTURE

THE ETHICS OF CULTURE.

I AM to speak to you on the ethics of culture. Because I teach the one and try to practice the other, it may perhaps be pardonable for me to think of them together, but I hope at least not to leave you without the conviction that the two are in a very vital and immediate way connected. In my judgment, the highest intellectual duty is the duty to be cultured. Ethics and culture are usually thought out of connection with each other— as, in fact, at the the very opposite poles. Particularly for our country, and the type of education which generally prevails, is this so. Quite unfortunately, it seems, duty toward the beautiful and the cultural is very generally ignored, and certainly, beauty as a motive has been taken out of morality, so that we confront beautiless duty and dutiless beauty. In an issue like this, it behooves education to try to restore the lapsing ideals of humanism, and to center more vitally in education the duty to be cultured.

It follows if there is any duty with respect to culture, that it is one of those that can only be self-imposed. No one can make you cultured, few will care whether you are or are not, for I admit that the world of today primarily demands efficiency—and further the only reward my experience can offer you for it is the heightened self-satisfaction which being or becoming cultured brings. There is, or ought to be, a story of a lad to whom some rather abstract duty was being interpreted who is said to have said, "If I only owe it to myself, why then I really don't owe it at all." Not only do I admit that culture is a duty of this sort, but I claim that this is its chief appeal and justification. The greatest challenge to the moral will is in the absence of external compulsion. This implies, young ladies and gentlemen, that I recognize your perfect right not to be cultured, if you do not really want to be, as one of those inalienable natural-born privileges which so-called "practical minded," "ordinary" Americans delight to claim and exercise. As a touch-stone for the real desire and a sincere motive, the advocates of culture would not have it otherwise.

Howard University Record 17 (January 1923): 178–185. An address delivered in the Freshman Lecture Course for 1922–23.

The way in which duty comes to be involved in culture is this: culture begins in education where compulsion leaves off, whether it is the practical spur of necessity or the artificial rod of the schoolmaster. I speak to a group that has already chosen to be educated. I congratulate you upon that choice. Though you have so chosen for many motives and with very diverse reasons and purposes, I fear that education for most of you means, in last practical analysis, the necessary hardship that is involved in preparing to earn a better living, perhaps an easier living. It is just such narrowing and truncating of the conception of education, that the ideals and motives of culture are effective to remove or prevent. Education should not be so narrowly construed, for in the best sense, and indeed in the most practical sense, it means not only the fitting of the man to earn his living, but to live and to live well. It is just this latter and higher function of education, the art of living well, or, if I may so express it, of living up to the best, that the word *culture* connotes and represents. Let me offer you, if I may, a touch-stone for this idea, a sure test of its presence. Whenever and wherever there is carried into education the purpose and motive of knowing better than the practical necessities of the situation demand, whenever the pursuit of knowledge is engaged in for its own sake and for the inner satisfaction it can give, culture and the motives of culture are present. I sense immediately that you may have quite other and perhaps more authoritative notions of culture in mind. Culture has been variously and beautifully defined. But I cannot accept for the purpose I have in view even that famous definition of Matthew Arnold's, "Culture is the best that has been thought and known in the world," since it emphasizes the external rather than the internal factors of culture. Rather is it the capacity for understanding the best and most representative forms of human expression, and of expressing oneself, if not in similar creativeness, at least in appreciative reactions and in progressively responsive refinement of tastes and interests. Culture proceeds from personality to personality. To paraphrase Bacon, it is that, and only that, which can be inwardly assimilated. It follows, then, that, like wisdom, it is that which cannot be taught, but can only be learned. But here is the appeal of it, it is the self-administered part of your education, that which represents your personal index of absorption and your personal coefficient of effort.

As faulty as is the tendency to externalize culture, there is still greater error in over-intellectualizing it. Defining this aspect of education, we focus it, I think, too much merely in the mind, and project it too far into the abstract and formal. We must constantly realize that without experience, and without a medium for the absorption and transfer of experience, the mind could not develop or be developed. Culture safeguards the educative process at these two points, and stands for the training of the sensibilities and the expressional activities. Mentioning the former as the neglected aspect of American education, former President Eliot contends that, since it is the business of the senses to serve the mind, it is reciprocally the duty of the mind to serve the senses. He means that properly to train the mind involves the proper training of the sensibilities, and that, without a refinement of the channels through which our experience reaches us, the mind cannot reach its highest development. We too often expect our senses to serve us and render nothing back to them in exchange. As a result they do not serve us half so well as they might: coarse channels make for sluggish response, hampered impetus, wastage of effort. The man of culture is the man of trained sensibilities, whose mind expresses itself in keenness of discrimination and, therefore, in cultivated interests and tastes. The level of mentality may be crowded higher for a special effort or a special pursuit, but in the long run it cannot rise much higher than the level of tastes. It is for this reason that we warrantably judge culture by manners, tastes, and the fineness of discrimination of a person's interests. The stamp of culture is, therefore, no conventional pattern, and has no stock value; it is the mould and die of a refined and completely developed personality. It is the art medallion, not the common coin.

On this very point, so necessary for the correct estimation of culture, most of the popular mistakes and misconceptions about culture enter in. Democracy and utilitarianism suspect tastes because they cannot be standardized. And if I should not find you over-interested in culture or over-sympathetic toward its ideals, it is because of these same prejudices of puritanism and materialism, which, though still typically American, are fortunately no longer representatively so. Yet it is necessary to examine and refute some of these prevalent misconceptions about culture. You have heard and will still hear culture derided as *artificial, superficial, useless, selfish, over-refined,* and *exclusive.* Let us make inquiry into the reasons for such attitudes. It is not the part of loyal advocacy to shirk the blow and attack of such criticism behind the bastions of dilettantism. Culture has its active adversaries in present-day life, indeed the normal tendencies of life today are not in the direction either of breadth or height of culture. The defense of culture is a modern chivalry, though of some hazard and proportional glory.

The criticism of culture as artificial first concerns us. In the mistaken name of naturalism, culture is charged with producing artificiality destructive of the fine original naturalness of human nature. One might as well indict civilization as a whole on this point; it, too, is artificial. But perhaps just a peculiar degree of artificiality is inveighed against— to which our response must be that it is just that very painful intermediate stage between lack of culture and wholesomeness of culture which it is the object of further culture to remove. All arts have their awkward stages; culture itself is its own cure for this. Closely associated, and touched by the same reasoning, is the argument that culture is superficial. Here we encounter the bad effect of a process undertaken in the wrong order. If the polished surface is, so to speak, the last coat of a consistently developed personality, it lends its final added charm to the total worth and effect. If, on the contrary, beginning with the superficial as well as ending with the superficial, it should be merely a veneer, then is it indeed both culturally false and artistically deceptive. No true advocacy of an ideal involves the defense or extenuation of its defective embodiments. Rather on the contrary, culture must constantly be self-critical and discriminating, and deplore its spurious counterfeits and shallow imitations.

More pardonable, especially for our age, is the charge of uselessness. Here we need not so much the corrective of values as that of perspective. For we only need to appreciate the perennial and imperishable qualities of the products of culture to see the fallacy in such depreciation. Fortified in ideas and ideals, culture centers about the great human constants, which, though not rigidly unchangeable, are nevertheless almost as durable as those great physical constants of which science makes so much. Indeed, if we count in the progressive changes of science through discovery, these are the more constant—the most constant then of all the things in human experience. Moreover, there is their superior representativeness by which posterity judges each and every phase of human development. Through their culture products are men most adequately represented; and by their culture-fruits are they known and rated. As we widen our view from the standpoint of momentary and partial judgment, this fact becomes only too obvious.

I take seriously, and would have you, also, the charge that culture is selfish. Being unnecessarily so is to be unduly so. Yet there is a necessary internal focusing of culture because true culture must begin with self-culture. Personality, and to a limited extent character also, are integral parts of the equation. In the earlier stages of the development of culture there is pardonable concentration upon self-cultivation. Spiritual capital must be accumulated; indeed, too early spending of the meager resources of culture at an early stage results in that shallow and specious variety which means sham and pretense at the start, bankruptcy and humiliation at the finish. Do not begin to spend your mental substance prematurely. You are justified in serious self-concern and earnest self-consideration at the stage of education. And, moreover, culture, even when it is rich and mature, gives only by sharing, and moves more by magnetic attraction than by transfer of material or energy. Like light, to which it is so often compared, it radiates, and operates effectively only through being self-sufficiently maintained at its central source. Culture polarizes in self-hood.

Finally we meet the criticism of exclusiveness, over-selectness, perhaps even the extreme of snobbery. Culture, I fear, will have to plead guilty to a certain degree of this: it cannot fulfill its function otherwise. Excellence and the best can never reside in the average. Culture must develop an élite, must maintain itself upon the basis of standards that can move forward but never backwards. In the pursuit of culture one must detach himself from the crowd. Your chief handicap in this matter as young people of today is the psychology and "pull" of the crowd. Culturally speaking, they and their point of view define vulgarity. As Professor Palmer says, "Is this not what we mean by the vulgar man? His manners are not an expression of himself, but of somebody else. Other men have obliterated him." There is no individuality in being ordinary; it is the boast of sub-mediocrity. Who in the end wishes to own that composite of everybody's average qualities, so likely to be below our own par? Culture's par is always the best: one cannot be somebody with everybody's traits. If to be cultured is a duty, it is here that that element is most prominent, for it takes courage to stand out from the crowd. One must, therefore, pay a moral as well as an intellectual price for culture. It consists in this: "Dare to be different—stand out!" I know how difficult this advice will be to carry out: America's chief social crime, in spite of her boasted freedoms, is the psychology of the herd, the tyranny of the average and mediocre; in other words, the limitations upon cultural personality. Strive to overcome this for your own sake and, as Cicero would say, "for the welfare of the Republic."

I am spending too much time, I fear, in pointing out what culture is when I would rather point out the way to its attainment. I must not trespass, however, upon the provinces of my colleagues who are to interpret culture more specifically to you in terms of the art of English speech, the fine arts, and music. I content myself with the defense of culture in general, and with the opportunity it gives of explaining its two most basic aspects—the great amateur arts of personal expression—conversation and manners. These personal arts are as important as the fine arts; in my judgment, they are their foundation. For culture without personal culture is sterile—it is that insincere and hypocritical profession of the love of the beautiful which so often discredits culture in the eyes of the many. But with the products of the fine arts translating themselves back into personal refinement and cultivated sensibilities, culture realizes itself in the fullest sense, performs its true educative function and becomes a part of the vital art of living. We too often estimate culture materialistically by what has been called "the vulgar test of production." On the contrary, culture depends primarily upon the power of refined consumption and effective assimilation; it consists essentially in being cultured. Whoever would achieve this must recognize that life itself is an art, perhaps the finest of the fine arts—because it is the composite blend of them all.

However, to say this is not to commit the man of culture to hopeless dilettantism, and make him a Jack of the arts. Especially for you, who for the most part work toward very practical professional objectives and who lack as Americans of our time even a modicum of leisure, would this be impossible. But it is not necessary to trouble much about this, for, even were it possible, it would not be desirable. There are, of course, subjects which are primarily "cultural" and subjects which are not, but I am not one of those who bewail altogether the departure from the old-fashioned classical program of education and the waning appeal of the traditional "humanities." Science, penetratingly studied, can yield as much and more culture than the humanities mechanically studied. It lies, I think, more in the point of view and the degree of intrinsic interest rather than in the special subject-matter or tradition of a subject. Nevertheless, to be sure of culture, the average student should elect some of the cultural studies; and, more important still, in his outside diversions, should cultivate a steady and active interest in one of the arts, aiming thereby to bring his mind under the quickening influence of cultural ideas and values. Not all of us can attain to creative productiveness and skill in the arts, though each of us has probably some latent artistic temperament, if it only expresses itself in love and day-dreaming. But each of us can, with a different degree of concentration according to his temperament, cultivate an intelligent appreciation of at least one of the great human arts, literature, painting, sculpture, music or what not. And if we achieve a high level of cultivated taste in one art it will affect our judgment and interest and response with respect to others.

May I at this point emphasize a peculiarly practical reason? In any community, in any nation, in any group, the level of cultural productiveness cannot rise much higher than the level of cultural consumption, cannot much outdistance the prevalent limits of taste. This is the reason why our country has not as yet come to the fore in the production of culture-goods. And as Americans we all share this handicap of the low average of cultural tastes. As educated Americans, we share also and particularly the responsibility for helping raise this average. A brilliant Englishman once characterized America as a place where everything had a price, but nothing a value, referring to the typical preference for practical and utilitarian points of view. There is a special need for a correction of this on your part. As a race group we are at the critical stage where we are releasing creative artistic talent in excess of our group ability to understand and support it. Those of us who have been concerned about our progress in the things of culture have now begun to fear as the greatest handicap the discouraging, stultifying effect upon our artistic talent of lack of appreciation from the group which it represents. The cultural par, we repeat, is always the best, and a group which expects to be judged by its best must live up to its best so that that may be truly representative. Here is our present dilemma. If the standard of cultural tastes is not rapidly raised in the generation which you represent, the natural affinities of appreciation and response will drain off, like cream, the richest products of the group, and leave the mass without the enriching quality of its finest ingredients. This is already happening: I need not cite the painful individual instances. The only remedy is the more rapid development and diffusion of culture among us.

It follows from this that it is not creditable nor your duty to allow yourselves to be toned down to the low level of average tastes. Some of you, many of you, I hope, will be making your life's work in sections of this country and among groups that are fittingly characterized as "Saharas of culture," that know culture neither by taste nor sight. You betray your education, however, and forego the influence which as educated persons you should always exert in any community if you succumb to these influences and subside to the mediocre level of the vulgar crowd. Moreover, you will find that, like knowledge or technical skill, culture to be maintained must be constantly practiced. Just as we saw that culture was not a question of one set of subjects, but an attitude which may be carried into all, so also we must realize that it is not a matter of certain moments and situations, but the characteristic and constant reaction of a developed personality. The ideal culture is representative of the entire personality even in the slightest detail.

I recall an incident of visiting with a friend a celebrated art connoisseur for his expert judgment upon a painting. He examined with a knife and a pocket magnifying glass a corner of the canvas. I perhaps thought for a moment he was searching for a signature, but it was not the signature corner. Without further scrutiny, however, he gave us his judgment: "Gentlemen, it is not a Holbein." The master painter puts himself into every inch of his canvas, and can be told by the characteristic details as reliably, more reliably even than by general outlines. Culture likewise is every inch representative of the whole personality when it is truly perfected. This summing up of the whole in every part is the practical test which I want you to hold before yourselves in matters of culture. Among cultivated people you will be judged more by your manner of speech and deportment than by any other credentials. They are meant to bear out your training and your heritage, and more reliably than your diplomas or your pedigree will they represent you or betray you. Manners are thus the key to personal relations, as expression is the key to intellectual intercourse. One meets that element in others which is most responsively tuned to a similar element in ourselves. The best fruits of culture, then, are the responses it elicits from our human environment. And should the environment be limited or unfavorable, then, instead of compromising with it, true culture opens the treasuries of art and literature, and lives on that inheritance.

Finally I must add a word about that aspect of culture which claims that it takes several generations to produce and make the truly cultured gentleman. Exclusive, culture may and must be, but seclusive culture is obsolete. Not all that are well-born are well-bred, and it is better to be well-bred. Indeed, one cannot rest satisfied at any stage of culture: it has to be earned and re-earned, though it returns with greater increment each time. As Goethe says, "What thou hast inherited from the fathers, labor for, in order to possess it." Thus culture is inbred—but we ourselves are its parents. With all of the possible and hoped for spread of democracy, we may say that excellence of this sort will always survive. Indeed, when all the other aristocracies have fallen, the aristocracy of talent and intellect will still stand. In fact, one suspects that eventually the most civilized way of being superior will be to excel in culture

This much, then, of the ideals of humanism must survive; the goal of education is self-culture, and one must hold it essential even for knowledge's own sake that it be transmuted into character and personality. It must have been the essential meaning of Socrates' favorite dictum—"Know thyself"—that to know, one must be a developed personality. The capacity for deep understanding is proportional to the degree of self-knowledge, and by finding and expressing one's true self, one somehow discovers the common denominator of the universe. Education without culture, therefore, ignores an important half of the final standard, "a scholar and a gentleman," which, lest it seem obsolete, let me cite in those fine modern words which former President Eliot used in conferring the arts degree, "I hereby admit you to the honorable fellowship of educated men." Culture is thus education's passport to converse and association with the best.

Moreover, personal representativeness and group achievement are in this respect identical. Ultimately a people is judged by its capacity to contribute to culture. It is to be hoped that as we progressively acquire in this energetic democracy the common means of modern civilization, we shall justify ourselves more and more, individually and collectively, by the use of them to produce culture-goods and representative types of culture. And this, so peculiarly desirable under the present handicap of social disparagement and disesteem, must be for more than personal reasons the ambition and the achievement of our educated classes. If, as we all know, we must look to education largely to win our way, we must look largely to culture to win our just reward and recognition. It is, therefore, under these circumstances something more than your personal duty to be cultured—it is one of your most direct responsibilities to your fellows, one of your most effective opportunities for group service. In presenting this defense of the ideals and aims of culture, it is my ardent hope that the Howard degree may come increasingly to stand for such things—and especially the vintage of 1926.

THE CONCEPT OF RACE
AS APPLIED TO SOCIAL CULTURE

In dealing with race and culture we undoubtedly confront two of the most inevitable but at the same time most unsatisfactory concepts involved in the broad-scale consideration of man and society. There is the general presumption and feeling that they have some quite vital and relevant connection, but as to the nature of this or even as to the scientific meaning of the individual concepts there is the greatest diversity of scientific opinion and theory. An analytic study of their highly variable meanings, confining this even to the more or less strictly scientific versions, would constitute two important and highly desirable treatises. But what we are here attempting is something quite more immediate and practical from the point of view of the use of these terms in the social sciences, and quite capable perhaps, if the analysis be successful, of settling some of these complexly controversial differences as to meaning by a process of elimination, namely an examination into their supposed relationship one to the other. For it seems that in the erroneous assumption of fixed relationships between the two, most of the serious difficulties and confusions lie. It will be our contention that far from being constants, these important aspects of human society are variables, and in the majority of instances not even paired variables, and that though they have at all times significant and definite relationships, they nevertheless are in no determinate way organically or causally connected. And if this should be so, whole masses of elaborately constructed social theory and cultural philosophizing fall with the destruction of a common basic assumption, that has been taken as a common foundation for otherwise highly divergent and even antagonistic theorizing. This position, differing from that of the school of interpretation which denies all significant connection between racial and cultural factors,[1] does not deny that race stands for significant social characters and culture-traits or represents in given historical contexts characteristic differentiations of culture-type. However, it does insist against the assumption of any such constancy, historical or intrinsic, as would make it possible to posit an organic connection between them and to argue on such grounds the determination of one by the other.

---

[1] Lowie, R. H.—Culture and Ethnology, Chap. II, 1923.

But the unwarranted assumption of race as a determinant of culture is still very current, and contemporary discussion, especially in ethnology, is still primarily concerned with the destructive criticism of this inveterate and chronic notion. We would by no means minimize the success and scientific service of such criticism as that of Boas in the field of anthropology and "race psychology," of Flinders-Petrie in archeology, of Finot, Babington, Hertz, and von Zollschan in social and political theory, and of Lowie and Wissler in ethnology,[2] in saying that as yet, however, we seem to be only at a transitional stage in the scientific consideration of the relationship of race to culture. In some revised and reconstructed form, we may anticipate the continued even if restricted use of these terms as more or less necessary and basic concepts that cannot be eliminated altogether, but that must nevertheless be so safe-guarded in this continued use as not to give further currency to the invalidated assumptions concerning them. It is too early to assume that there is no significant connection between race and culture because of the manifestly false and arbitrary linkage which has previously been asserted.

In the interval between these two stages of the discussion, as one might normally expect, there is considerable tendency to continue the corollaries of the older view even where the main position and hypothesis has been abandoned. Goldenweiser[3] is therefore quite justified in his insistence upon linking up these corollaries with the position of classical social evolutionism which gave them such vogue and standing, and disestablishing both by the same line of argument. For although this notion of race as a prime determining factor in culture was historically established by the theory and influence of de Gobineau,[4] its scientific justification has been associated with the doctrines of the strictly evolutionary interpretation of culture, especially with the influence of the social evolutionism of Spencer. The primary scientific use of this fixed linkage between race and culture was to justify the classical evolutionary scheme of a series of stepped stages in an historical progression of cultural development. In this connection it has been the analogue in the theory of society of the heredity factor in the biological field, and its stock notions of *race capacity* and *racial heredity* have had approximately the same phases of acceptance, repudiation, and revision. In their "classical" form they are now equally discredited by several lines of detailed evidence where the historical succession of stages does not coincide with those posited as the ground basis of the supposedly universal process of development,[5] and by the more intensive and objective study of primitive cultures which has shown how insidiously their consideration in the light of such evolutionary schemes has distorted their concrete facts and values. There is considerable warrant therefore for the position that wishes to exclude all further misinterpretation by a complete disassociation of the concept of race from the concept of culture.

---

[2] Boas, Franz—The Mind of Primitive Man. 1911. Flinders-Petrie, W. M. —Race and Civilization, Proc. Brit. Assoc., 1895. Finot, Jean—Race Prejudice (Trans. 1907). Babington, W. D.—Fallacies of Race Theories. Hertz—Moderne Rassentheorien. von Zollschan, I.—Das Rassenproblem, Vienna, 1912.

[3] Goldenweiser, A.—Early Civilization, Chap. I. pp. 14-15.

[4] de Gobineau—Essai sur l'inegalite des races humains. Paris, 1854.

This is the position of Lowie [6] who concludes after a brilliant and rigorous examination as to the inter-connection between culture and race that not only are cultural changes "manifestly independent of the racial factor," but that no race has permanent or even uniform alignment with reference to culture-type or cultural stages. His position, though one of the closest reasoned of any, is the most iconoclastic with respect to the assumption of any significant relation between race and culture, as may be estimated from the following passage: "With great confidence we can say that since the same race at different times or in different subdivisions at the same time represents vastly different cultural stages, there is obviously no direct proportional between culture and race and if great changes of culture can occur without any change of race whatsoever, we are justified in considering it probable that a relatively minute change of hereditary ability might produce enormous differences."

But the extreme cultural relativism of Lowie leaves an open question as to the association of certain ethnic groups with definite culture-traits and culture types under circumstances where there is evidently a greater persistence of certain strains and characteristics in their culture than of other factors. The stability of such factors and their resistance to direct historical modification marks out the province of that aspect of the problem of race which is distinctly ethnological and which the revised notion of ethnic race must cover. It seems quite clear that no adequate explanation can be expected from the factors and principles of anthropological race distinctions. In the light of the most recent and accepted investigations any attempt to explain one in terms of the other must be regarded as pseudo-scientific. Nevertheless though there is lacking for the present any demonstrable explanation, there are certain ethnic traits the peculiarly stable and stock character of which must be interpreted as ethnically characteristic. They are in no sense absolutely permanent, the best psychological evidence as yet gives us no reason for construing them as inherent, yet they are factors not without an integral relationship one to the other not satisfactorily explained as mere historical combinations. Indeed it seems difficult and in some cases impossible to discover common historical factors to account for their relative constancy. Few challenge the specific factuality of these peculiarly resistant combinations of group traits.

As Sapir [7] aptly says, "Here, as so often, the precise knowledge of the scientist lags somewhat behind the more naive but more powerful insights of non-professional experience and impression. To deny to the genius of a people an ultimate psychological significance and to refer it to the specific historical development of that people is not, after all is said and done, to analyze it out of existence. It remains true that large groups of people everywhere tend to think and to act in accordance with established and all but instinctive forms, which are in a large measure peculiar to it." The point that seems to be important to note and stress is that we do not need to deny the existence of these characteristic racial molds in denying that they are rooted in "inherent hereditary traits either of a biological or a psychological nature."

---

[6] Lowie, R. H.—Culture and Ethnology, p. 41.

[7] Sapir, E.—Culture, Genuine and Spurious, Amer. Journal of Sociology, Vol. XXIX. No. 4, p. 406.

If, instead of the anthropological, the ethnic characters had been more in the focus of scientific attention, there probably would have resulted a much more scientific and tenable doctrine of the relationship of race to culture. Race would have been regarded as primarily a matter of social heredity, and its distinctions due to the selective psychological "set" of established cultural reactions. There is a social determination involved in this which quite more rationally interprets and explains the relative stability or so-called permanency that the old theorists were trying to account for on the basis of fixed anthropological characters and factors. To quote again from Sapir:[8] "The current assumption that the so-called 'genius' of a people is ultimately reducible to certain inherent heredity traits of a biological and psychological nature does not, for the most part, bear very serious examination. Frequently enough, what is assumed to be an innate racial characteristic turns out on closer study to be the resultant of purely historical causes. A mode of thinking, a distinctive type of reaction, gets itself established in the course of a complex historical development as typical, as normal; it serves then as a model for the working over of new elements of civilization."

The best consensus of opinion then seems to be that race is a fact in the social or ethnic sense, that it has been very erroneously associated with race in the physical sense and is therefore not scientifically commensurate with factors or conditions which explain or have produced physical race characters and differentiation, that it has a vital and significant relation to social culture, and that it must be explained in terms of social and historical causes such as have caused similar differentiations of culture-type as pertain in lesser degree between nations, tribes, classes, and even family strains. Most authorities are now reconciled to two things,—first, the necessity of a thorough-going redefinition of the nature of race, and second, the independent definition of race in the ethnic or social sense together with the independent investigation of its differences and their causes apart from the investigation of the factors and differentiae of physical race. Of course eventually there may be some interesting correlation possible at the conclusion of these two lines of investigation, but up to the present they seem only to have needlessly handicapped and complicated one another and to have brought comparative ethnology and comparative anthropology both to a deadlock of confusion because of their incompatible points of view and incommensurable values. It is undoubtedly this necessity of a new start that Wissler[9] has in mind when he says, "So it is obvious that the relation between culture and race is a subject of more than passing interest, and though as yet not seriously investigated, the time is near at hand when its solution must be sought, if life is to be understood rationally and socially." Similarly we find Flinders-Petrie[10] in his address before the British Association saying "The definition of the nature of race is the most requisite element for any clear ideas about man," and then veering over to the strictly social definition of race by adding, "The only meaning a race can have is a group of persons whose type has become unified by their rate of assimilation and

---

[8] Ibid. pp. 405-06.
[9] Wissler—Man and Culture.
[10] Flinders-Petrie—Race and Civilization, Proc. Brit. Assoc., 1895.

affection by their conditions exceeding the rate of change produced by foreign elements." Evidently the thought here is that blood intermixture is only one of the conducive conditions to cultural assimilation and absorption and that therefore *culture-type* or *social race* is the important fact and concept. Race in the vital and basic sense is simply and primarily the culture-heredity, and that in its blendings and differentiations is properly analyzed on the basis of conformity to or variance from culture-type.

Gault,[11] discussing Stevenson's study, Socio-Anthropometry: An Inter-racial Critique and several studies of Indian cross-breeds, all of which draw conclusions that differences are due to blood-race factors. says: "There is always the possibility that the Indian of mixed blood owes a degree of his superiority (we should say 'difference') to the *social* stimuli of one or the other parent from earliest infancy: stimuli that from the beginning have induced a level of reactions that otherwise would have been lacking, and have built up personality complexes that are next to original nature as respects substantiality." Thus even in instances where physical assimilation is the condition responsible for cultural assimilation, the latter takes place in terms of social factors. Divorced then by every line of objectively considered evidence from the anthropological notion and criteria of race with which its distinctions rarely if ever coincide, ethnic race or what Gault calls "sociologic type" becomes the most scientifically tenable and useful concept.

Instead therefore of regarding culture as expressive of race, race by this interpretation is regarded as itself a culture product. Goldenweiser [12] puts the matter this way; he says: "Enough has been said to show that the view generally held of the relation between race and culture may well be reversed. According to the prevailing view, man is many and civilization one, meaning by this that the races differ significantly in potential ability and that only one, the white race, could have and has achieved civilization. The reverse view, forced upon the ethnologist and the historian by a more critical and open-minded survey of the facts, reads thus: *man is one, civilizations are many,* meaning by this that the races do not differ significantly in psychological endowment, that the variety of possible civilizations is great and of actual ones, considerable, and that many civilizations other than ours have achieved things of genuine and unique worth." Perhaps the revolutionary significance of this can only be realized when we see it applied to specific descriptive analysis as in the case of Rivers' [13] use of the term race solely in a sense which means the people who had such and such culture-traits, whose customs dominated this or that period and set the pattern upon which a certain culture-type was developed.

Nothing seems more likely than that there will gradually develop out of this new and more objective analysis of culture a series of relatively divergent and basic culture-types, for each of which perhaps some more or less organic principle of development or evolution can be worked out, so that we may eventually get a standard of value for relative culture grading. Meanwhile we must grant the logic of the position of Lowie which is that the most objective study at present gives no warrant for the relative scientific grading of cultures. Meanwhile each

---

11 Gault—Social Psychology, p. 104.

12 Goldenweiser—Op. cit., p. 14.

13 Compare Rivers—Psychology and Ethnology.

culture must be treated as specific and as highly composite, and each ethnic group as the peculiar resultant of its own social history. This is what we mean then by this reversal of emphasis, that instead of the race explaining the cultural condition, the cultural conditions must explain the race traits, and that instead of artificially extracted units representing race types, the newer scientific approach demands that we deal with concrete culture-types which as often as not are composite racially speaking, and have only an artificial ethnic unity of historical derivation and manufacture.

Confident that this is the correct scientific conception of culture and its most warrantable scientific basis of approach and study, we return to the consideration of whether or not by such interpretation the concept of race is not entirely relegated from serious consideration in connection with it. So considerable is the shift of emphasis and meaning that at times it does seem that the best procedure would be to substitute for the term *race* the term *culture-group*. But what has become absolutely disqualified for the explanation of culture groups taken as totalities becomes in a much more scientific and verifiable way a main factor of explanation of its various cultural components. Race accounts for a great many of the specific elements of the cultural heredity, and the sense of race may itself be regarded as one of the operative factors in culture since it determines the stressed values which become the conscious symbols and tradition of the culture. Such stressed values are themselves factors in the process of culture making, and account primarily for the persistence and resistance of culture-traits. For these determine what is the dominant pattern in any given culture, and it is toward these dominants as social norms that social conformation converges and according to which it eventually establishes the type. It is with respect to such principles of determination that the newer psychology of race must be worked out instead of with reference to assumed innate traits and capacities. The type itself may have been established by accident or fortuitous combinations of historical circumstances, but re-enforced by the sense of race as perhaps the most intense of the feelings of commonality, it becomes an accepted, preferred and highly resistant culture complex that seems to be and often is self-perpetuating.

Race operates as tradition, as preferred traits and values, and when these things change culturally speaking ethnic remoulding is taking place. Race then, so far as the ethnologist is concerned, seems to lie in that peculiar selective preference for certain culture-traits and resistance to certain others which is characteristic of all types and levels of social organization. And instead of decreasing as a result of contacts this sense and its accumulative results seems on the whole to increase, so that we get accumulative effect. It intensifies therefore with contacts and increases with the increasing complexity of the culture elements in any particular area. A diversity of cultural types temporarily at least accentuates the racial stresses involved, so that even when a fusion eventuates it takes place under the conditions determined by the resistance developed and the relative strength of the several cultural components.

Indeed, the evidence shows most cultures to be highly composite. Sometimes there seems to be a race relatively pure physically with a considerably mixed culture, sometimes, perhaps more frequently, a highly mixed race with a relatively fused culture. But in the large majority of cases the culture is only to be explained as the resultant of the meeting and reciprocal influence of several culture strains, several ethnic contributions. Such facts nullify two of the most prevalent popular and scientific fallacies, the ascription of a total culture to any one ethnic strain, and the interpretation of culture in terms of the intrinsic rather than the fusion values of its various constituent elements. Especially does this newer view insist upon the disassociation of the claims of political dominance and cultural productivity, and combat the traditional view that all or even the best elements of a culture are the contribution of the ethnic group which in a mixed culture has political dominance and is in dynastic control. Already a number of such politically proprietary claims have been disallowed and disestablished by the more intensive and objectively comparative study of culture-traits. Such procedure promises to redeem the fields of discussion which till recently have been so vitiated by racial and national bias that some ethnologists have been led to conclude the impossibility of the scientific evaluation of cultures. After all, the failure to maintain objective standards, relevant values, and parity of values ought not be taken as evidence that this is not possible. So great is the tendency to lapse back into the former positions of bias, that the rigid maintenance of objective description as the sole aim of the ethnologist may, however, be fully warranted for the time being.

But races may, and must eventually be compared with respect to their relative and characteristic abilities and tendencies with respect to cultural origins, cultural assimilation, cultural survival, and their concrete institutional contributions. But in every case absolute objective parity of condition and values must be maintained. An instance in point is Lowie's [14] own illustration in a discussion of the relative rating of cultures on the basis of cultural originality and assimilation. He says: "If the Japanese deserve no credit for having appropriated our culture, we must also carefully eliminate from that culture all elements not demonstrably due to the creative genius of our race before laying claim to the residue as our distinctive product." This seems simple enough to be axiomatic, yet as a principle of comparison one can find in treatise after treatise a score of breaches for every single observance of what ought to be a fundamental procedure. Irrelevant evaluation and invidious comparisons that do not even make the pretense of establishing either parity or equivalence of values abound, yet it is not to be corrected by excluding values, but rather through insistence upon the only properly scientific criteria—intrinsic values for the interpretation of any culture, and strictly commensurate or equivalent values as a basis of comparisons between them.

The chief source of error in the evaluation of cultures can be traced as the same source already described as responsible for the prevalent errors in the description of cultures. It is incumbent upon us to see clearly why the evolutionary formula has led in both these instances to such unsoundness of interpretation. It would seem that by putting all types and varieties into the same series, and this is the crux of the straight evolutionary point of view, the error of assuming basic common factors and commensurate values has almost irretrievably been made. Not that such factors may not exist, but that they are not to be dis-

---

[14] Lowie—Op. cit., pp. 32-33.

covered except from the point of view of a more objective and detailed comparison than has in most cases been attempted. Since the days of the Indo-Germanic myth, and its twin fancy the Aryan hypothesis, the desire and suppressed objective in many investigations has been to build a social pyramid of straight line progressive stages, and subtle variations of this point of view have been introducing error upon error into the interpretation of cultures, especially primitive and alien cultures which have naturally borne the brunt of the scheme through having been distorted and pinched into alignment with the pre-conceived formula.[15] We have a clear and succinct statement of the responsibility in this regard in the following passage:[16] "The earlier anthropologists and sociologists, swayed by the biological theories of evolution, posited parallel development in every people, following upon innate psychological tendencies. Complete systems, with stages of development culminating in our own particular type of civilization, were posited by such early writers as Morgan, Spencer, Tylor and others. However, it has been found that the other cultural mechanism, that of diffusion, constituted a grave stumbling block to this a priori scheme of stage development, and it is now known that independent origins of inventions are infinitely more rare than was believed, and that they are conditioned not by innate psychological tendencies, but by the cultural milieu in which they occur." Gradually it has become apparent that the procedure of using primitive cultures as the stock arguments and illustrations for societal evolution has disorganized the organic unity of these cultures, and merely used certain aspects of them as illustrating a comparative series which even if it were correct for the institution in question from which the accentuated culture-elements were taken, would not place correctly in scale as totalities the cultures respectively in question.

It follows then that the work of correction will have to begin at the very point where originally the errors and distortions have been introduced, namely, the more carefully objective study and organic interpretation of primitive cultures. This would be necessary from the purely corrective point of view, even if it were not also true as Wissler [17] says that "our clearest insight into the mechanisms of culture is attained when we examine the more primitive marginal cultures of the world." After the application of the reconstructed notion of race as social in manifestation and derivation, this would seem to be the most important and promising revision of idea and method in the entire field of our discussion. As a straight methodological question then we get the following as the only correct and acceptable procedure in the study of any given culture—first, its analytic and complete description in terms of its own culture-elements, second, its organic interpretation in terms of its own intrinsic values as a vital mode of living, combined if possible with an historical account of its development and derivation, and then finally and not till then its assignment to culture-type and interpretation as a stage of culture. Almost any culture so treated will be found to be radically different both in description and evaluation from that account which would have been given it if immediately submitted on

---

[15] Compare Goldenweiser—Chap. I and p. 125.

[16] Herskovits and Willey—The Cultural Approach to Sociology. Amer. Jour. of Sociology, Vol. XXIX, No. 2, p. 195.

[17] Wissler—Op. cit., p. 286.

first analysis to the general scale and to universal comparison. Let us call this the *principle of organic interpretation* and the other the *principle of cultural relativity,* and conclude that in combination with the dynamic and social interpretation of race, the three are the methodological foundation and platform of the newer science of social culture. Especially in connection with the concept of race are all of the biased and partisan points of view and scales of evaluation obviated by such procedure so that it becomes possible to continue the term scientifically and usefully in the context of discussion to which it is most relevant, but into which until recently it has introduced primarily serious errors both of fact and of value.

AMERICAN LITERARY TRADITION AND THE NEGRO

DOUBT if there exists any more valuable record for the study of the social history of the Negro in America than the naïve reflection of American social attitudes and their changes in the literary treatment of Negro life and character. More sensitively, and more truly than the conscious conventions of journalism and public debate, do these relatively unconscious values trace the fundamental attitudes of the American mind. Indeed, very often public professions are at utter variance with actual social practices, and in the matter of the Negro this variance is notably paradoxical. The statement that the North loves the Negro and dislikes Negroes, while the South hates the Negro but loves Negroes, is a crude generalization of the paradox, with just enough truth in it, however, to give us an interesting cue for further analysis. What this essay attempts must necessarily be a cursory preliminary survey: detailed intensive study of American social attitudes toward the Negro, using the changes of the literary tradition as clues, must be seriously undertaken later.

For a cursory survey, a tracing of the attitude toward the Negro as reflected in American letters gives us seven stages or phases, supplying not only an interesting cycle of shifts in public taste and interest, but a rather significant curve for social history. And more interesting perhaps than the attitudes themselves are the underlying issues and reactions of class attitudes and relationships which have been basically responsible for these attitudes. Moreover, instead of a single fixed attitude, sectionally divided and opposed, as the popular presumption goes, it will be seen that American attitudes toward the Negro have changed radically and often, with dramatic turns and with a curious reversal of rôle between the North and the South according to the class consciousness and interests dominant at any given time. With allowances for generalization, so far as literature records it, Negro life has run a gamut of seven notes,—heroics, sentiment, melodrama, comedy, farce, problem-discussion and æsthetic interest—as, in their respective turns, strangeness, domestic familiarity, moral controversy, pity, hatred, bewilderment, and curiosity, have dominated the public mind. Naturally, very few of these atti-

The Modern Quarterly 3 (May–July 1926): 215–222.

tudes have been favorable to anything approaching adequate or even artistic portrayal; the Negro has been shunted from one stereotype into the other, but in this respect has been no more the sufferer than any other subject class, the particular brunt of whose servitude has always seemed to me to consist in the fate of having their psychological traits dictated to them. Of course, the Negro has been a particularly apt social mimic, and has assumed protective coloration with almost every change—thereby hangs the secret of his rather unusual survival. But of course a price has been paid, and that is that the Negro, after three hundred years of residence and association, even to himself, is falsely known and little understood. It becomes all the more interesting, now that we are verging for the first time on conditions admitting anything like true portraiture and self-portrayal to review in retrospect the conditions which have made the Negro traditionally in turn a dreaded primitive, a domestic pet, a moral issue, a ward, a scapegoat, a bogey and pariah, and finally what he has been all along, could he have been seen that way, a flesh and blood human, with nature's chronic but unpatented varieties.

Largely because Negro portraiture has rarely if ever run afoul of literary genius, these changes have rather automatically followed the trend of popular feeling, and fall almost into historical period stages, with very little overlapping. Roughly we may outline them as a Colonial period attitude (1760-1820), a pre-Abolition period (1820-45), the Abolitionist period (1845-65), the Early Reconstruction period (1870-85), the late Reconstruction period (1885-95), the Industrial period (1895-1920), and the Contemporary period since 1920. The constant occurrence and recurrence of the Negro, even as a minor figure, throughout this wide range is in itself an indication of the importance of the Negro as a social issue in American life, and of the fact that his values are not to be read by intrinsic but by extrinsic coefficients. He has dramatized constantly two aspects of white psychology in a projected and naïvely divorced shape—first, the white man's wish for self-justification, whether he be at any given time anti-Negro or pro-Negro, and, second, more subtly registered, an avoidance of the particular type that would raise an embarrassing question for the social conscience of the period; as, for example, the black slave rebel at the time when all efforts were being made after the abatement of the slave trade to domesticate the Negro; or the defeatist fiction types of 1895-1920, when the curve of Negro material progress took such a sharp upward rise. There is no insinuation that much of this sort of reflection has been as conscious or deliberately propagandist as is often charged and believed; it is really more significant as an expression of "unconscious social wish," for whenever there has been direct and avowed propaganda there has always been awakened a reaction in public attitude and a swift counter-tendency. Except in a few outstanding instances, literature has merely registered rather than moulded public sentiment on this question.

Through the Colonial days and extending as late as 1820, Negro life was treated as strange and distant. The isolated instances treat the Negro almost heroically, with an exotic curiosity that quite gaudily romanticized him. At that time, as in the more familiar romantic treatment of the American Indian, there was registered in the emphasis upon "savage traits" and strange ways a revulsion to his social assimilation. The typical figure of the period is a pure blood, often represented as a "noble captive," a type neither fully domesticated nor understood, and shows that far from being a familiar the Negro was rather a dreaded curiosity. Incidentally, this undoubtedly was a period of close association between the more domesticated Indian tribes and the Negroes—an almost forgotten chapter in the history of race relations in America which the heavy admixture of Indian blood in the Negro strain silently attests; so the association of the two in the public mind may have had more than casual grounds. Two of the most interesting features of this period are the frank concession of ancestry and lineage to the Negro at a time before the serious onset of miscegenation, and the hectic insistence upon Christian virtues and qualities in the Negro at a time when the Negro masses could not have been the model Christians they were represented to be, and which they did in fact become later. As James Oneal has pointed out in an earlier article, the notion of the boon of Christianity placated the bad conscience of the slave traders, and additionally at that time there was reason at least in the feeling of insecurity to sense that it was good social insurance to stress it.

By 1820 or 1825 the Negro was completely domesticated, and patriarchal relations had set in. The strange savage had become a sentimentally humored peasant. The South was beginning to develop its "aristocratic tradition," and the slave figure was the necessary foil of its romanticism. According to F. P. Gaines, "the plantation makes its first important appearance in American literature in John Pendleton Kennedy's *Swallow Barn* (1832) and William Carruther's *The Cavaliers of Virginia* (1834)." As one would expect, the really important figures of the régime are discreetly ignored,—the mulatto house servant concubine and her children; the faithful male body-servant, paradoxically enough, came in for a compensating publicity. In fact, the South was rapidly developing feudal intricacies and their strange, oft-repeated loyalties, and was actually on the verge of a golden age of romance when the shadow of scandal from Northern criticism darkened the high-lights of the whole régime and put the South on the defensive. It is a very significant fact that between 1845 and 1855 there should have appeared nearly a score of plays and novels on the subject of the quadroon girl and her tragic mystery, culminating in William Wells Brown's bold exposè *Clothel; or, The President's Daughter* (1853), as the caption of the unexpurgated English edition of this black Abolitionist's novel read. Southern romance was chilled to the marrow, and did not resume the genial sentimental approach to race characters for over a generation.

With the political issues of slave and free territory looming, and the moral issues of the Abolitionist controversy coming on, Negro life took on in literature the aspects of melodrama. The portraiture which had started was hastily dropped for exaggerated types representing polemical issues. The exaggerated tone was oddly enough set by the Negro himself, for long before *Uncle Tom's Cabin* (1852) the lurid slave narratives had set the pattern of Job-like suffering and melodramatic incident. Apart from its detailed dependence on Josiah Henson's actual story, Mrs. Stowe's novel simply capitalized a pattern of story and character already definitely outlined 1845-50, and in some exceptional anticipations ten years previous. Of course, with this period the vital portrayal of the Negro passed temporarily out of the hands of the South and became dominantly an expression of Northern interest and sentiment.   In its controversial literature, naturally the South responded vehemently to the Abolitionist's challenge with the other side of the melodramatic picture,—the Negro as a brute and villain.   But the formal retaliations of Reconstruction fiction were notably absent; except for a slight shift to the more docile type of Negro and peasant life further removed from the life of the "big house," G. P. James and others continued the mildly propagandist fiction of the patriarchal tradition,—an interesting indication of how the impending danger of the slave régime was minimized in the mass mind of the South.   *Uncle Tom's Cabin*, of course, passes as the acme of the literature of the Abolitionist period, and it is in relation to its influence upon the issues involved.   But as far as literary values go, *Clothel* by Wells Brown and *The Garies and Their Friends* by Frank J. Webb were closer studies both of Negro character and of the Negro situation.   Their daring realism required them to be published abroad, and they are to be reckoned like the Paris school of Russian fiction as the forerunners of the native work of several generations later.   Especially Webb's book, with its narrative of a sophisticated and cultured group of free Negroes, was in its day a bold departure from prevailing conventions.   Either of these books would have been greater still had it consciously protested against the melodramatic stereotypes then in public favor; but the temptation to cater to the vogue of *Uncle Tom's Cabin* was perhaps too great.   The sensational popularity of the latter, and its influence upon the public mind, is only another instance of the effect of a great social issue to sustain melodrama as classic as long as the issue lives.   The artistic costs of all revolutions and moral reforms is high.

The Early Reconstruction period supplied the inevitable sentimental reaction to the tension of the war period.   The change to sentimental genre is quite understandable.   If the South could have resumed the portrayal of its life at the point where controversy had broken in, there would be a notable Southern literature today.   But the South was especially prone to sugar-coat the slave régime in a protective reaction against the exposures of the Abolitionist literature.   Northern fiction in works like the novels of Albion Tourgee continued its incriminations, and Southern literature became more and more propagandist.   At first it was only in a secondary sense derogatory of the Negro; the primary aim was self-justification and romantic day-dreaming about the past.   In the effort to glorify the lost tradition and balm the South's inferiority complex after the defeat, Uncle Tom was borrowed back as counter-propaganda, refurbished as the devoted, dependent, happy, care-free Negro, whom the South had always loved and protected, and whom it knew "better than he knew himself."   The protective devices of this fiction, the accumulative hysteria of self-delusion associated with its promulgation, as well as the comparatively universal acceptance of so obvious a myth, form one of the most interesting chapters in the entire history of social mind.   There is no denying the effectiveness of the Page-Cable school of fiction as Southern propaganda.   In terms of popular feeling it almost recouped the reverses of the war.   The North, having been fed only on stereotypes, came to ignore the

Negro in any intimate or critical way through the deceptive influence of those very stereotypes. At least, these figures Southern fiction painted were more convincingly human and real, which in my judgment accounted in large part for the extraordinary ease with which the Southern version of the Negro came to be accepted by the Northern reading public, along with the dictum that the South knows the Negro.

But the false values in the situation spoiled the whole otherwise promising school—Chandler Harris excepted—as a contrast of the later work of Cable or Page with their earlier work will convincingly show. Beginning with good genre drawing that had the promise of something, they ended in mediocre chromographic romanticism. Though the genteel tradition never fully curdled into hatred, more and more hostilely it focussed upon the Negro as the scapegoat of the situation. And then came a flood of flagrantly derogatory literature as the sudden rise of figures like Thomas Dixon, paralleling the Vardamans and Tillmans of political life, marked the assumption of the master-class tradition by the mass psychology of the "poor-whites." Reconstruction fiction thus completed the swing made quite inevitable by the extreme arc of Abolitionist literature; the crudities and animus of the one merely countered the bathos and bias of the other. In both periods the treatment of Negro life was artistically unsatisfactory, and subject to the distortions of sentiment, propaganda, and controversy. The heavy artillery of this late Reconstruction attack has shambled its own guns; but the lighter fussilade of farce still holds out and still harasses those who stand guard over the old controversial issues. But the advance front of creative effort and attack has moved two stages further on.

As a result of the discussion of the Late Reconstruction period "White Supremacy" had become more than a slogan of the Southern chauvinists; it became a mild general social hysteria, which gave an almost biological significance to the race problem. It is interesting to note how suddenly the "problem of miscegenation" became important at a time when there was less of it than at any period within a century and a quarter, and how the mulatto, the skeleton in the family closet, suddenly was trotted out for attention and scrutiny. From 1895 or so on, this problem was for over a decade a veritable obsession; and from William Dean Howells' *Imperative Duty* to Stribling's *Birthright* the typical and dominant figure of literary interest is the mulatto as a symbol of social encroachment, and the fear of some "atavism of blood" through him wreaking vengeance for slavery. While serious literature was discussing the mulatto and his problem, less serious literature was in a sub-conscious way no less seriously occupied with the negative side of the same problem;—namely, extolling the unambitious, servile, and "racially characteristic" Negro who in addition to presenting diverting humor represented no serious social competition or encroachment. The public mind of the whole period was concentrated on the Negro "in" and "out of his place"; and the pseudo-scientific popularizations of evolutionism added their belabored corollaries. But the real basic proposition underlying it all was the sensing for the first time of the serious competition and rivalry of the Negro's social effort and the failure of his social handicaps to effectively thwart it.

Many will be speculating shortly upon the reasons for the literary and artistic emancipation of the Negro, at a time when his theme seemed most hopelessly in the double grip of social prejudice and moral Victorianism. Of course, realism had its share in the matter; the general reaction away from types was bound to reach even the stock Negro stereotypes. Again, the local color fad and the naturally exotic tendencies of conscious æstheticism gave the untouched field of Negro life an attractive lure. The gradual assertion of Negro artists trying at first to counteract the false drawing and values of popular writers, but eventually in the few finer talents motivated by the more truly artistic motives of self-expression, played its additional part. But in my judgment the really basic factor in the sharp and astonishing break in the literary tradition and attitude toward the Negro came in the revolt against Puritanism. This seems to me to explain why current literature and art are for the moment so preoccupied with the primitive and pagan and emotional aspects of Negro life and character; and why suddenly something almost amounting to infatuation has invested the Negro subject with interest and fascination. The release which almost everyone had thought must come about through a change in moral evaluation, a reform of opinion, has actually and suddenly come about merely as a shift of interest, a revolution of taste. From it there looms the imminent possibility not only of a true literature of the Negro but of a Negro Literature as such. It becomes especially interesting to watch whether the artistic possibilities of these are to be realized, since thrice before this social issues have scotched the artistic potentialities of Negro life, and American literature is thereby poorer in the fields of the historical romance, the period novel, and great problem-drama than it should be. But the work of Waldo Frank, Jean Toomer, Walter White, Rudolph Fisher, and Du Bose Heyward promises greatly; and if we call up the most analogous case as a basis of forecast,—the tortuous way by which the peasant came into Russian literature and the brilliant sudden transformation his advent eventually effected, we may predict, for both subject and its creative exponents, the Great Age of this particular section of American life and strand in the American experience.

THE NEGRO'S CONTRIBUTION TO AMERICAN ART AND LITERATURE

THERE are two distinctive elements in the cultural background of the American Negro: one, his primitive tropical heritage, however vague and clouded over that may be, and second, the specific character of the Negro group experience in America both with respect to group history and with regard to unique environing social conditions. As an easily discriminable minority, these conditions are almost inescapable for all sections of the Negro population, and function, therefore, to intensify emotionally and intellectually group feelings, group reactions, group traditions. Such an accumulating body of collective experience inevitably matures into a group culture which just as inevitably finds some channels of unique expression, and this has been and will be the basis of the Negro's characteristic expression of himself in American life. In fact, as it matures to conscious control and intelligent use, what has been the Negro's social handicap and class liability will very likely become his positive group capital and cultural asset. Certainly whatever the Negro has produced thus far of distinctive worth and originality has been derived in the main from this source, with the equipment from the general stock of American culture acting at times merely as the precipitating agent; at others, as the working tools of this creative expression.

CULTURAL HISTORY

The cultural history of the Negro is as unique and dramatic as his social history. Torn from his native culture and background, he was suddenly precipitated into a complex and very alien culture and civilization, and passed through the fierce crucible of rapid, but complete adaptation to its rudiments, the English language, Christianity, the labor production system, and Anglo-Saxon mores. His complete mental and spiritual flexibility, his rapid assimilation of the essentials of this new culture, in most cases within the first generation is the outstanding feat of his group career and is almost without parallel in history. Costly as it was, it was complete and without reservations. And yet from the earliest efforts at crude self-expression, it was the African or racial temperament, creeping back in the overtones of his half-articulate speech and action, which gave to his life and ways the characteristic qualities instantly recognized as peculiarly and representatively his.

The materials were all American, but the design and the pattern were different,—in speech, social temper, song, dance, imagination, religious attitude. Some of these reactions were so vivid and so irresistible that they communicated themselves by contagious though condescending imitation to the general community and colored the temper and mores of the Southern whites. This generally unacknowledged influence was the Negro's first and perhaps most basic

Annals of the American Academy of Political and Social Science, 140 (1928): 234–247.

contribution to American culture. It is a fallacy that the overlord influences the peasant and remains uninfluenced by him; and in this particular case, with the incorporation of the Negro into the heart of the domestic life of the South, the counter-influence became particularly strong.

In humor, emotional temper, superstitions, nonchalance, amiability, sentiment, illogicality,—all of which were later to find expression in forms of folk literature and art,—the Negro colored the general folk-ways of the South. The Negro has exerted in no other way since so general an influence, but in passing, we must note a near approach to a similar influence, nation-wide though more superficial, in our own generation,—the contagious influence of the "jazz-spirit," a corrupt hybrid of the folk-spirit and modern commercialized amusement and art. Both these influences, we shall see, have direct relevance to formal art and literature, but have had their profoundest effect on the general background of life outside the boundaries of formal expression. It is on another plane, but it is just as important, perhaps more so, to color the humor of a country, or to influence its tempo of life and feeling, or to mould its popular song, dance and folk-tale, as it is to affect its formal poetry or art or music. This point will need to be borne in mind when, later, without detracting from his literary skill and service, we call Joel Chandler Harris a "kindly amanuensis for the illiterate Negro peasant." For Uncle Remus created himself, so to speak, and the basic imaginative background of his tales was African.

It was inevitable that the peculiar experiences of the American Negro should sooner or later find artistic expression. The history of the situation is that they did not wait for a control of the formal, civilized means of expression. They expressed themselves first in folk-ways and folk-arts. Notably, the folk-dance, folk-song, both the spirituals and the less known but equally abundant seculars, and the folk-tale and proverb,—the latter going over into colloquial modifications too rapidly for exact tracing. More and more, especially as the younger contemporary American and Afro-Ameri-

can artists turn back to this mine of folk material for artistic ore, we are coming to a new appreciation of its extent, quality, and originality. Paradoxically enough, it may be that in slavery the Negro made American civilization permanently his spiritual debtor.

The cultural history of the Negro himself in America may be broadly traced as falling into two periods,—a long period of sustained but unsophisticated expression at the folk level dating from his introduction to this country to half a generation after Emancipation, and a shorter period of expression at the cultural, articulate level, stretching back in exceptional and sporadic instances to 1787, but becoming semi-literary with the anti-slavery controversy from 1835–1860, and literary in the full sense only since 1890.

Between these two levels there is a gap, transitional only in the historical sense, when the main line of Negro expression was motivated by the conscious imitation of general American standards and forms, and reacted from the distinctive racial elements in an effort at cultural conformity. This was inevitable and under the circumstances normal; but the position of cultural conformity has since been reversed,—first by the dialect-folk-lore school of Negro expression of which Paul Laurence Dunbar was the leading exponent, and more lately still by the younger contemporary school of "racial self-expression,"—the so-called "New Negro movement," which, growing in volume since 1917, has in a decade produced the most outstanding formal contribution of the Negro to American literature and art. Among the latter are to be enumerated both the "race-realists" who follow the general technical trend of American realism, developing on the basis of local-color the native distinctiveness of Negro life and the "race-symbolists" who have made a cult of the revival of the traits of the race temperament, its philosophy of life, and the re-expression on the cultural level of the folk-spirit and folk-history, including the half-forgotten African background. The importance of this latter movement is not to be underestimated; for, apart from its own creative impulse, it has effected a transformation of race spirit and group attitude, and acted like the creation of a national literature in the vernacular upon the educated classes of other peoples, who also at one or another stage of their cultural history were not integrated with their own particular tradition and folk-background.

AMERICAN ATTITUDE

The general history of white American attitude toward the Negro cultural traits and elements may be similarly traced in broad outline. First a long period of unconscious absorption and exchange, beginning in sentimental curiosity and growing with institutionalized slavery into a sentimental, condescending disdain. Then a transitional period of formal revulsion, in part a natural reaction, in part a definite accompaniment of the Slavery-Anti-slavery controversy. This was an attempt to insulate the Negro culturally, to "put him in his place" culturally as well as socially,—the last hectic throes of which can be seen in the "Reconstruction" school of fiction of Cable, Thomas Nelson Page, and to a modified extent even Joel Chandler Harris.

Finally after a gap of disinterest, there began about 1895 in American literature a new more objective interest in the Negro which, with the growth of American realism, has since 1918 resulted in a serious preoccupation of many of the leading American novelists, dramatists, story-writers, musicians, and folk-lorists with the Negro folk-themes and materials. This movement, amounting at times to definite exploitation of this now highly prized material, has paralleled the Negro cultural movement described above, has given it from time to time encouragement, objective vindication (in the sense that majority attitudes always influence minority attitudes) and developed new points of coöperative contact between the intellectuals and artists of both races.

Some of the best expressions of Negro life in formal American art have in this decade come from such outside sources, like Eugene O'Neill's plays of Negro life, Du Bose Heyward's "Porgy," Mrs. Peterkin's "Green Thursday" and "Black April," Gershwin's adapted "jazz," the University of North Carolina studies in Negro folk-song and folk-lore, to mention some outstanding examples.

The more the cultural rather than the sociological approach to the Negro matures, the more it becomes apparent, both to white and black observers, that the folk-products of the peasant Negro are imperishably fine, and that they constitute a national asset of the first rank. They have survived precariously; much has been lost. Modern research may retrieve some. But Uncle Remus tales and the "Spirituals" are enough to assure one of the quality of the simon-pure product, and of the pity that the generation of 1840 to 1880 was blind to their value. The folk-story background was rescued by Thomas Cable and Joel Chandler Harris, but modern scholarship has yet to winnow out the sentimental additions which glossed over the real folkiness of the originals. The spirituals and other aspects of folk song and dance were saved by the Negroes themselves, beginning with the movement of the Fisk Jubilee singers for the preservation and vindication of the folk music. Their effort, beginning in 1878, has culminated since 1900 in the work of Negro musicians like Harry T. Burleigh, S. Coleridge-Taylor, Rosamond Johnson, Carl Diton, Nathaniel Dett, Lawrence Brown, Edward Boatner, Grant Still, C. S. Ballanta, and others; some in careful arrangement of the Negro folk-song in unvarnished transcription, others in more elaborate formal composition based upon its themes.

Meanwhile the secular Negro music, after a period of sentimental treatment culminating in the melodies of Stephen Foster, and one of minstrel balladry commencing about 1850 and climaxing in the eighties and nineties, has finally, as jazz in the contemporary period, exerted a constant, and at times, dominating influence on American popular music, light entertainment and popular dance figures. All of these popularizations have been somewhat debased versions of their original folk derivatives, even in the hands of their Negro professional exponents. The authentic things themselves, in surviving such treatment, prove their sterling worth; and modern scholarship is now coming to their rescue. Such work as Odum and Johnson's "The Negro and His Songs," Krebheils's "Afro-American Folk-Songs," Weldon Johnson's prefaces to the "First and Second Book of Negro Spirituals," Weldon Johnson's transcriptions of Negro ante-bellum folk-sermons in his "Seven Sermons in Verse" (God's Trombones), Ballanta's "St. Helena Spirituals" enable us now to judge the genuine worth and tone of the Negro folk-product. Finely representative as they are in their historical time and setting, they are now regarded as even more precious in their potential worth as material for fresh artistic development.

The modern scholar is, therefore, reverent where the older generation were patronizing, and painstakingly scientific where we were once sentimentally amateurish. We have learned to appreciate the poetic imagination as well as the music of

> Bright sparkles in de churchyard
> Give light unto de tomb

and the serene faith of "Dese bones gwine to rise again" and "De mornin'-star was a witness too." And grateful as we are for his far-sighted preservation of the most organic body of Negro folk-tale that American literature possesses, we cannot help wishing that Joel Chandler Harris had been a more careful and less improvising amanuensis of the mid-Georgian Negro peasant whom he knew and liked so well. Imperfect as the documentation is, emotionally the ante-bellum Negro has left, however, a satisfactory picture of his spirit. Slavery, which a brilliant ex-slave called "the graveyard of the mind," did not prove to be a tomb of the spirit; the Negro soul broke through to two ideals,—heaven and freedom,—and expressed these hopes imperishably. Although this was an expression of his own particular situation and his specific reactions, it was so profoundly intense as to become universalized; spiritually there are no finer expressions of belief in freedom and immortality, or of the emotional side of Christianity native to the American soil than these Negro folk utterances.

EFFECTS OF SLAVERY ON LITERATURE

If slavery moulded the emotional life of the Negro, it was the anti-slavery struggle that gradually developed his intellect and brought him to articulate expression. The pivot of thought and focus of inspiration with the two first Negro writers, both poets,—Jupiter Hammon (1787) and Phyllis Wheatley (1773),—was freedom, and the inconsistency of slavery, both with American revolutionary ideals and Christianity. There was in prose an anonymous arraignment of slavery by "Othello" as early as 1799, followed by Walker's famous "Appeal" in 1829. From this point on the growing anti-slavery movement developed necessarily the second-rate literature of controversy. Yet in this and the allied field of oratory, the Negro contribution was exceptional and at times up to the level of contemporary white talent, Garrison, Jay, Gerritt Smith, Sumner Phillips, as a critical comparison of the orations and essays of Martin Delaney, Samuel McCune Smith, Thomas Remond, Ringgold Ward, Henry Highland Garnett, Edward Wilmot Blyden, the West Indian scholar and abolitionist, and the greatest popular figure of the group, Frederick Douglass, will show.

These men all developed stages beyond literacy to forceful and polished oratory, and occasionally into matured scholarship. A synoptic view of their half-forgotten writings, such as Carter Woodson's carefully edited "Negro Orators and their Orations" affords, shows their contribution to American literature of this type and period to have been surprising in volume and quality, and also reveals the intellectual Negro in the rôle of an active and valuable collaborator throughout the whole range of the anti-slavery movement and its activities, 1831–1859.

From the literary point of view, anti-slavery literature by both white and black writers is admittedly second-rate, but no one can deny its representativeness of its historical period. In the main throughout this period the Negro was a conformist imitator; here and there characteristic notes cropped out, but not dominantly. The most original products of this period, therefore, are the so-called "slave-narratives,"—life stories of fugitive slaves, all of them picturesquely, some of them forcefully, written. Frederick Douglass's Narrative of "A Fugitive Slave" (1845), afterwards expanded into his autobiography, was one of the best known, Josiah Henson's life story (1858) was taken orally by Mrs. Stowe as the basis of her "Uncle Tom's Cabin" for characterization and a large part of the plot. The really most distinctive of these narratives are the early ones (1830–40), less known but also less tinctured with the tractate appeal of those later inspired directly by Abolitionist patrons, like Moses Roper's wonderful narrative of his escape (1837) or the story of Henry Bibb (1849). During this period there were two anti-slavery poets,—George Horton, a talented slave retainer of the University of North Carolina, who sold love lyrics to the Beau Brummel students at twenty-five cents a poem, and whose poems, "The Hope of Liberty," were published in 1829 by friends to raise funds for the purchase of his freedom; and a more versatile and trained person, Frances Ellen Watkins Harper of Baltimore, whose verses in the style of Dorothea Hemans made her really one of the most popular and best-selling poets of her day. ("Forest Leaves," 1855; "Collected Poems," 1854.)

Against the background of the naïve and winsome folk-expressions, and the powerfully self-contained "Sorrow-songs," these painfully self-conscious effusions of sentimental appeal and moral protest are tame, feeble, and only historically interesting. But they were the first necessary stage of articulate expression: they did open up the mastery of the whole range of the English language and bring the Negro mind out into the mainstream of practical and cultural contacts. In this period, too, there was considerable production of *belles-lettres* apart from that more practical polemical and propagandist work which, however, absorbed the major effort of the talented tenth who might otherwise have produced more creatively. Foremost among these more literary things were the essays of Martin Delaney and Henry Highland Garnett, the commentaries of William

Wells Brown, and the novels of Frank J. Webb (1857–59). Many of these works, like Phyllis Wheatley's Poems, were first published in London.

The Civil War in one sense drained the energies of the anti-slavery campaign; in another sense gave it a specious satisfaction. In this and the early Reconstruction period little was produced by the Negro intellectuals. The practical emergencies of emancipation and reconstruction absorbed their time and attention. Shortly after 1875, reconstruction fiction by white writers began to appear, and took the form of sentimental glorification of the old ante-bellum régime, with little protest or counter-statement by white Northern writers,—there was the notable exception of the prolific Albion Tourgée. Negro writers meanwhile were absorbed writing revisions of slave autobiographies or propounding panaceas for the solution of the race question. Memoirs and amateurish histories were the vogue, but a huge mass of valuable historical data got itself written down, beginning with Samuel Nell's "Colored Patriots of the American Revolution," and "The Services of Colored Americans in the Wars of 1776 and 1812," published in 1852–55, running through work like Frederick Douglass's "Life and Times" (1882) and Simmon's "Men of Mark" (1887), and culminating in 1883 with George Williams' epoch-making, two-volume "History of the Negro Race from 1619–1880."

Meanwhile, in literature the Southern protagonists had their innings in an uncontested field,—the enthusiasm of the North having spent itself in the furious and embittered campaign of Anti-Slavery. Reconstruction literature was in its first stage sentimentalist, and created the stereotypes by which the Negro is still popularly known in America; and then after Cable, Harris and Nelson Page, indeed before the end of their writing careers, became still more violently propagandist and caricaturist in its treatment of the Negro,—this phase culminating in the work of Thomas Dixon.

RECOVERY OF LITERARY EFFORT

Only in the late eighties did Negro literary effort recover itself, to succeed really only with two figures, Charles Waddell Chestnutt, the novelist and story writer, and Paul Laurence Dunbar, known as a dialect poet, but also considerably versatile as sentimental lyric poet, story writer and novelist. Chestnutt modelled his story style and technique upon Cable and Bret Harte, and achieved a real success in the *Atlantic Monthly*, which led to a series of publications by Houghton Mifflin and Scribner's. Stories like the "Conjure Woman," and "The Wife of His Youth" represent the modern breaking-through of the Negro man of letters after the gap of Reconstruction; but Mr. Chestnutt's more ambitious work has been the writing of period novels to counter the distorted picture of the Southern régime given by the Nelson Page school of fiction. Two of these, "The House Behind the Cedars" (1900) and "The Marrow of Tradition" (1901), are of documentary as well as literary importance.

Paul Laurence Dunbar is in the popular mind the outstanding Negro writer. This is because his poetry, heralded by William Dean Howells, started that increasingly popular school of Negro dialect poetry, about which there has been such controversy. There is no question about the representativeness of Dunbar's happy-go-lucky, self-pitying peasant; it is only a matter of realizing two things,—that he stands for the race at a certain stage of its history and a certain class at that stage. The Negro abolitionists were lecturing in Europe and J. C. Pennington preaching at the University of Heidelberg at the same time that Sam, Malindy, Dinah and Joe were making the plantation cook-house merry and the front porch gayer. Braithwaite, the critic, has the vital word on this question: "Dunbar was the articulate end of a régime, and not the beginning of a tradition, as most careless critics, both white and colored, seem to think. His work reflected chiefly the life of the typical Negro during the era of Reconstruction and just a little beyond, the limited experience of a transitional period, the rather helpless and still subservient era of testing freedom, of adjusting in the masses a new condition of relationship to the social, economic, civil and spiritual fabric of American civilization." Dunbar him-

self rebelled against this overemphasis upon his dialect poetry, and thought more both of his legitimate English lyrics and his fiction, in both of which fields he is not a negligible figure. In his "Ode to Ethiopia" and the sonnets to Robert Gould Shaw, Frederick Douglass, and Booker Washington, Dunbar reflected another side of the Negro soul than that delightfully rendered in "When Malindy Sings" or "When de Co'n Pone's Hot."

It was in this period (1895–1905) that the peasant cause and the mind of the Negro intellectuals became temporarily estranged because of a controversial feud over race programs and objectives. The cause of the masses found its protagonist in Booker T. Washington and his program of economic development, industrial education, and political and cultural *laissez-faire*. His autobiography, "Up from Slavery," since becoming an accepted American classic, made this wing of Negro thought articulate. "The Souls of Black Folk," by Dr. W. E. B. DuBois, equally a classic, though not so generally recognized, articulated the other cause of equal civic and educational and undifferentiated cultural ideals for the Negro.

The dialect school of poetry and all other strictly realistic arts were innocently caught in the dilemma of this controversy and aligned on the "segregationist" side. A considerable amount of controversial literature sprang up about this issue, most of it second-rate and negligible. Its effect was to delay pure art expression, to motivate Negro art temporarily upon an attempt to influence white opinion, and to retard the study of folk forms and tradition,— since the intellectuals capable of such study were for the time being out of sympathy with native and peculiarly indigenous things. A strain of dialect poetry trickled on, led by the ever-increasing popularity of Dunbar, but DuBois was followed by the majority of the talented class and himself undertook a semi-propagandist school of social document fiction, of which "The Quest of the Silver Fleece" (1911) is representative, and sentimental *belles-lettres* of which "Darkwater" is the classic expression. This literature of assertion and protest did perform a valuable service, however, for it encouraged and vindicated cultural equality, and at the price of much melodramatic sentimentalism, did induce a recovery of morale for purely cultural pursuits and self-expression. Meanwhile, the vogue of the school of Dunbar wrote into American literature, about a decade behind the general vogue of local-color sentimentalism, the important genre figure of the Negro peasant and troubador-minstrel.

Then from 1912–15 on, with poetry of the intellectual school leading, a new phase of Negro self-expression gradually began. Previously, we must recall, except as singer or rhymster poet, the Negro as artist was not taken seriously. In this new phase, important as was the influence of DuBois, perhaps even more influential was the indirect effect of the career and standing of William Stanley Braithwaite, who, in addition to his own verse publications in pre-Raphaelite and symbolist veins, became, by his scholarly anthologies and his advocacy of modern American verse, a figure in the general literary world. The effect upon the cause, poetry and art for art's sake among Negroes, cannot be overestimated; the "legitimate" poets took heart and the dialect school became obsolescent. James Weldon Johnson published "Fifty Years and After" in 1917, facing Dunbar in one direction and away from him in another. Later Mr. Johnson declared for a new interpretation of the dialect school, "for the idioms of the folk imagination" rather than the broken jingle of Negro patois, in his "Creation" published in 1920 (later expanded into Seven Negro Sermons in Verse, "God's Trombones" (1927)). Fenton Johnson, Charles Bertram Johnson, Roscoe Jameson, Georgia Douglas Johnson, and most important of all, Claude McKay, began to publish, so that between 1917 and 1922 a revival of first-class artistic production had set in.

The Negro experience was now taken as the starting point, but universalized and for the most part treated in traditional poetic forms and symbols. Real virtuoso technique was sought and in cases achieved. Part of this output continued in a more dignified way the note of social protest, as in Claude McKay's "To America":

Although she feeds me bread of bitterness,
And sinks into my throat her tiger's tooth,
Stealing my breath of life, I will confess
I love this cultured hell which tests my
    youth.
Her vigor flows like tides into my blood,
Giving me strength against her hate,
Her bigness sweeps my being like a flood.
Yet as a rebel fronts a king in state,
I stand within her walls with not a shred
Of terror, malice, not a word of jeer,
Darkly I gaze into the days ahead.
And see her might and granite wonders
    there,
Beneath the touch of Time's unerring hand,
Like priceless treasures sinking in the sand.

Another part, now the dominant note of the newer poetry, is a glorification of the racial background and of racial types of beauty, as in the same poet's lyric to "The Harlem Dancer":

Applauding youths laughed with young
    prostitutes
And watched her perfect, half-clothed
    body sway;
Her voice was like the sound of blended
    flutes
Blown by black players on a picnic day.
She sang and danced on gracefully and
    calm,
The light gauze hanging loose about her
    form;
To me she seemed a proudly-swaying palm
Grown lovelier through passing through
    a storm.

Some of this new crop of poetry indeed is quite general without reference to race situations or moods, which is particularly true of many poems by the three outstanding Negro women poets, Georgia Douglas Johnson, Angelina Grimke, and Ann Spencer, who range in technique from sentimental lyricism to ultra-modern free verse.

POETRY AND MUSIC

Obviously Negro artists had by this stage outgrown the fault of allowing didactic emphasis and propagandist motives to choke their sense of artistry. In music the same growth took place with a rediscovery of the artistic possibilities of the Spirituals and other folk music forms. Harry Burleigh, Rosamond Johnson, Carl Diton, Nathaniel Dett, and others led this advance of the Negro musician to classic control and general recognition. In fiction and drama realistic folk portrayal was being taken up, by imitation in the last two instances of such pioneering experiments with a purely artistic treatment of Negro themes by modernist white American artists as Stribling, Shands, Clement Wood, Ellen Glasgow, Julia Peterkin, DuBose Heyward in the field of the novel and short-story, and Ridgley Torrence, Eugene O'Neill and Paul Green in the drama. From the Negro side and point of view, however, the main motivation, instead of being a new realistic cult of utilizing native materials in American art, has established itself in a new desire for representative group expression, paralleling the quickening of the group life which increased education and economic prosperity have given. Additionally there were the factors of migration from the farms and the South generally, rapid urbanization, intensification of group feeling growing out of the World War, and a general resurgence of race-consciousness and group-pride.

In 1924-25, after it had focussed itself in advanced centers of culture like the Harlem Negro colony in New York, and somewhat in other centers like Chicago and Washington, and as it was running sub-consciously in the veins of the youngest school of Negro poets, the present writer articulated these trends as a movement toward racial self-expression and cultural autonomy, styling it the New Negro movement (Harlem issue, *Survey Graphic*, March, 1925). Since then the accumulated spiritual momentum of one knows not how many generations has suddenly precipitated in a phenomenal burst of creative expression in all the arts, poetry and music leading as might be expected, but with very considerable activity in the fields of fiction, race drama, Negro history, painting, sculpture and the decorative arts. It is a sound generalization to say that three-fourths of the total output is avowedly racial in inspiration and social objective, that a good part of it aims at the capitalization of the folk materials and the spiritual products of the group history; and equally safe to assert that more worth-while artistic output and recognition have been achieved in less than a decade than in all the range of time since 1619.

Coming concurrently with a distinct attention on the part of American writers and artists to the artistic possibilities of Negro life, this recent movement is momentous. And since it is based on a conscious revival of partly lapsed tradition and experience, particularly with reference to the African past, it is not ineptly termed "the Negro Renaissance." Its general social and cultural effects will not be apparent for half a generation yet, but in its literary and artistic course it has all the earmarks of other recent folk revivals like that of the Celtic tradition in the Irish Renaissance or of the Bohemian history and folk arts in the Czecho-Slovakian developments still more contemporaneously. And as a result already accomplished, we have a general acceptance of the Negro today as a contributor to national culture and a potential collaborator in national self-expression.

Since 1920, four Negro poets have appeared who, in addition to their significant extension of the gamut of Negro life and experience artistically expressed, must also be reckoned in any fair survey of leading contemporary American poets,—Claude McKay, Jean Toomer, Countee Cullen and Langston Hughes. Their poetry is racial on the whole, but in a new way. As Charles S. Johnson has aptly put it:

The new racial poetry of the Negro marks the birth of a new racial consciousness, and the recognition of difference *without the usual implications of disparity*. It lacks apology, the wearying appeals to pity, and the conscious philosophy of defense. In being itself it reveals its greatest charm. In accepting this life it invests it with a new meaning.

And in evidence he quotes the manifesto of Langston Hughes, whose poetry he rightly claims as

without doubt the finest expression of this new Negro poetry: "We younger Negro artists who create now intend to express our individual dark-skinned selves without fear or shame. If white people are pleased we are glad. If they are not, it doesn't matter. We know we are beautiful. And ugly, too. If colored people are pleased we are glad. If they are not, their displeasure doesn't matter either. We build our temples for tomorrow, strong as we know how, and we stand on the top of the mountain, free within ourselves.

A declaration of cultural independence,

this—and a charter of spiritual emancipation.

Yet as a cursory glance at Mr. Cullen's anthology of the younger Negro poet's "Caroling Dusk" will show, the field of poetic expression has at the same time so broadened technically as to have produced competent exponents of practically all the stylistic trends of contemporary poetry. Within the same period interest in Negro drama has also developed; on the metropolitan stage as a distinct Broadway vogue for serious acting by Negroes and for plays by and about Negroes, of which "Emperor Jones," "In Abraham's Bosom" and "Porgy" deserve outstanding mention. But Negro drama has still more importantly advanced in the direction of a movement for the development of a Negro theatre and a repertory of plays based on the folk tradition. Similarly in art, where five years ago one or two painters and sculptors of general note like Henry O. Tanner, Meta Warrick Fuller, May Howard Jackson were isolated exceptions, now centers like Chicago or New York can muster for special exhibit the work of younger Negro artists in all the media from illustration and applied art to formal painting, and count on a dozen to a score of contributing artists; among whom Archibald Motley, Aaron Douglas, William Edouard Scott, Laura Wheeler, Hale Woodruff, Edward Harleston, Palmer Hayden,—painters, and the sculptors Augusta Savage, Sargent Johnson, and Richmond Barthe must be mentioned. The work of some of these artists is in the general field, but much is racially interpretative, with some as a portrayal of folk types, with others as an attempt to base color and design somewhat more originally on the motives and technical originalities of primitive African sculpture and decoration.

FICTION

More significant still, sociologically, is the field of fiction. Here arrival at maturity represents more than emotional or technical control, resting as it does on the capacity for social analysis and criticism. Viewed in contrast with such masterfully objective and balanced portrayals of Harlem life as Rudolph Fisher's "The Walls of Jericho" and Claude McKay's "Home to Harlem," the Negro novel of ten or even

five years back seems generations less mature. For the work of DuBois, "The Quest of the Silver Fleece," and even his recent novel "Dark Princess," Jessie Fauset's "There is Confusion," and Walter White's "Fire in the Flint" and "Flight" are all essentially in the category of problem literature, and gain half or more of their value as "social documents." But the work of the younger generation stands artistically self-sufficient and innerly controlled. Beginning with the reaction from social interpretation in the pioneer artistic novel, Jean Toomer's "Cane" (1923), —a brilliant performance, and gaining momentum with some very competent short story portrayals by Fisher, John Matheus, Zora Hurston and Eric Walrond,—the younger school have swung round finally to an artistically unimpeachable combination of social and esthetic interpretation. In technical control and poise, we can now match the best contemporary writers of fiction in this field,—Van Vechten, Mrs. Peterkin, DuBose Heyward,—and promise shortly to overtake the same handicap in the field of drama, where as yet writers like Paul Green and Eugene O'Neill hold the preëminence. And this newly acquired mastery, in combination with the advantage of inside emotional touch with the facts and feelings of Negro experience, ought to give the young Negro writer and artist undisputed priority, though fortunately for American art as a whole, not an uncontested monopoly in this rich new field of the purely artistic expression of Negro life.

On the basis of evidence of this sort, it is warrantable to conclude that the advance-guard of Negro life has either reached or nearly reached cultural maturity after a hard and inauspicious transplanting; and it is difficult to know in advance which effects will be more far-reaching and important, those of the direct artistic products, or those of the cultural and social by-products. Apart from the great actual and potential effects of this self-expression upon group morale and inner stimulation, there is that equally important outer effect which may possibly bring about a new cultural appraisal and acceptance of the Negro in American life.

America, in fact, has never psychologically spurned the Negro or been cold to the spiritual elements of his temperament; it is simply a question now of what reactions their expression on a new and advanced level will generate in a situation where both products and producer must together be accepted or rejected, deprecated or recognized. The initial reactions to this phase are promising, which is in itself a significant and hopeful fact. In view of the dramatic yet integral character of the Negro's life with that of the dominant majority, and especially in view of the complementary character of the dominant Negro traits with those of the Anglo-Saxon Nordic, it would seem to be a situation of profitable exchange and real cultural reciprocity. For the Negro's predisposition toward the artistic, promising to culminate in a control and mastery of the spiritual and mystic as contrasted with the mechanical and practical aspects of life, makes him a spiritually needed and culturally desirable factor in American life. However, for the general working out of such a delicate interaction of group psychologies we cannot predict, but can only await the outcome of what is historically and sociologically a unique situation. All that we can be sure of in advance is the positive and favorable internal effect of such recent cultural development upon the course of Negro group life itself.

NEGRO LITERATURE

A SELECTED BIBLIOGRAPHY

I. EARLY WRITINGS (1775–1835)

Allen, Bishop Richard—Life of B. A., Philadelphia, 1793.

Banneker, Benjamin—Almanacks, 1791–96.

Coker, Daniel—The Journal of D. C., Baltimore, 1820.

Cuffe, Paul—Brief Account of Sierra Leone, New York, 1812.

Hammon, Jupiter—An Address to Miss Phyllis Wheatley, Hartford, 1778; An Address to the Negroes in the State of New York, New York, 1787.

Haynes, Lemuel—The Nature and Importance of True Republicanism, Rutland, Vt., 1801.

Minutes of the First Convention of Free People of Color, Philadelphia, 1831.

"Othello"—Slavery. By a Free Negro. 1789.

Vassa, Gustavus—Life and Letters of G. V., London, 1778–91.

Wheatley, Phyllis—Poems on Various Subjects, Religious and Moral, London, 1773.

II. THE PERIOD OF ANTI-SLAVERY (1835–1870)

A. *Early Biography and Slave Narratives*

Bibb, Henry—Narrative of the Life and Character of H. B., written by himself, New York, 1849.

Brown, William Wells—Narrative of W. W. B., a Fugitive Slave, Boston, 1847.

Craft, Henry and Ellen—Running a Thousand Miles for Freedom, London, 1860.

Douglass, Frederick—The Heroic Slave, Madison Washington, 1839; Narrative of F. D., a Fugitive Slave, Boston, 1845.

Henson, Josiah—Truth Stranger than Fiction, Cleveland, 1858.

Roper, Moses—The Escape of M. R., 1837.

Ward, Samuel Ringgold—Autobiography of a Fugitive Negro, London, 1855.

B. *Anti-Slavery Literature*

Delaney, Martin R.—The Condition, Elevation, Emigration and Destiny of the Colored People of the United States, Philadelphia, 1852.

Douglass, Frederick—My Bondage and My Freedom, New York, 1855.

Garnett, Henry H.—An Address to the Slave Population of the United States, Buffalo, 1843.

Pennington, J. W. C.—The Fugitive Blacksmith, London, 1849.

Walker, David—Appeal to the Negroes of the United States, Boston, 1829.

C. *Early Belles-Lettres*

Bell, J. Madison—Poems on Liberty; Emancipation Ode, 1865–1866.

Blyden, W. C.—Vindication of the African Race, 1857; The Negro in Ancient History, New York, 1872.

Brown, William Wells—Three Years in Europe, London, 1852; Miralda, or the Leap for Freedom, Boston, 1849; Clotelle, or the President's Daughter (Novel), London, 1853.

Crowther, Rev. Samuel—Journal of the Expedition up the Niger and Tschaddo Rivers, London, 1855.

Crummell, Rev. Alexander—The Future of Africa, New York, 1862.

Delaney, Martin R.—Principia of Ethnology, the Origin of Race and Color, Philadelphia, 1875.

Harper, Frances Ellen—Miscellaneous Poems, Boston, 1854; Forest Leaves, Baltimore, 1855.

Horton, George—The Hope of Liberty (Poems), Raleigh, 1829.

Nell, William C.—The Colored Patriots of the American Revolution, Boston, 1855; Services of Colored Americans in the Wars of 1776 and 1812, Boston, 1852.

Pennington, J. W. C.—A Text Book of the Origin and History of the Colored People, Hartford, 1841.

Webb, Frank J.—The Garies and Their Friends (Novel), London, 1857.

III. RECONSTRUCTION LITERATURE (1875–1895)

Blyden, W. C.—Christianity, Islam and the Negro, London, 1887.

Douglass, Frederick—Life and Times of Fred. D., New York, 1882.

Green, J. P.—Truth Stranger than Fiction, Cleveland, 1887.

Payne, Daniel A.—Recollections of Seventy Years, 1888.

Still, William J.—The Underground Railroad, Philadelphia, 1872.

Simmons, William J.—Men of Mark, 1887.

Williams, George W.—The History of the Negro Race from 1619–1880, New York, 1883.

Modern Literature (1895-1928)

A. *Biography*

Andrews, William McCants—John Merrick, Durham, N. C., 1920.

Brawley, Benjamin J.—Women of Achievement, Boston, 1919.

Bullock, Ralph W.—In Spite of Handicaps, New York, 1927.

Fauset, Arthur—For Freedom, Philadelphia, 1927.

Jones, Lawrence C.—Piney Woods and Its Story, New York, 1922.

Moton, Robert R.—Finding a Way Out, an Autobiography, New York.

Pickens, William—The Heir of Sleves, New York, 1911; Bursting Bonds, Boston, 1923.

Scott, Emmett J. and L. B. Stowe—Booker T. Washington, Builder of a Civilization, New York, 1916.

Walters, Alexander—My Life and Work, Chicago, 1917.

Washington, Booker T.—Up from Slavery, New York, 1901.

B. *Poetry*

Braithwaite, William S.—Lyrics of Life and Love, Boston, 1904; The House of Falling Leaves, Boston, 1908; Sandy Star and Other Poems, Boston, 1928.

Cullen, Countee—Color, New York, 1925; Copper Sun, New York, 1927.

Dunbar, Paul Laurence—Oak and Ivy, Dayton, O., 1893; Majors and Minors, Toledo, 1895; Collected Poems, New York, 1920.

Johnson, Charles Bertram—Songs of My People, Boston, 1918.

Johnson, Fenton—Visions of the Dusk, New York, 1915; Songs of the Soil, New York, 1916.

Johnson, Georgia Douglas—The Heart of a Woman, and Other Poems, Boston, 1918; Bronze, Boston, 1922.

Johnson, James Weldon—Fifty Years and After, and Other Poems, Boston, 1917; God's Trombones, Seven Negro Sermons in Verse, New York, 1927.

Hughes, Langston—The Weary Blues, New York, 1926; Fine Clothes to the Jew, New York, 1927.

McKay, Claude—Harlem Shadows, New York, 1922.

Toomer, Jean—Poems in "Cane," New York, 1923.

Poetry Collections:

Countee Cullen (Ed.)—Caroling Dusk, an Anthology of Verse by Negro Poets, New York, 1927.

Johnson, James Weldon (Ed.)—The Book of American Negro Poetry, New York, 1922.

Locke, Alain (Ed.)—Four Negro Poets—Pamphlet Poet Series, New York, 1927.

C. *Fiction*

Chestnutt, Charles W.—The House Behind the Cedars, Boston, 1900; The Marrow of Tradition, Boston, 1901; The Conjure Woman and Other Stories, 1899; The Wife of His Youth and Other Stories.

DuBois, William E. Burghardt—The Quest of the Silver Fleece, Chicago, 1911; Dark Princess, New York, 1928.

Dunbar, Paul L.—Sport of the Gods, New York, 190?; The Uncalled, New York, ?;

The Fanatics, New York, ?; The Love of Landry, ?.

Fauset, Jessie R.—There Is Confusion, New York, 1924.

Fisher, Rudolph—The Walls of Jericho, New York, 1928.

Johnson, James Weldon—The Autobiography of an Ex-Colored Man, New York, 1912.

Larsen, Nella—Quicksands, New York, 1928.

McKay, Claude—Home to Harlem, New York, 1928.

Toomer, Jean—Cane, New York, 1923.

Walrond, Eric—Tropic Death, New York, 1926

White, Walter—Fire in the Flint, New York, 1924; Flight, New York, 1926.

D. *Drama and Belles-Lettres*

Braithwaite, William S.—The Poetic Year, Boston, 1917; Anthologies of Elisabethan Verse, Boston, 1918; of Georgian Verse, Boston, 1918; The Anthologies of American Magazine Verse and Year Book of American Poetry, 1913-1928.

Brawley, Benjamin G.—The Negro in Literature and Art, New York, 1918.

DuBois, W. E. B.—The Souls of Black Folk, Chicago, 1898; Darkwater, New York, 1920; The Gift of Black Folk, Boston, 1924.

Grimke, Angelina—Rachel; a Drama, Boston, 1920.

Locke, Alain—The New Negro; an Interpretation, New York, 1925; American Literary Tradition and the Negro, Modern Quarterly, 1926.

—————— ———— and Montgomery Gregory (Ed.)—Plays of Negro Life, New York, 1927.

Nelson, Alice Dunbar—Masterpieces of Negro Eloquence, New York, 1914.

Woodson, Carter G. (Ed.)—Negro Orators and Their Orations, Washington, 1925.

E. *Historical and Sociological Works*

Brawley, Benjamin G.—A Short History of the American Negro, New York, 1919; A Social History of the American Negro, New York, 1921.

Cromwell, John W.—The Early Negro Convention Movement, Washington, 1904.

DuBois, W. E. B.—The Negro (Home University Library), New York, 1915.

Lynch, John R.—Facts of Reconstruction, New York, 1913.

Miller, Kelly—Race Adjustment, New York, 1909; Out of the House of Bondage, Chicago, 1914; The Appeal to Conscience, New York, 1918; The Everlasting Stain, Washington, 1924.

Pickens, William J.—The New Negro, His Political, Civic and Mental Status, New York, 1916.

Wesley, Charles H.—Negro Labor in the United States, New York, 1927.

Woodson, Carter G.—The History of the Negro Church, Washington, 1922; The Negro in Our History, Washington, 1923.

F. *Music and Art*

Ballanta, C. J. S., St. Helena Spirituals, Schirmer, N. Y., 1925.

Brown, Lawrence—Five Spirituals, Schott & Co., 1924.

Burleigh, Harry T.—Numerous Arrangements of Spirituals, Ricordi, 1917-26.

Dett, Nathaniel J.—Magnolia Suite, In The Bottoms, Summy & Co., 1920; Negro Spirituals, 3 vols., John Church Co., 1919; Religious Folk-Songs of the Negro, Hampton, 1927.

Diton, Carl R.—Four Spirituals, Schirmer, 1912; Four Negro Spirituals, 1914.

Guillaume, Paul, and T. Munro—Primitive Negro Sculpture, New York, 1926.

Hare, Maude Cuney—Six Creole Folk-Songs, Fischer, New York, 1921.

Handy, W. C., and A. B. Niles—Blues; an Anthology of Jazz, New York, 1926.

Johnson, James Weldon, and Rosamond Johnson—The Book of American Negro Spirituals, New York, 1925; The Second Book of American Negro Spirituals, 1926.

Locke, Alain—African Art, Special Issue Opportunity, May, 1925; The Negro in Art, Opportunity, September, 1926; African Art, The Arts, March, 1927.

Talley, T. W.—Negro Folk-Rhymes, New York, 1922.

Taylor, Samuel Coleridge—Twenty-Four Negro Melodies, O. Ditson, 1916; numerous orchestral and choral compositions, Augener and Novello, London, 1907–1919.

Trotter, William J.—Music and Some Musical People (Negro Musicians), Boston, 1888.

White, C. Cameron—Negro Folk Melodies, Presser & Co., 1927.

Work, John Wesley—Folk Songs of the American Negro, Nashville, 1915.

THE NEGRO'S CONTRIBUTION TO
AMERICAN CULTURE

After twenty years or so of continuous discussion, this subject of the cultural contribution of the Negro as a racial group has become trite and well-nigh threadbare. Having undergone much critical wear and tear, and having passed in the process from intriguing novelty to tawdry commonplace and from careful critical delineation to careless propaganda, the whole subject now obviously needs, even to the layman's eye, thoroughgoing renovation. Before we proceed to any further documentation, then, of the Negro's cultural contributions, let us address ourselves to this more difficult and more important task of its critical evaluation.

The crux of the whole issue from the critical point of view is basically the question of the propriety of applying race concepts to cultural products. What makes a work of art Negro, its theme or its idiom? What constitutes a "Negro contribution to culture," its authorship or its cultural base? Is there or should there be any such set of categories in our critical thinking or our creative living? Seldom do we ask such basic questions, and when we do, we too often run off, like Pontius Pilate, without waiting for an answer. Yet by and on some unequivocal answers to questions like these must our whole philosophy and practise of culture be judged and justified.

As an instance of this dilemma, we find James Weldon Johnson in his anthology, *The Book of American Negro Poetry*, cautiously accepting Negro authorship as the criterion of Negro cultural contribution in this field excluding both the folk poetry and the large body of American verse on the Negro theme,[1] but in his celebrated preface to the same, boldly claiming as Negro "contributions" Uncle Remus, with titular white authorship, jazz ragtime and American popular dance forms to the extent they are the derivatives of Negro idioms or source originals. Obviously here is a paradox. Which is the sound position? What is the proper and consistent claim?

Obviously culture politics has a good deal to do with the situation, often forcing both majority and minority partisans into strange and untenable positions. Granted even that the very notion of "Negro art" and of "Negro cultural contributions" is a sequel of minority status, and an unfortunate by-product of racial discrimination and prejudice, it by no means follows that an uncritical acceptance of the situation is necessary or advisable.

[1] Calverton's *Anthology of American Negro Literature* includes the folk poetry, and Sterling Brown's *Negro Poetry and Drama* treats the literature of the Negro theme by both white and Negro poets and dramatists.

Journal of Negro Education 8 (July 1939): 521–529.

There is, in fact, a fallacy in both of the extreme positions in this cultural dilemma. Although there is in the very nature of the social situation an unavoidable tendency for the use of literature and art as instruments of minority group expression and counter-assertion, there is a dangerous fallacy of the minority position involved in cultural racialism. Cultural chauvinism is not unique in a racial situation, however; a national literature and art too arbitrarily interpreted has the same unpardonable flaws. However, where as in the case of the Negro there are no group differentials of language or basic culture patterns between the majority and the minority, cultural chauvinism is all the more ridiculous and contrary to fact. Consistently applied it would shut the minority art up in a spiritual ghetto and deny vital and unrestricted creative participation in the general culture.

On the other hand, there is the majority fallacy of regarding the cultural situation of a group like the Negro after the analogy of a "nation within a nation," implying a situation of different culture levels or traditions, a system of cultural bulkheads, so to speak, each racially compartmentalized and water-tight. Like most fallacies, in explicit statement, they reveal their own inner self-contradiction and absurdities. However, hidden taint of both these fallacious positions is very common in our popular and critical thinking on this issue of Negro cultural expression and contribution.

Cultural racialism and chauvinism flatter the minority group ego; cultural biracialism not only flatters the majority group ego, but is the extension of discrimination into cultural prejudices and bigotry.[2] Both are contrary to fact, and particularly so in the case of the American Negro. What is "racial" for the American Negro resides merely in the overtones to certain fundamental

-----

[2] For a particularly trenchant analysis and criticism of this culture prejudice, see Buell Gallagher's *American Caste and the Negro College*, pp. 368-71.

elements of culture common to white and black and his by adoption and acculturation. What is distinctively Negro in culture usually passes over by rapid osmosis to the general culture, and often as in the case of Negro folklore and folk music and jazz becomes nationally current and representative. Incidentally, it is by the same logic and process that the English language, Anglo-Saxon institutions and mores, including English literary and art forms and traditions have become by differential acculturation what we style "American." In culture, it is the slightly but characteristically divergent that counts, and in most cases racial and nationalist distinctions are only shades of degrees apart. The Negro cultural product we find to be in every instance itself a composite, partaking often of the nationally typical and characteristic as well, and thus something which if styled Negro for short, is more accurately to be described as "Afro-American." In spite, then, of the ready tendency of many to draw contrary conclusions, there is little if any evidence and justification for biracialism in the cultural field, if closely scrutinized and carefully interpreted. The subtle interpenetration of the "national" and the "racial" traits is interesting evidence of cultural cross-fertilization and the wide general vogue and often national representativeness of the "racial contribution" is similar evidence of the effective charm and potency of certain cultural hybrids.

And so, we end up by being able to ferret out no other reliable criterion for what we style typically or characteristically "Negro," culturally speaking, than that cultural compounding and variation which has produced what we style "American" out of what was historically and basically English or Anglo-Saxon. This, if sound, destroys completely the "nation within a nation" analogy which has been so overworked a parallel, and makes Negro literature and art a vital, integral part of American cultural expression. Not even the notion of a cultural province will fit the facts, for the Negro variants have wide distribution and partake of the regional characteristics according to geographical distribution. The cultural products of the Negro are distinctive hybrids; culturally "mulatto" generations ahead of the mixed physical condition and ultimate biological destiny, perhaps, of the human stock.

This makes what is Negro in the truest sense, apart from the arbitrary criterion of Negro authorship, hard to define, no doubt; but fortunately in practise, it is easy enough to discriminate on close contact and comparison. Like rum in the punch, that although far from being the bulk ingredient, still dominates the mixture, the Negro elements have in most instances very typical and dominating flavors, so to speak. I know only one racial idiom with equal versatility combined with equally distinctive potency,—and even that with narrower cultural range since it has been almost exclusively musical; the idioms of Gipsy music and dance which blending with as diverse strains as Russian, Hungarian, Roumanian, Spanish, and even Oriental music, yet succeed in maintaining their own distinctive flavor. The Negro cultural influence, most obvious, too, in music and dance, has a still wider range,—in linguistic influence, in folklore and literary imagery, and in rhythm, the tempo and the emotional overtones of almost any typically Negro version of other cultural art forms. Let us consider a typical, perhaps an extreme instance of this characteristic dominance and its transforming force. Suppose we do laboriously prove the cultural ancestor of the Negro spiritual to be the evangelical hymn forms and themes of white Protestantism; suppose we even find, as the proponents of "White Spirituals" do, interesting parallels and close equivalents, that by no means counters or counteracts the uniqueness in style and appeal of the Negro spiritual, either as folk poetry or folk music. Indeed the formula

analysis, showing so many common ingredients, only adds to the wonder and credit of the almost immeasurable difference in total effect. We need scarcely go further to the acid test of comparing the continued spontaneity and fresh creativeness of the one strain with the comparative sterility and stereotyped character of the other. The one hardly moved its own immediate devotees and barely survives culturally; the other has been creatively potent at all musical levels—folk, popular and classical, has been vital out of its original context in instrumental as well as vocal forms, and has moved the whole world.

If this were a single exceptional instance, no weighty issue would be involved. But creative vitality and versatility, this contagious dominance seems in so many cases to be a characteristic trait of the Negro cultural product. This disproportionality of effect in culture contacts and fusions is becoming more and more obvious as we study the ramified influence of Negro cultural strains. Weldon Johnson no doubt had this in mind when he characterized the Negro genius as having great "emotional endowment, originality in artistic conception, and what is more important, the power of creating that which has universal appeal and influence." This truth will become axiomatic, I take it, when we broaden the scope of our studies of the influence of Negro cultural admixture geographically as is now beginning to develop. For the American Negro elements are but one small segment of the whole gamut of Negro cultural influence; there is the very pronounced Afro-Cuban, the Afro-Brazilean, the Caribbean Creole, the Jamaican, the Trinidadian, the Bahamian, the Louisiana Creole together with those better known to us,—the Southern Lowlands Carolinian, the Lower and Upper South and the urbanized or "Harlem" idiom, which it will be noted is in many respects the most hybrid and attenuated of all. In addition to a new perspective on the range and force of Negro culture contacts, such future study may give us important clues as to the basic African common denominators and some explanation of their unusual vitality and versatility.

It seems reasonable to maintain, therefore, that tracing an arbitrary strand of Negro authorship and narrowly construed race productivity not only does not do the Negro group cultural justice, but that more importantly, it does not disclose the cultural exchanges and interactions which are vital to the process. Following the latter pattern, criticism would teach us to view the cultural scene more in terms of what it actually is, and in addition cut under the superficial bases of the cultural partisanships and chauvinisms of both sides. An increasing number of critical studies and analyses are taking this more modern and more scientific point of view and approach; and a particular series[3] has recently taken as its basic viewpoint the analysis of the Negro idiom and the Negro theme in the various art fields as a gradually widening field of collaboration and interaction between the white and the Negro creative artists. Two schools or recent trends of American letters and criticism have also taken the same composite theory and practise, the one, regionalism—a growing school of critical thought, and Proletarian realism, also a popular and increasing vogue in fiction, drama, and criticism. The former of course is more congenial to the retention of the notion of racial idioms; the latter, over-simplifying the situation in my judgment, discounts and ignores almost completely in its emphasis on class status and class psychology, the idioms of race.

With this background, and with the now almost traditional precedents of claims like that of "Uncle Remus" (with titular white authorship) and jazz music, with its elaborate biracial production, it is to be hoped there will be little or no surprise, as we review

[3] *The Bronze Booklets.* Published by Associates in Negro Folk Education, Washington, D.C.

rapidly the epochs of Negro cultural activity, in having drama like *The Emperor Jones, The Green Pastures* and *Stevedore*, novels like *Green Thursday* and *Porgy*, poems like Lindsay's *Congo* or Bodenheim's *Jazz Kaleidoscope*, though by white authors, referred to in the context of the cultural influence of the Negro theme and idiom. In art, it is color, not the color-line that counts; and that not so much the hue of the author as the complexion of the idiom.

The cultural history of the Negro himself in America may be broadly traced as falling into two periods,—a long period of creative but unsophisticated expression at the folk level, dating almost from his introduction to this country up to half a generation after Emancipation, and a shorter period of expression at the cultural, articulate level, stretching back in exceptional, sporadic instances to Phillis Wheatley in 1787, but becoming semi-literary with the anti-slavery controversy from 1835-1860, and literary in the full sense only since 1890.

Between these two levels there is a gap, transitional only in the historical sense, when the main line of Negro expression was motivated by conscious imitation of general American standards and forms, and reacted away from distinctive racial elements in an effort at cultural conformity. This was inevitable and under the circumstances normal; most other literatures and art have passed through such imitative phases; even French and German literature and art; and of course American art itself in the colonial period. But in Negro expression the position of cultural conformity and the suppression of racial emphasis has since been reversed,—first by the dialect school of Negro expression of which Paul Laurence Dunbar was the leading exponent, and more lately still by the younger contemporary school of "racial self-expression," the so-called "New Negro Movement" which since 1917 or thereabouts has produced the most outstanding formal contributions of the

Negro to American literature and art.

The importance of this latter movement is not to be underestimated; for, apart from its own creative impulse, it has effected a transformation of race spirit and group attitude, and acted like the creation of a national literature in the vernacular reacted upon the educated classes of other peoples who, also, at one or another stage of their cultural history, were not integrated with their own particular tradition and folk-background.

There is a division of critical opinion about this so-called "Negro renaissance." In one view, it was a cultural awakening and "coming of age" pivoted on a newly galvanized intelligentsia; according to the other, it was a mass movement of the urban migration of Negroes during the war period, projected on the plane of an increasingly articulate elite. Both interpretations have their share of truth. What is more important than the interpretation is the fact of a new group dynamic acquired at this time and a steadily increasing maturity coming into the Negro's formal self-expression in the arts. The breadth of the cultural stream increased with its depth; for the traditional arts of music, poetry, and oratory were rapidly supplemented by increased productivity in drama, fiction, criticism, painting, and sculpture.

Cultural racialism, with its stirring dynamic and at times its partisan fanaticism, was the keynote of the Negro renaissance. In its first phase, it was naïve, sentimental, and almost provincial; later, under the influence of the World War principles of self-determination and the rise of other cultural nationalisms (Irish, Czecho-Slovakian, etc.) it was to become sophisticated and grounded in a deliberate revival of folk traditions and a cult of African historical origins. Poems, stories, novels, plays emphasizing such themes and glorifying race pride, race solidarity, folk-origins came in a crescendo of creative effort with the rising talents of Claude McKay, Jean Toomer, Countee Cullen, Langston Hughes, Rudolph Fisher, Jessie Fauset, Eric Walrond, Wallace Thurman, Zora Hurston, and others. This was the first generation of "New Negro" writers. They had their artistic, musical, and dramatic counterparts in Harry Burleigh, Roland Hayes, Paul Robeson, Charles Gilpin, Rose McClendon, the painters Archibald Motley, Aaron Douglas, Laura Wheeler, Edward Harleston, Palmer Hayden, Hale Woodruff, the sculptors—Meta Fuller, May Jackson, Augusta Savage, Sargent Johnson, Richmond Barthe, —to mention just the outstanding names.

But we have little time or space for names; what concerns us more are trends of style and schools of artistic thought. It was this significant decade, —1920-1930, that witnessed the collaboration of white dramatists like Ridgeley Torrence, Eugene O'Neill, Paul Green, and DuBose Heyward, with Negro acting talent like Cooper, Gilpin and Robeson which gave Negro drama its present vital position in serious native American drama; that saw the parallel developments of the new realistic and regional fiction of the liberal "New South" and the development of the Negro novel of both the Harlem and the folk-lore school; that from the world-wide recognition of the serious Negro singers from Roland Hayes to Marion Anderson threaded through first the vocal folk-song arrangements of Negro composers like Burleigh, Diton, Dett, Brown, Boatner, Hall Johnson and then gained audience for the orchestral and chamber music compositions of Coleridge Taylor, William Dawson, Dett and Grant Still. Comparable strides took Negro popular music on an upswing of popularity and influence, carrying the occasionally successful "rag-time composer" to the assured dominance of Negro dance and music in the jazz period. Here, too, was a collaboration and interchange of talent and effort,—perhaps the closest of all the cultural collaborations to date, and one profoundly influential on public opinion as well as upon the professional circles immediately involved. Indeed the competitive use, and sometimes exploitation, of the jazz idioms by the Whitemans, Gershwins and Goodmans on the one side and Fletcher Hendersons, Duke Ellingtons, Count Basies (over the common denominator, often as not, of the Negro jazz "arranger", the true composer for the non-improvising type of jazz orchestra) have made a demonstration of cultural reciprocity and mutual reenforcement that may be prophetic of similar developments in other artistic fields.

But to return to our tracing of literary trends; between 1925 and the present three schools of Negro cultural expression have in succession appeared. But they have overlapped and each has even at the moment its exponents and adherents, though of course with successively diminishing vogue. The first started the Negro renaissance with an enthusiastic cult of idealistic racialism. It made a point of the stressing of special traits of "race temperament," of a group philosophy of life, of the re-expression on the cultural level of the folk-spirit and folk history, including the half-forgotten African background. Many of this school were devoted, if slightly, too romantic Africanists. Toomer's *Cane*, Countee Cullen's *Color*, Langston Hughes' *Weary Blues*, McKay's *Harlem Shadows* were produced in the heyday of this enthusiasm. Social protest and ironic challenge had already had some embodiment, especially with Claude McKay and Fenton Johnson, but romantic and jazz exoticism still were dominant notes. As Harlem became a fashionable fad a certain amount of irresponsible individualism and eccentric exhibitionism inevitably followed, and some of the brightest of these younger talents were warped and diverted from the sounder courses of serious work and development.

Meanwhile, even before the disillusion of the depression became effective, a more serious trend of folk realism was gaining ground. It followed the general trend of American realism in poetry and fiction, and began to develop on the basis of serious local color portraiture the native distinctiveness of Negro life, first in the urban and then in the Southland settings. Hughes' soberer second book of verse *Fine Clothes to the New,*[*] McKay's *Banjo* and *Gingertown*, Sterling Brown's realistic and ironic folk poetry in *Southern Road* are typical of this latter trend. This was a more soberly toned and prosaic racialism, delineating the grimmer side of the Harlem scene, painting the Southern peasant in careful genre studies, exposing the paradoxes and injustices of race prejudice. A few problem novels saw the light,—not too successful because of lack of objectivity and too obvious indignation and indictment, but in drama and poetry some of the best folk portraiture by Negro writers was being produced.

Though not completely diverted, a good deal of this maturing realism has been channeled off, partly by the vogue of proletarian realism and partly by the deepening disillusionment of the Negro's sad economic plight, into a rising school of iconoclast protest fiction, poetry, and drama. *Stevedore* and Erskine Caldwell's novels and stories set the pace for this latest school of Negro expression, which closely parallels the general vogue in style, theme, and social philosophy. However, in poetry like that of Frank Marshall Davis, the latest work of Sterling Brown and Langston Hughes, and particularly in the brilliant fiction of Richard Wright, the Negro literature of social protest has some distinctive qualities of local color and idiom, quizzical irony, dashing satire, and freedom from unrelieved drabness, all of which make it somewhat distinctive in comparison with the parallel white authors. But the common factors of social reformism and relentless indictment are also there, as characteristic no doubt of the youngest trend in our serious literature.

Enough has been said to show

---

*[sic] *Fine Clothes for the Jew* [Editor's note].

clearly that Negro art follows no peculiar path of its own, but is, with slight differences of emphasis or pace, in step with the general aesthetic and social trends of contemporary American art and literature. As aestheticism, realism, regionalism, proletarianism become the general vogue, Negro art is apt to reflect it. But always, as might be expected, these reflections are caught up in the texture of a racially-determined phase of agreement with a difference, sometimes a difference of emphasis, sometimes of motivation, often also a difference of emotional temper and stylistic idiom. It is this that saves a good deal of our art from being a feebly echoed repetition of general situations and attitudes. At times, however, this is not the case, and then in reversion to the subservient imitativeness which it has so largely outgrown, the minority literature and art becomes really minor.

As for the counter-influence, an increasing vogue for Negro themes and materials has certainly been a characteristic feature of the unfinished decade in which we now are, in fiction, drama, and the classical use of Negro musical idioms particularly. A whole generation of younger Southern novelists, Robert Rylee, Hamilton Basso, William March, James Childers, Josephine Johnson, Julian Meade have succeeded the pathbreaking realists, Clement Wood, Stribling, Sherwood Anderson, Faulkner and Caldwell, with telling documentation recanting the Bourbon tradition and the contrary to fact romance of *Gone with the Wind* and *So Red the Rose*. A realistically portrayed and fairly humanized Negro is one of the vital pivots of this new Southern fiction; just as a new economic and social reconstruction is one of its basic creeds. In drama the folk realism of Paul Green and of DuBose Heyward has continued to give moving portraiture of Negro life, though no such level of truth or moving beauty has been reached in drama as has already been attained in fiction on the Negro theme. Jazz music has reached a level of serious cultivation and analysis unprecedented for any previous form of popular music, and in classical jazz, the great talents of Negro composers like Ellington, Dett, Still, Hall Johnson, Reginald Forsythe have been seriously challenged by Grofé, Gershwin, Gruenberg, Cesana, Lamar, Stringfield, and Morton Gould. Indeed the vogue and use of Negro themes and materials by white creative artists has grown so steadily as quite to challenge the Negro creative artist's natural spokesmanship for his own cultural materials. But this challenge should be stimulating, and the net result in event of any fair competition will doubtless be an enforced maturity of the Negro artist in several fields where he is yet immature, partly from lack of full cultural opportunity, partly through too little objectivity toward his subject-matter. It is to be frankly admitted that in the more objective fields of fiction, playwriting, descriptive portraiture, the white artist working in Negro materials has on the whole an advantage of objective control and technical maturity, while in the more intimately subjective and emotional activities of poetry, acting, music, and dance, the Negro creators and interpreters have their turn of the advantage. Such generalizations have, of course, their exceptions on both sides, but in passing they are typical of the present moment and tentatively true.

Benefiting, even because of the depression, by the Federal Arts Projects and their reasonably democratic inclusion of the Negro artists of various sorts, the growth and geographic spread of Negro art has been materially enhanced. Particularly a whole younger generation of promising painters and sculptors has been incubated by the Federal Art Project, almost too numerous for individual mention. Three Negro dramas, the *Macbeth, Haiti,* and the *Swing Mikado,* have been among the ranking successes of the Federal Theatre, a tribute to non-commercial management and in the case of the *Macbeth* and *Mikado* as refreshing and revealing "Negro versions" of familiar classics, almost living texts for the corroboration of the central theme of this discussion;—the compound gain of the distinctive cultural hybrid. Proof also, these experimental ventures of the powerful appeal of Negro idioms in dignified and unstereotyped contexts,—a lesson Broadway and Hollywood have yet to learn. Hollywood particularly, in spite of a new medium, is still snared in a reactionary groove and prostitutes genuine Negro talent to the perpetuation among the masses of reactionary social and racial stereotypes of character and situation. If the persuasiveness of the new art or the pressure of its new social creeds ever leaps the barricades and fences of the "movies" and the popular novel and the popular entertainment stage, as there is faint reason to hope, a revolutionizing force for liberalizing culture will have been set in irresistible motion. Up to this point we have been dealing mainly with the artistic cultural significance of Negro art, but here we sight what is probably the next objective and the next crusade in the ascending path of Negro art, its use as an instrument for social enlightenment and constructive social reform. This, too, is no racially exclusive job and has no racially partisan objective. It is perhaps, since it is the ultimate goal of cultural democracy, the capstone of the historic process of American acculturation. To be a crucial factor in so vital a general matter will be a cultural contribution of supreme importance.

THE NEGRO IN THE THREE AMERICAS

It seems fitting that our final consideration of the Negro in American
life should be set in the broadest possible perspective, and so I propose as
our final subject, *The Negro in the
Three Americas*. Even should we discover no further common denominators—though I think we shall—there
will be at least two of great contemporary concern and importance,—Pan-
Americanism and democracy, with
both of which the general situation of
the American Negro has, as we shall
try to show, some vital and constructive connection. Our opening lecture,

* This paper is the original English text
of the concluding lecture—"The Negro in
the Three Americas," from a series of six
public lectures on *The Rôle of the Negro
in the American Culture* delivered in Haiti
last Spring by Dr. Alain Locke, Professor
of Philosophy at Howard University, on
leave as Exchange Professor to Haiti under
the joint auspices of the American Committee for Inter-American Artistic and
Intellectual Relations and the Haitian Ministry of Education. The lectures were delivered in Port au Prince during May in
the Aula of the School of Law under the
sponsorship of the Council of The University of Haiti, the inaugural lecture under
the patronage of President Elie Lescot, and
were repeated in part at Cap Haitien at
the Lycee Phillipe Guerrier and the Salle
Municipale. They have recently been published, as delivered, in a French edition of
2,000 copies by l'Imprimerie de l'Etat, Port
au Prince, 1943 (pp. 141) under the title: *Le
Rôle du Nègre dans la Culture des Améri-
ques*. At the conclusion of his stay in
Haiti, Professor Locke was decorated by
President Lescot with the National Order of
Honor and Merit, grade of Commandeur.

indeed, suggested that the furtherance
of democracy in this Western hemisphere was bound up crucially with
basic social and cultural policies upon
which Negro life and its problems had
direct bearing. It is incumbent upon
us to justify such statements.

But before coming to the discussion
either of theory or policies, let us first
consider facts. In the United States
of North America, we are well aware,
sometimes painfully so, that the very
presence of a Negro population of
nearly ten per cent of the total population constitutes a race problem of
considerable proportions. I am aware,
of course, that under an Anglo-Saxon
regime of race relations ten per cent
may constitute, indeed does constitute, more of an active problem than
a considerably larger population ratio
would generate under the more tolerant Latin code of race which culturally predominates in Central and South
America. However, what may show
up very clearly on the surface of our
North American society as a race
problem may to a degree also be present under the surface of large areas of
Latin-American society as a class
problem, as we shall later see. At any
rate, as to the facts, a larger proportion of the Caribbean and South
American populations is of Negro racial stock than even our North Ameri-

Journal of Negro Education 13 (Winter 1944): 7–18.

can ten per cent. On a mass statistical average, by conservative estimates, the Negro population ratio of the Western hemisphere, the U.S.A. included, is 14 per cent, and the closer we come to the mid-zone of the hemisphere the higher that proportion becomes. For the Caribbean or West Indian islands, it is 46 per cent, for Brazil it is estimated at the lowest as 28 per cent, by some as high as 36 per cent. Columbia is more than one-sixth Negro, Ecuador fourteen and Venezuela more than eight per cent. The Central American republics, except Costa Rica, have their considerable Negro admixtures, Panama especially. Indeed of all the American nations, only Chile, the Argentine and Canada can be said to have a negligible concern in this particular issue of race relations. Indeed when we superimpose the figures of the Indian population—so considerable an element in all Central and South American countries—and then the large East Indian or Hindu populations of Trinidad and British Guiana, we begin to realize and appreciate more the polyracial character of our Continent and the fact that this phase of human group relations is more crucial and critical in our inter-Continental life and its progressive development than in even our respective national societies.

Fortunately, although different specific measures may be required, the same basic attitudes and principles of fully democratic living will resolve any of these problems, one as well as the other. They have different numerators and degrees in color differentials, but they have a common denominator of arbitrarily limited and unfulfilled cultural and economic democracy. Certainly for such a population situation, whether it be upon the basis of caste or of class, a hegemony of white or even the fairer elements of the population cannot be made to spell real or effective democracy. Nor can the group attitudes involved be forged into any really unified and durable hemispheric solidarity. It is in this way, to anticipate our analysis somewhat, that these matters condition Pan-Americanism almost as critically as they limit expanding democracy.

It is the common historic denominator of slavery which despite all other differences of national culture and social structure has determined both the similarity of condition and the basic identity of the problems which still so seriously affect the Negro population groups of the American hemisphere. For they are all the cultural consequences and economic aftermath of slavery, and like slavery itself they must eventually be completely liquidated just as that institution was itself abolished. Slavery in America was, of course, eliminated at different times and in quite different ways: here in Haiti, that came about by means of a slave rebellion; with us in the United States, it was Civil War; in still other American nations the process was legal emancipation, in some cases gradual, in others, immediate. But the lives of most persons of Negro blood and descent in America directly or indirectly, in one fashion or another or one degree or another are still seriously affected by the cultural, social and economic consequences of slavery. By an approximate estimate this involves at least 35 millions of human beings among the total American population of 266 millions, among these the 13 million Negroes of the United States, the 12 or more million Negroes in Brazil and the 8 or more million Negroes of the Caribbean.

To be sure, a considerable and an encouraging number of these Negroes have already attained the average level of cultural status, and a certain few have raised themselves considerably above the average levels of their respective cultures. But it should be clearly recognized that so long as the masses of these Negro groups comprise, even in part as a consequence of slavery so heavy a percentage of those who are illiterate, undernourished, ill-housed, underprivileged and in one way or another subject to social discrimination, just so long will it be necessary to give serious consideration both to the special causes and the specific remedies of such conditions, and to take stock, as well, of the undemocratic social attitudes and the antidemocratic social policies which invariably accompany these conditions.

Having now before us the fundamental historical reasons why so large a proportion of American Negroes enjoy less than their proper share of democracy, whether we take stock of the situation in Baltimore or Bahia, in São Paulo or in San Antonio, let us consider some basic common reasons why they must eventually share more fully and equitably in democracy's benefits than they do at present. The reasons which we have in mind to consider are not the uncontested and incontestable arguments of moral principle and abstract justice—important as these may be—but certain very particular and realistic reasons which it seems wise and opportune to stress at this critical hour of human history and social development. Doing so concretely, and on a hemispheric rather than a narrow nationalistic basis may reenforce their timeliness and urgency. One nation cannot directly solve the other's problems, but certain important international dimensions have lately come into the general area of these problems which should prove mutually reenforcing and helpful. It is profitable also to see the Negro position and its claims in the same perspective.

In the first place, in everyone of the countries where he constitutes a considerable proportion of the population, the Negro represents a conspicuous index by which the practical efficiency and integrity of that particular country's democracy can readily be gauged and judged. For the same high visibility which internally makes possible ready discrimination against Negroes makes the domestic practices of race externally all the more conspicuous and observable in the enlarging spot-

light of international relations. However fundamental the domestic issues of race may be, today and for the future we must all be particularly concerned about their international consequences. This holds in general on a world scale. Here the American treatment of the Negro can have and already has had serious repercussions on enlightened Asiatic and African public opinion and confidence. Or, for that matter, so will our treatment of any racial minority such as the treatment of the American segments of the Hindu or the Chinese resident among us. But this situation holds with intensified force as between the Americas and with particular reference to the widely distributed American groups of Negro and mixed Negro descent. For historical and inescapable reasons, the Negro has thus become a basic part and a conspicuous symbol of the cause of democracy in our Western hemisphere.

For the United States, especially interested in and committed to a program of broader and closer Caribbean cooperation as well as to a thoroughgoing furtherance of Pan-American solidarity, the foreign frontier of race, so to speak, has become more critical even than the domestic. Fortunately this is being seen and realized with increasing force and frequency by enlightened liberal opinion in the United States. Far-sighted statesmen and progressive race leaders alike realize that sounder and more consistently democratic practices of race at home are necessary for the successful prosecution of these important foreign programs and essential as well to complete conviction and moral confidence in our democratic professions and intentions. The *"Good Neighbor"* policy has worked a miracle of political and economic rapprochement between the Americas, but democratic race equality and fraternity, as its morally inescapable corollaries are practically necessary reenforcements of the *"Good Neighbor"* policy and principle.

This situation, as an acute observer has recently stated, is not altogether unilateral. Latin America has its part to play in the developing American democracy of race. This observer, my colleague, Dr. E. Franklin Frazier, has this penetrating view of the situation to offer on return from a year's study and observation of the Caribbean and Latin America. Although he finds that the race barrier to American solidarity stands to the credit side of the more favorable and democratic character of the typical Latin attitudes toward race, he also observes that Latin America has her important part to play in the achievement of racial democracy. "Differences between North and Latin America," he says, "in their attitudes toward race constitute one of the real barriers to American solidarity. This is a question that has not been faced frankly in most discussions of Pan-Americanism. "But," continues Dr. Frazier, "one might add that on the part of Latin Americans as well as of North Americans there has been a tendency to evade the issue, though their conflicting attitudes toward racial mixture are the basis of a real distrust and lack of mutual respect. In their dealings with North Americans, our Latin neighbors have often been careful not to offend our feelings with regard to color caste. This has been facilitated by the fact that the ruling classes, with some few exceptions, have been of predominantly light complexion. But (and I stress this but), as the masses of these countries begin to rise and as there is greater intercourse between the Latin-American countries and North America, such evasions in the long run will be impossible."

Professor Frazier has put his finger on the crux of the issue, but in a practical and constructive as well as acutely diagnostic way. For if at times class differentiation and its prejudices have contrived to aid and abet outright color caste prejudice, there is the obvious necessity of reenforcing democracy from both sides of this as yet admittedly unsolved social and cultural situation. The situation on either side needs and ultimately must undergo considerable democratizing. Almost all America, one way or the other and to one degree or another, suffers yet from the unhappy consequences of slavery, which in one situation has left us an undemocratic problem of class and in another, an even less democratic situation of color caste. We shall discuss this situation again a little further on, but it is worthwhile in passing to note the disastrous negation of democracy possible if, by way of the shortcomings of democracy either in the South or the North, fascism and its attendant racism should gain firm rootage in American soil. For then, as has been said already, racial and minority disabilities will have become a majority predicament and a general democratic catastrophe.

We must now hurry on, since ours in the constructive motive and interest, to sketch what favorable cultural trends are today coming to the aid of the cause of race democracy. But since slavery is the common root of our present difficulties, North as well as South, and in the Caribbean most especially, let us take one final backward glimpse at slavery itself in its most fundamental relationship to the whole American social scene. In the first place, it is salutary to recall that it was only historical accident that a white indentured servant class did not bear the brunt of the labor load of the European settlement of this continent, and thus become the victims, if not of slavery, certainly of its close equivalent. One need only remember the indentured servants, the convict debtors of the early United States colonies or the Jamaican Irish similarly imported as a laboring caste. However, through slavery and the slave trade, this hard fortune but constructive contribution fell to the lot of the Negro. In so doing slavery did two peculiar and significant things which have determined the course of American history and influenced the character of American civilization: *first*, American Slavery, since it was of the domestic variety, planted the Negro in the very core of the dominant white civilization, permitting not only its rapid assimilation by the Negro but its being, in turn, deeply and continuously counter-influenced culturally by the Negro; and *second*, it also planted the Negro—and that holds true for today as well as for the past, at the moral and political core of a basically democratic society, so that around him and his condition wherever there are undemocratic inconsistencies, must center the whole society's struggle for the full and continuous development of freedom.

As we shall more and more realize, the extension of American democracy must involve the reversal and eradication of these historical consequences of slavery, and it is more than appropriate, indeed it is morally inevitable that an historical American ill should have, in the long run, a typical and successful American cure. This is what I was thinking forward to when I said in the third lecture of this series that the majority stakes in the solution of the American race problem were nearly as great as the Negro minority's, and in the first lecture hinted that it would appear that the cause of the American Negro still had a constructive contribution to make to our current crusade for democracy.

We now come to some concluding considerations of ways and means. Especially important, it seems, are cultural developments, since they throw bridges of understanding and sympathy over the crevasses of the slow filling in of social reform and the still slower upbuilding of economic progress. They are essential, too, to the right and ready understanding of whatever group progress is being made along any other line. For some time now, undoubtedly, we have been aware of great Negro progress in our respective national areas, and have been taking national stock and pride in it.

Now however, it seems high time to become more aware of it, as of other aspects of our American life, in an inter-American perspective.

All along it has been the tragedy of Negro talent and accomplishment to be considered and discounted in its full meaning as a matter of exception. It is only when added up and dramatically collated that its proper significance is arrived at and its legitimate social effect brought to full realization. The cultural achievements and contributions of American Negroes, startling enough within their national boundaries, are from the approach of the whole hemisphere more than trebly inspiring and reassuring. In 1818 a French libertarian, Abbé Gregoire, inspired incidentally in great part by the galaxy of Haitian heroes of your Wars for Independence, wrote a small book on *De la litterature des Noirs*, which proved one of the most influential documents of the anti-slavery campaign. For to the conviction of the Negro's moral right to freedom, it added in intellectual circles, the demonstration that he had the capacity to fully use freedom's advantages. For so, in their brief day and as exceptions, these cases had previously been dismissed after the customary nine days' wonderment. But Gregoire added up a convincing total when he placed beside Toussaint L'Ouverture and Phyllis Wheatley and Benjamin Banneker, the Maryland inventor, mathematician and almanac maker of Jefferson's day, the lesser known figures of Juan Latino, the 16th century Spanish African poet, Pareja and Gomez, the Negro painter-apprentices of Velasquez and Murillo, Capitein, the Dutch African theologian, Gustavus Vassa, the English African essayist. Together they were convincing justification of the Negro's possibilities and rights.

Though needing, let us hope, no such extreme conversion today, the intelligent and forward thinking public of the Americas needs reenforcing evidence of the present cultural attainments and growing cultural influence of the American Negro. It must come, too, with that overwhelming effect that can only derive from corroborative evidence from every quarter and from every one of the American nations having any considerable Negro contingent. Certainly such evidence is rapidly coming in, and it seems to reflect only our naturally limited information if such cultural progress seems to be more developed in North or South or Mid-America. Someday, and as soon as possible, it is to be hoped the general record will be compiled in its hemispheric rather than just a narrow nationalistic scope. Someday, too, and as soon after the conclusion of the war as possible, it is also to be hoped that inter-American exhibits and visits will make wider known and reciprocally appreciated the contemporary personalities and contributions of this cultural advance of the various contingents of American Negro life.

Here only in barest outline can we begin to indicate them. But even that should prove enlightening and stimulating. Again, but this time on an inter-American scale, let us glance briefly at the Negro in music, art, folklore, literature and social leadership. Surprise is in store for any persistent student of the subject: I vividly recall my own, even after some years of reading, when I received unexpectedly the two volume study of Ildefonso Pereda Valdez of Uraguay on the influence of the Negro in the Plata Valley region, and again when Captain Romero turned up in Washington under the auspices of the Division of Cultural Relations of our State Department as an interested authority on the Negro in Peru.

To commence we may quote from a passage of Manuel Gonzalez, a statement that could easily be generalized to include also much of the Caribbean: "In Brazil, Cuba, Venezuela and other tropical localities, the Negro is the preponderant non-European race. The Negro is here, it is true, being slowly absorbed, but his deep inroads in the culture of these countries are today tantamount to a national characteristic and will persist for many generations to come."

In music, paralleling the North American developments with which we are now already familiar, there are, of course, those rich Negro contributions of Brazil, Cuba, Trinidad and the French Antilles. Blending with Spanish, French and Portuguese elements, they have produced an extraordinary crop both of folk and sophisticated American music. First, we encounter pure or almost pure African folk forms, manifested in rhythmic forms accompanied by percussion instruments or drums only. Then came what Gonzalez calls "the mulatto expression" —the hybrid "Creole" forms which are mostly of popular appeal and significance, diverting and useful as he says in the widespread service of dance and popular music. In this field today the outstanding creator is the Cuban, Ernesto Lecuona, a close analogue of our North American Gershwin. Finally we have what for the future is perhaps most important, the symphonic developments based on Negro motives and rhythms, but harmonized and orchestrated with all the skill of the modern European tradition. Here, it is hard to say whether Brazil or Cuba is outstanding, for in the one we have the important work of Villa Lobos, Fernandez, and Reveltas while in Cuba we have Amadeo Roldan, Caturia, Pedro Sanjuan and perhaps greatest of all, Gilberto Valdes. The Brazilian group combines Indian and Negro sources, but the Cuban work reflects, of course, predominantly Negro idioms. Indeed some think that serious Afro-Cuban music is one of the most promising strands of our whole contemporary American musical development, and it certainly would have already been so but for the untimely deaths of Roldan and Caturla.

Most of these composers cannot, of course, be claimed as Negroes, though several have mixed ancestral strains. That is not, indeed, the emphasis of our discussion: we are speaking primarily of the power and influence of the Negro materials. However, the situation does from time to time also yield a great Negro musician, like Gomez, or the Jamaican Reginald Forsythe, or one of the present musical lights of London, the Guiana Negro composer-conductor, Rudolph Dunbar. Add to this considerable accomplishment that of the North American Negro, and one has some idea of this incontestable domination for several generations both of American popular and serious music by Negro musical elements.

The situation in the field of art is also most interesting and promiseful. In the States we have undoubtedly among sculptors of front rank, Richmond Barthé, and of second magnitude Henry Bannarn and William Artis. The Cuban Negro, Theodoro Ramos-Blanco, is by general agreement one of Cuba's leading contemporary sculptors as is also his mulatto colleague, Florencio Gelabert. Professor of sculpture at the Havana School of Fine Arts, Ramos-Blanco is known both for his strong delineations of peasant and Negro themes and for his happy memorializations of Cuban heroes, among them his famous statue to the great patriot Maceo. Before an untimely death, Alberto Peña shared acclaim with Ramon Loy—companion figures in the sphere of Cuban painting. Indeed we may expect much of the development of the Negro subject and theme in Latin American art, whether it realizes itself in terms of the Negro artist or not. For already in Mexico, Rivera and Orosco have considerably emphasized the theme as has also Portinari, perhaps Brazil's leading painter. Gone completely, under the wide influence of these artists, is the over-Europeanization of sculpture and painting in progressive art circles

in Latin America, and that automatically means the glorification of the indigenous types and instead of cosmopolitan emphasis, the people's norms of beauty. In countries where the classical tradition still hangs on, and where the native artists are convention-bound and timid, as once indeed were the North American Negro artists, that subject matter hold-back may be expected slowly to disappear. With it always comes a freeing of technique and stronger and maturer accents of self-expression. Under the double leadership of North American and Mexican art that cultural revolution has already begun, and an art truly expressive of the polyracial elements in Latin-America, the Negro among them, may shortly be expected to show the effects of such influence.

It is in the field of letters that the Negro contribution has most generally expressed its unusual force in the Antilles and Latin America. Haiti, with its high and almost continuous tradition of authorship in *belles lettres*, with its successive schools of poets, usually far above provincial calibre and reputation, hardly needs to be told about this. Yet few of us, if any, realize the range and extent of the Negro's literary influence throughout the hemisphere, if for no other reason than the limited view imposed by four different major languages. But the record is formidable when we add up the Haitian, Cuban, Brazilian and North American contributions. Pereira Valdes *Anthology of Negro American Poetry* adds even an Argentinian Eusebio Cardozo and a Casildo Thompson and the Uruguayan Polar Barrios and Carlos Ferreira. Most general readers do know of Brazil's leading contemporary novelist, Mario de Andradé, and can also name such first magnitude Brazilian writers as the poet and abolitionist, Luis Gama, Manuel Alvarenga, Tobias Barreto, one of Brazil's greatest poets, Cruz e Sousa and Machado de Assis, founder of realism in Brazilian literature. We need only in passing mention the brilliant North American contingent of Paul Laurence Dunbar, James Weldon Johnson, Countee Cullen, Langston Hughes, Dr. DuBois and Richard Wright, to mention only the first-line representatives. And when we come to Cuban literature, only a book like Guirao's *Anthology of Afro-Cuban Poesie* will reveal the wide extent of the racial influence on both popular and academic poetry. But in addition, one has to take into account in the history of Cuban letters, Gabriel Valdes, better known as "Placido," Manzano, and especially the contemporary literary genius of Nicholas Guillen. With Marcelino Arozarena and Regino Pedroso, he almost dominates the present output of Cuban verse of distinction; surely, if we consider that the movement of folklorist expression is the product of the initiative and labor of these three Metizos. And then comes *Canapé Vert*[1] to swell the ranks of this growing current trend of literary interest and emphasis.

Nor has this creative literary expression lacked for critical support and backing. For years now in Brazil, Arthur Ramos and Gilberto Freyre have been issuing their scholarly studies of the Negro historical and cultural backgrounds, and similarly since 1906 in Cuba that tireless champion of Negro culture in Cuba's history and folklore—Fernando Ortiz, founder of the Society of Afro-Cuban Studies. For many of these years, too, Dr. Ortiz has been promoting an even more important project—the closer relation of Afro-Brazilian and the Afro-Cuban studies. In this way, then, the new American criticism is actively promoting the appreciation of the indigenous aspects of our American culture, Indian as well as Negro, and laying the foundation for a much more democratic cultural outlook.

Best of all, Cuba and Mexico have both marshaled the reforms of their

[1] The Pan-American prize novel by the Freres Thoby-Marcelin for 1943.

educational systems behind this movement, to the extent that in addition to a policy of wider public education, they admit the right of the people's culture to a recognized place in the program of studies. From such trends the various folk cultures must inevitably find greater representation in literature and the arts. So, if the folk yields have been as considerable as they have already been in spite of the discouragement of official philosophies of culture unfavorable to them, now that these policies have been reversed in their favor, they are doubly assured of enhanced influence and prestige.

Another factor needs, finally, to be noted. The cultural traffic that in the past has run so steadily from all our respective capitals back and forth to Europe now has swung around to a continental axis North and South. In these cultural interchanges, the native folk products and their representatives must be expected to play an increasingly important part. They are both more interesting, distinctive, and novel and, from the democratic viewpoint, more representative of the majority of the people. By the traditional exchanges in terms of the stereotyped European models, we got only to know our outstanding artists as individual talents; now if they come bringing the folk culture, we shall, in addition, really for the first time be able to foster sound international and interracial understanding. And I cannot emphasize too strongly that these interchanges must be interracial as well as international, if they are to bring about the calculated democratic result. Elsie Houston and Olga Coehlo, for example, have really brought Brazil to New York in bringing their marvelous renditions of the Afro-Brazilian folk-songs: almost for the first time, do we feel that we have sampled the distinctive flavor of the national culture. Marian Anderson at this moment is making her first Mexican tour, another happy augury. And certainly one of the greatest needs in the situation is the one we have been prosecuting together so pleasantly and helpfully, for Haitian-American rapprochement is both an interracial as well as international undertaking, happily so—not only for the two nations concerned, but for enlarging the democracy of the American mind throughout the entire American continent.

We might, indeed, close on this point of the radiant prospects for inter-American cultural democracy, but for a final, and let us say at the outset, more problematic point. Here, we must ask ourselves, finally, that other important question—what are the prospects for larger social democracy? Surely no one will claim that democracy can be complete or fully satisfactory without it!

Here the realism of the situation forces us to admit that unlike our cultural differences, which may even attract, our differences of social culture really do, in most instances, seriously divide. We know full well that there are great differences between the Anglo-Saxon and the Latin codes of race and the social institutions and customs founded on each. Not only do we have this as a matter of divergence between the Northern and the Southern segments of the hemisphere, but in the West Indies, we have these divergent traditions facing each other across the narrow strips of the Caribbean. But let us face the facts. Is there any way of looking at these differences constructively? Can we in any way relate them for the constructive reenforcement of democracy in America? At least, let us try.

The Latin tradition of race has, certainly, a happy freedom from a priori prejudice, looking at the individual first, and conceding him as an individual a reasonably fair chance. Triple heritage of the French Revolution, of Catholic universalism, and of Latin social tolerance, this is surely a basic democratic trait. The early and outstanding accomplishments of individual Negroes and their ready acceptance according to merit in Latin-American societies could never have taken place except on this foundation.

On the other hand, it is equally evident that the Anglo-Saxon code of race does base itself on a priori prejudice, and really, as the term itself indicates, pre-judges the individual on the arbitrary basis of the mass status of his group. It makes its exceptions grudgingly and as exceptions, and often cruelly forces the advancing segments of the group back to the level and limitations of the less advanced. Certainly no one would say it was justifiable either in principle or practise, no one that is, who believes basically in democracy. Nor can one say that it is democratic in intention: far from it.

However—and here I ask your patience for a moment—not as an apologist, God forbid, but as a philosopher, this hard code has had some unintended democratic consequences. In forcing the advance-guard of a people back upon the people, it has out of the discipline of solidarity forged mass organization for group progress. The successful individual in the majority of cases, still linked to the common lot, is not an élite released and removed from the condition of the rest of his people, but becomes as he advances an advance-guard threading through an increasingly coherent mass following. I am not condoning the circumstances which have brought this fact about; I repeat, I am merely describing objectively what has historically transpired.

Now let us put these separate pictures stereoptically together, to see if we can get a more three-dimensional view both of the situation and its prospects. The Latin-American code of race does more justice and offers less harm to the individual, but at the historical price of an unhappy divorce of the élite from the masses. The Anglo-Saxon practise of race seriously handicaps the individual and his chances for immediate progress, but forges, despite intentions to the contrary, a binding bond of group solidarity, an inevitable responsibility of the *élite* for the masses, a necessary though painful condition for mass progress. From the practical point of view, the more liberal tradition concedes but divides, while the other refuses to concede piecemeal, but by unifying, cannot possibly in the long run divide and conquer. This seems paradoxical, and is. But for one further moment, let us look at the history of the matter.

Both of these social policies of race, the Latin as well as the Anglo-Saxon, were laid down by slave-owning societies before the abolition of slavery. One saw in the more favorable condition and freedom of the mulatto a menacing advance that must be arbitrarily blocked by a solid wall of prejudice. The other for the most part, saw in the differential treatment of the *mestizo* the strategy of a buffer class, granting it considerably more than was allowed the blacks but always somewhat less than was standard for the privileged whites. Neither was democratic in intention or in the long run in basic historical effect. One produced an out-and-out race problem, the other, a tangential conversion of a large part of it into a class problem. Each respective group experience has something to teach, and the first common lesson is that you cannot expect to get democracy out of slavery or the institutional inheritances of slavery. We shall get along further and faster by the realization that democracy, as it must fully develop in America, cannot be developed either within the arbitrary and undemocratic traditions of color caste or fully within the less arbitrary but still undemocratic system of a racial *élite* split off, largely on the basis of a color class, from the race proletariat. Neither of these social race patterns of society is blameless, and to be fully democratic each needs radical improvement.

Obvious common sense teaches us that we shall only achieve fuller democracy in practise by democratizing further whichever system we have by historical accident inherited. However,

in these days of international intercourse and collaboration, there are just as obviously mutual lessons which can be constructively learned and applied. One system, the Latin, has vindicated a basic essential of social democracy —the open career for talent and unhampered mobility and recognition for rising individual achievement. The other, the Anglo-Saxon, has taught an increasingly important essential of a democratic social order—the responsibility of the *élite* for the masses. The basic necessity of the latter, even within the Latin-American framework has been distinctly corroborated by the organization in 1931 in Brazil—a country where there is almost no race problem as far as the individual is concerned, of a *National Union of Men of Color* for the improvement of the well-being of the Negro mass population. It is this organization, which sponsored the notable Second Afro-Brazilian Congress in 1937, and which, incidentally, in 1941-42 played an important political rôle in Brazil's anti-Axis alignment against Nazi racism and fascism.

Instead of heightened partisanship over our differences of race codes and practises, it is quite within the range of possibility that, looking at matters more broadly and objectively, we shall move forward in our democratic efforts with a sense of collaboration and a common ultimate objective. For the more democracy becomes actually realized, the closer must our several societies approach a common norm.

Slavery is one of the oldest human institutions, nearly as old as man and nearly as universal. But the longest, the most extensive and the most cruel chapter in the history of human slavery is that dark African chapter of the trans-Atlantic slave trade precipitated by the colonial settlement of the Americas. We must never forget how substantially it helped to make the colonial conquest of the New World possible, thus laying the foundation of that American civilization which we all enjoy today. The slave trade involved the Three Americas. It has affected permanently both the population and the culture of the Americas; especially Mid-America. It has influenced the life of the Americas both for good and evil, and almost everywhere in America, to one degree or another, the shadow of slavery's yet incomplete undoing still clouds the possibilities of a fully democratic American society. Not only for the sake of the Negro, but for the sake of that democracy, these consequences must be overcome. It is fitting and necessary that the inequities and human disabilities which came into our Western world by way of the exigencies of its colonial settlement should be liquidated through our collaborative efforts today to count as a representative American contribution to human freedom and democracy. That the Negro's situation in this hemisphere has this constructive contribution to make to the enlargement of the practise of democracy has been the main conviction and contention of these discussions. All segments of the Negro experience, that of the Latin as well as that of Anglo-Saxon society, must be focussed clearly and convincingly if America is to learn effectively the lessons which the Negro's history, achievements and social experience have it in their power to teach. And if the two wings of that experience teach that the open career for talent and the responsibility of the *élite* for the masses are both necessary for the full solution of the aftermaths of slavery, then the wisdom and uplifting force of both these principles must be effectively joined to enable democracy to rise and soar.

Only so can our whole American society, completely unshackled, fulfill our American institutions of freedom and equality. This, as I see it, is the constructive significance of the Negro to present-day America.

Again I thank all those who have so aided and added to the success of this series of lectures, but especially I thank those of you whose collaboration as a patient and responsive audience has given me such needed and welcome help and inspiration. It has been a great pleasure to have been among you and a great privilege to have been able to bring this message. All happiness, progress and prosperity to Haiti. Au revoir!

THE NEGRO IN THE ARTS

Shortly after the close of the Civil War, a Northerner observing with sympathetic curiosity the group life of the Negro freedmen in their refugee camps, made the momentous discovery that the American Negro had musical genius. He was William Allen, and in 1867 he published, as *Slave Songs of the United States*, a transcribed collection of the folk melodies he had heard. The Old South had been hearing this plaintive and rhapsodic folk singing for many generations before Allen, but because they listened only with cavalier condescension and amused bewilderment, it could all be dismissed as just their "darkie way of carrying on." Out of such superficial belittlement these "slave songs" rose to final recognition and universal acclaim as the "Negro Spirituals," now recognized as being not only the unique portrait of the Negro folk temperament and spirit, but also as being among the few native folk products of American culture.

Even in the Allen transcriptions these songs were inadvertently misconstrued, for he was unable to give proper notation to the unique folk way of singing them. Only in 1879 was this restored to them by the choral renditions of the Fisk Jubilee Singers, a Negro university group which was campaigning for funds by giving benefit concerts in the North and Midwest. They themselves were so much under the hypnotism of white disparagement of things wholly and primitively Negro, that they hesitated to put them on their regular programs and gave them as experimental encores on request. It was not until after the revelation of their profound effect upon enlightened American audiences, and European audiences, too, in an international tour resulting from their great singing success, that the spirituals were finally launched upon their triumphant career of the vindication of the folk genius they reflected.

Here in epitome is the story of Negro art and the Negro as artist. Decades before the debut of the spirituals, nationwide popularity had come to what were known as "minstrel songs"—diluted popularizations, often vulgarizations, of Negro secular folk song and dance. Not that in their genuine folk contexts this music was any the less representative, as was discovered a generation later when such undiluted folk seculars as the "blues" and the genuine folk balladry came through; but simply because in the minstrel role and idiom the Negro was a caricature of himself, whereas in the spirituals he was wholly himself and completely free in the intimate ecstasy of his group religious worship.

In the arts, then, as in matters political, economic, and social, the Negro road has been a slow and tortuous journey up from slavery to gradual freedom. Step by step, and from one art province to another, Negro genius and talent have worked a hard way to freer and more representative artistic self-expression. In many fields recognition has now been achieved; in some cases that of incontestable parity with the white artist, in others, with the acknowledged superiority of unexcelled uniqueness. I have been asked to give a panoramic sketch of these developments in music, dance, theatre, and the pictorial arts. The development has roughly followed this sequence, with overlappings, of course. The explanation is twofold. The conquest of the more sophisticated arts has naturally been slower: limited opportunity and cultural contact amply account for that. But a second and important reason also has been that,

United Asia: International Magazine of Asian Affairs 5 (June 1953): 177–181.

as might be expected, faster headway has been made where there existed a previous start in a well-developed folk art. It is interesting to note, for instance, that the Negro made a mark in vocal and choral music before he was successful in instrumental music and formal composition; and again, to notice how more powerfully expressive he has been in sculpture, an ancestral art, than in painting.

The spirituals are in musical form and folk poetry the acme of Negro folk expression. Although expressing an adopted religion, and remolded from the Protestant evangelical worship with which the Negro slaves were brought in contact, they were so transformed by the slaves' own inner experiences of suffering, and so transfused by the Negro yearning for freedom and salvation, that they are racial to the core. Other forms of the Negro's music, however, flowed beyond racial bounds to become in various hybrid varieties the basic popular music of America, ragtime and jazz particularly. But this, too, took a long period of some six or seven decades before the true and characteristic Negro idioms and moods became dominant through the gradual ascendancy of the Negro musician. When secular Negro music started to attract popular attention in the 1820s, it began as a thin shadow of itself concocted for comic, slapstick entertainment. The earlier minstrels were whites who blacked their faces with burnt cork and gave a variegated song, dance, and monologue entertainment that became popular as the "minstrel show." This stereotyped caricature of Negro life and character had such vogue that when Negro minstrels began to function in it they were forced to work within the set formula, even to the extent of the use of burnt cork makeup. Slowly the richer vitality and spontaneity of the Negro troupes gained advantage over their white competitors, and in the 1870s and 1880s began to dominate the field.

By an odd coincidence during this latter period, more genuine Negro secular music was rapidly becoming the vogue, but initially as entertainment music in low-life resorts from New Orleans up through the Mississippi Valley to Chicago. This was early ragtime and later jazz, performed by Negro pianists and singers principally. When this fresh stream of syncopation and improvised abandon struck the metropolitan centers, especially when in the late 1890s it crashed the New York stage, the heyday of the Negro singer, dancer, and entertainer had about arrived. From there on, with the dubious but profitable influence of commercial music vending one wave after another, Negro influence swept the field. It is no exaggeration to say that almost unremittingly since 1916–20, Negro idioms have dominated the popular music of America, and spread throughout the world as characteristic "American" music. It is not correct, however, to regard ragtime and jazz as one hundred percent Negro. The prototypal forms undoubtedly were, but they now represent the joint collaboration of white and Negro composers and performers in these idioms. Indeed, so many white musicians were among the earliest devotees that the jazz cult may be credited with a pioneer breaking down of the color-line in the entertainment and musical world.

By this time, the serious Negro musician and composer had also come to maturity and recognition, by a harder struggle but nevertheless with great ultimate success. The whole musical world knows the careers of such first-rank singers as Roland Hayes, Marian Anderson, Paul Robeson, Dorothy Maynor, and others; and with good warrant because, ironically, European audiences were destined to give them their first stellar acclaim. Even in the 1920s, prejudice was so much of a handicap to a top musical career for Negro artists. It can be reported now, three decades after Roland Hayes' pathbreaking success, that American Negro singers, musicians, and composers can claim almost immediate recognition proportional to their individual merit. Gradually, too, the discrepancy in instrumental music and composition is filling in, and such serious composers as Nathaniel Dett, Harry Burleigh, William Grant Still, William Dawson, and Ulysses Kay are winning fame in the symphonic, ballet, and concert music fields. Burleigh first broke the path for the "arranged" solo spiritual as a concert type of art song—a genre that has since added distinction to the program of all the major Negro singers, and has now become almost a national American vogue.

Much more could be said, but we must turn to a brief survey of the Negro dance. Many link the undisputed Negro virtuosity in this art to the influence of the African heritage. Be that as it may, even in plantation days, Negroes were noted for their community dancing. But here again, it was the jigging minstrel who first acquainted the general public with the originalities of the Negro dance forms; but, as might be inferred, in comic caricature. Slowly here, as in the other areas, the more genuine asserted itself, beginning with the artistic transformation of the "cake-walk," a minstrel favorite, by the Negro musical comedy teams of the late 1890s and 1900s. Ada Walker especially deserves credit; but soon, as in the Johnson and Cole and Will Marion Cook operettas, and in the pioneer jazz musical *Shuffle Along*, the full originality of Negro dance was revealed. From then on, in successive fads, one or another Negro dance step has dominated American stage, ballroom, and popular dance fashions, with brief intermittent importations from South America, like the "tango," "samba," or what not. And, of course, several of these are of Afro-Cuban or Afro-Brazilian derivation.

Finally, Negro dance crossed the jealous frontier of the ballet, with Grant Still's experimental African ballet of Sadjhi and the native African dance group that presented *Kykunkor*. The more general public knows the perennially popular dance group of Katherine Dunham, first American Negro to base her choreography on actual field study of native dances. She has had a number of successful followers, none more so than the now celebrated Pearl Primus, whose recent trip to Africa has introduced a new dimension into serious Negro dance recitals.

What is of special interest with regard to Negro dance patterns and their execution is the retention, except in a few choreographed ballets, of the basic folk habit of improvisation. This, also, is characteristic of the best of the jazz music, which in its purest strain is group improvisation by master musicians, whose technique is equal to the hard test of such a style of performance. In fact, all of the so-called jazz "tricks" originated as impromptu insertions designed to add variety. One by one they have become standardized to build up a formidable body of new musical patterns some of which have considerably influenced modernistic music in general. From Gershwin and Ellington on, this jazz invasion of formal music has been triumphantly proceeding; and it can be said that, in terms of dissonances, unresolved harmonies, and elaborate and eccentric rhythms, jazz and modern music have struck up a major alliance in a common cause.

Drama

After a promising start with the spectacular career of Ira Aldridge (1833–1866), serious Negro drama faded out with the waning interest of the general public in the dignified Negro actor. Aldridge's last days, as well as his most spectacular successes, were in Europe. Between 1860 and 1916 the Negro theme had to be content with sporadic melodrama and farce. Even when *Uncle Tom's Cabin* restored serious subject matter, all of the endless presentations of this *pièce de resistance* of the American stage were given by white actors.

Ironically enough, by the time the metropolitan stage was open to mature Negro acting, Negroes were out of the mood of acting as Topsy and Uncle Tom. In 1916 with *Three Plays for the Negro Theater* by Ridgeley Torrence, the Negro Hapgood Players ushered in the modern era of the Negro drama. But in spite of great pains to cultivate a single standard, literary and technical, for Negro plays, the effects of the long banishment were felt for a long time even after this. No seasoned tradition or craftsmanship has even yet been firmly established, in spite of the obvious fact of great native endowment in the histrionic arts, particularly if one may single out special factors, skill in emotional projection, facial and body pantomime, and unusual control of vocal timbre.

Broadway abdicated its ostracism with the great success of Charles Gilpin in *The Emperor Jones* by Eugene O'Neill, and from then on occasional distinction has accrued to Negro drama, notably in *The Green Pastures* by Marc Connelly, with its incomparable acting of the title role by William Harrison. There was also the distinctive success of DuBose Heyward's Charleston folk drama, *Porgy*. On the Broadway stage, however, the career of the all-Negro play is still fitful. There is no dearth of good Negro acting in plays calling for Negro characters: mixed casts are now common, both for serious plays and musical comedies, to the extent of seeming normal, although it was exceptional until a decade ago.

Development in the semi-professional stage has been somewhat steadier. For over twenty years one Negro repertory group, the well-known Karamu Players of Cleveland, Ohio, have carried out a program of high technical and dramatic distinction. The Howard University Players, the Atlanta University and several other collegiate groups, have achieved a high level of acting in a versatile repertory, including now and then an original play of Negro authorship. They enact plays of Negro life but not exclusively. Doubtless this policy was adopted on sound educational grounds, but necessity has added its weight, since the number of good plays on Negro themes is still limited. The Negro playwright still lags, probably because of limited contact and experience, with the professional theatre. One can cite several successful Negro playwrights, such as Willis Richardson, Randolph Edmonds, Langston Hughes, Theodore Ward, and Owen Dodson, but on the whole maturity comparable to that of the Negro actor and singer has not yet materialized.

A curious dramatic deficiency to date is very scarce use of satire and social comedy as a drama resource, due perhaps to the overseriousness of the Negro's approach to his own situation. Quite obviously, however, satire and comedy would be trenchant weapons. An interesting recent example of satirical dramas was the mixed-cast musical, *Finians Rainbow*. In heavier problem play discussion of the race question, there have been a moderate number of successes: *Stevedore*, a labor play; *Deep Are the Roots*, a problem play of an interracial romance; *They Shall Not Die*, based on the celebrated Scottsboro Case; and dramatizations of such problem novels as Lillian Smith's *Strange Fruit* and Richard Wright's *Native Son*. In view of several quite recent successes with pioneer advance-guard drama in the movies, such as *Home of the Brave*, *The Quiet One*, *Lost Boundaries*, and *Bright Victory*, there is some likelihood that the Broadway stage will take courage and follow suit.

The Pictorial Arts

We come finally to a field exhibiting not only more sustained activity, but very substantial achievement. Indeed, the appearance of Negro artists from very early times is a phenomenon of note, among them a representative society portrait painter of Baltimore in the early 1800s—Joshua Johnston. As might be expected, the middle phase was filled with a number of competent but not outstanding traditionalists: William Simpson, Rob Duncanson, and William Bannister among them. This academic tradition found a significant climax in the internationally successful career of a great traditionalist—Henry O. Tanner, outstanding Negro member of the Paris school of the 1900s.

Shortly before Tanner's death, however, the so-called "New Negro" movement came along, and swerved many of the younger artists into a racialist and later a social content mode of painting and sculpture. From 1925 on there has been a brilliant succession of such artists, who, although interested in racial types and situations, were also modernists, and therefore welcome company among their white fellow artists. Too numerous to mention exhaustively, typical names may be singled out among the painters: Aaron Douglas, Malvin Gray Johnson, Hale Woodruff, Eldzier Cortor, Charles Sebree, Horace Pippin, and Jacob Lawrence; and among the sculptors: Sargent Johnson, William Bannarn, and Richmond Barthé.

From the very beginning, as already mentioned, sculpture has been a forte. In the mid-nineteenth century Edmonia Lewis, a woman sculptor, became a pioneer in her art. Later, two other women sculptors—Meta Warrick Fuller, pupil of Rodin, and May Howard Jackson—achieved considerable recognition, to be followed by Augusta Savage and Nancy Elizabeth Prophet. But the most outstanding sculptor of the New Negro era was Richmond Barthé, whose acceptance in the art world has made him one of the leading contemporary Americans in the field. Similar claims can be made for the young painter, Jacob Lawrence, whose symbolically pictorialized abstractions of Negro historical materials have made him famous. In quick succession he painted a Toussaint L'Ouverture series, then one on Frederick

Douglass, and another on Harriet Tubman, climaxed by a Folk Migration series purchased by the Museum of Modern Art (New York). Lately, Lawrence has turned to more abstract and general themes with equal success.

Meanwhile, since realism and native themes have yielded to the present vogues of abstract modernism, many of the younger Negro artists are working without any sense of particular obligation to racial expression. One may expect, however, a return to further documentation of Negro life, such as the historical murals of Hale Woodruff and the growing portrait series of Aaron Douglas, whenever the vogue of the abstract declines. And even now certain centers in New York and Chicago, and Atlanta University with its annual special shows for Negro artists, keep fostering the racial theme and interest. In whatever vein of expression, the youngest generation of Negro artists are benefitting from the maturity of techniques and social insight made possible by superior opportunities and broader social contacts.

At the height of the New Negro phase there was promise that African art would exert a special influence on the work of Negro American artists. After some experimental flurries, this did not fully blossom. The contacts with African sculpture were not as direct as they could and should have been; and there is no doubt that a more informed development in this direction could still be fruitful. The possibilities, especially in sculpture, are revealed by modern African sculptors themselves, notably Ben Enwonwu.

For the moment the sense of integration has taken strong hold on many of our younger artists, and for that matter in other fields as well. This is warrantable, even though it may abate temporarily the more overt kind of racial self-expression. It is significant that Negro art moves out into the mainstream of American culture, and gains a sense of solidarity with its national fellow-practitioners and the general world of art. In time the return to native materials will occur in a context free of provincialism or propaganda; and the Negro artist will then find full and proper recognition and fraternal acceptance as a creative participant in the arts of America. Meanwhile, his future is bright: he can look forward to a beneficial relaxation of emotional tensions, conducive to a calmer flow of artistic effort and a deeper current of understanding.

ENDNOTES TO
EDITORIAL NOTES

Renaissance Apologetics

1. Alain Locke gave September 13, 1886, publicly as his birthdate. It seems certain, however, that he was born September 13, 1885, under the name Arthur Locke: Birth Certificate, "Arthur Locke" Department of Records, Vital Statistics, Philadelphia, Pa.; "Personal Astrology" (envelope), Folder—A. Locke, Box—"Additions to the Locke Papers," Alain Locke Papers, Manuscript Division, Moorland–Spingarn Research Center, Howard University (hereafter referred to as ALP, MD, MSRC, HU); Mary Locke to Alain Locke, n.d. (ca. February 17, 1906), Folder—1905, no month, Box 87, ALP, MD, MSRC, HU; Alain Locke to Mary Locke, February 15, 1906, Folder—February 1906, Box 96, ALP, MD, MSRC, HU; Alain Locke to Mary Locke, February 19, 1906, Folder—February 1906, Box 96, ALP, MD, MSRC, HU.

2. See Jeffrey C. Stewart, "A Biography of Alain Locke: Philosopher of the Harlem Renaissance, 1886–1930" (Unpublished Ph.D. dissertation, Yale University, 1979), pp. 33-1-3, 206–207.

3. Ibid., pp. 276–277.

4. W.E.B. Du Bois, "Opinion," *The Crisis* 19 (April 1920): 298–299.

5. Ernest Boyd, "Readers and Writers," *The Independent* 116 (January 16, 1926): 77; J.P. Whipple, "Letters & Life, In Which Books, Plays and People Are Discussed," *Survey Graphic* 56, No. 9 (August 1, 1926): 517–519.

6. Aubrey Bowser, "The Two Dollar Woman Out Again" (Review of *Harlem*, newspaper and date unknown), Scrapbook #3, Vol. 2, ALP, MD, MSRC, HU; W.E.B. Du Bois, "Criteria of Negro Art," *The Crisis* 32 (October 1926): 290, 292, 294, 296–297; Benjamin Brawley, "The Negro Renaissance," *Southern Workman* 56 (April 1927): 177–184; Allison Davis, "Our Negro Intellectuals," *The Crisis* 35 (August 1928): 268–269, 284–286.

Poetry

1. Alain Locke, *American Philosophy Today and Tomorrow*, ed. Horace Kallen and Sidney Hook (New York, 1968), p. 312 (Autobiographical sketch).

2. Alain Locke to Mrs. Charlotte Mason, September 14, 1932, December 21, 1932, April 11, 1933, January 21, 1934, Box 57, ALP, MD, MSRC, HU.

3. Darwin T. Turner, ed., *The Wayward and the Seeking: A Collection of Writing by Jean Toomer* (Washington, D.C., 1980), pp. 132–133; Claude McKay to Alain Locke, June 4, 1927, Box 148, ALP, MD, MSRC, HU.

Drama

1. Alain Locke to Mary Locke, April 7, 1908, Box 97, ALP, MD, MSRC, HU; Stewart, "A Biography of Alain Locke," p. 210; Constance Green, *The Secret City* (Princeton, N.J., 1967), p. 166.

2. Locke misspelled Max Reinhardt's name as R*h*einhardt.

Music

1. Mary Locke to Alain Locke, n.d. ("Sunday Night"), Folder—no month, 1905, Box 87, ALP, MD, MSRC, HU; "Order of Music for June, 1907, Trinity Church in the City of Boston," Scrapbook #5, Vol. 1, ALP, MD, MSRC, HU; "Sunday Evening Program," February 10, 1907, First Baptist Church, Boston, Scrapbook #5, Vol. 2, ALP, MD, MSRC, HU; Locke, "The Command of the Spirit," *The Southern Workman* 54 (July 1925): 296–297.

2. Locke, *The Negro and His Music* (New York, 1969), p. 70.

3. The announcement reads: "The Library of Congress and Gertrude Clarke Whittall Foundation present a Festival of Music and an Exhibit of Books, Manuscripts, Music, Paintings and Other Works of Art Commemorating the 75th Anniversary of the Thirteenth Amendment to the Constitution, December 18, 1940," Folder—Music, Groups, Box 27, ALP, MD, MSRC, HU.

African Art

1. Zowie Baber to Locke, June 21, 1927, Folder—Bab-Bak, Box 6, ALP, MD, MSRC, HU; Albert Barnes to Locke, January 25, 1924, Box 148, ALP, MD, MSRC, HU; Edith Issacs to Locke, November 1, 1926, Folder—Pareyn and African Art, Box 102, ALP, MD, MSRC, HU; Records of the Harlem Museum of African Art, 1927–1928, Box 217, ALP, MD, MSRC, HU; "A Note on African Art," Reprint in catalogue for exhibition of American Negro Art, The Weyhe Gallery, New York, 1940, Box 69, ALP, MD, MSRC, HU; Interview with Ladislas Segy, March 13, 1982.

2. Interview with Ladislas Segy, March 13, 1982; Ladislas Segy, *African Sculpture Speaks*, 4th ed. (New York, 1975), pp. 127–128.

3. Edith R. Issacs to Locke, November 8, 1926, Folder—Pareyn and African Art, Box 102, ALP, MD, MSRC, HU; Locke, "Memorandum February 25, 1928," attached to Locke to Mrs. Charlotte Mason, February 29, 1928, Box 56, ALP, MD, MSRC, HU.

Contemporary Negro Art

1. Locke, in *Twentieth Century Authors,* ed. Stanley Kunitz and Howard Haycroft (New York, 1942), p. 837 (Autobiographical sketch); Locke to Mrs. Mason, September 8, 1931, Box 56, ALP, MD, MSRC, HU; Locke, "Dedication," in *The Negro in Art* (Washington, D.C., 1940), p. 4.

2. A catalogue, "The Negro in Art Week," November 16, 1927, Folder—African and American Negro Art, Box 102, ALP, MD, MSRC, HU; a catalogue, Harmon Foundation's "Exhibit of the Work of Negro Artists" at the Art Center, New York, February 16–28, 1931, The Records of the Harmon Foundation, Manuscript Division, The Library of Congress, Washington, D.C.; Interview with Richmond Barthé, September 25, 1980. It appears that Locke first became associated with Miss Brady and the Harmon Foundation Art Exhibits in 1929.

3. Locke to Ernest Crichlow, n.d. (ca. 1939), Box 104, ALP, MD, MSRC, HU.

4. Phone interview with Helen Harrison, March 29, 1982. The subject of black artist participation in the New York World's Fair remains a subject for further investigation. For more information on the 1939 World's Fair, see *The New York World's Fair, 1939/40*: Selections, Arrangement and Text by Stanley Appelbaum (New York) and *Dawn of a New Day: The New York World's Fair, 1939/40*, The Queens Museum (New York).

Retrospective Reviews

1. Locke to Paul Kellogg, June 1925, Box 710, Paul Kellogg Papers, Social Welfare Archives, University of Minnesota; "Memorandum about Alumni Charges," F—Memoranda, Copies of, Box 4, ALP, MD, MSRC, HU; Locke to Mrs. Charlotte Mason, March 5, 1929, Box 56, ALP, MD, MSRC, HU.

2. Madeline Aldridge to Locke, December 10, 1928, Box 6, ALP, MD, MSRC, HU; Elmer Carter to Locke, December 22, 1931, F—Carter, Elmer Anderson, Box 9, ALP, MD, MSRC, HU.

3. Jessie Fauset to Locke, January 9, 1933 (mis-dated), Box 149, ALP, MD, MSRC, HU.

4. See Mark Naison, "Communism and Harlem Intellectuals in the Popular Front: Anti-Fascism and the Politics of Black Culture," *Journal of Ethnic Studies* 9 (Spring 1981): 1–25. Unfortunately the employment of blacks in the Federal Arts Projects outside of New York City and Chicago was very low; see Monty Noam Penkower, *The Federal Writers' Project* (Urbana, Ill., 1977), pp. 66–67.

5. Richard Wright, "Blueprint for Negro Writing," *New Challenge* 2 (Fall 1937): 53–65.

6. John A. Davis, "We Win the Right to Fight for Jobs," *Opportunity* 16 (August 1938): 232.

Race and Culture

1. Stewart, "A Biography of Locke," pp. 73–103, 178–195, 238–257; Dr. William A. Banner, "Alain Locke as a Philosopher," March 11, 1982, Howard University (Alain Locke Lecture).

FURTHER READING

Locke, Alain. *Negro Art: Past and Present and The Negro and His Music.* New York: Arno Press, 1969. (Originally published in 1936.)

————. *The Negro in Art: A Pictorial Record of the Negro Artist and of the Negro Theme in Art.* New York: Hacker Books, 1971. (Originally published in 1940.)

————. *The New Negro.* Ed. with new preface by Robert Hayden. New York: Atheneum, 1970.

————. *Plays of Negro Life. A Sourcebook of Native American Drama.* Westport, Conn.: Negro Universities Press, 1970. (Originally published in 1927.)

————. *When Peoples Meet: A Study in Race and Culture Contacts.* New York: Hinds, Hayden and Eldridge, 1946. (Originally published in 1942.)

Martin, Robert. "A Bibliography of the Writings of Alain Leroy Locke" in *The New Negro Thirty Years Afterward*, Washington, D.C., 1955, pp. 89–96. Edited by Rayford Logan et al.

Tidwell, John Edgar, and Wright, John S. "Alain Locke: A Comprehensive Bibliography of Published Writings," *Callaloo* 4, nos. 11, 12, 13 (February–October 1981): 175–192.

INDEX

Abraham, Peter, 339
Abraham's Bosom (Heyward), 24
Africa
  English views of, 209, 224, 254–5
  nation of Liberia, 234, 318, 392
  political critiques of, 254–5, 282, 307, 373
  Union of South Africa, 186, 266, 297, 307–8, 333, 338–9, 373, 392
Africa and the Rise of Capitalism (Williams), 281
Africa and World Peace (Azikiwe), 282
African
  anthropology, 255, 265–6, 283, 297, 317–8, 362, 393
  art, 15, 129–55, 166, 171, 177, 179, 183–4, 186, 204; photos of, 15, 133, 139–52 *passim*; see also Retrospective Reviews
  cultural development, 224–5, 234–5, 265, 348–9, 393
  dance, 243–4, 249–50
  drama, 85, 91
  effect on whites, 230, 247–8
  folklore, 204, 255, 282, 392–3, 440–1
  history, 210, 224, 233, 283, 335–6
  literature, 212–3, 219, 224–5, 247–8, 297, 348–9
  music, 107–8, 112, 114, 118, 135
  nationalism, 10
  religion, 125, 391
  slave trade, 286
  sociological investigations, 204, 224, 235, 254, 255, 282–3
  subjects for artistic portrayal, 163–9
  temperament, 439–40
Africanisms in the Gullah Dialect (Turner), 362
African Negro Sculpture (Kjersmeier), 344
African Sculpture Speaks (Segy), 392
Afro-American
  art, 159, 170–94, 447, 465, 474–5; see also Retrospective Reviews
  culture, 397–8, 412–3, 439–75
  drama, 69–98, 447, 455, 457, 473–4; see also Retrospective Reviews

education, 159, 162, 415–21; see also Retrospective Reviews
history, 439–49; see also Retrospective Reviews
literature, *passim*
music, 101–26, 440, 441, 445, 449–50, 453, 455, 457, 464, 471–3; see also jazz; Retrospective Reviews
nationalism, 6
poetry, 33, 39–66, 444–7, 454–5, 465–6; see also Retrospective Reviews
sociological investigations, 397–8, 407–13, 423–31; see also Retrospective Reviews
subjects for artistic portrayal, 160–8
temperament, 410–2, 439–41, 443, 451–8
Afro-American Symphony (Still), 113, 115
Afro-Cuban Folk Music (Ortiz), 349
After Freedom (Powdermaker), 292–3
Albany Institute of History and Art, 191–4
Aldridge, Ira, 71, 473
Alexander, L.M., 227, 229
Allen, J.S., 254, 264
All God's Chillun Got Wings (O'Neill), 23, 80, 93, 240, 341
Along This Way (Johnson), 223
American Caste and the Negro College (Gallagher), 281–2, 292
American Dilemma, An (Myrdal), 320, 358, 382
American Jazz Music (Hobson), 291
American Negro Spirituals (Johnson and Johnson), 303
American Youth Commission Studies, 313–4
Anderson, Marian, 120–1, 124, 186, 315, 455, 472
Annie Allen (Brooks), 357
Anthropology, 397–8, 407–13, 423–31, 439–42, 451–4; see also Retrospective Reviews
Anti-Slavery Origins of the Civil War (Dumond), 304
Aptheker, Herbert, 305, 391
Armstrong, Louis, 112, 250

483

art (visual), 129–94; see also African; Afro-American; Retrospective Reviews
Arts of West Africa, The (Sadler), 243
Azikiwe, Nnamdi, 282

Bach, Johann Sebastian, 101, 104, 105, 125, 250
Baldwin, James, 339
Baltimore Museum of Art, 159, 181–4, 186, 187, 188, 189
Banana Bottom (McKay), 222
Bannister, Edward M., 171, 191
Barnes Foundation, 15, 131, 133–4, 140, 149, 153; sculpture from, 15, 133, 134
Barthé, Richmond, 102, 177–9, 185, 186–7, 188, 189, 192; sculpture by, 102, 178, 185, 189
Barton, Rebecca, 55, 234, 345
Bearden, Romare, 193, 194
Bellegarde, Dantes, 255, 282
Belles Images (Maran), 249
Bennett, Gwendolyn, 45, 188, 289; poetry quoted, 289
Big Boy Leaves Home (Wright), 261, 274–5
Big Sea, The (Hughes), 301–2, 306
Big White Fog (Ward), 276, 304
Black Folk, Then and Now (Du Bois), 294
Black Jacobins, The (James), 279, 305
black literary magazines, 27, 203
Black Manhattan (Johnson), 207
Black No More (Schuyler), 212
Black Worker, The (Spero and Harris), 208, 210
Black Workers and the New Unions (Cayton and Mitchell), 293
Blesh, Rudi, 324–5, 368
Blondiau-Theatre Arts Collection, 129, 137–8, 139–48, 179
blues, 110, 231, 291, 316
Bond, Horace Mann, 234, 292
Bontemps, Arna
    Black Thunder, 260, 286
    Chariot in the Sky, 379
    Dream Keeper, The, 218
    Drums at Dusk, 286
    God Sends Sunday, 212
    Golden Slippers, 312
    Poetry of the Negro, The (with Langston Hughes), 343, 356
    Sad Faced Boy, 257, 260
    Story of the Negro, The, 347
    When the Jack Hollers (with Langston Hughes), 249
Book of American Negro Poetry, The (Johnson), 211, 451
Botkin, E.A., 209, 211
Bradford, Roark, 203, 206, 211, 222, 229
Braithwaite, William Stanley, 14, 248, 342, 368, 445

Brawley, Benjamin, 207, 219, 241, 253, 261, 262, 278
Brooks, Gwendolyn, 356, 357–8, 367; poetry, quoted, 357–8
Brothers Under the Skin (McWilliams), 382
Brown America (Embree), 210
Brown, Sterling, 33, 123, 228, 261, 289–90, 333, 356
    Negro Caravan, The (with Arthur Davis and Ulysses Lee), 310–1, 313
    Negro in American Fiction, The, 261
    Negro in Washington, The (Washington: American Guides Series), 264–5
    Negro Poetry and Drama, 261, 303
    Outline for the Study of Negro Poetry, 211
    Southern Road, 49–53, 212, 216, 217–8; quoted from, 50–2, 59–60
Brown, William Wells, 435, 436
Buckmaster, Henrietta, 313, 314–5
Bunche, Ralph, 255, 382
Burleigh, Harry, 111, 445, 455

Caballero, The (Courlander), 301
Cabin in the Sky (Root), 94, 95–7, 303
Caldwell, Erskine, 239–40, 258, 262, 301, 456
Candy (Alexander), 229
Caribbean arts, 279, 286, 301, 343, 349, 358, 379, 453, 459–69
Caste and Class in a Southern Town (Dollard), 264, 292
Caste, Class and Race (Cox), 347–8
Cather, Willa, 301
Catlett, Elizabeth, 193–4
Cayton, Horace, 293
Charles Waddell Chesnutt (Chesnutt), 389, 390
Chestnutt, Charles, 13, 389, 390, 444
Chestnutt, Helen, 389, 390
Chinaberry Tree, The (Fauset), 212
Clotel, or The President's Daughter (Brown), 435, 436
Collapse of Cotton Tenancy, The (Johnson), 242, 252, 292
Collapse of the Confederacy, The (Wesley), 280–1
Color and Conscience (Gallagher), 327
Color Blind (Halsey), 325–6
Colored Woman in a White World, A (Terrell), 302
Comedy, American Style (Fauset), 222
Connelly, Marc, 95–7, 206–7, 285, 290–1, 310
Cook, Will Marion, 111, 223, 268, 473
Courlander, Harold, 291, 301, 343
Covarrubias, Miguel, 168, 204, 313
Cowdery, Mae, 22, 248–9; poetry quoted, 22, 248–9
Creole Rhapsody (Ellington), 113–4

Crichlow, Ernest, 188, 193
Crite, Allan, 187, 188
Cry, The Beloved Country (Paton), 329, 333, 338–9, 351, 355
Culbertson, Edward, 75–6, 90
Cullen, Countee, 14, 24, 33, 52, 65, 230, 356
    Color!, 39–40
    "Fruit of the Flower," quoted, 39–40
    "Incident," 364
    Lost Zoo, The (illustrated by Charles Sebree), 303
    Medea, 241
    One Way to Heaven, 217, 249
    On These I Stand, 333, 357
    "Shroud of Color," quoted, 40
    other poetry quoted, 24, 45, 57
Cunard, Nancy, 231

Dahomey, An Ancient West African Kingdom (Herskovits), 282
Dark Princess (Du Bois), 202
Davis, Frank Marshall, 58, 241, 261, 276
Davis, John A., 198, 272
Dawson, William, 115, 472
Deep River (Wood), 229
Dett, Nathaniel, 107, 445, 455
Diplomatic Relations of the United States, The (Logan), 305
Diton, Carl, 108, 455
Divine Comedy, The (Dodson), 276, 291
Documentary History of the Negro People (Aptheker), 391
Dodson, Owen, 276, 291, 323, 363–4, 365
Dollard, John, 264, 292
Don't You Want to Be Free? (Hughes), 276, 290
Dorsey, Lillian, 176; painting by, 172
Douglas, Aaron, 177, 179, 188, 192, 475; illustrations by, 83–4
Douglass, Frederick, 315, 321, 345–6, 370
Dover, Cedric, 263, 297
Drama, 69–98; see also African; Afro-American; Retrospective Reviews
Drums at Dusk (Bontemps), 286
Du Bois, W.E.B., 3, 13, 251, 408, 412, 413
    Black Folk, Then and Now, 294–5
    Black Reconstruction, 223–4, 242
    Dark Princess, 202
    Dusk of Dawn, 302
    Haiti, 276
    Quest of the Silver Fleece, 444
    Souls of Black Folk, 107, 337, 381, 408, 444
    Star of Ethiopia, 72
    World and Africa, The, 335–6
Dumond, Dwight L., 304

Dunbar, Paul Lawrence
    biography of, 253, 313
    collection of writings by, 278
    significance of, 13, 43, 44, 268, 440, 444–5, 454
Duncanson, Robert S., 172, 191, 379
Dunham, Katharine, 97, 324
Dust to Earth (Graham), 313
Dvorak, Anton, 110, 111, 115, 123–4, 268

Edmonds, Helen, 382
Edmonds, Randolph, 231
Education, see Afro-American; Retrospective Reviews
Education of the Negro in the American Social Order, The (Bond), 234
Ellington, Edward Kennedy ("Duke"), 112–4, 456, 473
Ellison, Ralph, 385–6
Emperor Jones (O'Neill), 73, 80, 93–4, 475
    Aaron Douglas' illustrations of, 83–4
    Howard Players cast list for, 70
Europe, Jim, 111

Father Divine (George Baker), 253, 262, 343, 345
Father of the Blues (Handy), 316
Faulkner, William, 246–7, 299, 351–2, 355, 376
Fauset, Arthur, 278
Fauset, Jessie, 14, 24, 197, 212, 222
Fax, Elton Clay, 189; drawing by, 188
Federal Art Project, 183, 187, 192, 249, 457
Federal Theatre Project, 249, 262, 276–7, 457
Federal Writers Project, 261, 264–5, 274, 280, 293, 306, 316
Fighting Words (Stewart), 302–3
Fine Clothes for the Jew (Hughes), 456
Finkelstein, Sidney, 343
Fire!! (magazine), 24
Fisher, Rudolph, 14, 24
    Conjure Man Dies, 217
    Walls of Jericho, The, 202
Folk Culture on St. Helena Island (Johnson), 218
Folk-Say: A Regional Miscellany (Botkin), 211
Ford, James, 281, 297
Ford, Nick Aaron, 308
Foxes of Harrow, The (Yerby), 321–2
Franklin, John Hope, 198, 334–5, 347, 360, 369
Frazier, E. Franklin, 198
    Free Negro Family, The, 218
    Negro Family in Chicago, The, 218
    Negro Family in the United States, The, 293, 347
    Negro in the United States, The, 359
    Negro Youth at the Crossways, 307
    quoted, 462

Frederick Douglass (Quarles), 345
From Slavery to Freedom (Franklin), 334–5, 360, 369
Fuller, Meta Warrick, 14, 172–3, 176, 192, 474

Gallagher, Buell, 281–2, 292, 320, 327
Garvey, Marcus, 10, 345
Gershwin, George, 110, 111, 112, 473
Gilpin, Charles, 70, 71–3, 80, 96–7, 473
Gingertown (McKay), 217
Gloster, Hugh M., 343
God Sends Sunday (Bontemps), 212; book-jacket illustration, 212
Golden Hawk, The (Yerby), 341, 375
Gone With the Wind (Mitchell), 246
Goodman, Benny, 120
Gorleigh, Rex, 193
Graham, Shirley, 313, 321, 334, 361, 379
Green Pastures (Connelly), 95, 96, 206–7, 285, 290, 291, 310
Green, Paul, 23, 88, 90, 202, 211
    In the Valley and Other Carolina Plays, 204
    Native Son (with Richard Wright), 313; playbill from, 92
    No 'Count Boy, 90
    Roll On Sweet Chariot, 231
Gregory, Montgomery, 72
Grimke, Angelina, 13, 14, 88
Growing Up in the Black Belt (Johnson), 317
Guillaume, Paul, 15, 132, 134, 153, 166

Haiti, 243, 291, 296
    Black Jacobins, The (James), 279
    Caballero, The, (Courlander), 301
    Haiti (Du Bois), 97, 276
    Haiti and Her Problems (Bellegarde), 255
    Life in a Haitian Valley (Herskovits), 265
    literature about, 286, 381
    literature of, 349
    Locke lectures in, 459–69
    Masters of the Dew (Roumain), 329, 330, 353
    Nation Haitienne, Le (Bellegarde), 282
    Popo and Fifina (Bontemps and Hughes), 218
    Tell My Horse (Hurston), 279
    Voodoos and Obeahs (Williams), 219
Haitian culture, 219, 258, 265, 291, 301, 333
Halsey, Margaret, 320, 325
Handy, W.C., 316, 324, 389
Hare, Maud Cuney, 250
Harlem, 3, 5–6, 17–9, 29–30, 183, 306, 313, 340, 387–8, 446, 453
Harlem Artists Guild, The, 183, 188
Harlem Museum of African Art, 129, 174, 179, 204
Harlem Renaissance, 3, 5–30, 159, 198, 201, 205, 209, 217, 259, 268, 276

Harleston, Edwin A., 176; painting by, 170
Harmon Foundation, 159, 174, 179, 189, 192, 204
Harper, Frances Ellen Watkins, 443
Harris, Abram, 208, 210, 253–4, 372
Harris, Joel Chandler, 23, 229, 379–80, 437, 440, 441, 442
Harris, Rex, 390
Hayden, Palmer, 189, 192
Hayden, Robert, 308, 342, 356, 357; poetry quoted, 308
Hayes, Roland, 4, 14, 103–5, 124, 455, 472
Herskovits, Melville
    Dahomey, An Ancient West African Kingdom, 282
    Life in a Haitian Valley, 258, 265
    Myth of the Negro Past, The, 313, 314, 317–8
    Rebel Destiny (with Frances Herskovits), 234
    West African Civilization of the Negro, 255
Heyward, Du Bose, 23, 93, 211, 438, 447, 473
    Abraham's Bosom, 24
    Jasbo Brown, 212
    Mamba's Daughters (with Dorothy Heyward), 261, 290
    Porgy, 24, 94, 202, 203, 240, 441
    Star Spangled Virgin, 287
    quoted, 21
Hill, T. Arnold, 264
Himes, Chester, 331–2
His Eye Is on the Sparrow (Waters), 380
history, see Afro-American; Retrospective Reviews
History of Jazz in America, A (Ulanov), 390
Hoernle, R.A.F., 307–8
Home to Harlem (McKay), 202, 447
Horne, Lena, 371–2
Houseman, John, 92, 95
Howard Players, 30, 72, 73, 88, 474; cast list from program of, 70
Howard University, 3, 30, 70, 72, 73, 88, 204, 281, 296, 315, 474
How Britain Rules Africa (Padmore), 254–5
Hughes, Langston, 14, 33, 47, 53, 241, 333, 446
    Big Sea, The, 301–2, 306
    Don't You Want to Be Free?, 276–7, 290
    Dream Keeper, The, 218
    Fine Clothes for the Jew, 456
    Front Porch, The, 290
    Laughing to Keep from Crying, 388–9
    Montage of a Dream Deferred, 378–9
    Mulatto, 97–8, 240–1, 262, 290, 355, 368
    Negro Mother and other Dramatic Recitations, The, 212
    New Song, A, 276
    "Night Funeral in Harlem," quoted, 378–9
    Not Without Laughter, 206
    One Way Ticket, 357
    Poetry of the Negro, The, (with Arna

Bontemps), 343, 356
Scottsboro, Ltd., 56-7, 218; quoted from, 57,
   218
Shakespeare in Harlem, 312
Simple Speaks His Mind, 371, 372
Ways of White Folks, The, 229
Weary Blues, The, 41-2, 456
When the Jack Hollers (with Arna Bontemps),
   249
other poetry quoted, 24, 207
Huggins, Willis, 233
Hurston, Zora Neale
   Jonah's Gourd Vine, 229-30
   Moses: Man of the Mountain, 288
   Mules and Men, 239, 240
   Seraph on the Sewanee, 341-2
   Tell My Horse, 279
   Their Eyes Were Watching God, 260

I Am the American Negro (Davis), 261
In a Minor Key (Reid), 307
Infants of Spring (Thurman), 217
In the Valley and Other Carolina Plays (Green),
   204
Intruder in the Dust (Faulkner), 351-2, 355, 368
Invisible Man (Ellison), 385-6
Isaacs, Edith, 334

Jackson, May Howard, 172-3, 176, 192, 474
James, C.L.R., 255, 279, 305
James, William, 381, 397
jazz, 101, 110-4, 117-20, 250, 291, 316, 324-5,
   343, 368, 390, 455-7, 472-3
Jazz (Harris), 390
Jazz: A People's Music (Finkelstein), 343
Jazz: Hot and Hybrid (Sargeant), 291
Johnson, Charles
   and Locke, with Max Reinhardt, 77-8, 81
   Collapse of Cotton Tenancy, The, 242, 252, 292
   Growing Up in the Black Belt, 317
   Into the Main Stream, 335
   Negro College Graduate, The, 281
   Negro in American Civilization, The, 208
   Negro Personality Changes in a Southern
      Community, 232
   People vs. Property, 335
   Preface to Racial Understanding, A, 252
   Race Relations and Social Change, 294
   Shadow of the Plantation, The, 233
   quoted, 446
Johnson, Fenton, 52, 56, 456
Johnson, Georgia Douglas, 14, 45
Johnson, Guy B., 208, 218
Johnson, Hall, 113, 114, 207, 262
Johnson, Helene, poetry quoted, 45
Johnson, James Weldon, 13, 44, 52, 59, 111
   Along This Way, 223

American Negro Spirituals (with Rosamond
   Johnson), 303
Autobiography of an Ex-Colored Man, 24
Black Manhattan, 207, 225
Book of American Negro Poetry, 211
"Creation," 24, 47
Fifty Years and Other Poems, 44, 241
Negro Americans, What Now?, 233, 234;
   quoted, 233-4
Negro Sermons, 52
receipt of Du Bois literary prize, 225
St. Peter Narrates an Incident of Resurrection
   Day, 207
significance of, 52
"To America," 269
other poetry quoted, 9
Johnson, Malvin Gray, 173, 176, 182, 192;
   paintings by, 173, 187
Johnson, Rosamond, 111, 250, 261, 303, 445
Johnson, Sargent, 177, 178, 179, 189, 192;
   sculpture by, 178
Johnson, William H., 174, 176-7, 179, 188, 192,
   194; painting by, 174
Jones, Lois, 187, 188
Journal of Negro Education, 234, 242, 255, 281
Journey to Accompong (Dunham), 324

Karamu Theatre, The, 204, 290, 474
Kardiner, Abram, 376, 383
Kellogg, Paul, 3
Killers of the Dream (Smith), 360
Kingsblood Royal (Lewis), 329-31
Kjersmeier, Carl, 344
Knock On Any Door (Motley), 329-30
Know This of Race (Dover), 297
Kykundor or the Witch Doctor (Dafora), 96, 114,
   227, 249-50

Lafayette Federal Theatre Project, 249, 262
Larsen, Nella, 202-3
Last of the Conquerors, The (Smith), 339-40,
   354
Latin American history, 279, 296, 306, 459-69
Latin American literature, 279, 296, 456-67
Latin American music, 101, 112, 114-5, 349, 368,
   464-5, 473
Laughing to Keep from Crying (Hughes), 388-9
Lawrence, Jacob, 186, 188, 189, 193, 194
Lee, Canada, 92, 96, 97
Let My People Go (Buckmaster), 314-5
Lewinson, Paul, 216, 218
Lewis, Edmonia, 191
Lewis, Sinclair, 329-31
Life and Writings of Frederick Douglass, Vol. I:
   The Early Years, Vol. II: The Pre-Civil War
   Decade (Foner), 370

Life in a Haitian Valley (Herskovits), 258, 265
Lindsay, Vachel, 23
Lips, Julius, 265
Livingstone (Maran), 282
Lloyd, Arthur, 295
Locke, Alain, *passim*,
  and Du Bois, 3
  and Europe, 3, 101
  and Harvard University, 3, 397
  and Howard University, 3, 69, 197
  and New Negro Alliance, 198
  and patrons, 129, 159
  and poets, 33
  birth and education, 3, 397
  criticism of, 3, 197–8
  death, 398
  musical tastes, 101
  Negro and His Music, The, 250
  Negro Art: Past and Present, 250, 303
  Negro in Art, The, 303
  New Negro, The, 3, 271–3, 277–8, 358
  parents and family life, 159
  photo, frontispiece
  religious training, 101
  teaching, 3, 159, 197
  theater-going, 69
  When Peoples Meet (with Bernhard Stern),
    314, 382
Logan, Rayford, W., 305
Lonely Crusade (Himes), 331–2
Long Way from Home, A, 63–6, 262
L'Ouverture, Toussaint, see Toussaint L'Ouverture

McClendon, Rose, 80, 96, 97, 240–1
McKay, Claude, 9, 33, 44, 52, 56, 356, 445
  Banana Bottom, 222
  Gingertown, 217
  Harlem: Negro Metropolis, 306
  Harlem Shadows, 456
  Home to Harlem, 63, 202, 447
  Long Way from Home, A, 63–6, 262
  poetry quoted, 9, 45, 47, 381, 445
McWilliams, Carey, 382
Mambour, Auguste, 163, 165–6; painting by, 164
Man Called White, A (White), 346
Maran, Rene, 163, 249, 282, 381, 383
Mark of Oppression, The (Kardiner and Ovesey),
  376, 383
Marxism, 57–61, 239–40, 242, 251, 253–5, 264,
  281, 297, 305, 382
Masters of the Dew (Roumain), 329, 330, 333
minstrel tradition, 69, 72, 80, 203–4, 250, 472
Minty Alley (James), 255
Mis-Education of the Negro, The (Woodson), 224
Mitchell, George, 293
Mitchell, Margaret, 246

modernism, 33, 35–8, 131–2, 134–5, 147–8, 149,
  164–9, 179
Montage of a Dream Deferred (Hughes), 378–9
Moody, Ronald, 189; sculpture by, 187
Morton, "Jelly Roll," 324, 368
Motley, Archibald, 176, 182, 189, 192; painting
  by, 174
Motley, Willard, 330, 376–7
Mulatto (Hughes), 97–8, 240–1, 262, 290, 355, 368
Museum of Modern Art, 129, 149–55
Music, 101–26; see also African; Afro-American;
  jazz; Retrospective Reviews
Myrdal, Gunnar, 314, 320, 358, 382
Myth of the Negro Past, The (Herskovits), 313,
  314, 317–8

National Association for the Advancement of
  Colored People, 72, 242, 334, 366
Native Son (novel, Wright), 299–300, 302, 332,
  385
Native Son (play, Wright and Green), 93–8
  passim, 313; playbill of, 92
Negro, The (Cunard), 231
Negro and Economic Reconstruction, The (Hill),
  264
*Negro and Fusion Politics in the United States,
  The* (Edmonds), 382
Negro and His Music, The (Locke), 250
Negro and the Communist Party, The (Record),
  382–3
Negro Art: Past and Present (Locke), 250, 303
Negro as Capitalist, The (Harris), 253–4
Negro Builders and Heroes (Brawley), 262
Negro Caravan, The (Brown, Davis, Lee),
  310–1, 313; quoted, 310–1
"Negro Digs Up His Past, The," (Schomburg),
  quoted, 277–8
Negro Drawings (Covarrubias), 313
Negroes, see Afro-American
Negro Genius, The (Brawley), 261
Negro Immigrant, The (Reid), 294
Negro in American Civilization, The (Johnson),
  208
Negro in Art, The (Locke), 303
"Negro in Art Week" (1927), 174, 203, 204
Negro in Brazil, The (Ramos), 296
Negro in the American Revolution, The
  (Aptheker), 305
Negro Labor: A National Problem (Weaver), 327
Negro Professional Man and the Community
  (Woodson), 233
Negro Question, The (Allen), 254
Negro Renaissance, 3, 5–30, 63, 66, 159, 198, 201,
  205, 209, 215, 217, 259, 268, 276, 279, 342,
  446, 455

Negro Voices in American Fiction (Gloster), 343
New Art Circle, The, 137–8, 139
New Challenge (magazine), 261
New Negro, 7–10, 21, 29, 53, 63, 66, 183, 259, 268–9, 271–3, 446, 454, 474–5
New Negro, The (Locke), 3, 272, 277–8, 358
New York World's Fair (1939), 159, 186, 188

O Canaan! (Turpin), 288
Odum, Howard, 202, 211, 442
O'Higgins, Myron, 356–7; poetry quoted, 356–7
On Being Negro in America (Redding), 380–1
O'Neill, Eugene, 14, 73, 88, 89, 441
  All God's Chillun Got Wings, 23, 80, 88, 93, 240, 341
  Emperor Jones, 73, 80, 93–4, 475; Aaron Douglas' illustrations of, 83–4; Howard Players cast list for, 70
One Way to Heaven (Cullen), 217, 249
On These I Stand (Cullen), 333, 357
Orozco, José Clemente, 182, 465
Ortiz, Fernando, 349, 466
Ottley, Roi, 347, 381
Ovesey, Lionel, 376, 383

Padmore, George, 254, 282
Path of Thunder, The (Abraham), 338–9
Paton, Alan, 329, 333, 338–9, 351, 355
Patterson, Haywood, 370
Paul Robeson (Robeson), 207
Peterkin, Julia, 21, 23, 202, 207, 216, 222–3
Petry, Ann, 320, 322–3, 332–3
Pippin, Horace, 194, 334
poetry, 33–66; see also Afro-American; Retrospective Reviews
Poetry of the Negro, The (Bontemps and Hughes), 343, 356
Poitier, Sidney, 368
Porgy (Heyward), 24, 94, 202, 203, 240, 441
Porgy and Bess (Gershwin and Heyward), 240, 473
Porter, James, 379
Powdermaker, Hortense, 292–3
Presence Africaine (journal), 336, 349
propaganda, 27–8, 33, 55–61, 87, 218, 231, 238–9, 258–66, 267–70, 295
Puritanism, 24, 91, 126, 221, 222, 241, 438
Pushkin, Alexander, 249

Quarles, Benjamin, 345–6

Race, *passim*, 397–414, 423–75; see also Retrospective Reviews
Ramos, Arthur, 296, 466
Raper, Arthur, 222, 223, 252, 292, 316

Record, Wilson, 382–3
Redding, J. Saunders, 296, 364–5, 370, 380–1
Rehearsals of Discomposure (Scott), 389–90
Reid, Ira, 294, 316
Reinhardt, Max, 77–8, 81–2
Reiss, Winold, 17–20, 161–2, 204; drawings by, 4, 12, 17–20, 160
Renaissance, 3, 21–2, 28, 29–30, 63, 65–6, 148, 159, 198, 201, 205, 208, 209, 215, 217, 259, 268, 272, 276, 279, 342, 343–4, 446, 455
Renaissance in Haiti (Rodman), 343–4
Renascent Africa (Azikiwe), 282
Retrospective Reviews, 197–393
  anthropology, 207–8, 211, 218, 234–5, 243, 258, 260, 265–6, 313–4, 317–8, 324, 373
  art, 204, 243, 303, 334, 343–4, 373, 379, 392–3
  drama, 203–4, 206–7, 211, 231–2, 240–1, 249–50, 262–3, 276–7, 290–1, 303–4, 313, 334, 338, 355–6, 368
  education, 224, 234, 242, 281–2, 292, 294, 296, 315, 326, 348, 364
  history, 207, 210, 219, 223–4, 233, 241, 242, 253, 277–8, 279, 280–1, 294–5, 296, 304–5, 313, 314–5, 326, 334–6, 345–7, 359–60, 369–70, 372, 382, 391
  labor studies, 208, 210, 218, 254, 293, 327
  literature, *passim*
  music, 211, 231, 250, 291, 315–6, 324–5, 349, 368
  poetry, 203, 207, 211–2, 217–8, 230–1, 241, 248–9, 261, 276, 289–90, 308, 312–3, 333, 342–3, 356–8, 367, 368, 378–9
  race relations, 204, 233, 234, 251–2, 263–4, 294, 306, 317, 325–7, 359, 360–1, 382
  sociology, 204, 208, 210, 218, 223–4, 232–3, 242, 253–4, 264, 291–4, 306–7, 314, 316, 327, 335, 347–8, 372
Richard Allen (Wesley), 241
Richardson, Willis, 14, 88, 90
Richmond Peoples' Theatre, 276
Rivera, Diego, 182, 465
Robeson, Paul, 14, 80, 82, 124, 207, 290, 303, 472; Reiss drawing of, 12
Robinson, Jackie, 371
Robinson, Rev. James H., 371
Rodman, Selden, 343–4
Roll Jordan Roll (Peterkin and Doris Ulmann), 222
Roll On, Sweet Chariot (Green), 231, 240
Rose, Arnold, 360–1, 382
Rose McClendon Players of New York, 290–1, 304
Roumain, Jacques, 329, 330, 333, 349
Rowan, Carl, 391–2
Run Little Chillun (Johnson), 262, 276

Sadjhi (Still), 113, 473
Sadler, Michael, 243
Saracen Blade (Yerby), 389

Sargeant, Winthrop, 291
Sartré, Jean-Paul, 338
Savage, Augusta, 176, 188, 474
Savage Hits Back (Lips), 265
Scarlet Sister Mary (Peterkin), 202, 207
Schomburg, Arthur, 277–8
Schuyler, George
   Black No More, 212
   Slaves Today, 213; book-jacket illustration, 211
Schweitzer, Albert, 348–9
Scott, Cyril Kay, 177
Scott, Nathan A., 389–90
Scottsboro Boy (Patterson), 370
Sculptures of Negro Africa, The (Wingert), 373, 379, 392
Sebree, Charles, 193, 303
Segy, Ladislas, 379, 392
Seraph on the Sewanee (Hurston), 341–2
Sharecroppers All (Reid and Raper), 316
Sheldon, Edward, 87–8
Shining Trumpets: A History of Jazz (Blesh), 324
Shuffle Along (Noble and Sissle), 72, 81, 96, 473
Six Plays for a Negro Theatre (Edmonds), 231
Slavery Controversy, The (Lloyd), 295
Slave Songs of the United States (Allen), 471
Slaves Today (Schuyler), 213; book-jacket illustration, 211
Slave Trading in the Old South (Bancroft), 210
Smith, William Gardner, 339–40, 354, 365
sociology, 397–8, 407–13, 423–31; see also African; Afro-American; Retrospective Reviews
Songs From the Dark (Ford), 308
Souls of Black Folk (Du Bois), 107, 337, 381, 408, 444
South African Native Policy (Hoernlé), 307–8
southern literature
   black characters in, 206, 246–7
   black lifestyle in, 202
   compared to Afro-American literature, 222–3
   during Reconstruction, 436–7
   impact on black writers, 299
   realism and romanticism in, 216–7, 222–3, 228–9, 239–40, 285–7, 289, 301, 457
   reform novels of, 216–7
Southern Road (Brown), 49–53, 212, 217–8
Southern Youth Congress, 276
South of Freedom (Rowan), 391–2
Spero, Sterling, 208, 210
spirituals, 101–2, 103–5, 107–8, 123–6, 453, 471–2
Stevedore (Peters and Sklar), 97, 232, 240, 249, 262, 456, 474
Still, William Grant, 113, 115, 472, 473
Stolberg, Benjamin, 258–9, 262
Story of John Hope, The (Torrence), 346

Stowe, Harriet Beecher, 217, 231–2, 323, 351, 435–6, 443, 473; quoted from, 300
Stranger and Alone (Redding), 364–5
Street, The (Petry), 322
Survey Graphic (journal), 3, 161–2, 446
Sweeney, James Johnson, 149, 153, 392

Tanner, Henry O., 14, 172–3, 192, 268
Taylor, Coleridge, 110, 268
Tell My Horse (Hurston), 279
Terrell, Mary Church, 302
Their Eyes Were Watching God (Hurston), 260
There Was Once a Slave (Graham), 321
They All Played Ragtime (Blesh and Janis), 368
Three Plays for the Negro Theatre (Torrence), 72, 80, 88, 473
Tolson, Melvin, 367
To Make a Poet Black (Redding), 296
Toomer, Jean, 14, 33, 45, 47, 89, 218, 330, 385, 438
Torrence, Ridgely, 14, 23, 72, 80, 88, 346, 473
Toussaint L'Ouverture, 210, 255
Tragedy of Lynching, The (Raper), 222, 223, 292
Trial of Dr. Beck, The (Allison), 263
Turpentine (Smith and Morell), 249, 262
Turpin, Walter, 260, 288

Ulanov, Barry, 390
"Uncle Remus" (Harris), 14, 23, 229, 440, 454
Uncle Tom's Cabin (Stowe), 217, 232, 323, 351, 435–6, 443, 473; quoted from, 300
Uncle Tom's Children (Wright), 274–5, 385

Van Vechten, Carl, 23, 82, 107, 110, 189
vaudeville, 72, 77–81
Verhaeren, Emile, 33, 35–8
von Ruckteschell, Walter, 162, 167–8; drawing by, 11
Voodoos and Obeahs (Williams), 219

Walls Come Tumbling Down, The (Ovington), 334, 346
Walls of Jericho, The (Fisher), 202
Walrond, Eric, 14
Ward, Theodore, 276, 304
Waring, Laura Wheeler, 176, 192; painting by, 176
Washington, Booker T., 251, 316, 346, 372, 411, 413, 444
Waters, Ethel, 81, 95, 303, 368, 372, 380
Ways of White Folks, The (Hughes), 229
Weaver, Robert, 327, 347
We Fished All Night (Motley), 376–7
Welles, Orson, 92, 95
Wells, James Lesesne, 177, 189, 193; painting by, 175

Wesley, Charles, 241, 280–1
Wheatley, Phyllis, 43, 44, 55, 442
When Peoples Meet (Locke and Stern), 314, 382
White, Charles, 193, 194
White Man (Raphaelson), 240, 249
White, Walter, 14, 24, 346, 438
Williams, Eric, 281
Wilson, Dooley, 95–6
Wingert, Paul, 373, 379, 392
Witnesses for Freedom (Barton), 345
Wood, Clement, 229, 446
Woodruff, Hale, 177, 179, 188, 189, 192, 475;
    painting by, 175
Woodson, Carter G., 233, 347
  as publisher, 250
  Journal of Negro History, 369
  Mind of the Negro as Reflected in Letters
    Written During the Crisis, 1800–1860, 391
  Mis-Education of the Negro, 224
  Negro Orators and Their Orations, 442
  Negro Professional Man and the Community,
    233
  significance of his death, 359–60, 369
World and Africa, The (Du Bois), 335–6
Wright, Richard
  "Big Boy Leaves Home," 261; award for, 274
  "Bright Morning Star," 288–9
  "Ethics of Living Jim Crow, The," 261
  "How Bigger Was Born," 302; quoted, 300
  Native Son (novel), 299–300, 302, 332, 385
  Native Son (play, with Paul Green), 93, 94,
    97–8, 313; playbill from, 92
  poetry of, 241, 249; quoted, 58
  Twelve Million Voices, 309, 315
  Uncle Tom's Children, 274–5, 385

Yerby, Frank, 321–2, 341, 375–6, 389

Zola, Emile, 300, 322–3
Zulu Woman (Reyher), 348